UNDERSTANDING THE UK ECONOMY

MACMILLAN TEXTS IN ECONOMICS

This series presents a new generation of economics textbooks from Macmillan developed in conjunction with a panel of distinguished editorial advisers:

David Greenaway, Professor of Economics, University of Nottingham
Gordon Hughes, Professor of Political Economy, University of Edinburgh
David Pearce, Professor of Economics, University College London
David Ulph, Professor of Economics, University of Bristol

Published
Understanding the UK Economy (2nd edition): edited by Peter Curwen
International Finance: Keith Pilbeam

Future Macmillan Texts in Economics cover the core compulsory and optional courses in economics at first-degree level and will include:

Forthcoming
Business Economics: Paul Ferguson and Robert Rothschild
International Trade: Mia Mikic
Development Economics: Ian Livingstone
The Economics of the Labour Market: David Sapsford and Zafiris Tzannatos
Monetary Economics: Stuart Sayer
Macroeconomics: Eric Pentecost

In preparation
Introductory Principles
Comparative Economics
Development Economics
Econometrics
Environmental Economics
Financial Economics
Industrial Economics
Microeconomics
Public Sector Economics
Quantitative Methods
Welfare Economics

UNDERSTANDING THE UK ECONOMY

Edited by

Peter Curwen

Contributors

David Gowland and Stephen James
Keith Hartley and Nick Hooper
Paul Marshall

MACMILLAN

First edition 1990
Reprinted 1990
Second edition 1992

Published by
THE MACMILLAN PRESS LTD
Houndmills, Basingstoke, Hampshire RG21 2XS
and London
Companies and representatives
throughout the world

ISBN 0–333–57443–5 (hardcover)
ISBN 0–333–57444–3 (paperback)

A catalogue record for this book is available
from the British Library

Printed in Hong Kong

Series Standing Order (Macmillan Texts in Economics)

If you would like to receive future titles in this series as they are published, you can make use
of our standing order facility. To place a standing order please contact your bookseller or,
in case of difficulty, write to us at the address below with your name and address and the
name of the series. Please state with which title you wish to begin your standing order. (If you
live outside the United Kingdom we may not have the rights for your area, in which case we
will forward your order to the publisher concerned.)

Customer Services Department, Macmillan Distribution Ltd,
Houndmills, Basingstoke, Hampshire, RG21, 2XS, England.

To Benjamin and Alexandra

Contents

List of Figures

List of Tables

List of Abbreviations

ACAS	Arbitration, Conciliation and Advisory Service	EAP	Enlarged Access Policy	
ACT	Advance Corporation Tax	EAS	Enterprise Allowance Scheme	
AD	Aggregate Demand	EC	European Community	
AFBD	Association of Futures Brokers and Dealers	ECB	European Central Bank	
		ECU	European Currency Unit	
AMS	Aggregate Measure of Support	EDI	Electronic Data Interchange	
APC	Average Propensity to Consume	EEA	Exchange Equalisation Account	
ATM	Automated Teller Machine	EEC	European Economic Community	
BBC	British Broadcasting Corporation	EER	Effective Exchange Rate	
BES	Business Expansion Scheme	EFF	Extended Fund Facility	
BIS	Bank For International Settlements	EFL	External Financing Limit	
BoP	Balance of Payments	EFTPOS	Electronic Funds Transfer at Point of Sale	
BSA	Building Society Association	ELs	Eligible Liabilities	
BTEC	Business and Technician Education Council	EMCF	European Monetary Co-operation Fund	
CAP	Common Agricultural Policy	EMS	European Monetary System	
CBI	Confederation of British Industry	EMU	Economic and Monetary Union	
CCC	Competition and Credit Control	EPU	European Political Union	
CD	Certificate of Deposit	ERI	Effective Exchange Rate Index	
CFF	Compensatory Financing Facility	ERM	Exchange Rate Mechanism	
CFSP	Common Foreign and Security Policy	ESCB	European System of Central Banks	
		ET	Employment Training	
CGT	Capital Gains Tax	FES	Family Expenditure Survey	
CR	Concentration Ratio	FIMBRA	Financial Intermediaries and Brokers Regulatory Association	
CRT	Composite Rate Tax			
CSE	Consumer Subsidy Equivalent	FIS	Family Income Supplement	
CSO	Central Statistical Office	FMI	Financial Management Initiative	
CTT	Capital Transfer Tax	FRN	Floating-rate Note	
DCE	Domestic Credit Expansion	FSBR	Financial Statement and Budget Report	
DHSS	Department of Health and Social Security			
		GAB	General Agreements to Borrow	
DIB	Defence Industrial Base	GATT	General Agreement on Tariffs and Trade	
DIY	Do It Yourself			
DM	Deutsche Mark	GCSE	General Certificate in Secondary Education	
DTI	Department of Trade and Industry			
EAGGF	European Agricultural Guarantee and Guidance Fund	GDFCF	Gross Domestic Fixed Capital Formation	

GDP	Gross Domestic Product
GEMM	Gilt Edged Market Maker
GGE	General Government Expenditure
GNP	Gross National Product
HMSO	Her Majesty's Stationary Office
HP	Hire Purchase
IBA	Independent Broadcasting Association
IBELs	Interest Bearing Eligible Liabilities
ICCs	Industrial and Commercial Companies
IDC	Industrial Development Certificate
IFA	Independent Financial Adviser
IFS	Institute for Fiscal Studies
IGA	Inter-governmental Agreement
ILO	International Labour Office
IMF	International Monetary Fund
IMRO	Investment Management Regulatory Organisation
IPD	Interest, Profits and Dividends
IPR	Intellectual Property Right
ISDA	International Swap Dealers Association
ISE	International Stock Exchange
LA	Local Authority
LAUTRO	Life Assurance and Unit Trust Regulatory Organisation
LDC	Less Developed Country
LDE	London Derivatives Exchange
LDMA	London Discount Market Association
LFS	Labour Force Survey
LIBOR	London Inter-bank Offered Rate
LIFFE	London International Financial Futures Exchange
LTOM	London Traded Options Market
MCA	Monetary Compensatory Amount
MERM	Multilateral Exchange Rate Model
MFA	Multi-Fibre Arrangement
MLR	Minimum Lending Rate
MMC	Monopolies and Mergers Commission
MoD	Ministry of Defence
MPC	Marginal Propensity to Consume
MSC	Manpower Services Commission
MTFS	Medium Term Financial Strategy
NBFI	Non-bank Financial Intermediaries
NCVQ	National Council for Vocational Qualifications
NDP	Net Domestic Product
NES	New Earnings Survey
NHS	National Health Service
NI	National Income
NICs	National Insurance Contributions
NNDI	Net National Disposable Income
NNP	Net National Product
NSB	National Savings Bank
OECD	Organisation for Economic Co-operation and Development
OFGAS	Office of Gas Supply
OFT	Office of Fair Trading
OFTEL	Office of Telecommunications
OMO	Open-market Operation
OPEC	Organisation of Petroleum Exporting Countries
OTC	Over the Counter
PAYE	Pay As You Earn
PDI	Personal Disposable Income
PEP	Personal Equity Plan
PIBS	Permanent Interest Bearing Shares
PPP	Purchasing Power Parity
PPS	Perpetual Preferred Stock
PRT	Petroleum Revenue Tax
PSBR	Public Sector Borrowing Requirement
PSDR	Public Sector Debt Repayment
PSE	Producer Subsidy Equivalent
R & D	Research and Development
RDG	Regional Development Grant
RER	Real Exchange Rate
RPI	Retail Prices Index
RPM	Resale Price Maintenance
RSA	Regional Selective Assistance
RSSL	Recruitment Subsidy for School Leavers
SDR	Special Drawing Right
SEA	Single European Act
SEAQ	Stock Exchange Automated Quotation
SERPS	State Earnings Related Pension Scheme
SFA	The Securities and Futures Authority
SFF	Supplementary Financing Facility
SIB	Securities and Investments Board

SMU	Support Measurement Unit
SRO	Self Regulatory Organisation
TB	Treasury Bill
TDI	Total Domestic Income
TEC	Training and Enterprise Council
TESSA	Tax Exempt Special Savings Account
TFE	Total Final Expenditure
TPI	Tax and Price Index
TSA	The Securities Association
TSB	Trustee Savings Bank
UAA	Utilised Agricultural Area
USM	Unlisted Securities Market
VAT	Value Added Tax
VER	Voluntary Export Restraint
VSTF	Very Short Term Financing Facility
WIRS	Workplace Industrial Relations Survey
YES	Youth Employment Subsidy
YOP	Youth Opportunity Programme
YTS	Youth Training Scheme

Countries are abbreviated in tables and figures in accordance with the originals. The following abbreviations are used:

Belgium	B
Denmark	DK
France	F or FR
Greece	GR
Ireland	IRL
Italy	I or IT
Luxembourg	L
Netherlands	NL
Portugal	P
Spain	S or E
United Kingdom	UK
West Germany	FRG or WG or D

Preface to the First Edition

We very much hope that the justification for writing a book of this kind is self-evident. If this is not the case, then we simply wish to point out that economic literacy remains at far too low a level in the UK. In seeking to enhance this literacy we like to think that this book will be of interest to a very wide-ranging audience, but we recognise that, in practice, almost all those who read it will be studying a parallel course in economic principles, either at 'A'-level or as undergraduates, or will already be acquainted with economic issues either through their work or their reading of the financial press. We hope that the book is sufficiently challenging to interest readers who are already conversant with economics, but not so challenging as to prevent readers who are not conversant with economic theory from following the discussion.

We have tried to strike an acceptable balance between **analysis** and **description**. It is obviously necessary, in a book of this kind, to describe how the UK functions at the present time, and also how it has functioned in the past where this has been different. It is, however, unilluminating simply to explain what is done in policy terms without simultaneously explaining why, and the reasons why are also to be found in the book where appropriate. It should be noted that the kinds of models to be found in textbooks may often fail to explain why many policies are being pursued, because the real world may be evolving very rapidly and be using fairly crude rules of thumb whilst coming to terms with these changes. It is accordingly our intention to concentrate upon the real world, and to give short shrift to textbook models which cannot shed much light upon it.

Most readers familiar with economics will have been taught the subject as a succession of separate boxes labelled 'employment', 'inflation', and so on. There is, as a consequence, a preference for applications to be organised into similar boxes, to be dipped into one by one as appropriate. We do not care for this approach because, first, it fails to emphasise the **fundamental linkages** between the various parts of the economy; secondly, it fails to deliver a satisfactory **historical perspective**; and thirdly, it permits the authors covering the content of separate boxes to offer a **subjective interpretation** of events which conflicts with that to be found in other boxes. Rather oddly, some books consider this latter point to be a virtue, and express distaste for the imposition of monolithic structures. Our view is that this is very much a vice, and is indicative of lack of editorial control. This book is accordingly approached from precisely the opposite viewpoint – namely, that individual authors should work to a carefully predetermined structure and that stylistic differences should be kept to a minimum. In particular, each author has been asked to set out the pros and cons of every policy debate without prejudice. This does not mean that the authors do not have strong preferences concerning the conduct of policy, nor indeed that they have refrained from expressing them, but rather that they do not seek to persuade by omitting to mention what the counter-arguments are.

The issue concerning the need to provide a framework which integrates individual sections has been difficult to resolve. One innovative feature in this respect is the introductory chapter which seeks to provide both a philosophical basis and an historical perspective for all that follows. A second innovation is to set the discussion of fiscal and monetary policy at the end of the book, in Chapter 12, so that it draws together the macroeconomic threads from previous chapters, with Chapter 11 doing the same for the microeconomic threads.

The early chapters presume least prior knowledge, but where necessary they are extensively cross-referenced to later points in the text where the missing information is to be found. Issues which can broadly be said to concern welfare have been allocated a chapter of their own (Chapter 10), rather than ignored altogether or dispersed in brief and unrelated sections throughout the text.

Certain themes inevitably appear under several chapter headings – for example, the development of the Single European Market. Generally speaking they are left dispersed, but cross-referenced to other parts of the book where the same themes recur. However, in certain cases – for example, agriculture – it has made more sense to collect the themes together under one heading in order to avoid duplication and the loss of continuity in the discussion. For these reasons, the structure of the book may at first sight appear unusual, but we firmly believe that it does, in fact, make better sense than the structures to be found in other texts, and we leave it to the readers to judge for themselves (and hopefully to let us know their opinions on the matter in due course).

Whilst the book is essentially about the UK economy, it has a stronger international flavour than is commonly associated with books on this topic. This reflects a whole host of developments, such as the Single European Market and deregulation in general, which are making it increasingly inappropriate to view policy within the physical confines of the UK alone. Since this is very much a feature of ongoing policy we have deliberately set up our discussion so that it offers clear pointers towards the future, and we have chosen to compensate for this by saying much less than is usual about the more distant past.

In our opinion the election of the current government was a significant watershed in policy terms, for reasons set out in the Introduction. Each chapter is accordingly structured to say relatively little about the period before 1969; to provide a fairly detailed review of the decade 1969–79; and to focus primarily upon the decade 1979–89 and especially upon how it has compared with the decade which preceded it.

All this places great demands upon the handling of data. We have tried to introduce as much data as possible, and to locate it all within the appropriate context rather than relegate it to appendixes. Equally, we recognise that tabular material can be boring – and, at times, a poor means of communication – so where appropriate other methods of presentation have been used. A point to be emphasised is that data is expressed in the form normally used by government and reported in the media. Thus, for example, the Public Sector Borrowing Requirement (PSBR) is not simply stated as an absolute number but as a percentage of GDP. Much of the data is adjusted for inflation, and whenever space permits the comparable data for other countries is also included.

The contributors to this book (other than the editor) have been chosen because they are knowledgeable in their fields. However, too much knowledge can be a vice as well as a virtue when it comes down to the need to compress a great deal of information into a small space, and the authors are commended to you not so much because they are 'specialists' but because they have proved in their previously published work that they have the facility to communicate to the target audience for this book. We hope that it makes enjoyable reading. No doubt you will let us know if that is not the case. One way or the other the editor is more than happy to accept ultimate responsibility for the entire finished product, although individual authors are responsible only for the chapters which bear their name.

Finally, I would like to thank Gordon Hughes and the other five anonymous reviewers for their thorough dissection of the text in its varying stages of completion. There is a myth – propagated, one suspects, by those who write only short articles – that textbooks are not refereed adequately, but that has been far from the reality in this particular case. Whilst some suggestions for improvement have been set aside for this edition, it is anticipated that they will be incorporated in the second edition.

Any restructuring of the text in subsequent editions will be determined entirely by the suggestions of users, and these are accordingly welcomed by the editor.

PETER CURWEN

Preface to the Second Edition

Armed with reviews and a large number of questionnaires completed by teachers, we have set out to revise the text significantly for this second edition. Whilst not every suggestion for improvement has been adopted on this occasion, we are already considering how best to manage the book's evolutionary path.

It is important to begin by clearing up one particular misunderstanding. Although it is hoped that many readers will be able to enjoy the text without having previously learned economics in a formal way, we anticipated that most readers would use this book in conjunction with a basic text on economic theory, thereby allowing us to concentrate upon its applications in the real world. The text contains such models as are essential to assist both the general reader and students of economics who are reading ahead of their main text to understand the issues which we address, which can be very complicated, but it is simply impractical to try to combine detailed theory and applications in a single text.

We have attempted to keep the text as up to date as is humanly possible. To this end we have introduced a large amount of new data, particularly in the form of Figures, whilst removing a much smaller amount which appeared in the first edition. We believe that this database provides a truly comprehensive overview of the workings of the UK economy. In recognition of recent developments we have included a good deal of additional material on the European Community, and have sought wherever possible to draw comparisons between the performance of the UK and other member states.

The editor has chosen in this edition to take over responsibility for writing all of the first nine chapters in the book, two of which have been divided compared to the first edition as a result of the addition of much new material. This should ensure greater uniformity of approach, and also ease the burden of revision for future editions. The new material is generally intended to introduce developments which have taken place over the past two years, but completely new sections have also been added where it was thought that it would enhance the discussion in a material way. For example, there is a new section devoted to the housing market in Chapter 3, which is accompanied by a fuller discussion of the link between wealth, consumption and saving, and Chapter 2 contains a completely new version of the overall model of the economy.

It is hoped that these, and other, improvements have enhanced the usefulness of the text for a wide variety of readers. As before, the text has been thoroughly reviewed in draft form in order to ensure that this is so, and we would like to thank the reviewers for their extensive and helpful comments.

PETER CURWEN

Acknowledgements

The authors and publishers wish to thank the following for permission to use copyright material.

Bank for International Settlements for Table 6.5.
Bank of England for Tables 3.9, 3.10, 4.2, 6.1, 6.4, 6.10, 7.8, 12.2, 12.5 and Figures 2.7, 2.8, 3.3, 3.5, 3.8, 3.10, 4.2, 4.4, 6.3, 6.7, 6.8, 6.11, 6.15, 6.16, 12.1.
Barclays Bank for Table 6.11 and Figures 3.25 and 6.18.
Controller of Her Majesty's Stationery Office for Tables 2.1, 2.2, 2.3, 2.4, 2.5, 2.6, 2.7, 3.1, 3.2, 3.3, 3.4, 3.5, 3.8, 3.11, 5.1, 5.2, 5.3, 5.4, 5.6, 5.7, 5.8, 5.9, 5.10, 5.11, 6.2, 6.3, 6.6, 6.7, 6.8, 6.9, 6.10, 7.5, 8.1, 8.2, 8.4, 8.5, 8.6, 8.7, 9.1, 9.2, 9.3, 9.4, 9.5, 9.6, 10.1, 10.2, 10.3, 10.5, 10.6, 11.1, 11.2, 11.6, 11.8, 11.9, 11.12, 11.13, 12.1, 12.3, 12.4, 12.5, 12.7 and Figures 2.4, 2.5, 3.1, 3.2, 3.9, 3.12, 3.14, 3.15, 3.16, 3.17, 3.18, 3.19, 3.21, 3.22, 3.23, 3.24, 5.1, 5.2, 5.3, 5.5, 5.6, 5.7, 5.9, 5.10, 5.12, 6.1, 6.4, 6.5, 6.6, 6.10, 6.12, 6.14, 7.3, 7.4, 8.1, 8.2, 8.3, 8.4, 8.5, 8.7, 8.8, 8.9, 8.11, 8.12, 9.3, 9.4, 10.3, 10.5, 10.6.

Council of Mortgage Lenders for Table 4.4.
Dun and Bradstreet for Table 3.12.
Euromoney for Figure 4.8.
Financial Times for Table 10.9 and Figure 7.7.
Information Division, HM Treasury for Table 3.6 and Figure 3.13.
Institute For Fiscal Studies for Tables 10.7 and 10.10 and Figures 3.19 and 10.4.
Noel Alexander Associates for Tables 4.3 and 4.5.
Organisation for Economic Co-operation and Development for Tables 3.7 and 7.17 and Figures 3.6, 3.7, 3.20, 3.21, 8.12, 8.13.
The Economist for Figures 2.6, 4.7, 5.4, 5.13, 6.2, 6.9, 6.13, 6.17, 7.8, 7.9, 7.10, 7.11, 7.13, 8.10, 9.1.
UBS Phillips & Drew for Figure 8.14.

Every effort has been made to trace all the copyright-holders, but if any have been inadvertently overlooked the publishers will be pleased to make the necessary arrangement at the first opportunity.

■ Chapter 1 ■

History and Politics

Peter Curwen

■ 1.1 Introduction

Our purpose in this chapter is to set the scene for the detailed analysis of the UK economy which is the subject matter of this book.

Economics has become increasingly technical, in an attempt to build ever more sophisticated models which tend to lose touch with the behaviour of economic agents in the real world. This, in its turn, has tended to detract from the need to study the historical and political context within which policy-making actually takes place. This book, however, is entirely about the real world, and therefore requires the reader to have at least a rudimentary understanding of economic history and political systems. This chapter sets out to provide this understanding and may, therefore, readily be omitted by those already well versed in these fields.

Economic ideas, in common with those of many other disciplines, tend to pass through successive phases of **revolution** and **evolution**. The revolutionary phases are often associated with a particular event, such as the publication of a book, although the seeds of the ideas may have been sown a great many years earlier awaiting the ideal moment for germination. Furthermore, it is not altogether easy to pinpoint when a revolution is set in motion since there is inevitably a great deal of inertia before revolutionary ideas gain widespread acceptance. The subsequent discussion is concerned primarily with the Keynesian and monetarist revolutions. The former is generally associated with the publication of the *General Theory* in 1936, but for our purposes is more sensibly seen in policy terms as underpinning the significant changes which took place between 1944 and 1949. The monetarist revolution flowered during the 1970s and came of age in the UK during the early years of the period of Conservative rule commencing in 1979, and it is indeed for this reason that 1979 is treated as the watershed year for the text as a whole.

The evolutionary phase of Keynesianism lasted broadly from 1950 to 1970, at which point events (discussed below) conspired to bring about its steady demise until its official replacement by monetarism. Monetarism, on the other hand, barely had the chance to evolve at all before significant aspects were consigned to virtual oblivion, leaving the UK in a kind of policy limbo – part-monetarist, part-Keynesian and part whatever seemed to be a good idea at the time to deal with short-term problems.

It is important to appreciate, to begin with, that there are two quite divergent ways of looking at those economic models which are put into practice. The first, clearly enunciated by Keynes himself and generally favoured by the kind of intellectual circles in which he moved, is that the ideas of economists and political philosophers are the **driving force behind the implementation of policy**. Support for this viewpoint can be found in the influential doctrine of laissez-faire during the nineteenth century, and subsequently in the writings of Keynes himself. The opposing doctrine is that economists have a barely detectable influence on society as a whole, since the popularity of particular ideas ultimately depends upon their compatibility with economic and political circumstances at the time. In other words, the broad direction in which economic policy moves is determined by the ways in which **interest groups in society respond to changing economic opportunities,** and economic models are chosen because they lend intellectual support to the behaviour of those groups.

The debate between these two schools of thought will, naturally, never be satisfactorily resolved because it is hard to see how either case can be 'proved' to everyone's satisfaction. An interesting current illustration of this debate relates to the case of privatisation, where it is possible to argue, on the one hand, that the policy was adopted as a result of years of ear-bending in influential Conservative circles by the Institute of Economic Affairs and other like-minded groups and, on the other, that once the decision had been taken to reduce the role of government and to cut public expenditure, asset sales were simply one available means to achieve these goals.

A variety of economic models are analysed in the chapters which follow. However, it is at best unhelpful simply to model the economy at a specific point in time, as though it can be divorced from the historical and political context which shaped it over a period of many decades. Indeed, it is possible to argue that many of the key influences moulding the way the economy behaves today have their origins well back into the nineteenth century, but a shortage of space does not permit us to examine these other than in a fairly cursory way.

■ *1.2* The Neo-classical World

At the end of the nineteenth century the **forces of the market place** still largely held sway over economic life. Certainly, government had been taking on board ever wider responsibilities which needed to be financed through taxation, but macroeconomic management of the kind practised after 1945 was incompatible with the prevailing 'neo-classical' orthodoxy.

This held true, for example, with respect to unemployment. The mechanisation of agriculture at the turn of the century forced large numbers of people off the land and into towns and cities. There were, understandably, difficulties in absorbing this inflow of labour into the industrial workforce, and the prevailing orthodoxy therefore needed to explain the adjustment process whereby the level of employment would be restored to equilibrium. The line taken by the neo-classical school was that, in a competitive market system such as characterised the UK economy at the time, the **equilibrium condition was one of full employment.** In other words, any imbalances between the supply of, and demand for, a factor of production such as labour could be only temporary, since any imbalance between the two would automatically trigger forces in the market place which would bring them back into balance. The forces in question were **changes in relative prices,** such that if there was excess demand for a factor of production its price (its wage in the case of labour) would be driven upwards until the point was reached at which potential purchasers would be induced to switch over from demanding the new, relatively expensive, factor of production, to others which in the process had become relatively cheap. Likewise, the price of a factor of production in excess supply would be driven steadily downwards, until a level was reached at which all that was being supplied at the price level was purchased.

Given its resurgence in the modern context of **supply-side economics,** it is important to appreciate what interpretation this line of argument placed upon the concept of full employment. What the neo-classical model was effectively saying was that if the market for labour was left to its own devices, a wage rate would be established such that anyone who was willing to work would have a job to go to, and employment would in that sense be permanently 'full'. By implication, all unemployment could be treated as **voluntary** because the individuals in question must either be unwilling to work at **any** wage rate, or willing to work, but only at a wage rate higher than what the market was prepared to pay. There would always be enough potential jobs to employ everyone willing to work, it was simply a question of finding the market-clearing wage. However, if some individuals chose not to accept that wage, then clearly they were preventing the market from functioning smoothly, in which case they were themselves the **cause** of the problem of unemployment. Since they were the cause, and a cure was readily available were they willing to accept a reduction in their target wage rate, it could not by implication be anyone else's responsibility to deal with unemployment. Hence there was no need for governments to intervene in the labour market.

1.2.1 Real and Money Magnitudes

Within the neo-classical model a crucial distinction was made between **real** and **money** magnitudes. The total **volume** of labour – or of any other factor of production – in employment at any one time was regarded as a real magnitude, governed by the price of one factor relative to that of others. If all other things remain equal and if a unit of labour cost £1 whilst a unit of machinery cost £2, then labour was half the price of capital and would be employed in preference to capital. This would be wholly unaffected by a doubling of the **general price level**, with the prices above rising to £2 and £4 respectively, since labour would remain one half of the price of capital per unit employed, and indeed this would hold true were prices in general to rise by a multiple of 100 or 1000 times. The **volume** of labour would remain constant whilst the total monetary **value** of labour used would vary enormously.

It followed that there was no direct link between the general level of prices and the level of employment. Nevertheless, there had to be a reason why the general price level showed considerable volatility over time, and the reason was called the **Quantity Theory of Money**. The original, or 'old' version of the Quantity Theory was formulated within the context of a monetary system called the gold standard. This meant that the total amount of money available was directly related to

the available stock of gold – originally on a one-to-one basis but, subsequent to the widespread adoption of the principle of credit creation, in a fixed proportionate relationship. Hence, if more gold was put into circulation, but no more real goods and services, prices in general would be driven upwards in order to ensure that the available stock of money would remain just sufficient, **and no more**, to purchase the available stock of goods and services. This applied equally well in reverse, with prices falling when the output of goods and services increased but no new supply of gold became available.

1.2.2 Mass Unemployment

The return of the labour force from active military duty after 1918 coincided with a sharp downturn in economic activity resulting from a combination of matters such as an overvalued exchange rate, ageing technology and increased world-wide competition. Industries such as coal-mining suffered badly. Motive power was switching from coal to oil, and deep-mining in Britain was very expensive compared to the costs of newly-opened mines elsewhere. The coal-mine owners sought to resolve the problem by forcing their coal-miners to take a reduction in their wages. However, the miners resisted, going on strike in 1921 and triggering the General Strike of 1926. They were ultimately defeated (hindered, in part, by the lack of of a welfare system to fall back on in hard times) but many mines were nevertheless forced to shut down. This was paralleled in other industries and, as a result, there was widespread unemployment in the UK at a time when other economies were booming.

Although the depression which began in the UK in 1919 was by no means typical (the overvalued currency was a critical factor not found elsewhere), it did provide food for thought for many economists brought up in the neo-classical orthodoxy, amongst them John Maynard Keynes. The neo-classical model was steadily amended and refined, and within Keynes's *Treatise on Money*, published in 1930, one can detect a distinct step forward along the evolutionary path of the existing orthodoxy at precisely the point in history when events conspired to expose the model's inadequacies, for in 1929 there occurred the Wall Street Crash.

Unfortunately, the response of most governments after the Great Crash was to do all the wrong things. In particular, America rapidly introduced an era of trade protectionism to which other countries responded in kind, with the result that the total volume of world trade fell sharply. It has also been argued by writers such as Milton Friedman that the American Federal Reserve System deliberately engineered a shortage of liquidity, thereby making it very difficult for debtors to obtain the money they needed to settle their debts. Irrespective of the causes, the effects were straightforward enough. Unemployment rose sharply throughout the Western World, the impact falling particularly upon towns and regions overdependent upon traditional heavy industries such as shipbuilding.

In the face of mass unemployment the neo-classical orthodoxy effectively broke down. To argue that millions of people could be got back to work simply by lowering the wage rate, thereby restoring equilibrium in the labour market, seemed futile in the extreme. But on the subject of what else could be done the model was largely silent. The time was at last ripe for the seed of revolution to grow.

■ 1.3 The Keynesian Revolution

This revolution was associated with the work of Keynes, and in particular with the ideas expressed in the *General Theory of Employment, Interest and Money*, published in 1936. The *General Theory* is a book of baffling obscurity – which some argue was deliberately introduced in order to get the central, simple, propositions accepted whilst the arguments raged about interpreting the complexities. The standard textbook version essentially dates back to the model introduced after the Second World War, and it is certainly only fair to argue that Keynes himself, who died in 1946, would have made significant alterations to his text had he lived longer. Nevertheless, there can be little dispute about his main lines of attack upon the neo-classical orthodoxy.

In the *General Theory*, Keynes set out to demonstrate that the level of National Income – and hence effectively of output and employment – was determined by the **interaction of changes in both real and monetary variables,** and also that there was a direct link between decisions taken by **individual households and firms** and the effect upon the **economy as a whole**. The cornerstone of Keynes's work was the rejection of the reasoning which led in the neo-classical model to the automatic restoration of full employment; the creation of an alternative theory which in the general case would generate less than full employment; and the use of that theory to explain how unemployment could be cured.

One of the main innovations of the Keynesian model was its stress upon the role of **expectations in the face of uncertainty**. Keynes felt that decisions with respect to the expansion or curtailment of output were to a considerable degree dependent upon the prevailing set of expectations about the future held by households and firms. In the event, for example, that firms in general did not expect an early recovery from a period of recession, their natural reaction would be to hold back from producing output which they did not expect to be able to sell, and to lay off workers whom they could no longer gainfully employ. The consequence of such a policy would be significantly to reduce the amount of money which households had to spend since, insofar as it existed, State assistance was not as rewarding as full-time employment. The consequent cut-back in consumption spending would adversely affect retail outlets, which in turn would reduce orders from wholesalers, and the latter would cut back orders from manufacturers.

The curtailment of output and employment undertaken in the expectation of a fall in demand for goods and services would thus itself create the expected circumstances of reduced consumption. In other words, expectations have an in-built tendency to be **self-fulfilling,** and in so doing they inevitably help to generate a further set of **similar expectations**. The confirmation of a firm's expectations that it would not be able to sell what it produced would thus probably cause the firm to curtail output and employment still further. The link between decisions taken by households and firms, and their consequences for the economy as a whole were, therefore, plain to see.

This line of reasoning tended to imply that the level of employment was affected by the prevailing set of expectations. But there seemed little enough reason to suppose that the prevailing state of expectations would always be such as to secure full employment. The neo-classical model argued that full employment could always be restored by reducing the wage rate. But suppose the wage rate was indeed to fall as it recommended, the result would logically be a reduction in the amount of money available for current consumption, which in turn would lead inevitably to a reduction in sales and profits. The Keynesian model argued that firms would respond by **cutting** output and employment. Since this was exactly the opposite conclusion to that postulated in the neo-classical model, the inevitable conclusion was that full employment could not, in fact, be restored through changes in relative prices.

The one undisputed fact of the early 1930s was that the Great Crash and its aftermath had resulted in depressed expectations. It was not that firms did not want to expand on an individual basis, but if one firm produced more output, created new jobs and paid out more in wages at a time when other firms did not follow suit, then almost all of the extra wages would be spent on the output of other firms rather than that of the firm paying out the wages, thereby inevitably driving it into bankruptcy. Of course, if all firms chose to expand simultaneously there would be enough extra wages in circulation to keep them all in business, but that could happen only if their expectations were simultaneously to improve, and in the climate of the early 1930s that was simply not going to happen.

It followed logically from this that full employment could be restored if either households unilaterally decided to spend more money – for example, by running down accumulated savings – or firms decided to invest in more capital machinery. But if neither group was willing to behave in this way, the needed improvement in the climate or expectations would have to be engineered by some other party. Clearly, the only other party capable of achieving this was the **government**.

The implication was that full employment could be restored only if the government created a demand for goods and services. This, however, flew straight in the face of the neo-classical orthodoxy and, somewhat curiously, given the part played by Keynes in this tale, the UK government was particularly disinclined to accept the need for increased government spending.

□ 1.3.1 A Matter of Debt

But what other objections, apart from a simple-minded belief in the neo-classical model, were there to increased government spending? The answer was that increased spending not covered by increased taxation meant that the indebtedness of the government would have to increase. In general, public expenditure was not expected, unlike private investment, to be self-financing over time. Hence balancing the fiscal books was held to be the soundest way to behave.

In advocating government spending in excess of tax revenue, Keynes was not, however, suggesting that borrowing to get the economy on the move again was to be regarded as anything other than a temporary measure. The idea was that once public spending and the consequent increase in income and employment had generated more optimistic expectations, the simultaneous expansion of private sector organisations would once again be restored as the driving force behind economy activity, thereby allowing the government to cut back its own operations and to use revenue from the newly expanded tax base to redeem at least part of the outstanding debt.

In fairness to Keynes, it should be said that his view of the world was one in which a small group of public-spirited intellectuals would operate economic policy with wisdom, discretion and foresight. His was not a world of fiscal profligacy; debt was perfectly sensible so long as there was an intention to repay, to balance the books over the longer haul. But spending other people's money proved to be more enjoyable than spending one's own, especially as it helped to keep politicians in elected office, so acceptance of the belief that there was nothing particularly immoral about debt *per se* was turned around and used in evidence against him. Politicians in office all agreed that debt **ought** to be repaid, but they could not see any political advantage in doing so, especially as the interest payments might fall due during another political party's period in office.

In practice, it is probably fair to argue that it was the Second World War, rather than the *General Theory*, which accounted for the demise of neo-classicism in the UK. Elsewhere the Nazis in Germany were behaving in a thoroughly Keynesian way by the mid-1930s, and the New Deal was implemented in the USA, albeit with far less effect because the desire to help the disadvantaged had to compete with the desire not to run budget deficits. However, unemployment remained extremely high in the UK, especially on a regional basis (thereby providing further 'evidence' of labour market inflexibility), until the government was forced, despite itself, to rearm. Even then it was well into 1941, the second year of the War, before all of the unemployed could be absorbed into 'productive' work.

□ 1.3.2   *The New Order Cometh*

By the end of the Second World War the Keynesian revolution had inexorably entered into its 'orthodoxy' phase, common to all advanced Western economies for roughly 25 years. Not surprisingly, the sacrifices of the war years served to speed up enormously the process of social change. Under no circumstances was there to be a re-run of the 1930s, which meant that a clear priority had to be given to the eradication of unemployment. On the whole, the expectation was that, once the economy was restored to a peacetime footing, there would be considerable problems in switching the labour force into civilian occupations. The concept of 'full' employment was not, therefore, an immediate objective. The *White Paper on Employment* in 1944 talked in terms of something less ambitious, but for once the reality was an improvement upon the expectation. Naturally, the initial period of postwar reconstruction was bound to generate exceptionally high levels of demand in the short term. But the maintenance of demand in the longer term

would obviously need the government to play a more active role via demand management, which would have the characteristics established in the Keynesian model, namely short-term, counter-cyclical fiscal policy. Monetary policy would also need to be short-term and counter-cyclical, but would have little to do bar keeping down the interest rate in order to cheapen the cost of borrowing for investment.

But the Keynesian revolution was not simply an issue of macroeconomic objectives and instruments. It was an era in which voters turned away from markets, which were perceived as **efficient** but **inequitable**, in order to create a fairer and more just society. Although Churchill, who had led the wartime government, was a Conservative, there was nevertheless a massive swing towards the Labour Party, which had almost completely displaced the Liberals. The era of the Welfare State had arrived.

■ 1.4 Efficiency versus Equity

The postwar years have been characterised by contradictions within the processes of macroeconomic control, but one must not lose sight of the underlying debate about the role of market mechanisms. The Keynesian model effectively discarded the view that a modern advanced economy could be left to its own devices, and ushered in the era of the 'mixed economy'. But there are clearly an enormous variety of ways in which one can draw the boundaries between private and public sectors, and a great deal therefore hinges upon the balance between **efficiency and equity at the microeconomic level.** At the end of the day there are very few goods and services which cannot be supplied efficiently by the market mechanism – in the sense of maximising output for given inputs – but the amounts of goods and services produced, and their allocation between households, may be considered inequitable from a wider social perspective. One may naturally respond by arguing that concentration upon the issue of equity does not of itself necessitate any conflict with the objective of maximum efficiency, and indeed it is clear that the introduction of the Welfare State presupposed that no serious conflict would occur. But efficiency in the market is dependent upon the profit motive, and the profit motive has to be subjugated to the wider 'public interest' if equity issues are to be given greater priority.

This line of argument can best be clarified by a concrete example. Before the Second World War the health service largely required payment to be made at the point of consumption. Its size, therefore, depended upon people's willingness and ability to pay, but insofar as there was a demand for the service it could be provided very efficiently. The National Health Service (NHS) was introduced because this level of provision was felt to be both inadequate and inequitable, but equity – or so it was thought – could be maximised only by providing health care free at the point of consumption. Theoretically, there was no reason why this expanded provision could not be delivered as efficiently as before, but logically this would be true only if the motivation towards efficiency was generated as strongly by the pursuit of the public interest as by the pursuit of profit. At the time this was taken for granted, because it was felt that there was a consensus within society that the public interest should transcend private interests. In setting up the NHS, in expanding education and welfare services and in taking industries into public ownership, very little thought was thus given to the issue of objectives and how best to achieve them.

In retrospect this was, at best, unfortunate, but it reflected the widely held view at the time that a transfer of ownership from private to public sector would be sufficient to guarantee an improvement in performance. For example, there was bound to be a better relationship between managers and workers in an industry once it had been transferred to public ownership, since the owners would no longer be seeking to squeeze every drop of profit out of the workers. There would be no more General Strikes, no more trouble in the coal industry the long-term future of which would now be assured. Regrettably, hardly anyone observed that the coal-miners themselves had no greater personal stake in the industry post-nationalisation than had existed previously. Indeed, if anything, they had even less of a stake since wages and jobs were no longer directly related to the profitability

of the industry. It would thus be in their personal interests to try to raise their wages even if it resulted in the industry making losses. They might well prefer not to take this action because, for example, there was a government in power which had their wholehearted support. But if another, less appealing, government took power, or if the economic environment became so problematic that any government would be forced to try to control wages, then confrontation would almost inevitably occur. In such a situation it would be vital for someone to re-establish control, whether management or ultimately government. Yet to re-establish control there needed to be an **effective** system of control established in the first place, which even a cursory glance at the statutes governing the nationalised industries or the NHS demonstrates not to have been the case.

A further aspect of the 'efficiency versus equity' debate to which insufficient attention is paid relates to the distributions of income and wealth, and their implications for tax regimes. So far we have discussed the Keynesian orthodoxy largely from the expenditure side, but if public spending is to rise appreciably then it will be necessary to raise taxes, in which case one needs to stress the issue of **whom or what to tax**, and how onerously the individual taxes are to be applied. Once one starts out with the premise that a greater degree of equity is needed, it follows logically that the primary purpose of taxation, other than simply to finance expenditure, is to **redistribute**. That requires a strong element of progressivity to be present, most obviously in the income tax and inheritance tax schedules. But this in turn has implications for efficiency, since it affects the incentives to work and to take risks.

One further point is worth emphasising at this stage, before we return to the historical narrative. No matter what macroeconomic control system is adopted, it must send out both explicit and implicit signals at a microeconomic level. In a market system the signals are primarily in the form of **changing prices**, and this will remain true of many goods and services which are publicly provided even though the prices in question are not market prices. The **absence** of a price – as in the provision of health care – sends out an equally strong signal.

When one compares different societies with roughly equal wealth, one should **expect** to find different consumption patterns. This is because in one society a good may be taxed or subsidised where in the other society it is not. If, for example, mortgages and pension contributions are subject to tax relief, one should hardly be surprised to discover that the most popular forms of wealth are houses and pensions.

To summarise this part of the argument, what we are saying is that the macroeconomic model, whether Keynesian or otherwise, requires one to look deeply into its microeconomic implications, and this is why in later chapters we will be looking at tax regimes, industrial policy, welfare provision and other related matters.

1.5 Employment, Trade and Inflation

As we have indicated above, the primary focus of the Keynesian model was upon the level of unemployment. However, it followed logically that if there was insufficient demand for private sector goods and services, and a consequent falling off in the level of employment, then the new jobs created by public spending in order to maintain full employment would tend to be in the public sector – that is, in central government, local government and the nationalised industries. And if the prevailing orthodoxy held that any shortcomings in the operations of private sector bodies needed to be remedied by government in order to promote the cause of **social justice** (and sometimes **efficiency**), then the mix of the mixed economy was logically going to become weighted increasingly towards the public sector and away from the private sector. But the Keynesian model did not of itself imply a significant long-term shift, since public expenditure was meant to come to the fore only during recessions. When the economy was booming it could even be necessary for the public sector to be cut back in order to dampen down excess demand in the private sector.

So why did the upsurge in public spending happen in every major European economy? One obvious reason is that elected politicians saw themselves as elected to change things for the better, and this was bound to cost money. Furthermore, a consensus about the desirability of improving equity and welfare was incompatible with sharp cuts in public spending, since no element of such spending could be cut without causing someone somewhere to lose his or her job. Yet if the government could not bring itself to make cuts, the political opposition had little choice but to differentiate its product by promising to spend even more, and to resist any cuts which were on the agenda.

This argument had particular implications for employment policy. In principle, the objective of giving everyone a job could be fulfilled independently of locational issues. In other words, if an industry shut down in the North and another simultaneously expanded in the South, full employment could be maintained by moving the redundant workers to the new location. However, this inevitably meant both short-term hardship for those required to move and probably long-term decline in the areas where firms shut down. In countries such as West Germany these consequences did not trouble politicians overmuch, but in the UK they were considered to be unacceptable, and steps were taken, even by Conservative governments ostensibly dedicated to free market principles, to prevent them – through, for example, the rescue of lame duck industries.

The according of primacy to the objective of full employment also created other kinds of difficulty. The maintenance of high levels of demand in order to sustain full employment had implications for other important policy objectives, in particular for inflation and for the external trading position as reflected in the balance of payments. The existence of inflation and of deficits in the balance of payments needed to be examined from the point of view both of cause and of cure. Unfortunately, the Keynesian model had nothing useful to say about inflation because it had been formulated during an historical period when prices were tending to fall rather than to rise, and there seemed to be no obvious reason in theory why the demand for labour could not be expanded to absorb the available supply without bidding up its price.

Nevertheless, inflation did exist throughout the 1950s and 1960s, albeit at a fairly modest level, so in many ways the simplest thing was to do very little about it and to hope that it would go away. Every now and again prices would rise unusually sharply, and something would need to be done about it, but on the whole there were more important things to worry about. In particular, high levels of demand tended to be associated with high levels of imports, the more so as the UK became increasingly unable to compete internationally with respect to her manufactured goods. Now a balance of payments deficit can be dealt with in a number of different ways:

1 the **domestic economy can be deflated** (expenditure reducing) so that there is less demand to spill over into imports.
2 the **price of imports can be raised**, and that of exports lowered, via an alteration in the exchange rate (expenditure switching)
3 **artificial restraints on trade** can be introduced, such as tariffs and quotas on imports or subsidies to exports.

In the event the remedy mentioned in 3 was available on only a short-term emergency basis, because the UK was a member of GATT (General Agreement on Tariffs and Trade) which required free trade to be pursued whenever possible. Solution 2 was available within the terms and conditions of the adjustable-peg exchange rate regime introduced near the end of the Second World War (1944) at Bretton Woods. Unfortunately, it was considered to be a sign of failure for a country to lower its exchange rate, and so it was a policy to be avoided except as a last resort for fear that the government so doing would lose votes. But this left only solution 1, although its implementation meant that the level of aggregate demand would have to be cut back, thereby adversely affecting output and employment.

Given the higher priority assigned to full employment than to the external balance this could obviously be tolerated only for the minimum period compatible with restoring the balance of payments into better shape, whereupon demand would need to be expanded again in order to restore full employment. However, since this procedure had done nothing to deal with the underlying causes of the problem – namely an uncompetitive economy

– but only with its symptoms in the form of a balance of payments deficit, the symptoms were obviously going to recur once the economy was back at full employment again. A succession of periods of demand expansion to create jobs followed by demand reduction to control imports thus became the dominant characteristic, known as **stop-go**, of UK economic policy during the 1950s and 1960s.

1.5.1 Fiscal Versus Monetary Policy

As we have indicated, the level of aggregate demand was largely manipulated via **fiscal means**, and monetary policy had relatively little to do. However, its assigned role – namely, low interest rates to foster investment – was somewhat incompatible with a world in which inflation was a persistent phenomenon, since rising prices implied the need to **raise interest rates to deter consumption financed by credit**.

In the USA during the late 1950s, Professor Milton Friedman at Chicago University and others began publishing material which indicated that the money supply was the all-important monetary aggregate on which the authorities would have to concentrate their attention if they wished to have any meaningful control over economic activity. Friedman argued, in particular, that the role of monetary policy during the Great Depression had been widely misunderstood. The orthodox version of events held that the US monetary authorities had pursued aggressively expansionary monetary policies between 1929 and 1933, but that these policies had proved ineffectual. Friedman, on the other hand, contended that the monetary authorities had pursued highly **deflationary** policies. According to his research, the quantity of money in the United States fell by one-third during the course of the Depression, thereby providing clear evidence that monetary policy was extremely effective in regulating the level of economic activity rather than the reverse.

At the heart of Friedman's work lay the **New Quantity Theory** which represented a modernised version of the neo-classical model, linking the money supply to **money national income** (the volume of (real) output at current prices). In his model, most commonly known as **Monetarism**, real output resulted from decisions taken primarily by households and firms in the private sector, and could not be adjusted by demand management. Since real magnitudes were ultimately unaffected by the supply of money, the latter was directly linked only to the rate of inflation, and became its primary cause.

However, the fact was that in trying to elevate inflation to become the primary focus of economic policy Friedman's time had not yet arrived, particularly where the UK was concerned, although his ideas caught on more quickly elsewhere. Just as the Keynesian revolution had to wait for the neoclassical orthodoxy to break down in the face of mass unemployment, so the monetarist revolution had to wait upon a breakdown of the Keynesian orthodoxy. But for the moment at least, the Keynesian facade seemed impregnable. Quite simply, in an atmosphere of 'you've never had it so good', one does not seriously question the view that the prevailing orthodoxy has helped to bring this about. True, the UK economy had grown slowly by comparison with most other comparable countries, but growth was rapid by comparison with previous periods in the UK. True, there were periodic balance of payment crises which deflected the economy off course, and inflation was also ever-present. But jobs were freely available for those who wanted to work, and most people's standard of living was rising steadily. It was not a time for revolution, even in ideas.

The issue of inflation remained largely ignored, both in academic and political circles. This passive view of the problem was reinforced when, in 1957, A. W. Phillips published an article discussing what henceforth became universally known as the **Phillips Curve**. The Phillips Curve suggested that inflation need not be considered as an independent problem, but its real importance lay in the fact that up until that point in time the Keynesian model contained no theory of inflation. Given that inflation was treated with rather more indifference than it merited, this missing link did not prevent the model operating to most people's satisfaction. Neverthe-

less, the apparent message of the Phillips Curve that there was a predictable trade-off between employment and inflation (thereby offering, in effect, a 'menu' of choices between combinations of employment and inflation) appeared considerably to simplify economic policy. The government simply had to choose the particular **level of aggregate demand** which would generate the **target level of employment**, and a predetermined amount of inflation would simultaneously be generated. The price level could, therefore, be regulated to a lowly place in the pecking order of economic objectives, since in choosing the target value for the primary objective one could not be thrown off course by an unforeseen rate of inflation as one could by the balance of payments.

Unfortunately, at the end of the 1960s the situation began to deteriorate alarmingly. The rate of inflation began to rise sharply, and to register a value well above what had been predicted on the basis of the Phillips Curve. At first the authorities understandably treated this as an aberration, arguing that the original relationship between unemployment and inflation would shortly be restored. But when employment was allowed to rise slightly to help rein back inflation, it did not have the desired effect, and a new phenomenon appeared known as **stagflation** – namely, rising prices at the same time as rising unemployment. This phenomenon clearly needed to be explained within the context of the Keynesian model, but the model was found wanting. After 25 years its Achilles heel had been exposed.

Rather ironically, it was precisely at this point in time, at the beginning of the 1970s, that the exchange rate mechanisms introduced at Bretton Woods began to break down, to the point at which the UK felt obliged, in 1972, to move over to a floating rate (albeit a 'managed' one). This meant that balance of payments crises could now be dealt with via the exchange rate rather than via deflation (given the political will to accept currency depreciation), and thus allowed more freedom for demand to be managed in order to maintain full employment. But raising demand at a time when inflation was roaring ahead was not really a sensible option, and the quadrupling of oil prices by

OPEC helped send the inflation rate soaring to 24 per cent in 1975, as well as causing significant damage to the balance of payments. The Labour government in power at the time was unable to cope with these pressures, particularly as the foreign currency reserves were inadequate for the purpose, and turned for help to the International Monetary Fund (IMF), a body which was sympathetic to the monetarist doctrines now coming into vogue. The price exacted in return for assistance was that the UK economy would have to be subjected to a dose of monetarism, with tight control over the money supply and a tight fiscal policy keeping demand in check.

It was rather ironic that a Labour Government should be the first to apply monetarist doctrines, since its underlying philosophy was hardly right-wing. Nevertheless, it was as much imposition as choice at the time (or at least that was how the government excused its behaviour) and an inevitable effect was what, from the government's point of view, was a highly undesirable further upturn in unemployment. Indeed, the attempt to impose fiscal discipline, and to control inflation via a prices and incomes policy, ultimately led to the 'winter of discontent' and to the government's downfall. It was replaced in 1979 by the first Thatcher Government, which for the first time deliberately chose to make a version of monetarism the key plank of UK economic policy.

1.6 The Brief Reign of Monetarism

As previously indicated, the Keynesian orthodoxy collapsed in the face of a persistent rate of inflation well above the rate predicted by the Phillips Curve, and into the vacuum created by the failure of the model stepped the monetarist 'revolution'. It is important to remember that monetarism was a reworking of the neo-classical model rather than a totally new approach, and that it was not 'invented' after 1970. As with the Keynesian model, it had been advocated for many years prior to that, but few people were altogether persuaded by it. In particular, it must be borne in mind that its underlying philosophy placed particular emphasis upon **markets,** and played down very heavily the role of government as prime mover in the economy.

It would be fair to argue that the Conservative Government under Edward Heath was sympathetic to the doctrine of the free market, but at the end of the day it did not have the conviction to let markets have their head. Indeed, it is an interesting aspect of the Heath Government that it took Rolls Royce and British Leyland **into** public ownership rather than let them be destroyed by the forces of the market, thereby demonstrating that expediency was often a stronger factor than polemic in political manifestos. The Thatcher Government was different in that it set out determinedly to apply monetarism as a philosophy, relying heavily upon the evidence that the lax monetary policy introduced during the Heath Government's term of office had been responsible for the inflationary boom of the early 1970s. However, what the Thatcher Government did not at first realise was just how difficult this was going to be. Because monetarism is about markets, it is clearly much more than simply a statement about the money supply and the macroeconomy, and in that respect it becomes difficult to form a judgement as to its success or failure since some parts of the philosophy may work quite well whilst others may need to be discarded as unworkable. Whether what remains at the end of this process is still monetarism is, therefore, highly debatable, and we need to shed some light on this issue below.

Viewed in terms of macroeconomic policy monetarism is fairly straightforward. It contends that the price level is the most important economic objective because real variables such as employment can best be stimulated in the context of a non-inflationary environment. However, whilst zero (or near-zero) rates of inflation assist in the generation of employment through their positive impact upon the prospects of the private sector, demand management is either self-defeating (because of crowding out) or a recipe for accelerating inflation. The only way to control the price level is via the money supply. Hence it follows that the growth of the money supply should be geared to the expected growth rate of real output, which thereby makes it possible to buy any extra output at the **existing** level of prices. The balance of payments can be left to its own devices by allowing the exchange rate to float freely, thereby ensuring a tendency for it to self-equilibrate.

However, certain points flow obviously from the above. First, governments must resist the temptation to create money by **spending more than they earn** (running a PSBR), so fiscal policy must be viewed from the point of view of its consequences for the money supply rather than as a set of instruments to be managed in their own right. Fiscal policy becomes **subordinate** to money supply control, thereby reversing the logic of the Keynesian model. Fiscal conservatism means balancing government spending against taxation. But markets are much better at determining what people want to consume than the bureaucrats in local and central government, so public spending must be kept under tight control. This in turn will permit taxes to be cut, which will leave more of their incomes in people's pockets and provide the incentive for them to work harder, thereby generating economic growth. This growth will eventually provide new jobs in areas of the economy where there is genuine private demand, represented by direct spending by consumers, rather than an artificial demand generated by government spending designed, for example, to keep technologically backward and internationally uncompetitive industries in business.

This approach is generally known as 'supply-side economics' because it rests upon the assumption that **supply must be created before demand** if there is to be non-inflationary growth within the economy (see Chapter 2 for a fuller discussion of these matters). At the microeconomic level, the philosophy has far-reaching effects. Individual households and firms must be made to stand on their own feet, to succeed or fail as the market for what they provide dictates. Those who fail may need to be helped by the government within reason, but not to the point at which failure seems to be a soft option. In particular, the loss of a job is dependent upon the forces of the market. Jobs may need to be preserved by workers taking wage cuts, workers may need to retrain or they may

need to move to where the work is (possibly on their bicycles). If institutions such as trade unions are less than keen about these developments then their power to prevent them must be destroyed, and that applies to professional bodies as well as to craft unions.

Not surprisingly these doctrines seem firmly rooted in the neo-classical orthodoxy where the individual is responsible for his or her own predicament, and it is not the job of government to get him, or her out of it. In other words, the postwar swing from efficiency to equity must be put into reverse gear. Efficiency is once again to be king, and those who are productive will be allowed to enjoy the fruits of their labour. To be rich is no longer socially unacceptable; to be poor is unnecessary, so poverty must be pushed back into decent obscurity.

1.7 The Thatcher Years 1979–90

As will be discussed below, as well as in the body of the text, the Thatcher years in office are open to a variety of interpretations. On the one hand, there has been a renewed debate about the theoretical underpinnings of both the Keynesian and monetarist models, and on the other there has been an increasingly bitter debate about the picture presented by the statistical data generated both by the government and by other sources.

We have already referred to the debate between demand-siders and supply-siders, but there has also been a reinterpretation of the Keynesian model in order to make it more compatible with the observed phenomena of the 1970s and 1980s. The adherents of this approach are usually known as new, neo- or radical Keynesians. In addition, there has arisen a school of thought known as 'New Classical Economics', which has much in common with monetarism but which differs with respect to, for example, the role of expectations. It is also probably fair to say that may economists take an eclectic view of the proceedings, accepting parts but not all of any one viewpoint. Under the circumstances it is hardly surprising that the government receives conflicting advice, and that it is never exactly clear which model – if any! – of the economy it is trying to implement. At various stages in the main text these models will be introduced and analysed briefly, although it is not the primary purpose of an applied text such as this to analyse these models in detail. Accepting for the moment that economic policy may, therefore, be driven as often by short-term expediency as by the logic of a specific model, it is nevertheless desirable to provide a summary of recent experience in the light of the apparent switch to a monetarist orthodoxy in the early 1980s.

One unchanging point of reference, explored fully in Chapter 10, has been the priority accorded to the **control of inflation**. In the early Thatcher years this was seen as the task assigned to the money supply, but that has now altered insofar as control of the money supply is widely (but not universally) seen as a failure. Indeed, the government itself declared, in June 1989, that it no longer intended even to compile the money supply measure favoured during the early 1980s called M3. For some time now the government has relied upon the **interest rate** as its primary means of regulating demand, a policy which has brought many attendant problems in its wake and which may or may not prove to be successful. In this latter respect it is important to note that there is no unanimity about the meaning of the term 'success'. For example, it is possible to argue simultaneously that the UK's growth record was good because it remained high by international standards for many years, and that it was bad because the level of output barely rose above the level achieved at the time the government first took office. Equally, the inflation rate did fall to well below 5 per cent at one stage, the soaring money supply notwithstanding, but it never showed any sign of getting down to below 1 per cent and remained above that of many of the UK's main competitors.

The Thatcher Government certainly achieved its aim of fiscal conservatism, turning its borrowing requirement into a debt repayment. However, there remains a body of opinion which believes that such behaviour was inappropriate (see the discussion concerning the repayment of debt in Chapter 10), and it is significant to note that this did not result from the intended reduction in government spending combined with a lesser reduction in taxation. Rather, in absolute terms, even after allowing for inflation, government spending rose with tax revenue rising even faster due to the phenomenon known as **fiscal drag** (all of which matters are discussed in detail in Chapter 4).

The **exchange rate**, in particular, presented ambiguities. The one certainty is that it was never permitted to float freely as it should in a basic monetarist model – which permits the advocates of such a model to contend that it has never been properly tested. There was an increasingly acrimonious debate about whether the UK should join fully in the European Monetary System (EMS) (see Chapter 6) – and indeed, more widely, about the UK's role in Europe.

At the microeconomic level there was a real attempt to deregulate or free up markets – indeed the UK is generally acknowledged to be the world leader in this respect, although Americans might remark that it would have been better not to have created so many areas which needed deregulating in the first place. Unfortunately, it is also the case that some of the worst rigidities (such as are manifested in the housing market) were not addressed at all successfully, and perhaps more importantly that the overriding impression given by the Thatcher Government was its interventionist and centralising stance in a wide variety of markets. At heart this reflects one of the most awkward realities of economic life – namely, the fact that since free markets are subject to abuse, the more free the markets the more they need to be regulated. This issue is addressed at various points in the text, for example with respect to financial markets in Chapter 4, and particularly in Chapter 11.

At the macroeconomic level, as already indicated, the Thatcher Government came to suffer from a shortage of instruments to control the economy, and hence it came to overuse – and arguably abuse – those that were favoured. Here again it is much easier to explain where the government went wrong than to provide a convincing alternative approach.

As has been noted above, the Keynesian model broke down in the face of exceptionally high levels of inflation. It can just as easily be argued, however, that the most telling indictment of monetarism was its failure to reduce unemployment to acceptable levels. The fact that during the Keynesian orthodoxy governments chose to live with permanently rising prices, and that during the monetarist orthodoxy they chose to live with heavy unemployment, may be put down to the forces of democracy – at the end of the day the electorate must vote for one particular party – but even democracy can be made to mean all things to all men, and it is possible to argue that votes are not so much cast in favour of policy packages as against the alternatives which are viewed as wholly unacceptable. Some reflections on political processes are contained in the section which follows, and also in Chapter 11. For the moment it is necessary only to reflect that the movement away from any kind of established orthodoxy and towards what may best be termed pragmatism may be the only way forward. As will constantly be reiterated in the course of the text, the world's economies are evolving very rapidly, and the model of last year's behaviour may provide a poor guide to the current year, let alone to the future. In the UK, the Keynesian orthodoxy lasted for three decades whilst the monetarist experiment lasted for well under one decade. For the moment revolution is unfashionable and evolution is the name of the game.

The UK has a new leader in the guise of John Major – at least until mid-1992. Unlike his predecessor he is no visionary and hence his approach to policy-making can reasonably be termed pragmatic. With a General Election a necessity by the time this book appears, the absolute Conservative majority may no longer exist, and a new era of policy-making may have been set in motion. If so, this will form a significant component of the next edition of this text.

■ 1.8 The Political Context

It is a reasonable expectation of a so-called 'democracy' that its citizens will constantly consider it to be their right – and possibly their duty – to exhort the government to adopt this or that economic strategy. However, what they often fail to appreciate is that in order to deliver economic policies one must first create a **political system** with that end in mind, and since there are many ways of devising such a system, its precise form is ultimately of great consequence. One simple point to make in this context is to ask whether the 'Thatcher revolution' would have occurred in any of the other seven major industrial countries had it not occurred in the UK – to which the answer must be a firm negative because it was critically dependent upon the political context of the UK. When, in the course of time, Mrs Thatcher's full term in office is retrospectively compared with that, for example, of President Reagan, there can be no doubt as to which of them will be judged to have had a more profound impact upon their respective economies. However, as we shall argue below, the odds were stacked in her favour before she began.

A crucial – though by no means unique – feature of the UK political system is that it involves a race to be 'first past the post' between a very small number of very strong contenders and a number of 'also-rans'. Each constituency race produces a single Member of Parliament who may well fail to be supported by a majority of those casting their vote, let alone of those eligible to vote. However, the fact that the majority of voters do not actively support the government's policies is not the key issue, but rather that this system permits of a government being formed by a political party with more MPs than any other party irrespective of whether it has been supported by the largest aggregate number of voters, and that once a government has been formed the level of electoral support is technically a non-issue until the electoral terms is over.

On occasion, the combination of a strong opposition party and the also-rans may muster enough MPs to outvote the largest party, but again the key issue is that this generally is not the case in practice, and that even when it is, the opposition parties are generally less than fully united in their political goals. The style of political debate is also inevitably highly adversarial, but this should again not be allowed to conceal the key point that when the fire and fury has died down, and the vote is taken, a government with an **absolute majority of MPs is always the official winner**.

Clearly, this system delivers extraordinary powers to a majority government. Constitutionally, the monarchy has no power of veto, nor does the House of Lords (the upper chamber) which can only debate and recommend. A simple majority of one seat in the House of Commons is thus sufficient (provided, of course, every MP is available to vote) to permit the government to steamroller through any legislation that it wishes, irrespective of whether or not it was mentioned in the campaign manifesto issued to voters. It is true that individual MPs can refuse to vote in accord with their party line, but the rules disallowing the use of private monies to 'buy votes' effectively mean that an MP who rejects a 'three-line whip' will lose the support of the party machine and later, if not sooner, lose his seat. It follows that, especially when a party has a small overall majority, MPs toe the line almost without fail rather than bring down their own government. As a consequence, backbench MPs have little effective power over economic policy, whilst a small section amongst them, appointed to the Cabinet, have a great deal. Furthermore, a Prime Minister, elected from within the ranks of MPs and hence inseparable from the party in power, can exercise exceptional power by using the threat of dismissal from the Cabinet to force recalcitrant members to do what he or she wishes.

This ability to steamroller policy through Parliament is both a virtue and a vice. It obviously permits of very strong government, and there can be no doubt that voters prefer a government with a clear sense of purpose, and a determination to put it into practice, to one which is constantly vulnerable to losing on a vote of confidence. But such power can easily be abused, and it follows that other parties can appeal successfully to voters only by differentiating their policies to a considerable degree from those of the government. Irrespective of how it intends to behave in practice, a party must in principle appear to be either right-wing or left-wing, so voters have no opportunity to opt for a package containing combinations of the two. Thus if the party in power advocates public ownership, opposition parties may feel obliged to advocate denationalisation, and vice versa.

☐ 1.8.1 Other Political Systems

We will return subsequently to comment upon the performance of government in the UK, but first it is salutary to compare the above analysis to political systems elsewhere. In the USA, which has a two main party, first-past-the-post system, the President is not, however, the leader of the party in power in the House of Representatives (often called 'the House'), but elected independently, and may well belong to the other party. If the House is unsympathetic he may, therefore, find it very difficult to get his Bills enacted. He, in his turn, has considerable power to veto Bills emanating from the House, so one rebuff may well be repaid in kind. The upper chamber (the Senate) is a powerful body in its own right, and may well be controlled by the opposite party to the House. A President, House and Senate (which together constitute the Congress) belonging to the same party is possible, but unlikely. In any event, because election is as much a function of the wealth and prestige of the individual as of the party machine, individual Congressmen and Senators quite frequently vote against their own party line. All this prevents the accumulation of too much power in too few hands, as was precisely the original intention, but it is not exactly designed to deliver priorities, such as cuts in government spending, since every politician, irrespective of party, in an area adversely affected by such cuts will automatically vote against the strategy.

In continental Europe there is **proportional representation** (seats allocated in proportion to votes cast). This effectively prevents any one party from getting an absolute majority over all others, which on the face of it should lead to weak government. On the other hand it follows that, as a general rule, a coalition must reach agreement on priorities which are common to all parties if it wishes to avoid government by crisis, and the important policies may, therefore, get carried out with all-party support even when there is fundamental disagreement about other matters. The obvious drawback is that these shared priorities invariably sit somewhere near the political centre, and if voters are unhappy about that they can express their disapproval only by voting for someone or something on the extreme of the political spectrum (fascist or communist).

If, on the other hand, the UK government thinks that the electorate want, for example, privatisation or a poll tax, then they can be delivered by the system. Critics complain that this is all very well and good, but that it enables the government to deliver such policies **irrespective of whether** they are wanted by the electorate. As Joe Rogaly put it (*Financial Times*, 11 May 1990):

> Generally speaking, we are cursed with short-termism, unnecessarily adversarial politics, excessive prime ministerial power, a civil service whose contempt for the average Member of Parliament, senior ministers excepted, increases every year, and policies based on batty idealogical notions.

Nevertheless it is questionable whether adversarial politics in the UK are as 'adversarial' as one might imagine. As we have indicated, each party must differentiate its product in principle, but what happens in practice may be a totally different matter. When one examines the economic records dating back to the Second World War, it is very difficult to pinpoint the years in which there was a change in the party in power. This arises for a number of reasons. In the first place, many priorities are shared. Until recently, there was little dispute about the need to keep down unemployment to its lowest possible level. The Welfare State was not imposed against the wishes of any major party, nor is the current view that the public sector has failed to deliver the exclusive preserve of 'dry' Tories. There may be disagreement about causes and cures, but that is bound to be true even within the ranks of a coalition government. Secondly, governments are by no means all-powerful, and may be forced to take involuntary actions. This may arise simply because the UK is not a particularly big player on the world stage and cannot, therefore, be insulated from the forces which buffet the world economy. No matter how healthy the

underlying economy, the UK cannot expect to grow much – if at all – at a time when other advanced economies are sliding into recession. More generally, the government may find itself in a losing battle with the forces of the market place. The government may, for example, wish to see the exchange rate rise, but if the foreign exchange market wishes to see the exchange rate fall that may well prove to be the ultimate outcome.

To sum up this brief discussion, the overall picture with respect to the UK is that it has a political system with enormous potential power to direct economic policy. The system could result in enormous swings in the direction of policy as each successive government seeks to undo what its predecessor has done, but this is unlikely to happen because many priorities are shared, and the external environment may not permit it. It should finally be remembered that for a government to spend its time in office removing its predecessor's legislation from the statute book is not merely very unconstructive, but may leave little time to enact new policies. In any event, many policies which the political system requires the opposition party to oppose may privately be approved of. Thus, for example, the Labour Party currently have no desire whatsoever to undo all the trade union legislation put in place by the Conservatives, although they do intend to undo some of it on a very selective basis. It is equally true that some desirable policies are simply too expensive to implement. For example, no future government could possibly afford to repurchase the shares of privatised companies even if, as is unlikely, they were prepared to devote scarce parliamentary time to that end.

□ *1.8.2 A Caveat*

We have noted that the UK Government has considerably more power at the centre than comparable governments elsewhere, and that this gives it the power to bludgeon the economy into submission. In recent months it has been necessary to bludgeon the consumer rather hard in order to get him or her to behave in ways the government considers to be desirable for the health of the economy.

Adam Smith, who should be mentioned in all self-respecting books on political economy, knew all about this two centuries ago. 'Consumption is the sole end and purpose of all production', he wrote in *The Wealth of Nations*. Elsewhere, he noted that England was 'a nation that is governed by shopkeepers'. Perhaps what Adam Smith should have said was that England is a nation of **shoppers**. The British do not habitually take to the streets to protest. Indeed, they do not even rush out to vote, especially in local elections. They know that irrespective of who governs them the shops will be full, and that they can express their position in society by what they buy. Britain has an amazingly efficient system of retail distribution – just compare it with that of Japan, a country which is much more efficient at **making** things but hopelessly inefficient at **distributing** them (they even have a law preventing the spread of department stores). One cannot see the Japanese agreeing with Adam Smith's assertion that 'The interest of the producers ought to be attended to, only so far as it may be necessary for promoting that of the consumer'.

If readers have seen old newspapers they will know that their primary function was to spread information about what was on offer. It is, therefore, hardly surprising that the demand side of the economy came to dominate economic thought, as in the work of Keynes, rather than the supply side. When Macmillan expressed the opinion that the British 'had never had it so good', he was being quite serious – governments are elected in Britain by keeping consumers happy. What consumers want is low interest rates, rising real incomes and not much inflation. That some people are unemployed no longer seems to have much effect upon voting patterns. You do not go to the country when the housing market is flat, as Mr Major well knows. What he also knows is that the rampant consumer is a match for government unless the latter is willing to wield its policy weapons in a consumer unfriendly way. We will have much more to say about these issues as the story unfolds throughout the text.

■ *Chapter 2* ■

The Macroeconomy: 1

Peter Curwen

■ *2.1* Introduction

In the course of this book we will be examining a great many facets of the aggregate economy. Certain of these require detailed consideration, and hence have an entire chapter given over to their analysis. Others, however, require less detailed treatment, and it is our primary purpose in this and the subsequent chapters to bring them together at the earliest possible stage in the overall discussion. Whilst this necessarily means that these chapters are less cohesive than those which follow, they are essential pieces of the complete macroeconomic jigsaw puzzle. Indeed, one of the primary purposes of these chapters is to provide an overview of the entire jigsaw which must, of necessity, be put together in accordance with the picture on the lid. Unfortunately, as we shall soon discover, the picture on the lid is out of focus, so we can never be entirely sure that each piece is in its proper place!

The schematic figures which follow may well appear complex at first sight, especially to those with no prior experience of modelling the economic system. Nevertheless, it is worth observing that the 'Treasury' model which the government uses for forecasting purposes contains literally hundreds of equations, and there will, no doubt, be a number of 'academic' readers who feel that our schematics are far too simplistic. The only sensible response to this criticism is to point out that the recent record of both the Treasury and other models in forecasting such variables as the level of unemployment and the rate of inflation has been less than inspiring, so it is debatable whether accuracy is simply a function of the number of variables in the model. The obvious reason for this difficulty is that the behaviour of economic agents such as households and firms is constantly evolving, whilst forecasts are generally based upon measures of behaviour in past periods.

In the sections which follow we will be making use of the conventional distinction between **instruments**, **targets** and **objectives** of policy. It should, however, be noted that these will be treated in a more flexible manner than is the custom in introductory textbooks. The evolution of the UK economy over the past decade has turned many relationships upon their head, and engendered much controversy about the linkages – and especially the causality implied by these linkages – between different parts of the economic system. For example, it is clear that under certain circumstances both the interest rate and the exchange rate can be used as instruments (that is, as levers which, when pulled, set in train a sequence of changes in other variables, acting as intermediate targets, which ultimately cause changes in policy objectives).

However, interest rates and exchange rates are closely interrelated, as discussed below, so it is evident that one must be regarded as the instrument and the other as the target. Which is which depends upon how one sets up the system, so it is possible to argue that 'one model's instrument is another model's target'.

■ 2.2 The Internal Sector

The internal sector is modelled in **Figure 2.1**. It is essentially a Keynesian version of the model with the alternative version operating via the money supply discussed below. There are three objectives in the model, the rate of economic growth, the

Figure 2.1 *The Internal Sector: Demand*

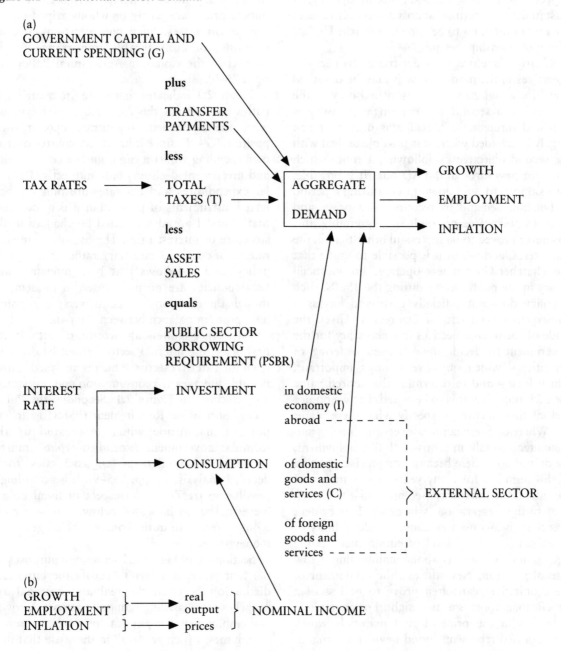

level of employment, and the rate of inflation. The route to all of these objectives passes through the box marked 'aggregate demand' (AD).

It is important, therefore, to consider whether an increase or decrease in aggregate demand will cause all three objectives to move simultaneously in the desired direction. Unhappily, this is not the case in practice. Whilst an increase in AD can be expected to increase the level of employment, at least in the short term, it almost always also causes the rate of inflation to become higher (the Phillips Curve relationship, see **pp. 74–5**).

Clearly, therefore, there are **trade-offs** between objectives in the model. Now it may be observed that, if one objective can be satisfied only at the expense of a second when a single pathway is followed through the model, this drawback can largely be avoided where it is possible to deal with the second objective by following a route which does not pass through the AD box. It is possible, for example, to hold down prices during a period of buoyant demand by recourse to a prices and incomes policy (see **pp. 464–5**). Regrettably, this has never proved to be successful other than in the short term, and whilst it is possible to argue that the Thatcher Government operated an unofficial policy in the public sector during the 1980s, such a policy does not officially exist and has as a consequence been left off Figure 2.1. Given the trade-off between objectives it is necessary for the government to decide upon a **rank ordering** of priorities – which objective is most important, which least – and to determine the **desired value** for each objective. It is to be noted that we do not seek at this juncture to specify what these might be. Whereas, for example, over-simplified arguments tend to talk in terms of 'full' employment, we do not do so here because the precise meaning of this term has for many years been a matter of considerable controversy (see **pp. 306–8**).

A further reservation is in order. It is evident that there is a consensus about the desirability of maintaining a 'high' level of employment in the UK, as indeed there is about maintaining a low rate of inflation. Nevertheless, the attainment of these objectives can often prove to be less of a benefit than appears at first sight. For example, a reduction in the price of raw materials which are imported represents 'good news' for a manu-

facturing nation such as the UK, since it helps to hold down costs, and hence inflation. It follows, however, that it must be very damaging to less-developed countries which export those materials. Such countries may subsequently prove unable to repay their international debts, which may partly be owed to the UK government and partly to UK banks (see **pp. 218–22**). But if there is a default on the debt any initial benefits derived from lower import prices are partly or wholly wiped out by subsequent losses. Such considerations are, for example, of considerable importance in the context of the Common Agricultural Policy (see **pp. 276–9**).

Figure 2.1 indicates that there are a variety of pathways through the AD box. In a Keynesian world the government concentrates upon its fiscal position (G – T) since it has direct control over its own spending whilst it can influence consumption and investment decisions only indirectly. Particular expenditures and tax rates are thus the preferred instruments of policy, but it is to be noted that C and I are also affected by changes in the structure of interest rates. The use of the interest rate is, of course, a monetary rather than a fiscal policy, and it follows that both monetary and fiscal policies are normally used in tandem, although there is constant controversy concerning the optimum balance between the two.

Two other matters are worthy of note. In the first place, the internal sector cannot be divorced from the external sector, which is analysed below. Possible linkages via consumption and investment are indicated in **Figure 2.1**. Secondly, the Public Sector Borrowing Requirement (PSBR) is an important magnitude which is created by the formula: government expenditure *plus* transfer payments *less* total taxes *less* asset sales (for a detailed analysis, see **pp. 165–9**). It is accordingly possible to treat it as an aspect of fiscal policy. Nevertheless, as indicated below, it is also commonly referred to in the context of changes in the money supply.

Section (b) of **Figure 2.1** serves two purposes. In the first place, it serves to clarify the important distinction between the **real** and **nominal** approaches to measuring economic activity. Growth and employment are physical measures, expressed as volumes, which are 'real' in the sense that they are measured independently of the prices at which they are sold. When a volume measure is multiplied by current prices it is converted into a money value, its 'nominal' counterpart. Hence the value of economic activity at current prices, or nominal income, changes because more activity is taking place (growth) at unchanged prices; because the same activity is taking place at higher prices; or because both output and prices are changing simultaneously.

Secondly, **Figure 2.1** serves to remind the reader of the feedback mechanisms which are ever-present in the model. As shown by the arrow at the foot, the level of consumption is itself determined in large part by the level of nominal income. Hence, when the level of consumption changes it changes the level of nominal income, as shown by the pathway through **Figure 2.1**, which in turn causes the level of consumption to change, which subsequently causes the level of nominal income to change and so forth (the multiplier mechanism, see **pp. 24–5**).

2.3 Money Supply and the Supply Side

As discussed in Chapter 1, the prevailing view that the UK economy is driven by demand in accordance with the Keynesian model became very unfashionable during the late 1970s, and was replaced by the view that the regulation of demand was more appropriately conducted via regulation of the money supply. The controversy this engendered is set out fully in Chapter 12, and need not concern us in detail here. What we do need to bear in mind is that a primary objective of economic policy during the 1980s was to reduce inflation, and that it was argued that this could be achieved via a tight regulation over the growth of the money supply.

This is illustrated in **Figure 2.2** where the direct link runs from aggregate demand to inflation, whereas the link from aggregate demand to growth and employment is shown as a broken link in-

Figure 2.2 *Money Supply and the Supply Side*

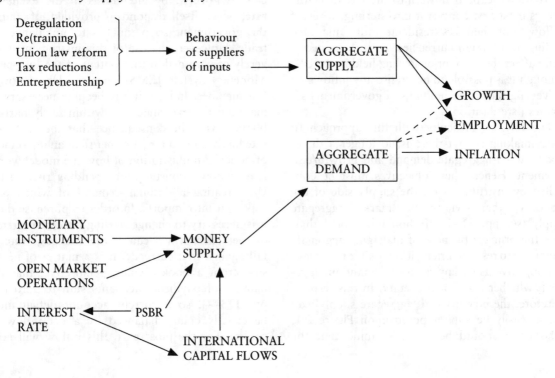

dicating that aggregate demand was not, in general, being manipulated in order to affect these variables. Given the perceived direct link between the money supply and aggregate demand, it is evident that the money supply now becomes an intermediate target of policy (see **pp. 466–9**). As such, it needs to be regulated via policy instruments such as open market operations, or other instruments such as credit controls or monetary base control (see **pp. 469–70**). However, it is also determined in part by the size of the PSBR insofar as this has implications for the way in which it is **financed** – that is, whether the method of financing creates new money or transfers existing money.

In other words, the fiscal stance which determines the PSBR has some bearing upon the money supply, as has the rate of interest which represents the cost of issuing or redeeming government securities (via an open market operation, for example). A sharp change in the size of the PSBR necessitates an adjustment to the structure of interest rates. When the interest rate changes it either attracts or deters a flow of international capital ('hot money'). This in turn affects the money supply, since if international capital flows into the UK then foreigners must first convert it into sterling, whilst if it flows out then UK residents must first turn sterling into foreign currencies. Both flows necessarily affect the amount of sterling held in the UK, although it is possible to neutralise any inflows by converting them into holdings of governments securities ('sterilisation').

The obvious difficulty with this approach to policy-making is that there is no longer a direct link between **aggregate demand** and **growth/employment**. Hence, these objectives must be controlled by instruments on the **supply side** of the economy – that is via the box marked aggregate supply (see **pp. 81–4**). It should be noted that, once the primary purpose of managing aggregate demand is to restrain prices, it is possible to achieve this objective using any form of demand management, whether fiscal or monetary. In this respect, therefore, the box marked 'aggregate supply' can just as easily be superimposed upon **Figure 2.1**, although it should be borne in mind that the general thrust of the Keynesian model is to enlarge AD whereas its role would have to switch to restraining AD if the objective were to control inflation.

■ 2.4 The External Sector

Let us now turn to the external sector, which is illustrated in **Figure 2.3**. This part of the model introduces additional complications, and it is evident that all kinds of difficulties can arise if policy is directed exclusively at resolving internal problems. Aggregate demand is increased by exports of goods and services, and reduced by imports of goods and services which form part of aggregate consumption in the internal sector. Exports can be subsidised (see, for example, the case of agriculture on **p. 264**) as a part of fiscal policy, whilst imports can be altered via the use of tariffs and quotas (not marked in **Figure 2.3** as they are currently of little significance, but see the discussion of the General Agreement on Tariffs and Trade on **pp. 257–9**).

More significantly, both imports and exports can be affected by alterations in the **exchange rate**, which itself responds – provided, of course, the government so permits – to imbalances in trade. However, the use of this instrument is severely constrained in the context of the European Monetary System (EMS) since the UK is now a full member. Indeed, it has become necessary to maintain the exchange rate within fairly narrow bounds with the consequence that the exchange rate has become a **target** rather than an **instrument** of policy. An illustration of how the model works is as follows: consumption spending rises in the UK, creating additional demand of which part leaks out into imports. In order to purchase these it is necessary to change sterling into the currency of the seller, which causes the exchange rate to fall against that currency. It is a matter of necessity, from a book-keeping perspective, that the balance of payments accounts sum to zero (see **pp. 173–4**), so a current account deficit must be exactly counterbalanced by a net inflow of capital. For the most part, this inflow will need

Figure 2.3 *The External Sector*

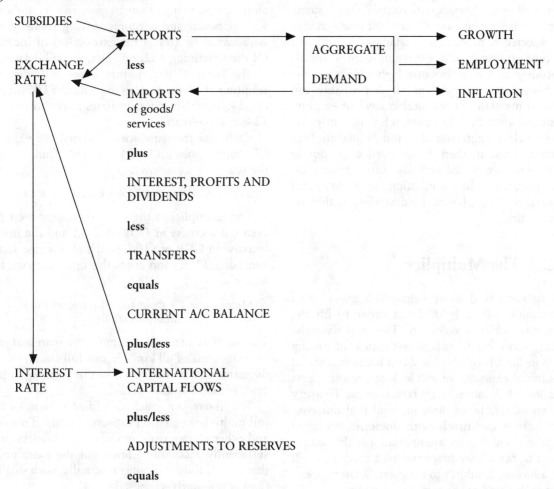

to be attracted in the short term by offering attractive rates of interest compared to those prevailing in the other financial centres, so a worsening current account deficit will result in an increase in interest rates in the UK.

As a consequence of these inflows the exchange rate is strengthened, and can be prevented from falling below the lower limit permitted under the EMS. The interest rate is thus the instrument and the exchange rate the target of policy. Unfortunately, the interest rate is also a primary instrument in the internal sector of the model, and by raising it a new disequilibrium is created in that sector. This, briefly, can be both beneficial and

detrimental. It is beneficial insofar as it will cause households to switch from consumption to saving, and hence help to eliminate the surge in consumption which probably created the original problem in the external sector. It is detrimental insofar as this, in turn, causes a fall in aggregate demand with consequent reductions in growth and employment. Furthermore, higher interest rates will deter investment and reduce aggregate demand yet further.

In the external sector this reduction in investment means that there is less need for medium- and long-term capital inflows to finance it, which sets off further changes in the system. The overall situation is clearly complex, but one conclusion above all others stands out, namely that a single instrument – in this case, the interest rate – cannot be expected to produce a satisfactory equilibrium in both internal and external sectors simultaneously. If it is sufficiently high to prevent the exchange rate from falling, it is probably too high to maintain an acceptable level of employment and growth. If, however, it is sufficiently low to stimulate aggregate demand, especially via more investment, then it may well exert downwards pressure on the exchange rate, causing import prices, and hence inflation, to worsen, and making it impossible to hold sterling within its EMS limits.

■ 2.5 The Multiplier

Let us suppose that we begin with government expenditure raised by £133 in order to lift the economy out of a recession. This will have the effect, according to official estimates, of raising GDP in the UK by roughly £100 because some of this initial expenditure will leak out into imports and some will immediately return to the Treasury as expenditure taxes. Bear in mind that our concern here is exclusively with **domestic** effects of spending, and that we are operating **at the margin** – that is, tax allowances have been used up so **all** extra income is subject to taxation. What happens next is depicted at the foot of the page.

As can be seen, the value of domestic output grows by £100, which in turn raises total factor incomes by £100. The major part of this is personal incomes, and of this part is saved and part goes in income taxation and national insurance. The residual part is profit which is partly distributed and partly undistributed. Profit is also subject

to taxation. At the margin, deductions from income are quite high in aggregate, and if combined with personal and corporate saving result in the withdrawal of £68 of the extra £100 of income. Of the remaining £32, one-quarter will disappear in the form of expenditure taxes and imports, resulting in an increase in the value of UK output of £24. This then raises incomes a second time by £24, and so forth.

Each time the sequence is repeated, the value of UK output goes up by 24 per cent. Thus, we get the sequence as follows:

£100 + £24 + £5.8 + £1.4 + £0.3 + . . . = £132

The **multiplier** is the relationship between the **eventual increase** in GDP of £132 and the **initial increase** in GDP of £100, which in this case has a value of 1.32. A short cut to this figure is to use the formula:

Multiplier = 1 ÷ the marginal propensity to withdraw (MPW)

The MPW is a technical term for the marginal rate of deductions of all kinds in one full circuit of the diagram, and is thus equal in this case to 76 per cent. Hence 1 ÷ 0.76 = 1.32.

The above is a much simplified version of the full multiplier equation expressed in the Treasury and other econometric models. Nevertheless, it is sufficiently accurate to bring out the basic point that the UK fiscal multiplier is actually much smaller than is popularly supposed.

■ 2.6 Crunchy Numbers

In what follows there is a great amount of data, wherever possible the most up-to-date available as at September 1991. Much of this data comes from

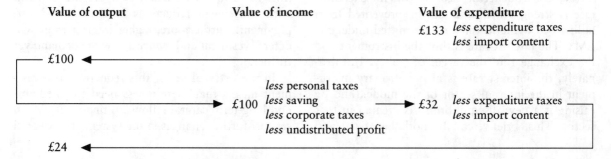

the Central Statistical Office (CSO). Over the past decade CSO statistics have become less reliable, primarily because the abolition of exchange controls has made it much more difficult to keep track of money moving in and out of the UK; because statisticians have failed to keep pace with the shift from manufacturing to services; and because the government has reduced the range of numbers it collects, partly to save money and partly to ease the burden of paperwork for business.

As a result the current figures published each month or quarter are subject to significant error. In many cases the practice is to insert a 'balancing item', which means that the money is known to exist, but for the time being (and perhaps for ever) it cannot be attributed to any particular category in a set of accounts. As time passes, missing money tends to turn up and it becomes possible to attribute balancing item money to specific categories. Hence, if we look back to 1979 we have a very good idea what was happening at the time. What we do not know too well is what is happening right now, yet that is precisely what we need to know if we are to manage the economy intelligently.

No doubt, by the time the next edition of this book comes out, the data in this edition will have been substantially revised, and it may be an interesting exercise for readers to look back to the previous edition and to compare the data for years up to 1989. Above all else, the reader should treat almost all the monthly data reported in the media with great caution since it is either inaccurate or distorted by non-recurrent items. The problem is that financial markets tend to be driven by the latest data, but the reader is advised to keep his or her knees firmly pressed against the table so that they cannot jerk in response to the often alarming but sometimes over-optimistic news about the state of the economy.

2.7 Introduction to National Income Accounting

It is possible to use some simple national income accounting to bring out a proposition of considerable importance to our later discussion. As a mat-

ter of definition, total spending on domestic goods and services (E) must consist of private sector final consumption (C) *plus* private sector investment (including houses) (I) *plus* government spending (G) *plus* spending on domestic goods by foreigners (exports (X)) *less* spending on imports (M).

Thus:

$$E \equiv C + I + G + X - M$$

In its turn, C is assumed to take place out of net-of-tax income (Y–T), and income which is not spent must, by definition, be saved (S).

Thus:

$$C \equiv Y - T - S$$

But Y and E are simply two alternative ways of measuring economic activity, as shown in the sections which follow.

Thus:

$$E \equiv Y \text{ and hence by substitution}$$
$$Y \equiv [Y - T - S] + I + G + X - M$$

Thus:

$$Y - Y + T + S - G - X + M \equiv I$$

Cancelling the Ys and rearranging the other elements gives

$$S + [T - G] + [M - X] \equiv I$$

In other words, **investment** in the UK economy must be **financed** either by domestic savings (S); a budget **surplus** (T – G); or by running a balance of payments **deficit** (M – X). In the latter case, this arises because the counterpart to such a deficit is an **inflow of capital** of equal size.

One element of this equation may appear to be puzzling, namely the assertion that a budget surplus can finance investment. Let us assume the external sector is in balance (X = M). If we also assume that savings are zero (Y = C + T), then some of the claims on income are transferred to the government in the form of taxes, and the only way in which the above equation can balance, which it must as a matter of definition, is if the government does not use up all of its claims on income – that is, T is greater than G – but makes some of them available for investment purposes.

■ 2.8 The National Accounts

□ 2.8.1 The Basic Building Blocks

The concept of 'aggregate economic activity' is clearly of fundamental importance for our understanding of how the economy works. Before any action is taken, the government needs to know what state the economy is in, and it needs to know retrospectively what difference was made by undertaking a particular course of action. In order to do these things we need a set of national accounts, and this is provided by the Central Statistical Office. It appears each year as the *UK National Accounts*, which is always known as the 'Blue Book' and which is published each September.

During the period between 'Blue Books', the CSO produces either monthly or quarterly data which appears in a variety of publications such as *Economic Trends*, the *Monthly Digest of Statistics* and *Financial Statistics*, and there are also periodic press releases. Unfortunately, the data appears under a wide array of definitions, and there is no choice but to explain what all the terms mean which the reader may come across in his or her reading, even though it may seem at times that they are infinite in number.

As with any system of accounts the 'Blue Book' records transactions in **money**. The value of a transaction can be approached in one of three ways, namely: the amount of money the buyer gives up to obtain a good or service (**expenditure**); the amount of money received by the seller (the value of **output** or **product**); the amount of money received in various forms by all those who contributed to the value of the end-product (**incomes**). These three figures must be equal *by definition*, since there is clearly only one sum of money involved in any given transaction.

If the value of all transactions is aggregated together we get the variable called **Gross Domestic Product** (GDP). This accordingly comes in three variants, namely GDP (E) where 'E' stands for expenditure; GDP (O) where 'O' stands for output, and GDP (I) where 'I' stands for income. It is important to bear in mind that the accounts are ultimately concerned with **final products** – for example, the sale of a desk in a shop to an end-user. However, there are a string of transactions prior to the final sales which might, for example, run as follows: raw materials sold to producer of semi-finished product; semi-finished product sold to producer of the finished product; finished product from factory sold to wholesaler; sold from wholesaler to retailer; and sold from retailer to customer. It would be seriously misleading to add all of these transactions together and to call them 'economic activity', since there would be elements of double, triple, quadruple, etc. counting involved. It is necessary, therefore, to use a **value-added** principle in counting. Beyond the raw material stage we add only the value added by each further stage en route to the end-user. In other words, we take the value of a transaction and **subtract** from it the value of the immediately preceding transaction in the above-mentioned sequence.

What we will end up with is the value of the final transaction at the price ruling at the time it takes place. This is known as the **nominal** or **money** value of the transaction. However, if precisely the same transaction takes place at a different point in time it is possible that the value of the transaction will be different because there has been a change in the price. In other words, the value of economic activity can go up over time because **more** goods and services are being sold at **constant** prices; because the **same number** of goods and services are being sold at **higher** prices; because **slightly more** goods and services are being sold at **slightly higher** prices, and so forth. In order to isolate the change in the **volume** of sales it is necessary to strip away the effect of rising prices by **deflating** the nominal value such that it leaves us with an inflation-adjusted magnitude. This so-called **real** value is thus measured in **constant-price** terms. It is necessary to select a base year for this purpose, which for most variables in this book is currently **1985**.

Measuring changes in the volume of output over time is a critical matter since this is the concept called **economic growth**. Obviously, therefore, the particular sequence of prices used to deflate money GDP is of some importance but, as we will discover below, there are many price indices which could be used for this purpose, and the reader must be careful to check which deflator is used when comparing, for example, growth rates in the media.

It is also the case that GDP and other measures of economic activity can be recorded in several ways. GDP at **market prices** is final output valued at the market prices at which it is sold. This is usually a greater magnitude than the sum of production costs (value added) because the government levies taxes such as value added tax (VAT) at the point of sale. In some cases the rate of VAT is zero so no difference will arise, and in some cases market prices are reduced below production costs because of subsidies paid by the government to producers. Thus we also need to take account of GDP at **factor cost**, which is equal to GDP at market prices *less* total **indirect taxes** and *plus* **subsidies**. In the national accounts, the sum of indirect taxes and subsidies is termed **Net Indirect Taxes**.

GDP, as the name suggests, is solely concerned with measuring the monetary flows generated by economic activity within the boundaries of the UK. However, UK residents may receive income from abroad, and there may be flows of money to foreigners as a result of domestic UK economic activity. GDP thus needs to be adjusted if it is to measure the total income available to UK citizens, which is called **Gross National Product** (GNP) and which is equal to GDP *plus* **Net Property Income from Abroad**.

Account must also be taken of the fact that part of the UK's stock of physical capital is used up over the course of a year. Buildings and machines may wear out through use (depreciation) or they may become outmoded by a technologically superior product and hence fall in value even though physically intact (obsolescence). **Capital Consumption** of these kinds must be replaced if the economy is to maintain its capacity to produce. When capital consumption is deducted from economic activity measured **gross** the residual is termed **net**, and GNP thus becomes Net National Product (NNP) whilst GDP becomes Net Domestic Product (NDP). These net figures express the value of resources generated in the course of a year which can be used either for consumption or to renew the stock of physical capital via investment. When NNP is expressed at factor cost it is customary to call it **National Income** (NI).

As noted previously, all three measures of economic activity must be equal as a matter of defini-tion. However, in practice, for each measure there are data limitations and measurement difficulties such that the estimates never do coincide exactly despite their conceptual equivalence. For this reason the CSO produces a definitive estimate known as GDP (A) where 'A' stands for average. For the period since the latest base year, GDP (A) is the unweighted arithmetic average of GDP (E), GDP (O) and GDP (I). If each of the measures of GDP is subtracted from GDP (A) it gives rise to a **statistical discrepancy** which is itemised in the accounts in order to bring all the individual definitions into line.

No matter how accurately economic activity is measured it is necessarily a flawed measure, insofar as it can take account of transactions only where a monetary flow is recorded – in other words, market activities. Where a transaction occurs, but no monetary flow is thereby generated, the transaction will not appear in the national accounts. Thus, for example, the accounts ignore all the activities of housewives; all do-it-yourself and all voluntary work. In the case of all illegal activity – and also where, for example, someone employed in the official economy 'moonlights' – there actually is a monetary flow when a transaction occurs but it is not declared to the authorities and hence does not appear in the national accounts. Such unrecorded flows are called the **black economy**. The national accounts hence substantially understate the true value of all economic activity, but provided the unrecorded part remains roughly the same percentage of the total then the rate of growth of recorded activity will still be correct. Problems could arise, however if, for example, reductions in tax rates caused unofficial activity to appear in the official market and hence to become recorded, since this would give the illusion that growth had suddenly taken off when in reality it was unchanged.

2.8.2 Measures at Market Prices: Effects of Introducing the Community Charge

GDP estimates for the year 1989 are affected by the abolition of domestic rates in Scotland and the introduction of the Community Charge there from April 1989. In the national accounts, domestic rates are classified as a tax on expenditure on housing services, and are therefore included in consumers' expenditure at market prices. The Community Charge, however, is classified as a separate category of transfer, which is treated as a deduction from income in calculating personal disposable income. It follows that the Community Charge is not part of consumers' expenditure.

Estimates of consumers' expenditure and of GDP at current market prices from 1989 are, therefore, marginally lower than they would have been if the Community Charge had not replaced domestic rates in Scotland. GDP at current factor cost is unaffected. Estimates at constant 1985 prices of consumers' expenditure and GDP are also unaffected. For a fuller description of the treatment of domestic rates and the Community Charge, and the impact of the switch from one to the other, see *Economic Trends* (August 1989).

2.8.3 The Expenditure Approach

The calculation of GDP, GNP and NI using the expenditure approach involves the measurement of all categories of expenditure in the economy. The sum of consumers' expenditure; investment – or, as it is referred to in the national accounts, gross domestic fixed capital formation (GDFCF); additions to work in progress; and general government final consumption – is equal to **Total Domestic Expenditure**. If total exports of goods and services is added to this, the total becomes **Total Final Expenditure** (TFE). However, not all of this expenditure is upon domestically produced goods and services, so in order to arrive at GDP it is necessary to deduct expenditure on imports.

It is conventional to value expenditure at the prices actually paid, which yields an estimate of GDP at market prices. If indirect taxes are subsequently deducted and subsidies added in, the end-result becomes GDP **at factor cost**. The further addition of net property income from abroad results in **GNP** at factor cost. Finally, the deduction of estimated capital consumption results in **NNP** at factor cost which is known as **National Income**

(NI) **expenditure based**. These relationships are set out sequentially in **Table 2.1**.

2.8.4 The Income Approach

Table 2.2 shows the alternative way of calculating GDP and NI in terms of income. Total Domestic Income is the sum of all incomes from employment; incomes from self-employment; gross trading profits of companies; the gross trading surplus of public corporations and general government enterprises; rent; and other (imputed) incomes. If the nominal increase in the value of stocks of raw materials and products is subtracted from TDI the residual becomes GDP (income based) and measures the income arising from economic activity during the year in question.

In order to reconcile the income-based measure of GDP with that based upon expenditure a statistical adjustment or residual error term is added, as noted previously. The resultant figure is measured at factor cost because it is literally a method of deriving GDP through the summation of incomes paid to factors of production. Further adjustments in order to calculate GNP, NNP and NI are exactly the same as for the expenditure-based estimate.

Tables 2.1 and **2.2** contain 'Blue Book' estimates of GDP for 1990 based upon both expenditure and income.

In 1990 GDP valued at current market prices was worth £550 bn. Much the largest share, at 63.5 per cent of GDP, consisted of consumers' expenditure. To this needs to be added government expenditure (19.9 per cent) and investment expenditure (19 per cent) in order to arrive at the share of GDP which is 'domestic'. The contribution of the external sector is counted net (–2.4 per cent) as the difference between exports (24.4 per cent) and imports (–26.8 per cent).

GDP at factor cost was valued at £477 bn in 1990, after adjusting market prices for the net impact of expenditure taxes and subsidies of £73 bn. Net indirect taxes thus accounted for 13.2 per cent of GDP at market prices.

The transition to GNP at factor cost requires the addition to GDP of net property income from abroad of £4 bn. In turn, GNP is reduced to NNP

Table 2.1 *1990 National Product by Category of Expenditure at Current Prices (£ bn)*

	Consumers' expenditure	349.4
plus	General government final consumption	109.5
plus	Investment expenditure	104.5
	of which:	
	Gross domestic fixed capital formation (105.2)	
	Value of physical increase in stocks and work in progress (–0.7)	
equals	Total domestic expenditure	563.4
plus	Exports of goods and services	134.1
minus	Imports of goods and services	147.6
equals	Gross domestic product (GDP) at market prices:	549.9
minus	Taxes on expenditure	79.1
plus	Subsidies	6.3
equals	Gross domestic product (GDP) at factor cost:	477.1
plus	Net property income from abroad:	4.0
equals	Gross national product (GNP) at factor cost:	481.1
minus	Capital consumption:	61.2
equals	Net national product (NNP) at factor cost or national income (expenditure estimate)	419.9
plus	Statistical discrepancy (expenditure adjustment)	0.7
equals	Net national product (NNP) at factor cost or national income (average estimate)	420.6

Source: UK National Accounts 'Blue Book' (CSO, 1991) Table 1.2.

at factor cost by the subtraction of £61 bn of capital consumption. This is the expenditure estimate of National Income, which can be converted to the 'average' estimate through the statistical discrepancy or expenditure adjustment.

GDP at current factor cost only for 1990 can also be calculated using the income approach, as in **Table 2.2** overleaf. Total Domestic Income (TDI) before deducting stock appreciation amounted to £484 bn. The largest share of this total (65.4 per cent) consisted of income from employment valued at £316 bn. After subtraction of £6.4 bn of stock appreciation from TDI we get an estimate of 1990 GDP at factor cost. This is fractionally different from the equivalent figure using the expenditure approach, so a statistical discrepancy or

income adjustment of £0.2 bn is needed to produce the estimated GDP (A) of £478 bn. The addition of net property income from abroad and the subtraction of capital consumption from GDP (A) produces the same figure for National Income as in **Table 2.1**.

□ 2.8.5 The Output Approach

As output has to be produced before either incomes are paid out or those incomes are spent, data on output is the first of the various estimates of economic activity to be published. It is customary to publish data on GDP (O), on a provisional basis, at quarterly intervals roughly three weeks

Table 2.2 *1990 GDP by Category of Income at Current Factor cost, £ bn*

Factor Incomes		
Income from employment		316.4
Income from self-employment		57.7
Gross trading profits of companies[1,2]		62.9
Gross trading surplus of pubic corporations and general government enterprises		4.3
Rent		38.4
Imputed charge for consumption of non-trading capital		4.3
Total domestic income[2]		484.0
minus	Stock appreciation	6.4
equals	Gross domestic product (income-based)	477.6
plus	Statistical discrepancy (income adjustment)	0.2
equals	Gross domestic product, at factor cost, average estimate	477.8
plus	Net property income from abroad	4.0
minus	Capital consumption	61.2
equals	Net national product at factor cost or national income (average estimate)	420.6

Notes:
[1] Before providing for (deducting) stock appreciation.
[2] Before providing for (deducting) capital consumption.
Source: UK National Accounts 'Blue Book' (CSO, 1991) Table 1.3.

after the end of the relevant quarter. Data is derived from estimates of physical output and survey returns from producers and is subject to considerable revision, partly in the light of subsequent and more detailed estimates of income and expenditure.

It is not customary to express output data in money terms, but rather as a series of index numbers, as in **Table 2.3**, which contains not only the series for GDP (O) spanning the period 1979–90 but also the series for various sub-categories of GDP (O). In the left hand column the total output in 1985 is assigned a weight of 1000, and each sub-category or part thereof is assigned a proportion of the total weight according to the proportion of GDP (O) which it contributed in 1985. Hence, it can be seen that the service sectors, with a weight of 578, accounted for 57.8 per cent of

1985 GDP (O), whilst the production industries accounted for 34.4 per cent and the manufacturing industries for only 23.8 per cent. This is not all that unusual for a major advanced economy where the service sectors are very unlikely to constitute less than one-half of total output. Indeed, the proportion is currently a lot higher in the USA.

It can be seen from **Table 2.3** that the service sectors as a whole rode out the 1980–81 recession without much difficulty at all, although distribution was hit fairly hard. By way of contrast, both manufacturing and construction fell back sharply. On the other hand, the 'other services' category grew at the same rate as manufacturing from 1981 onwards, despite their sharply contrasting experiences during 1979–81, and construction grew at the same rapid rate as transport and communications. The most unstable feature of the late 1980s

Table 2.3 GDP at Constant Factor Cost: Output Based Measure, Index Numbers of Output by Sector (1985 = 100)

	1985 weight in total output	1979	1980	1981	1982	1983	1984	1985	1986	1987	1988	1989	1990
Agriculture, forestry and fishing	19	76.8	85.3	87.5	92.3	87.3	104.7	100.0	97.4	98.2	97.8	101.3	104.4
Energy and water supply	106	82.5	82.6	86.5	91.6	96.8	88.8	100.0	105.0	10.39	99.3	89.7	88.8
Manufacturing	238	105.9	96.7	90.9	91.1	93.8	97.4	100.0	101.3	106.6	114.2	119.1	118.4
Total production	344	90.0	92.5	89.6	91.4	94.7	94.8	100.0	102.4	105.8	109.6	110.0	109.2
Construction	59	94.2	89.1	82.1	89.4	95.1	99.6	100.0	104.5	112.7	122.9	130.4	131.8
Services: Distribution, hotels, etc.	134	92.4	86.7	85.4	87.6	91.5	96.2	100.0	104.8	111.5	117.9	121.8	122.6
Transport and communication	70	92.2	90.5	90.7	89.6	91.6	96.1	100.0	104.3	112.5	118.5	125.3	128.0
Other	374	88.0	89.8	90.8	91.8	94.5	97.5	100.0	103.8	108.6	112.3	115.1	117.2
Total services	578	89.6	89.2	89.5	90.5	93.4	97.0	100.0	104.0	109.4	114.0	117.4	119.4
Gross domestic product (output based)[1]	1000	92.9	90.2	89.0	91.1	94.1	96.7	100.0	103.3	108.1	112.7	115.3	116.4

Note:
1 Adjusted for the statistical discrepancy this yields the index of the output of goods and services. This stood at 116.4 in 1990.
Source: UK National Accounts 'Blue Book' (CSO, 1991) Tale 2.4; Economic Trends, Tables 16 and 17.

has been the collapse of the energy and water supply sector which had breezed through the 1980–81 recession on the back of the discovery of North Sea oil. It can be seen that the agriculture, forestry and fishing sector barely affects total output, although it has a disproportionate effect upon policy making (as we will discover on **pp. 263–79**). Its poor performance since 1984 stands in stark contrast to the period 1979–84.

It is obviously possible to put a value upon the output of a given year, as is done for 1990 in **Table 2.4**. This has to be done on a **value-added** basis, as discussed previously, and this in turn requires that the data be collected on a factor cost basis which is recorded net of stock appreciation but before deducting capital consumption.

The level of disaggregation in **Table 2.4** is greater than in **Table 2.3**. Both contain a composite category for the energy and water supply industries, which in in 1990 was worth £24.3 bn and which represented 20 per cent of GDP (A). Of this total, the oil and gas industries contributed £7.7 bn. This can be compared with agriculture, forestry and fishing with its slightly smaller net output of £7.1 bn. In fact, this comparison is deceptive because oil and gas are sold in the free market whilst agricultural products are heavily subsidised, so the real contribution of the agricultural sector is much less than it appears to be on the basis of **Table 2.4**.

The contribution of financial services to GDP (A) is brought out clearly in **Table 2.4**. The figure of £26.7 bn indicates net interest receipts which need to be subtracted lower down **Table 2.4** because they do not contribute directly to net output. On a grossed-up basis the gap between the contributions of financial services and manufacturing is no longer all that large, and it can be expected to narrow further during the 1990s.

Table 2.5 serves to emphasise yet further the evolving nature of the UK economy. As can be seen in column (2), construction and services substantially outgrew production during the period 1980–90, with agriculture, forestry and fishing also performing rather poorly. It is true that the energy sub-category of production did especially badly in 1989 because of the closing down of North Sea oil capacity, but the trend to 1988 was not dissimilar.

Table 2.4   *UK GDP by Industry[1], 1990, £ bn*

Industry Category		Net Output
Agriculture, forestry and fishing		7.1
Energy and water supply		24.3
Of which:		
Extraction of mineral oil and natural gas	7.7	
Coal and coke	2.9	
Manufacturing		107.0
Construction		36.1
Distribution, hotels and catering; repairs		70.1
Transport and communication		34.0
Banking, finance, insurance, business services and leasing[2]		87.3
Ownership of dwellings (rent)		30.7
Public administration, national defence and compulsory social security		31.5
Education and health services		45.2
Other services		31.0
Total		504.3
Adjustment for financial services[3]		−26.7
Gross domestic product (income-based)		477.6
Statistical discrepancy (income component)		0.2
Gross domestic product at factor cost (average estimate)		477.8

Notes:
[1] The contribution of each industry to the gross domestic product (its value added), net of stock appreciation but before providing for (= deducting) capital consumption.
[2] Including net interest receipts by financial companies.
[3] The same as net interest receipts by financial companies.
Source: UK National Accounts 'Blue Book' (CSO, 1991) Tables 2.1 and 2.2.

Table 2.5 *GDP, Output-based Measure, Growth of Output by Sector, 1980–90*

	(1) 1985 Weight in Total Output[1]	(2) Percentage Change from 1980 to 1990	(3) Contribution to Change in Output 1980 to 1990 ((1) × (2))	(4) Percentage Share of Total Change
Agriculture, forestry and fishing	1.9	22.6	42.9	1.5
Production	34.4	18.1	622.6	21.4
Construction	5.9	42.5	250.8	8.6
Services	57.8	34.5	1994.1	68.5
Total Index of Output	100.0	29.1	2910.2	100.0

Note:
[1] Expressed as % of total weights in Table 2.3.
Source: UK National Accounts 'Blue Book' (CSO, 1991) Table 1.5.

After adjusting for the relative importance of the various sectors, as signified by column (1), it is possible to calculate, in column (4), the percentage share of the total change in output between 1980 and 1990 contributed by each sector. As can be seen, the service sector played a dominant role with the production industries lagging far behind. No doubt there are those who read into this dire implications for the future health of the UK economy, but it is worth observing that the 1980s were a very healthy decade for services, and that the issue is not merely whether the UK will be able to hold its own with respect to its residual manufacturing sector, but also whether the service sectors will be able to maintain their competitive advantage, especially in the field of financial services.

2.8.6 Real National Income 1978–90

The purpose of this section is to examine briefly real national income data spanning the full term of the three Thatcher Governments. This is presented in **Table 2.6**. **Table 2.6** culminates with an index of GDP (A) at factor cost. As can be seen, real GDP (A) fell back in 1980–81 before rising back to its 1979 level during 1983. Significant gains were made in every year from 1982 to 1989, but real GDP (A) rose only slightly in 1990 (subject to revision).

With real GDP actually falling during the latter part of 1990, and probably through most, if not all, of 1991, it is relatively easy to identify the roughly eight-year period during which the UK economy prospered in the course of an economic cycle lasting approximately one decade. During the upswing of the cycle real GDP rose by over one-quarter. In aggregate economic terms there clearly was no 'golden era' pre-Thatcher. As an economy, the UK is significantly wealthier than it was ten years ago.

Table 2.6 also demonstrates clearly that the economy was driven primarily by real consumers' expenditure, but the record on real investment, as discussed below, was excellent from 1983 onwards before subsiding back into the 1990–91 recession. Compare these figures with the proportionate increase in general government final consumption, and it also becomes evident that the 1980s were a decade when government turned its back on Keynesian demand management.

Table 2.6   *UK Real Domestic Product by Category of Expenditure at 1985 Prices[1], 1978–90, £ bn*

	1979	1980	1981	1982	1983	1984	1985	1986	1987	1988	1989	1990[2]
Consumers' expenditure	194.9	195.8	196.0	198.0	207.1	210.5	217.9	231.7	243.5	260.3	270.3	272.9
General government final consumption	69.9	71.0	71.2	71.8	73.2	73.9	73.9	75.3	76.2	76.6	77.1	78.4
Gross domestic fixed capital formation	56.5	53.4	48.3	50.9	53.5	58.0	60.3	61.5	67.6	77.2	80.2	78.7
Value of increase in stocks and work in progress	3.3	-3.4	-3.2	-1.3	1.4	1.1	0.8	0.7	1.2	3.7	2.2	-0.7
Exports of goods and services	88.8	89.0	88.3	89.0	90.8	96.8	102.5	107.3	113.4	113.7	118.8	124.5
Imports of goods and services	-84.0	-81.0	-78.8	-82.6	-88.0	-96.7	-99.1	-106.0	-114.3	-128.9	-138.3	-140.5
GDP (expenditure-based) at market prices	330.1	324.6	321.2	325.5	338.0	343.6	356.3	370.4	387.6	402.6	410.3	413.3
Statistical discrepancy	-0.2	-1.1	-1.9	-0.8	-1.2	0.4	-0.1	-0.6	-0.6	0.6	0.5	-0.2
GDP (average estimate) at market prices	329.9	323.5	319.3	324.7	336.8	344.0	356.2	369.8	387.0	403.2	410.8	413.1
Factor cost adjustment	-46.6	-45.3	-44.2	-44.9	-46.4	-48.4	-49.4	-52.0	-55.3	-57.6	-59.3	-59.8
GDP at factor cost	283.3	278.2	275.1	279.8	290.4	295.6	306.8	317.8	331.7	345.6	351.5	353.3
Index of GDP at factor cost, 1985 = 100	92.3	90.7	89.7	91.2	94.7	96.3	100.0	103.7	108.2	112.6	114.6	115.1

Notes:
[1]   For the years before 1983, totals differ from the sum of their components.
[2]   Forecast.
Source: UK National Accounts 'Blue Book' (CSO, 1991) Table 1.6; *Economic Trends.*

□ 2.8.7 *Exports and Imports*

Our discussion in this section is essentially concerned with matters internal to the UK, but it is worth picking up from **Table 2.6** a few pointers to the subject matter of Chapter 7 on international trade. As can be seen, the volume of exports remained almost totally static through the 1980–81 recession. It must be remembered that export demand is determined by spending power in other economies, and these did not nosedive anything like as steeply as the UK during this period. Furthermore, North Sea oil moved into excess supply and the UK was able to become a net oil exporter.

The effects of the recession on UK demand are clearly seen when one examines the real value of imports, which fell during 1980 and 1981. By 1983, however, imports had regained all this lost ground and were rising sharply once again as though nothing had happened. The rapid economic growth of the mid-1980s caused import demand to accelerate after 1985. In 1984 export and import demand were in balance after several years of exports exceeding imports. This balance continued up until 1987, after which import demand hugely outran export demand for two years. Some of the ground was recovered in 1990, but the gap remains too wide to be closed in the short term.

2.9 Sectoral Surpluses and Deficits

Insofar as it is of interest to take a periodic look backwards at the UK economy prior to 1979, an examination of sectoral surpluses and deficits is especially valuable. In part (a) of **Figure 2.4** the sectoral deficits of the overseas, public and personal sectors are plotted, **measured as a percentage of GDP** from 1970 to 1990. As can be seen, the **overseas sector** began the period modestly in deficit, ran up a big surplus at the time of the first oil price rise then settled around zero per cent until 1980. At the beginning of the 1980s, on the back of North Sea oil, it dropped sharply into deficit only to rise quickly back up to zero by the mid-1980s. From 1986 to 1989 it remained significantly in surplus, but that currently looks set to disappear by the end of 1991.

It should remembered that the overseas sector account tracks the movement of money and hence is the **mirror image** of the current account deficit or surplus. In other words, the current sectoral **surplus** represents a **deficit** on the **current account** of the balance of payments.

At the beginning of the 1970s the **public sector** was in surplus, but by the mid-1970s it had collapsed back into massive deficit. From 1975 to 1985 the situation was fairly stable, so the sudden upturn in 1984–85 was especially noteworthy given that it pushed the sector into surplus for the first time in fifteen years. Throughout the entire period the **personal sector** exhibited an almost exactly opposite pattern. It remained in surplus from 1972 to 1986, but from 1981 to 1988 the trend was almost continually downwards, amounting in all to a change of nearly 10 per cent of GDP. This was somewhat larger than the turnaround in the overseas sector, although the latter happened twice, firstly downward then upwards. The biggest turnaround of all was exhibited by the public sector, which exceeded 10 per cent of GDP, although this took much longer to complete.

In order to maintain clarity the industrial and commercial companies (ICC) sector is not plotted. From 1970 to 1982 this exhibited relatively little variability, oscillating regularly from a small positive to a small negative percentage of GDP. However, in 1982 it rose to 4.4 per cent of GDP and in 1983 began a decline which accelerated after 1986. By mid-1990 the turnaround represented 10 per cent of GDP.

It is evident from **Figure 2.4** that the various sectoral lines converged in 1986 for the first time since the turn of the 1970s. However, the 1986 convergence was more unusual in that all four sectors were in the throes of a significant unidirectional movement. For this reason the period from 1986 to 1991 is set out in more detail in **Figure 2.4 (b)**, where the graph represents the **absolute magnitudes** of each sectoral surplus/deficit (which would not be appropriate for the long-term series because of the distortions caused by inflation and the irregular growth of the economy).

Figure 2.4   *Financial Surplus/Deficit[1], by Sector*

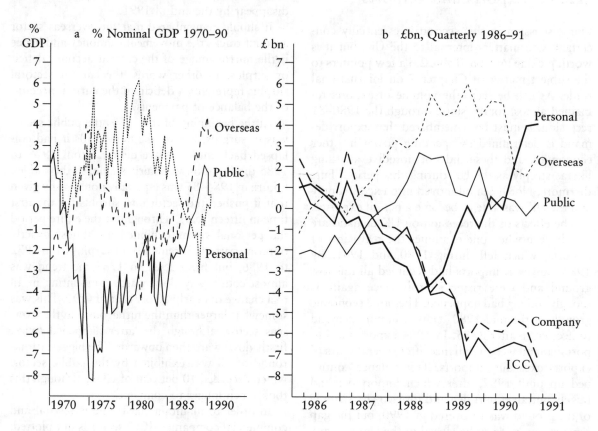

Notes:
[1]   This balance is equal to saving *plus* capital transfers *less* GDFCF *less* increase in value of stocks and work in progress.
[2]   Equals, apart from the change in sign, the current balance of payments accounts *plus* capital transfers.
Source: Economic Trends, Table 33.

☐ 2.9.1 Company Sector

The most remarkable feature of **Figure 2.4 (b)** is the collapse into deficit of the company sector. In 1990, industrial and commercial companies (ICCs) as a whole apparently spent £27 bn more on investment and stocks than they retained in earnings, after allowing for tax and dividend payments. This deficit managed to exceed even that of 1989, and was proportionately bigger than the crisis levels of 1974.

What is odd about this is that it was not reflected in the balance sheets of most large corporations which, whilst they deteriorated during 1990, were sufficiently strong to be able to sustain dividend growth. In fact, large companies continued to pay out dividends well in excess of what was warranted by their income growth, a policy which makes some sense as a smoothing device through the economic cycle but which obviously causes short-term problems. As the Bank of England noted, the ratio of dividends to post-tax profits reached 'an almost unprecedented' 62 per cent in the final quarter of 1989.

In 1987 the ICCs' net borrowing requirement stood at £23.6 bn, but it rose sharply to £44.9 bn in 1988 and to £49.1 bn in 1989 before falling back to £26.7 bn in 1990. During the period 1987–89 investment abroad remained fairly static at around £15 bn, whereas investment in UK company securities soared from £5.3 bn in 1987 (the year of the crash) to £18.5 bn in 1989. In all, the **gross** borrowing requirement (that is, including the acquisition of financial assets) rose from £23.3 to £63.0 bn, a by no means negligible sum by any standard. Not surprisingly, this latter figure fell back to 'only' £39.0 bn in 1990, with investment in UK securities down to £1.8 bn and investment abroad down to £5.8 bn (Bank of England, 1991b).

It is important to note that these figures must be treated with some caution. In the first place, we have the usual problem of a large balancing item (that is, unidentified flows). Secondly, unlike in 1974 and 1979, the large financial deficit was not triggered by a sharp decline in profitability. Total income was one-third higher in 1989 compared to 1987, and remained buoyant until the latter part of 1990.

It is possible to argue that the deficit reflected the confidence of the ICC sector, rather than the reverse. Fixed investment rose from £32.2 bn in 1987 to £45.3 bn in 1989 and to £50.1 bn in 1990. ICCs seemed quite happy to finance this with bank borrowing, thereby raising their 'gearing' (ratio of debt to equity). After the 1987 crash it became understandably difficult for ICCs to raise much money via the issue of ordinary shares (£2.3 bn in 1989 compared to £13.4 bn in 1987), and hence bank borrowing rose from £12.1 bn in 1987 to £33.3 bn in 1989. It would appear that interest rates were not expected to rise by much in the foreseeable future! It should also be noted, however, as discussed on **p. 128**, that increasing reliance was also placed on new financial instruments such as interest rate swaps.

Looking forward again to subsequent analysis it is interesting to reflect both upon the sharp upturn in the acquisition of UK company securities noted above, which indicated much increased activity in the merger/takeover market, and upon the maintenance of investment abroad, especially in the USA, well in excess of the acquisition of ICCs by foreign companies. In 1989, 80 per cent of all takeover bids were conducted in cash, which understandably make it necessary to resort to bank borrowing.

The financial deficit remained very high well into 1990, but so did the balancing item and the borrowing requirement clearly peaked in the 3rd quarter of 1989. Bank borrowing amounted to only £11 bn in the first three quarters of 1990. Amongst other factors was the almost complete disappearance of 'mega' takeover bids. In effect, the large corporations shut down the hatches and struggled to get their houses in order. In the majority of cases they were reasonably successful, and the 1991 company reporting season produced far fewer severe losses than had been expected (hence leading, in part, to a sharp upturn in share prices). There can be no doubt that the high interest rates in 1989 wreaked a fair amount of havoc in the property sector and among smaller companies, but the general view was that the 1990–91 recession would prove less severe than in 1980–2. This enhanced ability to ride out the downswing of the business cycle does provide some evidence that a decade of 'Thatcherism' has had beneficial effects in the company sector.

□ 2.9.2 *Personal Sector*

It is of interest to examine why the personal sector moved from a position of surplus to a position of deficit during 1987–89 and back into surplus in 1990. In point of fact, as shown in **Figure 2.4 (a)**, there was a reduction in the surplus during 1985 of almost equal size to the £6.5 bn switch from surplus to deficit in 1986, so the roots of the problem can be seen more clearly starting in 1985 in **Table 2.7**.

One prominent feature of the post-1985 period was a massive run down in personal holdings of UK company securities, particularly after the 1987 stock market crash. Whilst the situation improved in 1990 it is evident that, privatisation issues notwithstanding, the personal sector has lost its enthusiasm for direct holding of equities. On the other hand, it has continued to pump ever larger amounts into life assurance and pension funds which now play a dominant role in the market for company securities. Nevertheless, unit trusts have

Table 2.7   *Personal Sector: Financial Account, Main Changes 1985–90, £ bn*

	1985	1986	1987	1988	1989	1990
Loans for house purchase	−19.0	−27.0	−29.3	−40.0	−33.7	−32.2
UK company securities	−6.1	−6.8	−9.8	−12.4	−18.0	−8.7
Sterling bank lending	−6.0	−5.2	−8.5	−12.6	−13.2	−7.8
Unit trust units	+1.0	+2.0	+3.2	−0.5	+0.4	+0.3
Deposits with building societies	+13.3	+11.8	+13.6	+20.2	+17.5	+17.9
Sterling bank sight deposits	+6.5	+7.3	+7.4	+8.6	+11.0	+8.6
Sterling bank time deposits	−1.6	+1.1	+0.8	+8.1	+11.0	+7.0
British government securities	+1.5	+1.8	+1.8	−2.8	−4.2	+0.5
Life assurance & pension funds	+19.0	+21.0	+21.7	+22.3	+30.5	+31.0
Balancing item	−4.8	−8.6	−10.6	−8.8	−10.0	−12.2

Source: Financial Statistics, Table 1.11.

not prospered in recent years – again, perhaps, in the aftermath of the 1987 crash.

The latter end of the period also saw a run down in holdings of government securities, although this partly reflected the paucity of supply as a result of the repayments of the national debt after the Budget moved into surplus. It is evident from **Table 2.7** that a considerable part of the money forthcoming from the run down in these assets found its way into building society deposits, which soared after the 1987 crash. Such deposits are interest-bearing, and as can be seen there was also a huge transfer into interest-bearing bank deposits, mostly in the form of time deposits, but also to a much lesser extent in the form of newly-offered interest-bearing sight deposits.

The period of high interest rates clearly affected the balance of personal sector assets, but as **Table 2.7** shows it did little to suppress the demand for loans for house purchase. The sharp increase in 1988 not surprisingly went hand-in-hand with asset price inflation in the housing market. It is always well to bear in mind, however, that the large balancing items (that is, unidentified flows) shed more doubt over the individual magnitudes in **Table 2.7**.

■ *2.10* The Housing Market

It has become increasingly apparent over the past several years that the workings of the housing market play an extremely important role in the conduct of economic policy. The liberalisation of financial markets in the early 1980s led to much increased competition between banks, building societies and other intermediaries to make loans secured against housing. These were much less risky, as banks had discovered to their cost, than lending to sovereign states! The effects of liberalisation were to weaken prudential controls in the housing market.

Prior to the 1980s owner-occupation was subsidised, insofar as tax relief was given on mortgage interest (up to a loan limit of £25,000, which in the mid-1970s bought a splendid house outside London). Furthermore, they were not subject to capital gains tax. Not surprisingly, owner-occupation was very popular, as shown in **Figure 2.5**. However, most of the money provided in the mortgage market originated in retail deposits in building society branches, and so there were periodic famines and few feasts. As a result, mortgages were rationed and this made it almost impossible for borrowers to over-extend themselves. Deposits were needed, and a loan of 2.5 times income, or even less, was the norm.

After wholesale finance became available, and the market became competitive, prospective borrowers found it possible to demand reduced deposits and much higher income multiples (often taking second incomes into account as well). As a result, as shown in **Figure 2.6**, total mortgage debt in Britain, already high in 1982 (at 32 per cent of

Figure 2.5 *Stock of Dwellings by Tenure, UK, 1961–89*

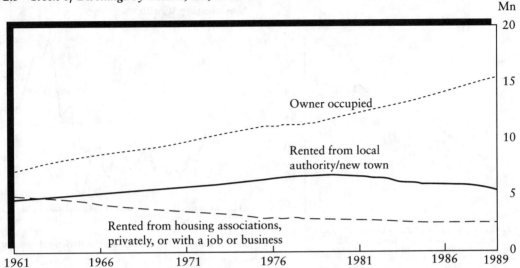

Source: Department of the Environment.

GDP) soared to 59 per cent of GDP in 1989, by far the highest ratio of the major economies. Only in the USA, where all mortgage interest is tax deductible, did anything like such a surge take place. In Germany, for example, where home loans cannot exceed 60 per cent of the value of a property, and where interest payments attract no tax relief, mortgage debt actually fell as a proportion of GDP.

As shown by the panel insert, house prices adjusted for inflation rose most rapidly as a consequence in Britain, and actually fell in Germany. **Asset price inflation** had arrived with a vengeance.

As indicated above, prudential controls were progressively relaxed. 100 per cent mortgages on new property became customary, and even bigger loans advanced in relation to income. This shows up clearly in **Figure 2.7** where the capital gearing of the personal sector is seen to have roughly doubled in the course of the 1980s.

After the economy moved out of recession in 1983, real personal disposable income began to grow strongly (as shown in **Figure 2.8**). At the same time asset price inflation in the housing market caused wealth in the form of housing to grow rapidly. The doubling of house prices in the late 1980s, in particular, caused the ratio of housing to non-housing wealth to shoot up, as shown in **Figure 2.8**. It also had the incidental

Figure 2.6 *Mortgage Debt as % of GDP*

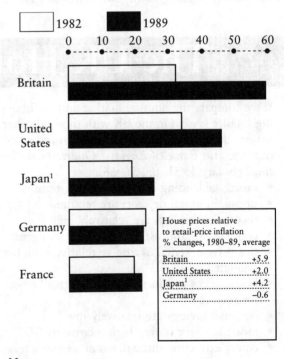

House prices relative to retail-price inflation % changes, 1980–89, average

Britain	+5.9
United States	+2.0
Japan[1]	+4.2
Germany	−0.6

Note:
[1] Land prices.
Source: The Economist.

Figure 2.7   *Personal Sector: Capital Gearing[1] %*

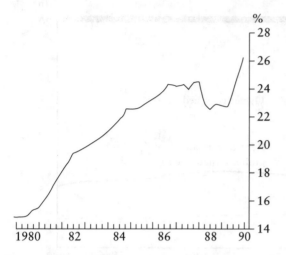

Figure 2.8   *Personal Sector: Ratio of Housing to Non-housing Wealth, %*

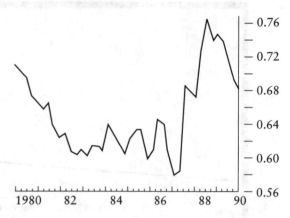

Source: Bank of England Quarterly Bulletin (February 1991).

Note:
[1]   Stock of lending to persons for house purchase as a proportion of the value of owner-occupied housing stock.

Source: Bank of England Quarterly Bulletin (February 1991).

The UK Housing Market

If we compare the housing market and the housing finance system in the UK with those of other major advanced economies, several features stand out (see also *Bank of England Quarterly Bulletin*, February 1991, pp. 56–66).

- mortgage lending is relatively long-term
- unusually small deposits are required
- income multipliers are relatively high
- controls on land use are relatively stringent
- the private rental sector is relatively highly regulated
- house prices run further ahead of retail prices on average
- personal savings are relatively low
- mortgage debt is very high relative to GDP
- equity extraction through remortgaging is relatively easy
- mortgages are subsidised which is uncommon
- there is relatively little tax on capital gains

The US housing market bears the closest resemblance to that of the UK, but things are quite different in Germany and Japan. In the latter countries, for example, it is not customary to lend more than 60 per cent of the value of a property, so it is not surprising that their inhabitants save much more than their counterparts in the UK, who expect to borrow up to 95 per cent of the value of a property (or even 100 per cent if lenders are competing fiercely for custom).

In the case of Japan, the high rate of saving also reflects the acute shortage of building land which results in such high prices that first-time buyers are frequently unable to enter the market until they are relatively old, if at all. It is also a demonstrable proposition that countries such as Japan, Germany and France, with the least developed systems of housing finance, have the highest personal saving ratios.

effect of making property more expensive in the UK compared to the USA at the ruling exchange rates.

As noted in the subsequent section on consumption, these developments appear to have triggered over-consumption and simultaneous reductions in saving, with the appearance of a huge personal sector financial deficit. This also reflected the phenomenon of **equity withdrawal**. As people live longer so they tend to pass on their assets, chiefly in the form of housing, to the next generation when the latter is already middle-aged and living in owner-occupied dwellings of its own. Hence, inherited property is usually sold, thereby releasing large amounts of liquidity into the economy. During the late 1980s, householders also discovered that because the value of their own houses had risen they were typically sitting on a large cushion of equity, and financial intermediaries competed to lend on the security of that equity (generally via second mortgages). Thus, even more liquidity was released in addition to that released via inheritance; and yet more was released because when people moved house they typically did not reinvest all their capital gains net of expenses, but rather increased their mortgages to reflect higher incomes and kept the rest as cash in hand.

The importance of this phenomenon cannot be over-emphasised because, as is evident, it has significant implications for macroeconomic management. Insofar as the interest rate is used as an instrument its main effects are going to be seen in the housing market. Raising interest rates is unlikely to deter consumption unless it forces up monthly mortgage repayments to the point at which householders' pips squeak loudly, and even that may operate with a lag because so many mortgages are currently readjusted only once a year.

The personal sector's balance sheet shows that the housing market is currently absorbing about £8 bn a quarter. What is rather astonishing about this is that it is insufficient to maintain house prices in nominal, let alone inflation-adjusted terms (although the average, which the Halifax BS claims to have risen by 0.5 per cent in 1990 but which the Nationwide BS claims to have risen by 11 per cent, disguises quite large regional variations). This is shown in **Figure 2.9**.

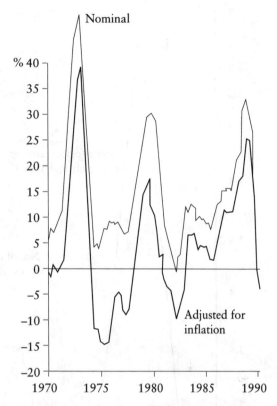

Figure 2.9   *Annual % Changes in Nominal and Real House Prices, Quarter on Quarter, 1969Q1–1990Q1, UK, %*

Source: Calculations based on official statistics by M. Fleming and J. Nellis (Fleming and Nellis, 1990).

According to the Nationwide the stock of owner-occupied houses was worth a 'mere' £850 bn at the end of 1990, some £100 bn less than a year earlier. Nevertheless, the debt secured on this property rose by only £30 bn to £290 bn, so there is lots more equity to withdraw if borrowers so desire. At the present time, as shown in **Figure 2.10** the house price–earnings ratio appears to be settling back to its long-run average of 3.5 after peaking at 4.8 in 1989 (subject to regional variations) but this adjustment resulted more from rising earnings than from falling prices.

Given that the government is intent upon a progressive lowering of interest rates, it obviously raises the question as to whether this will set off another house price spiral. In March 1991 the Governor of the Bank of England took the unusual

Figure 2.10   *House Price–Earnings Ratios 1969–91[1], and Number of Mortgage Loans (All Institutions) 1969–90[2], 000*

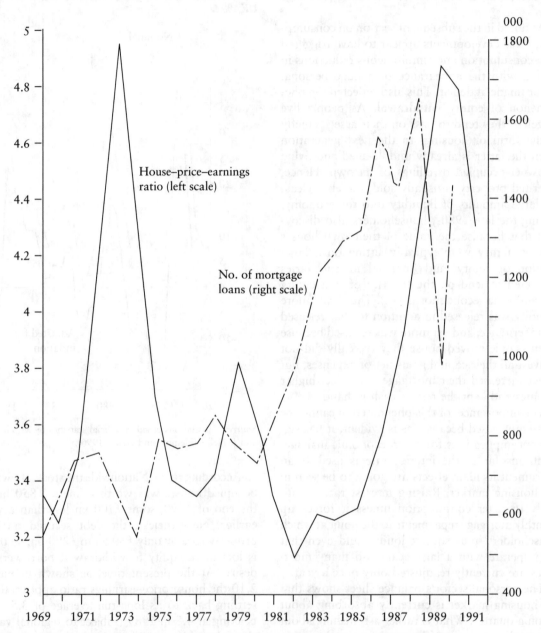

Sources: [1] Calculations based on official statistics by M. Fleming and J. Nellis (Fleming and Nellis, 1990).
   [2] *Housing and Construction Statistics* (HMSO).
   [3] Figures for 1989–91 taken from *Bank of England Quarterly Bulletin*.

step of suggesting that a minimum deposit level for mortgages might have to be introduced to curb excessive lending. As discussed on **pp. 469–70**, there is every reason to steer well away from credit controls and these are unlikely to become official policy. On the other hand, in such a competitive market the lenders are unlikely to revert back to the restrictive lending rules which they used in the 1970s.

Fortunately, asset price inflation is likely to be relatively subdued in the near future. In the first place, households are adjusting to the loss of wealth sustained as a result of falling house prices in 1990, and are unlikely to forget for a year or two that house prices do not necessarily rise all the time (static nominal prices anyway imply inflation-adjusted losses). Secondly, there is a large excess supply of housing to be cleared off the market. When prices cease to rise sellers prefer not to sell rather than to accept lower prices, hence there is a volume rather than a price adjustment (which is why the modest price reductions of 1990 are deceptive). Once the market picks up the supply reappears and serves initially to hold back price rises. Thirdly, the 1991 Budget saw the abolition of tax relief on mortgages at the higher marginal rate of tax. Fourthly, rising unemployment tends to suppress demand for housing. Finally, interest rates may be falling in nominal terms, but they remain higher in inflation-adjusted terms than in previous periods when house prices soared.

In the longer term they key question is the rate of new household formation. Pessimists believe that the low birth rate will cause household formation to be very limited by previous standards, and in time this will help to suppress the demand for housing. Optimists believe that older people, fewer of whom are owner-occupiers than among younger age groups, will move into the market and thus sustain demand. At this juncture there is no way of knowing who will be proved to be correct. It is also worth noting that the value of subsidies has fallen, not merely because of the loss of tax relief

at the higher rate but because the upper limit of £30,000 is being progressively eroded by inflation and no longer has much impact upon house purchase decisions in the South. In addition, the virtually tax exempt status of housing is no longer as unique as it was. Personal equity plans (PEPs), TESSAs and the Business Expansion Scheme all currently provide alternative ways of accumulating tax-relieved assets.

One final matter is worthy of note. Is asset price inflation not ultimately an illusion, since if all house owners tried to sell their properties at the same time would prices not collapse? Indeed they would, but it is possible to release huge amounts of liquidity via equity withdrawal even if only a small proportion of the housing stock is sold at any one time, and that is by no means illusory. Then why not conduct the discussion in terms of company shares, which underwent a long bull run during the 1980s, the 1987 crash notwithstanding? The answer here is that equity withdrawal is easy in the housing market, but much harder if shares are offered as collateral given that they often do fall in value on an individual basis. At an individual level, the housing market affects decisions about consumption and saving far more directly than the equity market.

References

Bank of England (1991a) 'Housing Finance – An International Perspective', *Bank of England Quarterly Bulletin* (February).

Bank of England (1991b) 'Industrial and Commercial Companies' Gearing', *Bank of England Quarterly Bulletin* (May).

Boleat, M. *et al.* (1991) *The State of the Economy 1991* (London: IEA).

Fleming, M. and J. Nellis (1990) 'The Rise and Fall of House Prices: Causes, Consequences and Prospects', *National Westminster Quarterly Review* (November).

■ Chapter 3 ■

The Macroeconomy: 2

Peter Curwen

■ *3.1* Personal Income, Consumption and Saving

□ *3.1.1 Personal Income*

Personal income consists of wages and salaries, employers' contributions, current grants from general government and other personal income. In total these constitute much the largest element of national income. However, the term 'personal' is somewhat ambiguous in that it refers not merely to individuals but to unincorporated businesses, private non-profit-making bodies and life assurance and pension funds. The latter three elements are largely excluded in data for 'household' incomes, but in making this distinction there are particular difficulties with, for example, the earnings of entrepreneurs who are, in effect, individual person and business rolled into one. **Figure 3.1** contains quarterly data for personal income before tax at current prices since 1977, and these show a steady upwards progression throughout the whole period at an average annual rate of around 10 per cent.

Personal income net of income taxes, social security contributions and transfer payments is called **personal disposable income** (PDI), which is also shown at current prices in **Figure 3.1**. Whilst this is understandably more volatile than pre-tax per-

sonal income given that tax regimes can be altered at specified points in time, the longer-term trend is very similar and exhibits an almost identical average rate of growth. The individual components of pre-tax personal income can mostly be measured quite accurately (± 3 per cent or less), and the same is true for income taxes and social security contributions. However, the subtraction of the latter from the former inevitably renders PDI less accurate than either (± between 3 and 10 per cent).

□ *3.1.2 Consumers' Expenditure*

Consumers' expenditure represents the consumption not merely of households but of the other non-household parts of the personal sector. Nevertheless, household consumption constitutes 90 per cent of the total, and it is reasonable to treat one as a close approximation of the other. Consumers' expenditure is plotted in aggregate at current prices in **Figure 3.1**, where the quarterly data are seasonally adjusted. This is necessary since consumption always surges in the final quarter of each year due to Xmas shopping, and the *unadju*sted data give the false impression that this heralds an ongoing upturn in expenditure.

Figure 3.2 breaks consumption down into a number of selected categories on an inflation-

Figure 3.1 *Personal Income, 1979–91, Quarterly at Current Prices*

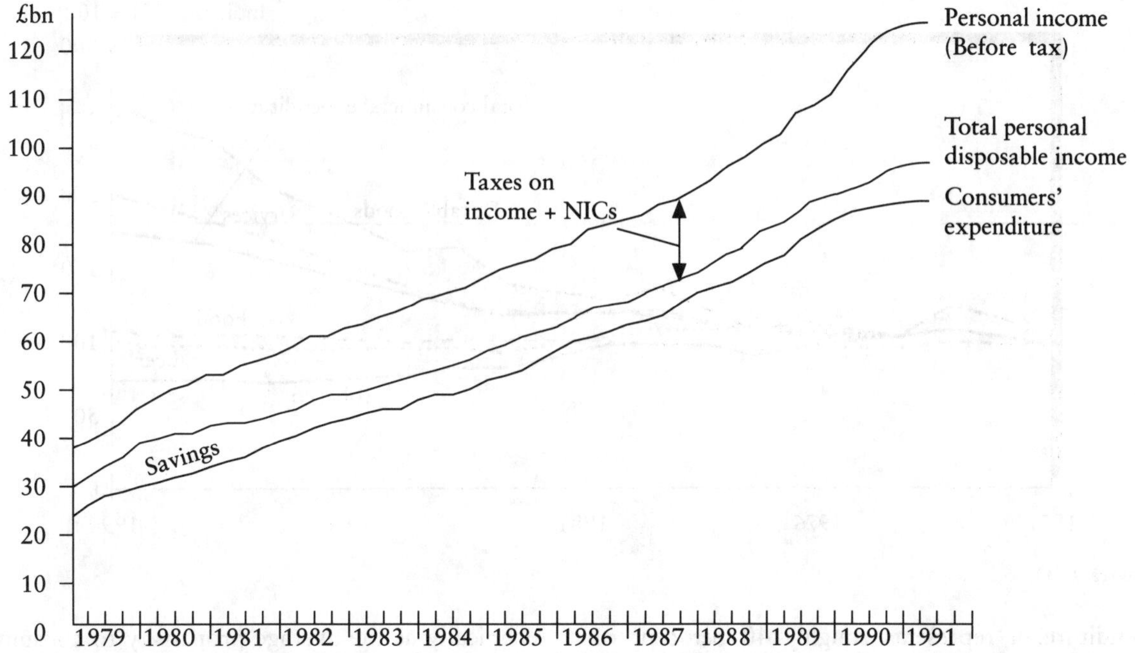

	1979	1980	1981	1982	1983	1984	1985	1986	1987	1988	1989	1990	1991	
	222.0	225.5	223.7	222.9	227.9	238.2	241.4	252.1	260.3	274.9	289.5	298.8		PDI at 1985 prices
	194.9	195.1	195.2	197.1	205.5	209.2	217.0	231.7	243.5	260.4	270.5	272.9		Consumers' expenditure at 1985 prices

Source: Monthly Digest of Statistics.

adjusted basis. Between 1971 and 1990 total consumers' expenditure rose by roughly 70 per cent in real terms. Nevertheless, tobacco consumption fell by over 20 per cent and beer consumption remained constant. Expenditure on food rose very slightly in real terms, which is not unexpected since people do not tend to eat all that much more as they get richer, especially if it is fashionable to be slim. On the other hand, real expenditure on durable goods rose sharply during the 1980s such that at the end of the decade 98 per cent of households had a TV (91 per cent colour); 84 per cent a washing machine; 77 per cent a deep freeze; 85 per cent a telephone; 53 per cent a video, and so forth. From the mid-1980s onwards real consumption of services also began to soar and, given that the market for durable goods must eventually reach saturation (although some households have a TV for every adult *and* every child), services are likely to provide the fastest growing sector in the 1990s.

Table 3 .1 indicates how these trends have affected the spending patterns of UK households. Food has become proportionately much less important (the Common Agricultural Policy notwithstanding), and there have been proportionate reductions in alcohol, tobacco, clothing and fuel and power (despite those rising gas and electricity bills). Transport has become more important, but it is the somewhat catch-all 'other goods and services' where the increase is most marked. The practice of eating out has increased enormously, but the biggest change of all since the mid-1970s has been in the practice of taking foreign holidays.

It is also worth noting that attention in the media is sometimes addressed to trends in **retail sales** as a guide to trends in consumers' expenditure, since the former are published on a provisional basis much earlier than the latter. However, it must be borne in mind that, for example, whilst food represents 12–13 per cent of consumers' ex-

Figure 3.2 *Consumers' Expenditure at Constant Prices, by Selected Item, UK 1971–90*

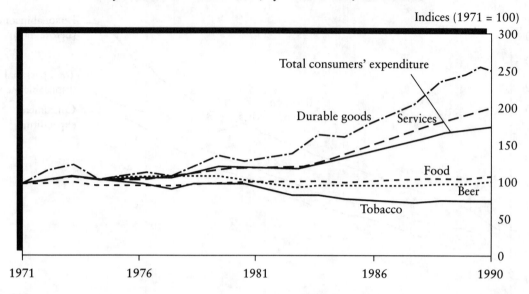

Source: CSO.

penditure, it represents roughly 40 per cent of retail sales which exclude energy, rent and rates and other services. Hence, in the short term, retail sales may prove a very unreliable guide to trends in the larger aggregate.

As can be seen from **Table 3.2** PDI is, by definition, either **consumed** or **saved**. The proportion saved (**saving ratio**) is specified in **Table 3.2**, and it follows that the proportion consumed, known

technically as the average propensity to consume (APC), is given by the formula (1 — saving ratio) Currently, this stands at over 90 per cent and, taking the official data at face value, has been high by historic standards since the mid-1980s.

It should be borne in mind that, because consumption is determined by PDI rather than gross income, savings tend to fall somewhat when the tax and national insurance burden rises. Between

Table 3.1 *Share of Total Household Expenditure at Current Prices, UK*

	1976	1981	1985	1986	1987	1988	1989	1990
Food	19.2	16.3	14.4	14.0	12.7	12.6	12.4	12.4
Alcoholic drink	7.6	7.3	7.4	6.9	6.5	6.4	6.3	6.4
Tobacco	4.1	3.6	3.3	3.2	2.8	2.7	2.6	2.6
Clothing and footwear	7.7	6.7	7.0	7.1	6.6	6.5	6.3	6.1
Housing	13.6	14.9	15.4	15.5	15.6	15.6	15.5	14.8
Fuel and power	4.7	5.1	4.9	4.6	3.9	3.9	3.6	3.6
Household goods and services	7.6	6.9	6.7	6.7	7.0	6.9	6.8	6.7
Transport and communication	15.4	17.2	17.4	17.1	17.7	18.0	18.5	18.3
Recreation, entertainment and education	9.2	9.4	9.4	9.4	9.4	9.4	9.6	9.7
Other goods, services and adjustments	10.8	12.5	14.1	15.5	17.8	18.0	18.4	19.4
Total	100.0	100.0	100.0	100.0	100.0	100.0	100.0	100.0

Source: UK National Accounts 'Blue Book' (CSO, 1991) Table 4.7.

Table 3.2　*Personal Income, Expenditure and Saving, 1984–90, £ bn*

	1984	1985	1986	1987	1988	1989	1990
Wages and salaries	155.5	169.1	183.9	200.0	223.4	248.0	275.3
Employers' contributions	25.3	26.5	27.6	29.0	31.6	35.2	39.6
Current grants	43.0	46.8	50.9	52.5	54.0	56.7	62.3
Other personal income	57.8	62.6	69.7	76.2	87.7	99.3	109.8
Total personal income	281.6	305.0	332.1	357.7	396.7	439.2	487.0
Less deductions:							
Taxes on income	34.7	37.7	40.8	43.4	48.2	53.4	62.0
Social security contributions	22.3	24.2	26.2	28.6	32.1	33.0	34.8
Transfers	1.5	1.7	1.9	2.1	2.4	2.4	2.6
Community charge	–	–	–	–	–	0.6	8.8
Personal disposable income (PDI)	223.1	241.4	263.2	283.6	314.0	349.6	378.8
Less consumers' expenditure	199.6	217.9	241.9	265.3	297.7	326.6	346.0
Balance: personal saving	23.5	23.5	21.3	18.3	16.3	23.0	32.8
Saving ratio %[1]	10.5	9.7	8.1	6.5	5.2	6.6	8.7

Note:
[1]　Saving as % of PDI.
Source: Monthly Digest of Statistics.

1983 and 1987, for example, total deductions rose from 21.20 to 21.45 per cent of total income, whereas the saving ratio fell sharply other than in 1984, the only year in which total deductions fell as a proportion of gross income. Whilst this relationship must be treated with caution, it does suggest that when the government removes demand from the economy via taxation, consumption steps into the breach to maintain demand. During the period covered by **Table 3.2**, consumers' expenditure rose by 73 per cent whilst PDI rose by 69 per cent. It appears that consumers have recently not merely spent the whole of their PDI, but borrowed in order to finance yet further consumption.

For the past decade, apart form a modest temporary fall in 1981–82, real PDI adjusted for inflation has risen. This is shown by the data for real PDI at the foot of **Figure 3.2**. Recent years have seen quite substantial increases, although none has been as large as occurred in each of the two years 1978 and 1979. Unfortunately, it is not altogether clear whether rising real PDI stimulates or depresses consumption. Evidence from the USA, where the saving ratio is exceptionally low, suggests that once real incomes rise to the point at which most people have satisfied their desire to own assets such as a house and some company shares, they see no further point in saving for the future and opt instead for additional current consumption. However, it is most unlikely that the UK has reached the same stage, as yet, and there was every sign in the booming housing market of 1988 that saving for asset accumulation was as popular as ever.

A related issue, of increasing importance given the present government's supply-side strategy, is the effect of reductions in the rates of income tax, especially those in excess of the standard rate. In the Keynesian model, taxing high income earners and redistributing the proceeds to those on low incomes is expected to raise the marginal propensity to consume (MPC) and to reduce the saving ratio. The recent reductions in the upper rates of income tax should thus have the opposite effect, given that they redistribute in favour of higher income groups. It is as yet impossible to form a judgement on the matter, but it will be a useful addition to our knowledge about consumption to discover whether this extra money will be spent or saved.

□ 3.1.3 Saving

National saving is the sum of private (personal and company) saving and public saving. **Personal saving** is the difference between PDI and consumers' expenditure. In principle it is equal to personal investment plus the personal sector's acquisition of financial assets *net* of personal borrowing. **Company saving** is the residual income of companies net of tax, profits remitted abroad, transfers and payments of interest and dividends. Company expenditure on durable goods in the form of fixed investment and stocks is **not** deducted from their income in measuring company saving, but depreciation is. **Public saving** is the difference between the public sector's current receipts and current expenditure, and is broadly equivalent to public sector net investment *less* public sector borrowing (or *plus* public sector debt repayment).

The discussion of saving in the media is concerned primarily with the personal sector, although as we will note later this may be misguided. Unfortunately, personal sector saving is a very unreliable statistic (potentially up to 20 per cent inaccurate in either direction) as it is the difference between two somewhat inaccurate figures for PDI and consumers' expenditure respectively. Furthermore, the distinction between consumption expenditure on durable goods and saving can be a fine one. Whilst, for example, the purchase of a car is treated as current consumption in the statistics, many purchasers would see the accumulation of a deposit and the repayment of the residual purchase price as an act of **saving**. On occasion, the CSO redefines consumption as saving (for example, DIY expenditure in 1984), and more generally the saving ratio tends to be retrospectively adjusted in each year's 'Blue Book'. The ratios recorded during the 1970s have in recent years thus been much reduced – with, for example, a downgrading of each of the previous seven years' ratios by almost 1 per cent in the 1987 'Blue Book'.

A further consideration bedevills the meaning of saving, namely that whilst personal payments into a private pension fund are counted as saving, contributions to the government's pension and social security schemes are not. Obviously, if the latter were not deducted from gross income both PDI and the saving ratio (including such payments) would be considerably larger.

Finally, it is evident that, whilst interest payments on a mortgage constitute consumption, that part of the monthly repayment which expunges part of the capital owed to the lender must enhance the wealth of the borrower, and in that sense is clearly an act of saving.

In many ways it is surprising that the saving ratio is treated with the reverence it is accorded in the media. As shown in Cullison (1990), the official saving ratio in the USA, which is even lower than in the UK, is widely regarded as a nonsense, with estimates of the true rate varying from twice the official rate to an astonishing six times the official rate.

As noted in *Barclays Bank Review* (February 1990, p. 17), the ratio derived from identified financial transactions is almost twice as high as the official ratio. When it comes to saving, therefore, the most sensible approach is, as usual, to take a long-term series defined on a consistent basis, so

Figure 3.3   *The Personal Saving Ratio, 1955–90, %*

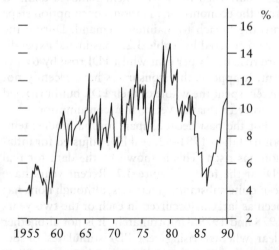

Source: Bank of England Quarterly Bulletin (February 1991).

that there is a clear view of the trend even if not of the absolute magnitudes.

Figure 3.3 illustrates the official saving ratio from 1985 to 1990. It is interesting to note that after a surge in 1960 it moved steadily upwards, on average, until 1980, peaking at roughly 15 per cent. From 1980 to 1989 it was almost downhill all the way, with the ratio bottoming out in 1988, and then entering the recession on a rising trend from a level last seen in the 1950s. It is evident, therefore, that there is at least one big difference between the 1980–82 recession and that of 1990–91, namely the saving ratio at the commencement of each period. This is unsurprising when one considers the changes in the personal sector's balance sheet during the 1980s. As we have noted, net wealth is much higher in relation to income compared to a decade ago and, more importantly, the personal sector is loaded up with liabilities which, being financial, are not subject to asset price inflation. **Figure 3.4** shows that between 1982 and the end of 1989 total credit outstanding (in addition to mortgage liabilities) in Great Britain rose in money terms from £16 bn to £48 bn, and to well over £30 bn in inflation-adjusted terms.

Possibly for the first time ever the personal sector now has more debts than assets at floating interest rates (in mid-1990 net floating-rate liabilities represented 15 per cent of disposable income). Not surprisingly, the vulnerability of the

Figure 3.4   Consumer Credit, Amount Outstanding, Great Britain, 1982–90, £bn

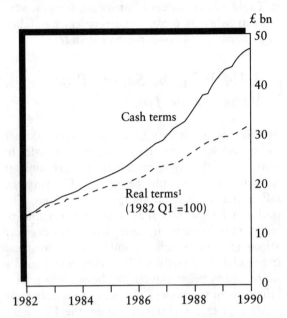

Note:
1   Real terms figures are the cash figures adjusted to 1982Q1 price levels by excluding the effect of general inflation as measured by the retail prices index.
Source: CSO.

personal sector to high interest rates on mortgages is accentuated by the huge amount of outstanding credit. No wonder the banks are finding that increasing numbers of people are repaying their credit

Table 3.3   *Composition of Consumer Credit, UK, % and £ bn, 1982–90*

	1982	1983	1984	1985	1986	1987	1988	1989	1990
Bank credit card lending	12.5	13.8	14.8	15.7	17.2	16.6	15.7	14.9	17.0
Bank loans[1]	66.3	64.6	63.2	62.1	61.6	62.7	64.6	63.5	63.4
Finance houses[2]	8.1	9.5	9.9	10.7	11.9	11.9	10.8	10.7	10.8
Insurance companies	1.9	2.1	3.1	2.7	2.6	2.2	2.1	2.1	2.1
Retailers	11.3	10.1	9.0	8.4	6.6	6.6	6.1	5.6	5.2
Building societies	0.0	0.0	0.0	0.0	0.0	0.2	0.7	1.2	1.5
Credit outstanding at the end of year (= 100%) (£ bn)	16.0	18.9	22.3	26.1	30.2	36.2	42.5	48.7	52.8

Notes:
1   Banks and all other institutions authorised to take deposits under the Banking Act 1987
2   Finance houses and other credit companies
Source: Financial Statistics, Table 9.3.

card debts on a monthly basis in order to avoid incurring interest charges. Nevertheless, as shown in **Table 3.3**, credit card borrowing remains very popular whereas credit from retailers has fallen away considerably over the past decade.

3.1.4 Why the Saving Ratio Varies Over Time

At this juncture it may be useful to pull together the strands of the previous discussion in order to analyse why the saving ratio may vary over time. It is useful to start with the relationship between inflation and consumption/saving behaviour. The traditional view was that once people came to realise that the value of money would be adversely affected by inflation, they would rush out to spend it as quickly as possible. This view was broadly supported by behaviour during the overseas hyper-inflations of the prewar period, but the relatively modest price rises manifested in the UK since 1970 appear to have stimulated more mixed behaviour, with the saving ratio rising during the high (by UK standards) inflation of the 1970s, then falling with inflation in the 1980s. There are a number of ways of explaining this, and their relative merits are unlikely ever to be satisfactorily distinguished since they are, in any event, significantly interdependent.

For example, if a person sets out to maintain the **real**, rather than the **nominal**, value of his savings, he or she will be obliged to increase the nominal value of those savings at the same rate as prices are rising. Furthermore, since high rates of inflation generally go hand in hand with rising unemployment, people who fear they may lose their jobs may try to build up a pool of savings in order to cushion their potential loss of income. Equally, if prices of consumer goods are rising so rapidly that people feel that they will never be able to afford to buy them, they may decide to give up trying to do so and save instead.

The role of interest rates in all this is hard to divine. Since interest rates, in nominal terms, tend to rise with inflation, the sacrifice in terms of interest foregone when buying consumer goods must itself be rising. However, the inflation-adjusted real rate of interest was negative during the mid-1970s at a time of very high nominal rates, and positive in the mid-1980s at a time of lower nominal rates, so one could have expected savings to be higher rather than lower in the latter period (assuming, of course, that savers were not suffering in the 1970s from **money illusion** – the illusion that nominal and real rates are the same). In fact, correlating savings against real rates of interest appears to indicate a rather weak relationship. This may, in turn, reflect the fact that financial deregulation has made it increasingly easy for people to borrow, and therefore, the principle that one has to save before one buys a costly item has been steadily eroded. Rather perversely at first sight, people may continue to put increasingly large sums of money into life assurance and pension funds and simultaneously borrow to finance additional current consumption. Savings are defined net of borrowing, so increased borrowing reduces the saving ratio. However, the borrower himself is unlikely to view borrowing as dissaving. Indeed, of course, pension fund contributions may well be compulsory rather than voluntary. In 1980, after adjusting for contributions to life insurance and pension funds, the personal sector still placed 30 per cent of its savings on a discretionary basis, but by 1986 this latter figure had become negative.

A broader view of these factors may be termed the **wealth effect**. Over the long haul – and, indeed, in most individual years – the value of property has tended to rise faster than prices in general. Equally, the value of company shares has easily outstripped inflation over the past decade, and more recently, though not previously, post-tax rates of interest have also outstripped inflation. As a result, people who own assets (currently in practice, the great majority) will tend to feel wealthier as time passes, and hence feel less need to convert current income into wealth via saving. This will also reflect the increased probability of inheritance.

The **age structure of the population** also links in with this analysis. The bulk of savings are accumulated by people between the ages of 45 and 65. Younger people have heavy outgoings incurred in setting up homes and raising families, whilst the elderly earn little and may need to eat into past savings. The high birth rate immediately after the Second World War has produced an exceptionally large generation approaching its period of high savings, which could well cause savings to rise again in the 1990s.

All this is, understandably, confusing enough, but it is additionally important not to interpret saving purely within the context of the personal sector. **Figure 3.5**, based on a somewhat different approach to the calculation of savings from that used previously, incorporates the savings of the personal sector, company sector and public sector, all expressed as a percentage of GDP at factor cost. As can be seen on the left-hand side of **Figure 3.5**, the decline in personal saving was offset by an increase in company saving from 1979 to 1988,

whilst the saving of the public sector remained consistently negative until 1987.

As a result, total savings at current prices showed a remarkable degree of stability from 1980 to 1988. Whilst this data is unavailable beyond 1988, statistics indicate that the public sector remained in surplus in 1988 and 1989 whilst the personal sector followed up a substantial deficit in 1988 with an even more substantial one in 1989. Clearly, these trends have offset each other to a considerable extent.

Adjusting the data for inflation, as shown on the right-hand side of **Figure 3.5**, has no effect upon this general proposition, although the sectoral shares are very different. This arises because, when inflation is rapid, a sector with positive net assets

Figure 3.5 *Total Domestic Saving*[1] *as % of GDP at Factor Cost*

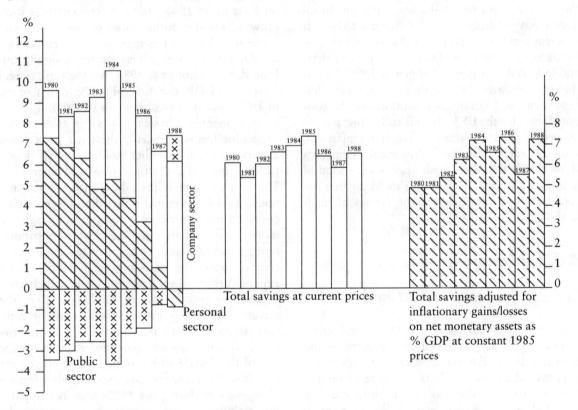

Note:
[1] After providing for stock appreciation and capital consumption at replacement cost and plus net capital transfers.
Source: *Bank of England Quarterly Bulletin* (May 1988) p. 234; (May 1989) p. 250; (May 1990) p. 229.

has an artificially increased income and saving rate, and vice versa. As result, the conventional national accounts misallocate savings among the sectors when inflation is high. The high nominal saving ratio of the personal sector in 1979 was thus in reality negative after adjusting for inflation, and exceeded 2 per cent only in the period 1982–84. In real terms the 1986 figure of 1 per cent was little less than the 1980 figure of 16 per cent. On the other hand, the real saving of the company sector was slightly higher than its nominal saving in every year except 1985 when it was identical. In the case of the public sector the real saving ratio was positive, but rapidly declining, between 1979 and 1982, and marginally negative thereafter.

Given the evident constancy of national savings the government has been a little ambivalent about the necessity to offer incentives to savers, although the pressure from the media was sufficient to induce a 'Savers' Budget' in 1990 (see **pp. 157–8**). It was reasonable to expect the personal saving ratio to rise again in the light of falling real house prices, and indeed that began to happen in 1990. Nevertheless, although the UK saving ratio may improve, and will doubtless remain above the (disputed) rate for the USA, there is still a long way to go before the UK citizenry save at German and Japanese rates. Mind you, historical documents show clearly that the British always were fond of indulging themselves, so why should anyone expect them to take on board the virtues of thrift at this point in history?

■ 3.2 Investment

□ 3.2.1 *Investment Defined*

The term 'investment' is used by the general public to refer to the acquisition of certain physical and financial assets. For our purposes, however, the purchase of an asset such as a picture or putting money into a building society account must be regarded as an act of **saving**. When we refer to **investment**, we mean that an addition has been made to the stock of productive capital machinery known as **fixed capital formation**. The existence of this capital stock is what enables the economy to produce output both in the current and in future periods.

Total investment, or **Gross Domestic Fixed Capital Formation** (GDFCF), consists of **replacement** investment and **net** investment. Replacement investment is simply that investment needed to make good any reductions in the capital stock due to depreciation and obsolescence. Net investment is any investment over and above that needed to keep the capital stock constant, and hence results in an increase in that stock. In general, net investment is the driving force behind economic growth and improved productivity. Nevertheless, this can be attributed in part to replacement investment insofar as this is technically superior to the capital stock which is being replaced.

Table 3.4 sets out the path of GDFCF over the period from 1979 to 1990, adjusted for inflation. The aggregate increase is at first sight impressive (at least up to 1989), but the economy was itself growing rapidly during most of the 1980s and hence if real GDFCF is expressed as a percentage of GDP the improvement is relatively insignificant. Indeed, it was not until 1988 that the ratio of real GDFCF to GDP rose noticeably above that ruling in 1977, and it has fallen again in 1990.

Investment in **physical assets** can take a wide variety of forms. Officially these are categorised as private dwellings, other building and work, vehicles, ships and aircraft and plant and machinery. The first of these is the odd man out because a house used for personal rather than business purposes cannot contribute to output, although the money spent on its purchase clearly contributes to aggregate demand. Hence, it is sensible to concentrate upon the ratio between GDFCF *minus* expenditure on dwellings and GDP, which constitutes the second row of **Table 3.4**. Here the picture is more promising, insofar that the ratio rose slightly above that prevailing during the late 1970s in 1984, and remained above it for the rest of the decade with a noticeable improvement in 1988. Nevertheless, the most notable feature of investment during the 1980s was its comparative stability. It was surprisingly resistant to the 1980–81 recession, and did not shoot ahead again until 1988.

1990 saw investment fall back as the recession took hold, but this was isolated in the second half

Table 3.4   *Investment (GDFCF) by Type of Asset and by Sector as % of GDP, at Market Prices, 1979–90*[1]

	1979	1980	1981	1982	1983	1984	1985	1986	1987	1988	1989	1990
GDFCF as a per cent of GDP	17.2	16.5	15.0	15.6	15.8	16.9	16.9	16.6	17.4	19.1	19.6	19.1
GDFCF excluding dwellings as a per cent of GDP	13.1	12.7	12.0	12.4	12.3	13.2	13.6	13.1	13.8	15.3	15.8	15.6
Private sector investment as a per cent of GDP	12.3	12.0	11.3	12.0	11.6	12.8	13.5	13.5	14.8	16.9	16.8	16.0
General government investment as a per cent of GDP	2.2	2.0	1.4	1.3	1.8	1.9	1.9	1.9	1.8	1.6	1.7	1.8
Public corporation investment as a per cent of GDP	2.6	2.6	2.4	2.4	2.5	2.2	1.6	1.4	1.1	1.1	1.0	0.8
Stocks and work in progress as a per cent of GDP	1.0	–1.0	–1.0	–0.4	0.4	0.3	0.2	0.2	0.3	1.0	0.6	0.5

Note:
[1] For the years before 1983, totals may not equal the sum of their components, because of the method used in rebasing to 1985 prices.
Source: Economic Trends, Annual Supplement (1990); *Economic Trends*, Table 9.

of the year, so the aggregate reduction for the year was not great. Both the CBI investment intentions inquiry and the CSO investment intentions inquiry are currently producing ominous responses through 1991 and well into 1992, so a sharp reduction in the ratio of GDFCF to GDP is very much on the cards. In the first quarter of 1991 investment was 20 per cent lower than in the corresponding quarter of 1990, the largest annual fall since the third quarter of 1981. It must be hoped that the upturn will arrive fairly early in 1992 if rapid economic growth is to be resumed.

In this respect it is important to remember that technological progress has become so rapid that simply maintaining the level of real GDFCF is insufficient to maintain the UK's ability to compete. Simply to return to the level of real GDFCF prevailing in 1989 when the recession ends would thus represent a long-term setback to the economy.

□ 3.2.2 The Pattern of Investment

The pattern of investment is revealed in the residual part of **Table 3.4** and the whole of **Table**

3.5. It is clear from **Table 3.5** that private sector investment was the driving force behind growth throughout the 1980s. After a patchy period at the beginning of the decade it moved solidly ahead from 1984 onwards. It peaked in the 1st quarter of 1989 at constant 1985 prices, but was at much the same value in the 2nd quarter of 1990, after which it began to decline very rapidly.

General government investment remained stable in real terms from 1984 to mid-1989, but this represented a reduction when expressed as a percentage of a growing real GDP, and by the end of the 1980s it resulted in a much smaller ratio than had existed during the 1970s. Rather curiously, the real value of general government investment rose in the final quarter of 1989, and remained much higher than in previous years throughout 1990.

In the case of the public corporations, the effects of asset transfers to the private sector, especially after the British Telecom sale in 1984, show up very clearly in **Table 3.4**. The total investment at 1985 prices has been stable since 1987, so the ratio to GDP is likely to continue to slide inexorably downwards so long as there are further

Table 3.5   *Investment by Type of Asset as % of GDFCF, 1979–90*[1]

	1979	1980	1981	1982	1983	1984	1985	1986	1987	1988[2]	1989[2]	1990
Investment in dwellings	23.7	23.2	21.1	21.4	22.9	21.6	19.6	21.0	21.0	20.5	19.6	18.1
Investment in other new buildings and work	28.7	28.7	30.8	32.2	31.1	31.3	30.2	31.1	31.9	32.6	32.9	35.5
Investment in plant and machinery	34.9	36.9	37.9	36.3	36.3	36.6	39.5	38.2	36.7	35.6	35.7	35.2
Investment in vehicles, ships and aircraft	13.3	11.8	10.1	9.8	9.7	10.5	10.7	9.7	10.4	10.2	10.8	10.2

Note:
[1] For the years before 1983, totals may not equal the sum of their components, because of the method used in rebasing the original data to 1985 prices.
[2] There is a statistical adjustment amounting to 1.1% of GDFCF in 1988 and 1.0% of GDFCF in 1989 and 1990.
Source: UK National Accounts 'Blue Book' (CSO, 1991) Table 13.2; *Monthly Digest of Statistics*, Table 1.8.

assets to privatise. Investment in stocks and work in progress have always been modest in relation to GDP.

Turning now to **Table 3.5**, the most notable feature is the initial ascendency of investment in plant and machinery at the expense of the other categories. The ratio to GDP stood at 32 per cent in 1977, but eight years later it had risen to 40 per cent. This was good news for the UK economy since it is clearly this category of investment which contributes most directly to economic growth. The decline since 1985 must come as something of a disappointment, but it has at least remained stable for several years.

In the light of our previous discussion, the decline in the ratio of investment in dwellings to GDP may come as something of a surprise. However, if this is broken down into private and public sector the picture is quite different. In real terms, for example, public sector investment in dwellings remained remarkably constant from 1984 to 1989, and hence declined quite rapidly in relation to GDP. Private investment, on the other hand, was 20 per cent higher in real terms in 1989 compared to 1984 (although it subsided in 1990). In real terms, some £100 bn was invested in private dwell-

ings during the 1980s, on average some 40 per cent of total investment in plant and machinery. It would doubtless have been better for the economy if the balance had been more in favour of the latter, and fortunately it did move in that direction as the decade progressed.

This can itself be explained in part, as previously noted, by the provisions in the 1984 Budget which lowered the rate of corporation tax (now even lower) and reduced first-year investment allowances. Equally, whilst property provides the ideal protection against the ravages of inflation during periods of rapid inflation, this is no longer the case when inflation subsides (as it did during the 1980s compared to the 1970s). Hopefully, therefore, the rebalancing in favour of productive investment will be the hallmark of the recovery when it in due course arrives.

Fluctuations in the level of investment have a considerable impact upon the business cycle. Over time, the level of investment determines the rate of growth of the stock of capital, and this is a major determinant of the rate of growth of real income.

Figure 3.6 shows that during the 1980s the UK grew on average at the same rate as France and West Germany, but needed two percentage points

Figure 3.6 *Growth Rates and Investment Ratios, OECD, 1979–90*

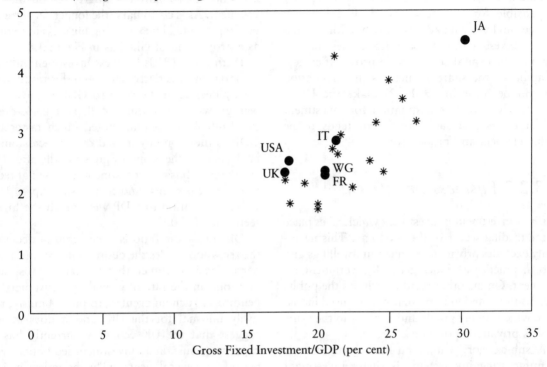

GDP Growth (average annual percentage rate)

Gross Fixed Investment/GDP (per cent)

Source: OECD.

Figure 3.7 *International Comparisons of Gross Fixed Capital Formation as a Proportion of GDP, 1979–90*

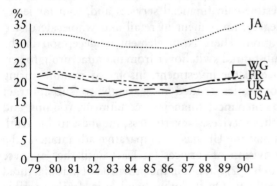

Note:
[1] OECD Estimates.
Source: OECD.

less investment to do so. Whilst this does not provide a full excuse for having such a low level of investment by international standards, as shown in **Figure 3.7**, it does show that the UK's record is no longer by any means as poor by EC standards as is often made out.

It is often argued, with some justice, that the **quality** of investment is a critical issue. For this reason, UK investment has been viewed as of questionable value because much more of it has traditionally been devoted to the defence industries compared to Japan and West Germany, and these industries have not been viewed as particularly beneficial for growth, exports and jobs. Equally, the poor performance of parts of the nuclear industry in which huge sums were invested, and the money wasted on prestige projects such as Concorde, have provided ammunition for critics of British investment performance. Nevertheless, **Figure 3.7** does suggest that the 1980s did not conform with this stereotype, and that investment

in, for example, West Germany, was overall noticeably less efficient.

Undoubtedly, government policy has been partly
responsible for this turnaround. Fiscal policy
changes no longer make it worthwhile for companies to invest mainly to save tax rather than to
enhance the capital stock and improve efficiency.
In addition, the sharp reductions in corporation
tax (33 per cent in 1991–92) make the UK a
particularly attractive destination for investment
by foreigners and such investment tends to be
highly efficient and productive.

☐ 3.2.3 Business Investment

Business investment is investment which takes place
in the trading sector of the economy. This necessarily excludes private investment in dwellings and
also in practice excludes general government investment. On the other hand it includes the public
corporations, and in particular nationalised industries, which supply goods and services in the same
way as private corporations.

A sub-category within business investment is
manufacturing investment. Business investment

currently accounts for roughly two-thirds of
GDFCF, and manufacturing investment currently
accounts for roughly one-quarter of business investment. As is customary, the longer-term trend is
best represented by expressing business investment
as a proportion of GDP, as in **Figure 3.8**.

During the 1970s business investment adjusted
for inflation was fairly static, and this resulted in a
steady decline in the ratio to GDP because GDP
was growing. Investment collapsed back during
the 1980–81 recession; surged much faster than
GDP as the economy moved out of recession; fell
back again as the economy grew rapidly after 1985
even though business investment was itself at record
levels in real terms; and finally shot up to levels
which in relation to GDP were much the highest
seen since 1970.

Obviously the ratio is once again in decline as
the recession erodes the desire to invest, but it is of
particular importance that the late 1980s' surge
even outran the rate of growth of consumers' expenditure. Such an event is, to put it bluntly, relatively unusual for the UK, and it does at least
suggest that the UK economy currently has the
capacity to sustain an investment-led boom over a
period of several years. (The boomlet in 1984
resulted from the bringing forward of investment
to avoid changes in the tax system intended to
discourage forms of investment undertaken primarily in order to obtain tax breaks.)

Manufacturing investment accounted for
roughly one-third of business investment in the
period to 1970. Subsequently it fell back to its
current one-quarter. Its place was taken by investment in financial services and, to a far lesser
degree, investment in retail and wholesale distribution. There is an element of deception in the
substantial switchover from manufacturing to service sector investment, insofar as manufacturing
companies tended increasingly to sub-contract
maintenance, financial, recruitment, training and
other services. Nevertheless, the inescapable truth
is that the UK has a comparative advantage in the
provision of services (at least until the Japanese
catch up?) but not in the provision of manufactured
products. On the other hand, it is clearly possible
to over-invest in services and to under-invest in
manufacturing.

Figure 3.8　*Business Investment* [1] *as % of GDP*

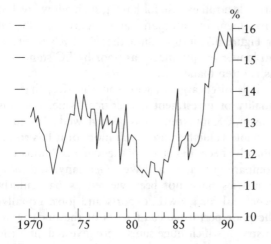

Note:
[1] Investment by industrial, commercial and financial
companies and public corporations as a percentage
of GDP (O).
Source: Bank of England Quarterly Bulletin.

☐ 3.2.4 Saving and Investment

Up until the 1980s the link between saving and investment was very strong. Countries such as Japan and West Germany, which saved a relatively high proportion of their GDP, also invested heavily, whereas the opposite was true for the USA and Britain. As we discovered previously, saving by the household sector can be absorbed by government or by companies overseas, and the removal of exchange controls after 1979 broke the link between domestic saving and domestic investment – but not completely.

During the latter part of the 1980s, the surge in investment in the UK could be accommodated by international borrowing without being constrained by a shortfall of domestic saving, but most domestic saving in OECD countries (61 per cent from 1980 to 1987) ended up as domestic investment. This proportion was 30 per cent lower than in 1960s, and a larger reduction was felt by EC mem-

ber states, except that in their case the reduction was from 74 per cent down to only 36 per cent. The tendency to rely on overseas saving is thus not limited to the UK, but it does expose the vulnerability of countries such as the UK to the possibility of a saving shortfall overseas which they are in no position to compensate for internally.

■ 3.3 Stocks

Fixed investment does not include investment in stocks or inventories. The scale of investment in stocks is small in comparison with GDFCF. Nevertheless, it is important both because it reflects changes in the level of demand and also causes such changes.

Although stocks play no part in the provision of services, they are clearly vital in overcoming imbalances between the supply and demand for raw materials and semi-finished and finished manufactures. When sales rise relative to production this

Figure 3.9 *Contribution or Stockbuilding to GDP Growth*

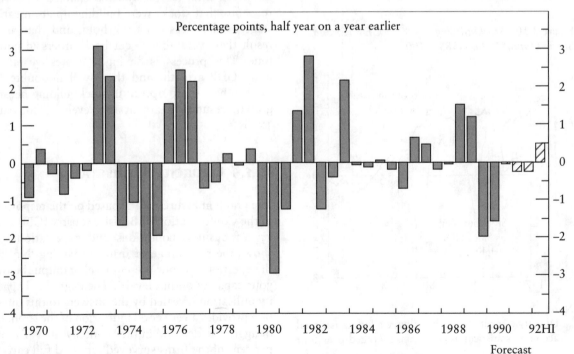

Source: FSBR 1991–92, Chart 3.9.

causes stocks to be run down, which acts as a signal to producers to increase output if the increased demand is expected to continue. Conversely, a rise in stocks relative to production, unless it is planned by producers in anticipation of a higher level of future sales, signals a reduction in demand and the need to cut back production if demand is expected to remain low.

As an economy slides into recession, producers cut back output severely and rely upon their cushion of stocks to meet demand. Destocking accordingly speeds up the rate of decline of output, and this phenomenon is very clear in the major post-war recessions, with destocking cutting output by over 3 per cent in 1974–75 and by 2.5 per cent in 1980 alone, as shown in **Figure 3.9**.

If GDP is growing erratically then this will cause the accumulation or run down of stocks to be erratic in its turn, and this will then feed through to cause further erratic movements of GDP. This pattern is clearly seen during the 1970s in **Figure 3.9**. It can alternatively be analysed in terms of stockbuilding in proportion to GDP or the **stock–output ratio**.

Figure 3.10 *Stockbuilding[1] as % of GDP (E) and Stock–Output Ratio (1985 = 100)*

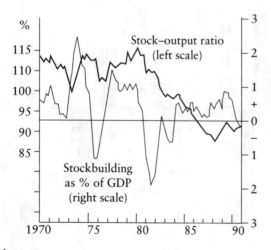

Note:

[1] Directly estimated stockbuilding, excluding national accounts statistical adjustments, averaged over four quarters.

Source: Bank of England Quarterly Bulletin (February 1991) p. 18; (August 1991) p. 365.

In the three years to 1980, as shown in **Figure 3.10**, stockbuilding was positive and the stock–output ratio rose accordingly, encouraged by negative real interest rates and a tax regime favourable towards stockholding. However, when in 1980 real interest rates rose sharply and demand collapsed, stocks were reduced sharply in order to maintain cash flow. The reduction in tax relief on stocks in 1981, combined with high real rates of interest and improvements in stock-control methods throughout the decade, served to stabilise stockbuilding at a modest positive rate which, given the rather faster rise in GDP, caused the stock–output ratio to decline until 1988. Since stockbuilding prior to the 1990–91 recession was significantly less than in 1980–81, the destocking which began in 1990 was on a relatively modest scale and hence, as shown in **Figure 3.9**, the effects upon GDP growth were also relatively modest.

At the equivalent of roughly three months' output, UK stockholding remains higher in 1991 than is customary for major competitors, but there is no longer much fat to trim. It would appear that improved information systems enabled firms to recognise that stocks were building up at an early stage as the recession took hold, and that as a result they were able to cut back orders in good time. This process is having a depressive effect upon GDP growth, and there will undoubtedly need to be a sharp upturn in stockbuilding before growth resumes again at the levels of the late 1980s.

■ 3.4 Capacity Utilisation

The graph in **Figure 3.11** is based on the responses to the Confederation of British Industry (CBI) survey of business conditions and expectations; it shows the percentage of firms answering 'No' to the question: 'Is your present level of output below your capacity output level?'. The degree of capacity utilisation revealed by the answers to this question provides a very good indication of the strength of aggregate demand in the economy. In 1979, 50 per cent of the firms surveyed reported full capacity working. While this may seem low, it indicates a low level of demand and represented the highest

Figure 3.11 *Capacity Utilisation, %*

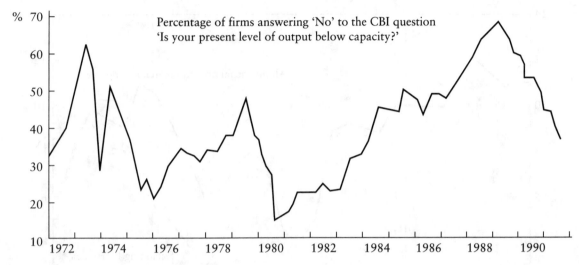

Percentage of firms answering 'No' to the CBI question 'Is your present level of output below capacity?'

Source: CBI.

level obtained since the 1970–73 boom. The rapid decline in the degree of capacity utilisation in 1980 was the sharpest recorded in the period 1972–90 and also the lowest level, with 85 per cent of firms reporting below-capacity output in 1980. The subsequent slow recovery to 1983 is clearly shown, as is the much stronger recovery in 1984–85. By 1985 capacity working was above the 1979 level, and this was followed by further continued growth of demand leading to the highest level of capacity utilisation (at 70 per cent) for the entire period from 1972. The level of capacity utilisation in 1988 indicated a very high level of aggregate demand in the economy, and hence the likelihood of both increasing inflationary pressure and a worsening balance of trade deficit.

These duly materialised, just as inflation speeded up after the previous cycle peaks in 1973 and 1979. It is possible to argue that improvements in management and on the supply side generally made it possible to run the economy nearer to capacity during the 1980s compared to previous decades without it boiling over, but the situation in 1988 was unsustainable on any measure, as was indeed that in 1979 when there was even less slack in the labour market than in 1988.

The downturn in 1979–80 was short but severe. So far the current downturn in capacity has been more gradual but also longer lasting, with an al-most identical aggregate reduction in the response rate. The graph should, therefore, bottom out in the 30–35 per cent range towards the end of 1991, at which point there should be enough spare capacity for an ensuing period of less inflationary growth.

■ 3.5 Company Profitability

Figure 3.12 presents a long-term view of companies' pre-tax profitability, adjusted also to take account of the North Sea oil sector after the mid-1970s. As can be seen, the profitability of all industrial and commercial companies (ICCs) sagged fairly continuously from 1962 to 1973, and then took a dive as costs rose sharply as a consequence of rising oil and other commodity prices. From this point there was nowhere to go but up – but not for long as there was a further sharp downturn after 1979 which, in the case of non-oil ICCs, depressed profitability below even the level prevailing in the mid-1970s.

The excellent profitability of the oil sector produced a somewhat better result for all ICCs, and as the economy grew rapidly out of the recession profitability surged with it. The improved climate for profits in turn fostered investment even though borrowing costs remained high, and additional

Figure 3.12   *Companies' Real Rates of Return on Capital, Pre-tax, 1962–90, %*

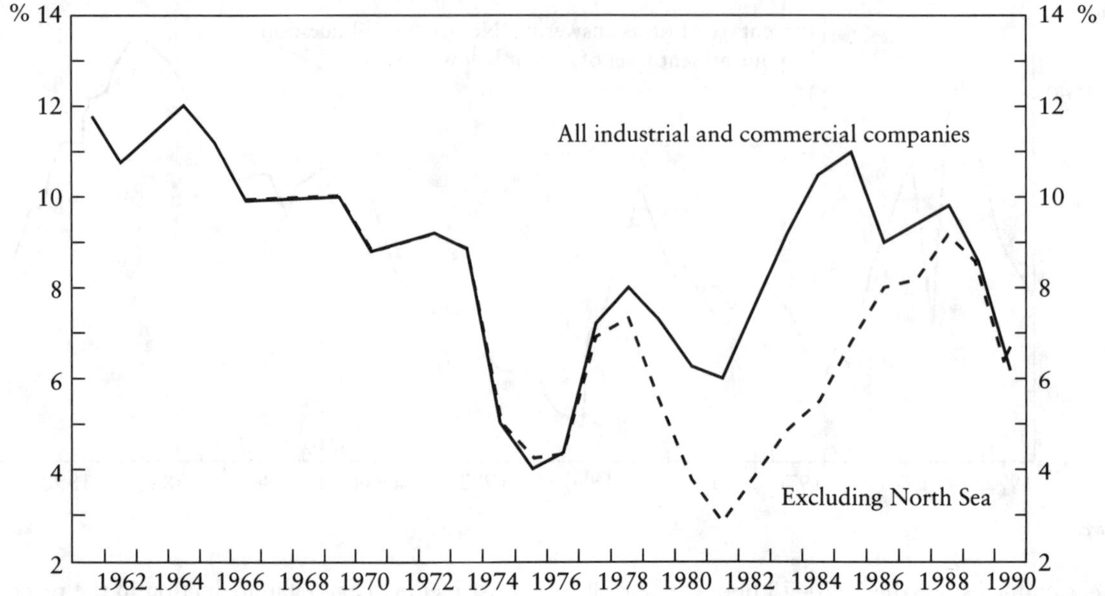

Source: Autumn Statement 1990, Chart 2.7.

investment helped to sustain profitability. By the late 1980s the situation looked healthier than it had been for two decades, but the onset of recession caused profitability to slump during 1990, and it has yet to turn up again.

It is not particularly easy to interpret the overall picture. One of the main thrusts of the Thatcher Government was to improve the workings of the supply side of the economy, as discussed below. This included, for example, reductions in corporate taxation and the removal of distortions in the tax system which encouraged investment for short-term financial gain rather than for long term. The power of organised labour was also eroded. Nevertheless, profitability collapsed after 1989 just as it had in previous recessions, so either these measures had no real impact upon profitability or they were offset by other supply-side problems as yet unaddressed.

■ **3.6 Growth and Productivity**

For a country to grow richer, it must first of all grow. In other words, it is the increase in the volume of goods and services (real GDP) which economic growth represents that underpins the improvement in a country's standard of living over time. It should be observed that there are quite a number of qualifications to be made when linking growth to living standards – for example, if the extra goods and services are all exported, domestic consumption will not be affected, and the fruits of growth may not be distributed at all equally so that some individuals may become worse off even when the economy is growing rapidly. Nevertheless, provided population growth does not outstrip economic growth – fortunately not the case in advanced societies – the only certain way for individuals to become steadily richer is for economic growth to be the rule rather than the exception.

It must also be remembered that growth is **compound**. In other words, if there is 10 per cent growth for three years, the index of real GDP will not rise in the sequence 100; 110; 120; 130 but in the sequence 100; 110; 121; 133. Whilst this makes little difference in any single year, it makes an enormous difference over several decades. At 10 per cent compound, real GDP doubles in 7½ years; triples 4 years later and is four times as large less than 3 years after that. At a growth rate of 5 per cent it takes 33 years to raise real GDP by a factor of 5 whereas at a growth rate of 10 per cent it takes only 17 years. No wonder Japanese growth rates look so attractive.

A word of caution is nevertheless necessary. If GDP is initially very low, high growth rates make little absolute difference. Thus, if a country with a GDP of £10 bn doubles its GDP, the absolute improvement is equivalent only to a 10 per cent growth rate for a country with an initial GDP of £100 bn. By and large, mature advanced economies do not, therefore, grow all that rapidly. Now that Japan falls into this category it also does not grow much faster than comparable economies, as we will see. The key issue about growth is, accordingly, not why the UK grows slowly (it is amazing, incidentally, after a decade during which the economy grew strongly in most years, how many critics claim that the UK is no better off **at all** than it was in 1979) but why it grows **more slowly** than comparable economies over the medium to long term.

For real GDP to grow year on year we strictly need only to keep increasing the size of the labour force and to maintain output per person employed at a constant level. However, if the labour force is not growing at all rapidly, what is needed is to make each worker more **productive**. Productivity is thus of crucial importance, and it is in respect of

productivity that a 'miracle' is alleged to have taken place in the UK during the 1980s.

But did it? The first difficulty is deciding exactly what the word 'productivity' means. As indicated above, most of the discussion centres around **labour** productivity as measured by **output per person employed** (or output per head). It can also be measured as output per person hour, but this produces an almost identical trend in practice. One could also refer to output per unit of capital, or **capital** productivity, but the most commonly utilised alternative is known as **total factor productivity** which is defined as output per unit of average input, where average input is a weighted average of capital (roughly 30 per cent) and labour (roughly 70 per cent).

It may be argued that none of these measures is a true measure of productivity because labour productivity, for example, can be responsive to changes in the quality of the capital stock, to the way work is organised and to the industrial relations climate. With such caveats in mind, what is the overall picture?

□ 3.6.1 Long-term Growth

It is useful to begin by taking a long-term perspective, as is done in **Figure 3.13**. Here the data has been used to calculate overlapping six-year period

Figure 3.13   *Average Growth for Six-year Periods, 1949–54 to 1982–87, %*

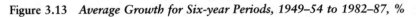
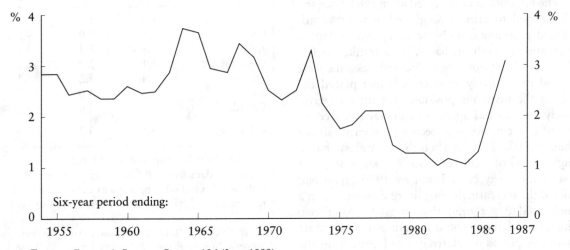

Source: Treasury Economic Progress Report, 196 (June 1988).

growth rates, rather than annual growth rates, in order to facilitate comparison with the high-growth period in the mid-1980s (here taken as 1981–87).

Figure 3.13 shows that during the 1950s and 1960s successive six-year periods had annual growth rates contained largely in the 2.5 to 3.5 per cent range. Nevertheless, the sharp improvements in the middle and end of the 1960s, and then again in 1973, are of particular interest in relation to the period post-1985, both in terms of the fact that they were short-lived and that each peaked at a successively lower level. Essentially, it was downhill all the way from 1965 to 1985, spanning the term of office of several governments of quite different political hues. The strength of the upturn after 1985 can be compared only to that during the early postwar recovery phase, but its starting point was a far lower rate of growth than at any point during the intervening period.

Taking the period 1960–87 as a whole, the UK's performance was poor by comparison with other advanced economies with the exception of the USA. During most of the 1960s it was worse even than that of the USA, although it was quite good compared to previous decades and better than the two subsequent decades. The downwards trend from 1974–79 was not, of course, a phenomenon unique to the UK as 'shocks' such as oil price rises affected other advanced economies to much the same extent, but that simply meant that the UK continued to grow relatively slowly (although the USA did even worse).

The big difference occurred after 1981 since the UK started to grow strongly whereas other advanced economies, with the exception of Japan, continued to perform badly. As a result, the UK shot up the growth league. Nevertheless, the long period of relatively slow growth had placed the UK in the invidious position of getting progressively wealthier at a time when every other country of consequence was becoming even wealthier than the UK. Even in 1966 the USA alone had a higher level of GDP per head. At that time Japan was a long way behind, but by 1980 Japan had joined the increasingly long list of countries with a higher GDP per head than the UK. After two decades of falling behind it obviously needs more than one period of relatively rapid growth for the UK to recover all of the lost ground. Nevertheless, at least the fatalistic view commonly voiced during the 1970s that the process of relative decline was irreversible has been proved to be false.

☐ 3.6.2 *Productivity*

Table 3.6 is concerned with labour productivity over the period 1960–88, divided into three sub-

Table 3.6 *Output Per Person Employed, Average Annual Percentage Changes*

Whole Economy	1960–70	1970–80	1980–88
UK	2.4	1.3	2.5
US	2.0	0.4	1.2
Japan	8.9	3.8	2.9
Germany	4.4	2.8	1.8
France	4.6	2.8	2.0
Italy	6.3	2.6	2.0
Canada	2.4	1.5	1.4
G7 average	3.5	1.7	1.8

UK data from Central Statistical Office. Other countries' data from OECD except 1988 which are calculated from national GNP or GDP figures and OECD employment estimates.

Manufacturing Industry	1960–70	1970–80	1980–88
UK	3.0	1.6	5.2
US	3.5	3.0	4.0
Japan	8.8	5.3	3.1
Germany	4.1	2.9	2.2
France	5.4	3.2	3.1
Italy	5.4	3.0	3.5
Canada	3.4	3.0	3.6
G7 average	4.5	3.3	3.6

UK data from Central Statistical Office. Other countries' data from OECD, except France and Italy which use IMF employment data. 1988 data for France and Italy cover first three quarters only.

Sources: CSO, OECD, IMF; Reproduced from *Treasury Economic Progress Report*, 201 (April 1989).

periods and covering manufacturing industry as well as the whole economy. The most notable feature is the significant reduction in productivity during the 1970s compared to the 1960s, and the rather modest improvement during the bulk of the 1980s.

Once again, the poor performance of the UK compared to the other major economies during the 1960s is plain to see, especially with respect to manufacturing. During the 1970s the general level of performance was much inferior, but the UK nevertheless managed to fall even further behind in manufacturing.

Figure 3.14 illustrates the relationship between output and labour productivity during the period 1975 to 1986, based upon 1980 = 100. **Figure**

Figure 3.14 *Output and Productivity*[1], *UK, 1975–86, (1980 = 100)*

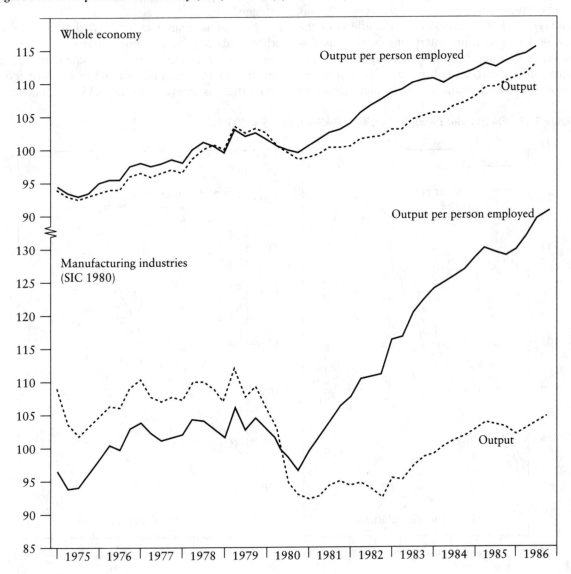

Note:
[1] Seasonally adjusted.
Source: Employment Gazette.

3.14 brings out very clearly the contrast between the 1970s and 1980s. In the manufacturing sector real output hobbled along during the second half of the 1980s with productivity following an almost identical trend but below that of output. The sheer inefficiency of labour use in manufacturing is scarcely credible in the light of the more recent discovery that UK workers are not necessarily bone idle by choice but can be motivated to work as hard as the Germans and Japanese.

The situation for the rest of the economy was scarcely much better. However, the effects of the 1980–81 recession are interesting in that, as discussed in Chapter 7, output and employment collapsed in manufacturing but not in the rest of the economy. Indeed, employment in manufacturing

collapsed so fast that productivity responded quite quickly and was back to its pre-recession level during 1981. Output in manufacturing barely budged from its nadir until 1983, and was still well below its pre-recession level even in 1986.

Elsewhere in the economy the situation was less serious in that the fall in output was short-lived, but it still took several years for output to regain its pre-recession level because few jobs had been shed and productivity growth was consequently sluggish.

Not so in manufacturing. With hundreds of thousands of jobs lost, productivity took off at a rate which previously would have come to a grinding halt in no time at all. But on this occasion it did not falter, as shown in **Figure 3.15** which is based

Figure 3.15   *Output and Productivity¹, UK, 1983–91, (1985 = 100)*

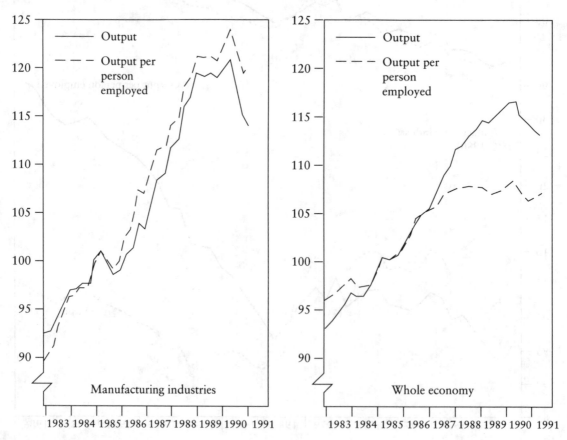

Note:
¹   Seasonally adjusted.
Source: Employment Gazette, Table 1.8.

upon 1985 = 100. As can be seen, from 1985 to the end of 1988 output in manufacturing rose by 20 per cent. Unemployment had ceased to grow much by 1985, and began to fall in 1986, so labour productivity only just kept ahead of output during this period. Elsewhere in the economy output continued to grow steadily but much more slowly than in manufacturing, and as employment picked up labour productivity ceased to grow at all from the end of 1986.

By 1988 the party was over, and after a period of marking time the hangover began. Not surprisingly it was much more painful in manufacturing, although as noted elsewhere, the pain was shared more equally by the service sectors than in 1980–81. So far we have yet to see either output or productivity bottom out.

In looking across both **Figure 3.14** and **Figure 3.15** it is possible to see why there is much acrimonious debate about whether one should examine the period from 1979 onwards or that from 1981 onwards. By the time the 1990–91 recession has bottomed out, manufacturing output will probably be back near where it began in 1979. In other words, a peak to trough (1979–1991) perspective can be made to provide a severe indictment of government policy towards the manufacturing sector. On the other hand, a trough to peak (1981–88) perspective can be used as evidence of a productivity 'miracle', with UK manufacturing outperforming the Japanese.

It may be noted that, both within the manufacturing sector and elsewhere in the economy, the performance of different sub-sectors has been very variable (Blackaby and Hunt, 1990). This may have resulted in an understatement of productivity. The current weights are based on 1985, which means that the shrinkage of sectors such as textiles is given too much weight and the expansion of other sectors too little. Furthermore, recent data on output per head have not reflected the greater incidence of part-time working and variations in overtime work.

The OECD provides data on productivity in the business sector (this is frequently revised when it appears in OECD *Economic Outlook*). As this is more broadly defined than manufacturing it provides a kind of halfway house between manufacturing and the whole economy. In respect of **labour** productivity the picture is the now familiar one, namely a poor performance throughout the 1960s and 1970s, followed by a performance improved upon only by Japan from 1979–88. In respect of **capital** productivity the UK was the only major economy to show a gain during the 1979–88 period, albeit a very modest one, whereas during the 1960s and 1970s the UK had performed in line with the OECD average. In respect of **total factor** productivity the performance during 1979–1988 was comparable with that of Japan and much better than the other major economies with the exception of France.

3.6.3 *Why did Productivity Improve?*

Improvements in productivity are related to plant closures. If the effect of the 1980–81 recession was to close down a large proportion of the least efficient plants in the UK, then that alone could account for much of the subsequent improvement in productivity as output became increasingly concentrated in efficient plants. Unfortunately, the evidence on this topic is ambiguous. A reasonable interpretation would appear to be that the rate of scrapping of the capital stock accelerated sharply at the beginning of the 1980s, and continued at levels some 50 per cent higher than in previous years.

This sounds impressive, but given that scrapping accounted previously for roughly 2 per cent of the aggregate capital stock each year, the acceleration accounted for only 1 per cent or thereabouts extra each year for possibly six years. This additional 6 per cent of scrapped capital would indeed have boosted productivity, but not significantly, especially when account is taken of the fact that during the 1980–81 recession plant closures were not concentrated among the least productive plants, but involved many larger plants with above average productivity.

It is more plausible to argue that the shock effect of the 1980–81 recession, both for management and workers, accounts for the productivity gains of the 1980s. During the 1970s labour was hoarded and hence productivity was repressed. The effect of North Sea oil upon the exchange rate, rendering UK companies increasingly uncompetitive, effectively forced them to improve productivity or go under, and this caused over 2 million workers eventually to lose their jobs. The government's deflationary policies, and its attack upon restrictive labour practices, all combined to force a reappraisal of work organisation which rapidly paid dividends. It is, however, slightly ironic that the government never intended the recession to be so severe, yet if it had been as mild as elsewhere in Europe the transformation of UK productivity would almost certainly not have occurred.

But this line of argument also implies that the easy productivity gains have been realised, and that unless there are continuing high levels of investment and training there will be severe difficulties in engineering a second productivity 'miracle' during the 1990s. In particular, there is the poor performance of manufacturing output to consider (the position is slightly better in other sectors). As can be seen in **Table 3.7**, the productivity improvement in the UK up to 1987 was entirely the effect of labour shedding whilst in the USA, and especially in Japan, it primarily reflected increases in output. Only in West Germany was the situation at all comparable to that in the UK, although the critical difference, as ever, shows up in the final column. In the UK, the productivity gains reappeared as higher real earnings. In the USA real earnings actually fell, and in Japan they absorbed only one-quarter of productivity gains.

Table 3.7 *Manufacturing Industry, 1979–87*

	Output per Worker	Employment	Output	Real Earnings[1]
		% Change in:		
USA	29.8	−6.3	21.6	−3.9
Japan	52.2	6.7	62.4	13.4
W. Germany	16.5	−7.5	7.6	10.4
UK	37.8	−27.5	0.0	25.8

Note:
[1] Hourly earnings deflated by consumer price index.
Source: OECD.

The lesson is fairly clear. The next productivity 'miracle' will need to be based upon a rapid expansion of output, preferably in manufacturing – Japanese style. A re-run of the 1980s 'miracle' offers no permanent solution to the problem of catching up the ground lost during the 1960s and 1970s.

■ 3.7 Inflation

Since the late 1940s the UK economy has experienced a succession of severe macroeconomic problems punctuated by short periods of more favourable economic performance. The same four main problems occur with a disturbing persistence even though at particular times one dominates. These are a low rate of growth of real GDP, high unemployment, persistent inflation and balance of payments deficits. The most serious and protracted problem in the 1970s was that of inflation. In 1975, at the height of the inflationary process, the annual rate of inflation exceeded 24 per cent. The seriousness of the problem is brought out by the fact that the inflation rate in 1975 was higher than at any other time this century. The economic performance of the economy in the 1980s was dictated by the measures adopted to eradicate the high inflation of the 1970s.

□ 3.7.1 Measurement of Inflation

'Inflation' refers to a rise in the general level of prices, or in an average measure of prices in the economy, rather than to the behaviour of the price of an individual good or service. Inflation becomes a serious problem when the general level of prices rises **persistently** and unpredictably. The rate of inflation is calculated using an index of the general price level, or some other relevant concept of prices, and the index is constructed as a weighted average of the relevant prices. The question of relevant prices highlights the fact that different groups of people are interested in the behaviour of different sets of prices; for example a manufacturer will be concerned about the rate of increase of the price of fuel and raw materials, while a consumer will be

Figure 3.16 *Structure of the Retail Prices Index.*

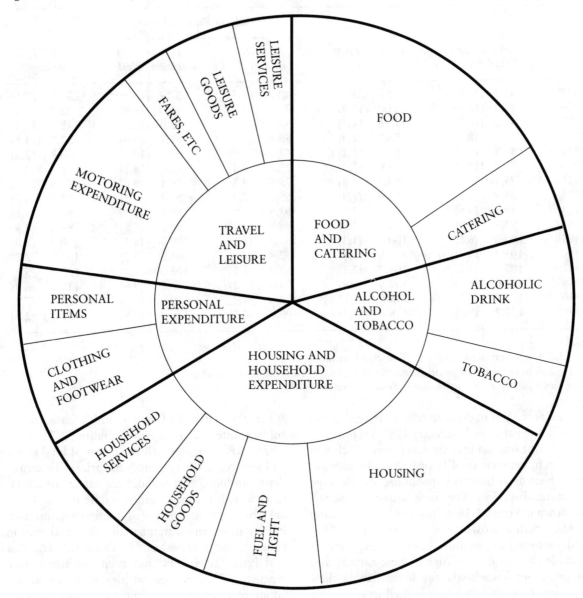

LEISURE SERVICES

LEISURE GOODS

FARES, ETC

MOTORING EXPENDITURE

FOOD

CATERING

ALCOHOLIC DRINK

TRAVEL AND LEISURE

FOOD AND CATERING

PERSONAL ITEMS

PERSONAL EXPENDITURE

ALCOHOL AND TOBACCO

CLOTHING AND FOOTWEAR

HOUSING AND HOUSEHOLD EXPENDITURE

TOBACCO

HOUSEHOLD SERVICES

HOUSEHOLD GOODS

FUEL AND LIGHT

HOUSING

Source: CSO.

more interested in retail prices. For this reason the CSO publishes several different price indices or measures of inflation.

The most widely used of these is the **Retail Prices Index** (RPI) which is published by the Department of Employment. This is a weighted average of prices for a basket of 600 goods and services consumed by a 'typical' household. The total

weights of 1000 are distributed so as to reflect the pattern of spending as revealed by the Family Expenditure Survey (FES), and a new set of weights is introduced at the beginning of each year, (see *Employment Gazette* June 1991, pp. 351–3). Over time the weights assigned to different groups of goods and services can vary considerably, and it is also necessary periodically to alter the main cat-

Table 3.8 *Assorted Price Indices (1985 = 100)*

Year	General Index of Retail Prices		Tax and Price Index		Producer Price Index				GDP deflator [1]	
					Materials and Fuel		Manufactured (Home Sales)			
1975	36.1	(24.1)[2]	37.7	(25.3)[2]	40.0	(11.7)[2]	37.9	(23.1)[2]	37.6	(27.6)[2]
1976	42.1	(16.5)	45.0	(19.4)	49.9	(24.7)	44.0	(16.1)	42.9	(14.1)
1977	48.8	(15.7)	51.6	(14.7)	57.5	(15.2)	52.0	(18.2)	48.2	(12.4)
1978	52.8	(8.2)	53.1	(2.9)	59.6	(3.7)	57.1	(9.8)	53.9	(11.8)
1979	59.9	(13.4)	59.5	(12.1)	67.3	(12.9)	63.3	(10.8)	60.8	(12.8)
1980	70.7	(18.0)	69.8	(17.3)	73.0	(8.4)	72.2	(14.1)	72.3	(18.9)
1981	79.1	(11.9)	80.1	(14.8)	79.7	(9.2)	79.1	(9.6)	79.9	(10.5)
1982	85.9	(8.6)	88.0	(9.9)	85.5	(7.3)	85.2	(7.7)	85.2	(6.6)
1983	89.8	(4.6)	91.5	(4.0)	91.4	(6.9)	89.8	(5.4)	90.1	(5.8)
1984	94.3	(5.0)	95.0	(3.8)	98.9	(8.2)	95.0	(5.8)	94.5	(4.9)
1985	100.0	(6.1)	100.0	(5.3)	100.0	(1.1)	100.0	(5.3)	100.0	(8.0)
1986	103.4	(3.4)	101.8	(1.8)	92.4	(−7.6)	104.3	(4.3)	102.7	(2.7)
1987	107.7	(4.2)	104.3	(2.5)	95.3	(3.1)	103.3	(−1.0)	107.9	(5.1)
1988	113.0	(4.9)	107.4	(2.9)	98.4	(3.2)	113.2	(9.6)	115.2	(6.8)
1989	121.8	(7.8)	115.0	(7.1)	104.0	(5.7)	119.0	(5.1)	123.6	(7.3)
1990	133.2	(9.4)	128.0	(11.3)	103.8	(−0.2)	126.0	(5.9)	127.2	(2.9)

Notes:
[1]   GDP at current factor cost ÷ GDP at constant factor cost.
[2]   Figures in brackets represent the percentage change from the previous year.
Sources: Employment Gazette; Economic Trends; Monthly Digest of Statistics.

egories of weights in order to reflect major changes in spending patterns. In January 1987 a significant amendment was made to the categories which had been in force since 1974 in order to take account of such items as holiday expenditure and the cost of financial services. The three largest categories, as shown in **Figure 3.16** in July 1991 were housing (192), which is growing continuously, food (151) and motoring expenditure (141). These weights exclude the spending of high income earners and of pensioner households, the latter having their own independent RPI which is used in order, for example, to index-link pensions.

The RPI for the period since 1975, based upon 1985 = 100, is shown in **Table 3.8**. However, most interest is focussed upon the ongoing rate of inflation, which is expressed most commonly as an annual rate of change. Thus, for example, the annual rate for calendar 1990 can be calculated from **Table 3.8** by the formula 133.2 − 121.8 ÷ 121.8 × 100 per cent which equals 9.4 per cent.

When this is repeated on a monthly basis the resulting pattern is as shown in **Figure 3.17**.

The RPI measures only the prices of final goods and services. It thus excludes the prices of intermediate products, but includes the effects of alterations in indirect taxes and in excise duties. There are obviously other ways of going about measuring inflation, and a number of other measures in common usage are set out in **Table 3.8**. **The Tax and Price Index** (TPI) has been published since August 1979. The general idea was to take account of changes in income taxes and National Insurance Contributions (NICs) which were expected to fall, thereby leaving households with more real spending power than appeared to be the case after adjusting gross incomes for changes in the RPI. This was expected to exert downward pressure on wage demands. However, as it turned out the TPI promptly rose more rapidly than the RPI as a result of the 1980 Budget, and was put into abeyance, a position it has continued to oc-

Figure 3.17 *Retail Prices Index, %*

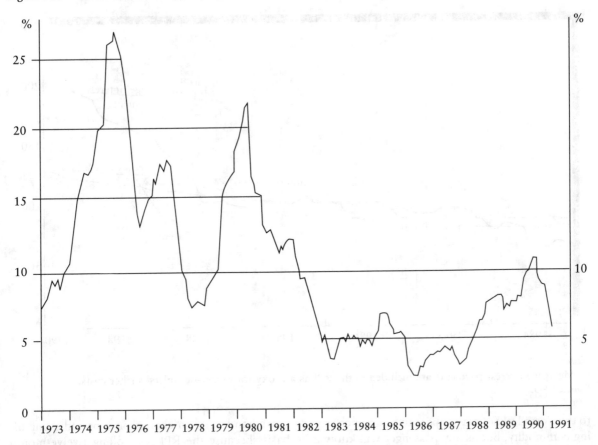

Source: Employment Gazette.

cupy ever since even though the TPI has risen somewhat more slowly than the RPI since April 1983. The **Producer Price Index**, previously known as the Wholesale Price Index, is divided into an index covering the prices of materials and fuel and an index covering the prices of home sales of manufactured products ('factory gate' prices). These indices respond to inflationary pressures earlier than the RPI and hence can be useful in providing prior warning of an upsurge in retail prices. As shown in **Table 3.8**, the RPI shadows factory gate prices very closely whereas the index for materials and fuel is relatively volatile and (as in 1986) can occasionally fall. As will be reiterated below, a combination of falling input prices and rising output prices is evidence of a sharp rise in profit margins.

Although these are the only price indices which are widely reported, much of the adjustment from

nominal to real magnitudes is done using so-called price 'deflators'. The best-known of these is the index of total home costs, commonly referred to as the **'implicit' price deflator**, which is also recorded in **Table 3.8**. This index measures the change of all prices in the economy as reflected in changes in the cost of producing all of the components of GDP.

As with so many other things, data on inflation must be treated with caution because inadequate account is taken of **changes in quality over time**. Companies are constantly turning out goods that are lighter, faster, more energy-efficient and more reliable than their predecessors. For example, one can buy a video for much the same price as five years ago, but it will have additional features. A basic office computer may even go down in price, yet that will disguise the fact that it will be vastly more powerful than its predecessor. A plane ride

Figure 3.18   *Housing, Selected Components of the Retail Prices Index (January 1987 = 100)*

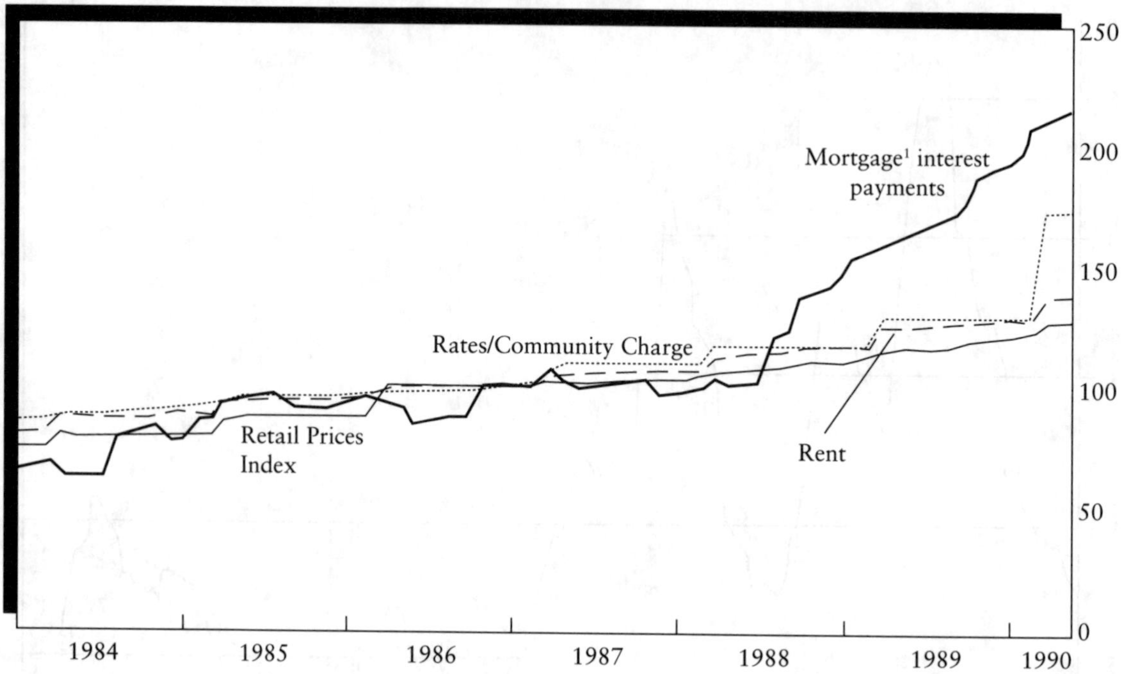

Note:
[1]   Mortgage interest payments are included in the RPI as a proxy for owner-occupiers' shelter costs.
Source: CSO.

to the Costa Del Sol may appear to be an unchanging commodity, but as any passenger will know a modern jet is faster and more comfortable than models in use a decade or more ago.

All of the main measures of inflation tell much the same story in the longer term, but monthly and quarterly figures can deviate quite appreciably (which is a good reason for not paying too much attention to them). Since the recorded figures for short-term inflation do have a significant impact upon financial markets there is political capital to be made out of the exclusion from the RPI of any components which are rising undesirably fast from the government's point of view. Controversy has recently surfaced in this respect concerning the treatment of housing and certain other costs in the RPI.

The key point to bear in mind in this respect is that inflation can be **persistent** only if something is persistently causing prices to rise – in other words it is **recurrent**. Wages, for example, tend to rise continuously. Interest rates or rates of tax, on the

other hand, tend to change on a periodic one-off basis. Because the RPI is a rolling twelve-month index an increase in, say, VAT in April 1991 will appear in the index [April 1991 – April 1990 ÷ April 1990] but not in the corresponding index for March 1991, and will cause the RPI to **rise** in April 1991. However, in April 1992, assuming VAT remains unchanged, the 1991 increase in VAT will have shifted in the formula [April 1992 – April 1991 ÷ April 1991] in such a way as to cause the RPI to **fall** to a lower rate. In effect, the RPI is as much dependent upon what happened to prices a year previously as upon what happens in the current month. Because of the formula it means, for example, that a series of interest rate increases will bump up the RPI very rapidly, but if they are followed by a series of reductions (as in 1990–91) the RPI will eventually fall back very sharply (as in May 1991).

As noted previously, housing constitutes the biggest single element in the RPI, and can therefore have a significant distorting effect in the short

Figure 3.19 *Alternative Measures of Inflation, 1987–91, %*

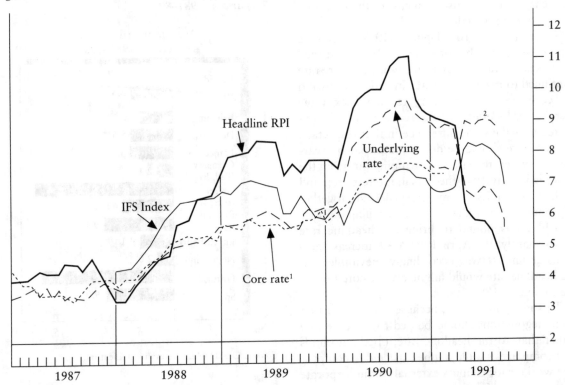

Notes:
[1] Excluding mortgage interest, Community Charge and oil.
[2] 'Underlying underlying' rate which reached its highest level for a decade in June 1991 of 8.9 per cent. The 1991 Budget 'exchanged' a rise in VAT for a reduction in poll tax. This caused the 'underlying' rate to follow the 'headline' rate, but the underlying underlying rate did not benefit from the poll tax reduction whereas it did incorporate the rise in VAT – hence it behaved perversely. Its behaviour is very similar to that of the core rate, and only one or the other has accordingly been depicted.
Sources: CSO, HM Treasury and Institute for Fiscal Studies.

run. As can be seen in **Figure 3.18**, this didn't happen prior to 1988, but became very important subsequently, especially when, on the advice of the Retail Prices Index Advisory Committee, the Community Charge was substituted for domestic rates in the RPI at the time the Charge was introduced. From the beginning of 1986 to June 1990, the RPI rose by 32 per cent whilst the rent index rose by 45 per cent and the rates/Community Charge index rose by 95 per cent (mostly between March and April 1990). The index of mortgage interest payments rose by 132 per cent over the same period, and in every month from May 1988 to June 1990, due partly to increasing mortgage balances caused by house price inflation.

These developments sparked off a furious debate about the 'proper' way to measure inflation (see, for example, the regular contributions by Samuel Brittan in the *Financial Times*). As a result, it is now customary to refer to the official **headline** RPI as well as to the official **underlying** rate, one version of which excludes mortgage interest payments whilst the other ('underlying underlying') rate also excludes the Community Charge. There is also the **core** rate which is the latter rate excluding oil. In addition, there is an index prepared by the Institute for Fiscal Studies (IFS) which adjusts indirectly for housing costs and hence, as shown in **Figure 3.19**, began to rise with house prices early in 1988 and to fall with house prices in 1990. By extension, now that VAT has been raised to 17½ per cent, it makes sense to measure the core rate also excluding the effects of VAT.

As can be seen from **Figure 3.19**, the headline rate soared above the core rate in 1988, but turned down sharply in 1990 at a time when the core rate continued to rise to a plateau. In order to unwind the core rate it is necessary to rein back wage increases. The effects of the recession can be expected to make some difference in that respect, so the core rate should be down somewhat by year-end. However, the effect of stripping out from the formula in May 1991 the rises in interest rates and in the Community Charge in April 1990, together with interest rate reductions and a falling oil price in 1991, was bound to bring the headline rate down sharply, the April 1991 VAT increase notwithstanding. It was accordingly inevitable that the headline rate would fall **below** the core rate by the middle of 1991.

This is slightly ironic, because it is argued that wage negotiations should be tied to the core rate rather than to the headline rate, on the grounds that companies should not be expected to compensate workers for changes external to the corporate sector such as higher interest rates.

□ 3.7.2 International Perspectives

It is understandable that, in addressing the problem of inflation, individual countries tend to judge their performance either against a norm based upon historical experience or, less probably, against an ideal set well below that norm. As a result, relatively little attention is paid to what is happening in other advanced economies even though, logically, some of the forces operating to raise prices in the UK will be operating in exactly the same way elsewhere. In other words, in judging just how much attention should be paid to the problem of inflation relative to, say, unemployment it is useful to know how inflation-prone the UK really is.

Such an issue is best addressed by recourse to the standardised data produced by the OECD, and this is illustrated in **Figures 3.20** and **3.21**.

Figure 3.20 produces data on inflation for the 12 EC members during the 1980s. As can be seen,

Figure 3.20 *Change in Consumer Prices, EC Comparison, 1981–89*

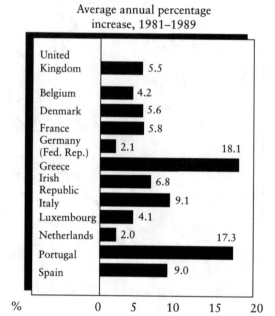

Average annual percentage increase, 1981–1989

United Kingdom	5.5
Belgium	4.2
Denmark	5.6
France	5.8
Germany (Fed. Rep.)	2.1
Greece	18.1
Irish Republic	6.8
Italy	9.1
Luxembourg	4.1
Netherlands	2.0
Portugal	17.3
Spain	9.0

Source: OECD Main Economic Indicators.

the UK was an average performer, but whilst the media are prone to make invidious comparisons with Germany and the Netherlands one can see that Greeks, Portuguese, Spaniards and Italians might pause to wonder what the fuss is all about.

Figure 3.21 takes a long view and concentrates upon the UK's main competitors. Here, as can be seen, the picture is less pleasing since the UK, apart from an interlude during the early 1980s, compares unfavourably other than with Italy. Nevertheless, there are clear similarities in the trends for individual countries. All six countries had a rising rate of inflation from 1966 to 1972, although the UK was the worst performer. All then suffered a significant increase in the rate of inflation, peaking in 1975 followed by a period of high but declining rates which, with the exception of the USA, lasted for several years only to turn up to a further peak in 1980.

The factor common to the experience of every country in the 1970s was the behaviour of the price of **crude oil**. This is illustrated in **Figure 3.22** on an inflation-adjusted basis. As can be seen it

Figure 3.21 *Consumer Price Indices, Selected Countries, 1975–90, %*

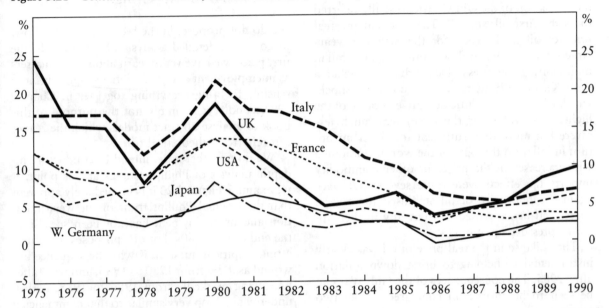

Sources: OECD Main Economic Indicators; *Employment Gazette.*

Figure 3.22 *Real Oil Price*[1], *$ per barrel, 1990 Prices*

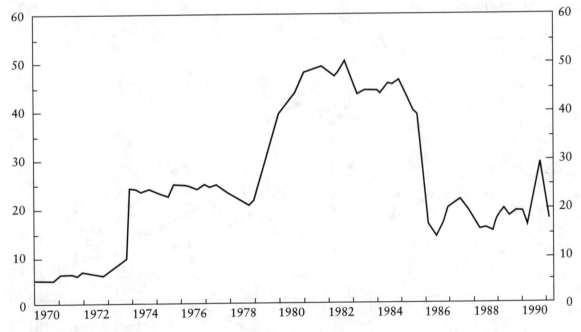

Note:
[1] OECD import price of oil to end-1988; average of Brent and Dubai thereafter.
Source: CSO.

rose by a factor of 4 in 1974 as a consequence of the formation of the OPEC cartel (usually referred to as the first oil 'shock'). The fact that the real price of oil held steady for the next five years largely explains why inflation rates began to fall in oil-importing countries (which at that time included the UK). In 1979 there was a second oil 'shock' which (the figure is a little deceptive because of the higher base value for the price) was much less severe but more than sufficient to trigger an upturn in inflation throughout the world. Combined with increases in the prices of other commodity imports the effects were quite severe, but once again the real price of oil stabilised for several years, and hence ceased to exert any further upwards pressure upon prices.

The collapse in the real price of oil was clearly instrumental in helping to bring down inflation after 1985. The consequences of the Gulf War can be seen to be short-term compared to the two previous oil 'shocks', and the breakdown of the OPEC cartel should mean that the price of oil will never again have the inflationary consequences seen previously.

□ 3.7.3 *Analytic Considerations*

We do not propose, in the sections which follow, to go into a detailed analysis of inflation. In the first place, we have yet to learn about such matters as unemployment and trade deficits, and it is more sensible to bring everything together in Chapter 12. Secondly, it is simply not the purpose of this book to analyse abstract models which the reader can refer to in theoretical texts.

We do not, therefore, intend to conduct an in-depth analysis of Phillips Curves at this point. If we examine **Figure 3.23** it is immediately apparent that the original Phillips trade-off between inflation and unemployment has not been seen since the end of the 1960s. For our purposes, the interesting empirical question is why the sequence unwound as it did from 1980 to 1986, and why, after improving markedly from 1986 to 1988, it then underwent a loop very similar to that commencing in 1978, but on a much reduced scale. Because at this juncture we have yet to meet concepts such as the 'natural' rate of unemployment (discussed in

Figure 3.23   *The Phillips Curve*

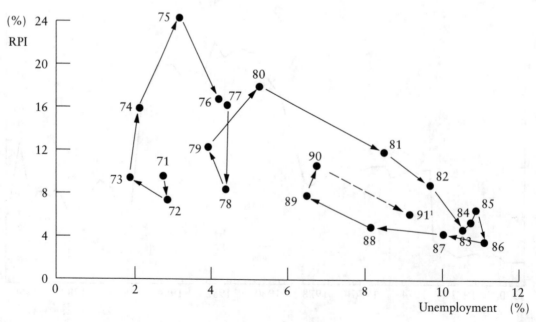

Note:
[1]   Author's estimate.
Source: Employment Gazette.

Chapter 9) we must accordingly conduct the discussion in fairly general terms.

It is evident that inflation is a **multi-causal phenomenon**. No doubt monetary policy has had a part to play, as discussed in Chapter 12. Undoubtedly, trade union militancy is a factor which must, at times, be taken into account, and the external sector, the subject of Chapter 6, cannot be ignored. It seems to the author (though others may disagree) that there is no reason to believe that the UK is inherently more inflationary than other countries, and that this opinion is supported by the evidence, discussed below, of the UK's inflation record during the past decade. What cannot be disputed is that in the early postwar period the UK was uncompetitive.

Attempts to deal with this problem were legion, but generally unsuccessful, in part because of the resistance of the workforce which was highly unionised compared to competitor countries. In good part, the pressure to introduce reforms floundered because governments of all political hues were locked into the belief that they had to maintain full employment. This meant running the economy with high levels of demand since this was adjudged an easier way to keep people in jobs than by increasing supply. However, it is evident that expanding demand in the face of fixed supply is an excellent recipe for the creation of inflationary pressure.

Some of this excess demand usually leaks out into the external sector, and results in balance of payments crises. In effect, these provide an alternative manifestation of an inflationary crisis, and hence are unlikely to disappear without triggering a resurgence of inflation unless something has been done to control the latter in the meantime. Certainly, the traditional expedient of lowering the exchange rate simply served initially to raise import prices, and fed through into domestic inflation as companies adjusted their prices to take account of increased costs. This process represented 'cost-push' rather than 'demand-pull' pressures, as text books were wont to label them.

Cost-push pressures also arise either if wages rise **independently** of the pressure of demand or if companies increase their profit margins **independently** of demand. In either case, the key issue is whether the government is willing to **validate these pressures** by recourse to an accommodating fiscal and monetary stance. During the heyday of the Keynesian model, governments were rarely willing to tolerate cuts in output and jobs – and if at all, only in the short term. Starting in the period after 1976, but more notably after 1979, governments adopted a tougher stance. Such an about turn in policy may at first be treated with scepticism, but if adhered to the message will eventually get through, as it did during 1980–81. But it was far more expensive than expected – or intended – in terms of the number of workers who lost their jobs in the process of persuading employers and employees that the government meant business.

Inflationary pressures which arise from other sources are more problematic. If, say, the price of imported commodities rises then the standard of living of UK residents must necessarily decline. If the labour market is competitive this will result in a reduction in wages, keeping total costs, and hence prices, unchanged. But probably wages will not fall, in which case there is renewed inflationary pressure and either the government reins back demand and uses job losses to suppress inflation or it accommodates the pressure and prices escalate. In the latter case, the tough stance is merely delayed in practice since the government will be forced to act once the inflationary pressure becomes severe.

The inflationary pressure described here is cost-push – that is, it occurs on the supply side of the economy – but its effects are clearly dependent upon the demand-side response by government. Given the above, it is a touch unfortunate that the UK government changed its stance from tough to accommodating during the so-called 'Lawson boom' in the latter part of the 1980s. Nevertheless, this permits us to adopt an optimistic view about future developments since the government **should** have learnt its lesson, although it is a commonly held view that governments never do learn the lessons of history.

One further point needs emphasising very strongly. It is clearly fallacious to argue that inflation cannot be reduced unless the economy stops growing, or that growth cannot be resumed until inflation is suppressed. As the data below shows clearly, periods of rapid productivity growth are periods when unit labour costs rise very little, if at all, in the high growth sectors (predominantly manufacturing). Where inflation emerges is in those sectors where productivity growth is low or non-existent, but which obtain roughly the same increase in wages on grounds of 'comparability'. Nevertheless, it is clearly impractical and inequitable to lock all the gains from productivity in the manufacturing sector.

What the government must guard against is attempts by workers to protect themselves against any erosion in their standard of living which arises **for external reasons**, such as higher oil prices. As we remarked earlier, there is scant sympathy in the UK for the view that when imported commodities go up in price this often represents the only means by which workers in much poorer societies can improve **their** standard of living.

□ 3.7.4 Inflation During the 1980s

It is possible to analyse what happened during the 1980s by reference to **Tables 3.9** and **3.10**. As shown in **Table 3.9**, the ongoing rise in labour costs, which have always been a characteristic of the UK economy, were largely compensated by rises in labour productivity with the result that unit labour costs rose comparatively little after 1982, at least in manufacturing. The biggest contributor to manufacturing output prices since 1982 has clearly been changes in domestic profit margins. These appear to have risen exceptionally sharply in 1986, although rather less subsequently. It has been argued that companies basically apply a mark-up to their expected long-run costs, which does explain the rise in margins in 1986 when oil import prices fell sharply, but is less plausible in terms of later years.

Table 3.10 takes into account the effects upon output prices of competitiveness and capacity utilisation, both of which are correlated with profit margins. The residual indicates that the specified contributions did not account exactly for the measured output prices, with the large residuals in 1986 and 1987 indicating that manufacturers took advantage of an unexpected fall in input prices. It is clear from **Table 3.10** that, for example, whereas companies were constrained in their ability to put up their prices because of competitive pressures in the early 1980s, they felt able to take advantage of

Table 3.9 *Contributions to Output Prices in Manufacturing[1], from Changes in Cost Components, %*

	Labour productivity (increase −) (1)	Labour costs (2)	Unit labour costs (3) = (1+2)[2]	Input prices (4)	Bought-in services[3] (5)	Margins (residual) (6) = (7 − (3+4+5))	Output prices (7)
1980	1.7	7.3	9.9	3.8	5.2	−3.5	15.4
1981	−1.9	6.5	4.5	2.9	2.8	−2.7	7.5
1982	−3.0	4.4	1.3	2.3	1.1	2.2	6.9
1983	−3.7	3.7	0.1	2.6	0.9	1.8	5.4
1984	−2.7	3.4	0.7	3.0	1.1	0.4	5.1
1985	−1.6	3.5	1.9	1.0	1.1	1.7	5.7
1986	−1.7	3.2	1.5	−3.4	0.8	5.2	4.1
1987	−3.1	3.4	0.3	1.7	0.9	1.5	4.4
1988	−2.8	3.6	0.7	1.6	1.9	0.6	4.8
1989	−1.9	3.9	1.9	1.8	2.4	−0.7	5.4
1990	−0.2	4.3	4.1	−0.3	2.4	−0.2	6.1

Note:
[1]   Excluding food, drink and tobacco.
[2]   Figures may not add up to totals because of rounding
[3]   Proxied by unit labour costs in the service sector.
Source: Bank of England Quarterly Bulletin (August 1991) p. 363.

Table 3.10 *Estimated Contributions to the Growth in Output Prices, %*

	Unit Labour costs	Input price proxy	Bought-in services	Competitiveness	Capacity utilisation	Residual	Output prices
1980	9.3	3.0	5.7	−2.3	−1.2	1.0	15.4
1981	8.7	1.3	7.1	−3.1	−3.6	−3.0	7.4
1982	2.7	0.8	5.0	−1.0	0.5	−1.1	6.9
1983	−0.4	0.2	2.1	1.1	1.6	0.8	5.4
1984	−0.6	1.1	1.1	1.4	2.4	−0.2	5.1
1985	1.3	1.0	1.4	1.0	1.7	−0.5	5.7
1986	2.7	−4.7	1.8	–	0.1	4.1	4.1
1987	0.8	−0.4	1.7	0.7	0.1	1.5	4.4
1988	0.6	0.9	1.7	0.3	1.3	–	4.8

Source: Bank of England Quarterly Bulletin (May 1989) p. 232.

their improved competitiveness thereafter. It is also clear that as spare capacity was used up, there was a tendency to take advantage of the shortage of supply by raising margins.

At the present time, it would appear that margins are roughly comparable with past experience. It is obviously possible to argue that inflation would have been rather lower if companies had resisted the urge to raise prices at every opportunity, but it must also be recognised that they could not have been expected to leave their margins at the depressed levels of the early 1980s. The most interesting lesson is possibly that UK manufacturers will have to emulate their Japanese and West German rivals in being prepared to cut margins in order to maintain competitiveness.

It is important to bear in mind that the manufacturing sector sells to a considerable degree in competitive international markets, whereas the services sector and public utilities sell predominantly in the sheltered domestic markets. There is thus greater pressure on manufacturing concerns to raise productivity and lower unit costs. As shown in **Table 3.11**, the index of labour costs per unit of output looks less impressive when it is measured across the whole economy, rather than just the manufacturing sector.

It is particularly interesting to examine the path of earnings, which is shown for manufacturing industries in **Figure 3.24** although, apart from being somewhat lower, the pattern is almost identical for the whole economy. The average earnings index in both cases fell progressively from the 12-month period ending in January 1981 to the 12-month period ending in January 1983. At this point they stabilised, and the index for the whole economy remained absolutely constant at 7.5 per cent for nearly three years. Subsequently, it began to move upwards again from mid-1987, remaining mostly in the 9–10 per cent band until the Spring of 1991. The trend for manufacturing only was slightly upwards from 1986 onwards.

In the mid-1980s the remarkable stability of the underlying rate of earnings was one of the most remarked-upon features of inflation although, as

Table 3.11 *Index of Labour Costs per Unit of Output*[1] *%*

	Manufacturing	Whole economy
1980	22.2	22.9
1981	9.3	10.6
1982	3.5	3.7
1983	−1.2	3.2
1984	2.4	3.8
1985	4.3	4.3
1986	4.5	5.0
1987	1.4	3.7
1988	0.4	6.5
1989	3.8	8.6

Note:
[1] % change from a year earlier.
Source: Employment Gazette.

Figure 3.24   *Earnings and Output per Head: Manufacturing Industries – Increases Over Previous Year, Great Britain, %*

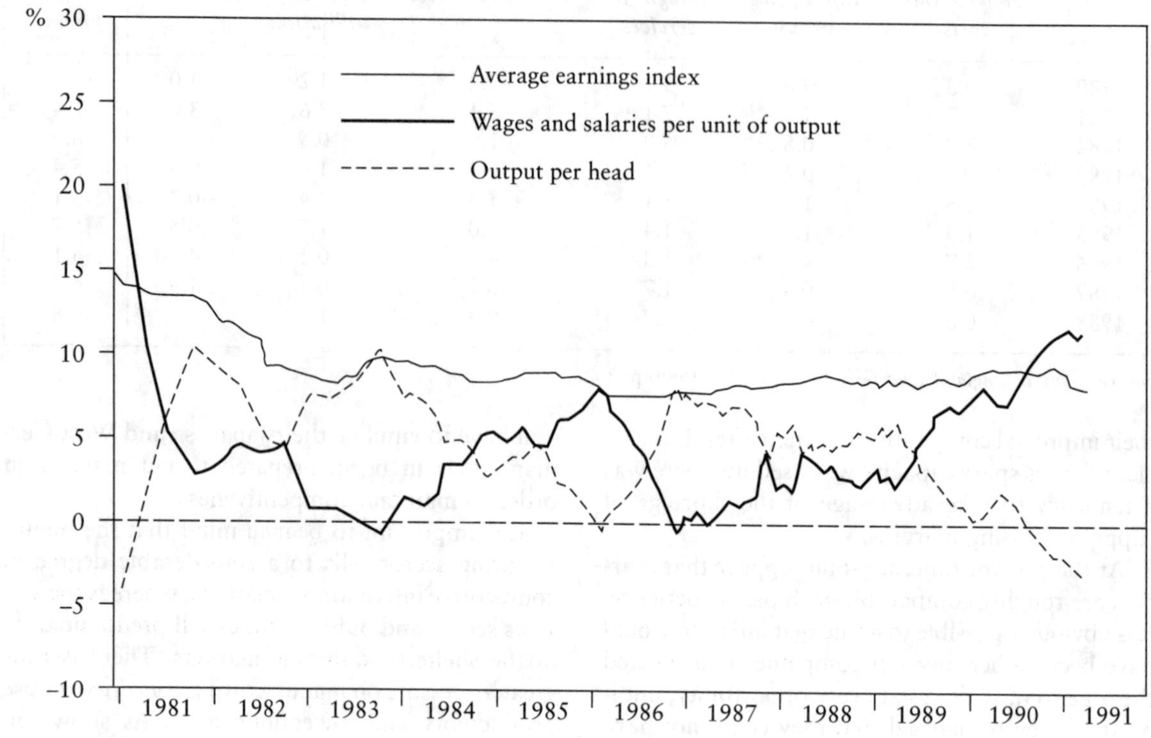

Source: Employment Gazette.

noted above, it was mostly matched by the underlying increase in productivity in the manufacturing sector. As can be seen in **Figure 3.24**, wages and salaries per unit of output in manufacturing fell back to zero in 1986 in response to a surge in output per head, and remained very low until 1989. The subsequent collapse of output per head, and the consequent sharp upturn in wages and salaries per unit of output, at a time of rising unemployment regenerated fears about the return of **stagflation** (rising prices in conjunction with rising unemployment). As competitor countries were keeping a tight grip on their unit labour costs at the time, this induced a wave of pessimistic forecasts about the future health of the UK economy.

What, therefore, is the prognosis for earnings at the end of 1991? There are three key determinants of wage inflation – namely the rate of price inflation, the level and rate of change of unemployment, and the level of profits. The first of these

peaked towards the latter end of 1990, and the headline rate subsequently began to fall sharply. In its industrial trends survey of March 1991 the Confederation of British Industry reported that fewer British manufacturing companies expected to raise their prices in the next four months than at any time in the previous 16 years. Unemployment had been rising for 17 consecutive months by September, but the rate of increase was decelerating. Finally, the corporate reporting season was fairly dismal.

This combination eventually had to have some impact upon pay deals. In fact, in April 1991 the Industrial Relations Services research group recorded the sharpest fall in the level of pay settlements for five years. True, this represented only a fall from 9.5 to 9.0 per cent, but the downwards trend continued as the year progressed, and in September there was a full percentage reduction relative to the previous month to 7.5 per cent.

Since the statistical series charting the underlying increase in earnings began in January 1981, the increase had never previously dipped below 7.5 per cent. In all probability this floor will be breached, but it may not be long before earnings are back above it again.

■ *3.8 Credit Crunch*

A 'credit crunch' exists when financial intermediaries, and especially banks, become unwilling to lend to the private sector. They may try to widen the gap between the interest rate at which they borrow and the rate at which they lend (as, for example, early in 1991 when despite four reductions in base rates the overdraft rate to personal customers actually **rose**). Alternately, they may toughen the criteria to be met before a loan is sanctioned. If crunch becomes crisis, lending may dry up altogether.

In **Figure 3.25** the left hand triangle represents a credit crunch, whilst the full figure represents a financial crisis. In the high era of Keynesian demand management the expansionary phase of the business cycle was set off via a loosening of fiscal policy. This did not happen during the 1980s, however, when as previously noted, the upswing was based primarily upon the free availability of credit. This was similar to what happened in the 19th century when there were a series of booms and recessions driven by the behaviour of the financial markets. A credit crunch presupposes a prior boom based upon credit. The indebtedness of the personal and company sectors grows sharply and bank lending becomes directed increasingly towards more speculative types of activity, such as junk bond financed management buy outs and property development, where returns are potentially very high.

When the slow down inevitably arrives there is a rash of company failures which in turn damages the banks' balance sheets when the loans have to be written off. This causes the banks' credit rating to be lowered and hence raises their cost of finance. The banks respond not merely by raising the cost of their other lending to recover their own higher costs, but also widen the spread between

Figure 3.25 *Financial Crisis and Credit Crunch.*

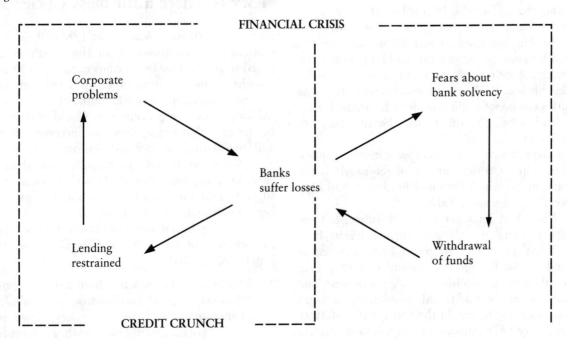

Source: Adapted from *Barclays Bank Review* (November 1990).

borrowing and lending rates. They also dispose of their collateral when payments secured by that collateral cease to be made, and shut down companies which in better times they would have been willing to tide over a bad patch. This may cause their credit rating to be downgraded yet further.

The step from credit crunch to financial crisis requires that depositors become afraid that their deposits will be put at risk by the banks' problems and consequently withdraw their funds, thereby precipitating a run on the banks. In practice, deposit insurance can be expected to prevent this later step, especially if combined with assurances by the authorities that they will maintain the liquidity of the system.

It is, therefore, more appropriate to ask whether there is currently a credit crunch in the UK. In practice, the banks have sailed through their 1991 reporting season without serious damage, and whilst they have been downgraded (see **pp. 96–7**), they seem perfectly capable of raising new equity finance and their existing share prices have been fairly buoyant.

Corporate failures are running at a very high level, but to some extent this simply reflects the unusually high rate of new business formation during the mid-1980s. In April 1991 the Bank of England announced that bank and building society lending had risen by just 0.1 per cent on the month to take the annual rate to 11.1 per cent, the weakest since records began 15 years previously. Nevertheless, the Bank commented that there was 'little evidence of credit crunch in the original sense of lenders being unable to lend because they are unable to raise funds'.

Credit crunch or no, there were more company failures in 1990 than in any of the previous ten years during which Dun and Bradstreet had kept records, as shown in **Table 3.12**.

When Mrs Thatcher first took office, failures were running at only half current levels. It is notable that 11,000 failures in 1990 occurred in London and the south east, and that they rose sharply in the previously booming south west. The situation in the traditional manufacturing areas was much less severe. In the first quarter of 1991 there were 5478 liquidations, so it is fairly certain both that the 1985 record will be exceeded in the

Table 3.12 *Business Failures in England and Wales, 1980–90*

Year	Liquidations	Bankruptcies	Total Failures
1980	6 814	3 814	10 651
1981	8 227	4 976	13 203
1982	11 131	5 436	16 567
1983	12 466	6 821	19 287
1984	13 647	8 035	21 682
1985	14 363	6 580	20 943
1986	13 689	6 991	20 680
1987	10 644	6 761	17 405
1988	9 276	7 286	16 652
1989	10 197	7 966	18 163
1990	13 611	10 831	24 442

Source: Dun & Bradstreet.

full year, and that the increase on 1985 will exceed the 15 per cent increase in the number of companies operating since then.

Given the predictions of an upturn by the year-end, it therefore seems reasonable to conclude that a credit crunch has on this occasion been averted.

■ 3.9 Is There a Business Cycle?

During the Vietnam War era of 1961–69 the US economy grew continuously for 106 months compared to the average in previous expansions of 35 months. Before turning down in 1990, the US economy logged up over 90 months of expansion, the longest ever in peacetime. It would appear to be the case that expansions have become longer and downswings shorter and shallower; the average US downswing now seems to last less than a year. Evidence from Britain, Japan and Germany suggests that the severity of cyclical swings has been much reduced since 1975.

There may be a number of reasons for the relative stability of the cycle (see *The Economist*, 9 June 1990, p. 85).

1   Manufactured products exhibit a strong cyclical effect, in good part because of variability in investment and stocks; services, however, are less volatile, partly because they cannot be stored. Advanced economies have switched

progressively from manufacturing to the provision of services.

2 Government spending, which acts counter-cyclically, has grown as a proportion of GDP. Automatic stabilisers have also become more important.

3 Stock control methods have become more sophisticated, so stockbuilding has less impact upon the cycle.

4 Improved financial management, as manifested after the October 1987 crash, has tended to avert panic responses to severe malfunctions in the world economy which serve only to make the problem worse.

In respect of the long expansion of the 1980s, it would appear that this was assisted by the modest levels of inflation endured by most countries compared to the 1970s. Governments tend to respond to a sharp rise in prices by pressing on the monetary brake, and this has frequently brought an upswing to a grinding halt during past cycles. In addition, the collapse of the oil price in 1986 gave a boost to the major advanced economies just as the expansion was running out of steam.

One of the curiosities of the current cycle is that there no longer appears to be a synchronised cycle for all major economies. Both the USA and UK relapsed into recession in the middle of 1990, at a time when both Japan and Germany (on the back of reunification) were still buoyant. As a result, international trade did not collapse and the world economy as a whole remained comparatively prosperous for such a late phase in a major expansion. The drawback is that there is an inevitable disagreement about the common policy stance to be adopted. Countries sagging into recession prefer interest rates to be lowered to help pull themselves out, whilst countries which are still expanding are afraid of the inflationary consequences of lower interest rates, and prefer to keep their rates relatively high. This explains why a country such as the USA, bedevilled by a large budget deficit and current account deficit but in the midst of recession, can end up with lower interest rates than a country such as Germany with a significantly better budget and trade position but in the midst of a period of rapid economic growth.

■ *3.10* Supply-side Economics

During the long period of Keynesian orthodoxy it was widely accepted both that government intervention was desirable *per se* and also that the purpose of macroeconomic intervention was primarily to maintain demand during recessions in order to boost output and employment. In terms of a standard economic model this is best viewed as a shift to the right of the aggregate demand curve. However, it follows that if prices are to remain stable (as measured in aggregate by a price index) then aggregate supply must increase at the same rate as aggregate demand. In a recession, with machinery and men lying idle, this seems a reasonable proposition, but in practice it is open to a number of objections. In the first place, the labour supply may be inflexible because it is geographically located in a different place to where the demand is being created, or it may possess skills which are unsuitable or alternatively no skills at all. It is possible to argue that regional policy can resolve the former difficulty by moving work to the workers, although as we shall see (on **pp. 411–2**) this may be both inefficient and expensive, but the latter problem is likely to prove more intractable. Equally, there is the issue of 'crowding out' whereby government spending may to a greater or lesser degree simply displace private sector spending.

But if aggregate supply is inflexible then a surge in aggregate demand is almost certainly going to create excess demand and hence drive up prices, thereby creating the kind of trade-off between employment and inflation enshrined in the Phillips Curve. Faced with this phenomenon, the logical response might be to try to suppress the inflationary pressure whilst maintaining high levels of aggregate demand – in which case inflation cannot be suppressed by reducing aggregate demand itself. This suggests that a prices and incomes policy should be used in order to prevent, by law, the onset of both price and wage inflation, but since this does nothing of itself to reduce the excess demand it is unlikely to have lasting effects (see **pp. 464–5**).

This being so, logic indicates that if output and employment are to be fostered without creating inflationary pressures, then the model must be made to work the other way around – that is, by holding aggregate demand in check in order to prevent it spilling over into higher prices, whilst simultaneously increasing aggregate supply. Indeed, if aggregate supply increases whilst aggregate demand remains constant, then not only do output and employment rise but downwards pressure is also exerted on prices. It may, of course, be argued that aggregate demand cannot be held back that successfully in the face of rising aggregate supply, at least not in the context of the UK, but so long as supply moves first and demand merely keeps pace with it, rising output and employment are compatible with stable prices. It is possible to set some of the subsequent discussion in the context of this simple model. In particular, monetarism can best be viewed as the attempt to **rein back aggregate demand** after 1979 in order to **control inflation** whilst supply-side economics got on with the task of **creating output and jobs**. It is clear that both needed to work in tandem, or alternatively that some other mechanism for reining in demand **such as high interest rates** be introduced instead of money supply control.

The Achilles heel of such an approach is straight-forward – if demand moves ahead of supply, which could most easily happen when supply runs up against capacity constraints, then rising output and employment will be accompanied by rising prices, and if prices rise too quickly demand may have to be reined in so sharply that a recession is caused. The issue of whether demand can be adequately reined in is discussed in detail in Chapter 12. For the moment, the concern is to address how a supply-side policy has been introduced in the UK since 1979.

It is important to appreciate that aggregate supply is dependent upon supply at a microeconomic level. The bottom line is that individuals must be given **incentives to work harder** and to behave in an **entrepreneurial manner**. This can happen only if markets are allowed to work as freely as possible, hence the main task of government is to create an environment in which effort is rewarded rather than to take decisions on behalf of individuals. From this it follows that governments should reduce their share of total expenditure and so

reform the fiscal system that the total tax burden is reduced and disincentive effects are kept to a minimum.

Lower tax rates encourage saving, investment, work effort and risk-taking. Consumption, leisure, the use of tax shelters and the black economy cease to be as attractive as before. As supply increases in response, the consequent rising incomes, profits and wealth provide an increase in the tax base which returns to the Treasury revenue lost as a consequence of the tax reductions. Savings also rise, thereby providing additional investment funds.

At least, that is the theory. It is often objected that work effort and savings are unresponsive at best to reductions in tax. Further, that the 'substitution' effect will come into play whereby, if it is possible to earn a given net-of-tax sum with less work effort once tax rates are lowered, then less work will be done. But whilst this could be true for individuals, it cannot be true in the aggregate since if everyone worked less, total output and incomes would fall and people would have to work harder to restore their post-tax incomes to their previous level.

The effect upon work effort may be difficult to measure directly. One way in which workers have traditionally responded to what they perceive as an insufficient net-of-tax reward for work effort has been to work more slowly, absent themselves, take longer vacations and move jobs more frequently. In other words, it may be that the supply-side effects will show up as much in the **quality of work** as in the number of hours worked.

It is, however, slightly ironic that, at least in the medium term, it is incumbent upon the government to take a great deal of (often legislative) action in order to get the supply side of the economy to work. Thus, for example, the failure of the private sector to deal adequately with the training of the labour force has left the government with much of the responsibility for improving the quality of the labour supply. Equally, deregulation of markets has generally brought regulation hard on its heels. There is a wide range of governmental initiatives which may reasonably be considered as supply-side policies, and it is not possible to comment on all of these in detail, but it should be noted that some, for example, are directed at removing the 'unemployment trap' – that is, the tendency for certain people to find themselves no better off financially when in employment than when out of employment; some at encouraging workers to price themselves back into jobs, mainly by curbing the power of trade unions to push up wages; some to improve the quality of the labour force; some to deregulate markets; and some to transfer activity back from the unofficial (black) economy to the official economy.

It is extremely difficult to judge whether these policies have been successful, as few unambiguous econometric studies have as yet been published.

Obviously such indicators as the rate of growth offer some support for the efficacy of supply-side measures, and there is widespread agreement that the labour market works rather better than it did 10 years ago. But whether cuts in tax rates have achieved anything is at best open to doubt, particularly since, as will be shown on **p. 144**, the aggregate tax burden remains rather high.

Appendix: Say's Law, the Laffer Curve and the Gutman Effect

Say's Law

Supply-side economics has its roots in the work of J. B. Say (1767–1832) who is best-known for coining the expression 'supply creates its own demand', an opinion shared by many neo-classical economists. Say's basic argument was that if there was an increase in the numbers of those seeking work then competition among the suppliers of labour would drive down the real wage to the point at which employers would be willing to buy any available labour which had not already chosen to be self-employed. In the process of using these labour inputs to make products, payments would have to be made for both labour and other inputs in the form of interest, dividends and profits. The value of output is thus exactly matched by an equal amount of factor payments sufficient to buy everything which has been produced. Hence **supply creates its own demand**.

During the Keynesian orthodoxy Say's Law came to be held in low esteem once it became widely accepted that there could be a deficiency of effective demand (see discussion in the Introduction). Say's Law came back into fashion along with the Quantity Theory when a solution was sought to the problem of 'stagflation'.

The Laffer Curve

The Curve, associated with the work of A. Laffer in the mid-1970s but which can be traced back to the ideas of Adam Smith (1776) among others, correlates tax rates with tax revenue. The Curve begins with zero revenue at a zero rate of tax, rises to a peak at some positive rate of less than 100 per cent (which can be determined only empirically) and subsides back to zero revenue at a tax rate of 100 per cent. This latter point is supposed to be the consequence of the total disincentive effect of such a tax rate, although it seems extremely implausible once one accepts that most tax revenue is returned to workers as benefits of one kind or another. However, the key issue is that if tax rates are raised continuously then eventually tax revenue will begin to fall, which implies the need to keep the rate below the threshold rate that triggers the fall in revenue. It follows logically that if tax rates start above this threshold then lowering them will increase tax revenue. Just what is going to happen if tax rates are lowered when they are already below the threshold is somewhat less clear-cut, but the benefits are likely to be rather greater if tax-deductible allowances such as mortgage interest relief are simultaneously phased out. In the case of the UK there is considerable disagreement about the exact shape of the Laffer Curve.

The Gutman Effect

This phenomenon, named after P. Gutman, essentially arises when reductions in the rate of tax induce transactions occurring previously in the black economy, and hence generating no tax revenue, to enter the official economy because the possibility of fines or imprisonment is no longer warranted given the relatively small deduction in tax if transactions are declared to the tax authorities. Hence the tax base is widened if tax rates are reduced and tax revenue rises accordingly. This effect will operate in conjunction with the Laffer Curve.

References

Blackaby, D. and L. Hunt (1990) 'An Assessment of the UK's Productivity Record in the 1980s: Has There Been a "Miracle"?', *Economics* (Autumn).

Boleat, M. *et al.* (1991) *The State of the Economy 1991* (London: IEA).

Cullison, W. (1990) 'Is Saving Too Low in the United States?', *Economic Review* (May/June).

Eltis, W. (1991) 'United Kingdom Investment and Finance', Chapter 3 in M. Boleat *et al, The State of the Economy 1991* (London: IEA).

Feinstein, C. and R. Mathews (1990) 'The Growth of Output and Productivity in the UK: the 1980s as a Phase of the Post-War Period', *National Institute Economic Review* (August).

Feldstein, M. and P. Baccheta (1989) 'National Saving and International Investment', *National Bureau of Economic Research, Working Paper,* 3164.

Gilbert, C. (1990) 'Primary Commodity Prices and Inflation', *Oxford Review of Economic Policy* (Winter).

Layard, R. and S. Nickell (1989) 'The Thatcher Miracle?', *American Economic Review, Papers and Proceedings* (May).

Lee, C. and W. Robinson (1990) 'The Fall in the Savings Ratio: the Role of Housing', *Fiscal Studies* (February).

Lipsey, R. and I. Kravis (1987) 'Is the US a Spendthrift Nation?', *National Bureau of Economic Research, Working Paper* 2274.

Nickell, S. (1990) 'Inflation and the UK Labour Market', *Oxford Review of Economic Policy* (Winter).

Oulton, N. (1990) 'Labour Productivity in UK Manufacturing in the 1970s and in the 1980s', *National Institute Economic Review* (May).

Roberts, P. (1989) 'Supply-side Economics', Chapter 3 in J. M. Buchanan *et al.* (eds), *Reagonomics and After* (London: IEA).

■ *Chapter 4* ■

The Financial System

Peter Curwen

■ *4.1* Financial Intermediation

In a primitive economic world those who have saved part of their income and who wish to **on-lend their savings** (the ultimate lenders), will meet together with those who wish to **borrow** for various reasons (the ultimate borrowers) and arrange a mutually agreeable price for the transfer of funds between them. However, in a sophisticated world such transfers are beset with difficulties. The lenders and borrowers may be geographically dispersed; the amounts which lenders wish to make available may not match the amounts which borrowers wish to borrow; and the term to maturity of funds on offer may not match borrowers' requirements. In principle, the price charged for transfers of funds – **the interest rate** – can be adjusted to overcome most of these difficulties, but in many cases a mutually agreeable interest rate will not be forthcoming, and the transfers will not take place even though lenders wish to lend and borrowers wish to borrow. Financial intermediaries are needed to overcome this problem.

Any lender who has decided to hold a portfolio of financial assets has to balance a number of considerations in deciding which assets to hold. In the first place, he or she is concerned with the **risk** element in the loan, which arises because the loan may not be repaid at all; because he or she may need cash prior to an asset's redemption date; or

because even if an asset can be redeemed before maturity this may involve a partial capital loss. Furthermore, if relatively small sums are involved, these can generally be turned into only one or two different types of asset, thereby preventing the lender from holding a sufficiently diversified portfolio of assets to protect against a particularly bad performance by one type of asset held. Secondly, the lender is unlikely to want to lend for long periods, partly for the reasons mentioned above, and partly because it constrains his ability to spend as the opportunity arises.

Finally, the individual lender is unlikely to be well-informed. It may prove a time-consuming and expensive process to find a borrower willing to match the characteristics of the loan, and indeed the lender may ultimately fail to do so.

It is equally true that a potential borrower may be unable to find a lender willing and able to match his requirements – which generally include a desire to borrow for long periods of time. At the end of the day these considerations, combined with the fact that the lender obviously wants to maximise the interest rate whilst the borrower wants to minimise it, severely constrain the volume of funds transferred directly between individuals.

It is also necessary to take account of **liquidity considerations**. Liquidity is concerned primarily with the speed with which any financial instrument can be turned into cash, or wholly liquid, form. But it is also important that the value of the instrument is preserved in the process. It is possible to sell most financial instruments in the open market for cash, but there is no guarantee that the exact face-value of the instrument will be repaid to its holder unless it is held to maturity. If it is sold prior to maturity, then its face-value will be determined by the face-value of newly-issued instruments having the same characteristics with respect to – for example – yield, maturity and risk. An early sale of any instrument may thus result in either a capital gain or a capital loss. Conventionally, any instrument issued with an original lifespan of no more than 91 days is considered to be liquid, and this term also applies to any instrument which, irrespective of its original term to maturity, has less than 91 days left to maturity.

These matters can be addressed by an intermediary. The **law of large numbers** operates such that, whilst some liabilities to depositors need to be kept in cash or near-cash form to meet daily cash withdrawals, the rest can be on-lent to borrowers as long-term lending. As a consequence, the intermediary, unlike an individual, can create a balance sheet with its liabilities in relatively liquid forms and its assets (representing its claims on those to whom it lends) in relatively illiquid forms. Because it handles large numbers of loans, an intermediary must expect some borrowers to default. However, such defaults are very unlikely to put the intermediary at risk of going out of business. Hence, whilst the ultimate lender, in lending directly to one or a few individuals, faces the possibility of a total default, he generally runs the risk of losing no more than a small proportion of his funds if the intermediary he deposits them with gets into difficulties. Furthermore, the rate of interest can be adjusted to take account of different degrees of risk when lending to different intermediaries.

It is important to note from this discussion that when funds are deposited with an intermediary the money is not, in the majority of cases, on-lent in exactly the same form to the ultimate borrower. Instead, the process of **funds transformation** takes place whereby the intermediary creates liabilities, in the form of claims against itself by the ultimate lender, having different characteristics to its assets

in the form of its own claims against the ultimate borrowers. Sometimes one intermediary may on-lend to another, with the result that funds transformation takes place on more than one occasion as funds flow through the financial system, and in the process the ultimate lender becomes increasingly separated from the ultimate borrower.

In summary, the process of intermediation is as beneficial to lenders as it is to borrowers. On the one hand, as discussed above, the lender faces a reduced risk; he can withdraw his money on demand or by giving relatively short periods of notice; he has no need to choose between a host of ultimate borrowers but between only a small number of intermediaries; and he effectively obtains a share in a much more diversified portfolio than he could hold as an individual. On the other hand, the borrower knows where to go to get funds, and there are more funds available.

One final point which should be noted is that whilst in principle the use of an intermediary might be expected to cause interest rates paid to depositors to fall, and those charged to borrowers to rise (since the intermediary exists to make a profit by selling its services), this may well not happen in practice. The depositor faces a reduced risk of default, and therefore should accept a lower reward for the risk-taking element of the loan, so that even after adding the intermediary's mark-up, the cost to the borrower may be lower than for a direct transfer from the ultimate lender.

4.2 Classifying Financial Intermediaries

The range of financial intermediaries in the UK is unusually varied. The first task is, therefore, to determine the most coherent way to arrange them in classes for further analysis. There are two main considerations here. In the first place, monetary controls operate through intermediaries, and it would seem helpful to divide up intermediaries into those which are affected by controls (particularly over the money supply) and those which are not. In this respect it was traditionally argued that intermediaries which can create credit (**banks**) should be distinguished from those which cannot create credit (**non-banks**). In practice, however, such divisions are always rather unsatisfactory. Let us assume, for example, that an individual transfers money from his or her bank deposit account to a building society, and that this money is then redeposited by the society into a current account at the same bank. Since its total deposits are unaffected the bank can create as much credit as previously, but in addition the building society can now offer additional mortgage loans on the basis of its new deposits.

The second consideration is that it is necessary to lay down in law what, for example, is or is not a bank so that appropriate prudential supervision can be exercised by the Bank of England (see discussion of the Banking Act 1987 below). Historically, these considerations did not create particular difficulties, but the 1980s witnessed much blurring of traditional distinctions between intermediaries, partly as a result of attempts to regulate particular institutions in the pursuit of money supply control. The Banking Act 1979 created a now obsolete distinction between banks and licensed deposit-takers, but in September 1983 the Bank of England introduced a new classification system for banks which created three categories of **British bank**. The first category comprises the **retail banks**, as listed below. The second, categorised as **other British banks**, comprises primarily the subsidiaries of the clearing banks, whilst the third category comprises the **British merchant banks**. All other banks are categorised as **overseas banks**.

The banks can also be divided into those which conduct business primarily in the **retail** market – that is, branch banks handling vast numbers of small accounts – and those which conduct **wholesale** business involving small numbers of very large transactions. The retail banks are all British, whilst the wholesale banks are primarily foreign. Most banks fall partly into both categories, so their classification is determined by their predominant form of business. The **discount houses** retain a separate classification.

However, many intermediaries are not banks as defined above. Whilst these can be lumped together as **non-bank financial intermediaries** (NBFI), some closely resemble banks in that they take in deposits, often via branch networks, and indeed may in individual cases ultimately need to be re-

Table 4.1 *Financial Intermediaries*

Banks	
Retail banks:	London clearing banks (5)
	Scottish clearing banks (3)
	Northern Ireland banks (4)
	Trustee Savings Banks (3)
	Co-operative Bank plc
	Yorkshire Bank plc
	Girobank plc
	Bank of England Banking Department
Wholesale banks:	Other British banks
	British Merchant banks
	Overseas banks
Discount houses	
Non-bank financial intermediaries	
Other deposit-takers:	Building societies
	National Savings Bank
	Finance houses
Other NBFI:	Insurance companies
	Pension funds
	Investment trusts
	Unit trusts

classified as banks as discussed below, whilst others conduct their business in quite different ways. **Table 4.1** shows the full classification.

We now need to examine, albeit briefly, the individual components of the monetary sector. At the heart of the sector lies the Bank of England, so we will start by discussing its role, subsequently moving on to look at the banks, both retail and wholesale, and the non-bank financial intermediaries. We will then examine the capital market where equities and bonds are traded, before completing the discussion with an overview of how the sector has evolved in recent years and the changes that can be expected to take place in the near future.

■ 4.3 The Bank of England

The Bank of England (the Bank) is the central bank of the UK. It started life as a joint stock company in 1694, and in return for a large loan to the government was put in a privileged position which enabled it to become the largest private bank. It was subsequently authorised to hold the gold reserves of the banking system. In 1844 note issuing powers were terminated other than via the Bank, which gradually became a monopoly supplier (other than in Scotland). It also increasingly stood prepared to maintain liquidity in the banking system. Whilst not technically a public sector body until the passing of the Bank of England Act 1946, it had long been under the control of the Treasury (Chancellor of the Exchequer). It still retains today the residual part of its private sector clientele. It is managed by a Court of Directors, headed by the Governor, who are appointed by the Crown.

The Bank's balance sheet has since 1844 been somewhat artificially divided into two halves, namely the **Issue Department** which is concerned with the issue of notes by the Bank, and the **Banking Department** which is concerned with everything else. Issue Department liabilities consist of £18 bn of notes in circulation, and its assets consist of an equivalent amount of government and other securities. Banking Department liabilities consist of public deposits (accounts of the government), bankers' deposits and reserves and other accounts. Bankers' deposits are either **operational** and used for inter-bank clearing; to equalise cashflows between banks and the government; or to pay for the purchase of notes and coin, or **nonoperational** cash-ratio deposits to comply with monetary control requirements. Banking Department assets (of £8 bn) consist of government securities; advances and other accounts; and premises, equipment and other securities which are primarily in the form of commercial bills.

4.3.1 Functions of the Bank of England

The Bank performs a wide variety of functions. It:

(a) is responsible for the issue of notes and coins
(b) acts as banker to the central government
(c) acts as banker to the banking system
(d) manages the Exchange Equalisation Account (EEA)
(e) advises the government on, and on behalf of the government carries out, its monetary policy
(f) supervises the financial system.

These days notes and coins are the proverbial 'small change' of the financial system, and are produced to meet demand rather than to implement policy. As banker to the government the Bank handles the daily net balances of government departments, financing them when they show a deficit and converting any surplus into repayments of debt. The balance sheet item 'public deposits' is normally kept as small as possible in order to minimise the need to issue – and pay interest on – new national debt. The Bank is responsible not only for debt transactions which arise in the present period, but also for managing all the outstanding debt from previous periods. This requires a continuous stream of transactions in both the bill market and in the market for longer-dated government securities, known as **gilt-edged** (or gilts for short). All government debt instruments can be freely traded on the Stock Exchange and money markets, and can therefore be controlled for policy purposes as set out below.

All clearing banks keep an account at the Bank through which pass, first, daily transfers of funds between public deposits and the accounts of the banks' customers and, secondly, daily transfers of funds from one bank to another for bank clearing purposes (plus the occasional purchase of notes and coins). These transfers utilise the bankers' operational balances at the Bank, which do not need to be particularly large as all daily cash flows are netted out.

The **Exchange Equalisation Account** contains the UK's gold and foreign currency reserves. These reserves are used periodically for intervention purposes in order to maintain the value of the exchange rate for sterling in accordance with the wishes of the government. If sterling is considered to be too low the Bank will buy sterling and sell other currencies as appropriate, and if it is considered to be too high the Bank will sell sterling and buy foreign currencies. Sterling required for this purpose is obtained from the National Loans Fund which forms part of the public deposits. The Bank therefore needs to keep accounts with a large number of overseas central banks.

Altogether, the Bank operates in three separate markets – gilt-edged; **discount**; and **foreign exchange**. These operations collectively constitute the government's **monetary policy**. The Bank has always had the right to use its expertise to give advice to the government concerning the conduct of monetary policy, but it is nevertheless only the **government's agent**, and it is the Chancellor of the Exchequer, acting via the Treasury, who has ultimate responsibility for such policy. Confusion may arise in this respect because it is inevitably reported in the news that the Bank has taken particular actions in the gilt-edged or currency markets, but in so doing it is simply following instructions. Market interventions are, however, best performed at particular times and on a particular scale, and the Bank has considerable discretion in this respect since the Chancellor cannot be expected personally to keep the markets under continuous scrutiny.

The Bank has an important role to play in the gilt-edged market. The Bank not merely issues gilts on behalf of the government, but underwrites the issues in that any unsold gilts are bought in by the Issue Department for future resale. It buys and sells on a daily basis in order to ensure that there is a receptive market for large-scale holders of gilts, especially insurance companies and pension funds, which may wish to adjust their portfolios. The Bank's operations also inevitably affect gilt-edged prices, and hence long-term interest rates. Until recently this was considered of great importance, because sales of gilts reduce the liquidity of the private sector and hence help to control the money supply.

The final, but increasingly vital, role for the Bank is to **supervise the financial system**. With such vast sums at stake confidence is all-important, and it is the Bank's job to set the rules and ensure fair play. There has never been any need to question the Bank's ability to achieve this in the banking sector, but the increasing sophistication and diversity of non-banking activity has recently forced the Bank to permit other regulatory bodies to take over some of its responsibilities, for example the Securities and Investments Board (SIB) under the terms of the Financial Services Act 1986 (see **pp. 123–5**).

Banking supervision was first formalised under the Banking Act 1979 which allowed the Bank to authorise recognised banks and licensed deposit takers (which offered a narrower range of services). However, the collapse of Johnson Matthey Bankers in September 1984 set in train a reappraisal which resulted in the passing of the **Banking Act 1987**, which now treats all banks as a uniform category. In order for a bank to be authorised, it is required in particular that every director, controller and manager shall be a fit and proper person to hold his position; that the business of the bank be conducted prudently especially in respect of capital adequacy, liquidity, and bad and doubtful debt provision; that proper systems of accounting and control are maintained; and that net assets are at least £1 mn. If necessary, required standards can be adjusted in individual cases. The Bank can object to takeovers and mergers involving banks, and has done so recently on several occasions. The Bank must be notified if a bank becomes over-exposed (borrowing in excess of 25 per cent of bank capital) to an individual borrower. A Board of Banking Supervision has been set up to give guidance on the development of the supervisory system.

Traditionally monetary policy was heavily dependent upon **liquidity ratio controls**. This is no longer the case, and since 1982 no such controls have been enforced by the Bank. Individual banks are expected to maintain what they themselves consider to be a prudent level of liquidity, but the Bank requires that banks maintain systems for keeping proper checks on liquidity, and reserves the right to check up that this is the case.

In 1988 the Bank issued a consultative paper which contained a new set of tough proposals concerning bank liquidity. However, banks objected to being told what type of assets they had to hold, particularly since the Bank wanted them to include low-yielding Treasury bills. In addition, foreign banks complained that they were already subject to liquidity controls in their home countries. As a result, the Bank dropped the proposals in April 1990 on the grounds that the banking system was too diverse to be subjected to a common liquidity regime, and that the EC might soon be proposing its own regime.

The **Financial Services Act 1986** also led to a more formal regulation of the wholesale money markets. To become an approved institution a bank must pass a 'fit and proper' test covering ability to manage and capital adequacy, and agreement to abide by the 'London Code of Conduct'. The Bank also runs the scheme which insures depositors against the failure of an authorised bank.

In October 1990 the Bank issued a set of procedures which it wished banks to adopt when dealing with companies in a liquidity crisis. In particular, it encouraged creditor banks 'jointly [to] ensure that (a troubled company) has sufficient liquidity to continue trading until a considered view of its prospects can be reached'. The Bank was, however, at pains to emphasise that its purpose was to remind banks of traditional procedures rather than to recommence the interventionist policies forsaken during the 1980s.

4.3.2 Should the Bank be Independent?

As noted previously, the Bank is essentially an arm of government, and as such is one of the least independent central banks in the developed world. In recent months many voices have been raised in favour of granting more independence to the Bank. The main justification for so doing is that it will provide credibility to programmes for restraining inflation. Alesina (1989) ranked central banks according to an index of independence, taking into account characteristics such as the formal institu-

Figure 4.1   *Central Bank Independence and Inflation*

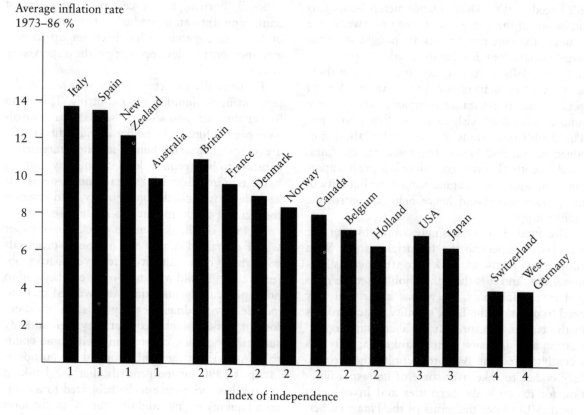

Source: Alesina (1989).

tional relationship between the government and the central bank; the presence of government officials on the bank's board; and the existence of rules forcing the central bank automatically to print money to finance budget deficits.

Figure 4.1 illustrates that over the period 1973 to 1986 the least independent central banks (graded 1) were in Italy and Spain, whilst the most independent (graded 4) were in Switzerland and West Germany. Britain was included amongst those central banks with only a modicum of independence (graded 2). As can be seen, there was a close correlation between the index of independence and the rate of inflation. During the period studied, banks graded 1 had an average inflation rate of 12.5 per cent whilst banks graded 4 had an average rate of 4 per cent. Furthermore, unemployment also tended to be lower in banks graded 4 than in banks graded 1.

This suggests that inflation is affected by expectations as to whether the central bank means what it says when it adopts a tough anti-inflationary stance, or whether it is expected to be told to relax its stance by politicians anxious to protect jobs. Given the position of Britain in **Figure 4.1**, it is understandable that there is a credibility problem in respect of monetary policy.

■ 4.4 Banks in the UK

As previously discussed, there are two ways in which the banking sector can usefully be divided up for analytic purposes – namely, British/overseas and retail/wholesale. **Table 4.2**, parts (**a**) and (**b**), sheds considerable light on why these distinctions are useful. As shown in part (**a**), the total deposit liabilities of banks in the UK at the end of 1990 were £1270 bn. Of this total, over £1150 bn was recorded separately either as sterling or foreign currency liabilities, whilst the rest was in a mixture of currencies. To those unfamiliar with the Eurocurrency markets (discussed below), it may come as a surprise to note that roughly 55 per cent of the £1150 bn was in the form of non-sterling deposits.

The proportions are in practice somewhat variable, because they are a snapshot of the picture on

one particular day which may be unrepresentative of the days which both precede and follow it. One reason for this is that wholesale banking tends to **respond to demand** – in other words, if there is a potential borrower for a very large sum of foreign currency at a particular point in time, the wholesale banks will go out and attract deposits of the same magnitude. One must also bear in mind that the valuation of foreign currency deposits varies according to movements in the exchange rate. It is thus quite possible to find the ratio between sterling and non-sterling deposits registering a much lower order of magnitude.

This ratio disguises the fact that the retail banks, which are primarily British banks with branch networks, conduct much more of their business in sterling than the wholesale banks. As shown in part (**b**) of **Table 4.2**, sterling deposits were fairly equally divided between retail and wholesale banks, whilst the latter took in over 90 per cent of foreign currency deposits. It is somewhat surprising to learn that wholesale banks took in 70 per cent of all deposits in the UK. Since the wholesale banks are mostly subsidiaries of foreign banks, it follows that the latter must take in the majority of all deposits, and as shown in **Table 4.2** the proportion was roughly 72 per cent of the total. Here again, the distinction between British banks taking in most of the sterling deposits, and overseas banks taking in an even bigger proportion of the foreign currency deposits, is particularly notable.

□ 4.4.1 Retail Banks

The retail banks comprise primarily the clearing banks in England, Scotland and Northern Ireland. There are also the Trustee Savings Banks and the Girobank which became clearing banks in the late 1980s and provide very similar services. The odd man out is the Bank of England Banking Department, which gets included in the statistics despite its quite different role which has been discussed above.

The typical retail bank is a clearing bank which provides services to individuals and firms through a branch network. The traditional side of the business is represented by current (sight) and deposit

Table 4.2   *(a) Banks in the UK[1], Deposit Liabilities at 30 December 1990*

	Sterling deposit liabilities (a)		Foreign currency deposit liabilities (b)		Total deposit liabilities
	£ bn	%[2]	£ bn	%	£ bn[3]
Retail banks	298.5	83.0	61.3	17.0	426.1
British merchant banks[5]	34.9	67.4	16.9	32.6	59.4
Other British banks	39.0	83.7	7.6	16.3	56.5
American banks	18.1	16.9	88.9	83.1	110.1
Japanese banks	40.0	15.9	211.4	84.1	254.5
Other overseas banks[4]	97.6	27.9	251.8	72.1	360.1
Total	528.1	45.3	637.9	54.7	1266.7

Notes:
[1] As a result of the changes in the monetary sector culminating in the conversion of the Abbey National Building Society into a bank on 12 July 1989, the term 'monetary sector' was replaced by 'banks in the United Kingdom' or simply 'banks'.
[2] Expressed as percentage of (a) + (b) only.
[3] Including items in suspense and transmission, capital and other funds.
[4] Including consortium banks listed separately prior to August 1987.
[5] Members of British Merchant Banking and Securities Houses Association (formerly the Accepting Houses Committee).
Source: Calculations based on data in *Bank of England Quarterly Bulletin.*

(b)

	% Banks in the UK sterling deposits	% Banks in the UK foreign currency deposits	% Banks in the UK total deposits[1]
Retail banks	56.5	9.6	30.8
Wholesale banks	43.5	90.4	69.2
British banks	70.5	13.5	27.5
Overseas banks	29.5	86.5	72.5

Note:
[1] Excluding items in suspense and transmission, capital and other funds.
Source: Calculations based on data in *Bank of England Quarterly Bulletin.*

(time) accounts; provision of cheque books; clearing of cheques; overdraft facilities and personal loans; small currency transactions; and a wide range of financial advice. In the 1980s there has been considerable innovation in the way that traditional services are provided, such as cheque-guarantee cards; automated teller machines; Eurocheques; and most recently new lines of business have been developed such as large-scale mortgage lending on a regular basis; managed unit trusts; and share dealing services.

All retail banks publish balance sheets to a set pattern, and their combined balance sheet as at 31 December 1987–90 is set out in **Figure 4.2**. Retail

Figure 4.2 *Retail Banks: Balance Sheet*

	31/12/88 £ mn	31/12/89 £ mn	31/12/90 £ mn
Sterling Liabilities			
Notes Issued	1 407	1 560	1 678
Deposits: UK banks	20 165	25 158	27 830
UK public sector	4 185	4 844	4 550
UK private sector	137 362	197 761[5]	218 053[5]
Overseas	17 609	23 060	26 730
Certificates of deposit[1]	11 965	15 599	21 354
Other Currency Liabilities			
Deposits: UK banks	6 373	6 589	6 903
Other UK	6 883	10 042	10 371
Overseas	26 437	40 353	37 346
Certificates of deposit[1]	3 549	6 499	6 690
Sterling and Other Currencies[2]	47 038	60 030	64 609
TOTAL LIABILITIES[3]	282 974	391 495	426 114
Sterling Assets			
Notes and Coins	3 375	3 861	3 926
Balances with Bank of England[4]	749	1 064	1 032
Market loans: Secured money with LDMA	5 220	6 952	7 375
Other UK banks	17 639	29 396	31 748
UK bank CDs	4 201	6 047	8 469
UK local authorities	738	293	226
Overseas	3 573	4 800	5 258
Bills: Treasury bills	1 502	1 631	2 469
Eligible local authority bills	388	62	31
Eligible bank bills	6 060	9 093	10 064
Other	137	204	150
Advances: UK public sector	702	370	527
UK private sector	147 920	207 579[5]	234 239[5]
Overseas	5 284	5 492	4 599
Banking Dept. lending to central government (net)	956	1 321	1 657
Investments: British government stocks	3 547	3 719	3 226
Others	5 122	8 806	10 785
Other Currency Assets			
Market loans and advances: UK banks	10 007	9 483	9 395
UK bank CDs	178	108	736
UK public sector	–	28	18
UK private sector	7 648	12 120	10 980
Overseas	30 391	46 538	38 020
Bills	436	563	1 153
Investments	6 198	7 938	11 675
Miscellaneous (all currencies)	20 999	24 025	28 355
TOTAL ASSETS	282 974	391 495	426 114

Notes:

[1] And other short-term paper issued.

[2] Items in suspense and transmission, capital and other funds.

[3] Of which eligible liabilities amounted to £127bn at end-1987; £160bn at end-1988; £221bn at end-1989[5]; £249 bn at end-1990.

[4] Including cash ratio deposits.

[5] These figures were affected significantly by the reclassification of existing business with Abbey National Group at 1 July 1989. This added roughly £30bn to UK private sector sterling deposits, sterling advances and eligible liabilities.

Source: Bank of England Quarterly Bulletin.

banks do an increasing amount of wholesale business, as discussed below, but this is not distinguished separately in the balance sheet.

The balance sheet ultimately represents a trade-off between a number of contradictory forces. On the one hand, retail banks are, with minor exceptions, obliged to make profits for shareholders, and high rates of return can be earned only by lending for longish periods of time and by taking a certain amount of risk. On the other hand, account holders constantly require cash to be made available, and other low return assets may need to be held either for prudential reasons to avoid a possible loss of confidence by depositors, or because it is so required by the Bank of England.

The balance sheet, both liabilities and assets, is divided into sterling and foreign currency categories. **Sterling deposits** are heavily dominated by the sight and time deposits of individuals and companies in the UK. Traditionally, the latter paid interest whilst the former did not, but sight deposits remained in the majority because they offered instant access whilst time deposits required notice of withdrawal. However, factors such as the provision of interest-bearing instant-access accounts by building societies eventually persuaded large numbers of depositors that only minimum sums should be kept in bank current accounts, and the banks were forced to respond by offering to forgo charges on such accounts provided, typically, they were kept in credit. As a result, time deposits lost their appeal, and sight deposits once again became equally popular.

In 1987 the Midland Bank introduced a **Vector account** which paid interest on accounts held in credit, but attracted few customers because interest earned was largely offset by account charges. The decision by Lloyds Bank in October 1988 to offer all of its customers an interest-bearing current account came as a considerable surprise, but once the Midland, Barclays, Royal Bank of Scotland and TSB followed suit, this process became unstoppable. Indeed, in January 1989 Barclays went one stage further by abolishing charges for transactions on current accounts such as standing orders and cheques even if they go into overdraft. The distinction between sight and time deposits will eventually appear to be no more than an historical anachronism, especially when it is borne in mind that the retail banks' wholesale business largely comprises interest-bearing sight deposits.

Wholesale deposits and deposits from overseas in sterling are currently of equal value. Wholesale deposits have fixed terms to maturity varying from days to years, and are paid a market-determined rate of interest which may therefore differ considerably from interest rates paid to individuals. Whilst wholesale deposits are still fairly modest, it must be recognised that there is intense competition for retail deposits and the retail banks, like all other intermediaries, can no longer rely on a sufficiently large inflow of retail deposits to meet their needs for on-lending particularly in, for example, the mortgage market.

Certificates of Deposit (CDs) are fixed-term deposits which are exchanged for a certificate issued by the bank which can be traded in the open market. Hence, although the deposit itself cannot be withdrawn before maturity, the original depositor can get at his cash much earlier by selling his CD, although he may well be obliged to sell it for less than its face value if interest rates have risen.

The large item 'sterling and other currencies' includes items in suspense because, for example, of uncertainty about ownership; items being transferred between accounts; and the capital injected into the banks by shareholders *plus* liabilities to bond holders. It is also the custom to itemise 'eligible' liabilities. These comprise all sterling deposits from non-bank sources with an original maturity of no more than two years; net interbank lending in sterling; sterling CDs issued *less* sterling CDs held; any net deposit liabilities in sterling to overseas offices; and any net liabilities in currencies other than sterling – *less* 60 per cent of the net value of transit items. Eligible liabilities were first introduced in 1971 for the purposes of monetary control, and since August 1981 all banks with eligible liabilities in excess of £10 mn must hold 0.5 per cent of their eligible liabilities in the form of non-interest bearing balances at the Bank of England. Whilst these were originally intended to operate as a cash-ratio monetary control mechanism, they currently serve only to provide the Bank of England with a free source of income to pay for its functions as the central bank.

Overall, the preponderance of instant-access or short-notice deposits means that retail bank liabilities are exceptionally liquid, and this inevitably has to be reflected in their asset portfolios. The liquid assets category includes, first, notes and coins (till money) plus balances at the Bank of England – which are partly involuntary to finance the Bank, and partly voluntary to facilitate inter-bank clearing. Sterling market loans represent short-term money market lending, either (**a**) to the discount houses, (**b**) to the inter-bank market, (**c**) to another bank in return for that bank's CD, (**d**) to local authorities, or (**e**) to overseas individuals and banks.

Of these, inter-bank lending is by far the most important, although it is only in recent years that it has become so dominant. It represents transfers from banks which temporarily have an excess of liquidity to those which are temporarily short of funds (an especially useful practice in the days when monetary controls operated on bank liquidity, although this is no longer of any relevance). There is a speculative element, insofar as any bank which expects interest rates to rise can borrow for long periods in the hope that the money can be on-lent for an initial short period at current interest rates, and then relent subsequently for successive periods at higher rates, thereby earning a speculative profit. If interest rates are expected to fall, successful speculation would require the bank to borrow short, and subsequently to reborrow more cheaply, whilst lending long at current rates.

Eligible bank bills are also prominent in the balance sheet. An eligible bill is one which the Bank of England will buy, via the discount houses, in order to make good a shortfall of cash in the banking sector. Only the bills issued by private companies, called **commercial bills**, which have been 'accepted' (guaranteed to be redeemed at face value) by major banks which fulfil specified requirements laid down by the Bank of England, acquire the status of eligible bank bills. The government's own bills (Treasury bills) are obviously also eligible, as are certain bills issued by local authorities.

It is worth noting that when a bank buys a bill it is not redeemed at face value *plus* interest by its issuer, but rather the bank buys the bill at a discount to its face value and when it matures its issuer redeems it at face value. The difference between the price paid and the face value can then be divided by the price paid in order to convert the discount into a conventional rate of interest. Any discounted bill can be rediscounted any number of times – that is, it can be resold at a different price to another party who subsequently is paid the bill's face value if it is held to maturity. By rediscounting bills a bank can, therefore, hold a portfolio of bills some part of which matures on any given day of the year.

The bulk of bank lending to private individuals and firms is represented by UK **private sector advances**. Public sector advances are insignificant because lending to the government and local authorities is largely via discounting their bills, money market loans and the purchase of long-dated government securities (gilt-edged). Private sector advances are linked to bank base rates where modest sums are involved, but large loans are commonly linked to the central money market interest rate known as the London Inter-Bank Offered Rate (**LIBOR**). It is important also to note that traditionally the pattern of private sector sterling deposits and advances was one where the deposits of individuals were recycled into loans to firms. In 1978 individuals deposited three times as much as they borrowed. By 1988 these deposits had trebled, but their borrowing had risen nearly tenfold, and marginally exceeded these deposits. Since 1983 they have borrowed more than firms in aggregate.

Banking Department lending to central government represents the net contribution to the retail banking sector of the Banking Department of the Bank of England. As it retains certain long-standing private individual accounts these do need to be itemised as retail bank assets, but the major part, which represents transactions with government departments, is something of an anachronism in the balance sheet. This item is quite often negative, which simply means that government departments have more money on deposit than they are borrowing at that point in time.

Foreign currency assets are almost entirely in the form of inter-bank lending within the UK and of lending to overseas residents, companies and especially banks. It may finally be noted that the fixed assets of retail banks, in the form primarily of property, are not separately itemised because of their relatively modest value.

In conclusion, we may note that the pattern of the retail banks' balance sheet is constantly evolving. In particular, the difficulty of attracting adequate retail funds has driven banks into the wholesale markets where interest rates are linked to LIBOR, and this has to be balanced by increased LIBOR-linked lending. The problem is accentuated by the need to pay interest on sight deposits which were traditionally a free source of funds. Furthermore, the retail banks are obliged to hold some non-interest earning assets in the form of bankers' balances. These factors, combined with a very expensive branch network and with severe losses on many of their loans to sovereign countries (see pp. 99–100), have understandably made considerable inroads into their profitability, and they have increasingly seen the solution as a movement away from traditional banking services and towards other financial services – that is, banks as financial supermarkets.

Amongst the retail banks three organisations warrant a brief individual mention.

Girobank plc

This started out life in 1968 as the National Giro in an attempt to get at those without bank accounts, comprising some 25 per cent of the adult population. Since these individuals were accustomed to using Post Offices on a regular basis, the existing very large branch network seemed ideal for the purpose of providing money transmission services at a modest price. However, whilst there was considerable initial growth in deposits, there were a number of serious hindrances in the form of a competing bank giro; current account facilities at the TSBs; increasing use of credit cards; and a continuing desire on the part of a very large number of individuals to deal only in cash transactions.

During the 1970s the range of banking services steadily improved, and deposits gradually built up to a current value of over £1½ bn held in 2 mn accounts. However, this is still a very small-scale operation. Renamed the National Girobank in 1978, the organisation subsequently became Girobank plc in 1985 and in April 1989 was sold off to the Alliance and Leicester, the fifth biggest building society. It has had full clearing bank status since 1983, and should be able to hold its own on a modest scale in future years.

TSB Group plc

Originally there were large numbers of local savings banks which were administered by the National Debt Commissioners, and which provided depositors with a simple money in-money out service. Even cheque books did not come into use until 1965, and the Central Trustee Savings Bank was then established as a member of the Bankers Clearing House to clear cheques on behalf of all the individual banks. The TSB Act 1976 authorised the development of a full range of banking services, subject to a requirement that the smaller banks merged together. Subsequently, the decision was taken to privatise the remaining banks, and although the sale proceeds were arguably the entitlement of the government, they were put straight into the TSB Group plc balance sheet. This is rather unusual compared to other retail banks in that, for historical reasons, most of the deposits are time deposits and a disproportionate share of the assets are held in the form of public sector debt. The TSB Group has found it difficult to find creditworthy borrowers so advances are relatively low as a share of assets, and there is no sovereign country debt.

Yorkshire Bank plc

For nearly eight decades the Yorkshire bank was owned by a consortium of big clearers. The Midland dropped out in the early 1950s, leaving the National Westminster, Barclays, Lloyds and the Royal Bank of Scotland as its owners. In 1989 it was sold to the National Australia Bank.

□ 4.4.2 Retail Banks in Transition

Retail banks have acquired an unenviable reputation for losing money. It all began when they decided that sovereign states would not default on their debts. Unfortunately, the rulers of many of these states decided that they could do as they pleased, which in many cases was not to repay. Then the banks decided that property lending must be sound because it was secured by real assets, which in many cases subsequently proved to be unsaleable except at bargain basement prices. Then they advanced money for highly leveraged management buy outs in the expectation that the junk bonds (very high yielding but risky) they obtained in return would indeed yield a high return once the company taken over was broken up and resold. In many cases, wrong again.

So then they decided to engage in devices to abolish risk such as swaps (discussed below), only to discover that they **shifted risk** – in the case of local authority swaps onto themselves – but they did not **abolish** it. And they decided to create financial services empires by buying estate agency chains – just in time for the housing market to collapse – and insurance companies. Whilst it is theoretically possible to make a loss in the life and pensions business if too many customers die at the wrong time or surrender their policies, if expenses go out of control or if investment returns deteriorate, it had always been difficult to do so in the past. Nevertheless the TSB paid £227 mn for Target Life in August 1987 only to end up selling it for a loss in excess of £200 mn to Equity and Law in January 1991. It then followed this up by shutting down its centralised mortgage lending arm Mortgage Express (the third largest of its kind established in 1986) in April 1991 because it was unsaleable.

To single out the TSB is unfair, if only because there were two dozen other mortgage books on the market at the time so riddled with non-performing mortgages that their owners were prepared more or less to give them away – if only they could find any takers.

Some idea of the severity of the provisions which are having to be made against bad debts is shown in **Figure 4.3**. The consequences are fairly predict-

Figure 4.3 *UK Clearing Bank Total Provisions, £ mn*

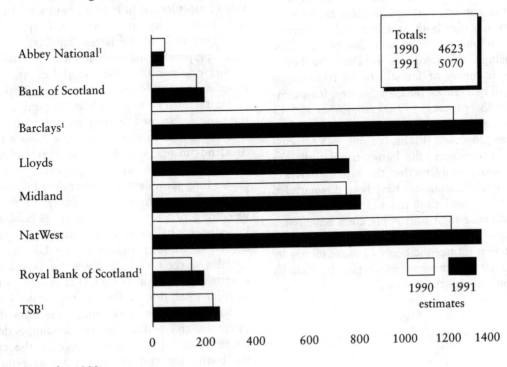

Note:
[1] Actual figure for 1990.
Source: Morgan Stanley.

able in that the banks are having to slash their staff by between 30,000 and 50,000 all told by the end of 1992, according to internal estimates. Barclays expects to shed up to 7000 jobs by natural wastage; the Midland 4000 jobs by the end of 1991; National Westminster 17,000 jobs by 1993 (although they are simultaneously recruiting in certain areas); Lloyds up to 6000 jobs by the end of 1991. They are also having to rethink their global strategies. In November 1990, for example, the Midland withdrew from the market its finance house, Forward Trust Ltd, because there were no acceptable offers. In December, its proposed merger with the Hong Kong and Shanghai bank fell through due to losses suffered by both parties. In March 1991, it sold its French mortgage lending business to the Woolwich Building Society.

In February 1991, National Westminster decided to withdraw from Belgium. Meanwhile Barclays continued to try to sell the consumer division of Mercantile Credit. Nevertheless, Barclays bought Compagnie Européene de Banque in December 1990 and thereby doubled its retail presence in France to more than 70 offices with 100,000 customers. Barclays has now become the UK market leader both at home and in Europe where it is one of the three major players (the others being Crédit Lyonnais and Deutsche Bank).

There is plenty of fat still to be trimmed in banking. The Halifax Building Society, for example, has 753 branches, 17,000 employees and 13 mn customers, whereas Barclays has 2600 branches, 85,000 employees in Britain but only 6.5 mn customers. Furthermore, the banks tribulations are creating more problems for the future. Barclays and National Westminster have been downgraded from AAA status by the main credit rating agencies, and hence their borrowing costs have risen. More importantly, many blue chip companies now have a higher rating, and hence can save money by going directly to the money markets rather than by operating through the banks.

4.4.3 Basle Capital Convergence Accord

In July 1988 the Governors of the Group of Ten central banks signed the Basle Capital Convergence Accord, thereby making banking the first industry to be regulated on a world-wide basis. The central purpose of the Accord is to force all international banks to comply with minimum capital requirements, and thereby to **ensure fair competition between them**. However, the Accord covers only credit risk and, whilst it is true that non-repayment of domestic and international loans has been the biggest risk faced by banks, other sources of risk such as those associated with exchange rate and interest rate variability will need to be added to the Accord at a later date.

The Accord essentially lays down a definition of **capital** and a formula for working out how much of it banks must have, depending upon the **riskiness** of their assets. The definition was complicated by different practices in different countries, but needed to identify capital **permanently available to meet losses**. In the UK, banks are financed with both equity and debt, but German banks have very little of the latter. Equally, US banks issue 'perpetual preferred stock' (PPS) which is neither one nor the other. In the event, a compromise was reached whereby **at least 50 per cent** of capital must be tier 1 or 'core' capital, comprising equity, disclosed reserves and PPS (but only if it is non-cumulative, meaning that failure to pay dividends in one year must not create an obligation to make them up in later years). Tier 2 includes long-term debt and other debt instruments.

The other complication concerned the 'risk weighting' of assets. Risk assets are all bank assets, including off-balance sheet commitments, weighted according to their riskiness. The UK, as a full member of the OECD, is deemed to be a low-risk borrower, as are other OECD members (with the possible exception of Turkey) plus Saudi Arabia.

Bank lending to other countries is deemed to be at greater risk. All commercial lending is deemed to be at equal risk, irrespective of the size of the borrowing company, in order to avoid vast numbers of individual decisions about creditworthiness.

Every bank has until 1992 or early 1993 to meet its minimum 'risk asset ratio', which may be imposed at a level higher than that of the Accord if individual countries so wish. The Accord itself requires that capital must be equivalent to at least 8 per cent **of a bank's risk-weighted assets**. This ratio is sometimes known as the BIS (Bank for International Settlements) ratio. The Bank of England decided, however, not to leave matters to chance and to a last-minute cleaning up of bank's balance sheets, and accordingly announced in November 1988 that UK banks would have to meet the Accord stipulations by the end of 1989, well in advance of most other signatories.

In practice, UK banks have had little difficulty in meeting their ratios via retained earnings and modest rights issues. At the end of 1990 the Midland's ratio was above 10 per cent and the other main clearers were clustered around 9 per cent, and they are currently above these levels. Oddly enough, it is the big Japanese city (commercial) banks which have got problems. At the end of the 1980s 9 out of the biggest 10 banks in the world and 23 out of the biggest 30 were Japanese. Several were bigger, in market capitalisation terms, than the entire British banking industry. They were permitted to count 45 per cent of the investment gains on shareholdings as capital, and the booming Tokyo Stock Market was viewed as an effective guarantor that their ratios would be easy to safeguard. The enormous fall in the Nikkei index during 1990 proved how vulnerable they in reality were.

There is still room for improvement in implementing the ratio. It makes little sense to treat all commercial loans as equally risky since this may incline banks to divert scarce capital away from blue-chip companies to others where the capital is, in reality, much more at risk. Also, the fact that loans secured on residential property require only half as much capital as commercial loans will inevitably make it harder to suppress asset price inflation.

☐ 4.4.4 Directives

As with other parts of the financial system the banks have had to come to terms with a stream of EC directives. On 3 January 1991 the Bank of England adopted two directives which govern banks' capital and the size of their balance sheets. The directives also affect building societies, but in that case implementation is the responsibility of the Building Societies Commission.

The **Solvency Ratio Directive** takes effect for all EC members in 1991. It lays down a formula for calculating how large a balance sheet a bank can run, based on the riskiness of its assets and the size of its capital. It sets a minimum ratio of capital to assets of 8 per cent.

The **Own Funds Directive** states how a bank's capital is to be calculated. This directive does not need to be implemented until 1 January 1993, but the Bank intends to implement it during 1991. The two directives are essentially a reiteration of the Basle capital adequacy provisions, and hence will not require major policy changes since the banks have been operating under the Basle provisions for two years. However, there may be some adjustments required on account of the high risk weighting accorded to mortgage-backed securities as compared to actual mortgages.

☐ 4.4.5 International Debt and the Banks

The analysis of the international debt problem is more appropriately left to Chapter 6. At this juncture it is appropriate simply to clarify the previous reference to its impact on banking practice. It was clear by the early 1980s that a good deal of the money lent to LDCs would never be repaid even if these countries did not officially renege on their debts (see **pp. 219–22**). However, banks which had become heavily involved in this lending, possibly because of the fanciful idea that sovereign country debt is more secure than lending to households and firms, but also because it gives a measure of status to a bank to be the banker to a sovereign State, were unwilling to write the debt off their balance sheets for fear that it would expose their inadequate capital structure. Initially, the common practice was to convert short-term loans into long-term loans, and to set aside some of the profits earned on other business into a reserve fund to cover international bad debts. Where possible, the capital base of a bank was replenished by an additional issue of equity (see discussion of rights issues on **p. 120**), and it was possible to offset some losses against tax liabilities.

In 1987 the international banks, following the example set in America, decided to bite the bullet and write a significant part of the debt off their balance sheet. Rather interestingly, the Stock Market took a fairly positive view of this new sense of realism and bank share prices rose rather than fell. Nevertheless, it remained understandably difficult for banks to raise new capital in the markets, especially in the aftermath of the October 1987 crash. The decision by Brazil to delay repayment of foreign debts in July 1989 raised the possibility either that further provisions for bad debts would have to be made or that the loans to those countries least likely to repay would be written off once and for all. The Midland and Lloyds both had outstanding loans of £4.2 bn in 1988, followed by National Westminster and Barclays at £2.5 bn, so the write-off alternative appeared to be more realistic in respect of the latter than of the former pair.

However, in late July 1989 Lloyds reported that 15 out of the 29 problem debtor countries which owed it money were in arrears with their repayments, and accordingly announced a massive £483 mn provision of which £183 mn was set against specific countries' debts. This caused the bank's net profits to slump to a loss of £88 mn for the first half of 1989, but as previously the share price rose sharply on the news. Lloyds' cover for problem country debts was accordingly raised to 47 per cent, well above that for the other three which stood at between 31 and 33 per cent in 1988. Since that time all the banks have seen fit to make additional provisions, so that by 1992 there will be no further need to make major provisions against defaulting sovereign debt, although as previously mentioned there are plenty of other non-performing loans to take its place.

☐ 4.4.6 *Wholesale Banks*

As shown in **Table 4.2 (a)** at end-1990 the total deposit liabilities of the wholesale banks amounted to some £840 bn, of which some £720 bn was held

at overseas banks. Collectively, therefore, wholesale banks greatly outweigh retail banks, but as there are 600 or so such banks currently in operation in the UK, their individual portfolios are on average much smaller than those of the typical retail bank.

Wholesale banks concern themselves with small numbers of large-scale transactions. Deposits of less than £100,000 are unlikely to be accepted, and these deposits are often parcelled up into even larger loans. Deposits are not normally withdrawable on demand, so there is no need to keep anything like the same degree of cash and near-cash reserves as retail banks. Furthermore, it is possible to supplement liquidity by borrowing in the interbank market or through issuing certificates of deposit, with the result that, for example, British merchant banks keep only some £80 mn, and other British banks some £120 mn, in the form of notes and coin and of balances with the Bank of England. Because each deposit is in a specific currency (mostly non-sterling – see **pp. 116–18** for a discussion of the Eurocurrency markets), and the depositor can specify the term to maturity, wholesale banks need to find borrowers who want the same currencies for as near as possible the same periods of time. A perfect match between assets and liabilities is, however, rarely possible because of the preference among lenders to lend for periods of time which are shorter than the periods over which borrowers prefer to borrow, and there are obvious problems in matching currencies. The characteristic transaction of a wholesale bank is, therefore, quite different from that of a retail bank, but this has led to the main retail banks setting up wholesale banking subsidiaries in order to diversify their pattern of business, so there are in practice more links between the two banking sectors than may at first seem apparent.

British Merchant Banks

The British Merchant banks are distinguished from other British wholesale banks by virtue of their membership of the British Merchant Banking and Securities Houses Association. Their former name of 'accepting houses' arose from the traditional practice of 'accepting' commercial bills, which effectively guarantees repayment in full upon maturity and hence both makes the bills easier to market and reduces the interest rate which needs to be offered. Some bills are retained for their own portfolios, but this type of agency business is no longer all that important, acceptances representing only some 12–15 per cent of total liabilities at the present time.

The now more significant banking activity is almost entirely wholesale rather than retail. The total deposit liabilities of £60 bn are modest by wholesale banking standards, and are generally divided between sterling and foreign currencies in approximately a 60:40 ratio. Both deposits originating overseas and from the inter-bank markets (UK monetary sector) have become increasingly prominent. Assets are correspondingly distributed, with the bulk of sterling assets in the form of loans to the UK inter-bank market and advances to UK borrowers, and the greater part of foreign currency assets in the form of lending abroad, especially to foreign banks. Lending to non-bank customers is relatively unimportant and, as indicated above, very little cash is held.

British Merchant banks are also significant providers of financial services. Many undertake responsibility for all the administrative aspects of issuing new equity; provide a wide range of banking services for companies and some wealthy individuals; act as management consultants with respect to, for example, mergers and takeovers; and provide portfolio management services for pension funds and, in certain cases, unit trusts and investment trusts.

Other British Banks

The typical other British bank, so categorised because whilst registered in the UK it does most of its business with overseas clients, is considerably smaller than the typical British Merchant bank. Of the 200 or more such banks, the core group comprises long-standing institutions originally set up to facilitate retail banking in British colonies. This has understandably not been a growth area for some time, and this category now includes a number of the smaller UK banks which offer a restricted range of services, including some which, although not officially Merchant banks, provide almost identical services. Since the Banking Act 1979 took them within its provisions, many former finance houses have also operated in this category, competing directly with organisations listed separately under that heading.

The total deposit liabilities of other British banks are no longer greater than those of the British Merchant banks, and there are considerable similarities in the respective balance sheets. Other British banks do not, however, hold many acceptances.

□ 4.4.7 Overseas Banks

A number of American and European banks have had a London office for many decades in order to provide services for their customers whilst in the UK. However, the number of overseas banks has grown enormously over the past two decades, initially as a result of the growth of Eurocurrency markets, and more recently as a result of financial deregulation.

As shown in **Table 4.3**, there were 478 overseas banks in London in 1990, a gain of roughly 100 on the figure a decade previously. The invasion was originally spearheaded by American banks although their numbers peaked in 1983 and are now barely greater than those of Japanese banks, which have more than doubled since 1980 with only two recent departures.

As shown in **Table 4.2(a)**, whilst the American banks alone still have deposit liabilities of £110 bn, equal to over 95 per cent of the combined liabilities of British Merchant banks and other British banks, this represents only 40 per cent of the liabilities of the Japanese banks which are mostly comparative newcomers to London. The Japanese banks in 1988 had deposit liabilities virtually equal to those of the retail banks and it was thought that they would soon overtake them, but in the event the sterling liabilities of the retail banks shot up as did deposits at other (non-American) overseas banks. The latter currently exceed the deposits of Japanese banks by a wide margin. As **Table 4.3** indicates, this has resulted from the huge influx of European banks (82 net in

Table 4.3   Foreign Banks in London

	US			Europe			Japan			Arab			Others			Summary		
	Total	Out	In	Total	Out	In	Total	Out	In	Total	Out	In	Total	Out	In	Total	Out	In
1980	71	2	1	141	3	21	24	0	0	19	0	1	128	3	12	383	8	35
1981	73	1	3	147	2	8	25	0	1	23	0	4	131	5	8	399	8	24
1982	77	0	4	153	0	6	29	0	4	26	0	3	144	1	14	429	1	31
1983	76	2	1	165	3	15	31	0	2	28	0	2	145	2	3	445	7	23
1984	75	1	0	168	6	9	35	0	4	35	0	7	146	2	3	459	9	23
1985	70	7	2	169	0	1	38	0	1	34	2	1	143	5	2	454	14	9
1986	68	3	1	184	3	18	40	0	2	34	2	2	136	8	1	462	16	24
1987	64	5	1	190	5	11	46	0	6	33	1	0	131	6	1	464	17	19
1988	59	8	3	201	5	16	50	0	4	36	1	4	132	3	4	478	17	31
1989	57	4	2	205	5	9	50	0	0	35	1	0	134	3	5	482	12	16
1990	53	4	0	207	10	13	51	2	3	34	1	0	133	6	3	478[1]	23	19
Total 1980–90		37	18		42	127		2	29		8	24		44	56		132[2]	254

Notes:

[1] Comparable figures for Paris and Frankfurt were 277 and 247 respectively.

[2] Many of these departures were due to mergers of foreign banks.

Source: Noel Alexander Associates.

all, between 1979 and 1989), with a significant surge after the Single European Act in 1986.

The Eurocurrency markets are discussed separately below, and it is necessary to note at this stage only that the enormous growth in **international money** (for example, dollars traded outside America) was particularly centred in London, so all the important overseas banks necessarily had to open an office there to participate on any scale in these markets. American banks, in particular, were drawn to London by a desire to avoid the much tighter regulations in their domestic market. Because American and Japanese banks have been at the forefront of developments in electronic banking, they have been particularly well placed to take advantage of the recent deregulation of financial services, and their recent movement into, for example, the mortgage market has had profound effects upon traditional practices in the UK. No doubt overseas banks will steadily encroach upon other areas of business, such as corporate finance, and given that their deposits are backed by the vastly greater assets of the parent companies, they look set to play an increasingly dominant role.

As shown in **Table 4.2 (a)**, the overseas banks do the vast bulk of their business in **foreign currencies**. Their deposits, unsurprisingly, largely come from overseas, and mostly from parent organisations. Around one-third of their sterling deposits also come from overseas, and most of what remains is borrowed in the UK inter-bank markets which also provide over 15 per cent of foreign currency deposits. On the assets side of the balance sheet there are minimal amounts of cash and balances held at the Bank of England, but massive amounts of foreign currency lending to overseas residents, a great deal of which is routed via overseas banks. Inter-bank lending is very important, both in sterling and foreign currencies. As with other categories of wholesale banks, almost exactly the same amount is borrowed from the inter-bank markets as is lent to them. Apart from the modest net effect of retail bank operations in the inter-bank markets, it is simply a matter of definition that total lending must be equal to total borrowing, and the very large sums being transferred represent either portfolio adjustments by individual banks (for example, adjustment of maturity pro-

files) or simply opportunities which individual banks have to borrow from other banks with no immediate customers and to on-lend at a profit. Because wholesale banking is in aggregate so much larger than retail banking, the small proportion of assets held in sterling still represents a far from modest amount of lending. Whilst they are clearly more than happy to compete for sterling business in the UK, they do not as yet show any real interest in moving out of London, and this is why one gets the impression, even in the largest provincial cities, that the UK retail banks are the only major banking intermediaries.

Since August 1987 the other overseas banks category has included the operations of the **consortium banks**. These are independent banks, jointly owned by other banks and/or financial intermediaries located in a variety of countries, with no single parent body having a majority share in the consortium. They were often set up because individual small banks could not afford a London operation, and the combined status of the parent bodies could be expected to attract more business than their individual operations added together. By combining together they could move into areas of business beyond their individual means, and also operate outside the control of their domestic regulations. They operate entirely in wholesale markets, and 80 per cent of their assets are in foreign currencies. It is no longer worth listing consortium banks separately because, unlike other overseas banks, their growth is insignificant. Many consortium members have become a strong enough to stand alone, whilst others have grown reluctant to let other banks involve them in overly risky ventures. There is also no longer the need to avoid regulations in many domestic markets. Nevertheless, there are always small institutions wishing to have a share in a London-based operation, so as consortium members withdraw others take their place, and the number of consortia has tended to remain stable at a figure of 23 since 1981.

□ 4.4.8 The Discount Market

The discount market is a money market, the membership of which was until very recently restricted to the eight (currently nine) discount houses which were members of the London Discount Market Association (LDMA). The nature of their business can be clearly seen in the LDMA balance sheet, which at 30 December 1990 showed total liabilities of £14.9 bn, of which sterling liabilities constituted £14.5 bn. Of these £13.2 bn were funds borrowed 'at call' (recallable without notice) and overnight. These funds, as we have seen, represent the most liquid asset bar cash itself in the retail banks' balance sheet. On the assets side of the balance sheet are to be found very little bar sterling denominated short-term assets, largely in the form of commercial bills (£58 bn) and bank and building society certificates of deposit (£7 bn).

It logically follows that the functions of the discount market are to make a market in bills of all kinds; to give the banking sector a means by which they can replenish their cash holdings virtually on demand; and to assist in the financing of short-term trade debts through the purchase of discounted commercial bills from banks and their customers. The discount houses are also committed to tender for the whole of every issue of Treasury Bills (TBs) in order to guarantee that government departments can pay their way, but they can be out-bid, and indeed holdings of TBs have fallen to quite modest levels (£415 mn at the end of 1990).

The LDMA, in essence, exists to maintain liquidity in the financial system. There are vast amounts of short-term instruments in existence, and the LDMA effectively guarantees that they can be bought and sold freely, thereby greatly reducing the need for cash holdings. At the end of daily cheque clearing, for example, some banks will have cash surpluses which can earn interest, albeit at very low rates, by being placed in the discount market, whilst the others can find the cash on the spot which is needed to settle deficits.

The discount market also has an important role to play in the conduct of monetary policy. Every day, money flows between government departments and the clearing banks via accounts held at the Bank of England. On any given day this may result in a very large net cash flow in one direction or the other. If government departments have drawn heavily on cash held at the clearing banks, the banks will have to go immediately to the discount market to replenish their cash holdings. With cash in short supply, short-term interest rates will have to rise rapidly to attract sufficient cash into the market. Conversely, if the clearing banks are flush with cash, which is then deposited in the discount market, the LDMA will have to bid for short-term assets, causing their prices to rise and their yields (face value *less* price paid) to fall.

If short-term interest rates become very volatile, this will quickly be transmitted to longer-term interest rates and to the exchange rate. In order to avoid this, the Bank of England stands ready to smooth cash flows between government departments and the clearing banks. If the banks have too much cash the Bank will mop it up by selling eligible bills to the LDMA, whilst if there are cash shortages the Bank will buy eligible bills in return for cash. This is called an **open-market operation** (OMO). Whilst it is the case that the Bank of England is willing on occasion to deal directly with financial intermediaries other than the LDMA, it is formally the case that only the LDMA may go to the Bank for funds when they cannot be obtained from any other source.

An OMO in the discount market therefore provides the means whereby the Bank can influence short-term interest rates. Since August 1981 the procedure has been as follows. When cash is in short supply the Bank will invite the LDMA to sell eligible bills. If their selling price, and hence the associated discount (rate of interest), is acceptable to the Bank it will buy the bills and relieve the cash shortage. However, if the price is unacceptable, it will ask the LDMA to re-offer at a different price, thereby raising or lowering the interest rate as appropriate. The same procedure can be used if the Bank offers to sell eligible bills in order to mop up surplus cash.

If the Bank was, exceptionally, to refuse to buy bills at any price offered by the discount houses, then it would leave them with no option but to ask for a 'lender-of-last-resort' loan from the Bank, and the Bank would be able to charge any interest rate which it wished as a condition for making the cash available. The significance of this procedure is that the money markets cannot know for certain, in advance of the Bank's response to an offer to buy or sell eligible bills, what the Bank's views are about the appropriate level for short-term interest rates. The money markets are constantly nudging short-term interest rates up and down, but the Bank can signal its desire either to see these rate movements go beyond the limits set by the market, or the restoration of rates previously prevailing. By behaving in this way the Bank does not seek to dominate the markets on a continuous basis, as was the practice throughout most of the period prior to 1981, but rather to give clear guidance to the markets as and when it is considered to be appropriate.

As of June 1988 the Bank published a draft document which reassessed the decision made at the time when capital markets were deregulated ('Big Bang', October 1986) to allow other bodies to become members of the discount market. Whilst previously the discount houses had to be independently capitalised, it was now proposed that a gilt-edged market-maker would be able to incorporate a discount house within its other operations without separate capitalisation. However, its total operations would be limited to dealing in sterling debt, sterling money market instruments and related futures and options, and capital adequacy and other requirements would need to be met (see *Bank of England Quarterly Bulletin.* August 1988, pp. 391–402). Prior to 1986 the discount market was kept adequately financed by making it a condition for 'eligibility' status that a bank keep at least 2.5 per cent of its eligible liabilities (ELs) with the LDMA, and at least 5 per cent of its ELs with the LDMA, money brokers and gilt-edged jobbers. It is hoped that the new proposals will guarantee sufficient capital adequacy for the really quite modest operations of the discount market to be expanded. In January 1989 it was revealed that two new intermediaries had applied to join the discount market, potentially increasing its capitalisation by only £25 mn to £375 mn, but only one joined in February. This poor response obviously reflected the post-Big Bang fallout.

4.5 Non-bank Financial Intermediaries

Taken in aggregate the non-bank financial intermediaries (NBFIs) currently hold a much more valuable portfolio of assets than the banks. In 1989 the largest group was the pension funds (£224 bn, up from £30 bn), followed by the insurance companies with assets of £214 bn (up from £42 bn in 1977); the building societies (£190 bn, up from £35 bn); the unit trusts (£55 bn, up from £3 bn); and the investment trusts (£24 bn, up from £6 bn). Pension funds and unit trusts have grown very rapidly, with the other groups some way behind. The NBFI also include the National Savings Bank and the Finance Houses.

4.5.1 Building Societies

The building societies began life as terminating societies, which lasted as long as it took to build houses for all of the members. Over time they became permanent, and came to monopolise a particular form of financial service. Modern societies are **mutual organisations**, which bring together the generally modest savings of large numbers of individuals and parcel them up into a much smaller number of mortgages. Savers' accounts are known as **shares** and **deposits**. Shareholders do not, however, share in a society's profits, but by virtue of being society members can vote at annual general meetings on such issues as conversion to banking status (see below). Interest rates are slightly lower on deposit accounts, which have the balancing advantage of priority in repayment if a society goes bankrupt. This is not generally thought to be much of a risk, so there are understandably many times as many shareholders as depositors.

During the 1970s the societies faced little competition from the banks, which thought mortgage lending too long term; did not enjoy the composite tax rate arrangement which cheapened the cost of funds to societies; had, unlike the societies, to build a profit margin into the interest rate charged; and had their aggregate lending constrained by monetary controls. The societies chose to avoid competition amongst themselves by operating an

Table 4.4 *Building Society Statistics, End-year*

	1960	1970	1975	1980	1985	1988	1989[1]	1990[1]
Number of societies	726	481	382	273	167	131	126	117
Number of branches	N/A	2 016	3 375	5 684	6 926	6 912	6 236	6 055
Number of shareholders (mn)	3.9	10.3	17.9	30.6	40.0	43.8	36.8	37.0
Number of depositors (mn)	0.6	0.6	0.7	0.9	2.1	4.3	4.5	4.3
Number of borrowers (mn)	2.4	3.7	4.4	5.4	6.7	7.4	6.7	6.7
Number of advances in year (mn)	0.4	0.6	0.8	0.9	1.7	2.0	1.6	1.5
Volume of advances in year (£ bn)	0.6	2.0	4.9	9.5	26.5	46.9	42.3	44.3

Note:
[1] Excludes Abbey National plc.
Source: Housing Finance (formerly the *BSA Bulletin*) (August 1990).

interest rate cartel, and mortgage lending was heavily constrained by the inflow of retail funds in the absence of access to wholesale markets.

None of these considerations any longer apply. Building societies both compete amongst themselves for business, and are under attack not merely from the 'clearing' banks, but also from the foreign banks and the mortgage corporations which keep down costs by having no branch network. When funds were in short supply, large-scale borrowing attracted an interest rate penalty. These days the larger the loan the cheaper it tends to be, as funds from the wholesale markets appear to be almost limitless. Faced with bank encroachment upon their traditional business, the societies have responded by encroaching on the business of the banks.

Table 4.4 provides an interesting historical snapshot of the building society sector. The number of societies has dropped dramatically since 1960, and although the rate of reduction has necessarily slowed down, the process of merger is still continuing. Assets are thus concentrated in the hands of a relatively small number of societies, many of which are huge by historical standards. As the number of societies shrank so they snapped up sites in every High Street in the land, a process which peaked in the mid-1980s when there were twice as many branches as a decade earlier. This process is now beginning to reverse itself as societies seek to economise on their operations, but the big reduction in 1989 resulted from the transfer of Abbey National's branches to the banking sector.

This also cut back the number of shareholders, which peaked at 44 mn in 1988. This is rather astonishing given the size of the population, but many people hold accounts at several societies. In a given year only a fraction of these accounts are active, and many lie dormant for years on end, but the number of active accounts has nevertheless risen sharply since the passing of the Building Societies Act 1986. The number of borrowers has grown more steadily (adjusting for Abbey National), but whilst the amount borrowed only rose by a factor of less than 5 during the highly inflationary 1970s because inflows to societies were limited, it trebled during the first half of the 1980s alone in the face of much tougher competition from other lenders. This reflected much sharper increases in house prices than in prices generally, together with an enormous influx of money into the mortgage market. Had it not been for the exclusion of Abbey National, the sums advanced would probably have doubled again by the end of the decade.

Not surprisingly, this was financed mainly from share and deposit account liabilities. These stood at £50 bn in 1980, and at the time this represented over 90 per cent of total liabilities. By 1988 deposit liabilities stood at £151 bn, but even so this represented less than 80 per cent of the total.

This is accounted for by the fact that in 1979 wholesale borrowing from the money markets was non-existent, yet by 1990 a total of £37 bn was being borrowed, representing some 17 per cent of the total. One can anticipate the continuance of

Figure 4.4 *Building Societies, Assets and Liabilities, 1990* [1]

	£ mn	%
Assets		
Commercial[2]	182 454	82.7
Cash & bank deposits	23 766	10.8
British government stocks	3 789	1.7
Other investments	3 014	1.4
Other assets	4 244	1.9
Other public sector debt	3 415	1.5
Total	220 682	100.0
Liabilities		
Shares and deposits	160 842	72.9
Wholesale	37 425	17.0
Other liabilities & reserves	22 415	10.1
Total	220 682	100.0

Notes:
[1] From July 1989 figures exclude Abbey National plc.
[2] Of which 173,193 are Class 1 assets, namely advances to individuals secured on land for the residential use of the borrower which must also be first charges on the property.
Source: Bank of England Quarterly Bulletin, Table 6.2.

this reduction in reliance upon retail deposits into the future.

The asset side of the balance sheet is dominated by mortgage lending (see **Figure 4.4**), the traditional business of the societies. In future years we are going to see the long-term effects of the relaxed personal lending rules set out in the Building Societies Act 1986. Immediately after the Act there was a portfolio adjustment. Over £1 bn of local authority investments were sold off and after a significant build up of British government securities between 1980 and 1983, these were also heavily depleted between 1986 and 1989.

The liquidity of the societies is hard to explain. The Chief Registrar of Friendly Societies used to require that cash plus investments be maintained at a minimum of 7.5 per cent of total assets. As the balance sheet shows, it is the custom for the societies to keep well in excess of that amount. His-

torically, it was just about possible to argue that, if inflows dried up, commitments to mortgage lending could be maintained by running down these reserves, but with wholesale funding now freely available that hardly any longer seems necessary.

Building Societies Act 1986

As most deposits are effectively withdrawable upon demand, whilst mortgages are mostly granted for 25 years, the **liquidity mismatch** between assets and liabilities is very striking. However, the average life of a mortgage is in reality only 7 years (which partly explains the belated enthusiasm for mortgage lending by the banking sector); there is a constant inflow of capital and interest repayments; very little bad debt; and almost all borrowing and lending is at floating interest rates, so there is always a margin between them to cover expenses and leave room for profit.

The Building Societies Act 1986 has operated since January 1987, and has subsequently been amended to relax its rules which, whilst allowing societies to move some way from their traditional business both in terms of methods of raising finance and of disposal of funds, are nevertheless regarded as overly restrictive.

For example, the original 20 per cent limit on the amount of funding to be raised from wholesale sources was doubled with effect from 1 January 1988. The Building Societies Commission has operated an informal 25 per cent limit and in practice the aggregate ratio has not exceeded 20 per cent, with none of the largest societies exceeding 24 per cent. Nevertheless, the societies want the 40 per cent limit to be raised.

One of the most important new powers gained by societies in the 1986 Act was the ability to undertake limited unsecured lending. Three classes of commercial asset were introduced. Up to 7.5 per cent of commercial assets can be in the form of class 3 assets (unsecured advances, investment in land and investment in subsidiaries), but only provided societies have commercial assets in excess of £100 mn. This has permitted qualifying societies to issue credit cards, to provide overdrafts and to provide unsecured loans for non-housing-related purposes. Once again, societies have not used these powers all that fully so far, but that has reflected the buoyancy of mortgage lending and societies chafe against the restrictions.

The review of building society powers completed in June 1988 resulted in their being able to offer a wide range of banking and housing-related services; to take up to a 100 per cent stake in life assurance companies and up to a 15 per cent stake in general insurance companies, to undertake fund management; and to take up to 100 per cent stakes in stockbrokers.

There was also a provision in the Act for designating bodies with wide powers in which societies may invest which has been used on several occasions. From 1 July 1989 appropriate mortgage companies were designated as suitable for investment or support by a society. These may buy, administer or sell the existing mortgage books of other lenders as well as making mortgage loans on their own account. Furthermore, since 1 January 1988 societies have been permitted to establish subsidiaries to operate in other EC member states.

With some societies eager to expand their range of financial services even faster than the rules evolved, the issue inevitably arose as to whether any of them might wish to convert to banking status. The government adopted a neutral stance, and introduced draft rules governing conversion on 28 July 1988. The Abbey National, the second largest society, obtained the necessary majority to convert in April 1989, and was given the authorisation to proceed by the regulatory body set up by the 1986 Act, the Building Societies Commission. It became a plc in July 1989. Support for conversion by Abbey members was so high that other societies were thought to be almost certain to follow suit. In the event, however, no other society has yet followed the Abbey's example, in good part because they are now permitted to do so many new things under their own relaxed rules.

Perhaps this is just as well, because they have not shown themselves to be particularly astute in expanding into new spheres of operation.

The Halifax, for example, built up a chain of 700 estate agency branches, starting only in 1988. It lost £27 mn on these operations in 1989 and now has only 585; it hopes the housing market will recover soon. The Nationwide Anglia acquired 434 estate agencies of its own, but subsequently needed the Guardian Royal Exchange insurance company to help out by taking a 29 per cent stake. In January 1990 the Woolwich chose to increase its own chain to more than 400 branches by acquiring two regions of the Prudential's loss-making agency, but at least they only cost one-quarter of the peak prices paid by the Halifax. The Woolwich also decided to launch a unit trust company just when the industry had moved into the doldrums.

Such moves may retrospectively prove to have been more astute than earlier forays by the societies, as may the Alliance and Leicester's acquisition of Chase Manhattan's British credit card operation to supplement that acquired when it bought Girobank. Its immediate reward was, however, a downgrading by credit rating agencies, thereby raising the cost of its borrowing.

Because building societies cannot easily issue shares, they have to raise capital by increasing their retained earnings. This makes it difficult to finance acquisitions and other forms of expansion. The Building Societies Commission has therefore proposed that societies should be permitted to issue **Permanent Interest Bearing Shares** (PIBS) which, like non-voting shares, would yield interest rather than dividends.

Cross-border Activity

It is now regarded as inevitable that some societies will be taken over by outside institutions. Large numbers of UK and foreign intermediaries such as Citicorp and Crédit Agricole are allegedly eager buyers. In December 1990 the Bank of Edinburgh was set up on the basis of £26 mn in equity, with Scottish Amicable as a 39 per cent stakeholder, in the hope of persuading societies to give up their mutual status and become part of a plc. So far, societies have declined to play ball.

The implementation of the Single European Market (see **p. 224**) has made little progress with respect to the integration of housing finance systems in the EC. Levels of owner-occupancy are highly variable in member states, and the legal procedures, institutions and financial instruments are often incompatible. As a result the creation of a mortgage finance directive is unlikely to be realised. However, the Second Banking Coordination Directive, published at the end of 1988, permitted mortgage lenders to operate outside their home country in the same way as they operate at home.

The 'mutual recognition of techniques' has so far failed to lead to a plethora of cross-border activity. Part of the difficulty lay in the necessity to establish a subsidiary elsewhere in the EC before conducting business there, and UK legislation will need to be amended before funds can be transmitted through societies' UK branches. The most active society in recent times has been the Woolwich, which established an Italian subsidiary at the end of 1990 and currently sells its mortgage products through 500 Italian bank branches. In March 1991 it also acquired Midland Bank's mortgage subsidiary in France, the Banque Immobilière de Crédit, to be renamed Banque Woolwich.

□ *4.5.2 Insurance Companies*

The business of life insurance is often conducted by large composite insurers which also insure general risks such as damage to house and car. Our concern here is primarily with **life insurance**, which may also be provided by specialist insurance companies. The business of life insurance has little to do with liquidity. The commonest form of policy is where the individual makes regular monthly payments which entitle him or her to a lump sum at a specific future date (an **endowment**). If the endowment is 'with profits', then bonuses will be added in line with the profitability of the company. If the policy holder dies before the policy matures, then a lump sum will be paid to the next-of-kin or specified beneficiary.

An endowment may alternatively be purchased via a single, large, lump-sum down-payment. Special forms of endowment are increasingly linked to mortgages, either 'low cost' endowments or mortgage protection policies which simply guarantee to repay the outstanding mortgage upon the death of the mortgagee (term insurance). Unit-linked endowments are also available, and indeed there is the now customary proliferation of new forms of life insurance in this exceptionally competitive market. Endowments can be cashed in before maturity, although this may result in a repayment of less than the total amount paid in, since insurance brokers are frequently paid the first year's premium as a fee for arranging the endowment.

Life insurance companies hold roughly half of their long-term assets in the form of UK and overseas equities, and the rest mostly comprises gilts and UK land, property and ground rents. Equities are even more prominent in the assets structure of pension funds, because fixed-yield assets would not keep pace with commitments to make payments based upon rapidly-rising incomes. These institutions clearly, therefore, play a dominant role in the equity and gilt-edged markets.

Like the commercial banks, the insurance companies are often less than astute investors on behalf of their policy holders. In May 1991, for example, the Prudential Corporation decided that it was 'emotionally unsuited' to being a residential estate agent, and completed the sale of its 500-branch operation which it had built up a total cost of £338 mn. Total receipts from branch sales were £30 mn. General Accident did equally badly with its ill-fated acquisition of its New Zealand subsidiary, NZI Corporation. A prudent Scottish institution which rarely strayed further south than Yorkshire until the mid-1980s, General Accident bought its majority stake in NZI in 1988 and 1989 for £460 mn. Its losses on the NZI banking operations are expected to total around £200 mn. At least the Guardian Royal Exchange lost only £70 mn on its Italian non-life venture which folded in January 1991. So much for global ambitions.

In 1990, Eagle Star sold its French general insurance subsidiary and Prudential disposed of its Belgian subsidiary. Spurred on by these notable successes, companies such as Commercial Union and General Accident have recently started new ventures in France where competition is especially fierce. The life insurance companies have cause to be very grateful for the decision to introduce personal pensions, discussed below, since it provided them with a huge source of new business. It is to be hoped that they have learned their lesson from the 1980s, namely that it is not easy to cross-sell life insurance and other similar policies with the products of other types of financial intermediary.

Lloyd's of London

The cornerstone of UK's insurance market is Lloyd's of London. Traditionally one had to be very rich to join a syndicate and become a 'name' since 'names' were subject to 'unlimited liability'. From 1967 to 1987 Lloyds made substantial profits and the risk attached to unlimited liability seemed of little account. As a result large numbers of modestly wealthy middle class individuals signed up as 'names'. However, this proved to be a case of very bad timing.

Lloyd's is very slow to declare its results because syndicates cannot close their accounts for any year in which there are unknown outstanding claims. Heavy and unremitting pollution claims from the USA, together with a series of severe natural disasters and events such as the explosion on the Piper Alpha platform in the North Sea, have plunged Lloyd's into the red since 1988 to an extent that can only be guessed at. Many outstanding claims relate to policies written decades ago to cover pollution and diseases unforeseeable at the time (such as asbestosis). As a result a 'name' may ultimately be liable for 20 to 30 times the original investment.

Unsurprisingly, many 'names' are now taking legal action, claiming that Lloyd's was lax in its regulation of the market and that they are victims of negligence. In its turn, Lloyd's has instigated a wide-ranging review of its procedures, to include the issue of 'unlimited liability', but by the time it reports a large proportion of the 'names' may be technically bankrupt as annual losses are likely to exceed £1 bn for 1989 and 1990.

Pension Schemes

A **pension** cannot be paid out to anyone other than the person in whose name the monthly payments are made, irrespective of who pays the premiums, nor in part to anyone other than his or her spouse or children upon the death of the pensioner. Most pension schemes involve payments both by the individual and the company he or she works for. Until recently, this has meant that if the individual moved jobs the pension in the old job would be frozen until retirement, and the individual would have to start up a new one with the new company. In certain circumstances, however, pensions are now 'portable' between jobs. The self-employed must buy personal pensions for themselves, and it is now possible for individuals to top up existing pension rights by buying additional personal pensions.

Pension, or superannuation, funds make payments for as long as a pensioner lives after reaching pensionable age. In certain cases these payments were index-linked before 1990. Thus while life insurance is primarily a means of buying protection (for dependents) in the event of early death, a pension fund exists to cover the risk of living too long without an income. The popularity of life insurance and pension funds has traditionally been fostered by the existence of tax concessions both to individuals and to companies. Tax relief on life insurance premiums was, however, discontinued in the 1985 Budget. During the late 1980s many company pension funds had a 'contributions holiday' since they already had more than sufficient income from investors to cover pension liabilities due to the bull market in equities during the 1980s.

At the end of 1990, the average UK scheme had assets equal to 122 per cent of pension liabilities. This appears to be a comfortable cushion, but the 1990 Social Security Act which requires inflation-proofing of pensions, and the European Court of Justice ruling concerning sex discrimination in pensions (discussed on **pp. 337–8**) will both cost quite a lot of money to implement.

Furthermore, pension funds had a dreadful year in 1990. The previous negative return on assets was in 1974, and the average rate of growth from 1979 to 1989 was 15 per cent. The losses on overseas (especially Japanese) equities in 1990 resulted in a 10 per cent negative return. Fortunately, this is unlikely to recur in 1991, so the long-term effects upon the size of pensions will be negligible.

The State Earnings Related Pension Scheme (Serps) was once compulsory for all, and financed, at least in principle, by National Insurance contributions (NICs). In 1985 the decision was taken to allow people to opt out by contracting a personal pension for themselves. This was expected to reduce the burden on the National Insurance Fund, although this was to be more than offset by the 5.8 per cent NICs' rebate, the special incentive of 2 per cent of relevant earnings payable until April 1993 and tax relief on the employee's part of the rebate.

It was estimated that 500,000 people would immediately take out personal pensions, with numbers eventually peaking at 1.75 mn. But by April 1990 4 mn personal pensions had been taken out. As a result, the net cost to the Exchequer was estimated by the comptroller and auditor-general to reach an eventual figure of £5.9 bn at April 1988 prices (when the new pensions were first introduced). In 1990–91 the net cost was estimated at £1.8 bn, equivalent to a 1.5p rise in the rate of income tax.

One serious misjudgement, apart from the cost, was to allow those who opted out of Serps to rejoin at any time they chose. The nature of the rebates made it exceptionally attractive to opt out when employees were in their twenties, and to opt back in twenty years later – hence the large numbers who chose to opt out. The government is now stuck with the problem of how to keep the cost to the Exchequer under control without simply inducing everyone to opt back into Serps in 1993.

□ 4.5.3 Unit Trusts

Direct investment in equities has never been popular among individuals in the UK. This is partly because it is not possible to obtain a diversified portfolio of shares if there is only a modest amount of capital to invest. Unit trusts and investment trusts pool the savings of large numbers of individuals, and by giving them a share in a diversified portfolio of assets, reduces the risk element in equity-related saving. Nevertheless, as with any equity-linked portfolios, those of trusts can fall heavily in value when the Stock Exchange is depressed.

In the case of unit trusts there is a legally binding trust deed. A trustee, normally a large financial intermediary, holds the trust's assets on behalf of unit holders, and the trust is independently managed by another company within the terms of the trust deed. Units can be bought and sold only with the trust itself. New units are created as desired,

Figure 4.5 *Unit Trusts, £ bn*

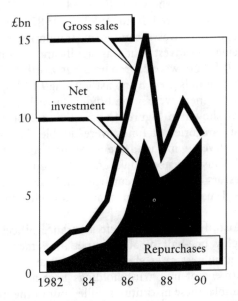

Source: Unit Trust Association.

and old ones eliminated when units are sold back to the trust. The trust repays such units by disposing of investments. There has recently been considerable dispute about the rules for calculating the purchase and sale price of units, and it is permissible for a unit trust to refuse to repurchase under specified circumstances.

Figure 4.6 *Unit Trust Index*

	Index 2.01.91	1 year ago	2 years ago	5 years ago
UK Equity	190.5	226.1	184.0	117.1
International	150.4	204.1	150.4	113.4
North America	115.0	148.3	106.5	107.0
Europe	238.9	312.7	202.7	153.8
Japan	191.3	318.4	228.9	105.8
Australia	102.5	161.0	134.8	85.3
Far East	164.5	241.8	171.5	96.3
Av of all trusts	169.3	221.7	168.6	112.8

Note:
1   Unweighted and based on 2 January 1985 = 100.
Net income has been reinvested.
Source: OPAL/IDC.

The 1980s were a very successful decade for unit trusts. As shown in **Figure 4.5**, the value of gross sales soared from 1982 to 1987, and although there was a significant amount of repurchasing, net investment was significantly positive. In 1985 there were 2.5 mn holdings worth £20 bn. In 1986 funds grew by an astonishing £12 bn, and by 1988 there were 5 mn holdings worth £42 bn.

As shown in **Figure 4.6,** by the end of 1989 most categories of funds were double their end-1985 levels – in Japan the index had risen threefold. This was not, however, such good news for investors since 6 per cent front end sales charges plus 1 per cent annual charges ate into capital gains.

Also, funds relied on life assurance offices for roughly one-half of all new net investment, but when interest rates shot up in 1990 and the tax treatment of unit trust holdings became less favourable, these institutions pulled out of the funds and put the proceeds in interest-bearing accounts. Although private investors did not follow suit, and indeed put over £0.5 bn in unit trust-linked Personal Equity Plans, net new investment sank in 1990 to a mere £400 mn, the worst for over a decade. The number of units held declined to 4.6 mn. The unit trust index took a severe dive, most notably in the case of Japanese funds.

With 1400 trusts in existence, compared to only 500 a decade before, the customer is understandably rather bewildered. The number of management companies has nevertheless sunk to 160, but as there is a clear advantage for larger groups in terms of costs, there are likely to be a spate of mergers among management companies.

1991 has so far proved to be much more successful, and there are plans under consideration to create four new categories of authorised unit trusts: lower-risk futures and options funds; higher-risk or 'geared' futures and options funds; warrant funds; and property funds.

☐ 4.5.4 *Investment Trusts*

Investment trusts are much the smallest group of NBFIs in terms of assets. They operate rather differently from unit trusts in that they are public companies rather than legal trusts, and sell shares in the trust itself. The money received is then invested in other equities and securities. Their own shares are quoted in the Stock Exchange and can be fully traded.

☐ *4.5.5 National Savings Bank (NSB)*

The NSB, which had its origins in the need for wartime financing and which is now under the control of the Department of National Savings, is important primarily as a route for channeling private sector savings directly into the hands of the government. In this way the PSBR can be financed without the need to issue an equivalent amount of public sector debt. National Savings were unpopular in the decades prior to 1975, but it has subsequently been possible to widen their appeal by deliberately making them attractive compared to deposits at banks and building societies. This is done primarily either through index-linking, which guarantees that a specified real rate of interest, adjusted for inflation, is earned, or through a reduction in the tax burden to be borne by such savings. The great reduction in government borrowing in recent years has in turn much reduced the need for a National Savings movement.

☐ *4.5.6 Finance Houses*

The finance houses are no longer of much importance in the financial system because there has been a tendency for the largest houses to convert into banks, included statistically in the 'other British banks' category. Funds are raised in the wholesale markets and by issuing bills. They are used to provide loans to individuals (to be repaid in instalments) and to private companies, together with leasing finance whereby a finance house buys a machine or factory and leases it to a company. This type of business is also done by retail banks, but many finance houses have special relationships with large manufacturers and retail chains.

■ 4.6 Money Markets

□ 4.6.1 A Brief History

We have already referred, when discussing individual groups of financial intermediaries, to the existence of money markets, and it is now necessary to say something about these markets in general, and specifically about those of them not previously mentioned.

The movement of huge sums of short-term funds around the financial system is historically a relatively new phenomenon. Up until the early 1960s organisations acquired short-term funds either from the commercial banks in the form of overdrafts and loans or as trade credit from suppliers. The banks' ability to lend was itself determined largely by the value of retail deposits, and they did not complete amongst themselves as their interest rates were uniformly linked to the central Bank Rate. Furthermore, direct controls on lending were frequently imposed by the Bank of England.

However, commencing in the early 1960s, large amounts of dollars began to be deposited in London (see discussion of Eurocurrency markets below), and these deposits were totally independent of the existing banking system. They could, therefore, be handled by any institution willing to make a sufficiently attractive offer to depositors, and they could be handled flexibly because they did not fall within the compass of existing monetary controls. As a result, large numbers of foreign banks came to London, each intent on grabbing as big a share of the business as possible, and this in turn meant that competition for deposits was so intensive as to exclude the possibility of interest rate cartels. Once in the UK, they also began to compete for sterling deposits, previously the exclusive preserve of the UK banks, which were obliged to match their interest rates.

The Bank of England acknowledged the desirability of competition on an equal footing between institutions when it introduced the Competition and Credit Control (CCC) document in 1971. This detached bank interest rates from Bank Rate, which was abolished, and allowed each bank to set its own **base rate**. The replacement of Bank Rate by the market-determined **Minimum Lending Rate**

(MLR) was, however, more apparent than real in practice, as the government found it increasingly difficult to forgo the use of the interest rate as a major instrument of monetary control. Furthermore, base rates have tended to fall back into line. However, this disguises the fact that whilst retail banking is still operated as a virtual cartel, wholesale banking is not. If one has a large sum of money to sell then it can be offered around to the highest bidder. One interesting consequence is that **asset management** whereby, as discussed above, financial intermediaries and especially banks must maintain part of their asset portfolio in liquid forms, becomes matched by **liability management** whereby liquidity can be supplemented via borrowing in the money markets. Precisely the same argument applies for governments and commercial organisations. Cash, which does not earn interest, can no longer be left lying idle, even overnight. It is hardly surprising, therefore, that retail banking, where small accounts are handled at considerable expense, is increasingly viewed as simply a means whereby a captive audience is acquired for the sale of profitable financial services, and the primary concerns of liquidity, risk and profitability are juggled in the money markets.

□ 4.6.2 Types of Money market

The primary money market is the **discount market**. This has already been discussed, and nothing further needs to be added at this juncture. In addition to the discount market there are currently five other significant sterling money markets known, collectively as the **'parallel' or secondary markets**. These are the inter-bank market; the certificate of deposit market; the local authority market; the finance house market; and the inter-company market. They are called 'sterling markets' to distinguish them from the Eurocurrency market discussed below.

The inter-bank market has also been mentioned previously. It is the largest parallel market and, as the name indicates, is the market in which **banks lend to one another**. Having started in 1955, the local authority market is the oldest of the five, and is where local authorities issue their own debt instruments which are sold to banks and other investors. Loans are unsecured, so the reputation of the borrower is all-important. Until recently local authorities, with their right to levy rates, were regarded as low-risk borrowers, but the financial practices of certain authorities such as Liverpool have altered that somewhat. The inter-company market, which began in 1969, is where **large companies lend directly** to one another. It is a low-key affair because there are alternative ways to lend with security at much the same rate of interest. The finance house market is also fairly insignificant because of the transfer of many of the largest houses to the banking sector. The sterling CD market, started in 1968, consists of a **primary** market in which new CDs are issued, and a **secondary** market in which they are subsequently bought and sold, thereby enhancing their liquidity and hence desirability. The market has grown rapidly, but it is totally dwarfed by the foreign currency CD market.

It is not always possible to distinguish to which market a particular transaction should be assigned, since many types of intermediary operate in several of them simultaneously. Supervision is accordingly exercised largely over participants' banking activities although, as discussed above, the Bank of England is involved in the discount market on a daily basis. In the parallel sterling markets **supervision is light**. Participants are expected to join the Sterling Brokers Association and to adhere to the Bank's issued code of practice. The Bank also checks on the various instruments issued to ensure that they are of the highest quality. This lightness of touch has provided a suitable environment for rapid growth, but the Bank must occasionally wonder why it fosters markets which make its monetary controls much harder to implement.

4.6.3 Financial Futures and Options

So far, we have been exclusively concerned with transactions involving a current payment in exchange for the current delivery of some kind of asset such as a share or bond. However, a large number of contracts involve either the delivery of an asset at some **future date** in exchange for a payment made **in the present,** or the purchase of the right to buy or sell (or to decline to buy or sell) an asset at some **future date** at a price **agreed when taking out the option.** The former are traded on the London International Financial Futures Exchange (LIFFE) and are known as **financial futures,** and might involve, for example, a contract to buy an amount of gilts in three months' time at a current price which reflects the expectations of the parties to the contract about the future trend of interest rates. Currencies can also be traded in this way. The latter are traded on the London Traded Options Market (LTOM) and are known as **traded options** (as distinct from the similar but less-commonly purchased **traditional** options). These involve the outlay of a modest sum today for the rights to buy or sell in the future at an agreed price, known as 'calls' and 'puts' respectively. If the market price moves in such a way as , for example, to rise above the agreed price for a call option, then the option will be enforced by the buyer. Where the writer of the option (the seller) does not have the asset to hand it will have to be purchased in the market and immediately resold at a loss (which is partly offset because the seller has received the price of the option in cash). If, however, the market price has fallen below the price agreed at the time of buying the option (in other words, the asset can be bought more cheaply in the open market) then the option will be allowed to lapse, and the writer of the option gets to keep the money paid for the option *less* trading costs.

Financial futures and traded options clearly involve risks for both buyer and seller. Almost invariably **one must gain at the expense of the other.** However, there is a sound rationale behind this kind of behaviour. When a buyer agrees to buy an asset at some future date he runs the risk that he could have bought it more cheaply in the future compared to the present. On the other hand, he avoids the risk that he would have had to pay well above the agreed price. Traded options are thus a mechanism for **financial leverage.** In other words, for the downpayment of a modest sum a buyer of call options can guarantee himself the chance to make a profit by buying and instantly reselling a

Figure 4.7 *Trading in Derivatives*

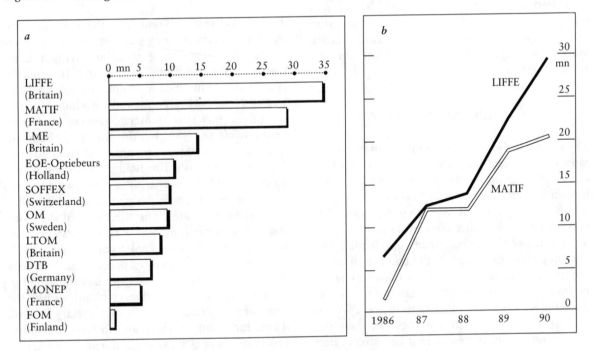

a   European Futures and Options Markets, 1990 Trading Volume, Contracts mn.
b   Futures Trading Volume, No. of Contracts, mn.
Source: The Economist (16 March 1991).

very expensive portfolio of assets which he could not have afforded to pay for in full at the time of buying the option. Equally, the most he can lose is the total cost of the options should he decline to take them up, even if the price of the asset has fallen disastrously in the meantime.

Traded options also provide a hedge against share movements which would be disadvantageous to a shareholder. Thus, for example, a shareholder whose shares have risen sharply in value can protect at least part of his capital gain by taking out an option conferring the right to sell the shares at a price of his choosing.

If this is the current share price then the maximum loss is the cost of taking out the options *plus* trading costs, irrespective of how much the shares subsequently fall in value.

It was intended that in March 1991 LIFFE and LTOM would merge to form the **London Derivatives Exchange** (LDE). The name was chosen partly in the hope that the other Exchanges – International Petroleum; International Freight Futures; London Metal; and Futures and Options (the FOX covering soft commodities and now property) will eventually combine together to form an overall exchange capable of challenging the pre-eminent position of Chicago.

LIFFE will initially be the dominant partner in the LDE. In 1989 its volume soared by over 50 per cent to 24 mn lots. The total for 1990 of 34 mn lots (up 44 per cent) was well ahead of the MATIF, as shown in **Figure 4.7**, and it grew to 39 mn lots in 1991. The 1990 Budget was a big boost for trading in derivatives because it permitted institutions to avoid paying tax on any of their transactions without having to prove that they were not 'trading' in the market.

The LDE should emerge some time in 1992. Before it does a mini-'Big Bang' would appear to be on the cards, with 'open outcry' on the Stock Exchange floor almost wholly replaced by screen-based trading. This may help to bring back retail clients who constitute only 30 per cent of business compared to 70 per cent at Chicago, but fees remain high and it is the usual Catch 22 situation in which fees cannot come down until trading volume picks up, but trading volume will not pick up until fees come down.

☐ 4.6.4 Eurocurrency Markets

The size of the Eurocurrency markets in the UK, as indicated in **Table 4.2 (p. 92)**, is much larger than one might expect. At the present time the assets held in dollars alone amount to some $500 bn, to which should be added more than the equivalent of $200 bn in other currencies. Eurocurrency transactions are **wholesale** borrowing and lending in a currency other than that of the country in which the transactions take place. Thus Eurosterling can be transacted anywhere other than in the UK, and Eurodollars anywhere other than in the USA and so forth. The term 'Eurocurrency' is, therefore, something of a misnomer since it can involve non-European currencies and be transacted outside Europe. It arose because, as previously stated, the markets began with dollars deposited in Europe. At present London is the biggest Eurocurrency market, accounting for approximately 30 per cent of all transactions by value.

There is normally a lower limit of $1 mn set for each transaction, and also often an upper limit since loans are unsecured. Whilst much of the lending is very short-term, sometimes for as little as a day, there are longer-term loans in the form of Eurocommercial paper (the total market for which rose from $4 bn in early 1986 to $45 bn in early 1988), and especially of Eurobonds which are largely fixed-interest securities or floating-rate notes (FRNs) denominated in a Eurocurrency. FRNs are attached to LIBOR in the UK, and may be convertible to equity. They are issued by multi-national firms, foreign governments, local authorities and public corporations. There is also a great deal of inter-bank lending. Eurobonds are not usually traded on the Stock Exchange, but rather certain international banks and security houses 'make a market'. There are sufficient market-makers to ensure that Eurobonds can be freely traded at competitive prices.

Origins

The central role of London in the Eurocurrency markets reflects the long-standing provision of finance for foreign trade combined with a large number of international banks and an efficient system of communications links throughout the world. New York was originally excluded by virtue of the fact that transactions were in dollars held **outside** the USA, but this inevitably begs the question as to why Americans (and subsequently everyone else) wished to hold their domestic currency somewhere other than in their own country.

The answer is particularly to be found by reference to **interest rates**. The sheer size of the sums transacted is itself important as it keeps costs per unit of currency transacted to an absolute minimum, but more importantly, because Eurocurrency does not constitute part of any individual country's money supply, it does not fall within the remit of any country's system of monetary control. Thus, for example, there are no **reserve requirements** as there are on dollars held in American banks or sterling held in UK banks. Reserve holdings do not earn interest, and the savings which accordingly arise if they are not applicable can be passed on to depositors in the form of higher interest rates. Furthermore, there have periodically been upper limits placed upon domestic interest rates. In the American case the Federal Reserve Board rule, known as Regulation Q, twice imposed upper limits on bank deposit interest rates during the 1960s, and as a result dollar deposits came to earn a higher rate of return outside the USA where Regulation Q could not be enforced.

Exchange controls have also played a major role. Again, in the American case, large outflows of dollars resulted from the adverse balance of payments of the USA during the 1960s. Exchange controls were, therefore, introduced to stem the outflow, albeit somewhat ineffectively, but as the dollar was the most favoured currency for settlement of international trade transactions the demand for dollars did not disappear, but was simply turned aside into the Eurodollar market. This caused the rate of return on Eurodollars to rise, and most of the dollars received outside the USA were accordingly placed into the Eurodollar market, together with dollars transferred from the accounts of anyone in the USA whose status made their deposits exempt from the controls (including some central banks). As Eurodollar balances rapidly built up, it became clear to the US authorities that the controls were counter-productive and they were abolished in the mid-1970s.

The growth of the Eurocurrency markets has also been affected by the behaviour of particular groups of countries. A significant part of the huge OPEC surpluses of the late 1970s found its way into the markets, and Eastern European countries, when buying American products, prefer to deal in the markets rather than hold dollars in the USA.

The abolition of exchange controls in the USA and elsewhere led to a significant readjustment of Eurocurrency holdings between financial centres. In the heyday of exchange controls many 'offshore' centres such as the Bahamas prospered by the simple expedient of offering an uncontrolled environment. However, once a much freer environment is created near to home, the desirability of such centres is bound to wane.

Consequences

The Eurocurrency markets have, as noted above, been an important source of funds for inter-bank lending. This has had the effect of bringing together banks throughout the world into an informal network, and there can be no doubt that

international liquidity has been enhanced in the process. However, it is clear that there are dangers in moving around vast sums of money without there being any institution in overall control of proceedings. This can arise first with respect to individual banks. Eurocurrencies tend to travel through a succession of banks on their route between ultimate lender and ultimate borrower. An individual bank cannot, therefore, know to what extent its lending may end up with any particular borrower, and therefore how vulnerable it is to that borrower's financial health.

Secondly, from the point of view of sovereign states, it is clear that domestic monetary policy may be rendered ineffectual by the Eurocurrency markets. The movement of 'hot money' has, for example, recently been of considerable concern to the UK government. It should be noted, in particular, that interest rate differentials between countries are critical in determining the direction of flow of hot money, and hence that no individual country can set its interest rate structure in isolation.

The loss of control implied by these developments is inevitably a considerable irritant to banks and governments alike, but attempts to regulate Eurocurrency markets would simply result in their replacement by other markets not subject to the new regulations. The steady growth of the Eurobond market has, perhaps fortunately in view of

Figure 4.8 *Eurobond Issues by Currency*

1990 Rank	Currency	Total Raised ($ bn)	No. of Issues	1989 Rank	Total Raised ($ bn)	No. of Issues
1	US$	69.10	346	1	119.05	558
2	Yen	21.39	269	4	14.54	273
3	Sterling	20.65	89	2	19.92	109
4	Ecu	17.47	79	5	12.23	114
5	D Mark	15.45	104	3	15.24	125
6	FFr	9.18	53	8	4.52	46
7	C$	6.34	55	6	11.05	109
8	Lira	5.85	34	9	3.67	31
9	A$	5.01	95	7	6.66	118
10	Guilder	1.35	10	10	1.95	23

Source: Euromoney.

the above, faltered somewhat in recent years. The removal of regulations has led to some of the funds returning to their country of origin, particularly dollars to the USA. The international debt problem has also made lenders wary of channelling funds to high-risk borrowers, and there are no longer any OPEC surpluses to be invested. In 1990, trading of dollar denominated Eurobonds in the new issue market fell to $69 bn, as shown in **Figure 4.8**.

The position of London is increasingly vulnerable. The big growth sector in the late 1980s was in Japanese equity warrants, but given that the issuers and the bulk of the investors are Japanese it will take only a dose of deregulation in Tokyo to induce much of the business to return home. In any event, this sector has lost its buoyancy because the collapse of the Nikkei meant that most of the outstanding warrants to purchase at specified share prices would not be worth exercising at prices higher than those ruling in the open market.

ECU Securities

In 1981 a market developed for Eurobonds denominated in European Currency Units (ECUs, see **pp. 235–6**). As shown in **Figure 4.9**, the market built up rapidly in 1985, then subsided. An initial problem was the absence of any parallel market in short-term (up to six-month) ECU bills. The market picked up again in 1988, as the Single European Market began to exert an influence. In August 1988 the UK government launched a series of ECU Treasury bill tenders, partly as a pre-emptive measure to concentrate the ECU markets in London.

These and other issues were hugely successful. By the end of 1990 there were $60 bn of fixed-rate ECU bonds outstanding in the international bond market, making it the fifth ranking currency by value of outstanding bonds. In 1990 ECU 14 bn of bonds were issued, the fourth most popular currency, exceeding issues in Deutsche Marks. In the first two months of 1991 alone a further ECU 10.9 bn of bonds were issued, so the total for the year is estimated at over ECU 60 bn. In February the UK government issued ECU 2.5 bn of bonds, partly to foster business in London. The Japanese

Figure 4.9 *Growth of the ECU Bond Market*

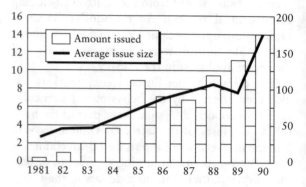

Source: Paribas Capital Markets.

are believed to hold around 10 per cent of the outstanding bonds, preferring them to bonds issued in individual currencies on the grounds that they combine relatively high yields with relatively low risk.

A futures contract in ECU Bonds has recently been launched by LIFFE and also in France. With the possibility of a single European currency now increasingly on the minds of investors, it seems that the ECU will be playing a major role in the international bond market by 1992.

■ 4.7 Capital Markets

When companies need more medium- and long-term capital than is available from retained profits, and when the government cannot cover its expenditure from its tax revenue, they make up the shortfall by recourse to the capital markets. These thus encompass both the **institutions** which provide medium- and long-term finance, illustrated in **Figure 4.10**, and the **forms of financial instrument** which are traded there.

4.7.1 New Issue and Secondary Markets

There are two basic markets; the first, called the **new-issue or primary market**, is where new securities are offered to investors; the second, called the

Figure 4.10 *The Capital Markets*

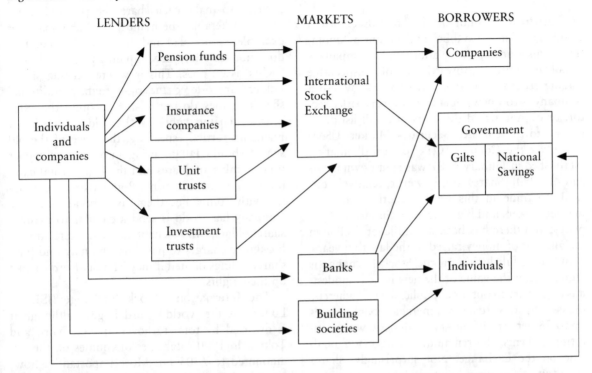

secondary market, is where existing securities are traded. The securities traded fall into two basic categories. Equity, or shares, are issued by companies and pay dividends, usually half-yearly, which are variable and linked to profitability. Most shares carry voting rights at the annual general meeting, although these are rarely exercised in practice. The value of a share is also variable, being determined by the forces of supply and demand, and a shareholder may, therefore, make either a capital gain or loss over time. Interest-bearing securities (stocks) come in a variety of forms. They are mostly issued by the government in the form of **gilts**. Those issued by companies are called **debentures**. There is also an active market in **Eurobonds** as outlined earlier. Stocks almost universally become redeemable at a specific future date, and yield a fixed rate of return. However, some are convertible into equity, and others are in the form of floating-rate notes, or are index-linked to guarantee their return in real rather than money terms. Stocks may also be subject to capital gains and losses as interest

rates vary when sold before maturity.

The secondary market is essential if the primary market is to operate successfully. In other words, stocks and shares are regarded as liquid assets by investors although they are frequently held for long periods of time by the original purchaser, and it is essential that there is a mechanism for rapid trading (see the discussion of 'Big Bang' below). The International Stock Exchange, as it is now known, lies at the centre of the capital markets, but it is by no means necessary to use its services in order to raise longer-term capital. This is related to the role of financial intermediaries which hold the bulk of all stocks and shares in the UK. Whilst it is quite easy for individuals to deal in shares, personal portfolios are still, despite privatisation, very modest. In the UK most investors prefer to save with pension funds, insurance companies and unit trusts where there have normally been tax advantages whilst there are none for personal shareholdings (other than special concessions for privatisation issues).

□ *4.7.2 Raising Funds*

In order to raise funds on the Stock Exchange a company must 'go public' and obtain a 'quotation'. This is an expensive affair, and a company is usually expected to show evidence of a respectable trading record over a period of years. Where a company is too new, operates in a very risky sector, or cannot afford the costs of a full listing, it can go to the **Unlisted Securities Market** (USM) (the **Over the Counter** (OTC or 'third') market established in January 1987 was shut down at the end of 1990). Shares are, however, relatively difficult to trade in this market as there are few market-makers and big differences in buy and sell prices, and there has been a significant decline in the amount of money raised in the last two years.

Where a full listing on the Stock Exchange is required, but the value of the new issue is modest, it is customary to opt for a 'public placing' whereby the issuing house (usually a merchant bank) places up to 75 per cent of the shares directly with institutional clients, the remainder being made available on the Exchange. Not surprisingly, shares issued in this way tend to end up concentrated in a very few hands. For major issues an Issue by Prospectus or an Offer for Sale is preferred, the difference being that in the latter case the issuing house first acquires the shares and then sells them to the public (favoured where the company is obscure but the issuing house is well known).

These methods are expensive because a prospectus has to be drawn up containing a full financial history of the company. The issue must be advertised nationally, and the issuing house and other advisors paid a commission. If oversubscribed a system of allocation will have to be chosen and implemented. In the great majority of cases the issue will be underwritten for a further fee as a precaution against an undersubscription, the underwriter then being obliged to purchase the outstanding shares. An Offer for Sale may be either at a fixed price, or less commonly by tender at (or above) a predetermined minimum price. The latter prevents the shares being seriously underpriced with attendant capital gains for 'stags' who immediately resell, but will almost certainly leave virtually all of the shares with the institutions.

Occasionally there are 'scrip' issues whereby, perhaps to make each share cheaper and hence more marketable, the number of shares may, for example, be doubled and their price halved. This does not raise any new capital as such, whilst a 'rights' issue does. This is where existing shareholders are offered the right to buy additional shares. If they do not wish to acquire the extra shares then the rights can be sold on the Stock Exchange. Strictly speaking, the price of the old shares should fall to bring into line the higher total number of shares and the higher total capitalisation of the company. Rights issues are popular with companies themselves because all the company has to do is send a circular to existing shareholders, who benefit because there are no brokerage charges to pay, but who may find their shareholdings diluted if they cannot afford to take up their rights.

The International Stock Exchange (ISE) in London is the world's third largest, although it is dwarfed by total turnover in New York and Tokyo. In 1990 total sales of equities on the ISE amounted to £305 bn. More importantly, however, the ISE was the world's biggest foreign equity market where more than two-thirds of reported trading of equities outside their country of origin took place. In 1990 this amounted to £150 bn of equity sales, compared to £4.3 bn in Frankfurt and £2.5 bn in Paris. Even Tokyo accounted for only £7.3 bn, but then a good part of foreign equity turnover is in Japanese shares. The advantage of the ISE lies in its low trading costs and in its structure, with market makers taking positions between buyers and sellers, and thereby providing superior liquidity for large wholesale trades.

The existence of **SEAQ International** is important in this respect. This is a lightly regulated, computerised arena in which more than 50 large securities' firms, mostly British, American and Japanese, trade huge blocks of shares among themselves and with institutions. SEAQ (Stock Exchange Automated Quotation System) was founded in June 1985, and now accounts for roughly 40 per cent of the volume in many major European stocks. Sales doubled in 1989 compared to 1988 as interest in shares connected with the Single European Market was sparked off by the realisation that 1992 was no longer far off. If SEAQ continues to gain ground it is possible that there will eventually be a two-tier market with smaller investors operating through domestic exchanges.

☐ 4.7.3 Gilt-edged Securities

The issue of **gilts** is the responsibility of the Bank of England, and the total value outstanding grew rapidly as a result of net borrowing by the government in the majority of postwar years. However, in the Autumn Statement of November 1988 the Chancellor declared that he would 'fully fund' the Public Sector Debt Repayment (PSDR, see **p. 167**), the effect of which was to withdraw £9 bn of gilts from the market during the financial year 1988–89. This not merely had the effect of altering considerably the shape of the yield curve which relates short-term to long-term yields, but caused problems for institutions such as pension funds which like to hold long-dated assets which match their long-dated liabilities. Indeed, given a shortage of alternative long-dated securities denominated in sterling offering an attractive rate of return, institutions turned increasingly to invest in foreign bonds, holdings of which rose by £5.5 bn during the first half of 1988. The Chancellor followed this up in December by announcing that, commencing in January 1989, the Bank of 'England would conduct reverse gilts auctions, concentrating on short-dated gilts. The first auction of £500 mn of gilts was 3.2 times oversubscribed.

There were no new issues of gilts during 1990, and as a consequence of redemptions totalling £8.6 bn the total nominal value outstanding, adjusted for index-linking, fell from £128 bn at end-1989 to £122 bn at end-1990. Official operations in the market in 1990 were directed largely towards market management.

In the light of the shrinking market, a reduction in the number of actively traded stocks was brought about in 1990 by inviting investors in small, less-liquid issues to convert into larger, more liquid issues. Somewhat surprisingly, the number of market-makers (GEMMs) remained constant at 19 throughout 1990, the first full year post-Big Bang not to have seen any withdrawals. As a group, the GEMMs approximately broke even in 1989,

and actually made a £40 mn post-tax profit in 1990 despite the lack of new issues. From October 1986 to the end of 1988 the capitalisation of GEMMs had fallen by £175 mn (see *Bank of England Quarterly Bulletin*. February 1991, p. 50), but it stabilised in 1990 at £395 mn.

In January 1991, faced with the certainty of the reappearance of the PSBR in 1991/92, the Treasury began issuing new gilts. The first issue of £500 mn of 5-year tap stock was initially left largely unsold because it was marginally overpriced, but within two days it was all taken up. Given redemptions of existing issues, about £1 bn per month will need to be issued throughout 1991.

■ 4.8 'Big Bang' and its Aftermath

The term 'Big Bang' is the colloquial name for the **deregulation of the Stock Exchange** in October 1986. A variety of circumstances conspired to bring it about at that particular point in time. Historically, there were two major groups of participants in the Exchange. The first, the **stockbrokers**, acted on behalf of clients, both personal and institutional, who paid a commission for stockbroking services. Brokers primarily traded equity, but also gave advice on portfolios. In order to obtain shares the brokers had to go to a **jobber** who acted as a **market-maker** – that is, he held a portfolio of shares which he bought and sold on his own account. His income came from the 'split' – the difference between the price at which he would buy and the price at which he would sell any given share. Since jobbers could not deal directly with the general public, they were independent of the brokers in a so-called 'single capacity' system. The Stock Exchange's own rules enforced the system, the main attractions of which were superficially that there were always jobbers willing to trade and that, since the brokers had nothing personally to gain by using one jobber rather than another, they would get the best deal they could for their clients.

However, the system had two particularly serious defects. In the first place, the scale of commissions paid to brokers was fixed by the Exchange. An institution buying shares worth £10 million had thus to pay virtually the same rate as a personal investor buying shares worth £1000. Secondly, the Stock Exchange would not allow individual member firms to grow at the expense of others. Prior to 1970 no member firm could become a limited company, and only 10 per cent at most of the share capital could subsequently be held by anyone outside the Exchange. This was raised to 29.9 per cent in 1982, but did little to resolve the problem of undercapitalisation because the aggregate capital base could expand only if the internal shareholders were simultaneously adding to their investment. But as individual members of the Exchange were personally liable if their firms made losses, they understandably did not often want to add to their exposure by taking on too much additional business.

The single capacity system was out of line with normal practice in competing centres, and was causing considerable difficulties in the UK because, for example, of a shortage of jobbers in many stocks. This largely reflected the fact that with institutions trading huge parcels of shares, the jobbers had to hold large blocks on their own account, and they could raise the capital to do so only by merging, causing the number of jobbers to halve between 1968 and 1984. Furthermore, the New York stock market was already deregulated, and had expanded considerably as a consequence. Competition there kept commissions lower than in the UK, and most international shares were accordingly cheaper for institutions to buy and sell in New York than in London. New York trading was done electronically, so information was available more quickly and accurately than on the Stock Exchange floor in London. Whilst previously the cross-subsidy from institutions to personal clients implicit in the fixed commission rate had been justified by the quality of research done on behalf of the institutions, the lure of cheaper prices for heavily traded shares in New York was proving irresistible.

At the same time (1979) the new government was casting its eye over the Stock Exchange rule book, and not much liking what it saw. The Restrictive Practices Act 1976 was clearly being contravened, and the Stock Exchange was given an ultimatum – to bring its rule book into line with the Act or face an investigation in the Restrictive Practices Court (pencilled in for 1984). In 1983

the Stock Exchange agreed to **forgo fixed commissions and single capacity trading** as from 27 October 1986. Commencing in March 1986 any Stock Exchange firm could be **wholly taken over by outsiders**. This also held true in the gilt-edged market which had previously been dominated by only two firms of jobbers.

One obvious question which may be asked is why Big Bang occurred in London rather than, say, in Frankfurt. There were already two very large exchanges in New York and Tokyo, but one shut well before the other opened so it was not possible to trade 24 hours around the clock. To connect them up a European exchange was needed. London had a long financial tradition, it was true, but in many respects the UK did not seem as ideal as Switzerland or West Germany. Probably a major factor in London's favour was the relatively light regulation of its financial markets. Also English (of a kind) was spoken there, making it an easy environment for Americans and English-speaking Japanese to work in, and London was regarded as a pleasant city with good educational facilities for children.

As Big Bang approached there was a mad rush to organise the new 'dual-capacity' market-making firms which stood ready to deal directly with investors, to trade on their own account, and to make markets in as many shares as they wished. Brokers and jobbers were taken over by UK and foreign banks, thereby **destroying the historic distinction between banking and security trading** in the UK. The number of trained personnel was understandably totally inadequate, and vast sums of money were offered to attract qualified staff.

One significant problem related to **technology**. Very few old-style jobbers had modern electronic dealing rooms, so there was also a mad scramble to obtain new premises and to get them wired up. The system for transmitting data throughout the Exchange known as **SEAQ** (Stock Exchange Automated Quotations), was only just about up and running in time for Big Bang. Once the electronics were in place, the Stock Exchange floor suffered a virtual mass desertion.

Some idea of the altered scale of operation post-Big Bang can be seen in the gilts market where the two main jobbers were replaced by 27 primary dealers licensed by the Bank of England. It was generally realised that not all could survive unless the volume of business rose dramatically, but all were individually confident that their expertise would win through. As predicted, commission rates for institutions fell, but for private clients they rose, and some brokers ceased to deal with such clients altogether because of the paperwork costs of executing small transactions.

For a year, all went very well. The stock market boomed and the volume of business rose to new heights. However, in October 1987 there was a market collapse which made even the Wall Street Crash of 1929 look insignificant. The authorities in the UK and elsewhere reacted positively on this occasion, making large amounts of liquidity available to prevent market-makers going to the wall, and in the event remarkably little damage was done. The real economy carried on working pretty much as before. The enormous cuts in the capitalisation of firms did not make any real difference because, at the end of the day, share prices simply reflect the use of capital which has already been invested. One thing that understandably was affected was the amount of new equity capital which could be raised, because that is not normally allowed to exceed a given proportion of the value of existing capital. The issue of 'rights' came to a grinding halt, and has yet fully to recover although there have been a number in Spring 1991.

Equally, on paper, investors became less wealthy, which might have caused them to cut consumption and save more with consequent effects upon GDP. However, this did not discernably taken place. What happened is that many personal and institutional investors stayed out of the equity market until early 1991 and the daily volume of shares traded fell well below 1987 levels. As a result, many market-makers and brokers struggled to break even and there were eventually extensive redundancies in the City. In the gilts market five firms had withdrawn by July 1988, although two Japanese firms had applied to join. Personal investors switched back to the building societies which regained much of the mortgage market share previously lost to the banks, whilst the institutions remained highly liquid, by previous standards, until recently.

As can be seen in **Table 4.5**, twice as many foreign securities houses set up shop in London in 1986 compared to 1984 and 1985, and even more in 1987. This increase in capacity neatly coincided with the cyclical down turn after the October 1987 crash, and caused the members of the International Stock Exchange to lose £27 mn in 1987 and

Table 4.5 *Foreign Securities' Houses in London*

	US			Japan			Europe			Other			Summary		
	Total	In	Out	Total	In	Out	Total	In	Out	Total	In	Out	Total	In	Out
1980	43	4	1	21	1	0	13	3	0	27	1	0	104	9	1
1981	45	2	0	23	2	0	13	0	0	30	3	0	111	7	0
1982	47	2	0	25	2	0	15	2	0	31	1	0	118	7	0
1983	52	5	0	25	0	0	17	2	0	33	2	0	127	9	0
1984	51	0	1	27	2	0	17	1	1	35	3	1	130	6	3
1985	51	0	0	29	2	0	17	1	1	37	3	1	134	6	2
1986	52	1	0	34	5	0	18	1	0	39	5	3	143	12	3
1987	54	2	0	41	7	0	21	3	0	39	1	1	155	13	1
1988	54	0	0	41	0	0	24	3	0	37	2	4	156	5	4
1989	55	1	0	42	1	0	24	1	2	38	1	0	158	4	2
1990	54	2	3	44	2	0	29	5	0	34	1	5	160	10	8
Total		19	5		24	0		22	4		23	15		88	24

Source: Noel Alexander Associates.

£265 mn in 1988. Subsequently, market activity peaked and the ISE returned to profit in 1989, but the volume of trading in UK and foreign equities, government securities and other fixed income stocks has yet to rise above levels prevailing before the crash.

What is surprising is not the reduction in the number of new entrants in 1988 and 1989, but rather that there were as many as there were and that they exceeded the negligible number of departures. Those departures, either of UK or overseas houses, as did occur received much publicity, but they were in fact atypical, and in the year up to mid-1989 the capitalisation of the ISE rose by a quarter whilst the number of employees rose by 20 per cent in the three years to the end of 1989, although there were subsequently widespread redundancies.

This was not, however, merely the triumph of hope over experience, since the ISE managed to replace much of its sagging domestic business with trading in international securities. As a result, there is currently intense pressure from other European houses such as Paris and Frankfurt to attract this business from London.

This necessarily raises a question mark over London's trading rules. These require immediate publication of most trades and a delay of only 90 minutes in the publication of the very biggest, which market makers claim leaves them insufficient time to make a profit. It is also argued that the quota-driven system is a boon for those (mainly institutions) who trade large blocks of shares, but is expensive and cumbersome for small investors.

In his 1991 Budget the Chancellor appealed to financial institutions to produce ideas for marketing and trading shares through their high street branches so as to 'provide a cheap and accessible way' for individuals to invest, but this is unlikely to make any difference in the foreseeable future.

■ 4.9 Investor Production

In the run up to Big Bang it became clear that deregulation on the intended scale could have highly adverse effects upon investors. The government therefore appointed Professor Gower to look into the issue of investor protection, and his Report was published in 1984. Gower raised a good many objections to existing practices, which were generally based upon the principle of letting the professionals look after their own because only they were competent to do so. With more and more cases of practices such as insider dealing coming to light, and wholly inconsequential punishments being meted out by the professionals, the government decided to build many of Gower's criticisms into a Financial Services Act which became law in 1986.

4.9.1 Financial Services Act 1986

The Financial Services Act is intended as a **system of regulation covering the entire investment sector**, from the largest bank to the smallest investment advisor. It is intended to ensure that financial services are provided only by those who are fit and proper to do so; that legitimate complaints can be laid before the relevant authorities; and that compensation is available where appropriate. For the past four years the regulatory framework has been painfully pieced together. At its centre lies the Securities and Investments Board (SIB) whose powers are delegated to it by the Secretary of State for Trade and Industry. The SIB is a private company, financed by levies on its members, whose original Chairman was Sir Kenneth Berrill. The main responsibility of the SIB is to oversee the Self Regulatory Organisations (SROs) of which there were originally five (now four).

AFBD	Association of Futures Brokers and Dealers
FIMBRA	Financial Intermediaries, Managers and Brokers Regulatory Association
IMRO	Investment Management Regulatory Organisation
LAUTRO	Life Assurance and Unit Trust Regulatory Organisation
TSA	The Securities Association The TSA and AFBD have now merged to form the
SFA	The Securities and Futures Authority

The SIB's first task was to draw up its rule-book. Each SRO then had to draw up its own rule-book which had to be at least as rigorous as that of the SIB. All professional bodies have to register with the appropriate SRO. Failure to register is a criminal offence. The SIB can investigate any alleged malpractice, and apply sanctions as appropriate, and in certain circumstances bring legal proceedings.

The SROs were slow in putting their rules together, and were mostly hard pressed to get them agreed by the SIB before the deadline of February 1988. The deadline for professional bodies to register with the SRO was put back until April 1988, but even then there was a massive backlog of applications to be assessed, so 'interim authorisation' had to be granted to any firm which had applied in time.

The construction of rule-books created a good deal of controversy. In the case of the SIB it was argued that the rule-book was unnecessarily complicated, and as a consequence Berrill was replaced by David Walker as Chairman of the SIB in 1988. Several SROs disputed their rule-books with the SIB, and the protracted argument about how to price unit trusts was especially acrimonious. The key elements of all rule-books are that:

1   clients' money must be kept separate from that of professional bodies
2   written contracts must be provided to clients specifying agreed services
3   there must be 'polarisation' (see below)
4   investigations of clients' needs must be undertaken and the best possible advice given in the light of their findings
5   clients should be advised to go elsewhere if expertise is lacking
6   an established complaints procedure must be followed.

Polarisation requires all registered bodies to state clearly whether they are acting as a salesman or agent for the services of only one intermediary (such as one insurance company's endowments), or as independent advisors choosing the best services on offer. There is no middle ground. If a bank elects to be an independent advisor then it cannot recommend its own services (life insurance, endowments or whatever) although a client can expressly ask for them. Polarisation has caused particular controversy because of differences between the amount of information on commissions which has to be disclosed to clients by salesmen in each category.

The compensation scheme has operated since August 1988. It pays out a maximum of £48,000 to any investor who loses money when a registered firm goes into liquidation. Complaints must be taken up with the appropriate SRO as plans for an ombudsman have fallen through.

Interim authorisation gave cause for concern because it was necessary to issue interim licences to many firms which had no real hope of ultimate acceptance. During 1988 a series of investigations had to be launched into dubious operators, which did at least indicate that the regulatory powers would be used, but with the ambiguities subject to interpretation in the courts such operators had little incentive to fade away for the time being.

The crucial question for David Walker was whether the degree of regulation was pitched about right. On the one hand, too much regulation would drive business away to less regulated markets elsewhere in the EC. On the other hand, too little regulation would foster abuse and fraud. Eventually, the SIB came up with the 'new deal', comprising 10 principles (**tier 1** introduced in July 1990) and 40 'core rules' (**tier 2**, introduced in January 1991) all written in clear, straightforward English. The principles are along the lines of 'A firm should observe high standards of integrity and fair dealing'. The core rules are designed to draw a clear distinction between business carried out between professionals and the sale of investment products to the general public.

Unfortunately, the key to the regulatory edifice lies in the SRO's 'third-tier' rules which are expected to be far from simple and easy to comprehend. Those of the TSA, issued in draft form at the end of 1990 for implementation in 1991, were mostly simple, but those of IMRO are known to be highly complex. The SIB must judge the 'adequacy' of the SRO's rule-books, and will be under pressure to 'derogate' exemptions from its own core rules, which it is most reluctant to do. In any event, interpreting simple rules is much harder than writing them, and the TSA's notes and appendices are longer than the rule-book itself. Life will be made slightly easier by the fact that on 1 April 1991 the TSA and AFBD merged to form the **Securities and Futures Authority (SFA)**, so there are now only 4 SRO rule-books.

4.9.2 Disclosure of Life Assurance Commissions

Polarisation created independent financial advisers (IFAs) and tied agents selling the products of one company. IFAs were to rely upon commissions for their income. As some life companies could be tempted to bias proceedings by offering excessive commissions, a maximum commissions agreement (MCA) was introduced by LAUTRO. The Office of Fair Trading promptly struck this down as anti-competitive, causing commissions to rise by 20 to 30 per cent. This did at least keep some agents as IFAs, given that direct-selling life assurance companies had previously managed to induce large numbers of IFAs to become their tied agents by offering commissions well in excess of the MCA.

The trouble was that the remaining IFAs were told to disclose more about their commissions to clients, which they could fudge as IFAs but did not need to do at all as tied agents, so virtually every bank and building society ceased to be an IFA. This caused FIMBRA's income to fall drastically and it got into financial difficulties. The IFA share of the life and pensions market is probably less than 40 per cent at the present time, yet the SIB had originally set out to ensure that there would be a strong independent sector.

Disclosure has become a critical issue. A personal pension plan can carry as many as seven different layers of charges and first-year payments in endowments mostly go as commission. IFAs are subject under SIB rules to 'soft' disclosure of commissions. That is, at the time of sale the client must be told the method by which the IFA is paid for his services. The insurance company provides details of the commission after the sale takes place, hidden among the small print. Tied agents need not disclose commissions. The playing field is not level, and the client rarely gets to know the truth.

In March 1991, the SIB announced a new review of the regulatory system, with especial emphasis upon disclosure. The Financial Services Act was supposed to usher in a new era of clearly defined relationships. It would appear that this was optimistic.

4.10 Financial Intermediation in the Future

Let us turn, by way of summary, to pick out from the above discussion the most important themes which will determine how the financial system will evolve during the final decade of this century.

4.10.1 Deregulation and Regulation

A particularly interesting issue is the balance between **deregulation** and **regulation**. Historically, the financial system in the UK was heavily regulated by the government acting through the Bank of England. In addition, specific kinds of financial assets and liabilities were favoured by tax concessions to lenders and/or borrowers. As a result, certain parts of the financial system grew rapidly whilst other parts stagnated. This imbalance was recognised in the UK when the present government came to power and, starting with the abolition of exchange controls in 1979, it set in train a process of freeing up the system. Most of the monetary controls were subsequently terminated or put into abeyance; public corporations were sold, partly to small shareholders; the Financial Services Act (1986) and Building Societies Act 1986 became law; the Stock Exchange was reformed via Big Bang; portable pensions were introduced as were personal equity plans, and so on.

However, these processes have been incomplete, and the government has been forced to recognise that free-for-alls in financial markets are a recipe for widespread abuse, and hence **deregulation has dragged regulation in its wake**.

Whilst the Financial Services Act and Building Societies Act, for example, have allowed NBFIs to provide services previously forbidden to them, they have also made it necessary to set up regulatory

Figure 4.11 *The Framework for Financial Regulation in the UK*

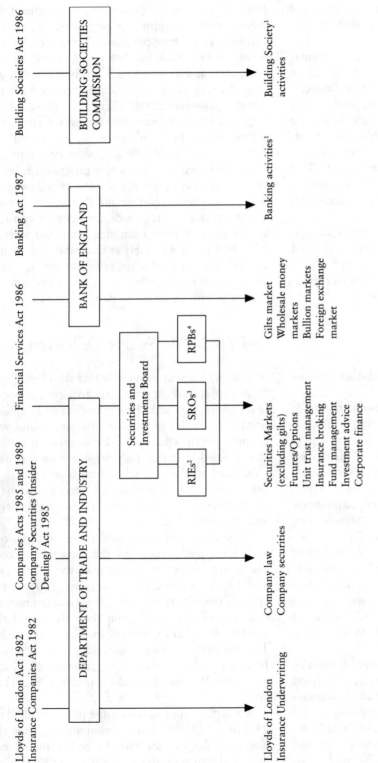

Notes:
1. The investment business of banks and building societies is supervised within the Securities and Investments Board regime.
2. RIEs = Recognised investment exchanges.
3. SROs = Self-regulatory organisations.
4. RPBs = Recognised professional bodies.
Source: D. Goacher (mimeo).

bodies to ensure that the new services are provided by fit-and-proper intermediaries, and that the new rules are obeyed to the letter. This in turn has caused many disputes about what kinds of regulatory bodies are needed, and how they should be financed. It must be recognised that financial markets always have been regulated in the sense that, for example, the Stock Exchange imposed a rule-book upon its members, but this kind of self-regulation is bound to be treated with considerable scepticism by outside parties who read about scandals, and their resolution behind closed doors. However, it is clear that other existing bodies such as the Bank of England and Monopolies and Mergers Commission do not have the resources to cope with the huge increase in regulatory work, and hence other bodies have had to be created.

The full current framework for financial regulation in the UK is set out in **Figure 4.11**.

□ 4.10.2 Innovation

At the present time these new regulatory systems are beginning to settle down, but it is too early to form a judgement about their success or failure. It is reasonably to be expected that many amendments will be forthcoming in the years to come. Indeed, this is almost inevitable in the face of ever more rapid **innovation** in financial markets. Regulations can ultimately be applied only to cover existing practices, and it is clear that a rule-book set up to cover existing practices in 1980 would by now be looking totally out of date. Financial innovation is driven by a variety of forces, including most obviously changes in monetary control systems; the desire to avoid regulation; vast increases in the total sums being transacted; a wider variety of both lenders and borrowers; and increasing sophistication on the part of both in specifying their needs.

We have already referred to the rapid growth of Eurobonds. It is worth nothing that, hand in hand with these, it is increasingly common to find transactions in the **swaps** market. According to the International Swap Dealers Association (ISDA) the nominal principal involved in interest rate and currency swaps was in excess of $1,500 bn in mid-1989. Despite their superficial complexity, at the

heart of any swap lies simply an agreement between two institutions receiving or paying interest income to exchange payments or receipts. For example, if one bank has borrowed in dollars at a fixed rate, and a second bank has borrowed in yen at a floating rate, each then agrees to meet the interest payments of the other. Their decisions are influenced by different expectations concerning the future path of both the currencies and the interest rates in question. Whole sequences of swaps can be placed end-on-end in a single programme. However, most swaps currently involve simple swaps in dollars between fixed-rate and floating-rate notes. Currency swaps carry more risk than interest rate swaps because both exchange rates and interest rates may move adversely at the same time. Banks accordingly runs a 'swaps book' in which swaps are matched up, thereby limiting their exposure to exchange rate or interest rate movements.

□ 4.10.3 The Swaps Debacle

In 1989 a case was brought before the High Court by a district auditor who, on checking the books of a London borough, Hammersmith and Fulham, uncovered £6 bn of interest rate swaps and was unsure of their legality. On 1 November the High Court ruled that not only were the swaps *ultra vires* (that is, the council had no legal powers to engage in swaps) but that any interest rate management contracts with any council were illegal and unenforceable.

Some 78 banks had traded swaps and options with local authorities. All the outstanding contracts were frozen at the time of the judgement, and the banks stood to lose at least £500 mn. On appeal, the Court of Appeal ruled unanimously that legality depended upon the objective of the council official at the time of the deal. If the objective was money management, then the deal was in order since this was a proper function of a local authority. If it was to make a profit, it was *ultra vires*.

On further appeal, the House of Lords ruled on 14 January 1991, again unanimously, that the Court of Appeal was wrong and annulled not merely Hammersmith's swaps but over 1000 other local authority swaps dating back to 1982. The banks were appalled. After all, both the Bank of England and the Audit Commission had sanctioned swaps as tools for managing interest rate risk. The banks and the Bank appealed to the government to introduce retrospective legislation to validate the illegal transactions. Early in May the government refused to do so, partly because it would have caused Hammersmith's residents to pay extra poll tax bills of at least £1250 each. The banks were recommended to issue writs for repayment. These were expected to recover about £125 mn, and with the Treasury meeting 35 per cent of the residual losses through tax repayments the banks were expected to suffer a net loss of £275 mn.

☐ *4.10.4 Disintermediation*

It is important to note that much innovative activity such as swaps is **off-balance sheet**. In other words, the bank concerned in a transaction does not lend to the borrower funds which the bank has itself previously borrowed, which would cause both transactions to appear on its balance sheet, but rather acts as the agent organising a loan directly between ultimate lender and ultimate borrower. The process in which funds flow from lender to borrower other than via the banks is known as **disintermediation,** and has obvious consequences for monetary controls which are intended to operate via regulations imposed upon specified intermediaries (traditionally banks). It also involves the process known as **securitisation**, whereby conventional bank lending is replaced by other forms of financial instruments. A Eurobond, for example, is a 'securitised' debt, which means that it is sold by a borrowing institution to a lender without the money being either lent to, or by, a bank. The purchaser may subsequently resell the debt in the secondary Eurobond market, and the debt may be resold any number of times before maturity. The obvious consequence of securitisation is that the issuer of the security has no real idea who actually holds it as an asset at any given time. However, securitised debt is set to become increasingly popular as top quality borrowers such as 'blue chip' companies take advantage of the fact that they can actually borrow more cheaply in their own names than through the intermediation of a bank, the

credit rating of which may have suffered as a result of underperforming LDC debt.

On the fact of it financial innovation should permit independent groups of intermediaries to carve out their own market niches, and indeed specialist intermediaries are often successful as niche operators. However, a successful niche operator with a limited capital base is sooner or later going to attract the attention of an intermediary in another part of the system which has spare capital and limited capacity to expand in its major lines of business. Historically, the process of merger and take-over between different kinds of intermediary was heavily restricted, but in a deregulated environment the key issue is simply whether the merged company will be a fit-and-proper operator in every market in which it wishes to operate. The process of merger and take-over may allow an intermediary to reduce the risk inherent in its exposure to a single or very small number of markets. It may provide a short cut, via merger with another intermediary overseas, to becoming an international as against a national operator. There are also going to be circumstances in which a company outside the financial system will want to merge with a financial intermediary, especially if it wants, for example, to provide credit facilities to its customers.

It is unclear where the adjustments implied by the above will end. It is certain that for many companies the process of merger will prove to be an unhappy and costly business, and parts of the merged organisations may subsequently need to be shut down or resold. It was clear at the time of Big Bang, for example, that there were too many players and too little talent in almost every part of the equity and bond markets. The crash of October 1987 caused the process of readjustment to be speeded up, but it is by no means complete as yet. The link between economic efficiency and concentration in the financial markets cannot be determined by historical precedent. There is much evidence of a 'clash of cultures' when different kinds of intermediary are brought together. At the end of the day the authorities must also form a judgement both about their ability to oversee the system and also the compatibility of different kinds of financial system with the pursuit of their major objectives.

☐ *4.10.5 Internationalisation*

One of the trickier issues is raised by the **internationalisation** of the financial system. Predominantly national intermediaries still exist in the UK, particularly the building societies, but the process of merger and take-over is increasingly international in scope. Big Bang specifically encouraged the inflow of foreign capital, but it would be wrong to suppose that this can be interpreted as a completely laissez-faire attitude on the part of the authorities. They have indicated that there are distinct limits beyond which internationalisation will not be permitted to go – the UK clearing banks, despite the rather modest level of their share capital, are not going to be allowed to fall into foreign hands (nor indeed into the dubious hands of non-financial companies in the UK if the abortive bid by Saatchi and Saatchi for the Midland Bank in 1988 is anything to go by).

☐ *4.10.6 New Technology*

To be a major international intermediary it must be possible for the head office to know what is going on in the farthest-flung outposts of the company. This has increasingly been made possible by the introduction of **new technology**, and especially of computers, which can communicate information instantaneously over vast distances. However, the introduction of computers has had much more widespread effects, because it has permitted an individual intermediary to handle an enormously increased range of data, and therefore made it possible for it to compete in many more markets than in previous periods when a lack of skilled manpower could not produce enough detailed information for rational decisions to be made. Dealing with a multiplicity of currencies is no longer more than a technicality, and the full spread of interest rates can be arranged on a screen at the touch of a button. Much of the software is marketed commercially, so it is not even necessary for organisations to develop their own software before joining in a new market. It should, however, be borne in mind that computers cannot think for themselves, so if information is mistakenly or

fraudulently inserted, serious consequences can easily arise involving losses on a scale which would have been spotted much more quickly in less-sophisticated systems.

Dealing in equities and gilts is so dependent upon modern technology that the Stock Exchange floor was deserted almost immediately after Big Bang, and face-to-face transactions have become a virtual anachronism. Most readers will be familiar with modern dealing rooms through the media and especially such films as 'Wall Street', but this technology barely touches upon the everyday lives of individuals. However, automated teller machines (ATMs) are now in widespread usage, and the National Westminster Bank, for example, has spent £1 bn in order to create a computerised system which will allow it to deal with deposits, cash dispensing and account information at branches entirely through machines.

EFTPOS (electronic funds transfer at point of sale) has become popular very quickly. EFTPOS is a system whereby, for example, a supermarket uses an individual's debit card to debit his or her purchases direct to a bank account, thereby rendering unnecessary the use both of cash and cheques.

By the end of 1990, 45 per cent of adults in Britain owned a debit card, and the number of debit card transactions grew by 400 per cent in 1989 alone. Switch and Visa cards are expected to be used ten times as often as credit cards by the year 2000. In January 1991, the big five clearing banks announced that they had agreed upon a pilot scheme that would eliminate paper for corporate customers and replace it with electronic messages. Inter-bank electronic bank interchange (EDI) will enable companies to make payments by sending messages directly from their computers to their banks. The banks will then transfer the funds and notify the recipient electronically.

In 1992, the much delayed ISE system called TAURUS, which will replace share certificates with electronic records, will come on stream. The latest delay was a consequence of disquiet about the proposed compensation ceiling to cover losses by shareholders in the event of electronic failure, error or fraud. The ISE is keen on a low ceiling in order to reduce trading costs, whilst the government wants a high ceiling.

Other recent innovations are electronic gadgets which allow an individual sitting at home to access his bank account or a share dealing service via a telephone link, with the information shown on a home computer screen. The Midland Bank has set up First Direct, a retail bank that has no branches. All transactions are done over the telephone on a 24-hour a day basis. For other innovations see the *Financial Times* (3 January 1991).

This takes us one further step towards a cashless society, but as noted above there remains, and will remain for the foreseeable future, very large numbers of the 'unbanked'. Furthermore, the use of ATMs requires relatively large amounts of cash to be held, so what is being replaced is not so much cash as cheques – which makes the banks happy as cheques are expensive to process.

■ *4.11* Conclusion

It is clear from this discussion that the circumstances of the financial markets post-Big Bang are somewhat different from those anticipated in 1986. There was an almost universal belief that the markets would be transformed by the quest for globalisation, and that in order to compete a financial supermarket would have to be created.

This would require the elimination of the weakest players from the markets, leaving the survivors with profitable businesses with significant shares of each market. The reality has been a fascinating illustration of the forces of competition, which in this case are dependent upon information flows. The quest for globalisation was based upon the assumption that the market players with the most sophisticated, and by implication most expensive, communications would have an advantage over the less-well capitalised players. Regrettably for those companies who spent vast sums of money following the path mapped out by this line of reasoning it proved possible for all the players, even those operating on a small scale and with relatively little capital, to access the necessary information on equal terms. Furthermore, the customer has found himself able to shop around at the touch of a button on a computer screen. He is largely indifferent from whom he buys, so he may simply opt continuously for the cheapest (and prob-ably not very profitable) bargain such as is offered by a basic share dealing only service. Alternatively, he may be willing to pay a premium for high quality advice, but if this fails to meet expectations he can readily transfer his allegiance elsewhere.

Building up allegiance is largely a matter of personal relationships and trust. This is why, following American precedents, department stores began to offer a limited range of financial services. Marks and Spencer obtained a banking licence and started to market investment products, most recently unit trusts in October 1988. Most department stores offer credit cards and personal finance. Given the rather poor image of banks, there is every reason to suppose that many people will be at least as happy to deal with M & S. In any event, it is evident that most functions performed by a clearing bank can be done satisfactorily by a different type of financial intermediary such as a building society.

It is also probable that many of the new ventures in financial services by non-financial companies will be at least as successful as diversification by existing financial intermediaries. As has been recounted at various stages in the preceding analysis, there is a good deal of licking of wounds going on, and the financial sector is still some way from reaching a post-Big Bang equilibrium. The winners have undoubtedly been the stockholders and estate agents who were bought out by financial intermediaries for highly inflated prices in the belief that there would be lots of energy to tap. Some of these fortunate sellers have recently been able to buy back their old companies for a fraction of their selling price. If there is one lesson to be learned above all others, it is that there is no substitute for local knowledge of the customer.

References

Alesina, A. (1989) 'Politics and Business Cycles in Industrial Democracies', *Economic Policy* (April).

Callen, T. and J. Lomax (1990) 'The Development of the Building Societies' Sector in the 1980s', *Bank of England Quarterly Bulletin* (November).

■ Chapter 5 ■

Spending, Taxing and Borrowing

Peter Curwen

■ 5.1 Introduction

Our purpose in Chapter 5 is to describe the components of the UK fiscal system and to provide an up-to-date statistical analysis of government expenditure, taxes and borrowing. We do not seek to discuss the philosophy and mechanics of fiscal policy as such, which is left to the concluding chapter because it is unhelpful to discuss fiscal policy independently of monetary policy. Furthermore, it is impractical to discuss the use of policy instruments until all of the relevant policy objectives have been thoroughly reviewed, and their interrelationships assessed.

Our first task is to examine the available data on public spending. Whilst the government has shown some ambivalence about the presentation of its policy objectives since 1979, its public spending plans have always been an important element of its strategy. At the present time the government's stated objective is to hold the rate of growth of public spending below the growth of the economy as a whole, and thus to reduce public spending as a proportion of national income. This should then make it possible to ease the burden of taxation without any accompanying increase in the overall burden of the National Debt, and from this should flow the enterprise and efficiency which leads to growing output and employment. Once our discussion of public spending is complete we will move on to examine, first, the burden

of taxation, and subsequently the government's borrowing requirements and their impact upon the National Debt.

■ 5.2 Public Expenditure

☐ 5.2.1 The Growth of Public Expenditure

As shown in **Figure 5.1**, public expenditure has grown enormously during the twentieth century, a phenomenon common to all advanced industrial economies, albeit to varying degrees. As will be discussed subsequently, it is very difficult to reduce public expenditure once it has taken root, so it is of considerable interest briefly to review the origins of the growth of public expenditure in the UK.

At the microeconomic level it is first possible to argue that governments are constantly intervening in order to offset the undesirable side-effects of free markets. In the case of what are known as **public goods**, such as national defence and street lighting, there is unlikely to be adequate provision in a private market since the provider will be unable to obtain payment from beneficiaries of his provision. Equally, in the case of **merit goods**, the provision in a private market of such things as health and education will be limited to those with the ability to pay.

Figure 5.1 *The Planning Total and General Government Expenditure: How it is Planned and Spent, 1990–91, £bn*

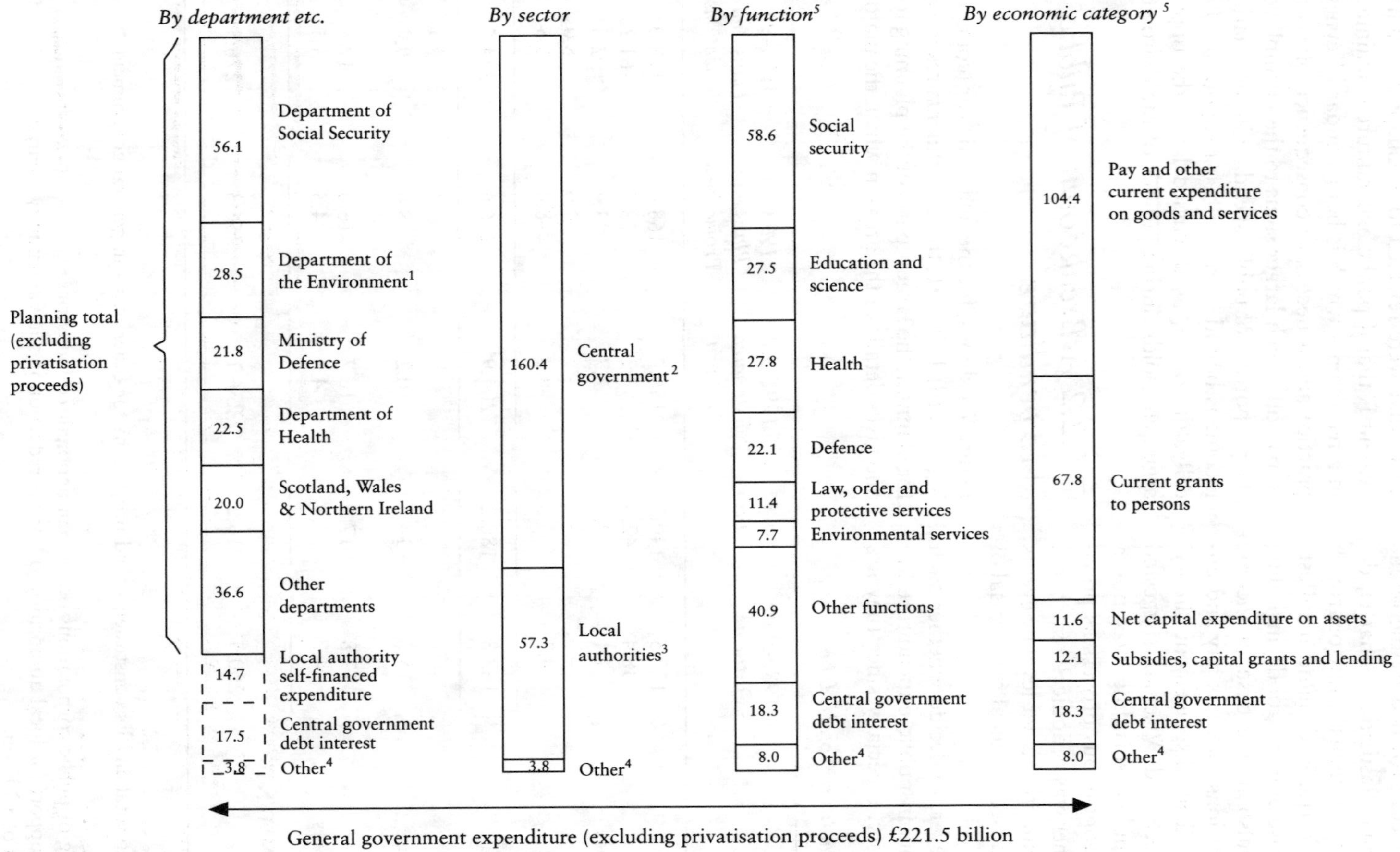

By department etc.

Department of Social Security	56.1
Department of the Environment[1]	28.5
Ministry of Defence	21.8
Department of Health	22.5
Scotland, Wales & Northern Ireland	20.0
Other departments	36.6
Local authority self-financed expenditure	14.7
Central government debt interest	17.5
Other[4]	3.8

Planning total (excluding privatisation proceeds)

By sector

Central government[2]	160.4
Local authorities[3]	57.3
Other[4]	3.8

By function[5]

Social security	58.6
Education and science	27.5
Health	27.8
Defence	22.1
Law, order and protective services	11.4
Environmental services	7.7
Other functions	40.9
Central government debt interest	18.3
Other[4]	8.0

By economic category[5]

Pay and other current expenditure on goods and services	104.4
Current grants to persons	67.8
Net capital expenditure on assets	11.6
Subsidies, capital grants and lending	12.1
Central government debt interest	18.3
Other[4]	8.0

General government expenditure (excluding privatisation proceeds) £221.5 billion

Notes:

1. Includes revenue support grants and non-domestic rate payments and certain transitional grants to local authorities in England. Comparable items are included in the figures for Scotland and Wales.
2. Includes grants, subsidies and net lending to public corporations, including nationalised industries. It also includes central government debt interest (£17.8bn).
3. The total is made up of £42.7 billion financed by support from central government and £14.5 billion financed from local authorities own resources. It includes local authority debt interest (£5.2bn).
4. Includes the national accounts adjustments. The differences in these figures reflect the different treatment of local authority debt interest and market and overseas borrowing of public corporations in the analyses of GGE by function and economic category.
5. These are unrevised figures and therefore do not sum exactly to the total.

Source: Autumn Statement (November 1991); *Statistical Supplement to the 1990 Autumn Statement*, Chart 1.3.

At the macroeconomic level the basic premise is that goods and services provided by the public sector have **high income elasticities** – that is, demand for them grows faster than the rate of growth of incomes. This sharp rise in demand manifests itself not only in the case of merit goods, including public housing, but also in the case of income support, including pensions, sickness pay and unemployment benefits. The 'displacement theory' put forward by Peacock and Wiseman suggested that the growth in public spending was not a broadly smooth and continuous process as previously thought, but rather was periodically ratcheted upwards onto a permanently higher level by events such as wars, which caused a radical reappraisal of the existing order.

It is difficult, however, to decide whether such upwards displacements in public expenditure are permanent or transitory, especially since they are divorced from the more general political influences that were referred to in Chapter 1. What is evident is that if public expenditure is maintained in a recession – which is both standard Keynesian practice and a necessary consequence of needing to pay out much larger sums to the unemployed – the proportion of public spending in total national income is bound to rise, albeit temporarily. Logically, of course, as discussed later, the opposite argument holds during periods of rapid growth.

5.2.2 A Breakdown of Public Expenditure

Figure 5.1 shows, for the financial year (commencing 5 April) 1990–91, the departments responsible for planning the largest parts of the planning total, and gives details of the areas in which the majority

Table 5.1 *Public Expenditure Totals, £ bn*

	1989–90 Outturn	1990–91 Outturn	1991–92[1] Estimated Outturn	1992–93 Plans and Projections	1993–94 Plans and Projections
Central government[2]	127.5	140.7	156.7	168.6	178.0
Local authorities	38.4	42.5	53.2[3]	58.6	61.2
Nationalised industries	1.1	2.3	2.7	3.4	2.8
Reserve	–	–	–	4.0	8.0
Privatisation proceeds	–4.2	–5.3	–8.0	–8.0	–5.5
PLANNING TOTAL	162.8	180.2	204.9[4]	226.6	244.5
Local authority self-financed expenditure	15.2	14.7	10.2	8.6	9.0
Central government debt interest	17.8	17.5	16.7	16.6	17.5
Accounting adjustments	4.7	3.8	4.3	4.5	5.5
GENERAL GOVERNMENT EXPENDITURE	200.5	216.2	236.1	256.3	276.5

Notes:
1. Plans for the planning total and its constituents, and projections for other items in general government expenditure.
2. Includes the financing of public corporations other than nationalised industries.
3. Includes additional support for local authorities to finance reduction in the Community Charge.
4. Including adjustment of £300 mn.
Source: Statistical Supplement to the 1991 Autumn Statement.

of general government expenditure is incurred. It also shows who spends the money and what it is spent on.

There are different ways of defining 'public spending', and different aggregates are relevant for different purposes. The measure which is used for the formulation of macroeconomic policy and the Medium Term Financial Strategy (MTFS) is **general government expenditure** (GGE), consisting of the combined capital and current spending of central and local government including debt interest. This represents the amount which needs to be raised by taxation and borrowing. However, for the purposes of planning and control of programmes, the public expenditure **cash planning total** is the relevant figure, since it is built up from the control totals for departmental programmes including public corporations.

Table 5.1 illustrates GGE and the planning total over a five-year period. 1990–91 is retrospective and is known as an outturn. 1991–92 is an estimated outturn. The figures are published in the Financial Statement and Budget Report (FSBR), known as the 'Red Book' and published in the Spring at the end of each financial year, and are subsequently revised in the Autumn Statement in November. The Red Book and Autumn Statement also contain estimates for the ongoing financial year and forecasts for the three subsequent years. These latter figures will be subject to extensive revision over time, and should be treated as indicative rather than as gospel.

As can be seen, the major difference between the planning total and GGE is interest on debt instruments issued by the central government. This amount depends both upon the total debt outstanding and upon interest rates, so it is very difficult to forecast accurately. Its size is related to the historic and current borrowing needs of government which are discussed in a subsequent section. In practice, it has been stable in nominal terms for some years, implying that it has been falling in both inflation-adjusted terms and as a percentage of GDP. The other major difference between the two halves of **Table 5.1** did not exist at the time of the first edition, and is therefore discussed in detail below.

Meanwhile it is worth observing that it is customary to insert a rolling reserve of £4.0 bn in the planning total. In a year of recession such as 1991–92 this is consumed by unforeseen demands upon the public purse almost as soon as the financial year begins.

5.2.3 *Local Government Financing*

The approach to the calculation of public spending contained in this discussion dates back to the original surveys of public spending which were set up in accordance with the recommendations of the Plowden Committee (Cmnd 1432, 1961).

However, in a White Paper entitled *A New Public Expenditure Planning Total* (Cm 441, 1988), the government proposed a change in the coverage of the planning total, to take place when the new arrangements for local government financing came into operation in England and Wales in 1990. Under this proposal the planning total now includes (**1**) spending on the government's own programmes; (**2**) grants, current and capital, paid to local authorities; (**3**) credit approvals issued by government for local authority borrowing for capital expenditure; (**4**) payments to the local authorities from the proceeds of the national non-domestic rate; (**5**) the external financing limits of public corporations; (**6**) privatisation proceeds; (**7**) a Reserve. Data collection in the appropriate form could not be integrated into the 1988 Public Expenditure Survey because it was already in progress, but commenced with the 1989 Survey.

The underlying purpose of this change is to distinguish that part of local authority spending which is the responsibility of central government from that part which local authorities determine and finance for themselves. Public spending control is enhanced in a number of ways – for example, by including grants in the planning total for the first time. Furthermore, since this requires the grants to be planned for three years ahead, it helps the local authorities to plan their own expenditure more effectively.

Table 5.2 *Public Expenditure, 1970–71 to 1993–94*

	Planning Total[1]		*General Government Expenditure*			*General government expenditure (excluding privatisation proceeds)*			*Money GDP*	
	£ bn	*Real terms*[2] *£ bn*	*Spending on goods and services £ bn*	*Total £ bn*	*Privatisation proceeds £ bn*	*£ bn*	*Real terms*[2] *£ bn*	*% of GDP*[3]	*£ bn*	*Adjusted series, Index (1990–91 = 100*[3]*)*
1970–71			11.9	21.6		21.6	148.1	41¼	53.2	9.4
1971–72			13.4	24.4		24.4	153.6	41¾	59.3	10.4
1972–73			15.2	27.6		27.6	161.1	41¾	67.6	11.9
1973–74			17.9	32.0		32.0	174.3	43½	75.0	13.2
1974–75			22.9	42.9		42.9	195.3	48¾	89.4	15.7
1975–76			29.4	53.8		53.8	195.3	49¼	111.2	19.6
1976–77			32.9	59.6		59.6	190.5	46¾	130.1	23.0
1977–78			35.2	63.9	−0.5	64.4	181.1	43¼	151.4	26.8
1978–79			39.0	75.0		75.0	190.1	44	173.8	30.7
1979–80			46.5	89.9	−0.4	90.3	196.4	44	208.6	36.9
1980–81			56.7	108.6	−0.2	108.8	199.9	46½	237.8	42.1
1981–82			61.1	120.5	−0.5	121.0	202.6	47¼	260.9	46.2
1982–83			67.4	132.6	−0.5	133.1	208.1	47½	285.7	50.5
1983–84			72.9	140.4	−1.1	141.7	211.7	46½	309.8	54.8
1984–85	127.0	180.7	78.6	150.8	−2.1	152.9	217.5	47	331.5	58.7
1985–86	130.7	176.2	82.6	158.4	−2.7	161.1	217.2	45¼	363.1	64.2
1986–87	136.0	177.5	87.4	164.6	−4.5	169.1	220.8	44	390.6	69.1
1987–88	142.6	176.6	94.5	173.2	−5.1	178.4	220.9	42	432.3	76.5
1988–89	145.6	168.2	99.7	179.6	−7.1	186.7	215.6	39½	480.9	85.1
1989–90	162.8	176.6	112.6	200.5	−4.2	204.8	222.1	40	521.5	92.4
1990–91	180.1	180.1	123.8	216.1	−5.3	221.5	221.5	40	555.1	100.0
1991–92	204.9	191.5	(4)	236.1	−8.0	244.4	228.1	41½	588.0	
1992–93	226.6	202.7	(4)	256.3	−8.0	264.3	236.4	42	631.0	
1993–94	244.5	210.8	(4)	276.5	−5.5	282.0	243.1	41¾	675.0	
1994–95	258.0	215.9		291.1	−5.5	296.6	248.2	41¼	718.0	

Notes:

1 Figures for the planning total are available on a consistent basis only for the years shown. Figures are estimated outturn for 1991–92 and plans for 1992–93 onwards.

2 Cash figures adjusted to 1990–91 price levels by excluding the effect of general inflation. The deflator series used is that for GDP at market prices adjusted to remove the distortion caused by the abolition of domestic rates.

3 Based on money GDP figures adjusted to remove the distortion caused by the abolition of domestic rates.

4 Figures are available on a consistent basis for outturn years only.

Source: Statistical Supplement to the 1991 Autumn Statement.

It should be noted that this change has no effect upon the total for general government expenditure. The effect, in accounting terms, is to remove local authority self-financed expenditure from the planning total and to place it, in terms of **Table 5.1**, together with debt interest and other adjustments.

In the 1991 Budget, the Chancellor announced that additional central government support would be provided to local authorities in order to reduce the Community Charge, to be financed from central taxes. The Government will pay a new grant called the Community Charge Grant which will reimburse authorities for the gross cost of reducing charges in 1991–92 by £140, estimated at some £5.6 bn. It will not be possible to finalise the exact amount payable until after the end of the financial year, so it is proposed to pay 90 per cent of the estimated grant in 1991–92, with the remainder to follow in 1992–93.

The net cost of the measure will be lower than payments of the new grant because the reduction in the Community Charge will bring down the costs of the Community Charge reduction scheme, announced on 17 January 1991, and of Community Charge benefit. It is estimated that these savings may bring down the cost of the measure by nearly a quarter, to a net level of some £4.3 bn. Provision for support to local authorities in 1992–93 and 1993–94 has also been increased by an amount equivalent to the new grant, uprated in line with the GDP deflator, *less* estimated savings on the Community Charge reduction scheme and community charge benefit. The public expenditure planning totals for all three years have been increased to take account of these changes and of the Community Charge reduction scheme and the other measures announced on 17 January 1991.

5.2.4 Trends in Public Expenditure

Table 5.2 provides an overview of public expenditure spanning the period 1963–64 to 1993–94. Various aspects of the overall picture are picked up in the subsequent discussion. For the moment it is necessary merely to remark upon the missing data for the planning total. This arises because it has not proved to be possible to recalculate the local authority element in the planning total on the current definition for the years pre-1984–85.

Figure 5.2 illustrates the path of general government expenditure (excluding privatisation proceeds) in real terms and as a percentage of GDP from 1963–64 to 1993–94. This is drawn on a log scale in order to demonstrate the rate of growth of spending which is denoted by the slope of the line. As can be seen, this was exceptionally rapid from 1963–64 to 1967–68, and then again from 1969–70 to 1974–75. After a setback during the first OPEC crisis, it moved upwards again until 1984–85, albeit not quite as fast as during the previous two upturns. Subsequently, it barely grew at all until the end of the decade, but is now once again growing quite strongly.

For ease of comparison **Figure 5.2** also indicates real spending as a percentage of GDP at various points along the growth path. As can be seen, the initial surge in spending was much faster than GDP growth and the percentage rose by 6¼ points. The second surge resulted in a further 8¼ point rise, with an overall effect, allowing for the setback at the end of the 1960s, of 12½ points. There were a few countries such as Sweden where this figure was easily exceeded, but the OPEC crisis forced real spending down at a time when GDP continued to rise, thereby clawing back 6 points within only two years.

Although much of this was recovered once the crisis was over, the governments post-1976 never showed as much enthusiasm for public spending as their predecessors. Nevertheless, it is notable that the 1980–81 recession prevented the first Thatcher Government from getting to grips with spending. Only after 1985–86 did the ratio of real spending to GDP start to fall rapidly, yet even at its lowest level in 1988–89 the ratio was back only to the level of 1966–67 and it is currently back to the levels customary in the early 1970s.

As shown in **Figure 5.3**, which reflects the discussion at the beginning of the chapter, this is less of an achievement when viewed over the long term. Furthermore, for reasons discussed below, there is no foreseeable likelihood that the ratio of GGE to GDP will unwind to levels customary pre-

Figure 5.2 *General Government Expenditure (Excluding Privatisation Proceeds) in Real Terms*[1], *and as % of GDP, 1963–64 to 1993–94*

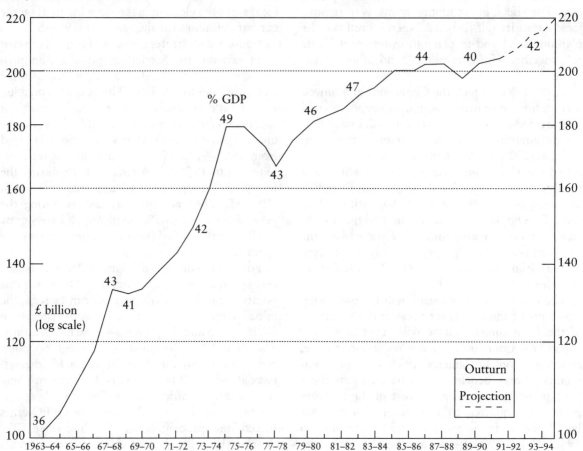

Note:
[1] Cash figures adjusted to 1989–90 price levels by excluding the effect of general inflation as measured by the GDP deflator adjusted to remove the distortion caused by the abolition of domestic rates.
Sources: Statistical Supplement to the 1990 Autumn Statement, Chart 1.2; *FSBR 1991–92.*

1970. It is interesting to note, however, the difference between the two lines shown in **Figure 5.3**. GGE includes transfers, and shows the extent to which the government has to raise taxation and to borrow on the financial markets to finance its activities. The narrower measure, which covers goods and services only, shows the extent to which the nation's resources are being directly absorbed by the government. It is very evident that the latter has changed remarkably little over the past four decades. In other words, it is transfer payments of all kinds which have largely accounted for

the much enlarged role of central government in people's lives.

Given that the government does not itself consume transfer payments, there are those who prefer to discuss the role of government in terms of the lower rather than the upper line. On the other hand, taxes and social security levies must be raised to cover the entire sum spent by government, so there are also those who believe that the upper line is the critical one. This is the kind of (never-to-be-resolved) debate which keep the letters page of the *Financial Times* and its ilk in business.

Figure 5.3 *General Government Expenditure as % of GDP, 1890–1994*[1]

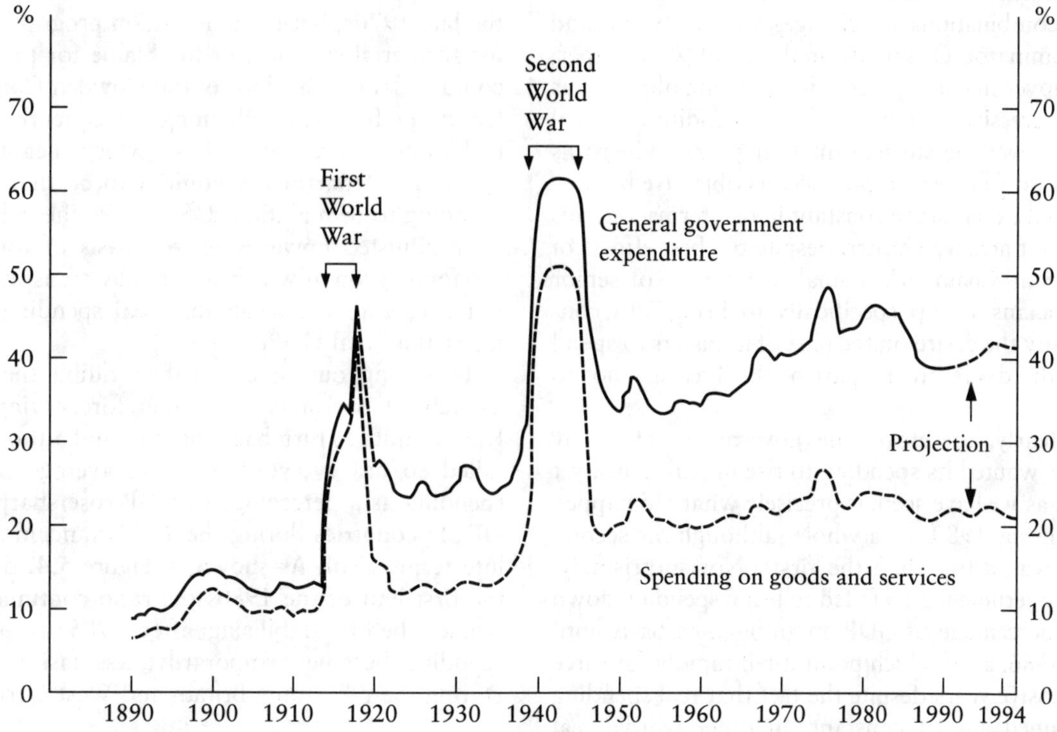

Note:

[1] Excluding privatisation proceeds and adjustments to remove the distortion caused by the abolition of domestic rates.

Sources: Economic Trends (October 1987); *Statistical Supplement to the 1990 Autumn Statement*; *FSBR 1991–92*.

□ 5.2.5 *Public Expenditure Targets*

In the course of the Autumn Statement for 1990 the government restated its position in relation to both expenditure and taxation as follows:

> The Government's medium term objective for public spending is that, over time, it should take a declining share of national income, while value for money is constantly improved. This is consistent with the policy of maintaining a balanced budget over the medium term and reducing taxation when it is prudent to do so. The public spending objective is expressed in terms of the ratio of general government expenditure (GGE), excluding privatisation proceeds, to gross domestic product (GDP). GGE is

the main spending aggregate used in the Medium Term Financial Strategy (MTFS).

Throughout the 1980s it was the custom for the government to produce figures for its expenditure which showed a clear downward trend over time as a percentage of GDP. Initially, the planned percentages were consistently over-optimistic by a wide margin. By the mid-1980s the outturns were proving to be only modestly worse than the plans, and by the end of the decade the outturns were an improvement on the plans.

During the current recession public spending will inevitably rise as a percentage of GDP, but the government is proud of its record, claiming that unlike its predecessors it has got to grips with public spending. But has it? In the first place, it must remembered that we are dealing here with a **ratio**, which can fall in value for a variety of different combinations of changes in numerator and denominator. Originally, in the 1980 White Paper, the government expressed its spending objective as a progressive reduction of its expenditure in real terms over the subsequent four years. When this failed to transpire in practice, its objective became to hold expenditure constant in real terms, but this was not achieved either, despite the best efforts of the 'Star Chamber', a small committee of senior politicians set up specifically to bring into conformity the desire on the part of ministers to spend and the desire on the part of the Treasury not to spend.

Clearly, therefore, the government expressly never wanted its spending to rise in real terms, yet that, as we have seen, is precisely what did happen taking the 1980s as a whole (although the second half was better than the first). Not surprisingly, the government also failed to bring spending down as a percentage of GDP on an ongoing basis until 1985–86, after which point it fell rapidly for three successive years despite the fact that real spending remained almost constant. In other words, real spending as a percentage of GDP fell **not because real spending was itself falling but because GDP was rising rapidly**, as shown in **Table 5.2.**

Our conclusions from the above discussion are that **(1)** in terms of its **original** public spending targets the government has been a failure; **(2)** by moving the goalposts the government did manage, during the late 1980s, to hit its targets; but **(3)** this could not be ascribed to successful curbs on real spending but rather to the effects of rapid economic growth; and hence **(4)** the government will be unable to hit its targets again until the recession is over, and possibly not for some time after that.

It is evident that the government puts a favourable gloss on its spending performance, as it does in other matters such as unemployment. It is also evident that the government has, as in other matters such as the money supply, missed its spending targets more often than not. But has it **failed**? It must be recognised, first of all, that the government took office at the end of the era of profligate public spending which not merely rose sharply in real terms but as a percentage of GDP – up from

36 per cent in 1964–65 to 49 per cent in 1975–76. True, the Labour Government stemmed the tide in the late 1970s, but the longer-term prognosis was for further rises. Some of the blame for that rise could be laid at the door of the Plowden Committee. In the first place, planning subsequently came to be done on a volume basis which meant that spending Departments could expect their real spending to be maintained. Secondly, the volumes were adjusted upwards on the basis of forecast economic growth which never fully transpired in practice, with the result that real spending rose faster than real GDP.

In setting out to cut real spending the first Thatcher Government was, therefore, trying like King Canute to turn back the tide, and although it failed **so did everyone else**. On average public spending as a percentage of GDP rose sharply in OECD countries during the 1970s (and in absolute terms also). As shown in **Figure 5.4**, during the first half of the 1980s the ratio continued to worsen before stabilising after 1985 as public spending became, temporarily, less fashionable. During the 1980s only Britain and West Germany

Figure 5.4 *Government Spending, % of GDP, OECD 1979 and 1989*

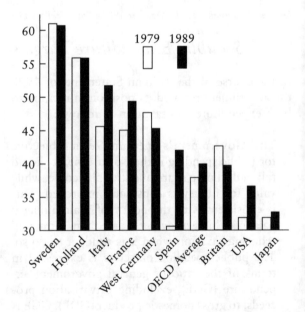

Source: The Economist.

managed to rein back their ratios at all significantly. Elsewhere in Europe high spenders such as Sweden and Holland made negligible progress overall, although quite sharp reductions towards the end of the decade more than offset rising ratios at the beginning. Spain deteriorated seriously and even the USA moved up towards European levels of spending, Reagan notwithstanding.

It was fortunate for Britain that its difficulties in the mid-1970s brought the desirability of spiralling public spending into question at a relatively early point in history. Gradually, expenditure was transformed onto a cash basis, a process completed in 1981, and this was accompanied by a more determined pursuit of value for money in public spending during the Thatcher years. The government's **efforts** could not be denied, but such progress as was made has to be set against a decade of Thatcherite determination. A recession followed by a 'wetter' government (or a higher spending Labour Government) will probably serve to unwind most of the gains made in the late-1980s.

5.2.6 Functional Analysis of Expenditure

In trying to analyse why even a decade of Thatcherism failed to make any inroads into the level of real public spending we need to disaggregate public spending into its main functions, as in **Figure 5.5**. The key lesson of **Figure 5.5** is that roughly 70 per cent of public spending is accounted

Figure 5.5 *General Government Expenditure by Function, % Share of Total, 1978/79 to 1990/91*

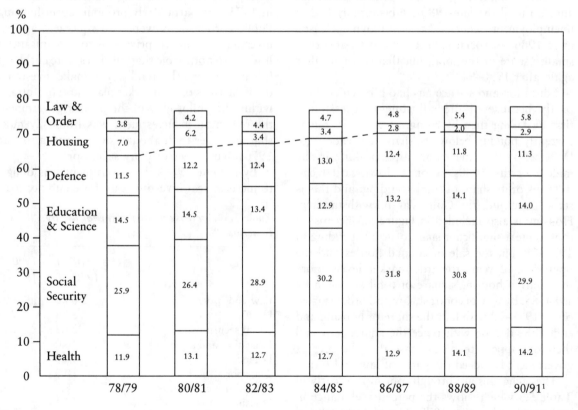

Note:
[1] Estimated outturn.
Source: Statistical Supplement to the 1990 Autumn Statement, Table 2.2.

for by only four functions, namely health, social security, education and science and defence. Over the period 1978–79 to 1988–89 these four functions absorbed an increasing share of total spending, as shown by the dotted line.

It is important to remember that real spending rose during this period by £20 bn, so this was an **increasing share of an increasing real total**. In other words, any increase in the share necessarily means that additional **real** (not simply nominal, but inflation-adjusted) resources are being pumped into the function in question, and this may still be true even if the share declines slightly. Given the current controversy over health care, it has been put at the foot of each column in order to bring out the essential reality that the government has **pumped a good deal of additional real resources into health care over the past decade**. The biggest share has long been taken by social security, reflecting in particular long-term growth in pension liabilities and, up until the late-1980s, substantially higher unemployment benefits. As unemployment eased after 1986, so social security began to absorb a smaller share of the total, but that is set to alter again after 1990–91.

Education and science has had a patchier time, partly because of the adjustment necessitated first by falling then by rising school rolls, but is currently not far below its share a decade ago. Defence, on the other hand, after peaking in the middle of the 1980s, is on a downward trend in terms of its share of total spending, and this is set to continue, the Gulf War notwithstanding. Housing is also included in **Figure 5.5** because it took quite a significant share of total spending in 1978–79, but the sale of council houses and the upgrading of rents towards market levels more than halved housing's share of total spending by 1984–85. By way of contrast, law and order started off in 1978–79 with half the share of housing and ended the decade with twice the share. It would therefore appear to be the case that the present government is indeed the party of law and order.

These changes are brought out more clearly in **Table 5.3** which shows the percentage change in real spending between 1979–80 and 1990–91 and also between 1980–81 and 1990–91 (in order to avoid disputes about whether the government

should be held responsible for spending during its election year). In either case the biggest increase was in spending on law and order, with both health and social security showing substantial increases. With real spending on health up by over a quarter it is, frankly, rather **unrealistic to accuse the government of undermining the national health service**.

On the other hand, education and science did less than half as well, and real spending on defence was only slightly larger at the end of the decade. The really significant reduction, as can be seen, was in real spending on housing.

These developments can also usefully be re-expressed in terms of capital (investment) versus current spending. In 1973, investment constituted 12 per cent of general government expenditure whereas by 1986 it constituted only 4.5 per cent. The reduction in the real level of fixed investment by roughly one-half during the decade beginning in 1975 was particularly pronounced in housing. Public corporations were also squeezed, as were investment grants to private sector organisations. It was also noticeable that subsidies were cut sharply, but although this tendency to make investment obey the rules of the market place sits comfortably within the philosophy of the present government, the reduction in investment was ironically much sharper under the Labour Government in the late 1970s than under its Tory successor.

By the late 1980s the government was obliged to increase real investment in, for example, roads

Table 5.3 *Increase in Real Expenditure by Function, %*

	1990–91 / 1979–80	1990–91 / 1980–81
Law and order	65.6	60.6
Health	37.4	26.6
Social security	35.2	32.5
Education and science	16.0	12.9
Defence	10.8	7.9
Transport	0.0	1.4
Agriculture & fisheries	8.0	–3.6
Housing	–53.1	–45.4

Source: Statistical Supplement to the 1990 Autumn Statement, Table 2.3.

and prisons (because it was increasing the jail population), but it is trying to involve private capital in these and other areas in order to keep its own capital investment under control. An incoming Labour Government would be likely to bring up capital spending quite sharply.

One obvious conclusion to be drawn from the above discussion is that the government's efforts to control real spending during the 1980s were successful only in areas which did not absorb a big share of its spending – trade and industry was another in this category. Now these functions have been cut back to the bone there is no more fat to trim. Hence, further reductions can occur only in major heads of spending – yet as we have seen those are precisely the areas where even the current government has had little or no success. The number of pensioners cannot be reduced; unemployment will remain high by 1970s' standards; the number of school children and college students is set to rise; and the health service is impervious to cuts.

□ 5.2.7 The Spending Conundrum

It is surely one of the greatest ironies of Mrs Thatcher's decade in power that, having claimed for many years that a major objective was to **cut** public spending (but having failed in real terms to do so), it eventually became politically expedient to claim to the **contrary**, for example in the case of the health service. But by that time the propaganda machine had been so successful that no one would believe the government, even though what it claimed was true!

We already know that real spending on the health service rose significantly during the 1980s, yet the medical establishment has complained endlessly that the health service is under-resourced and (prospective) patients certainly believe that the service they receive (or cannot obtain) is deteriorating. How can this be?

Many categories of public expenditure, such as health and education, are currently labour-intensive. This means that the public expenditure debate has been directed primarily towards **inputs** rather than **outputs**. The GDP deflator, which

is used to express spending in real terms is, however, output-based and is therefore inappropriate for evaluating the **volume** of provision of **labour-intensive services**. This suggests that an own-cost deflator should be used in such circumstances, namely one based upon the **costs of inputs used** in each spending category. A study by Levitt and Joyce (1987) has demonstrated what a difference this can make. In the case of health, real GDP-deflated spending rose by 25 per cent between 1979 and 1986, whilst own-cost deflated spending rose by only 9 per cent. Since population growth absorbed over half of this latter increase, and technological advances absorbed the rest, the actual volume of health care delivered *per capita* was **effectively identical** throughout the entire period. Thus, when the government claims to have increased real spending on the NHS, and the medical profession categorically denies that the resource base has improved, they are **both in their respective ways telling the truth!**

The obvious difficulty this creates is that, if real spending has to be constantly increased simply in order to deliver an unchanged volume of provision in crucial labour-intensive areas such as health, the only painless way to cut public spending as a percentage of GDP is to make GDP grow rapidly. One could alternatively, of course, move public spending into the private sector, so it is hardly surprising that educational loans rather than grants, and the tendering out of NHS services, are being actively promoted. However, these changes are very difficult to deliver politically even for a government with a big majority.

The demand for more resources in, for example, the NHS is inevitably couched in terms of **inputs** – too few nurses, hospital beds and so on. However, this tells us nothing about how **efficiently** these resources are going to be used, so the government has understandably tried to switch the emphasis of the public expenditure debate onto **outputs and productivity**. It introduced the Financial Management Initiative (FMI) in 1982; the programme of scrutinies of efficiency by the Cabinet Office under Lord Rayner in 1979; and the publication of performance indicators in the Autumn Statement. The drawback here is that one can, for example, show an increase in the number of in-patients treated per available bed by discharging patients more quickly than before! If, as a consequence, this means that many of them need to be readmitted, then they count as new patients and productivity remains high. There is also an inevitable tendency to use readily accessible measures of performance such as the size of GP's lists, the pupil-teacher ratio in schools or the crime clean-up rate per police officer. However, there is no guarantee that reducing either of the first two will improve the quality of output, which would need to be measured by the ratio of cured patients per doctor or examination passes per teacher.

■ 5.3 The Overall Tax Burden

Between 1948 and 1985, in money terms, the gross receipts from taxation rose by 3200 per cent. Starting from 1948 it took 14 years to double tax revenue. It doubled again in eight years, and again in five. This acceleration was clearly associated with a sharp rise in the rate of inflation, and since 1975 the rate of increase has slowed down. However, prices rose by a total of only 1200 per cent during the equivalent period, which means that gross tax receipts more than doubled in real terms. As the population has remained fairly constant the gross real burden of taxes *per capita* has also clearly more than doubled.

However, individuals are not simply interested in their total tax bill but also in the **proportion of their total earnings which is taxed away.** This makes it sensible to express the tax burden in the form of total taxation as a percentage of GDP. Interestingly, this has shown no long-term continuous tendency to rise. Taxation as a percentage of GDP fell from 1948 to 1960, admittedly from the high percentage required for postwar reconstruction. However, it was back to the 1948 level by 1970. Having fluctuated somewhat during the 1970s, it rose sharply after the election of the present government in 1979, as shown in **Figure 5.6.**

Figure 5.6   *Taxes and Social Security Contributions*

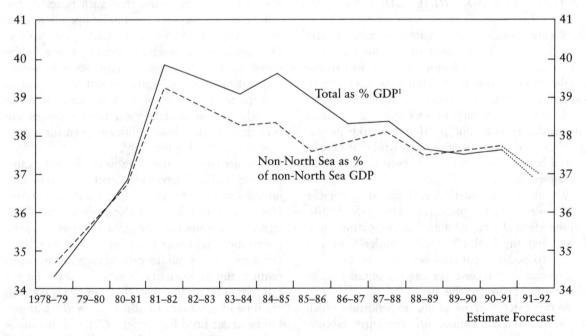

Note:
[1] Includes the Community Charge with taxes from 1989–90.
Source: FSBR 1991–92, Chart 6.2.

As in the case of public expenditure, there are various methods which can be used to calculate the tax burden, but the trends have been almost identical so it is sensible to stick to the definitions which match up with the government's expenditure data. It is very interesting to note that on that basis the tax burden levelled out somewhat at the end of the 1980–81 recession, and particularly during the period 1985–86 to 1990–91 when the two measures used in **Figure 5.6** became effectively one and the same. Thus, **at no time since 1979–80 has the tax burden fallen below that prevailing at the time the first Thatcher Government was elected**, nor indeed below that prevailing when the last Labour Government was in power!

Fiscal drag, discussed below, is clearly a more powerful phenomenon than is commonly understood. In fact, the most markedly cyclical effect is shown by corporation tax receipts which soared with rising profitability during much of the 1980s. In 1989–90 corporation tax accounted for 10.9 per cent of total tax revenue, but this has fallen to a forecast of only 8.6 per cent in 1991–92 as profitability has collapsed back much faster than GDP. This accounts in good part for the projected fall in the tax burden for 1991–92, but as this is a cyclical phenomenon the tax burden is likely to rise again as soon as the recession is over.

5.3.3 The Marginal Rate of Tax

The tax burden represents the **average** rate of direct tax – that is, total direct tax divided by total GDP. Given the existence of tax allowances, it is evident that the rate levied on an **extra** £1 of income, the **marginal** rate of direct tax, will be **higher**. Suppose, for example, an employer wishes to pay an extra £1 to a worker. In every case he must himself pay 10.4p in National Insurance Contributions (NICs). The employee may, or may not, pay 9p in NICs (because they are levied only up to a maximum income, see **p. 151**) and will pay either 25p or 40p in income tax. Out of what is left, the employee will subsequently incur VAT, excise duties and other indirect taxes.

Thus out of every additional £1 earned a higher income tax payer will initially pay 40p (income tax) but the employer will also pay NICs of 10.4p – a total tax bill of 50.4p. For a standard rate payer it will be either 25p + 10.4p + 9p = 44.4p or, without employee NICs, 35.4p. The Labour Party promise to uncap NICs – that is, to make the 9p apply in all cases. Under such circumstances we get 59.4p for the higher rate payer and 44.4p for the standard rate payer. They also propose to raise the higher income tax rate to 50 per cent, thereby raising total direct tax when £1 is earned by the higher rate payer to 69.4p. And this remember, only relates to **direct** tax. When what remains is spent all kinds of additional **indirect** taxes are incurred.

The Labour Party argues that this will yield sufficient extra revenue to finance improved child benefits and State pensions, but this is most unlikely to occur. In 1978–79, the last Labour Government's final financial year in power, with higher rates of income tax **alone** rising to 83 per cent, the highest-paid 10 per cent of the working population contributed 34 per cent of all income tax collected. In 1989–90, with the higher rate set at 40 per cent, the highest-paid 10 per cent contributed 42 per cent of all income tax. On the other hand, the share contributed by the bottom 70 per cent of income tax payers (including almost all Labour voters) fell from 38 per cent to 32 per cent. It is widely recognised that when higher income tax rates go up almost everyone in a position to do so **looks for ways to avoid them**, so the tax burden will simply be redistributed back from the highest paid to the lowest paid and **little or no extra spending will be financed**.

Opinion polls consistently reveal that UK residents **prefer** more public spending to tax cuts. But for the past twelve years they have just as consistently **voted** for governments who have promised tax **reductions**. Readers may draw their own conclusions.

■ 5.4 Fiscal Drag

It may come as something of a surprise, in view of the sharp reduction in the marginal rates of income and other taxes in recent years, that the burden of taxation has shown no consequent tendency to fall. This can primarily be explained by the phenomenon of **fiscal drag** which arises because, whilst the Rooker–Wise–Lawson amendments to the 1977 Finance Bill provided that tax allowances be raised in line with inflation unless the Budget specifically provided otherwise, the index used to adjust for inflation is for **prices** rather than **incomes**.

When the economy is growing strongly incomes tend, on average, to grow noticeably faster than prices. Hence, even if tax allowances are adjusted to compensate for rising prices, an increasingly larger proportion of total income is subjected to tax. In 1987–88 this caused tax revenue to be some £2 bn higher than forecast, and this was comfortably exceeded in 1988–89. In fact, despite the raising of allowances by more than the rate of price inflation in almost every recent Budget, and despite the reductions in the marginal rate of tax, the tax burden has merely been stabilised – indicating that without these concessions it would have risen sharply. As a rule of thumb, each 1 per cent rise in real income increases the average personal tax rate by between 1.5 and 1.75 per cent.

Though not technically fiscal drag, precisely the same effect will occur for corporate taxation when profits are rising much faster than GDP. Equally, spending tends to rise with real incomes, with the result that indirect tax receipts rise sharply.

Figure 5.7　*Taxes and Social Security Contributions as a % of GNP at Factor Cost, 1988*

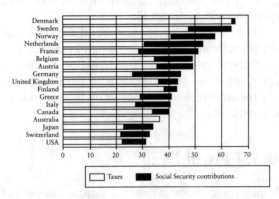

Source: CSO.

■ 5.5 International Comparisons

The CSO calculates the tax burden for OECD member countries on a standardised international definition used by the OECD, as shown in **Figure 5.7**. This reveals, first, that in 1988 the overall tax burden in the UK as a percentage of **GNP at factor cost** was exactly half-way down in the list of countries illustrated, well below the Nordic countries and France and similar to West Germany, albeit appreciably above Japan and the USA.

For studies of the UK alone, **GDP at market prices** is often used as a denominator, as in **Figure 5.5**. This has the effect of reducing the size of all

Table 5.4　*Taxes and Social Security Contributions as a % of GDP at Market Prices by Rank*

	1978		1983		1988	
	Percentage and Rank		*Percentage and Rank*		*Percentage and Rank*	
Including social security contributions						
Sweden	50	1	51	1	55	1
Denmark	43	4	46	4	52	2
Norway	49	2	48	2	49	3
Netherlands	45	3	48	3	48	4
France	39	8	44	6	44	5
Belgium[1]	43	5	44	5	44	6
Austria	42	6	42	7	42	7
FR Germany	41	7	41	8	41	8
United Kingdom	34	10	38	9	37	9
Finland	35	9	34	11	37	10
Italy	29	13	35	10	37	11
Greece[1]	29	14	33	12	35	12
Canada	30	12	32	13	34	13
Switzerland[1]	31	11	31	14	32	14
Japan	23	17	27	17	31	15
Australia	27	16	29	15	31	16
USA	28	15	28	16	29	17

Note:
[1]　Calculations based upon current system of National Accounts except for Belgium, Greece and Switzerland which are based upon the pre-1968 SNA.
Source: CSO.

the ratios in **Figure 5.7**, but it does not affect the UK's ranking as shown in **Table 5.4**.

Clearly, therefore, the UK is **not over-burdened by taxation relative to most other industrialised countries**. As shown in **Figure 5.7**, many of the misconceptions about the burden of taxation arise because of the very different balance between what are officially called 'taxes' as against 'social security contributions' in different countries. The 'tax' burden in the UK is relatively high but the overall deductions in relation to GDP are nothing exceptional.

Unfortunately, what this means in policy terms is that there is equal ammunition (**a**) for those who believe that taxation should be at Japanese or American levels in a free society and (**b**) for those who believe that the UK can afford to expand public expenditure, financed out of taxation, without raising the tax burden above that commonly ruling elsewhere in the EC, or indeed in Europe generally.

■ 5.6 The Tax System

□ *5.6.1 Introduction*

The tax system in the UK is somewhat out of line with that typically found elsewhere in the OECD.

Only in the UK, between 1955 and 1985, did the importance of income tax, measured as a percentage of GDP, fall rather than rise. However, the UK has been typical in its increased emphasis upon National Insurance (or its equivalent) which, though not technically a tax, has precisely the same effect as income tax upon disposable income.

The UK tax system has been developed in an **evolutionary** rather than a **revolutionary** manner since 1948. Whilst no Chancellor has chosen to institute a major programme of tax reform (unless, as some believe, Nigel Lawson is to be regarded as the exception in this respect), the long-term consequence of continuous small adjustments has been to alter the relative importance of different taxes quite dramatically. The preference for evolution is unsurprising from a political perspective since it has been calculated that, as a rule of thumb, tax reform is politically acceptable only if the beneficiaries outnumber the losers by a ratio of four to one. Furthermore, it is much easier to sweeten a reform which hurts the pockets of a large number of voters by giving them back bigger sums via tax cuts elsewhere in the system, and this can be done only if tax revenue is buoyant. In any event, the Inland Revenue are never keen on major administrative changes.

The structure of the tax system since 1948 is laid out in **Table 5.5**.

Table 5.5 *The Structure of the UK Tax System Since 1948*

Ongoing Taxes	New Taxes	Repealed Taxes
Beer duty	Selective employment tax (1967)	Profits tax (1965)
Customs and protective duties	Capital gains tax (1967)	Selective employment tax (1972)
Hydrocarbon oil duty	Corporation tax (1967)	Purchase tax (1973)
Income tax	Value added tax (1973)	Estate duty (1974)
Local authority rates	Capital transfer tax (1974)	Capital transfer tax (1976)
National insurance	Petroleum revenue tax (1978)	Community charge (1993)[1]
Stamp duty	Inheritance tax (1986)	
Tobacco duty	Community charge (1989)	
Vehicle licences	Council tax (1993)[1]	
Wine and spirits duties		

Note:
[1] Announced on 23 April 1991.

☐ *5.6.2 Taxes on Income*

Income Tax

Income tax remains the most important element of the tax system, but its importance has declined since 1979. In general, income tax is charged **on all income which originates in the UK** (including, since 1987, the earnings of overseas entertainers and sportsmen), and on **all income arising abroad of people resident in the UK**.

However, every tax payer, is entitled to a **personal allowance** to set against his or her gross taxable income (which is itself taken net of any pension fund contributions). There is currently a separate allowance for the single and for the married (but see discussion of personal allowances reform below). This is generally referred to as the **standard rate tax threshold**. It may also be supplemented by a whole variety of other allowances, of which the most common is tax relief on interest paid on mortgages. Currently this is almost always paid direct (at source) to the building society or bank acting as mortgagor by the Inland Revenue, with the mortgagee paying a net-of-tax relief monthly figure (the MIRAS system), so it does not normally affect an individual's tax code. Tax relief may also be given for such things as covenants, or for payments under the Business Expansion Scheme (BES). Once all allowances have been deducted the residual sum becomes the **taxable income**.

Historically, income tax was designed to be **progressive** – that is, to take a higher proportion of income in tax as income rises. This was based upon the principle of **ability to pay**, and provided the main mechanism whereby the redistribution of spending power between households could be effected (see **pp. 349–51**). Progressivity was thought to require a significant number of different tax rates, although in practice there is progressivity if there is a single tax threshold below which the tax rate is 0 per cent and above which it is positive. During the early postwar period the standard rate rose sharply, and was held at over 40 per cent throughout the period from 1948 to 1968, although until 1971 two-ninths of earned income was exempt from tax so that the effective rate was lower than the nominal rate.

The higher rates were raised to punitive levels, and predictable consequences followed. During the 1970s everyone in a position to do so earned 'income' in the form of legitimate tax-relieved 'perks', and taxable income fell to half the total income declared to the Inland Revenue. Furthermore, a good deal of income was undeclared (the black economy). But with the tax base shrinking in leaps and bounds, the only way to maintain total tax revenue was assumed at the time to be to raise tax rates even higher, setting off the vicious circle yet again.

The disincentive effects of high tax rates on hard work understandably did nothing for economic growth, and in recognition of this the standard rate had been brought down to 33 per cent by the beginning of the present government's term of office. The government declared its intention of bringing down the basic rate as part of the MTFS, and managed to reduce it steadily to 25 per cent by 1988–89. In so doing, it reduced the rewards of non-declaration relative to the drawback of a possible prison sentence, and the benefits of perks compared to cash. At the same time many perks were either abolished (for example, tax relief on life insurance premiums) or were held roughly constant in money terms thereby reducing their real-value (for example, mortgage interest relief). As a result, taxable income rose to two-thirds of total income by 1987–88.

The possibility of moving to a 25 per cent standard rate, which the government had declared to be its ultimate goal but which was widely regarded at the time as little more than a pipedream, arose as a result of the immense fiscal drag in 1987–88. Chancellor Lawson was very keen to emulate the USA which had already moved to a two-rate system of 15 per cent and 34.7 per cent (adjusted for local income tax), in the process abolishing a whole host of tax reliefs as a quid pro quo. The Chancellor had always been ambivalent about perks, inventing new ones such as the Business Expansion Scheme whilst abolishing existing ones. However, he found himself able in the Budget of 1988 not merely to fund higher levels of spending and to reduce the PSBR, but also to produce his own two-rate structure with the standard rate set at 25 per cent and the higher rate at 40 per cent (compared to the five higher rates ranging from 40 per cent to 60 per cent only the previous year). Furthermore, he did not need to eat heavily into perks. The effect of this reform upon the income tax/benefit schedule can be seen in **Figure 5.8**.

Compared to other major industrialised countries the standard rate tax threshold in the UK still remains low (at £5015 for a married couple in 1991–92), and the standard rate itself is almost the highest. However, the top rate is lower than all except that of the USA (although it bites at the very low threshold of £23,700). There is, therefore, still considerable scope for further rate reductions, but fiscal drag will be needed to provide the means to achieve them. Indeed, in his 1988 Budget

speech Nigel Lawson stated that the objective was to be a standard rate of 20p.

Two issues do, however, need to be carefully noted. In the first place, the sharp reduction in the top rate of tax inevitably transferred huge sums of money to the highest income earners without offsetting reductions in perks, whilst the minor reduction in the standard rate made little difference to the bulk of the working population. This inevitably made the distribution of post-tax income less equal. Against this can be set the benefits of a simplified tax structure and the hoped-for incentive effect on work effort and entrepreneurial activity, but it is doubtful whether the balance between equity and efficiency can be pushed even

Figure 5.8 *Income Tax/Benefit Schedules, 1978 and 1989[1]. Marginal Tax Rates[2].*

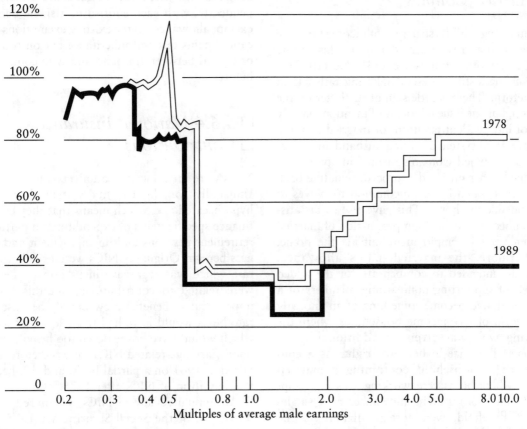

Notes:
[1] Wife not working and two children aged 4 and 6 years.
[2] Loss of benefit is treated as equivalent to a tax. If a £1 increase in weekly earnings results in a loss of £1 in benefits this represents a 100% marginal tax rate.
Source: NEDO.

further towards the latter by repeating the exercise. Secondly, the very high levels of consumer spending during 1988, and their consequences for overheating and inflation, made Lawson wary of anything that smacked of fiscal give-aways in his 1989 Budget, and his successors, Major and Lamont, have chosen to follow suit even in the face of a deepening recession.

Nevertheless, the 1991 Budget undoubtedly represented a move back towards more progressivity in the income tax structure. In particular, the abolition of tax relief on mortgage interest payments at the higher rate of tax imposed additional burdens only upon high income households.

5.6.3 Independent Taxation for Married Couples

Recent changes in the structure of income tax have altered it to a greater degree and at a faster rate than at any other time since 1945. Nevertheless, these changes still represent tinkering rather than true reform. There is little sign of the latter on the horizon, but one issue is worthy of mention, namely that of independent taxation for married couples. The pre-1990 system of taxing husband and wives treated a married woman's income in law as if it belonged to her husband, a procedure dating back to the time when it was uncommon for wives to earn outside the home. This gave rise to dissatisfaction because such a high proportion of married women were in employment outside the home. Furthermore, the married man's allowance, originally intended to compensate for the added burden of supporting non-earning members of a household, had become something of an anomaly in a world of two-income households where the working wife was given an additional single person's allowance in her own right. As a consequence, a household containing a married couple where both were working was in receipt of 2½ times as much in allowances as a single-person household. Even more anomalous was the fact that if the wife alone was at work she was entitled to the full set of allowances, whilst if the husband alone was at work he was entitled only to the married man's allowance.

Green Papers, published in 1980 and 1981, considered how to eradicate these anomalies, and in his Budget speech in 1988 the Chancellor announced that, from 6 April 1990, husbands and wives would be taxed independently on their income and chargeable capital gains. This has meant that (a) husband and wife become independent taxpayers, each with their own allowances to set against their own income from whatever source, and each responsible for dealings with the Inland Revenue; (b) every taxpayer receives the single person's allowance; (c) in addition, a married couple receives the difference between the current single allowance and married allowance, which is set first against the husband's income but any unused amount may be transferred to the wife; (d) special arrangements apply for those aged over 65; (e) a husband and wife's capital gains are taxed independently, with each entitled to a single person's exempt allowance; (f) the existing exemptions from capital gains tax and inheritance tax on transfers of capital between husband and wife continue as before.

5.6.4 National Insurance Contributions

NICs were introduced as a universal tax in 1948. Unusually for the UK tax system they are a hypothecated tax, which means that they exist to finance specific items of expenditure, in particular retirement pensions and unemployment and sickness benefit. Originally NICs were levied at a flat rate which was regressive in its impact. Benefits were related to contributions, but this became impractical as benefits grew rapidly because flat-rate NICs would have had to be levied at a level which would have borne down too heavily on the poor. Earnings-related NICs were therefore introduced in 1961 on a partial basis, and this became the only form of NICs after 1975.

An annual review of NICs is required by the provisions of the Social Security Act 1975. It is necessary to comment briefly on this because from the taxpayer's point of view both income tax and NICs have the same effect since they are deducted at source on Pay As You Earn (PAYE), which

Table 5.6 *National Insurance Contributions, 1991–92*

Weekly Earnings	Percentage NIC Rate	
	Employees	Employers[1]
Below £52	0	0
£52 to £85	2% of £52	4.6
£85 to £130	plus	6.6
£130 to £185	9% of earnings	8.6
£185 to £390	between £52	10.4
Above £390	and £390[2]	10.4

Notes:

[1] Rates apply to all earnings.

[2] For 1992–93 the respective figures are £54 and £405, and the intermediate bands are set at £90, £135 and £190 for employers' contributions.

Source: Autumn Statement 1990, p. 65.

applies to all except the self-employed in the UK. Whilst the income tax structure was simplified in the 1988 Budget, the structure of NICs retained the perverse principle that once a threshold was triggered the relevant rate was applied not only to income between the thresholds but to all income, thereby generating very high marginal rates at the threshold points.

The reform of NICs introduced in the 1989 Budget took effect in October 1989. This simplified the system in that those with earnings below £52 per week in financial year 1991–92 continue to pay nothing, whilst those with earnings at or above £52 per week pay 2 per cent on the first £52 (104p) and 9 per cent on the rest up to the upper earnings limit of £390 per week.

Removal of all except a very modest NICs' liability on the first £52 of weekly earnings undoubtedly benefits the low paid (and helps to off-set fiscal drag), but it remains the case that the lower earnings limit is indeed very low (below that for income tax) and also that, once earnings rise above £390 per week, the combined rate of income tax plus NICs falls back at the margin from 34 per cent to 25 per cent. This can hardly be called a progressive structure, and it must also be borne in mind that it is only those whose incomes are high enough to provide spare cash who can afford to spend money in tax-deductible ways (by

taking out a £30,000 mortgage, for example). Furthermore, employee benefits do not attract NICs. Despite the 1989 reform the employer continues to pay NICs on all employee earnings at the rates shown in **Table 5.6**.

The government has come under pressure to make employee NICs open-ended in terms of income, which would have the effect of a permanent marginal rate of deduction of either 34 per cent or 49 per cent on earned income alone. This is Labour Party policy, but has so far been ignored by Conservative Chancellors. Instead, in the 1991 Budget, Chancellor Lamont made employers pay NICs on the benefit of cars provided for the private use of employees, based on the scale charges set for income tax. Employees are, however, exempted.

□ 5.6.5 Corporation Tax

During the 1970s corporation tax, which is levied on company profits, had much in common with income tax. On the face of it the marginal rate was high, but deductible allowances were so extensive, particularly those concerned with capital investment, that large companies were able to adjust their balance sheets so as to incur little or no tax liability.

As a result, Nigel Lawson reformed the tax in 1984 by phasing out many of the allowances and by simultaneously cutting the tax rate progressively from 52 per cent to 35 per cent. The matching rate for small companies earning profits below £100,000 per annum was initially set at 29 per cent (to match the existing income tax basic rate), and was reduced to 25 per cent for their financial year 1988–89. By international standards, company taxation in the UK thereby became modest.

However, care must be taken to **adjust for the phasing out of capital allowances**, and for the **failure to inflation-adjust** those that remained. Furthermore, the abolition of tax relief on the increase in the value of stocks due to inflation, which seemed non-controversial at the time because inflation had fallen rapidly, became a problem when inflation rose again towards the end of the decade. Hence, many companies actually found themselves paying more tax than before even though the rate was much lower.

With the onset of recession in 1990, the need for a Budget to assist businesses resulted in the retrospective reduction in the rate of corporation tax in the 1991 Budget to 34 per cent for the 1990–91 financial year and to 33 per cent for 1991–92. In addition, companies were to be allowed to carry back trading losses for three years instead of one year and the profits limit for the small companies' corporation tax rate of 25 per cent was raised from £200,000 to £250,000 for 1991–92.

The remaining allowances of any consequence are concerned with **depreciation provisions**. These exist in order to permit companies to build up a stock of money (often itself confusingly called 'capital') which can be used to replace their worn-out or obsolete physical capital stock. Since money set aside for this purpose is needed merely to keep the company in business as a going concern, it is clearly not 'profit' and should not be taxed as such. There are basically two ways of calculating how much money can be set aside each year without incurring a tax liability on the equivalent amount of gross profit. The first is the straight-line method whereby a given proportion of the original capital cost is set aside each year, for example 15 per cent each year for four years. Alternatively, the declining-balance method is used whereby a specified proportion of the original outlay is set against tax liability in Year 1, and the same proportion of the residual amount is written down in Year 2 and so on. This has the effect of setting aside the largest absolute amount of tax liability in Year 1, and successively smaller absolute amounts in successive years. It is up to the tax authorities to determine which depreciation method is to be applied. Historically, when inflation was unusually high, adjustments also needed to be made for the fact that the replacement cost of a unit of capital was much higher than the original cost, but this is no longer considered to be necessary.

Prior to 1984 it was customary to allow a very high proportion of all capital expenditure to be set against corporation tax liability in the year of purchase, but since 1986 these provisions have been made much less generous in view of the much lower rates of tax. Each year 25 per cent of the cost of plant and machinery can now be set against corporation tax liability on a declining-balance basis, whilst only 4 per cent of the cost of industrial or agricultural buildings and hotels can be written down on a straight-line basis each year (since buildings last much longer than machines). Short-life machinery and plant may be wholly written down over its lifetime. These provisions are universal because it would be far too difficult and expensive to deal with companies on an individual basis. However, it remains possible for the government to make exceptions, usually in the context of **regional policy**.

Corporation tax is levied on all profits, whether retained within the company or distributed to shareholders. However, if a company wishes to distribute profits in the form of dividends, then these are paid in a net-of-tax form. The company is obliged to pay the tax liability arising on the gross dividends at the standard rate of **income tax** on behalf of the shareholders. This is collected by the tax authorities in advance of the time when dividends are paid out and is therefore known as advance corporation tax (ACT). ACT, which is strictly not a corporation but an income tax, currently represents one-third of the value of distributed profit (tax rate of 25 per cent: net dividend equals 75 per cent of gross dividend). The shareholder receives his dividend together with a 'tax credit' which he can pass on to the Inland Revenue in order to show that the tax liability on his dividend has already been discharged (although he will have to pay extra tax if his marginal rate is 40 per cent). Any shareholders exempt from income tax can claim a refund.

The company then subtracts the ACT payment from the total corporation tax liability on its profits, and the outstanding sum is paid over at the end of the relevant financial year in the form of **mainstream** corporation tax.

☐ 5.6.6 North Sea Taxes

North Sea taxation consists of royalties, petroleum revenue tax (including advance payments)

Table 5.7 *North Sea Revenues, £ bn*

	1989–90	1990–91		1991–92
	Outturn	1990 Budget	Latest Estimate	Forecast
North Sea corporation tax[1]	0.8	1.0	0.8	0.9
Petroleum revenue tax	1.1	1.1	0.9	0.0
Oil royalties	0.6	0.7	0.6	0.5
Total North Sea revenues	**2.4**	**2.8**	**2.3**	**1.4**

Note:
[1] *Before ACT set off of:*   *0.5*   *0.5*   *0.4*   *0.5*
Source: FSBR 1991–92, Table 6.3.

and corporation tax from North Sea oil and gas production (before advance corporation tax set off). In 1984–85 these amounted to £12 bn, but in 1986–87 there was a very sharp fall to £4.8 bn, a figure which was halved again by 1989–90. The recent decline shown in **Table 5.7** indicates how unimportant this element of the tax system has become. Fortunately, as we have seen, this reduction in North Sea taxation has coincided with fiscal drag elsewhere in the system, and has therefore had far less impact than could reasonably have been predicted in the early 1980s.

Royalties are levied on the production of oil and gas fields on an individual basis. However, in order to induce oil companies to explore for oil and gas in less accessible – and hence more costly – tracts of the North Sea, the government first abolished royalties on newly-developed fields in the central and northern sectors in 1982, and in the 1988 Budget subsequently abolished royalties on post-1982 oil and gas fields in the Southern Basin and onshore areas. The latter development was primarily intended to stimulate gas production.

As a consequence North Sea taxation is now almost entirely dependent upon profit-related taxes. Petroleum revenue tax (PRT) is charged at a rate of 75 per cent on profits (net of royalties) from the production, as opposed to the refining, of oil and gas under licence in Britain and on its Continental Shelf. Various allowances can be set against PRT, in particular certain costs incurred in oil explora-

tion. The 1988 Budget reduced the oil allowance from 250,000 tonnes to 100,000 tonnes for a chargeable period, thereby causing tax to become payable earlier than previously where profits are being earned. Corporation tax is payable on profits in the usual way, but is levied on profits net of royalties and PRT.

Events in the North Sea, such as the Piper Alpha fire, and the instability of oil prices due to the Gulf War have had an erratic effect upon recent North Sea production. With investment in the North Sea expected to increase significantly in 1991–92, short-term losses are likely to be sustained by some operators, and as a consequence PRT will need to be repaid. As a consequence, it is expected to yield no net revenue at all in 1991–92, and North Sea revenues are forecast to fall to less under 1 per cent of total tax revenue – a far cry from the 9 per cent which they represented at their peak in 1984–85.

5.6.7 Customs and Excise Duties

Customs duties are charged on imported goods in accordance with the Common Customs Tariff of the European Community. This exempts community goods imported from other EC member states, and provides a uniform EC-wide tariff barrier against goods from elsewhere in the world. Special arrangements apply for agricultural products in accordance with the Common Agricultural Policy

(CAP). As these duties are an EC rather than a purely national policy, their proceeds are transferred to Brussels to help finance the EC.

Excise duties, on the other hand are not concerned with controlling trade flows but purely with raising revenue from goods and services which are either in inelastic demand (their consumption varies less than in proportion to price) or antisocial, or both. They apply to oils used for road fuel (and for other uses at a reduced rate); to alcoholic drinks (taxed largely in accordance with alcoholic strength); to tobacco products (in accordance with number, price or weight); to betting; and to gambling machine and casino licences. Road usage is additionally taxed through vehicle licences.

These duties are very unpopular, but have the virtue (from the Chancellor's viewpoint) that consumers are really aware only of how much they are going up and not of how much has cumulatively been levied in the past. Each increase therefore causes great aggravation at the time, but very rapidly gets forgotten as consumers get used to the new levels of prices, which are anyway constantly adjusting for other reasons. Furthermore, as they are levied in incremental amounts expressed in pence, their incidence is very erratic. VAT receipts automatically rise in money terms when product prices rise, but excise duties do not and therefore can – and often do – fail to keep pace with inflation. Surprisingly, some products, such as whisky, are currently very cheap by historical standards once inflation is taken into account, partly as a result of a move to uniform taxation of alcohol content.

Alcohol and tobacco products bear VAT on the total cost after levying excise duties – that is the tax is taxed! In the case of cigarettes EC harmonisation proposals (see below) resulted in a specific tax of 3.2p per cigarette **and** a special *ad valorem* tax of 21 per cent of retail price. As a result roughly 75 per cent of the retail price of a packet of cigarettes consists of tax of one kind or another whereas it is only roughly one-third for a pint of beer.

In recent years increasing attention has been paid to the wider social costs associated with the misuse of alcohol, tobacco and vehicles by individuals, but there has been no clear attempt to force a reduction in consumption via the price mechanism. This may partly reflect the desire to maintain revenue, since sharp increases in prices may, at least temporarily, cause demand (and hence revenue) to fall disproportionately. Perhaps more importantly, excise duties feed straight through to the rate of inflation, control of which is the primary macroeconomic objective.

One recent innovation, in the 1988 Budget, was the introduction of a reduced rate of duty on unleaded petrol which causes less pollution than its leaded equivalent.

□ 5.6.8 Car Tax

New cars, motor cycles, scooters, mopeds and some motor caravans, whether made in the UK or imported, are also chargeable with car tax at 10 per cent on the wholesale value. VAT is charged on the price including car tax.

□ 5.6.9 Taxes on Wealth

For the most part, income has to be **earned**. By saving part of this income a pool of wealth can be accumulated. However, a very large proportion of the total pool of wealth currently results from capital gains (especially rising house values) and from inheritance, neither of which requires much effort to acquire. Thus, in principle, one would expect wealth to be taxed much more harshly than income on grounds of equity.

There are however, a number of practical difficulties. Much wealth is, for example, tied up in physical assets (houses, businesses, farms, etc.) and to pay a wealth tax in cash could require a part of these assets to be sold. This could be very damaging to efficiency (for example, farms could become progressively smaller). Equally, the incentive for an entrepreneur to build up a business would be much reduced were it to be necessary for the business to be sold off by his heirs in order to pay wealth taxes since it is reasonable to suppose that the entrepreneur is often driven by a desire to build up a business dynasty. Furthermore, it is inequitable and impractical to force widows to sell up their family homes upon the death of their husbands. As a result, wealth taxes have never accounted for more than a very small proportion of total tax revenue.

Inheritance Tax

It is possible to value assets on an annual basis and to tax their value on an ongoing basis. Annual wealth taxes are levied elsewhere in Europe, but have never been implemented in the UK. Instead, wealth is liable to tax only upon its **transfer from one individual to another,** whether in the form of a gift during the donor's lifetime, or upon the donor's death. This is administratively convenient since estates must anyway be valued for probate purposes when a person dies.

Inheritance taxes have been levied in the UK since 1894. Until 1974 they were known as Estate Duty (or death duty) and applied only to transfers at death. The Labour Government introduced Capital Transfer Tax (CTT) in 1974 in order to incorporate certain lifetime gifts. These were accumulated over time, with the tax rate being applied to each gift being determined by the cumulative total. However, transfers of property between husbands and wives both during life and at death, were tax-exempt, together with gifts and bequests to charity. Tax-exempt thresholds also applied to transfers upon death, and to gifts both to individuals and in total during any one year.

In practice, CTT proved to be scarcely more punitive than its predecessor because of the widespread exemptions and the low rates levied on lifetime gifts. When elected in 1979 the Conservatives nevertheless set about 'drawing the teeth' of CTT by raising thresholds, lowering rates and reducing aggregation periods during which lifetime gifts were accumulated (those made pre-1979 being exempt). In 1986 CTT was renamed Inheritance Tax. The period of accumulation was reduced from 10 to seven years and the rate of tax was lowered. Anyone making a 'potentially exempt transfer', and living for a further seven years, could subsequently expunge that transfer from their cumulative lifetime total of taxable gifts. If that person lived on for between four and

seven years, a proportion of the tax would become payable, ranging from 100 per cent for deaths occurring within three years of making a gift to 20 per cent in the seventh year.

Between 1979 and 1988 prices in general less than doubled. However, the tax threshold for inheritance tax (CTT) rose from £25,000 in 1979 to £110,000 in the Budget of 1988, representing a more than doubling in real terms. Furthermore, the multiple rate structure of previous years was abolished, and a single rate of 40 per cent introduced. The threshold and rate changes in 1988 had little effect upon modest estates, but reduced the tax bill on an estate of £1 mn by £145,000 (and by even more where legitimate tax shelters had been used). The additional 50 per cent tax relief for family businesses means that they cannot be taxed at a rate in excess of 20 per cent. The 1991–92 threshold stands at £140,000.

In 1965 annual wealth taxes and capital transfer taxes accounted for 1.6 per cent of the total tax revenue of OECD countries, with the UK well above that figure. In 1985 the OECD average was down to 0.7 per cent with the UK below average at 0.5 per cent. It is therefore fair to conclude that, whilst becoming wealthy is problematic (although becoming progressively easier as houses are inherited), staying wealthy is no problem at all.

Capital Gains Tax (CGT)

This tax is levied on the difference between the purchase and sale price of any asset. This price difference might occur entirely because of inflation, and capital gains tax has accordingly been index-linked since 1982 so that only **real gains** are currently taxed. Were there no CGT it would pay those with spare income to invest it almost entirely in assets with potential for capital gains rather than in those which accrue interest or other forms of unearned income.

It has to be said that this tends to occur anyway because a large variety of assets are exempt from CGT, including principal private residences (but not second houses), agricultural property, winnings from the football pools and other forms of gambling, motor cars, National Savings instruments and so forth. Furthermore, there is a threshold below which gains are tax-exempt, and a provision to set losses against gains before tax liability is assessed.

Before April 1988 the tax threshold stood at £6600, and the tax rate at 30 per cent. However, the tax was based on any assets acquired since 1965, and the high threshold existed partly to adjust for the fact that gains between 1965 and 1982 were not index-linked. In April 1988, the threshold was reduced to £5000, and raised again to £5500 from April 1991. Gains are currently taxed at the individual's highest income tax rate, either 25 or 40 per cent. However, any gains accruing prior to April 1982 are wholly tax-exempt.

The similar tax treatment of earned income and capital gains is at variance with the traditional view that earned income is morally superior to unearned income, and should accordingly be less-heavily taxed. However, the widespread exemptions allowed under CGT have made rather a mockery of this principle, and the government effectively wish it to be known that for tax purposes 'income' is henceforth simply income irrespective of source (it was never exactly clear whether a capital gain was wealth or unearned income although CGT has been listed here as a tax on wealth for convenience). This view is also consistent with the change made in 1987 for companies. Since 17 March 1987 companies' gains have been taxed at normal corporation tax rates (25 and 35 or 34 per cent) rather than 30 per cent. Gains of life assurance companies attributable to policy-holders remain taxable at 30 per cent, and the exemption of gains on business assets or on shares in family companies has been increased.

Stamp Duty

Transfers or sales of property (other than of stocks and shares) above a value of £30,000, are subject to stamp duty of 1 per cent on the entire purchase price. Transfers of stocks and shares are subject to stamp duty of 0.5 per cent, regardless of the amount. This will be abolished on 1 April 1992 as will stamp duty on transfer of property other than land and buildings.

□ 5.6.10 *Taxes on Expenditure*

Value Added Tax (VAT)

VAT is the most wide-ranging tax on expenditure, and has been in force since the UK joined the EEC in 1973. It is levied in one instalment directly by the retailer upon the customer. The standard rate of VAT was raised sharply to 15 per cent in 1979 as part of the switch by the first Thatcher Government from direct to indirect taxation (initially with predictably inflationary consequences). It was raised to 17½ per cent in April 1991 as a quid pro quo for the £140 per head reduction in the Community Charge. There is also a zero rate. These rates are not uniform throughout the EC, and this is therefore one of the areas where harmonisation has yet to be achieved. However, this represents a highly elusive goal in practice because of the enormous problems which would need to be overcome if it became necessary to switch some of the burden of taxation back on to income taxes.

VAT is collected at each stage in the production and distribution of goods and services by taxable persons (running a business with a turnover in excess of £35,000 per annum in fiscal year 1991/92). The burden of the tax is ultimately borne by the consumer as part of the final purchase price, but the tax is built up in stages. When a taxable person purchases taxable goods or services (say at £10), the supplier adds VAT to the supply price. This is called the taxable person's input tax (£1.75). When the taxable person subsequently adds value to the good or service, and sells it on to another taxable person, he adds VAT to the price charged (say at £20 which includes the input tax). This is known as the output tax (£3.50). Since the input tax has already been paid by the original supplier, it is necessary only for the taxable person to pay over to the Customs and Excise the difference between the output tax and the input tax, or in other words the tax on the **value which has been added to the good or service**. Since the final price in our example is £23.50 of which £3.50 is tax, the taxable person has added £10 to the supply price of £10 and paid a second instalment of £1.75 in tax.

There will normally be several such instalments before the final customer is reached, once account is taken of both wholesalers and retailers. VAT is further complicated by the fact that not all goods and services are taxable. This arises primarily because everyone pays 35p in tax on a taxable item costing £2.35 irrespective of income, so the tax bears down more severely on the low-paid than on the high-paid. In order to offset this there are two methods by which goods and services, especially those heavily consumed by the relatively poor, can be tax-relieved. The first method is where a taxable person does not charge any VAT to a customer and also reclaims any VAT paid to his supplier. In this case total VAT is zero. **Zero rating** applies, *inter alia*, to most food; reading matter; fuel other than for road use; construction of new buildings; exports; public transport fares; young children's clothing and footwear; prescription medicines; and caravans.

The second method is where a taxable person does not charge any output tax to a customer, but is not entitled to deduct or reclaim the input tax. In this case total VAT is not zero and the final good or service is said to be **VAT-exempt**. Exemption applies, *inter alia*, to land (including rents); insurance; postal services; betting; finance; education; health; and burial and cremation.

□ 5.6.11 *Taxing Savings*

In the UK savings have not generally been encouraged by the system. First income is taxed and then the savings set aside out of net-of-tax income are frequently taxed as well. This is not universally the case because, for example, pension contributions are deducted from gross income without incurring a tax liability, but it is sufficiently common to be a matter of considerable contention in tax-reforming circles.

It has often been argued that only **spending** should be taxed, which would provide an incentive to save more. However, most of the recent discussion has been concerned with tax **neutrality** – that is, the desire to treat all savings in the same way by taxing **all of them** either once or twice (see

Robinson, 1990). In the 1990 Budget the then Chancellor, John Major, moved several steps towards single taxation by extending tax exemptions on savings. This was in the form of TESSAs (Tax Exempt Special Savings Accounts) which could be added to the PEPs (Personal Equity Plans) introduced by Nigel Lawson. It is important to bear in mind, however, that Lawson was concerned primarily with the abolition of tax breaks for savers such as tax relief on insurance premiums, and that both PEPs and TESSAs were expected to divert savings out of one channel and into another, more tax efficient, one rather than to increase substantially the total level of saving.

Personal Equity Plans

PEPs were first announced in the 1986 Budget and brought into operation in January 1987 as a simple way to invest in shares, especially for small savers and first-time investors unfamiliar with the stock market. The amount which could be invested in any one year was originally £2400. In 1987, 270,000 PEPs were taken out and £480 mn invested. 1988 was a very poor year for PEPs, but in 1989, 300,000 PEPs were taken out and £750 mn invested. In the 1990 Budget the requirement that investors had to keep their investments in their PEPs for at least a complete calendar year to qualify for tax benefits was abolished; up to £6000 in total could be invested in any one year; up to £3000 of this total could be invested in investment and unit trusts; and new issue shares could be transferred into plans.

In the 1991 Budget investors were further permitted to place up to £9000 in two separate PEPs a year with returns free from both income and capital gains tax. As from 1 January 1992 the extra £3000 limit can be invested only in the shares of a single company.

Tax Exempt Special Savings Accounts

TESSAs were introduced in the 1990 Budget to become operational as from 1 January 1991. A taxpayer is permitted one TESSA which confers the right to receive interest on building society and bank deposits tax-free. A maximum of £9000 can be deposited over a five-year period, either in lump sums or in irregular amounts, up to £3000 in the first year and then up to £1000 a year for the subsequent years subject to the overall limit. If capital is withdrawn early all tax relief is lost, but interest earned can be withdrawn at any time at the net-of-tax rate. At the end of five years the TESSA is wound up, although a new TESSA can be started with up to £3000 transferred into it from the previous one.

Composite Rate Tax

CRT was a special low rate of tax charged on interest paid to individual savers by building societies, banks and certain other intermediaries. It could not be repaid to savers such as children and pensioners who were not liable to tax. Effectively, therefore, low income savers were subsidising those who would otherwise have paid tax at their full marginal rate. By 1990 some 14 mn individuals were caught out by CRT and it was abolished in the 1990 Budget to take effect from April 1991.

5.6.12 Hybrid Taxes: The Community Charge

The UK tax system has long been dependent upon taxes raised within the confines of a local authority rather than of the UK as a whole. These taxes were traditionally based upon property – whether domestic or commercial (but excluding farms). The calculation of tax liability required that each property be given an imputed rental value, called a **rateable value**, in accordance with a complex formula devised by the responsible local authority to take into account location, size, amenities, provision of public services and so on. The LA then levied a uniform rate per pound of rateable value, with a small rebate for domestic as against commercial property. A supplementary rate was then added to cover water, sewerage and environmental services.

The **rates**, as they were known, were a hybrid tax in the sense that whilst they were wholly divorced from a property occupier's income and

clearly therefore not an income tax, they were not based directly upon the market value of a property and hence not exactly a wealth tax either. Obviously, house prices varied considerably over time, thereby making it necessary to revalue periodically in order to preserve equity between different properties. The sheer cost of the exercise militated against intervals of less than 10 years, but this in turn meant that some people would find their rateable values sharply increased, to their immense annoyance, whilst those who had seen their bills reduced thought this no more than their just deserts. The political ill-will engendered by the revaluation of 1973, coming as it did at the end of a period of sharply rising house prices, discouraged a repeat of the exercise in both 1978 and 1983. The Scottish revaluation of 1985 was blamed for the severe loss of Conservative electoral support in the subsequent General Election.

The failure to alter rateable values did not, however, imply a failure to raise the yield from the rates. The ruling political party in a local authority could impose any rate poundage that it thought fit, although it would have to subject itself to periodic re-election. However, a number of local councils, especially in the larger towns and cities, had such large majorities that they could do virtually anything they liked and make their ratepayers, including local businesses (with no right to vote independent of the rights of their employees to vote as individual ratepayers if eligible), and also the government (which supplied over one-half of all local authority revenue via a **rate support grant**), foot the bill. The ability to charge high taxes, yet remain politically popular, reflected the high proportion of the total bill laid at the door of government and businesses (over 75 per cent by 1970 and higher still by 1980), and also the fact that domestic rates took no account of the number of individuals living in a property. Large, underoccupied, properties in expensive areas could be made to pay very high rates, whilst small, overoccupied, properties were frequently exempted from rates altogether because their main occupier was entitled to a rate rebate on account of his or her low income.

Not surprisingly, those who paid heavy rates wanted services to be cut and rates to be reduced, whilst those who paid little or no rates demanded more and more services regardless of expense. In the bigger towns the latter were often in a clear majority and elected a council committed to ever higher expenditure. When the Conservative Government was elected in 1979 on a platform of reductions in public spending, their attention was inevitably drawn to the alleged profligacy of the local authorities. Since the highest spending local councils were almost all Labour controlled the issue inevitably became political as well as economic. The power of such councils, democratically elected though they were, had, in the government's view, to be subjugated to the constitutionally superior power of the democratically elected central government.

But how was this to be achieved? For several years the government sought desperately for a foolproof method of keeping local authority spending in check. However, the fatal flaws in most schemes were either that the local authorities could raise the rate poundage to substitute for reductions in revenue supplied by central government, or that, if

prevented from so doing by **rate capping**, they could introduce increasingly innovative methods of raising finance such as sale and lease-back deals on local authority-owned assets and swaps. The government's position was that all local voters had to be made to pay personally for increases in spending if that was what they wanted and voted for. The chosen solution was (**a**) to take the **non-domestic (business) rate** away from the local authorities and transfer it to central government which then sets it nationally at a uniform level. The revenue is then distributed to local authorities as a *per capita* grant; and (**b**) to introduce a **Community Charge** (often referred to as the **poll tax** because it requires everyone above the minimum voting age of 18 to register with their local authority) to be paid by all voters either in full or in part (if eligible for a rebate) at a **flat-rate**. The changes were introduced in Scotland in April 1989 and in England and Wales in April 1990.

This solution was not without its drawbacks. It clearly implied a major redistribution of the bur-

Table 5.8 *Local Authority Income by Source, UK, % and £ mn*

	1961	1971	1981	1986	1988	1989	1989 (£ mn)
Current grants from central government							
Rate support grants and other non-specific grants	23.3	33.3	38.7	32.7	30.6	28.3	15 466
Specific grants	7.3	3.7	8.8	16.1	16.0	15.8	8 640
Total current grants from central government	30.6	37.0	47.5	48.8	46.6	44.1	24 106
Rates	30.8	27.0	31.9	34.1	37.0	36.2	19 790
Community charge						1.1	615
Rent	9.3	9.1	10.3	6.9	6.3	5.8	3 163
Interest, dividends and other current income	7.2	6.3	6.7	6.1	6.4	7.0	3 808
Capital grants from central government	1.7	2.3	1.0	1.8	1.8	4.3	2 322
Borrowing requirements	17.6	17.8	0.8	1.5	1.2	1.1	585
Other financial receipts	2.8	0.6	1.8	0.8	0.7	0.4	203
Total (= 100%) (£ mn)	2 702	7 725	31 969	44 690	50 369	54 592	54 592

Source: CSO.

den of taxation, both from the single-adult house-hold to the multiple-adult household, and from the well-off to those previously considered too poor to pay any rates at all. It was also going to be a problem to get all those who should be paying the Charge to register for that purpose, and to track them down if they refused to do so. This did not necessarily imply that spending on the rump of services left in the hands of local authorities would fall, because voters could opt for as many such services as they were willing to pay for, but the underlying assumption was that spending would indeed fall in order to keep the Charge as low as possible. However, it would still be the case that most spending by local authorities would be covered by central government grants and the apportioned non-domestic rate, as shown in **Table 5.8**.

As can be seen, the LAs raised only 27 per cent of their total spending via the rates (domestic + business) in 1971. From a low point of 24 per cent in 1975–76, the proportion rose to 37 per cent by 1989, but throughout the 1980s well over 40 per cent of their spending was financed by central government grants.

The way the poll tax system works is (**1**) for each local authority to be given a spending target according to its needs; (**2**) the central government sets a 'community charge for standard spending' or 'headline' charge (£278 per charge-payer in 1990–91); (**3**) non-domestic rate income is distributed (£293 per charge-payer in 1990–91); (**4**) the

difference between (1) and (2 + 3) is supplied as a grant. Although any LA can exceed its standard spending, the extra spending falls **entirely** on local charge-payers. This can raise the local tax sharply, but so can a miscalculation by civil servants of local needs.

As part of the 1991 Budget the government sought to reduce the political fall-out of the poll tax by reducing the headline Community Charge by £140 per charge-payer in Britain (down from £385 to £245), to be financed by a 2.5 per cent increase in VAT. Net of rebates and reliefs, the average charge was expected to be roughly £175. As a result, local authority revenues for 1991–92 are as forecast in **Table 5.9**.

It may be observed that this left only 11 per cent of LA spending to be raised locally, inducing many commentators to wonder why the central government did not simply scrap local taxes and be done with it. But on 23 April 1991 the Environment Secretary, Michael Heseltine came up instead with a new **Council Tax**, the main features of which, subject to revision, are as follows:

1   it will replace the poll tax in April 1993
2   it will reflect the capital value of a property occupied by two adults and give a 25 per cent discount to single people
3   properties will be assigned to eight bands based upon value
4   payment in the top band will be limited to 2 times that levied on an 'average-priced' house
5   there will be a single bill for each household
6   the poor will be protected by discounts
7   there will be no minimum contribution
8   second homes will receive a 50 per cent discount.

Given the potential for revision, and also for the election of a Labour Government which would scrap the tax, there is little point in discussing the merits of the proposal in this edition.

As indicated above, the poll tax has proved to be a costly blunder, both politically and economically. As early as April 1989 the government was obliged to produce a £500 mn package of adjustment to income-related social security benefits. To this must be added the £1.7 bn poll tax reduction package of January 1991, transitional

Table 5.9   *Local Authority Revenues, 1991–92[1]*

	£ bn	*% of Total*
Poll tax[2]	7.3	11.0
Business rates	14.1	21.2
Current and capital grants from central government	38.3	57.4
Other sources	6.9	10.4
Total	**66.5**	**100.0**

Notes:
[1]   Forecast.
[2]   Net of all rebates and reliefs financed by central government.
Source: FSBR 1991–92.

reliefs, extra collection costs and at least £1 bn of extra non-payment each year. If the shift to higher VAT is added on, the extra annual cost compared to the rates for the final two years of the Community Charge will amount to roughly £7 bn.

In the end, the poll tax had to go because at realistic levels in relation to local authority spending it would impose a crippling burden on millions of households, whereas at realistic levels in relation to household incomes it would contribute an unacceptably small proportion of local authority finance.

5.6.13 The EC and Tax Harmonisation

The UK is obliged, as a member of the EC, to contribute tax revenue to cover EC expenditure in the areas of agriculture, social policy and regional policy. The EC Budget is financed by its 'own resources', comprising the proceeds of the common external tariff (*less* 10 per cent to cover national collection costs); the proceeds of agricultural import duties and levies (*less* 10 per cent); a share in national VAT proceeds and a share of GNP (see **pp. 230–3**). EC members have compiled a collection of goods and services known as the *common assessment base*. The UK calculates the total value of sales of the base every year, applies VAT, and remits the EC's share to Brussels. This share is currently 1.4 per cent. In practice, the UK has always argued that its contribution is excessive compared with that made by other EC members, and has had part of it returned each year (see **p. 233**). It is also obviously the case that some of the money is returned in the form of EC expenditure in the areas set out above.

Under the terms of the Single European Act 1985 (see **pp. 224–7**) there is supposed to be *fiscal harmonisation* in the EC. Initially, progress towards this objective achieved very little since, whilst VAT is levied in every country, each member state wished to impose its own preferred rates upon the others. The only progress of any note arose in that, since taxes within the EC are not supposed to favour domestic as against imported goods, the European Court of Justice felt obliged periodically to implement this principle in a piecemeal way by, for example, obliging the UK to reduce excise duties on wine (largely imported) relative to beer (largely domestic).

However, the debate about tax harmonisation has become considerably more heated now that 1992 is approaching. The original blueprint was proposed by the then European Commissioner, Lord Cockfield, on behalf of the EC in late 1987. In the Single European Act 1985 the internal market is defined as 'an area without internal frontiers'. What the Cockfield plan proposed was that all border controls within the EC should be abolished by 1992, and it concluded that this could not be achieved without first harmonising rates of VAT and excise duties within the EC. It thus proposed that the wide array of VAT rates (the 'standard' rate alone currently ranging from 12 per cent in Spain and 22 per cent in Denmark), should be grouped into two 'bands', comprising a **standard rate band** at 14–20 per cent, and a **reduced rate band** at 4–9 per cent covering goods which member states wished to keep cheap for social reasons.

The Cockfield plan also recommended a single EC-wide excise duty for alcohol, petrol and tobacco. This arose because VAT is levied on the price of goods **inclusive of** excise duty, and were excise duties to vary the proposed VAT bands would be distorted. This is an important consideration because, like VAT, excise duties currently vary enormously within the EC, being very low in the south – where, for example, most wine is produced – and high in the north for health and environmental reasons.

It is hardly surprising that the Cockfield proposals were contentious. On the one hand, if existing VAT rates are retained, but frontier controls are abolished, the citizens of high-VAT-rate countries will pour across their frontiers with countries where VAT rates are lower in order to shop there, which is unacceptable to the former countries. On the other hand, harmonising tax rates will force prices up in those countries where rates are below the designated minima whilst causing tax revenue to fall in those countries where rates are above the designated maxima.

The need for either group of countries to suffer an unacceptable adjustment can be avoided by setting maxima and minima close to existing levels, but this would be insufficient to forestall the cross-border flows. Once frontier controls are abolished, and duty-free allowances with them, such flows will force rates into closer convergence. The UK government's position has always been that competition should be used to force tax rates down towards the lowest rate available. This implies that there should be no maxima or minima. Indeed, competition requires a free market in rates in order to ensure that convergence is downwards rather than upwards.

Unfortunately, this view is not shared by other EC members, all of whom favour a minimum rate in order to protect their tax revenue (and hence their ability to spend). Reflecting this majority view, the European Commission came up with a proposal to set a legally binding 15 per cent minimum standard rate of VAT together with a number of special lower rates where their abolition would be politically damaging. Ironically, given that the UK would be less affected by these rates than almost any other country, the UK used its veto on tax matters (which require unanimity) to stop the proposal. Its position on market convergence could not be faulted on economic grounds, but its previous adherence to the doctrine of fiscal sovereignty was looking slightly shaky given that the UK had accepted the principle of a minimum for excise duties on alcohol and tobacco. Clearly, an (unspoken) consideration was that a minimum rate of VAT would make it impossible to rebalance the tax system from indirect to direct tax on a future occasion should it be politically expedient.

In June 1991 the Council of Ministers declared that they would all apply a minimum standard rate of VAT of 15 per cent from 1 January 1993. This was a political agreement only, because the UK would not have it otherwise. The Council also agreed that there should be one or two optional reduced VAT rates of not less than 5 per cent to be applied to an as yet to be agreed list of goods and services. For member states with existing VAT rates below the reduced rate minimum, a super-reduced rate may be retained during a transitional period which is expected to last until 1 January 1997, from which date VAT is to be levied in the country of origin with goods despatched on a tax-paid basis.

However, the wrangling over excise duties is by no means resolved. The UK prefers to have high domestic rates for health and environmental reasons, but is less supportive of high minimum rates elsewhere since these will affect exports of, for example, Scotch whisky. Elsewhere in the EC there is controversy over excise duties on wine. If differential duties are to be permitted then cross-border tax evasion will need to be monitored very carefully, but there are considerable doubts about the competence of southern countries in this respect.

Attempts to harmonise VAT are only a relatively modest step along the path towards tax harmonisation because, by virtue of the fact that VAT is payable only in the country of sale, there can be no biasing effect on the location of firms. This is not, however, the case if one considers taxes on unearned income. At the present time the London Stock Market is much larger than all other EC stock markets added together, but there are drawbacks for foreign residents and institutions wishing to invest in UK companies in London. There is, for example, the widespread inability to set payments of advance corporation tax against dividends received, in the manner described above, which applies to UK residents. In certain cases part of ACT is currently refunded, but even so the unrefunded part may prove sufficient of a deterrent to would-be investors. In the absence of tax harmonisation the Chancellor is unlikely to make any concessions which would result in a reduction in total tax revenue, so there is at least a possibility that other financial centres may ultimately grow at London's expense.

It must also be recognised that differing corporation tax schedules do affect location, although it is doubtful whether tax considerations often play a dominant role in commercial decisions. The European Commission originally proposed that there should be a uniform EC rate of between 45 and 55 per cent, but the rate in the UK is currently only 33 per cent and rates elsewhere are likely to fall rather than rise, so this will need to be amended. The issue of harmonisation is, as usual, bedevilled by the fact that firms in countries with special concessions are most reluctant to give them up in the cause of greater European harmony (see Kay and

King, 1990, p. 218). As for harmonisation of income tax, that is too far off even to worry about.

■ 5.7 The Budget

□ 5.7.1 Budgetary Changes

The Budget is an annual event, in either March or April, which exists both to set out the government's proposals for changes in taxation and to provide an occasion for the annual review of economic policy. The proposals are announced to the House of Commons by the Chancellor of the Exchequer in the Budget Statement, and are published in the *Financial Statement and Budget Report* (FSBR).

The Budget statement is followed by the moving of a set of Ways and Means resolutions embodying the Budget proposals, and these form the foundations of the **Finance Bill** which goes forward for debate in Parliament. The Ways and Means resolutions exist so that taxes can be levied at the new levels set out in the Finance Bill pending its enactment. The Finance Bill, subject to any amendments volunteered by, or forced upon, the Chancellor during debate, is then passed as the **Finance Act,** usually in July.

Tax proposals are concerned primarily with changes in the rate or coverage of taxes, the introduction of new taxes and the abolition of existing ones, or changes in methods of administration. Most taxes are permanent, but in the case of income tax and corporation tax the Finance Act is needed every year to keep them in existence, which ties the Budget to the beginning of the fiscal year in April. It is, however, perfectly proper either to have a mini-Budget at any other time of year,

Figure 5.9 *Sources of Revenue, 1991–92*[1]

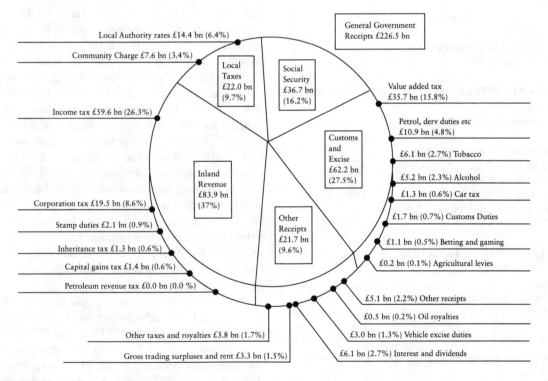

Note:
[1] Forecast in Autumn Statement 1991.
Source: FSBR 1991–92, Table 1.2.

which necessitates amendments to the Finance Act, or simply to operate the Regulator which permits VAT to be varied by up to 25 per cent, and the main excise duties by up to 10 per cent between Budgets.

Budgetary changes are made both with a view to their effects upon **tax revenue** and also to their effects upon the **performance of the economy**. These are detailed in the FSBR which contains a review of recent developments in the economy; an economic forecast updating that contained in the Autumn Statement; and an overview of the MTFS.

Figure 5.9 represents the breakdown of total government revenue forecast for 1991–92. As can

Table 5.10 *Direct Effects of Budget Measures 1991, £000*

INLAND REVENUE (17 changes) of which[1]	−1 870
Increase in personal allowance of £290	−1 420
Increase in basic rate limit of £3 000	−470
Reduction in corporation tax main rate to 34%	−380
CUSTOMS AND EXCISE (17 changes) of which[1]	+6 125
Increase in VAT standard rate to 17.5%	+3 900
Increase in tobacco taxes by 15%	+735
Increase in leaded petrol duty by 15%	+665
Increase in unleaded petrol duty by 15%	+470
TOTAL CENTRAL TAXATION + NICs (37 changes)	+4 175
less	
Reduction in Community Charge by £140	−4 345
TOTAL RECEIPTS	−170

Note:
[1] Separate listing where effect is at least ± £300 mn.
Source: FSBR 1991–92, Table 4.1.

be seen, 37 per cent of all revenue comes under the control of the Inland Revenue, whilst a further 27.5 per cent is handled by Customs and Excise. It is not generally appreciated how dependent tax revenue is upon a narrow range of taxes. NICs account for slightly more than VAT, which is itself exceeded only by income tax. Not so long ago, in 1985, duty on petrol/derv plus petroleum revenue tax (PRT) were the next most important, followed by corporation tax, but the effects of the fall in the price of oil and of fiscal drag (both discussed below) have resulted in corporation tax currently yielding almost twice as much as the other two combined. No other taxes individually account for as much as 5 per cent of total revenue.

The Budget contains an array of changes to the tax system. It is clear, however, from the above discussion, that very few of these have other than marginal effects upon total revenue, whilst changes in income tax of an apparently modest kind (for example, a 1p reduction in the marginal rate) have quite dramatic effects (altering revenue by more than £1 bn). This is shown in **Table 5.10**.

The purpose of raising revenue is primarily to fund expenditure, so it is a little curious that the Budget was traditionally divorced from the two main discussions of public expenditure set out in the Autumn Statement and the Public Expenditure White Paper. The Treasury do not like making statements about revenue in the Autumn because tax receipts can alter sharply between November and April (perhaps due to fiscal drag). On the other hand, public expenditure needs to be planned well in advance and does not have to be financed solely through tax receipts. The drawback to the separation in time is that any increases in expenditure made in the Autumn have been largely forgotten by April, so any buoyancy in tax receipts immediately leads to demands for yet further spending.

Since 1980 it has been possible to see how revenue and expenditure are linked by recourse to the discussion of the MTFS in the FSBR, since this necessarily examines both the aggregates and the difference between them. However, it is this difference, the PSBR which tends to form the focus for discussion rather than the aggregates themselves.

5.7.2 *What is a 'Budget for Business'?*

The 1991 Budget was 'sold' to the electorate as a 'Budget for business'. Was this because the business sector was a major beneficiary of the fiscal changes made in the Budget? Not exactly. There were indeed gains such as a reduction of 1 per cent in corporation tax for 1990–91 and a further 1 per cent for 1991–92; a higher VAT registration threshold; and VAT relief on bad debts. But there were also losses such as NICs paid by employers on company cars; higher VAT payments by companies providing services that are VAT exempt which cannot reclaim VAT on inputs; and companies which have to absorb higher rates of VAT out of profits because the weakness of demand does not make it possible to pass VAT on. Overall, the business sector may therefore end up paying more tax than previously, which is an odd way to structure a Budget for business.

5.8 The Public Sector Borrowing Requirement and Public Sector Debt Repayment

The public sector consists of central government, local government and the public corporations. The global figure for the PSBR does not, therefore, show flows between the three sectors, normally from central government to the other two and on

Table 5.11 *Borrowing Requirements of Central Government (CGBR) and Public Sector (PSBR)* [1], *£ bn, cash*

	1989–90	*1990–91*	*1991–92*	*1992–93*	*1993–94*	*1994–95*
General government expenditure	199.4	216	235	252	266	279
General government receipts	206.0	217	226	240	260	281
Fiscal adjustment from previous years	–	–	–	–	0	1
Annual fiscal adjustment [3]	–	–	–	0	1	1
CGBR [2]	–6.6	–1	8	12	7	0
Public corporations' market and overseas debt repayment	–1.4	0	0	0	0	0
PSBR [2]	–7.9	–1 [5]	8 [6]	12	7	0
Money GDP at market prices [4]	509.9	547	580	624	668	710
PSBR [2] as % of GDP	–1½	–¼	1¼	2	1	0

Notes:
[1] Rounded to the nearest £1 bn from 1990–91 onwards.
[2] Negative figures denote a debt repayment (CGDR and PSDR).
[3] Means lower taxes or higher expenditure than assumed in lines 1 and 2.
[4] Figure for 1989–90 adjusted for the distortion caused by the abolition of domestic rates.
[5] In April 1991 this was adjusted to a PSBR of £0.4 bn.
[6] In the Autumn Statement (November 1991) this was adjusted to a PSBR of £10.5 bn and the PSBR as % of GDP to 1¾. Figures for subsequent years are also likely to be exceeded in practice.
Source: FSBR 1991–92.

Figure 5.10   *PSBR as a % of GDP*

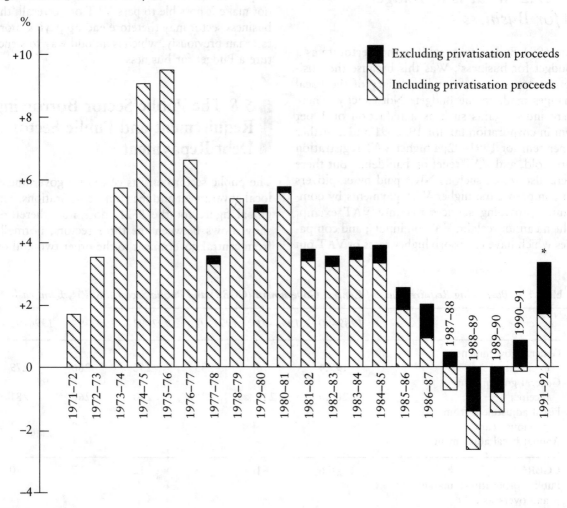

Note:
* Forecast.
Source: FSBR 1988–89, 1989–90 and 1991–92.

a very large scale, but does include public corporations' borrowing from the money markets and overseas. The figures for the past two years, and projections for the next four are to be found in Table 5.11. These are in cash terms, and the PSBR is also expressed as a percentage of GDP.

The longer-term trend of the PSBR can be seen in **Figure 5.10**, again expressed as a percentage of GDP. During the oil crisis in the mid-1970s the percentage came close to reaching double figures and, despite some subsequent improvement, rose back to 5 per cent when the present government was elected.

It is important to note at this point the accounting convention used for privatisation proceeds. As shown earlier, in **Table 4.1**, these are recorded as **negative spending**. The government argues that, since the purchase price appears as public expenditure when assets are taken into public ownership, it is only logical to treat any monies arising when they are sold back to the private sector as negative spending. A more cynical view might be that the purpose of this exercise is to reduce the declared amount of public spending in order to reduce the difference between that total and total tax revenue – the PSBR. Certainly, it is undeniable that the government actually does spend the amount indicated before privatisation proceeds are subtracted, and it therefore seems to be more sensible to treat the PSBR as the excess of gross public expenditure over total tax revenue, and to treat privatisation proceeds as a means of **financing the shortfall**. Were this alternative convention to be adopted then the PSBR data in **Figure 5.10** obviously look markedly worse.

During the major part of the present government's period in office the PSBR remained stubbornly higher than forecast, for reasons familiar from our previous discussion. In five of the seven years after 1981–82 public expenditure exceeded its forecast value, and bettered the forecast only in 1983–84. Four of the five overshoots were serious, exceeding £4 bn. On the other hand, tax revenue exceeded its forecast value on four occasions, falling short only in 1986–87 because of a sharp drop in North Sea taxes. However, these overshoots were generally more modest than those for spending, and the PSBR consequently did no better than

hit its target value for the six consecutive years beginning in 1981–82.

5.8.1 Public Sector Debt Repayment

The dramatic turnaround came in 1987–88 when tax revenue overshot the forecast by an astonishing £7.5 bn, with the result that, despite a serious £4 bn overshoot in spending, the PSBR became negative for the first time since 1971. It became the custom to refer to the PSDR – public sector **debt repayment**. Strictly speaking, a PSDR did not arise **excluding** privatisation proceeds until 1988–89. The then Chancellor, Nigel Lawson, never did, however, advocate the desirability of a PSDR as such. Indeed, he formally advocated the desirability of a **balanced budget** only in the FSBR of 1988, and did so then only on the grounds that 'it provides a clear and simple rule, with a good historical pedigree'.

Table 5.12 *General Government Lending (+) or Borrowing (–) as a % of GDP, 1974–92*

	1974–82	1983	1984	1985	1986	1987	1988	1989	1990	1991[3]	1992[3]
B	–7.2	–11.3	–9.0	–8.5	–9.1	–7.0	–6.6	–6.7	–6.0	–6.4	–6.1
DK	–2.3	–7.2	–4.1	–2.0	3.4	2.4	0.5	–0.5	–1.5	–1.3	–1.1
D[2]	–3.1	–2.5	–1.9	–0.9	–1.3	–1.9	–2.1	0.2	–2.2	–4.7	–3.9
GR	–	–8.3	–10.0	–13.8	–12.6	–12.4	–15.5	–19.2	–18.9	–15.4	–10.7
E	–1.8	–4.7	–5.4	–6.9	–6.0	–3.2	–3.3	–2.7	–3.7	–2.7	–2.0
F	–1.2	–3.1	–2.8	–2.9	–2.7	–1.9	–1.8	–1.2	–1.6	–1.6	–1.5
IRL	–10.9	–11.8	–9.8	–11.2	–11.2	–9.1	–5.2	–3.5	–3.4	–3.8	–3.5
I	–8.9	–10.6	–11.6	–12.5	–11.7	–11.1	–10.9	–10.1	–10.6	–10.0	–10.0
L	1.4	2.0	3.3	5.3	3.3	1.2	2.1	3.3	4.2	1.7	1.6
NL	–3.4	–6.4	–6.3	–4.8	–6.0	–6.6	–5.2	–5.0	–5.7	–4.8	–4.9
P	–	–9.0	–12.0	–10.1	–7.2	–6.8	–5.4	–3.4	–5.8	–5.5	–5.0
UK	–3.6	–3.3	–3.9	–2.8	–2.4	–1.3	1.1	1.0	–0.5	–2.2	–3.1
EUR[1]	–3.9[1]	–5.3	–5.3	–5.2	–4.8	–4.2	–3.7	–2.9	–4.1	–4.6	–4.4
USA	–1.7	–4.9	–2.8	–3.3	–3.5	–2.4	–2.0	–1.7	–2.4	–1.8	–2.4
JAP	–3.6	–3.7	–2.1	–0.8	–1.0	0.7	2.1	1.8	2.2	1.7	2.0

Notes:
[1] EUR without Greece and Portugal up to 1983.
[2] Including current transfers to East Germany and the deficit of East German territorial authorities.
[3] Forecasts based upon individual countries' national accounts.
Source: European Economy, Supplement A (May 1991).

Figure 5.11   *Gross Public Dept as a % of GDP*

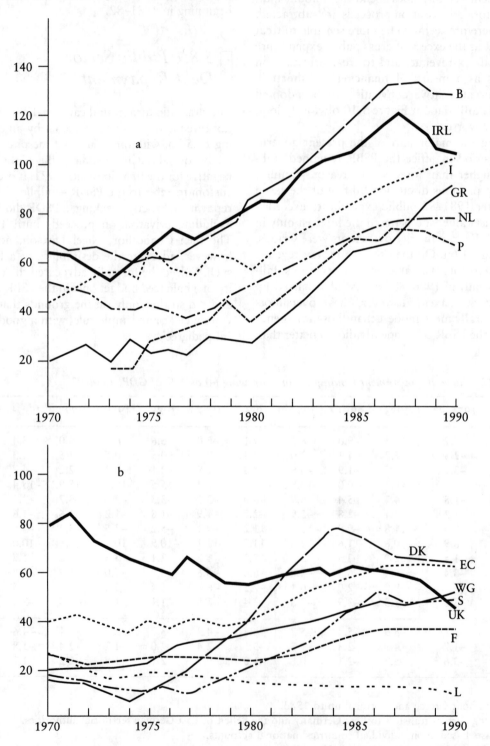

Source: European Commission.

In the event, his avowed strategy could not cope with the buoyancy of tax revenue, and on either definition there was a PSDR In 1988–89 and 1989–90 – quite substantial ones if privatisation proceeds are included. As the economy sank into recession during 1990, the original forecast of a further substantial PSDR gradually gave way to less optimistic views about the eventual outturn. Currently, this stands at a PSDR of £0.5 bn including privatisation proceeds, (or a £4.8 bn PSBR if excluded) but this may be revised downwards yet again. On either definition 1991–92 is going to show a PSBR, currently projected at £10.5 bn including privatisation proceeds and £18.5 bn if excluded. 1992–93 will unquestionably be worse.

There can be no doubt that the turnaround from massive and apparently uncontrollable PSBRs in the 1970s to PSDRs in the late 1980s was an extraordinary achievement. Indeed, in achieving a PSDR the UK could be compared only with Japan among the major industrialised nations as shown in **Table 5.12**. As can be seen, the ongoing fiscal situation in Italy and Greece is ultimately untenable, and that of Ireland and Belgium a cause for concern, so the EC as a whole is clearly no paragon of fiscal virtue.

■ *5.9* The National Debt

As noted previously, the first claim on tax revenue is interest on the national debt. Were there to be no such debt, public spending on real goods and services could be increased by £17 bn without any need to raise further taxes. Whilst this may appear to be a pipedream, there was much discussion of

Figure 5.12 *General Government Debt Interest Payments*

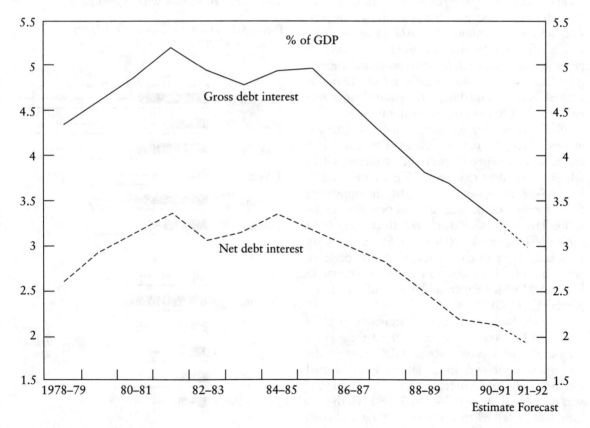

Source: Autumn Statement 1990.

such an outcome as a result of the succession of debt repayments at the end of the 1980s.

The ability to repay debt exists provided there is an excess of taxation over expenditure adjusted for privatisation proceeds. This, as we have seen, occurred during the financial years 1987–88 to 1990–91 inclusive, and although the government was not obliged to use the surplus to repay the debt, it chose to do so, thereby wiping out well over £20 bn of debt in 1988–89 and 1989–90 alone. At the beginning of the financial year 1991–92 the outstanding **net** debt was accordingly worth a 'mere' £150 bn. It is also possible to treat total debt in its **gross** form, in which case the equivalent figure was £190 bn. The transformation from gross to net debt requires the deduction of liquid assets held by the public sector, of which well over one-half is currently in the form of gold and foreign exchange reserves.

It has been claimed that the national debt is in reality nearly twice as large as is officially admitted. This arises because certain public sector pension schemes are notionally rather than actually funded. The government borrows the excess of pension contributions over expenditure and dummy gilts are created (but not actually issued). This, it is alleged, is the national accounts equivalent of off-balance sheet borrowing by corporations.

With this proviso in mind, we will continue the analysis using the official figures. The gross debt currently represents 35 per cent of money GDP, whilst the net debt represents 28 per cent of GDP. In 1985–86, prior to the first PSDR, the equivalent figures were 54.5 per cent and 46 per cent, so the ratios have both fallen by almost 20 per cent from their mid-1980s peaks (see Bank of England, 1990). It is fascinating to compare the UK's experience with that of comparable countries, as shown in **Figure 5.11** which illustrates **gross** public debt as a percentage of GDP.

Over the twenty-year period beginning in 1970 only two EC countries have reduced their gross public debt as a percentage of GDP, namely the UK and Luxembourg. In the latter case, it started out relatively low whereas the ratio for the UK was the highest in the EC in 1970. By 1990 the UK ratio had halved whereas the EC average had risen by 50 per cent and even that for Germany had

more than doubled. The increases for Belgium, Italy and Greece show what happens when fiscal policy is excessively loose.

The precise implications of changes in the absolute size of the debt for **debt interest payments** is complicated by such matters as interest rate volatility and the effects of inflation on index-linked debt. The situation for the UK over the past decade, again expressed as a percentage of GDP, is shown in **Figure 5.12**.

Here again, it is salutory to make international comparisons, as in **Figure 5.13**. As can be seen, Britain had the highest ratio of the countries covered in 1970 but one of the lowest in 1989. Obviously, a wealthy country can afford to service its debt, but as in the case of Belgium and Italy to use up around 10 per cent of GDP in the process should be worrying these countries' citizens very badly. Nothing short of a sequence of big PSDRs can stop the rot whereas Britain can afford to run a sequence of PSBRs with equanimity.

Figure 5.13 *General Government Interest Payments as a % of GDP/GNP*

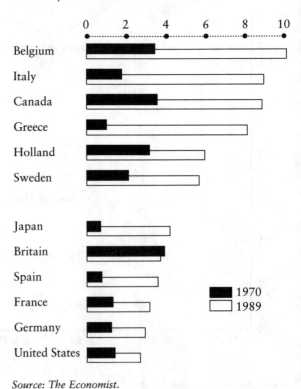

Source: The Economist.

References

Bank of England (1990) 'The Net Debt of the Public Sector: End-March 1990', *Bank of England Quarterly Bulletin* (November).

Cmnd 1432 (1961) *Control of Public Spending* (London: HMSO).

Cmnd 9714 (1986) *Paying for Local Government* (London: HMSO).

Cm 441 (1988) *A New Public Expenditure Planning Total* (London: HMSO).

Cm 1520 (1991) *Public Expenditure Analyses to 1993–94. Statistical Supplement to the 1990 Autumn Statement* (London: HMSO).

CSO (1990) 'International Comparison of Taxes and Social Security Contributions in 20 OECD Countries 1978–1988', *Economic Trends* (November 1990).

House of Commons (1991) *Financial Statement and Budget Report 1991–92* (London: HMSO).

Jackson, P. (1990) 'Reflections on the Growth of Public Expenditure', *British Review of Economic Issues* (June).

Kay, J. and M. King (1990) *The British Tax System* (Oxford: OUP) 5th edn.

Levitt, M. and M. Joyce (1987) *The Growth and Efficiency of Public Spending* (London: NIESR).

Local Government Act 1988.

Local Government Finance Act 1988.

Local Government and Housing Act 1989.

OECD (1991) 'The Public Sector: Issues for the 1990s', *OECD Working Paper No. 90* (Paris: OECD).

Robinson, W. (1990) 'How Should Savings Be Taxed?', *National Westminster Bank Quarterly Review* (November).

■ Chapter 6 ■

External Transactions

Peter Curwen

■ 6.1 Introduction

There are enormous differences in the extent to which individual nations are dependent upon transactions with the outside world. The UK has always been an 'open' economy, both importing and exporting on a massive scale. Superficially this may simply be seen to reflect the difficulties which any nation the size of the UK must inevitably face in trying to be self-sufficient across the whole range of goods and services, but it is important to note both that the UK's degree of openness has been increasing steadily over the past several decades (as has also been true elsewhere in the EC), and that external transactions increasingly involve one-way flows of capital which are unrelated to the immediate consumption requirements of UK residents.

In recent years the value of both imports and exports has grown to exceed 30 per cent of the UK's GDP, and it is obvious that these trade flows impact significantly upon the UK's industrial structure, the level of employment, the standard of living of UK nationals and so on. In other words, the **internal and external sectors are inextricably**

linked, and it is impossible to control internal macroeconomic objectives such as the level of employment and the rate of inflation without taking into account their links with the external sector. Indeed, as we shall see, much of the postwar history of UK macroeconomic policy can be viewed in terms of a struggle to find **acceptable trade-offs between the internal and external objectives of policy.**

Economic policy is frequently focussed upon the **balance of payments,** and our first task is, therefore, to set out the accounting system used to measure it, and to explain how policy objectives are expressed in relation to these accounts. The other central task is to examine the primary instrument used to achieve this objective, namely the **exchange rate.** However, as we will discover, these apparently straightforward tasks are in practice greatly complicated by the need to take account of other related policy objectives and instruments; of the behaviour of other countries insofar as it impinges upon the UK; of international institutions; and of the whole plethora of arrangements which govern the conduct of the world economy.

6.2 The System of Balance of Payments Accounts

□ 6.2.1 Recording Transactions

The Balance of Payments (BoP) may be defined as a **systematic record over a given period of time, of all transactions between residents and non-residents of the UK**. The term 'resident' covers both individuals living permanently in the UK, and corporate bodies located therein, but not their overseas branches and subsidiaries. It also includes government agencies and military forces located abroad. 'Permanent' residence is determined by the intention to remain in the UK for at least one full year.

The object of the accounting system is to record these transactions in a way which is suitable for analysing the economic relations between the UK economy and the rest of the world. The transactions may represent **resources** provided by or to UK residents (imports and exports of goods and services, and the use of investments); **changes** in the UK's **foreign assets or liabilities**; or **transfer payments.**

In principle, transactions are recorded when the ownership of goods or assets changes and when services are rendered. In practice, however, trade flows are recorded on a **shipments basis**, and the payments which match these shipments are not only almost invariably delayed, but the length of this delay is quite erratic from one period to another. In the longer term all the shipments and monetary flows can be matched up, but the short-term picture is almost inevitably quite heavily distorted. This is important because, first, both foreign exchange markets – and indeed sometimes the government – respond in a volatile way to monthly or quarterly BoP statistics and, secondly, because the annual accounts are constantly being adjusted retrospectively to a degree that can turn surpluses into deficits, or vice versa. In other words, the short-term picture can conflict with the longer-term perspective, yet by the time the latter is visible it is too late to take appropriate action.

A further element of ambiguity is introduced by the need to **convert currencies**. The general rule in international trade is that the exporter dictates the form in which payment is made – which, in the case of a developed nation like the UK, is mostly in its own currency. A much smaller proportion of UK imports will also be paid for in sterling. All non-sterling payments must then be converted into sterling at the ruling exchange rates, but these may fluctuate enormously during the course of a financial year, with the result that the valuation of imports and exports can be influenced by the **precise timing of currency conversion.**

□ 6.2.2 Double-entry Accounting

The BoP accounts are, like any accounting system, constructed according to the **double-entry principle**. Every transaction involves equal credit and debit entries but, instead of arranging these in separate columns, all BoP entries are arranged in a single column, and given different signs so that they sum to zero. It is therefore the case that the BoP accounts **must balance by definition**. (This should not be confused with the concept of **equilibrium**, which is discussed below.) This method accommodates account items which are generally recorded only on a *net* basis.

Under the conventions of the accounts all credit items are entered with a **plus (+) sign**. The credit relates to the **flow of currency** and not to the flow of resources. If resources are provided in the form of exports of goods or services, then the payment in currency thus **flows into the UK** and is recorded with a plus sign in the accounts. Where resources are provided to UK residents – for example, as imports of goods or services – payment **flows out of the UK** and is recorded with a **minus (–) sign** in the accounts.

Every positive entry must, as indicated, have its matching negative entry, but this may appear in a variety of forms. For example, an export of goods may be matched by either (**a**) an increase in the foreign assets owned by UK residents (where the export receipts are, for example, deposited in a bank outside the UK); (**b**) a reduction in non-residents' holdings of sterling in the UK (which are transferred to the exporter's bank account); or (**c**) a direct exchange for imports of equal value (bar-ter trade). It is undoubtedly rather confusing, at first, to regard an **increase in foreign assets** as a **negative** item in the accounts, but it makes sense in terms of identifying **where the currency goes**. The above example works exactly in reverse where one starts with a negative entry for an import of goods.

To make things somewhat easier to follow, the BoP accounts are currently divided into two halves. This division is relatively recent, and whilst the accounts have been recalculated in this format going back as far as is necessary for the purpose of this book, it should be recognised that variants of the accounts published before 1987 are in the original format which is difficult to match up with the new and should, therefore, no longer be used. The upper half of the accounts is called the **current account**. In this are to be found transactions covering exports and imports of goods and services, investment income, and transfers. The lower half of the accounts is called **transactions in UK external assets and liabilities**. In this are to be found inward and outward investment; external transactions by banks in the UK; borrowing and lending overseas by other UK residents; drawings on and additions to the official reserves; and other capital transactions. For simplicity this will be referred to as the **capital account**.

Where there is a positive entry in the current account – arising, for example from the export of goods – the corresponding negative entry is, as indicated above, normally to be found in the capital account as in (**a**) or (**b**) above. However, it must also be noted that corresponding plus and minus entries may both appear in the capital account, as would be the case if a UK resident borrowed from a bank in France in order to buy shares in a French company.

It is also necessary to remind ourselves about the difficulties of estimation with respect to items in the BoP accounts because, as previously noted, the accounts must balance as a matter of definition (for every plus a corresponding minus). The two entries made in respect of each transaction are generally derived from separate sources, and the methods of estimation are neither complete nor precisely accurate. Hence the two entries either may not match precisely, and/or may fall within different recording periods. It is also possible

that two entries, both in the same foreign currency, have been converted at different exchange rates. Hence, when all the entries in the accounts are added together, they never actually do sum to zero, and in order to make them do so the **balancing item** has to be added at the foot of the accounts.

6.3 The Structure of the Accounts

☐ 6.3.1 *The Current Account*

The full set of accounts is set out for the period of 1983 to 1988 in **Figure 6.1**. The first part of the accounts covers exports and imports of goods, and the **net** figure is called the visible balance. It is more commonly referred to as the **balance of trade**. Note that both exports and imports are entered as positive amounts, but the net figure is plus or minus as appropriate. The next entry relates to credits and debits generated by trade in services, which are again entered as positive amounts with the net figure, called the **invisibles balance**, signed as appropriate. This net balance is then broken down into its three component parts – services (primarily sea transport, civil aviation, tourism and financial); interest, profits and dividends; and transfers (primarily central government grants to overseas countries and contributions to the EC Budget and to international organisations, and private transfers of assets by migrants). It should be noted that only the services part of the invisibles balance arises from trading, whilst the larger part arises as a result of movements of money.

The sum of the visible and invisibles balance, signed as appropriate, is called the **current balance**. Adjustments to the current balance usually occur as a result of changes in national income both at home and abroad; the proportion of it which is spent; and the proportion of that spending which goes on domestic as against overseas goods and services. A sharp deterioration in the current balance is usually taken to indicate an upturn in consumption (either private or public) which has spilled over into imports, but an alter-

Figure 6.1 *UK Balance of Payments Accounts, 1985–90*

	1985	1986	1987	1988	1989	1990
CURRENT ACCOUNT	£m	£m	£m	£m	£m	£m
Visible trade						
Exports (fob)	77 991	72 627	79 153	80 346	92 389	102 038
Imports (fob)	81 336	82 186	90 735	101 970	116 987	120 713
Visible balance	–3 345	–9 559	–11 582	–21 624	–24 598	–18 675
Invisibles						
Credits	80 022	77 273	79 896	88 041	108 465	117 350
Debits	73 799	67 507	72 473	81 937	104 271	113 055
Invisible balance	6 222	9 747	7 423	6 103	4 195	4 295
of which:						
Services balance	6 687	6 808	6 745	4 574	4 685	5 201
Interest, profits and dividends balance	2 646	5 096	4 078	5 047	4 088	4 029
Transfers balance	–3 111	–2 157	–3 400	–3 518	–4 578	–4 935
Current balance	2 878	187	–4 159	–15 520	–20 404	–14 380
TRANSACTIONS IN EXTERNAL ASSETS AND LIABILITIES						
Investment overseas by UK residents						
Direct	–8 456	–12 038	–19 215	–20 880	–21 521	–11 702
Portfolio	–16 755	–22 095	7 201	–8 600	–31 283	–12 587
Total UK investment overseas	–25 211	–34 133	–12 014	–29 480	–52 804	–24 289
Investment in the United Kingdom by overseas residents						
Direct	3 865	4 987	8 478	10 236	17 145	18 997
Portfolio	9 671	11 785	19 210	14 387	13 239	5 070
Total overseas investment in the United Kingdom	13 538	16 772	27 688	24 623	30 384	24 067
Foreign currency lending abroad by UK banks	–20 209	–47 861	–45 787	–14 890	–24 113	–33 327
Foreign currency borrowing abroad by UK banks	25 295	58 568	43 143	20 403	33 012	34 000
Net foreign currency transactions of UK banks	5 086	10 707	–2 644	5 513	8 899	673
Sterling lending abroad by UK banks	–1 815	–5 817	–4 640	–4 625	–2 919	–3 919
Sterling borrowing and deposit liabilities abroad of UK banks	4 148	5 559	9 457	13 815	10 875	12 179
Net sterling transactions of UK banks	2 333	–258	4 817	9 190	7 956	8 260
Deposits with and lending to banks abroad by UK non-bank private sector	–1 305	–3 019	–4 632	–3 980	–9 473	–5 722
Borrowing from banks abroad by:						
UK non-bank private sector	2 618	3 817	2 035	3 971	7 081	7 916
Public corporations	64	–31	–166	–253	–1 132	–127
General government	87	100	104	–10	–65	–461
Official reserves (additions to –, drawings on +)	–1 758	–2 891	–12 012	–2 761	5 440	–77
Other external assets of:						
UK non-bank private sector and public corporations	528	1 656	254	1 201	1 611	–3 740
General government	–730	–509	–796	–891	–942	–1 227
Other external liabilities of:						
UK non-bank private sector and public corporations	732	567	1 448	1 682	13 710	5 649
General government	–64	78	1 725	841	2 251	1 158
Net transactions in assets and liabilities	–4 082	–7 234	5 810	9 645	12 916	12 081
Balancing item	1 204	7 047	–1 651	5 875	7 488	2 299

Source: UK National Accounts 'Pink Book' (CSO, 1991) Tables 1.3 and 1.4.

native, and more beneficial, interpretation is that it indicates the importation of capital goods for investment by UK companies to improve their productive capacity. Unfortunately, it is very difficult for analytical purposes to distinguish in the short term between these interpretations.

□ 6.3.2 *The Capital Account*

The rest of the accounts can be distinguished by virtue of the fact that no goods and services flow in the opposite direction to the flows of currency. What are being acquired are foreign assets such as shares and securities. When such flows of currency are recorded they can be attributed to a number of basic influences. The first – of critical importance in recent years – is the **structure of interest rates** in the UK compared to that overseas. If interest rats are higher in the UK than elsewhere, after adjusting for any risk of default, currency will tend to flow into the UK in very large amounts. For the most part, such currency flows will be **short-term** (colloquially called **hot money**). The second is the **rate of return on investment**. If a UK company takes over a foreign company, it does so in the belief that the investment will yield a higher rate of return than would result from the takeover of another UK company. Equally, private investors in the UK will buy shares in foreign companies if they believe that the dividend yield and/or the prospect of capital gains is better than that to be achieved in the UK. These currency flows are mostly **long-term**. If interest rates are relatively low in the UK, or rates of return in the UK are relatively low, the flows cited above will operate in the reverse direction.

It should be noted that the distinction between short-term and long-term capital flows is much easier to establish in principle than it is in practice. The capital account is not divided up specifically to illustrate this distinction, and we will accordingly be using the term 'hot money' to refer to highly mobile international capital.

The third influence is the **exchange rate**. All capital flows must take place in a particular currency, the value of which can vary quite considerably over time. Whilst long-term investment is not much affected by this influence, given that exchange rate movements in the longer term are impossible to predict and that the investor can anyway hedge against changes in currency value within reason, hot money flows are a different matter. Even where the interest rate on offer is higher than in other financial centres, a financial asset denominated in a currency the value of which is expected to fall sharply will be unpopular, whilst that denominated in a currency the value of which is expected to rise sharply will prove popular, even if its yield is very poor, as this will be more than compensated by the prospect of a capital gain on the asset. This proposition is developed in more detail on **p. 207**.

Direct investment primarily comprises net investment by overseas companies in their UK affiliates, including the reinvestment of retained profits, and by UK companies in their overseas branches, subsidiaries and associates.

Portfolio investment by UK residents comprises net purchases and sales of overseas government, municipal and company securities, whilst portfolio investment in the UK primarily comprises net purchases and sales of UK company securities and government stocks. These flows clearly affect the **net asset/liability position** of the UK relative to the rest of the world. In principle, one simply adds or subtracts the net annual change to the existing cumulative net value of assets, but in addition there may be capital gains and losses arising from, for example, changes in share prices which cannot show up in the BoP accounts until such time as an asset is sold. The scale of financial asset acquisition by UK residents resulted in the UK becoming one of the world's three largest net creditor nations in 1989 as shown in **Table 6.1** (expressed in dollars). This is obviously balanced by growing net indebtedness elsewhere and, although it is hard to accept, the USA appears to have become a net debtor, indeed the world's largest net debtor. This is a highly contentious issue and it is discussed in some detail on **pp. 194–5**.

Net foreign currency transactions of UK banks consist of changes in deposits of foreign currencies made with UK resident banks by non-residents, and loans by the banks in those currencies to non-residents. **Net sterling transactions** of UK banks

Table 6.1 *International Comparisons of External Net Assets* [1,2]

End-years	1980	1981	1982	1983	1984	1985	1986	1987	1988	1989
United States										
$ bn	95	130	126	78	–8	–122	–285	–389	–542	–675
% of GNP	3	4	4	2	—	–3	–7	–9	–11	–13
% of exports[3]	35	44	47	30	–3	–43	–97	–114	n/a	n/a
Japan										
$ bn	10	10	24	36	74	129	179	240	291	292
% of GNP	1	1	2	3	6	8	9	8	10	11
% of exports[3]	6	5	13	19	37	50	65	66	n/a	n/a
West Germany										
$ bn	26	24	26	27	36	46	90	162	203	254
% of GNP	3	3	4	4	6	6	9	13	17	19
% of exports[3]	12	11	12	14	19	17	26	39	n/a	n/a
United Kingdom										
$ bn	30	53	59	72	87	110	151	134	140	174
% of GNP	6	11	13	16	23	21	26	20	16	21
% of exports[3]	20	41	50	61	81	70	101	84	83	87

Notes:
[1] Excluding gold holdings.
[2] The data underlying this table are taken from national sources which may use disparate methodology.
[3] Gross exports of goods and services
Source: Bank of England Quarterly Bulletin (November 1989) p. 521 and (November 1990) p. 492.

consist of sterling advances and overdrafts (net of repayments) provided to overseas residents (including banks abroad) by UK banks, sterling commercial bills discounted, acceptances, and sterling borrowing and deposit liabilities abroad.

Deposits with, and lending to, banks abroad by UK non-bank private sector consist of UK residents' deposits with banks in the Bank for International Settlements (BIS) reporting area *plus* assets held in the custody of banks in the USA. **Borrowing from banks abroad** covers predominantly borrowing from commercial banks in the BIS reporting area, the European Investment Bank and the United States Export-Import Bank.

Lastly we come to changes in the **official reserves**, which are also analysed in more detail below. Other external assets include identified trade credit between unrelated companies, inter-government loans by the UK and subscriptions to international lending bodies, whilst other external

liabilities include broadly the same items. Special Drawing Rights (SDRs) are reserve assets created by the International Monetary Fund (IMF) (See **pp. 217–18**), and the balancing item has already been discussed above.

■ 6.4 The Accounts in Retrospect

In taking a retrospective view of the BoP accounts it is clearly not practicable to operate at the detailed disaggregated level presented in **Figure 6.1** except insofar as it is needed to shed light on the peculiarities of recent policy *vis-á-vis* the external sector. **Table 6.3**, which covers the period prior to the present government's election and its full period in office, accordingly treats transactions in external assets and liabilities only in the aggregate. This accords with the customary presentation of the accounts in the media.

6.4.1 The Meaning of Equilibrium

Before proceeding we need to consider first the meaning of the term 'equilibrium' in the context of the accounts. As we have explained, the accounts as a whole must balance by definition, but to achieve that it is not necessary for any individual component of the accounts, for example the current balance, to have a zero value. The main issue is how to express the objective of policy concerning the balance of payments. The messages sent out about the state of the economy by the current and capital accounts are rather different, and the focus of concern about the accounts has always been upon the **current balance**. It is, therefore, often argued that this should be equilibrium in the sense that it should have a value of zero.

However, since historically the UK has been predominantly a manufacturing nation, it is sometimes argued that attention should be focussed more narrowly upon the **visible balance**, and that this should be kept in equilibrium with a value of zero.

Occasionally, reference is made to the **basic balance**, which is the sum of the current balance plus the balance of long-term capital flows (i.e. it excludes hot money). It can be argued that hot money merely 'accommodates' the basic balance which gives a true insight into the current and longer-term prosperity of the trading sector. However, as we have noted, the basic balance cannot be estimated accurately because of the difficulty of separating out short-term from long-term capital flows.

The first important lesson from the above is that when the word 'equilibrium' is encountered, it requires one to look carefully to see to which part of the account it is being applied. In the second place, there is clearly a time dimension to the issue. The current balance might sum to zero over a period of years, and hence yield an equilibrium, albeit possibly more by chance than by design. This may be preferable to the requirement that it be in equilibrium over a period of months, or in any given year, since it will allow for cyclical adjustments and the problems of data collection

discussed above. But unless a government is prepared to state in advance that it is pursuing a set of policies intended to achieve equilibrium within a specified period, the fact that it can retrospectively identify such an equilibrium cannot be said to prove anything one way or another about its policies.

In any event, the whole issue is clouded by the choice of a particular exchange rate regime. Without discussing this in detail here as it is covered below, the essential point is that it is possible to choose a regime which will, other than in the very short term, keep the visible balance in equilibrium. However, it will not keep the other components of the accounts in equilibrium, and there are also likely to be conflicts with other objectives of policy which rule out this approach to the achievement of equilibrium. It is finally worth reminding ourselves that it is current practice to isolate the balancing item from both the current and capital account balances. But if, as has generally been the case, the balancing item is large, and if it is unclear how it should be divided between current and capital accounts, one may reasonably enquire how on earth one is supposed to know whether either account is anywhere near, let alone specifically at, its equilibrium value, whether in the short or the longer term.

6.4.2 The Balancing Item

The balancing item is a very volatile item in the accounts. Some part of it will be permanent insofar as, for example, the data collection system consistently fails to record certain transactions. Other parts will be erratic and arise because, for example, the data collection system either becomes able to record transactions in the capital account which could not previously be attributed to any of its headings, and therefore had to be lumped into the balancing item, or ceases to be able to do so, with the reverse effect. Large balancing items (whether plus minus) have been a feature of the 1980s in the accounts. This is partly because, since 1982, a substantial proportion of trade credit between unrelated companies, required to bridge the gap between the time goods are shipped and the settlement of the invoice, has been switched from the capital account to the balancing item. Furthermore, in 1986, the high level of capital flows during the period leading up to and following 'Big Bang', created difficulties of attribution to appropriate headings in the capital account.

Hopes that the balancing item would settle down, as it did in 1987, have unfortunately been confounded. This is more important than it seems because, if the balancing item is large, and if it is not known whether it is created by under- or over-recording in the current account and/or capital account, it is difficult to know how seriously to take the recorded data.

Since 1975 the balancing item has been positive in every year except 1982 and, possibly, 1987 where the most recent revision sets it (temporarily, no doubt) at −£1651 mn. A positive balancing item implies either unrecorded net credits in the current account or unrecorded net inflows in the capital account or both. In practice, the balancing item is highly volatile on a quarterly basis (see Bank of England, 1990, p. 497), and individual quarters have been as large as +£10 bn and −£5 bn in recent years. Nevertheless, the Bank of England considers that of late the under-recording of inflows has become a structural problem. Transfers from the balancing item to portfolio inflows in the accounts has ameliorated the situation somewhat (the cumulative balancing item was, at the time, shown as £35 bn for 1986–88), but it remains unclear exactly where the problem lies.

The Bank believes that the recording of visible trade should be highly accurate. (This author, who tracks the flow of books – bulky and easy to count items – and discovers that there are huge discrepancies between what the UK reckons to export and import and what the country at the other end of each transaction reckons to be trading, is highly sceptical). It believes that there are problems with data on services, but does not see how these errors could account for more than a small part of the overall balancing item. Hence, 'it seems likely that the explanation for the majority of the balancing item lies in the capital account' (Bank of England, 1990, p. 498). In particular, the Bank considers that 'the bulk of omission may be in portfolio inflows'.

There is an additional factor to consider. Taking the world as a whole, whilst as a matter of simple definition total world exports must equal total world imports, they fell short in practice by a wide margin as shown in **Figure 6.2**. It therefore follows that in many parts of the world exports are significantly under-recorded. The situation is fluid because the discrepancy for a given year tends to decline over time as the data are improved (the 1987 estimate was $45 bn two years ago), but as **Figure 6.2** shows they remain large.

The International Monetary Fund indicate where they believe the problem arises, and in recent years their preference has been to attribute it to under-recorded investment income flows in industrial countries.

Figure 6.2 *World Current Account Imbalances, $bn*

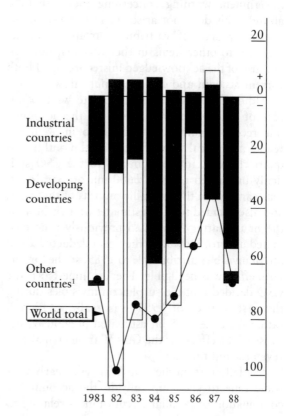

Note:
1   Mainly USSR and Eastern Europe.
Source: The Economist.

The CSO version of events thus has it that the balancing item consists of under-recorded capital account **inflows** and, taking the IMF line, that missing world exports are predominantly not of goods and services and anyway do not originate at all from the UK. If they are right then this has, as we shall see, serious implications for the value of the UK's net overseas assets. The sceptics' view, on the other hand, is that a significant part of the balancing item is unrecorded exports of goods and services, and that these also exist for the UK as part of the black hole in the world's trading accounts. If the sceptics are right then the trading account is considerably healthier than it appears to be.

In many ways the most surprising aspect of the above debate is that both politicians and currency dealers set so much store by the monthly data on the balance of payments which clearly carry a government warning concerning their use (and abuse). This does not arise solely because of the constant process of reattribution from the balancing item to other items in the accounts, but also because of the acknowledged misrecording of both current account and capital account flows.

Although recent history is replete with examples of extraordinary revisions in the accounts, one recent example will suffice to instil in the reader a sceptical view of the official monthly and quarterly data. In December 1990 the CSO suddenly unearthed roughly £600 mn of extra overseas earnings in the first nine months of that year, and also decided to raise estimates of invisibles for the final quarter which had previously been estimated at zero. However, they also deducted £500 mn of invisibles attributable to 1989, so the longer-term effect was negligible. Then, in June 1991, the CSO decided that the surplus on invisibles during the first quarter of 1991 was really £230 mn, rather than the £1.5 bn estimated previously, because of the effects of the Gulf War on civil airline revenues and the like.

The fallout from the Gulf War will clearly take some time to show up fully in the accounts. A combination of peculiar circumstances relating to airlines, tourism, fluctuating oil prices, contributions to the EC and foreign contributions to UK Gulf War costs resulted in both the first quarterly deficit (estimated at £650 mn) since 1980 on interest, profits and dividends and the smallest quarterly deficit (estimated at £79 mn) on transfers since the beginning of 1986 – or not, as the case may be once the figures have been revised.

6.4.3 *Index Numbers of UK Visible Trade*

It must be recognised that when one has become used to regarding a current account deficit of £10 bn as giving cause for concern, there is a tendency to be dismissive of historic deficits of a 'mere' £1 bn, let alone those of £100 mn. Yet these figures, in their historic context, were regarded with equal dismay because of their size in relation to the then value of GDP. The escalation in the numbers partly reflects the effects of economic growth, but primarily those of continuous – and in many individual years very rapid – inflation. It is possible to give a general impression of the relative effects of growth and inflation by the use of index numbers, as in **Table 6.2**.

The volume index for visible exports rose by roughly 60 per cent between 1970 and 1980, a markedly better performance that for the volume of imports. However, from 1982 to 1989, but with the exception of 1985, as shown in **Figure 6.3**, the volume of imports easily outstripped that of exports. Nevertheless, the growth differential was shrinking from 1987 onwards and became positive in 1990. The effects of the 1990–91 recession has yet to be seen. Over the period 1970 to 1980 the **value** of both visible exports and imports roughly quadrupled, so prices of both exports and imports were clearly rising rapidly, but faster for imports than for exports. The unit value index continued to outrun the volume index until 1985, although prices of imports and exports were rising in unison during this period. However, from 1986 to 1990 the situation reversed itself with volumes outrunning unit values by a substantial margin.

If the unit value of visible exports is divided by the unit value of visible imports we get a measure of the *terms of trade*. As can be seen, these worsened sharply between 1971 and 1974, but

Table 6.2 *Index Numbers, UK Visible Trade (1985 = 100)*

	Volume indices[1]						Unit value index[2]		Terms of trade ((a)/(b))
	Exports				Imports		(a) Exports	(b) Imports	
	Manufactures		Share of world exports of manufactures	Total	Total	Manufactures as % Total Final Expenditure			
	Semi	Finished							
1970				52.9	54.9		18.2	17.0	107.0
1971				56.1	57.4		19.2	17.8	108.0
1972				55.9	64.1		20.3	18.6	109.2
1973				63.4	73.0		22.8	23.7	96.3
1974				68.0	73.3		29.0	34.6	83.7
1975				65.2	66.9		35.6	39.5	90.2
1976				71.7	71.3		42.6	48.4	88.1
1977				77.6	72.8		50.5	55.9	90.3
1978	97	91	117	79.6	76.1	11.4	55.5	58.0	95.5
1979	99	88	110	83.1	83.5	11.8	61.4	61.8	99.4
1980	93	89	105	84.1	79.0	10.8	69.9	67.8	103.1
1981	85	86	96	83.3	75.8	10.1	76.2	73.7	103.4
1982	86	87	102	85.6	80.1	10.7	81.4	79.9	101.9
1983	91	84	99	87.6	87.0	11.7	88.0	87.6	100.5
1984	97	93	98	94.7	96.9	12.7	95.0	95.3	99.6
1985	100	100	100	100.0	100.0	12.8	100.0	100.0	100.0
1986	106	102	102	104.0	107.2	13.0	90.2	95.4	94.5
1987	113	112	105	109.8	114.8	13.3	93.9	97.7	95.9
1988	120	120	103	113.0	131.2	14.1	94.0	96.7	97.2
1989	126	136	105	118.0	141.6	14.6	101.3	103.2	97.9
1990	133	148	107	126.0	143.8	14.2	106.9	107.1	99.5

Notes:
[1] Seasonally adjusted.
[2] Unadjusted.
Sources: UK National Accounts '*Pink Book*' (CSO, 1991). *National Institute Economic Review; Economic Trends; Monthly Digest of Statistics*, Table 15.8.

subsequently improved more steadily until 1981. They worsened sharply again in 1986, before climbing back to their 1985 level by 1990.

The terms of trade must be treated with care. On the face of it, an improvement, resulting perhaps from relatively high inflation in the UK, enables the same volume of imports to be bought in exchange for a lesser volume of exports than before. However, much depends upon the price elasticity of demand for exports and imports. If demand for UK visible exports is elastic, as is generally the case, an increase in price results in

a reduction in revenue. Equally, if demand for visible imports is inelastic, as is generally the case, a reduction in price results in an increase in payments. Thus, overall, the balance of trade (visible exports *less* visible imports) will worsen rather than the reverse. In other words, a dose of domestic inflation in the UK is likely to cause serious damage to the visible trade balance, and is also likely to damage invisibles trade in an increasingly competitive world. The, albeit modest, improvement in recent years has not, therefore, been beneficial to the UK.

Figure 6.3   *The Differential Between Export and Import Growth* [1]

Note:

[1]   Growth of non-oil export volume *less* growth of non-oil import volume (3-month moving average).

Source: Bank of England Quarterly Bulletin (February 1991) p. 25.

It is of particular interest to examine the other columns in **Table 6.2** in the light of the alleged collapse of manufacturing capability in the UK. What the first two columns show is that at the end of the 1970s, and through the 1980–81 recession, the volume of semi-manufactures and finished goods suffered a setback, particularly as the exchange rate was driven up by North Sea oil coming on stream. There was a sharp recovery in 1982 and 1983 respectively, with both categories back to their 1978 volumes in 1984. From that point on to the end of the decade export volumes rose rapidly, demonstrating that the manufacturing capability which survived the 1980–81 recession was well capable of selling competitively in international markets.

The consequences for the UK's share of world exports of manufactures are important because so many attacks on government policy include a claim that this is continuously falling – but it is not. It did indeed fall rapidly at the end of the 1970s, but once the 1980–81 recession was over it stabilised

Figure 6.4   *UK Share of World Trade in Manufactures, %*

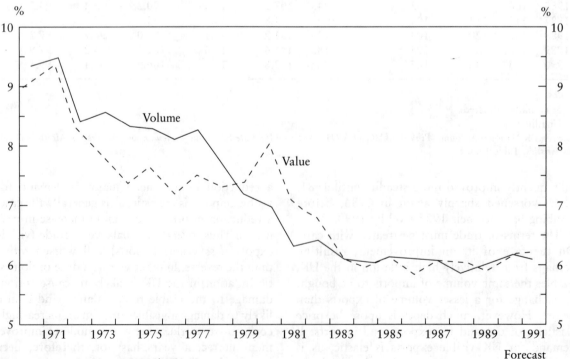

Source: Autumn Statement 1990, Chart 2.10.

around its 1980 level. This can be seen more clearly in both volume and value terms in **Figure 6.4** which covers the period 1970–90. Bearing in mind the export success of, for example, Japan and Taiwan, this was a creditable performance, and it would be unreasonable to expect a mature economy like the UK to gain much market share in the intensely competitive environment of international trade in manufactures.

On the import side the picture is less rosy, with manufactured imports rising as a proportion of TFE from 1981 onwards. The fact that import and export volumes of manufactures rise together is a commonplace of advanced countries which, for example, trade different makes of car and electronic goods. The purchase of cheap, high quality, imports is not to be deplored as such – provided, of course, one believes more or less in free trade. The key issue is whether or not a country can compensate by maintaining exports of goods and services in order to keep the current account balance in rough equilibrium.

☐ 6.4.4 *Visible Trade in Retrospect*

Prior to 1967 the UK managed to keep the current balance in surplus but, with the exception of 1956 and 1958 when the visible balance was positive, the pattern of a negative visible balance more than compensated by a positive invisible balance was already well-established. There was considerable volatility with respect to short-term capital flows, but long-term capital flows were mostly outflows, and hence negative in the accounts. In looking at the current situation one might be tempted to believe that nothing much had changed since the 1960s. However, as we shall see, this is not the case because of differences in the exchange rate regime in operation; in the UK's reserve position; and in the contribution of North Sea oil.

The steady deterioration in the UK's share of world trade in manufactures, exacerbated by an uncompetitive fixed change rate and combined with a tendency for hot money to pour out of the UK whenever a crisis loomed, thereby draining the

inadequate reserves, was an unsustainable situation. The BoP accounts gave every appearance of being in 'fundamental disequilibrium' and only a reduction in the value of the pound could remedy the situation. This duly took place in November 1967, and a programme of domestic deflation was set in hand. The combination proved successful, albeit not immediately and not soon enough to prevent a change of government. Starting from a balance of –£286 mn in 1968, the current account moved to +£460 mn in 1971. Whilst long-term capital continued to flood out of the UK, an even larger amount began to flood in after 1969, and this was paralleled by net inflows of hot money sustained by the belief that the UK was making a determined attempt to restore sound finance. It was true that the domestic deflation was taking its toll in terms, for example, of rising unemployment, but this was of less concern at the time than the symbolic value of the deflationary measures.

From this point on fundamental disequilibrium never reappeared in the same guise as before. One major factor was the abandonment of the fixed exchange rate regime in 1972, which subsequently permitted the exchange rate to be used more positively to regulate the current balance. A second factor, which was initially of much less help, was the sharp increase in the price of North Sea oil. The subsequent picture is spelt out by **Table 6.3**. From 1975 to 1979 the visible balance remained heavily in deficit. The invisibles largely offset the damage, although the negative transfer component (including contributions to the EC) grew too rapidly to allow for a substantial current account surplus other than in 1978 at the end of a long period of oil price stability. The exceptionally high rate of inflation, partly triggered by the first oil price rise (see **pp. 69–71**) was ultimately the key problem, because although long-term capital was flowing into finance the development of the North Sea oilfields, international confidence in the UK's ability to deal with its domestic problems caused a massive outflow of hot money. This caused the then Labour Government both to deplete the reserves and to borrow from the IMF (agreeing in return to deflate the economy along 'monetarist' lines), as shown in **Table 6.4**.

Table 6.3   *Balance of Payments of the UK, 1977–90, £ mn*

	1977	1978	1979	1980	1981	1982	1983	1984	1985	1986	1987	1988	1989	1990
CURRENT ACCOUNT[1]														
Visible Balance	−2 322	−1 592	−3 342	1 357	3 251	1 911	−1 537	−5 336	−3 345	−9 559	−11 582	−21 624	−24 598	−18 675
Invisibles:														
Services	3 238	3 700	3 895	3 653	3 792	3 022	4 064	4 519	6 687	6 808	6 745	4 574	4 685	5 201
Interest, profits and dividends	265	806	1 205	−182	1 251	1 460	2 831	4 357	2 646	5 096	4 078	5 047	4 088	4 029
Transfers	−1 128	−1 791	−2 210	−1 984	−1 547	−1 741	−1 593	−1 730	−3 111	−2 157	−3 400	−3 518	−4 578	−4 935
Invisibles Balance	2 375	2 715	2 890	1 487	3 496	2 741	5 302	7 146	6 222	9 747	7 423	6 103	4 195	4 295
CURRENT BALANCE	53	1 123	−453	2 843	6 748	4 649	3 765	1 811	2 878	187	−4 159	−15 520	−20 404	−14 380
TRANSACTIONS IN EXTERNAL ASSETS AND LIABILITIES[2]														
Net Transactions	−3 892	−2 871	−742	−3 940	−7 436	−2 519	−4 562	−7 766	−4 082	−7 234	5 810	9 645	12 916	12 081
Allocation of SDRs[3]	0	0	195	180	158	0	0	0	0	0	0	0	0	0
Balancing Item	3 839	1 748	1 000	917	530	−2 130	797	5 955	1 204	7 047	−1 651	5 875	7 488	2 299

Notes:
[1] Seasonally adjusted.
[2] Assets: increase −/decrease +. Liabilities: increase +/decrease −. Not seasonally adjusted.
[3] Special Drawing Rights.
Sources: Financial Statistics, Table 10.2. UK National Accounts *'Pink Book'* (CSO, 1991) Table 1.1.

Table 6.4   *UK Official Reserves, 1973–90, End-year Values [1,2], $ mn*

	Gold	SDRs	Reserve position at IMF	Convertible currencies	TOTAL
1973	887	724	140	4 725	6 476
1974	888	830	248	4 823	6 789
1975	888	840	366	3 335	5 429
1976	888	728	—	2 513	4 129
1977	938	604	—	19 015	20 557
1978	964	500	—	14 230	15 694
1979	3 259	1 245	—	18 034	22 538
1980	6 987	560	1 308	18 621	27 476
1981	7 334	1 048	1 513	13 457	23 347
1982	4 562	1 233	1 568	9 634	16 997
1983	5 914	695	2 168	9 040	17 817
1984	5 476	531	2 110	7 577	15 694
1985	4 310	996	1 751	8 486	15 543
1986	4 897	1 425	1 820	13 781	21 923
1987	5 792	1 229	1 579	35 726	44 326
1988	6 466	1 341	1 694	42 184	51 685
1989	5 457	1 125	1 610	20 453	38 645
1990	5 235	1 142	1 534	30 553	38 464

Notes:
[1]   The level of the reserves is affected by changes in the dollar valuation of gold, SDRs and convertible currencies as well as by transactions.
[2]   The total in July 1991 was 44 631.
Source: Bank of England Quarterly Bulletin.

With confidence restored by the IMF intervention, the reserve position took a dramatic turn for the better, and although the reserves remained fairly volatile they never again fell to a level which suggested further recourse to the IMF would be needed.

☐ 6.4.5 Visible Trade in the 1980s

With North Sea oil coming on stream, the visible balance actually returned to surplus from 1980 to 1982, and the oil surplus itself grew steadily from £0.3 bn in 1980 to £8.1 bn in 1985. Under the circumstances it seems extraordinary that the visible balance should have returned to deficit, but whilst non-oil visibles were £1 bn in surplus in 1980, they had collapsed to show a deficit of £11 bn by 1984 as depicted in **Figure 6.4**. The decimation of the UK manufacturing sector when the

present government first took office, resulting from a combination of a deliberate policy of domestic deflation, the UK's relatively high rate of inflation and the high value of the effective exchange rate (see **pp. 450, 69, and 210** respectively) was largely to blame, since the damage done at that time has never been fully rectified. Whilst the effective exchange rate fell to an historic low by 1986, and the rump of the manufacturing sector performed very creditably in export markets, the growth in the UK economy sucked in vast amounts of foreign manufactures, many of which could no longer be produced at all in the UK (see **Table 6.2**). Individual events such as the coal-miners' strike in 1984–85 added to the difficulties, and it is possible to argue that although many UK products were highly competitive on price alone, they fell down with respect to non-price factors such as quality and speed of delivery.

It is also necessary, in looking at the visible balance, to appreciate a peculiarity of the way in which exchange rates work. In practice many products, and especially raw materials including oil, are priced in dollars. Thus if the pound rises in value against the dollar these become cheaper in sterling and vice versa. However, exports to the EC are affected by the rate at which the pound is exchanged for EC currencies. If the pound rises against these currencies then UK exports become expensive and vice versa. The worst combination for the UK is, therefore, for the pound to fall against the dollar, making raw material imports expensive, and to rise simultaneously against EC currencies, making exports expensive. From 1979 to 1985 this combination broadly held true (see **p. 210**) and the visible balance was salvaged only by North Sea oil coming on stream.

From 1980 to 1985 the invisibles balance remained very healthy. The balance on private services was a major contributory factor. Equally, whilst interest payments needed to be made on outstanding government borrowings from abroad, the long-term capital outflows in the 1970s mentioned above resulted in a sharp upturn in private sector interest, profits and dividends (appearing, note, in the **current** rather than the capital account).

Because of its diversity the capital account is much more difficult to interpret. Account must be taken of the lifting of exchange controls in October 1979, which resulted in a sharp upturn in investment overseas by UK residents (rising from £12.6 bn in 1983 to £34.4 bn in 1986 as shown in **Figure 6.1**). These were offset by large amounts of foreign currency borrowing by UK banks and, as already mentioned, short-term inflows were heavily influenced by sterling's new status as a petro-currency and by the government's determined attack upon inflation via its 'monetarist' policies, and, more recently, high interest rates. UK companies continued to perform creditably in export markets, but **Table 6.2** indicates the scale of the problem. From 1985 to 1987 the volume of visible exports rose by roughly 10 per cent, but the volume of imports rose by 15 per cent, and the gap continued to widen during 1988. If the comparison is linked only to manufactured goods, then the margin of difference was considerably wider. The consequences, taken in conjunction with the collapse in the price of North Sea oil, show up clearly

in the visible balance which worsened sharply in 1986 to record a deficit of £9.5 bn. This would have been worse had the £ not risen against the dollar, thereby cheapening raw material imports, and fallen against EC currencies, thereby cheapening UK exports. The invisibles balance, on the other hand, improved sharply in 1986, and just matched the visible balance overall. However, the behaviour of the balancing item, which was initially larger than both visible and invisibles balances, inevitably leaves a question mark over the value of these statistics.

☐ 6.4.6 Recent History

It is helpful at this stage to examine the trend in the visible balance with the erratic effects of oil stripped out, expressed as a percentage of GDP as in **Figure 6.5**.

In 1987 the visible balance deteriorated further to show a deficit of £11.2 bn. The invisibles balance registered a surplus of £6.9 bn resulting in a current account deficit of £4.3 bn for the year, the first major deficit since 1979. 1987 also seemed at first to be exceptional in relation to earlier years in the decade in that net transactions were recorded in the 1988 'Pink Book' as being only marginally negative, a turnaround of £13 bn in one year. This was widely thought to be due to the appreciation of sterling which lowered the sterling value of assets priced in other currencies, and also because UK residents ran down their overseas investments, mainly after the stock market crash in October. The attraction of the UK as a haven for hot money grew even stronger because of the combination of fiscal rectitude and high nominal interest rates. The year was accordingly also unusual in that the balancing item appeared to fall sharply. However, the revisions published in subsequent 'Pink Books" vacillated from a £7 bn outflow on net transactions to the latest £5.8 bn inflow, and from a +£11 bn balancing item to the latest estimate of a negative balancing item. No wonder the government has set in hand a major overhaul of the statistical service!

In 1988 the current account deteriorated rapidly. The visible balance recorded an unprecedented

Figure 6.5   *Non-oil Visible Balance as % of GDP*

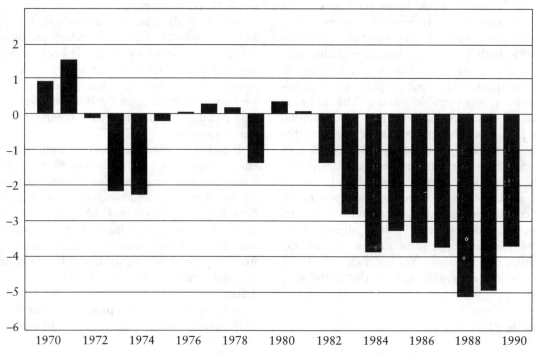

Source: CSO.

deficit of £21 bn, which was only partially compensated by an invisibles surplus that was itself falling sharply from its 1986 peak. Hence the current account deficit was an alarming £15.5 bn which even the large positive balancing item could not explain.

One factor, apart from the general surge in imports of all kinds, was a sharp decline in the oil surplus as domestic industry increased its oil consumption and the Piper Alpha platform disaster affected supplies. This appeared to herald the end of an era for North Sea oil and gas insofar as it affects the balance of payments, an issue addressed in the next section.

The visible trade deficit worsened in 1989, and with the invisibles surplus shrinking further, so did the current account deficit. The enormous balancing item of £7.5 bn undoubtedly gives cause for caution in interpreting these data, although it goes without saying that in many quarters they were taken as evidence that the obsolete ship SS. Great Britain was sinking without trace. As a result the government was forced to scratch around with increasing desperation to explain why they were merely a 'blip' rather than a trend.

In practice, the situation did improve in 1990 as the recession began to take hold, and it is worthwhile at this stage examining a number of subsectors of the accounts in order to gain some insight not, as above, solely into the past but also into the future.

Trade in Cars

The most notable improvement on the balance of trade during 1990 resulted from an end-year surge in exports of cars and commercial vehicles. In the whole of 1990, 414,000 cars were exported with the final quarter figures up 60 per cent on 1989. Overall, the motor trade account remained in deficit to the tune of £4.6 bn, but this was much better than the 1989 deficit of £6.6 bn. Ford and Vauxhall resumed large-scale exports to the Continent for the first time in over a decade and the Nissan factory in Sunderland became the first Japanese plants to create 'UK' exports of cars.

The trading position in 1991 is likely to be difficult. Nevertheless, the longer-term perspective is much rosier. Nissan is expected to be exporting 100,000 cars a year by 1993–94 and up to 300,000 by 1999. Both Toyota and Honda will also have the capacity to export at this time. Furthermore, these companies' cars will displace existing imports to a considerable extent. The ultimate impact of these developments is dependent upon such factors as the growth in demand on the UK home market and the proportion of UK content in both exports and imports of cars (Rhys, 1990). There is reason to doubt that the motor trade deficit will ever completely disappear, but as it constituted roughly one-quarter of the total visible trade deficit in 1990 (and slightly more in 1989) it does offer some support for the expectation that the visible trade deficit will shrink to a more manageable size in the fairly near future.

Trade in Electronics

The process described above is by no means confined to cars. Even though, for example, there are no longer any UK-owned TV manufacturers, colour TV exports exceeded imports in both 1989 and 1990. Ferguson, the last substantially UK-owned manufacturer of TV sets was bought by Thomson of France in 1987, but once again it is primarily the Japanese who have spear-headed the attack on overseas markets. Sony, the largest UK-based manufacturer, has won three Queen's Awards for Export Achievement since it established its factory in South Wales in 1974. Needless to say all this has provided an intense debate about whether ownership 'matters', but in simple balance of payments terms the consequences for the visible balance are undoubtedly positive. We will return to this issue in our subsequent analysis of the commodity composition of visible trade (on **pp. 201–4**).

In examining the reasons for the UK's poor performance in manufacturing trade such as poor education and training, bad design and quality and too little research and development, it is salutary to remember that the sectors in which the UK trades successfully such as chemicals, pharmaceuticals and aerospace, operate in exactly the same domestic environment as the sectors such as cars in which the UK trades unsuccessfully. It is possible to hypothesise that sectors which are currently successful are successful precisely because they always had to operate in international markets, whereas those such as white goods and motor cycles which relied upon the home market proved easy pickings for internationally competitive overseas producers.

If this is so, then the situation should be more stable than in the past, especially given the partial substitution of uncompetitive UK-owned business by Japanese-owned subsidiaries as in the case of cars. It is not the case that the UK's problems are particularly in high-technology sectors since the aerospace industry trades successfully. Indeed, it is in areas such as white goods, which are essentially low-tech, that the worst problems have typically arisen.

It is slightly ironic that part of the 'problem' lies in the exceptionally efficient UK retail sector. The inefficient system of retail distribution in Japan is undoubtedly one of the subtle protectionist devices used to keep out imported manufactures, whereas the ease with which such products find their way into British stores, and the ease of 'comparison shopping' in such outlets has ruthlessly exposed price and quality shortfalls in domestic products.

6.4.7 Balance of Payments Effects of North Sea oil

The BoP effects of the North Sea show up in four ways. The first two are current account items, appearing mainly in the visible balance. First, there is the balance of trade in oil and gas. This, as discussed above, was heavily in deficit during the 1970s, but showed a healthy surplus during the 1980s until the more than halving of the price of oil in early 1986. This surplus is no longer of sufficient size to warrant the level of attention accorded to the oil balance over the period to 1987. The second item relates to the net purchase of goods and services required to discover and extract the oil and gas. This was a significant deficit item in the early 1970s, but is no longer of any consequence. One of the other two effects appears in the capital account, namely capital inflows to finance the discovery and extraction activities. These basically can be set against the cost of purchasing goods and services, and like them have been inconsequential for a good many years. However, in the usual way, these inflows of capital generate the final effect, namely a requirement to pay interest, profits and dividends at a later date, which have accordingly been a negative item in the invisibles during the 1980s.

If this is set against the worsening in the balance of trade in oil and gas, it is clear that net revenue from the North Sea is unlikely to be able to offset any further deterioration which may occur in trade in manufactures. It is possible to speculate that this offset will continue because the price of oil will rise a good deal in the future, but this is less than probable. It is equally possible to argue that the output of oil and gas will rise rapidly, and the change in the tax regime should assist in this respect, but even if true this is likely to hold down prices and it has adverse fiscal effects in the short term. Indeed, the North Sea sector in general no longer provides anything like as much tax revenue as it did in its heyday.

If the BoP benefits of North Sea oil and gas have now largely come to an end, but the non-oil variables are showing larger deficits, it is certainly possible to argue that the existence of North Sea resources has simply been used as an excuse for not tackling some of the most deep-rooted problems of the economy. On the other hand, it has to be asked whether the huge increase in the net overseas assets of the UK, shown in **Table 6.1**, has anything to do with the use of the money generated by the onset of North Sea oil. If so, then it is unreasonable to regard the money as 'wasted' even if it has not been put to the purpose preferred by all parties.

Furthermore, it is possible to argue that the UK's net trading position with respect to manufactures has been permanently damaged by the effects of North Sea oil on the exchange rate. As noted elsewhere, the willingness of the government to let the exchange rate appreciate rapidly at the beginning of the 1980s in response to both the current account benefits of oil and the boost to foreign confidence in the UK which accompanied it made it very difficult for many firms to sell in export markets. The subsequent decline in the oil balance was not, however, accompanied by a parallel resurgence in manufactured exports.

☐ 6.4.8 The Invisibles Balance

The invisibles balance has for some time been a cause for concern. In money terms it is static, and hence its real value is falling. Traditionally, an invisibles surplus offsets a balance of trade deficit, but on a monthly and quarterly basis there are now invisibles deficits and the short-term prognosis is poor because of the effects of the Gulf War. It is useful, as ever, to express the balance as a percentage of GDP as in **Figure 6.6** to bring the trend out more clearly.

The UK remains the world's largest exporter of financial services (the Cayman Islands, interestingly, is the main rival), so it is tempting to see the problem as an excess of foreign transfers – primarily to EC institutions. Given the political unanimity concerning the UK's membership of the EC, and given the fact that the UK has wrung whatever concessions it is likely to get from other EC members, the long-term negative impact of such transfers upon the invisibles balance is best treated as a simple fact of life. The issue is thus whether the other elements in the balance can rise to compensate for this difficulty.

It is hard to be optimistic on this matter. The raising of virtually all barriers to the free flow of international capital cannot help but put the City of London under increasingly competitive pressure, and whilst it looks certain to hold its own it cannot be expected to make much headway. Equally, the British have become rather fond of their holidays abroad, and there seems little prospect (especially in summers like 1991!) of them staying at home for the sake of the invisibles balance. The key issue probably relates to interest, profits and dividends (IPD). The very large (apparent) holdings of overseas assets should be generating a substantial inflow of capital, but there is no need for such capital to be repatriated. If, for

Figure 6.6   *Invisibles Balance 1970–90, % of Money GDP*

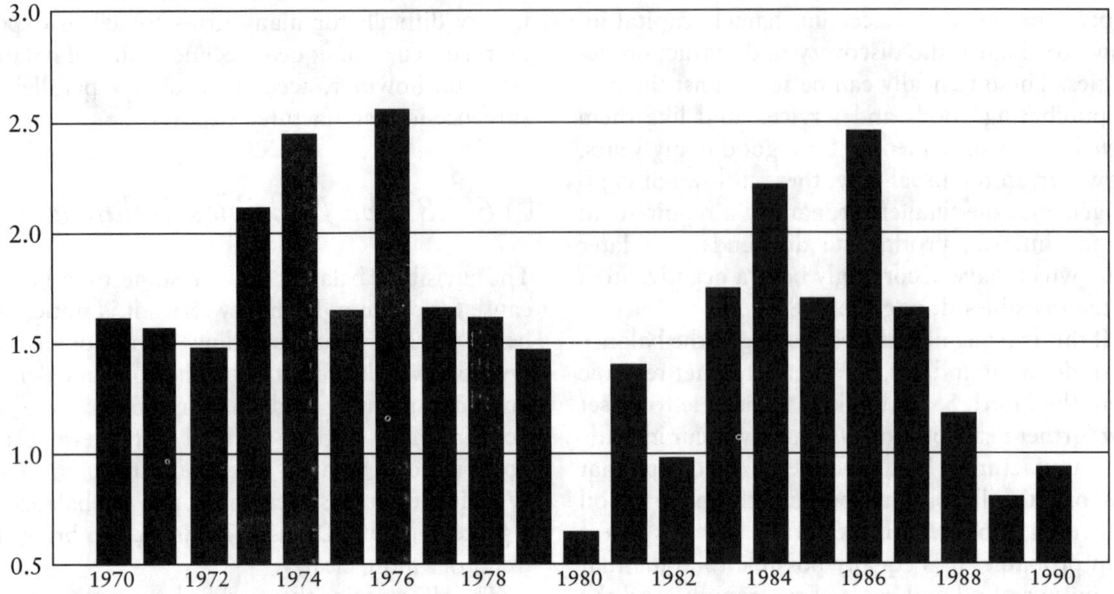

Source: CSO.

example, it is reinvested abroad then the short-term effect is a deterioration in IPD although the longer-term outlook is clearly improved.

It is also significant that the large deficits of 1988 and 1989 have necessitated an inflow of hot money which has caused UK banks to become net borrowers from overseas rather than the reverse. Furthermore, interest rates are considerably higher in the UK than in most other advanced economies, so these borrowings are expensive to service. As the visibles balance improves the IPD should improve with it, but the best thing that could happen would undoubtedly be an agreement under GATT auspices to lift barriers to trade in services in which the UK has a comparative advantage. Failing that, fewer natural disasters would be a boon to the insurance sector which has taken a hammering over the past year at a time of softening premiums.

☐ 6.4.9 Prognosis for 1991–92

The effects of the Gulf War have made it difficult to discern the longer-term trend hiding beneath the short-term volatility. Furthermore, there is as yet no clear evidence concerning whether or not the trough of the recession has been passed. The effects of recession upon the balance of trade can be seen more clearly in **Figure 6.7**.

By the end of 1990 the growth of import volumes was negative after a period of two years during which it had once again shot ahead of export growth. Initially the buoyancy of exports, resulting from continued growth overseas, especially elsewhere in the EC which lagged the UK in the economic cycle, opened up a big gap between export and import volume growth. This has yet to disappear, but it is possible that once the UK picks up a new head of steam the import volume growth line will rise to meet, and perhaps cross, the export growth line. Much depends upon consumer demand in this respect, and fortunately it remains smuggish relative to manufacturing for export as of July 1991. How big a deficit will ultimately appear in value terms is uncertain. We have already commented on the improvement in certain parts of the trading accounts and the situation is unlikely to return to pre-1990 levels. It is interesting to look at the geographic pattern of trade, as in

Figure 6.7 *The Volume of Exports and Volume of Imports, % Change, 3 months on a year earlier*

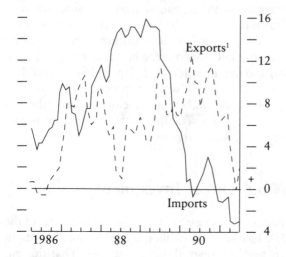

Note:
[1] Excluding oil and erratics.
Source: Bank of England Quarterly Bulletin (May 1991) p. 196.

Figure 6.8 which shows that the big improvement has come relative to other EC countries against which the exchange rate is semi-fixed. The deterioration relative to North America is unsurprising given the almost 20 per cent reduction in the value

Figure 6.8 *The Visible Trade Balance* [1], *1986–90, £mn*

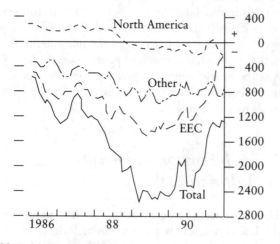

Note:
[1] 3-month moving average at monthly rate.
Source: Bank of England Quarterly Bulletin (May 1991).

of the dollar against the pound in 1990, but this has now reversed itself which should be to the UK's advantage once the USA also begins to pick up from recession.

On the whole, the evidence indicates that the trade and current account deficits will remain with us for the foreseeable future, but not on the scale of 1988 and 1989 and probably not on a scale sufficient to influence the outcome of the 1992 general election.

■ 6.5 International Perspectives

□ 6.5.1 *The Current Deficit*

The deterioration in the domestic current account balance needs to be seen in a wider context, as in **Figure 6.9**. This indicates (1) that the current deficit is not unusually large as a percentage of GDP

Figure 6.9 *Current Account Balances as % of GNP/GDP*

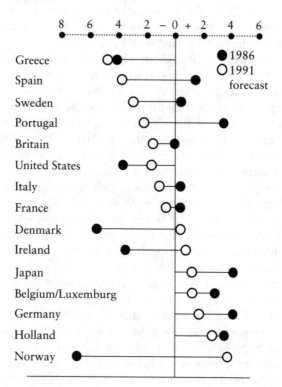

Source: The Economist

(2) that the recent deterioration is nothing unusual and far less severe than that of Spain and Portugal (3) that it is possible to produce an equivalent swing in the opposite direction as in the case of Norway, Ireland and Denmark (currently in surplus for the first time in three decades).

□ 6.5.2 Trade With Japan

From the beginning of 1987, until the third quarter of 1990, Japan's plans to reduce its trade surplus were widely acknowledged to be succeeding. Imports grew, on average, by 17.7 per cent whilst export growth slowed down to average 2.9 per cent. Furthermore, Japan exported capital on a much increased scale, thereby easing the adjustment problems of countries with which it was running big current account surpluses.

The overall current account surplus for 1990 was the lowest for five years at £18.3 bn, in particular because of a big rise in the deficit on invisibles. As a proportion of GNP this represented 12 per cent compared to 4.4 per cent in 1986, and Japan was loudly proclaimed to be behaving like a model world citizen.

However, throughout the latter half of the 1980s Japan's trading relationship with the USA continued to deteriorate, and the USA made it increasingly clear that it would use the provisions of the 1988 Omnibus Trading Act to resist further Japanese incursions into the US market. As a consequence, Japan began to search for alternative markets, and found them in Asia and Europe. Had the Japanese current account deficit continued to shrink this would not have mattered, but in the fourth quarter of 1990, despite the recession in the USA and Canada, Japan exported $81 bn of goods, the largest ever quarterly amount by value. By end-1990 the surplus was a third higher on a monthly basis than a year earlier, but more importantly the surplus with the EC exceeded that with the USA for the months of April and May 1991.

Hence, not merely is there once again the distinct probability of a massive Japanese current account surplus in 1991, but for the entire decade. Furthermore, this surplus will increasingly be with the EC. Edith Cresson, the French prime minister

appointed in 1991, was quick to voice her disapproval of this development, but in practice the EC member with the worst trading imbalance with Japan is currently the UK. Indeed, not all members are even in deficit. It is unsurprising, therefore, that the UK government has also voiced its concern about its trade with Japan, but it would be surprising if this were to produce any concrete response unless, as in the case of USA, the UK adopts a belligerent approach, presumably as part of an EC-wide response.

■ 6.6 Direct Investment

For centuries past an unfailing characteristic of the UK has been the willingness of its inhabitants to engage in foreign direct investment. That this enthusiasm has continued in recent years is not, therefore, altogether surprising. What is surprising is that it reached unprecedented levels during the latter half of the 1980s, as shown in **Figure 6.1**. As a consequence, the gross stock of UK-owned foreign assets grew very rapidly and is currently second only to that of the USA.

The second surprise is that, after dipping below zero in 1984, **inward** investment first rose sharply to £8 bn in 1987 and then, after marking time in 1988, shot up from 1989 onwards to such an extent that it not merely constituted a much higher proportion of GDP (over 4 per cent) than for any other equivalent economy, but also exceeded outward investment by a significant margin for the first time in several hundred years. Indeed, the UK was the world's most popular destination for direct investment in 1990, surpassing even the USA as shown in **Table 6.5**.

⃞ 6.6.1 Foreign-owned Multinationals

The existence of foreign-owned multinationals in the UK is not a new phenomenon. Indeed, many US companies such as Ford and General Motors have been around for so long that their cars are widely regarded as British rather than foreign.

Table 6.5   *Capital Movements for Large Industrial Countries*[1], *1975–90, $ bn*

	1975–79[2]	1980–84[2]	1985	1986	1987	1988	1989	1990
Outward portfolio flows (ie movements of share capital and other securities).								
Total outflows	17.0	45.7	119.6	180.3	122.7	197.0	266.7	157.6
US	5.8	5.8	7.5	4.3	5.3	7.9	21.9	26.7
Japan	2.6	13.8	59.8	102.0	87.7	87.0	113.1	39.7
EC nations	3.8	18.7	43.8	62.9	20.8	85.6	116.0	83.0
France	0.9	1.2	2.5	6.0	3.3	4.2	6.7	6.8
Germany	1.5	4.3	11.0	9.7	13.5	41.4	26.7	14.6
UK	0.8	10.8	24.7	34.0	−6.7	17.8	58.8	28.5
Direct inward investment								
Total investment	18.4	34.2	33.4	58.7	92.0	120.5	155.0	114.9
US	6.1	18.6	19.0	34.1	46.9	58.4	72.2	25.7
Japan	0.1	0.3	0.6	0.2	1.2	−0.5	−1.1	1.8
EC nations	10.6	13.3	12.2	17.1	34.0	49.5	69.8	72.2
France	1.9	2.2	2.2	2.8	4.7	7.2	9.7	8.1
Germany	1.3	0.8	0.5	1.1	1.9	1.0	6.8	1.5
UK	4.2	5.3	4.7	7.3	14.1	18.3	28.8	31.6

Notes:
[1]   Includes EC plus Group of Ten leading industrial nations.
[2]   Annual averages.
Source: Bank for International Settlements, *Annual Report 1991.*

The more recent influx of investment has been particularly associated with Japan, for example the takeover of ICL by Fujitsu and the car plants being set up by Honda and Toyota to join that of Nissan already operating at Sunderland. During 1988–90 some 80 Japanese manufacturers set up in the UK, but their role should not be exaggerated since at the end of 1988 the USA accounted for 40 per cent of all foreign-owned assets in Britain (with £25 bn), Holland for another 18 per cent and Japan for only 4 per cent, as shown in **Figure 6.10**.

It is unsurprising that the imminent arrival of the Single European Market (see **pp. 224–6**) has triggered an influx of foreign direct investment into the EC. It exceeded that into the USA for the first time in a decade in 1990 as shown in **Table 6.5**. Nevertheless, the fact that 60 per cent of US investment in the EC is in the UK, as well as 40 per cent of Japanese EC investment, indicates that the net inflow of direct investment is set to be an ongoing rather than a temporary characteristic of

the balance of payments accounts. Indeed, if the Uraguay Round ultimately breaks down (see **pp. 276–9**) and the USA becomes more inhospitable to inward Japanese investment, the Japanese may turn

Figure 6.10   *Direct Investment into Britain, Book Value of Net Assets, End-1988 as % of Total*

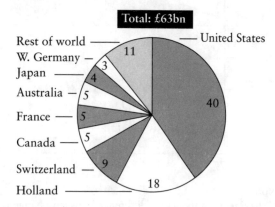

Total: £63bn

Rest of world — 11
W. Germany — 3
Japan — 4
Australia — 5
France — 5
Canada — 5
Switzerland — 9
Holland — 18
United States — 40

Source: CSO.

increasingly to the UK as their preferred investment location.

Such a development is not welcomed in all quarters. It is often argued that the balance of payments will deteriorate as a consequence, since the Japanese will use the UK as a glorified assembly plant whilst manufacturing high value-added products in Japan and exporting them to the UK. Furthermore, profits made in the UK will subsequently be repatriated. This argument is less than convincing for several reasons. In the first place, it is evident that if the Japanese do not, for example, set up car plants in the UK and use them as a base for exporting to other EC countries, then there will be no substitute exports for UK-originated products which no longer sell overseas. The same applies for any products no longer manufactured at all by UK firms. Secondly, as a result of infighting between the EC and Japan, the Japanese have conceded the need to create much more value-added in the EC then they had originally intended.

Finally, their imposition of much higher quality standards compared to UK manufacturers has caused some UK suppliers to improve their products to the point at which they are attractive in export markets.

6.6.2 *The External Balance Sheet of the UK*

We have already met the external balance sheet of the UK in the form of **Table 6.1**. This is analysed in great detail in Bank of England (1990). The first point to note is that because it is denominated in dollars, the equivalent sterling value can be highly variable. This can be seen in **Figure 6.11** where the net capital flows (above the line is an outflow and below the line is an inflow) are rather small (well below £10 bn) whilst the effects of revaluation due to exchange rates changes and the movement of security prices are very large.

Figure 6.11   *Contributions to the Change in UK Net External Assets, £bn*

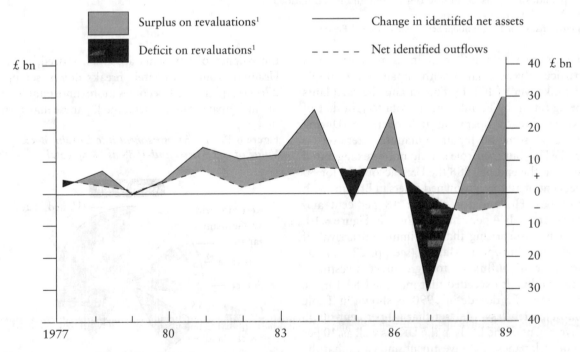

Note:
[1]   Residual component – difference between change in recorded net stock and net identified outflows.
Source: Bank of England Quarterly Bulletin (November 1990) p. 488.

In 1987, 1989 and the first half of 1990 the revaluation was primarily due to the exchange rate effect – when the £ rises against the dollar the value of external assets falls in dollar terms and vice versa – whereas in 1988 it was almost entirely due to revaluations of share and bond prices. The collapse of the dollar in the second half of 1989, followed by its equal and opposite rise during the first half of 1991 will obviously cause the external balance sheet to fluctuate widely in value even though net capital flows remain small.

As we have seen in **Figure 6.1**, the biggest shifts between 1988 and 1989 took place firstly in inflows of direct investment (up from £10.2 bn to £17.1 bn, and up again to £19 bn in 1990), and secondly in UK financial intermediaries' purchases of overseas portfolio investments (up from £8.6 bn to £313 bn). Direct investment overseas remained at its previously high level. This latter item collapsed back by one-half in 1990 whilst portfolio investment overseas collapsed to 40 per cent of its 1989 level as did portfolio investment into the UK, although the absolute difference was much smaller.

The acquisition of £107 bn of overseas assets in the course of 1988–90 is really rather extraordinary for a country running large current account deficits and – in the mistaken view of many critics – allegedly brought to its knees by a decade of Thatcherism. One obvious consequence of this capital outflow at a time of current account deficits (which, added together, constitute the **basic balance**) has been the need to borrow to cover the gap at high interest rates (see Davies, 1990, pp. 34–9). This, in turn, has a detrimental impact upon the interest, profits and dividends item in the invisibles account, causing the current balance to worsen further in subsequent years. Given that the dividend yield on overseas investments is lower than the interest costs of financing those investments, this might appear to be irrational behaviour on the part of UK investors.

It has to be borne in mind, however, as argued by Cliff Pratten (*Financial Times*, 18 July 1990, p. 15) that no account is taken of **capital gains** in this respect. It has been the case in almost every year during the 1980s that part of the return on investments has taken the form of capital gains

which **do not appear in the current account** of the BoP. Pratten estimates the total capital gains during the 1980s as £95 bn and during 1990 as £12 bn (adjusted for inflation). Pratten's conclusion is thus that the current account deficit is largely offset by capital gains but that, since they are mostly unrealised, there is a **liquidity** problem resulting from short-term borrowings to cover the capital outflows.

This view is not universally shared. Coutts and Godley (1990), for example, conduct their own analysis of the accounts and conclude that, first, only £3 bn of the £20 bn current account deficit in 1989 can be compensated by adjustments for capital gains and inflation and, secondly, that if the balancing item represents under-recorded capital inflows rather than under-recorded net exports, then the net stock of overseas assets is much smaller than official estimates suggest and hence that Britain will become a debtor nation if the balance of trade is not restored to a surplus in the near future.

According to a calculation by Keith Skeoch, the chief economist at James Capel, adjusting for capital gains on foreign assets in Britain which he assumes to have accumulated as a result of, first, officially identified investments and, secondly, under-recorded capital inflows, means that Britain already is a net debtor. The official data, published in the 1991 'Pink Book', now show a significant reduction in the value of net assets, down from £83.7 bn at the end of 1989 to £29.6 bn at the end of 1990 (equivalent to roughly $50 bn in relation to **Table 6.1**). This reduction was a consequence entirely of lower asset values as the value of liabilities remained unaltered from 1989. Interestingly, this meant that both assets and liabilities were exactly four times as large in 1990 as in 1980.

All of this may, understandably, leave the reader wondering just what is the real truth of the matter. If so, he or she is not alone since by the same reasonings it has been alleged that the USA is not really a net debtor at all but a net creditor. The US Government actually refuses to publish the official (horrendously large) figure for the net debt, claiming that it is erroneous and misleading. Nevertheless, respected US analysts claim that a proper revaluation of both assets and liabilities leaves the net position almost unchanged.

□ 6.6.3 A Final Caveat

Measured in constant 1980 dollars, the value of direct foreign investment was roughly ten times as large at the end of the 1980s as it had been at the beginning of the 1970s. The effect of these enormous overseas investments has been to change the ownership structure of business in many countries, and at the same time to cast doubt upon the conventional way of calculating trade balances.

For example, an increasing amount of trade takes the form of transfers between the domestic operations of a multinational business and its overseas subsidiaries. On an 'ownership-based' accounting system these would not be counted as international trade. In addition, some sales in a domestic market are to the subsidiaries of foreign businesses which it may be argued are analagous to exports, as are the sales of overseas subsidiaries in overseas markets. On the other hand, it may be argued that domestic purchases from the subsidiaries of foreign-owned businesses are analagous to imports, as are purchases by overseas subsidiaries in overseas markets.

Until the 1980s rejigging trade flows onto an ownership basis would not have made much overall difference, and it currently makes relatively little difference in the case of, for example, Japan. In the case of the USA, however, it totally transforms the trade balance, converting a very large deficit into a modest surplus. The effects upon the UK accounts are not known, but given the surge in outward investment during the 1980s an ownership-based system of trade accounts would presumably look much more favourable today than it did a decade ago and thus help to allay fears about the overall trading position.

■ 6.7 Competitiveness

□ 6.7.1 Measuring Competitiveness

It is appropriate to refer, at this point in our discussion of trade performance, to the 'competitiveness' of the UK. 'Competitiveness' is impossible to measure in any absolute sense, so it must be judged by compiling indices of **relative performance** compared to other relevant countries. Even this is fraught with data collection difficulties, because we need to take some relevant characteristic of the UK economy, measure it over time as an index, and compare that index with the corresponding indices for other countries. Since no single index can be expected to tell the whole story, we need to provide as wide a variety as possible. However, whilst some of these should incorporate non-price characteristics, these cannot realistically be measured, so indices must concentrate upon **cost and price competitiveness**, on the assumption that price and non-price factors are interdependent.

Many goods are in practice sold almost entirely on the home market, so the indices need to incorporate only those goods which are internationally traded on a major scale. As manufactured goods comprise the large element in both UK imports and exports, they are used exclusively for the indices. Additionally, because competitiveness is affected by the exchange rate, all the costs and prices need to be converted into a common currency, in this case dollars, at the ruling spot rate. With every country's index valued in a common currency, the ratio expressing one relative to another can then be measured as an absolute number.

Figure 6.12 illustrates the most important measures of competitiveness on a quarterly basis for the past 10 years. These measures represent changes in the degree of competitiveness over time. The ratios are compiled as follows:

- **Import price competitiveness:** UK wholesale price index for home market sales of manufactures (other than food, drink and tobacco) divided by the unit value index of imports of finished manufactures (SITC sections 7–8, Revision 2).
- **Relative normal unit labour costs:** index of normal labour costs per unit of output in the UK divided by a weighted geometric average of competitors' normal unit labour costs adjusted for exchange rate changes.
- **Relative producer prices:** UK wholesale price index for home sales of manufactures (including food, drink and tobacco) divided by weighted average of the indices of competitors' wholesale prices.

Figure 6.12 *Measures of UK Trade Competitiveness (1985 = 100)*

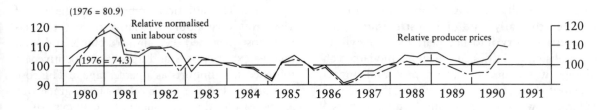

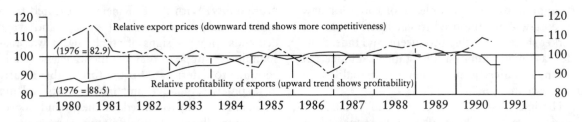

Source: Economic Trade, Table 26.

- **Relative profitability of exports:** ratio of the UK export unit value index for manufactured goods (SITC sections 5–8, Revision 2) to the UK wholesale price index for home market sales of the products of manufacturing industries (other than food, drink and tobacco).
- **Relative export prices:** unit value index of UK exports of manufactured goods divided by a weighted average of competitors' export price indices for manufactures.

All of these indices are subject to data measurement problems (see *Economic Trends*, No. 304 (February 1979) and No. 319 (May 1980) for details). However, the various measures of competitiveness do appear to follow the same pattern, so the overall picture can be taken as acceptably accurate.

□ 6.7.2 *The Historical Pattern*

During the 1970s, as shown in **Figure 6.16** sterling's effective exchange rate (EER) fell steadily, thereby cheapening exports and making imports more expensive. Unfortunately, this did not, as we have seen, prevent the trade balance from remaining firmly in deficit. The reason can partly be seen in the data for relative normal unit labour costs, where the index, standing at 74.3 in 1976, rose sharply to 100.0 in 1980, and actually peaked at over 120.0 in the first quarter of 1981. Irrespective of non-price factors, which in any event were unfavourable for the UK, it is understandable that the UK's relatively high costs caused relative export prices to move unfavourably despite the advantage of a falling exchange rate. Equally, even though this caused import prices to rise, domestic prices also rose steadily, albeit less dramatically, relative to import prices. The only positive feature was that the steady rise in relative export prices maintained the relative profitability of exports on an even keel, although it was showing clear signs of sagging at the end of the decade.

A generally similar picture is shown in **Table 6.2**. The UK's share of world exports of manufactures had been falling throughout the post-war period. This, of itself, was only to be expected since the initially very high share held by the UK reflected the early date of industrialisation, and progressive entry into her markets by newly industrialising countries, using more modern technology, was bound to have a profound impact. The disturbing aspect was, however, that the total volume of world trade in manufactures was itself rising very rapidly, commonly at over 10 per cent per annum, so there was plenty of room for new entrants without the need to eat heavily into the market share of existing producers, and indeed the UK was unique amongst the established industrial nations in suffering more than a marginal loss in market share.

The increased share of imports in Total Final Expenditure (TFE) was also to be expected as industrialised nations increasingly trade manufactured goods with one another, and indeed was characteristic of all such nations. Again, however, the disturbing aspect was the relatively rapid pace at which this occurred in the UK, reflecting in part the UK's relatively high income elasticity of demand for imports.

The overall picture during the period from 1981 to 1984 was a generally much happier one. As shown in **Table 6.2** the UK's share of world exports of manufactures appeared to have reached an equilibrium situation.

Figure 6.12 shows that relative normal unit labour costs declined steadily, and with the effective exchange rate moving sharply downwards, relative export prices became significantly more competitive, and the relative profitability of exports rose slowly but steadily. Despite the rise in import prices, the competitiveness of imports also improved, albeit understandably more slowly, and the visible balance showed several years of surplus. The major problem was, however, the fact that imports as a share of TFE had bottomed out

in 1981, and by 1984 was up 2.6 percentage points. The visible balance in 1984 was accordingly back in substantial deficit.

During 1985 competitiveness suddenly deteriorated, in particular because of a sharp rise in relative normal unit labour costs and in the EER, and although the following year witnessed a recovery, it was clear that the first quarter of 1985 was going to prove difficult to emulate, let alone improve on. The situation from 1985 to the end of 1988 was very gloomy. Relative normal unit labour costs resumed their upward climb, and both relative export prices and import competitiveness followed suit. Imports as a percentage of TFE rose yet further, but the one modest saving grace was an increase in the UK's share of world exports of manufactures and the resilience of relative export profitability. With the EER being prevented from falling much as a matter of policy, and wage demands showing signs of escalating, it was reasonable to suppose that competitiveness would continue to deteriorate for the foreseeable future.

In practice, relative unit labour costs did dip again in 1989 only to concede all the ground gained, and more, during 1990. Relative export prices followed suit and relative export profitability dipped at the end of 1990 for the first time in four years. With inflation rising relative to its trading partners, the UK inevitably suffered a loss of competitiveness in 1990, but this looks to have reversed itself by the end of 1991 so the past two years have undoubtedly been volatile by previous standards. It can only be hoped that a favourable sequence such as occurred after the 1980–81 recession will recur after the current recession is over. One clear difference is, however, that the EER will be fairly constant rather than falling, which will make the restoration of competitiveness that much harder than a decade ago.

As ever, it is important not to get too fixated with domestic problems taken in isolation. Compared to most OECD advanced countries Britain managed to remain relatively competitive during the latter part of the 1980s, as shown in **Figure 6.13** which measures the growth of manufacturing exports relative to the growth of their export markets (measured as a weighted average of the import growth in each exporting country's markets).

Figure 6.13 *Relative Export Performance¹*

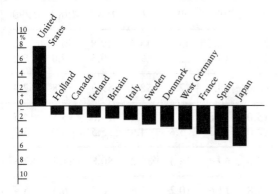

Note:
¹ Manufacturing export growth (volume) *minus* export market growth, 1985–88 average.
Source: The Economist.

The likes of Taiwan and Hong Kong were the real exporting successes of the decade, but Britain held on to its markets better than Japan and most of the EC.

6.8 Area Composition of UK Visible Trade

During the nineteenth century circumstances conspired to create a pattern of trade in the UK consisting essentially of the importation of raw materials and the exportation of finished goods. This arose in the first place because the UK was the earliest country to industrialise, and in the second place because most of the trade was conducted with former or existing colonies. The latter was to a considerable extent a consequence of the former, since other newly-industrialising countries erected barriers against imports from the UK in order to protect their infant industries, but in any event the existence of a common language facilitated trade even with ex-colonies such as the USA.

Trading links with Europe developed gradually during the twentieth century, but as **Tables 6.6 and 6.7** indicate, Europe accounted for only one-quarter of UK imports and a slightly higher proportion of her exports even in 1955. At that time the LDCs accounted for roughly 40 per cent of both UK imports and exports, of which very little

was contributed by the Eastern bloc countries. Over the past three decades the UK has come to trade increasingly with other developed countries. In the case of exports the share has risen to over 80 per cent, although there was a marked temporary dip in the mid-1970s due to the oil-price effect discussed below. In the case of imports the growth in the share taken by the developed countries has been much steadier, with no comparable mid-1970s effect, and the current figure of over 85 per cent is, as a consequence, even higher than that for exports. It is clear that this growth cannot continue for much longer if the UK is to maintain any meaningful trade links with the LDCs, and **Tables 6.6 and 6.7** give some reason to believe that the ultimate equilibrium between developed and less developed countries has just about been reached of late.

The increased share of both imports and exports taken by developed countries has not, however, been evenly distributed. The UK joined the EC in 1972 at a time when trade links with Western Europe were already significantly outweighing those with developed countries outside Europe. Exports to America were still fairly buoyant, whilst imports had only very recently begun to decline, but a marked reduction in trade with other English-speaking ex-colonies had by then become evident.

Prior to 1972 the switch from non-EC to EC countries was already quite marked, but the sharp increase in the share of UK imports from the EC between 1970 to 1975, and the even bigger increase in the share of UK exports taken by EC countries between 1975 to 1980, can reasonably be attributed to UK membership. The share of UK exports taken by EC countries appears to be rising, but the situation in 1990 was in good part a reflection of a rise in the value of the £ compared to the $ which damaged exports to North America and also drew in imports, although this had little effect upon the share coming from the EC which has been stable for several years. The rest of Western Europe provides much the same share of imports as it did in 1955 (albeit well below its 1975 peak) but it has been in decline as an export market since the UK joined the EC. The quadrupling of the share of UK imports originating from the EC has undoubtedly been the most dramatic ad-

Table 6.6 *Area[1] Composition of UK Exports, f.o.b., 1955–90, % Total Value*

	1955	1965	1970	1975	1980	1985	1987	1989	1990
EC	15.0	26.3	28.9	32.2	45.4	48.6	49.8	50.8	53.2
Rest of Western Europe	13.9	15.5	17.1	15.9	12.1	9.7	9.5	9.0	9.2
TOTAL EUROPEAN	28.9	41.8	46.0	48.1	57.5	58.3	59.3	59.8	62.4
North America	12.0	14.8	15.0	11.8	11.2	17.0	16.0	15.5	14.5
Other developed[2]	20.5	14.8	12.0	9.5	5.6	4.9	5.5	6.0	5.7
TOTAL DEVELOPED	61.4	71.4	73.0	69.4	74.3	80.2	80.8	81.3	82.6
Oil exporting	5.1	5.6	5.8	11.6	10.2	7.6	6.5	6.3	5.4
Other developing	31.8	20.1	17.5	15.7	12.5	9.8	10.8	10.5	10.3
TOTAL LESS DEVELOPED	36.9	25.7	23.9	27.3	22.7	17.4	17.3	16.8	15.7
Centrally planned	1.7	2.9	3.7	3.3	3.0	2.4	1.9	1.9	1.7

Notes:
[1]   The 1990 breakdown is the last in this format.
[2]   Japan, Australia, New Zealand, South Africa.
Source: Annual Abstract of Statistics.

Table 6.7 *Area Composition of UK Imports, c.i.f., 1955–90, % Total Value*

	1955	1965	1970	1975	1980	1985	1987	1989	1990
EC	12.6	23.6	28.3	36.5	45.1	50.0	52.9	52.9	52.6
Rest of Western Europe	13.1	12.2	14.9	14.9	13.0	14.3	13.8	12.9	12.6
TOTAL EUROPEAN	25.7	35.8	43.2	51.4	58.1	64.3	66.7	65.8	65.2
North America	19.5	19.6	20.9	13.3	14.9	13.5	11.6	12.6	13.2
Other developed[1]	14.2	11.9	10.1	7.7	6.2	7.3	7.8	7.7	7.5
TOTAL DEVELOPED	59.4	67.3	74.0	72.4	79.2	85.1	86.1	86.1	85.9
Oil exporting	9.2	9.8	7.2	13.5	8.4	3.2	1.8	1.9	2.4
Other developing	28.7	18.4	14.7	11.4	10.0	9.5	9.9	10.1	9.9
TOTAL LESS DEVELOPED	37.9	28.2	21.9	24.9	18.4	12.7	11.7	12.0	12.3
Centrally planned	2.7	4.5	3.9	2.7	2.4	2.2	2.2	1.9	1.8

Note:
[1]   Japan, Australia, New Zealand, South Africa.
Source: Annual Abstract of Statistics.

justment to UK trade patterns over the past three decades, and it is hardly surprising that the UK economy has been reorientated geographically, swing around from north-west (feeding trade with America) to south-east (feeding trade with Europe).

As previously mentioned, the oil price has affected the pattern of UK trade with the LDCs. The effect of the sharp increase in the oil price in 1974 was to transfer huge sums to OPEC countries, and as **Table 6.6** shows this resulted in a doubling of the share of UK exports to oil exporting countries in 1975. Imports did not follow suit on the same scale because only one product was involved, but in the short-term the low price elasticity of UK demand for oil did result in a marked increase in the value of oil imports. The oil price rose sharply again in 1980, but by then the UK was becoming self-sufficient. Subsequently, imports from OPEC have virtually disappeared, although exports remain high compared to the 1960s because the OPEC countries have much greater spending power.

The reasons behind some of the changes described above are fairly obvious, but the heavy dependence upon imports from other developed countries is less so, given that they must consist primarily of finished manufactures which traditionally formed the bulk of UK exports. However, it is increasingly a phenomenon of advanced industrial countries that they simultaneously import and export the same types of product such as cars and electronic apparatus, and there has also been a marked reduction in the dependence of the UK economy upon the exportation of finished manufactures.

6.9 Commodity Composition of UK Visible Trade

As indicated above the UK was traditionally an importer of raw materials and an exporter of manufactured goods. Even in 1955, as shown in **Tables 6.8 and 6.9** raw materials constituted some 75 per cent of UK imports, whilst over 80 per cent of UK exports consisted of semi-manufactured or finished manufactured goods. However, the switch towards

European markets documented above went hand-in-hand with a sharp change in the nature of imports during the 1970s, such that raw materials currently constitute only one-fifth of the total value of imports.

As can be seen in **Table 6.9**, the steady decline in this share disguised some volatile behaviour among the sub-aggregates. In particular, fuel imports shot up as a result of OPEC during the mid-1970s, only to decline sharply thereafter as the UK became self-sufficient in oil.

The share of semi-manufactured imports has also been rather volatile, whilst that of finished manufactured imports has shown a steady rise. As a result, the two parts of **Table 6.9** currently stand in approximately the inverse ratio to that of 1955. The shares are of a total value which has grown steadily in money terms throughout the period examined, but it is difficult to assess whether the current position is near to its ultimate equilibrium because sharp changes in sub-aggregates – such as the virtual halving of fuel imports in money terms during 1986 – have introduced an element of instability which may prove either to be an aberration or the beginning of a new long-term trend. It may be argued that the UK is no longer much dependent upon imports of food, beverages and tobacco. Nevertheless, this sector currently presents major trading problems, as noted below, once exports are taken into account.

The situation with respect to exports has generally been much more stable until relatively recently. However, from 1980 to 1985 the share of exports taken by manufactured goods of all kinds declined quite sharply. This was not altogether surprising given the effects of the recession brought on by the MTFS combined with an overvalued exchange rate, and it reflected in part the sharp increase in the share taken by fuels.

Fuel exports collapsed after 1985, and their share of total exports was entirely taken up by manufactures on the back of rising productivity and a sustainable exchange rate in relation to other EC countries.

Overall, the situation bears a remarkable resemblance to the position pre-1980, although the balance between semi-manufactures and finished manufactures is somewhat different.

Table 6.8   *Commodity Analysis of Exports, % Total Value*

	1955	1965	1970	1975	1980	1985	1987	1989	1990
Food, beverages and tobacco	6.0	6.6	6.2	7.1	6.8	6.3	7.0	7.0	6.8
Basic materials	3.9	4.0	3.2	2.7	3.1	2.7	2.8	2.5	2.2
Fuels[1]	4.9	2.7	2.2	4.2	13.6	21.5	11.0	6.6	7.5
Total	14.8	13.3	11.6	14.0	23.5	30.5	20.8	16.1	16.5
Semi-manufactured	36.9	34.6	34.4	31.2	29.6	25.6	28.3	29.9	27.5
Finished manufactured	43.5	49.0	50.2	51.0	44.0	41.2	48.1	51.6	53.8
Total	80.4	83.6	84.6	82.2	79.6	66.8	76.4	81.5	81.3
Unclassified	4.8	3.1	3.8	3.8	2.9	2.7	2.8	2.4	2.2

Note:
[1]   Roughly 95% oil.
Source: Annual Abstract of Statistics; Monthly Digest of Statistics, Table 15.1.

Table 6.9   *Commodity Analysis of Imports, % Total Value*

	1955	1965	1970	1975	1980	1985	1987	1989	1990
Food, beverages and tobacco	36.9	29.7	22.6	18.0	12.2	10.6	10.8	9.5	9.8
Basic materials	29.0	19.3	13.7	8.4	7.4	6.0	6.0	5.4	4.8
Fuels	10.6	10.6	8.3	17.5	14.2	12.8	6.5	5.2	6.2
Total	76.5	59.6	44.6	43.9	33.8	29.4	23.3	20.1	20.8
Semi-manufactured	17.9	23.8	29.2	23.9	27.3	24.8	26.7	27.8	26.2
Finished manufactured	5.3	15.4	24.6	29.9	36.6	44.0	48.8	50.9	51.7
Total	23.2	39.2	53.8	53.8	63.9	68.8	75.5	78.7	77.9
Unclassified	0.3	1.2	1.6	2.7	2.3	1.8	1.2	1.2	1.3

Source: Annual Abstract of Statistics; Monthly Digest of Statistics, Table 15.1.

The aggregates disguise some significant switches between industrial sectors. Amongst the semi-manufactured exports the share taken by chemicals rose steadily throughout the period from 1955 whilst that of metals fell by almost one-half and that of textiles by three-quarters. The chemicals industry has been a major success story for UK exports, with 12.7 per cent of total exports in 1990, although this share has risen only slightly since 1985.

Engineering products constituted roughly one-third of all exports in both 1955 and 1985. However, its share peaked some 10 per cent higher in 1970, and there has been a steady decline since that time. A good part of this was in the road motor vehicles classification. This accounted for only 1.5 per cent of total exports in 1984, but its share has subsequently more than doubled.

It is also of interest to look at the visible balance for each of the aggregates as depicted in **Figure 6.14**. Throughout the period 1967–90 imports of food, beverages and tobacco consistently exceeded exports, although the size of the deficit in money

Figure 6.14 *Visible Trade Balance, Current Prices*

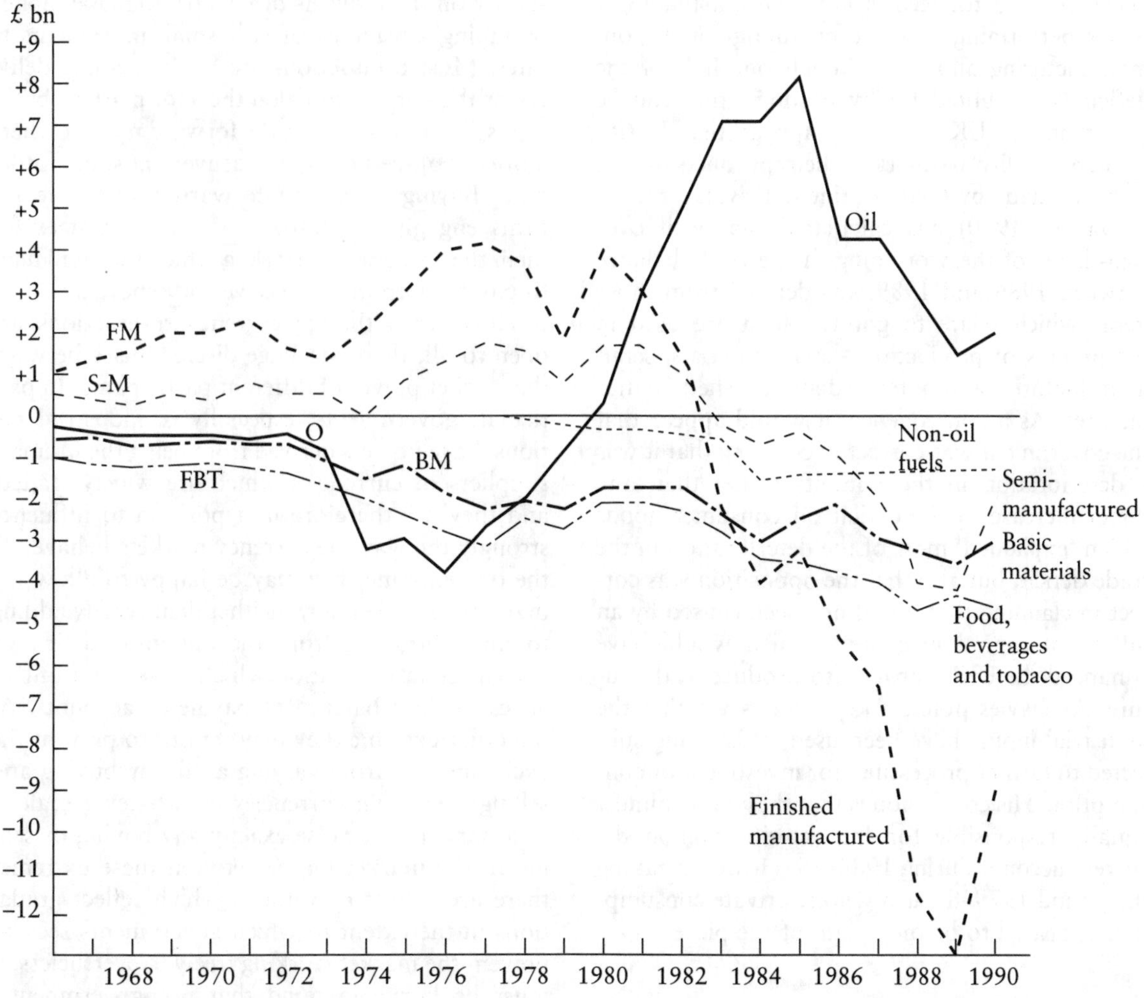

Source: 'Pink Book' (CSO, 1991) Table 2.3.

terms has crept up over the past decade. This has also been the case for basic materials.

The oil aggregate fell to a record deficit of £4 bn in 1976, but moved into surplus by 1980. The record surplus of £8 bn in 1985 therefore represented a turnaround of £12 bn over a 10-year period, but the surplus remained at half that value for the next two years and fell sharply again in 1988 and 1989. Semi-manufactured goods remained in surplus until 1983, but recorded deficits thereafter, and the problem has become significantly worse since 1985.

However, even this is insignificant compared to the situation with respect to finished manu-

factured goods, which also remained in surplus until 1983 before moving sharply into deficit thereafter. The surplus of £4 bn in 1980 was transformed into a £6 bn deficit in 1987, a somewhat smaller turnaround than for oil (though larger if the oil figure for 1987 is taken) but accomplished in half the time. In 1988 the deficit soared to £11 bn. Not surprisingly, much of the policy debate over the past year or two has focussed on this phenomenon.

For most of the 1980s the sector which contributed most to the deficit in manufactures was motor vehicles. As we have noted this sector is on the mend, and is unlikely ever to play that undesirable role again. What is rather alarming is that food, beverages and tobacco is now the outstandingly worst performing sector even though it is non-manufacturing and even though one half of the deficit is accounted for by products that can be grown in the UK. It would appear that British farmers' ability to market their products is put into the shade by their continental rivals.

Davies (1990) has calculated that well over two-thirds of the worsening in the trade balance between 1986 and 1989 was derived from those items which relate to goods which are used in the process of production – raw materials, semi-manufactures and intermediate finished manu-factures. As a consequence, it would appear that the government was correct in claiming that it was a deterioration in these inputs rather than any direct increase in the deficit on consumer goods which 'explained' most of the deterioration in the trade deficit, but also that the opposition was cor-rect in claiming that it had not been caused by an inflow of capital machinery which would have enhanced the UK's capacity to produce in the fu-ture. As Davies notes, a key issue is whether the industrial inputs have been used, after being sub-jected to further processing, for investment or con-sumption. His conclusion is that these were almost equally responsible for the deterioration in the current account during 1986–89. However, taking the period 1979–89 as a whole, private consump-tion appeared to be the villain of the piece.

■ *6.10* Exchange Rates

□ *6.10.1 Introduction*

An 'exchange rate' is the **price of one currency**, for our purposes the £ sterling, **in terms of another currency or set of currencies**. As such it is in prin-ciple determined in the market place for curren-cies, and moves up or down in accordance with the relative forces of demand and supply. In this case the market place is no longer physical, since currency transactions are these days conducted on electronic screens, and this in turn means that anyone can deal in currencies at any time of the day or night anywhere in the world. Not surpris-

ingly, exchange rates are as a consequence con-stantly on the move as dealers try to make money by taking advantage of very small movements in rates. Most transactions are for immediate deliv-ery at the current price on the **spot** market, but it is possible to transact in the **forward** market where a price is agreed today for delivery **at some future date**. Buying or selling forward is valuable for firms engaging in trade, since it guarantees for them the amount of £ sterling which they will have to pay for imports or receive for exports.

However, although currency transactions are open to all, there are huge discrepancies between the market power of different participants. In par-ticular, governments, especially of industrial na-tions, have powers derived from being the ultimate suppliers of currencies which are widely traded, and they are therefore in a position to influence strongly the way the currency markets behave. At the one extreme they may be happy to allow the markets to trade freely, neither deliberately adding to, nor subtracting from, the amount of their own currencies in circulation which arise from imbal-ances in their balance of payments accounts. At the other extreme they may set out to prevent the exchange rate from varying at all, by buying and selling their own currencies on whatever scale is necessary to neutralise exactly any buying or sell-ing in the market place. Between these extremes there are a host of variants which reflect grada-tions in the extent to which governments seek to prevent the market working freely. Nevertheless, it must be borne in mind that non-governmental traders are **in aggregate** also very powerful, and it is not altogether clear in principle whether they, or governments, will be the dominant influence on exchange rates. A reasonable view might be that whilst traders in aggregate can dominate **individual** governments (the average *daily* gross trading in the foreign exchange markets in London, New York and Tokyo exceeds $500 bn), they cannot dominate the major industrial nations **acting in concert** over extended periods of time. Since in practice, as we will see below, this latter eventual-ity is very uncommon, it is fair to say that in the long term exchange rates are broadly determined by market forces irrespective of which exchange rate system is nominally in operation.

The very appearance of the authorities in the foreign exchange markets is potentially an encouragement to speculation. In the absence of intervention, a speculator can make gains only at the expense of other speculators and hence tends to tread a little carefully for fear of being outwitted. However, once the authorities enter the markets to buy a particular currency it becomes obvious to all speculators that this currency cannot otherwise be held at its desired level, and they realise that they can all become sellers and impose losses upon the authorities rather than upon others of their kind.

Furthermore, if they can create sufficient selling pressure then the authorities may have to withdraw from the markets in order to avoid using up scarce foreign currency and/or suffering too great a trading loss, whereupon the currency will drop sharply in value and produce huge speculative gains for sellers.

It follows that half-hearted inventions by the authorities are largely counter-productive. Intervention is only successful **insofar as it imposes losses on speculators**. If the authorities in several major economies, acting in concert, suddenly enter the markets with large-scale buy orders for a particular currency which speculators are selling on a modest scale, or vice versa, speculators will get their fingers burned and act more circumspectly on future occasions.

However, it may strictly be necessary only to **threaten** such behaviour to discourage a good deal of speculation, since if one group of speculators is selling heavily another group may move to buy in anticipation of similar behaviour by the authorities should the rate fall too far (which, naturally, does not then happen).

When the forces of the market are dominant, and the exchange rate is constantly on the move in response either to excess demand or supply, an upwards movement is called an **appreciation** and a downwards movement is called a **depreciation**. Where, however, the government engineers a **unilateral change** in the rate from one value to another, an upwards adjustment is called a **revaluation** and a downwards adjustment is called a **devaluation**. The action of the government may, however, not be intended to alter the rate, but rather to halt its upward or downward movement.

When it intervenes in the foreign exchange market in order to prevent sterling from rising, it is obliged, via the Bank of England, to sell sterling and to buy foreign currency in exchange. This is then mostly deposited in the official reserves. When, however, the government wishes to prevent sterling from falling, it is obliged to buy sterling and in exchange to sell foreign currency which is withdrawn from the official reserves.

As suggested above, the government may, or may not, be successful in its endeavours. To some extent this is conditioned by whether or not the government has openly declared the value of the £ at which it wishes it to be stabilised, since this is bound to affect market expectations. Even if there is no official upper or lower limit to the value of the £, the currency markets can work out the unofficial policy by retrospective inspection of changes in the reserves. Clearly, if there has been, for example, a rise of $1 bn in the monthly reserves figure, it follows that the Bank of England must have been intervening heavily in order to prevent the value of the £ from rising against the $ (by selling £s and buying $s).

It is reasonable to suppose that, officially or unofficially, the government will usually have a clear view about the appropriate level for the exchange rate because of its effects upon the balance of payments.

In any event it must be recognised that the currency markets are not interested in the official position other than as a pointer as to whether to buy or sell a currency at a particular point in time. They do not necessarily agree with the government about the consequences of its economic policy, and having formulated their own view about the probable direction of change of the £ will be looking for signals from the Bank of England in order to determine whether they will be allowed to push the rate to what they believe it should be, or whether – and to what extent – they are likely to be thwarted by intervention.

The view about the exchange rate, whether governmental or market, will be influenced by a whole host of factors, of which the following are the most important: the rate of inflation compared that the major competitors; the structure of interest rates compared with that of major competitors;

and the balance of payments on current account. In addition the market view will, as indicated, be influenced by its forecast of how the government will respond to these factors. Clearly, in order to form an opinion about these matters their underlying causes will themselves have to be studied with care – including, for example, the rate of growth in the economy; capacity constraints; unit labour costs; the fiscal and monetary aggregates and so on. Under the circumstances it is hardly surprising that there should be disagreement about the 'proper' value for the exchange rate.

6.10.2 *The Theory of Purchasing Power Parity (PPP)*

This theory, which dates back to the 1920s, has traditionally been used to explain long-term trends in the exchange rate. PPP states that the exchange rate between two currencies depends upon the **purchasing power of each currency in its country of origin**. If both the UK and USA can produce a set of identical products, in the former case for £100 and in the latter for $100, PPP dictates an exchange rate of £1 = $1. If, however, the set of products in the UK rises in price to £200, but the price of the set in the USA stays unchanged, then PPP dictates an exchange rate of £2 = $1.

The change in the exchange rate comes about through adjustments to trade flows. In the above example, at the original exchange rate, it would pay UK residents to buy US exports for £100 in preference to identical domestic products at any higher price, and that would continue to be the case until the £/$ exchange rate had fallen in value (by one-half if UK prices had doubled). Unfortunately, this is an oversimplified view of the real world in which sets of identical products are difficult to identify, and are certainly less than comprehensive. In addition, allowance must be made for **trading costs** including transportation costs when comparing prices in domestic and foreign markets. In any event, these matters relate only to **visible trade flows**, and the exchange rate is likely to be affected by capital flows which fall outside the confines of the theory.

A looser – and hence by implication a more accurate but at the same time less analytically helpful – definition of PPP is that the currency of a country which has a **higher inflation rate** than its main trading partners will **depreciate**, and vice versa. Such testing of the theory as has been undertaken (and even that has to be treated with care because of problems with respect both to the measurement of the price level and of the exchange rate and to the choice of countries) indicates that, starting at any particular year, the exchange rate eventually reaches an equilibrium level compatible with PPP, but that in the intervening period it may deviate significantly from it in either – and probably both – directions. It follows, therefore, that PPP is of little value of itself, but it does have the virtue of focussing attention on the reasons why deviations of the exchange rate from PPP actually occurred.

6.10.3 *Interest Rates*

We have already remarked upon the fact that hot money is attracted to countries which, after allowing for risk, offer the highest short-term rate of interest. This is also true, but on a much lesser scale, where non-residents with to hold longer-term interest-bearing securities. If UK interest rates exceed those in the USA, West Germany and Japan there is going to be a high demand for £s to invest in the UK, and hence upwards pressure upon the exchange rate. The sums involved can best be thought of in terms of billions rather than millions, but there is fortunately a limiting device in operation.

This arises because, when a non-resident buys sterling at the current or 'spot' exchange rate in order to acquire an interest-bearing asset, he or she may wish to protect against a capital loss, should interest rates rise further, by arranging to sell the asset 'forward' at an agreed price. Buying in the present pushes the spot rate up, whilst selling in the future pushes the forward rate down. The greater the volume of sterling being bought and sold, the greater the difference between purchase and sale prices. Hence, beyond a certain point, the extra interest earned by investing in the

UK is in principle entirely offset by the loss resulting from the need to sell at an exchange rate lower than that at the time of purchase. The **interest rate parity theory** argues that the difference between spot and forward rates will automatically adjust to neutralise differences in short-term interest rates between countries, thereby greatly limiting flows of hot money. However, this argument may be defeated by the sheer volume of hot money, since it follows that a flood of hot money will drive up the exchange rate even higher, and hence even though forward rates are below the matching spot rates at any point in time, they will be rising above the spot rates which ruled in the preceding period. If sterling becomes a 'one-way bet' to continue rising, there is thus no necessity to accept a forward rate until it has risen above the spot rate at the time of purchase, or even perhaps to trade forward at all, since the spot rate at the time of sale will almost certainly be higher than any forward rate contracted previously.

In practice, the above effect is frequently stronger than any influence which the current account surplus or deficit may have upon the exchange rate. This is not to argue that the latter cannot be significant, but it follows logically that if the exchange rate is driven by the current account, then the current balance should be perpetually close to, or at, equilibrium. Since this has rarely been the case for the UK it follows that, particularly in the short-term, **the exchange rate is more responsive to capital flows**. The obvious exceptions are where the current account deficits become so large that even after adjusting for offsetting capital inflows the reserves will run out unless the exchange rate is devalued. Where this is not at issue, it is quite possible that even a massive current account deficit will have less influence upon the exchange rate than hot money responding to rising interest rates, and hence that the **exchange rate will itself continue to rise**.

6.10.4 Interest Rates and Exchanges Rate Risk

Let us assume that:

A US investor has $100 to invest

The interest rate is 5% in the USA and 10% in the UK

The exchange rate is initially $1 = £1 and does not vary

Hence:

If $100 is converted into £s it becomes £100 (ignoring transaction costs)

After earning interest in the UK at 10% it becomes £110

And when converted back into $s it becomes $110

This then compares **favourably** with the $105 which would have arisen in the USA.

However:

Suppose the value of sterling can vary, and it **falls** by 10% (i.e. £110 = $100)

Then the £110 earned in the UK will convert back to $100

This then compares **unfavourably** with the $105 which would have arisen in the USA.

On the other hand:

Suppose the value of sterling can vary, and it **rises** by 10% (i.e. £100 = $110)

Then the £110 earned in the UK will convert back to $121

This represents a return of 21% compared to only 5% if the money is left in the USA.

It follows, therefore, that whether a higher nominal interest rate in one country compared to another is sufficient to attract an inflow of capital depends upon **expectations** of changes in exchange rates. If a country is expected to have a strengthening exchange rate then it will not need to have a high nominal interest rate. This was traditionally the situation for Japan and Germany, but in Spring 1991 it applied, unusually, to the USA.

This can be seen in **Figure 6.15**. At the end of 1990 the US Government was determined to reduce interest rates in order to offset the recession. The Germans, on the other hand, were anxious to raise interest rates in order to offset the inflationary impact of reunification. Ordinarily this would have caused the DM to surge against the $, whereas precisely the opposite happened because the post-Gulf War euphoria and hopes of recovery made

Figure 6.15 *Short-term[1] Interest Rates, 1981–91, %*

Note:
[1]   3-month money market rates.
Source: Bank of England Quarterly Bulletin.

investors buy the $ whilst fears about the cost of reunification made investors sell the DM. Once it was clear that this was going to continue well into 1991 it became possible for the US Government to cut interest rates even further without triggering a run on the $. Meanwhile, in the UK the government refused to follow suit, only reducing interest rates slowly and by small increments, for which they were much criticised.

Where a country's exchange rate is expected to weaken, it will normally need to have a much higher nominal interest rate than elsewhere. The only way to eliminate exchange rate risk is to lock exchange rates together, a factor which underlay the decision to enter the Exchange Rate Mechanism (ERM) (see **pp. 241–2**), but even the current wide band is clearly sufficient to create expectations of exchange rate variability in the UK, and to create worries in the minds of the government that interest rate reductions will trigger a sharp fall in the value of the £.

Once the above is understood, it is possible to unravel the mystery posed on **p. 57** as to why the correlation between saving and investment in any given country is stronger than one would expect in a world of freely mobile capital. At the end of the day, no matter how high the nominal interest rate on offer in, say, the UK, the fear of capital losses on the exchange rate will be enough to deter the more timid investor who will keep his or her money firmly at home. This is borne out by the astonishing size of capital flows during the era of the gold standard when exchange rate risk did not exist. When the topic of capital flows is under discussion, few remember that prior to 1915 the UK ran an average current account surplus of 5 per cent of GDP over a period of three decades, and that the money was exported all over the world to finance development in, for example, North and South America.

It would appear, therefore, that talk of a global capital market is a touch premature, and this is anyway not a new concept. As EC countries lock their currencies closer together, and exchange rate risk is reduced, capital will tend to flow more freely.

6.10.5 Measuring the Exchange Rate

It is such a commonplace to read about movements in 'the' exchange rate that few non-economists ever bother to question whether it is always the **same exchange rate** which is moving. In fact it isn't, so we must consider below the appropriate ways to measure exchange rate movements.

It is clear, to begin with, that there is an exchange rate linking sterling to every other currency belonging to a country with which the UK conducts trade. Naturally, some of these are much more important than others, either in terms of the pattern of UK trade or because of their significance for world affairs. For both these reasons it is customary to place most attention, in terms of individual exchange rates, upon the dollar, and it is indeed the £/$ rate which is most often quoted in the media. However, as shown in the section on the area composition of trade, the UK now trades increasingly with the EC, and within the EC the German currency, the Deutsche Mark (DM), plays a central role, so there are often good reasons to concentrate upon the £/DM rate. Whilst Japan is also very important from the point of view of its share of total world trade, the yen has less significance than the $ or DM specifically in terms of UK trade patterns. Nevertheless, it must be recognised that if the $/yen rate alters sharply, then this is bound to have some repercussions for the £/$ rate as well.

Measuring exchange rates in terms of individual currencies does, however, have drawbacks. In the first place, such rates can be very volatile, as the discussion of recent history below will demonstrate. But this volatility is much greater in certain cases, such as the $, compared to others such as the DM, and individual rates may not simply move in the same direction but at **different speeds** and in **opposite directions**. Clearly, to concentrate exclu-

sively on the $ when it is rising against the £, at a time when the DM is simultaneously falling against the £, may prove highly misleading in terms of consequences for the UK economy.

In order to adjust for this, the sensible procedure is to measure the exchange rate in terms of a **basket of currencies** which includes all those of any significance in terms of UK and, by implication, of world trade. One could simply take the arithmetic average of all the rates included in such a basket, but it also seems sensible to make adjustments for the **relative importance of different countries in terms of UK trade** through a system of **weights**. Such a weighted average is in use, and is called the **effective** exchange rate (EER), where the weights used represent the share of total UK world trade conducted with each country whose currency is included in the basket. It follows that, if a volatile currency is highly weighted, as is true of the $, then the EER will itself show a tendency to be volatile, albeit on a much reduced scale. However, a low-weighted currency will have little effect upon the EER, no matter how volatile it is.

Unfortunately, because the EER measures the £ in relation to other **currencies**, it may be a poor guide to changes in the **competitiveness** of UK goods and services. For this reason, it is preferable for certain purposes to use a **real** exchange rate (RER), which measures the price of UK goods (and hence of UK exports) relative to the average price of foreign goods (and hence of UK imports). Since the latter need to be converted into sterling, the average price of foreign goods is multiplied by the EER for this purpose, and the RER is given by UK price index ÷ overseas average price index × EER. If the RER **falls** then UK competitiveness **improves** because, converted to sterling, imports have become more expensive relative to exports. One obvious drawback to the RER is that not all UK and foreign goods are traded, so the formula is something of an approximation as a measure of competitiveness in the traded goods sector, but it provides a useful supplement to other exchange rate measures.

Table 6.10 sets out the data for the three most important bilateral exchange rates, for the EER and for the ECU. During the period 1975–88 the DM and the yen were the world's strongest cur-

Table 6.10 *Selected Sterling Exchange Rates and Effective Exchange Rate Index (ERI), 1975–90, Annual Averages*

| | Exchange value of sterling in | | | | Sterling effective exchange rate index,[1] (1985 = 100) |
	US$	DM	Yen	Ecu	
1975	2.220	5.447	658.1		124.8
1976	1.805	4.552	535.4		107.0
1977	1.746	4.050	467.7		101.2
1978	1.920	3.851	402.6		101.0
1979	2.123	3.888	465.6		107.0
1980	2.328	4.227	525.6		117.7
1981	2.025	4.556	444.6		119.0
1982	1.749	4.243	435.2		113.7
1983	1.516	3.870	359.9	1.740	105.3
1984	1.336	3.791	316.8	1.694	100.6
1985	1.298	3.784	307.1	1.700	100.0
1986	1.467	3.183	246.8	1.495	91.5
1987	1.639	2.941	236.5	1.420	90.1
1988	1.780	3.124	228.0	1.506	95.5
1989	1.638	3.080	225.7	1.489	92.6
1990	1.786	2.876	257.4	1.400	91.3

Note:

[1] The weights used for the ERI used to be calculated by the IMF using its Multilateral Exchange Rate Model (MERM). However, as from January 1989, the index is that published in the IMF *International Financial Statistics*, where the weights reflect the relative importance of other countries as competitors to the UK in both domestic and overseas markets. The base year is 1985. The weight of the $US in the new ERI has fallen compared to the old ERI, whilst that of the DM has risen.

Source: Bank of England Quarterly Bulletin; Economic Trends.

rencies, and as can clearly be seen, the £ depreciated steadily against both currencies other than during 1980 and 1981 and, more recently, against the DM in 1988 and the yen in 1990. However, the £/$ rate was much more volatile, with peaks in 1972, 1980 and 1988, and troughs in 1977, 1985 and 1989. As these are annual averages they obviously understate the daily high and low values for each year, some of which are also referred to in the following sections. Again, it is important to remember in the wider context that, even if the £ is falling against the DM whilst simultaneously rising against the $, the DM is not necessarily also rising against the $, and so forth.

The EER is also plotted graphically, on a quarterly basis, in **Figure 6.16** since the annual averages are a little misleading. As can be seen, the EER stood at 120 in mid-1975 in the midst of a

massive depreciation lasting from early 1972 to the end of 1976, with only one temporary abatement in 1974–75. From early 1977 to early 1981 it subsequently appreciated steadily to stand once again at a value of 120, only to collapse back to a value of 95 at the end of 1984. On an annualised basis the EER continued to fall until the end of 1987, but as the graph in **Figure 6.16** shows, the quarterly pattern was actually quite volatile, and showed a rising tendency from 1986 to 1988 before falling sharply again in 1989. During the latter half of 1990 the EER rose sharply (gaining 15 per cent against the $ alone), but the sudden recovery of the $ against the £ at the beginning of 1991 promptly reversed the sequence.

It is worth noting that the UK's EER has in general shown considerably less volatility than that of other major countries, especially Japan and the

Figure 6.16 *Sterling Exchange Rate Index, 1972–91, Quarterly Averages (1985 = 100)*

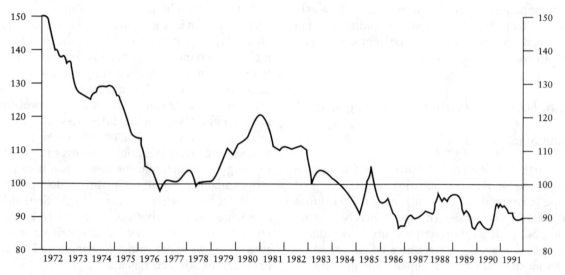

Source: Bank of England Quarterly Bulletin.

USA, as can be seen in **Figure 6.17**. Hence a quite different perspective is gained in the longer-term when comparing volatility in the EER with volatility in, say the £/$ rate. In the short term the EER shows little volatility, even though bilateral rates may be highly volatile, which might be taken as a lesson for financial markets that what you see depends upon where you look.

The RER is rarely mentioned in the media, so detailed figures are not given here. By and large the RER is affected mostly by the EER in the short-term, and mostly by relative inflation rates in the longer term, much as one would expect. Since the UK has almost continuously suffered more inflation than her main competitors since 1975, this has exerted constant upwards pressure upon the RER and led to a corresponding loss of competitiveness. During those periods in which the EER has risen sharply, for example in 1979–80, this has combined with the relative price effect to produce a disastrous loss of competitiveness. The same combination, albeit on a lesser scale, was evident in 1988 and 1990. At other times, however, the decline in the EER has more than outweighed the relative price effect, and the RER has fallen (as in 1986–87). It is finally worth noting that a country which is undergoing a strong

Figure 6.17 *Effective Exchange Rates (1985 = 100)*

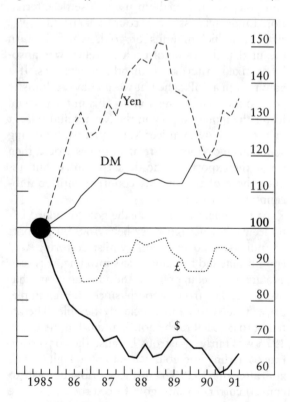

Source: The Economist.

currency appreciation need not necessarily become uncompetitive. As the Japanese have shown in recent times, the RER can still be induced to fall provided domestic prices can be kept down relative to world prices.

□ 6.10.6 *Exchange Rate Regimes*

Gold Standard

Although there is no realistic prospect of an equivalent exchange rate regime being restored, it is of some importance to explain briefly the workings of the old **gold standard** which involved strict rules, but which did not require any international co-operation since each country could apply the rules independently of the others. The gold standard operated in the UK from 1821 to 1914, and from 1925 to 1931. During these periods the UK money supply was determined by the gold reserves, and gold was the medium used to settle international indebtedness. Each country's currency was fixed in value in terms of gold, which in turn meant that the value of each currency was absolutely fixed in terms of all other currencies. If a country ran a BoP deficit, it would have to transfer gold to the country in surplus. This in turn would lower the money supply in the former and raise it in the latter, with prices subsequently following suit. This movement in relative prices would then boost the exports of the deficit country, and reduce those of the surplus country, until equilibrium was restored.

At the time, the fact that the gold standard left no leeway for discretionary behaviour on the part of individual governments, whilst restoring BoP equilibrium and bringing prices into line, was seen as a great virtue. In practice, the adjustment mechanism was far from smooth since, for example, prices tended to be insufficiently flexible. The attempt to go back to the gold standard in the UK in 1925 was fairly disastrous because the conversion rate of sterling into gold was set at too high a level, and after the 1929 Crash the worldwide rush to convert currencies into gold forced the UK, whose gold reserves were limited, to suspend convertibility and to float the £ in 1931.

From a more modern perspective, a gold standard type of mechanism is sometimes advocated because it provides a strong brake upon inflation. However, against this has to be set the fact that an individual country cannot **choose** its rate of inflation; it cannot use money supply control as an instrument of demand management; and it cannot vary the exchange rate to deal with BoP problems arising either because of differences in national inflation rates, or because of unforeseen external shocks. The fact that it might no longer be possible to use gold to underpin the mechanism because it is unavailable in sufficient quantities does not rule out the use of the mechanism as such. Something else which is available can quite easily be used instead. This could either be an existing currency such as the $, or an artificial currency linked to a basket of existing currencies.

Bretton Woods 1944–71

At the end of the Second World War a new set of rules was introduced for controlling the world's monetary system. These included a fixed exchange rate mechanism harking back in many respects, but in a less rigid manner, to the gold standard. All members of the IMF had to peg their currencies to the $, which was in turn pegged to gold at a rate of $35 per ounce. However, this peg was not immovable, but 'adjustable'. Any individual currency could freely move up or down by up to 1 per cent in relation to its $ par value, but beyond that point the relevant central bank would have to intervene, and to use its reserves in order to keep within the permitted variance about the par value. In addition, any country could, without seeking the permission of the IMF, unilaterally lower (devalue) or raise (revalue) its currency by up to 10 per cent. If a larger alteration was thought to be necessary, then the permission of the IMF had to be sought, but this was certain to be forthcoming provided the country could demonstrate that its BoP was in 'fundamental disequilibrium'. Since no specific definition of this term existed, it was hard to see how the IMF could refuse a country which claimed that such a condition was indeed in force.

For the most part the adjustable peg worked quite well until the later 1960s. It was a period of generally sustained growth, and the gold reserves of the USA were sufficient to settle trade imbalances in the few cases where dollars, effectively as good as gold, were unacceptable. Compared to the gold standard, inflation control was weakened because currencies could be realigned, but the widespread adoption of fiscal policy as an instrument of demand management overcame a serious deficiency of the gold standard in that it had no instruments for demand management.

However, the Bretton Woods system came under increasing pressure, primarily because (1) countries arguably in fundamental disequilibrium, such as the UK in the 1960s, were afraid to admit it and to devalue, since their governments feared the political consequences of being seen as unable to manage their economies. Whilst devaluations did occur, as in the UK in 1967, these were always by too little and too late. (2) Since such countries preferred instead to deflate their economies by fiscal means, their growth was held back. (3) Countries in surplus generally refused to revalue, arguing that this would stimulate spending on cheap imports and impart an inflationary bias to their economies. (4) But this in turn meant that speculators could be fairly certain that a fundamental disequilibrium would be resolved by a devaluation, effectively yielding a one-way bet which in turn put further pressure on deficit countries' reserves. (5) The dollars needed to maintain international liquidity, and to allow for BoP deficits to be paid for, had to come as a result of the USA running a BoP deficit and paying its debts in its own currency (which no other country could do). Eventually these dollar holdings outside the USA grew larger than the value of the gold reserves held in the USA to which they were fixed, and the whole system became overdependent upon US macroeconomic policy. Confidence in this policy could not be restored, and as a result, attempts were made to convert dollars into gold at the fixed parity, and the USA was forced to suspend convertibility in August 1971. This signalled the end of the era during which gold played an important role in international trade.

In an attempt to salvage the adjustable peg, agreement was reached at the Smithsonian Conference in December 1971 to increase the permitted fluctuation around par values from ±1 per cent to ± 2.25 per cent; to revalue certain strong currencies; and to raise the $ price of gold (which was worth far more in the free market than when held in reserves). However, the situation could not be salvaged, and in the particular case of the UK the BoP problems of the early 1970s forced the government to float the £ in June 1972. One year later, floating exchange rates were the norm rather than the exception.

Managed Floating

The floating exchange rate system adopted after 1973 was 'dirty' rather than 'clean'. Even so, it was considered that a number of advantages would follow compared with the adjustable peg, many of which were compatible with the newly popular monetarist doctrines. In this latter respect it was argued that the adjustable peg had necessitated the use of monetary instruments to manage demand, with a view to keeping the BoP in equilibrium. Once the exchange rate was floating, equilibrium would automatically be restored by appreciation or depreciation of the currency, and as a result monetary instruments could be transferred to their proper use, namely control of inflation. Strictly speaking, this required the float to be clean if it was to work properly, but even a dirty float would free up the hands of the authorities to some extent.

In principle, any country experiencing relatively rapid inflation should not suffer a permanent competitive disadvantage. As prices rise faster than in competing countries, so the exchange rate should depreciate to offset this. The nominal exchange rate thus adjusts to keep the real exchange rate constant. But this should not create unemployment in uncompetitive countries. As their currencies depreciate, the price of imports – and hence retail prices in general – will begin to rise. Provided nominal wages stay more or less unchanged, real wages will therefore fall and bear the brunt of the adjustment rather than the number of jobs on offer. Furthermore, there should be much reduced scope for destabilising speculation compared with the adjustable peg. By buying cheap and selling dear, speculators actually move the currency towards its equilibrium value, and hence reduce the opportunities for further speculation.

Unhappily, the era of managed floating was not an unqualified success, and a number of serious drawbacks manifested themselves in practice. Most importantly, (1) certain currencies remained overvalued in relation to the current account, which accordingly remained heavily in deficit with the deficit financed by capital inflows. (2) Monetary policy often did not succeed in controlling domestic inflation because, for example, of the problems of defining the monetary aggregates for this purpose, and so the exchange rate needed to be depreciated further, once again driving up import prices. Where domestic wages rises were demanded by way of compensation, further damaging effects upon inflation and employment ensued. (3) Exchange rates were much more volatile than could be accounted for by differences in inflation rates, leading to large fluctuations in real exchange rates which had damaging effects upon world trade flows. (4) Speculation at times was very heavy. Whilst it is clear that if one party gains £1 another party must have lost £1, it does not necessarily follow that winners and losers come from the same group. Professional speculators may gain continuously at the expense of the ill-informed.

In essence, acknowledgement of these difficulties led to two distinct developments. Firstly, the EC countries introduced the European Monetary System (EMS), discussed in detail in Chapter 7, which harks back to the adjustable peg in that it requires much the same degree of co-operation between participants, but in the context of a somewhat less rigid set of rules. Secondly, the USA under President Reagan attempted to move away from unco-ordinated floating towards a system, centred essentially upon the dollar, the yen and the Deutsche Mark (and hence linking in to the EMS), requiring progressively more co-operation and the adherence to progressively more specific rules. Before discussing this, it is worth noting that the UK has been party to both these developments, either as a member of the EC or as a member of the Group of 5 (G5) or 7 (G7) major industrial countries, but has until recently remained on the sidelines pursuing a policy of an essentially ad hoc nature.

There have been a large number of minor milestones along the road which may perhaps best be labelled 'informal' management of the world's major three currencies. However, the more notable ones were the **Plaza Agreement** of September 1985, the **Louvre Accord** of February 1987 and the Group of Seven Statement of December 1987 (issued in the absence of a formal meeting).

In March 1985 the $ stood at ¥260 and DM3.4, a rise of roughly one-half in its RER since 1980. This was viewed in the USA as a virtue insofar as it reflected the strength of the US economy, and simultaneously as a vice insofar as it produced huge BoP deficits and stirred up strong protectionist sentiments. The $ then began to fall of its own accord, but only temporarily. The Plaza Agreement (between the members of G5 including the UK) was designed to talk it down a further 10 per cent or so, essentially by stating that it was too high. The sum of $18 bn was made available for supportive intervention, 30 per cent contributed by the USA, 30 per cent by Japan and 40 per cent by European countries. By October the $ had fallen to its desired level, but it continued to fall sharply, thereby raising fears in Japan and Germany that it was not going to achieve a 'soft landing' – with consequent undesirable effects upon their competitiveness. Eventually this led to the Louvre Accord in early 1987, which agreed 'reference rates' for the $ of ¥153.50 and DM1.825. A 2.5 per cent fluctuation on either side could be ignored, but if it increased to 5 per cent then there would need to be obligatory consultations. These consultations should be distinguished from an obligation to intervene, and implied only a modest increase both in co-operation and in the establishment of rules compared with the Plaza Agreement.

However, a substantial amount of buying intervention to stabilise the $ did take place, roughly of the order of $100 bn, and with considerable initial success. But the G7 summit in Venice in June, which reaffirmed the Louvre Accord, failed to instil confidence in the financial markets that the USA was determined to deal with its twin Budget and BoP deficits. This was the trigger for the stock market Crash in October 1987, subsequent to which the $ fell sharply. The G7 Statement in December sought to re-emphasise that the Louvre Accord was alive and well, and in order to demonstrate that there was a clear intent to keep the $ at a reference level of around ¥125 the authorities intervened heavily to punish speculators who were attempting to drive down the $.

All this did not bode particularly well for international co-operation. The Japanese were very keen to prevent the $ falling sharply against the yen until they realised, in early 1988, that their exporters had learned to live with a high yen value. As a result, active intervention is no longer high on their agenda. The West Germans never showed much interest in reference ranges in the first place, and have always been unhappy at being attacked by the USA for not expanding their economy in order to increase imports and hence raise the DM/$ rate, arguing that this would be inflationary and that the USA was, after all, the source of the problem. The oddest aspect of all this is, perhaps, that the USA is the country least able to keep its promises about exchange rate co-operation, because the US Treasury Secretary controls neither fiscal policy nor monetary policy, respectively the responsibilities of Congress and the Federal Reserve.

As previously stated, the UK was not actively locked into the above manoeuvres insofar as there was no official reference range for sterling against the $, yen or DM. However, after a period of floating wherever the Chancellor saw fit, sterling was first managed more like an adjustable peg in the sense that attempts were made to keep the £ broadly constant in terms of DM, thereby effectively shadowing the EMS without making this an explicit objective, and subsequently locked into the ERM at a central party of £1 = DM2.95.

■ *6.11* Exchange Rate Issues

It is helpful at this stage to summarise some of the threads with run through the preceding discussion. We may note, for example, that each exchange rate system can be designated according, first, to the rigidity of its rules, and secondly to the degree of co-operation required of participants.

The post-war years have witnessed a considerable diversity of systems, all quite distinct from the prewar gold standard. This, as explained above, required currencies to be fixed in terms of gold,

with no discretion to alter the rate and with each country able to fix its rate wholly independently of other countries. Subsequently, countries have periodically reimposed either fairly rigid rules or adopted an independent stance, but never both together. The Bretton Woods 'adjustable peg' allowed for some variation around par values, and also for periodic realignment of currencies, so it was less rigid than the gold standard, but it differed from the latter primarily insofar as it could only operate successfully through co-operative behaviour. However, the willingness to set supranational interests above national interests was distinctly limited, and indeed the system ultimately faltered because of a general unwillingness to adopt co-operative solutions.

The EMS, discussed in detail in Chapter 7, is essentially a more flexible version of the adjustable peg, but like that system it allows participants to behave in somewhat different ways. The country at the centre of the system, Germany, has more room for manoeuvre than any of the others. Those participants which peg themselves to the Deutsche Mark, such as Holland, are relatively rule-bound compared with those which are willing to realign their currencies. Spain has even more discretion than these because of its wider permitted variation around its par value, and this also applies currently to the UK.

The UK, from 1979 to 1990, largely did its own thing. It avoided becoming rule-bound by pegging sterling neither to the EMS nor to any other currency, but periodically showed some enthusiasm for shadowing the Deutsche Mark as a possible prelude to eventual ERM membership, as in 1988. For much of the earlier period the dollar was also managed very independently, but the recent agreements such as the Louvre Accord indicate a growing preference for more co-operation combined with adherence to some loosely defined rules which require the G7 central banks to limit the volatility of the major currencies.

Countries which are eager to grow more quickly tend to prefer an undervalued exchange rate, since this keeps down export prices. Equally, if control of inflation is the primary concern, an overvalued exchange rate becomes more desirable since it keeps down import prices. It is difficult to prove that exchange rates are deliberately managed in order to pursue national interests (at the expense of other countries), since governments are overtly dedicated to better co-operation. But insofar as it does occur, it prevents rather than enhances the move towards equilibrium in international trade.

This returns us, finally, to the issue of credibility underlying our remarks in the introduction to this chapter. We noted there that whilst governments, acting in concert, have considerable leverage over their exchange rates, they cannot defeat the forces of the market once these are pushing uniformly in one direction. The implication is that if the international capital markets believe, for example, that the G7 countries have no clear-sighted long-term strategy, then they will continue to drive rates up and down in search of a speculative profit.

G7 countries can seek to persuade the markets that they do indeed have a clear view on the appropriate level for the $ and DM by sudden interventions on a massive scale which inflict heavy losses on speculators. The issue for the markets is then to decide whether the rate is being held at the 'right' level. But this is difficult to define. In general it may be interpreted as the rate which is neither so high as to make UK exports uncompetitive, nor so low as to raise the rate of inflation via rising import prices.

▌6.12 The International Monetary System

☐ 6.12.1 International Liquidity

As has become clear from our previous discussion, it is impossible to isolate an individual country such as the UK from the economic forces which affect the rest of the world. The UK is, hence, not merely linked into these forces via the institutions which try to control them, but through the flows of international liquidity which are the physical manifestation of these forces.

International liquidity is the stock of assets which is held by the appropriate body in each country, on behalf of its government, in order to settle BoP

deficits and to defend its exchange rate. The assets in question must obviously be acceptable throughout the non-Eastern bloc world, and at any point in time the great bulk of them are to be found in the official reserves of the major industrialised countries. However, since few individual countries are either able – or, indeed, wish – to hold sufficient reserves to cover every eventuality, existing reserves need to be supplemented by a variety of sources, whether money markets or international institutions, from which additional liquidity can be obtained as required.

International liquidity is no different from domestic money in terms of its functions, such as acting as a medium of exchange or unit of account, but is much more restrictive in its physical forms. A greatly expanded volume of trade has caused a dramatic escalation in the need for such liquidity since the 1970s. This is to be expected, because it is obviously a precondition for international liquidity that it is acceptable not merely within an individual country, but well beyond its boundaries.

International liquidity takes three basic forms – namely, gold; the domestic currencies of individual countries which are acceptable as 'reserve' currencies; and non-domestic currencies created by international bodies such as the IMF. The holdings of gold and reserve currencies are largely to be found in the reserves of individual countries, but substantial quantities are also held by the IMF quite independent of its own 'artificial' currency.

Until fairly recent times gold was the most favoured form of international liquidity, since it has always been universally desired for its intrinsic qualities. Given that its value has always greatly exceeded its production costs, those countries which mine it – mainly the USSR and South Africa, and hence not the most popular of sources – have profited enormously from its supply, but the main economic issue is that its supply is inflexible even in the face of a rapid increase in its price. Hence the enormous increase in the demand for international liquidity after 1945 could not be met by an increase in the supply of gold at its existing price. Whilst it would have been possible to raise the value of the existing stocks to the required level, this would have seriously affected the world economy because of the very unequal distribution of gold stocks between countries. Thus, so long as gold was fixed in terms of dollars, as was the case until 1972, the increasing demand for international liquidity had to be met in other ways, although gold still constitutes a very significant proportion of the value of reserves held by industrialised nations.

The use of domestic currencies as 'reserve' currencies has many advantages. Paper money is cheap to produce and to store; it can be supplied on any scale that can conceivably be required; and there is widespread familiarity with its use. It is also worth noting that reserves do not have to be held in the form of currency as such. Rather, the currency can be placed on deposit and hence earn interest, or be converted into financial instruments denominated in the relevant currency.

Most international liquidity has been held in the form of reserve currencies since 1945. The obvious drawback is that no-one wishes to hold reserves in the form of a currency which is subject to capital losses. Until 1972 the US$ was pegged to gold, and hence was a universally popular reserve currency (unlike the £ which was devalued in 1949 and 1967). Since 1972 the volatile behaviour of the $ has considerably undermined its desirability, and the yen and the Deutsche Mark (and more recently the £) have tended to displace the $. However, the vast $ reserves built up over the years (issued to settle US balance of payments deficits with the rest of the world), mean that international liquidity will remain dominated by the $ for the foreseeable future.

There are clear advantages accruing to a country whose currency is used for reserve purposes, not least of which is its ability to settle its debts in its own currency (which it can print at virtually no cost to itself). The main drawback is that if there is a severe loss of confidence in the currency – arising perhaps as a result of large and ongoing BoP deficits – attempts by foreigners to switch into other, stronger, currencies may have severe implications for the domestic economy. When there is a run on a currency it is unlikely that the country whose currency it is will by itself have the resources to stem the tide. Hence international co-operation between the central banks of industrial nations

is a prerequisite for stability in the international monetary system.

6.12.2 Special Drawing Rights (SDRs)

The shortage of gold, and the increasing overdependence upon the dollar, stimulated moves towards the creation of an 'artificial' form of currency (that is, one controlled not by the monetary authorities of an individual country but by an international body). As part of the Bretton Woods agreement discussed above, the IMF had been set up to oversee the adjustable peg mechanism and to help countries in BoP difficulties to set their houses in order. In order to do this it received funds from member countries, varying according to their ability to pay. Originally, these funds were paid as a quota, of which 75 per cent constituted the domestic currency of the contributor and 25 per cent constituted gold. The funds were then lent in the same form by way of temporary loans to countries in difficulties, in the expectation that they would be repaid within three to five years once the difficulties had been resolved (following guidelines determined by the IMF).

In 1969 the IMF managed to obtain international agreement for the introduction of an international currency called **Special Drawing Rights** (SDRs), and these first began to circulate in 1970 following an amendment to the IMF's Articles of Agreement. The SDRs are not put into circulation in the form of banknotes, but rather exist as **credits in ledgers to be drawn on as required in relation to members' quotas**, as explained below.

The creation of SDRs was certainly a major improvement on preceding arrangements because it offered a permanent solution to the shortage of international liquidity which existed at the time, rather than the kind of ad hoc arrangement previously adopted. In particular, the General Agreements to Borrow (GAB) had been brought into being in 1962 whereby members of the Group of Ten (major industrial countries) agreed to increase allocations of their domestic currencies to the IMF if other members of the group needed to withdraw larger amounts than the IMF had in stock. The UK was itself able to utilise GAB during its periodic BoP crises in the 1970s, and especially in 1976. Over the years, the sums allocated to GAB have been periodically revised, with Switzerland joining the other ten members in 1984, and the possibility of access to GAB being extended beyond its immediate membership.

Like GAB, SDRs are available only temporarily (the World Bank being the appropriate body to approach for more permanent financing). Each country paying over its quota to the IMF is guaranteed a borrowing facility related to the size of that quota, which is measured in terms of SDRs. Furthermore, this facility rises in value over time as the size of the quotas is periodically raised.

A country seeking to borrow from the IMF obviously desires reserve currencies and/or gold. It purchases these with its SDRs, acquired either in return for its quota payments or as a loan from the IMF, thereby transferring the SDRs to the country supplying the currency which is being borrowed.

The IMF expects to influence a borrowing country's macroeconomic policy in order to ensure that the borrower creates the capacity to repay. However, no conditions are imposed where the borrower seeks a loan no greater than 25 per cent of its quota. This is called its **reserve tranche** and is contained in the figure for the borrower's official reserves (denoted 'reserve position at IMF' in **Table 6.4**). Conditions begin to be imposed when a loan exceeds this figure, and are made increasingly stringent as the size of the loan increases. Loans in excess of the reserve tranche are available in four equal instalments, each amounting to 25 per cent of a country's quota. These **credit tranches** can thus bring total borrowings up to a maximum of 125 per cent of a country's quota, but unlike the reserve tranche they are recorded, where relevant, in the BoP accounts as 'allocation of Special Drawing Rights' (**see Table 6.3**).

The conditions placed upon credit tranches are understandably somewhat unpopular in the borrowing country. When the UK was forced to borrow in 1976, the IMF demanded that public spending be sharply reduced and that the growth of the money supply be curtailed, neither policy being likely to appeal to the Keynesian Labour Government of the time. Inevitably, borrowers are wont to place the blame for austerity measures at the IMF's door, since this avoids explaining why the problems arose in the first place, so the IMF has something of an image problem. It also has something of a credibility problem, because it is dealing in an artificial currency on a scale which is deliberately restricted by the major industrial countries wielding large blocks of votes on its Governing Board.

The size of quotas is subject to five-yearly reviews, but the initial intention steadily to replace reserves held in other forms by SDRs has never found favour with the major industrial countries, which are understandably wary of handing over control over monetary matters to a supranational body. Certainly, some attempts were made over the years to bring the SDR into increasing prominence, including the partial or full payment of increases in quotas in the form of SDRs rather than gold, and the payment of attractive rates of interest to countries receiving SDRs in exchange for their currencies, but a major consideration has been the ready availability of dollars arising from the huge US BoP deficits of the mid-1970s and 1980s. SDRs thus currently account for only some 5 per cent of world reserves.

Throughout the 1980s the UK reserve position was relatively sound, and the need to borrow from the IMF has become a non-issue. Whilst, therefore, the SDR is of some relevance insofar as it constitutes a small part of total UK reserves, and also insofar as the £ is one of the five currencies on which the value of the SDR is based (as a weighted average), it has to be recognised that the UK is currently far more affected by the remarkable rise in international currency reserves which has occurred since 1985.

6.13 The International Debt Crisis

□ 6.13.1 Origins of the Crisis

During the period prior to the early 1970s, the volume of world trade was growing rapidly, to the mutual benefit of both developed and less-developed countries. Lending to the LDCs, whether via the banks or bodies such as the IMF, was not considered to be a widespread risk of default since these countries were, with occasional exceptions, generating sufficient national income to service the interest payments on their debts. However, the sudden sharp rise in the price of oil engineered by OPEC in 1974 severely affected not merely the non-oil LDCs but some of the more developed countries as well, and so reduced their national income as to prevent full payment of outstanding debt interest. The second oil price rise in 1979 worsened their situation yet further – partly via increased costs of production, and partly via the resultant recession amongst their industrialised customers.

During the 1970s the IMF provided very limited assistance. The largest sum lent in any one year was $3 bn, and that included loans to the developed countries in difficulties. The burden of lending accordingly fell upon the commercial banks in industrialised countries which, rather foolishly in retrospect, were happy to offer short-term loans tied to floating interest rates. At the time, such behaviour did not appear to be quite so foolish. In the first place, the borrowers were sovereign states which, unlike industrial concerns, were not thought to be in any danger of bankruptcy. Secondly, the recycled OPEC surpluses were swilling around the banking system looking for a profitable home, and with industrial profitability falling sharply in domestic markets, the number of customers wishing to borrow expensive money was on the decline.

With interest rates floating upwards rather than down, it gradually became clear that sooner or later a major default on interest payments was going to occur, and that this could have a disastrous impact if such a default threatened to bankrupt commercial banks, which would then call in other loans to LDCs, and so on. In 1982 the three largest debtors, Mexico, Brazil and Argentina, between them owed $220 bn in debt, with an annual interest bill of $13 bn. Since it was clear that countries such as these literally – for the time being, at least – lacked the capacity to repay, some kind of debt rescheduling operation was clearly required.

Between them, the IMF and the banks devised a way to proceed. The IMF stood prepared to make further loans available, albeit on a relatively modest scale, through a variety of programmes such as the extended fund facility (EFF); the supplementary financing facility (SFF); the compensatory financing facility (CFF); and the enlarged access policy (EAP). Most of the loans were not merely made 'conditional' upon changes in the macroeconomic policies of the debtor nations but also conditional upon the creditor banks accepting a **restructuring of those debts** and, if necessary, further increases in their lending. In other words, the banks needed the reassurance of an IMF-imposed austerity programme, whilst the IMF needed the banks' co-operation in order to induce the debtor countries to accept such a programme. It has to be said that the debtor countries were somewhat ungrateful, arguing that their sovereignty was being undermined (which, in truth, it had to be), whilst the creditor banks complained about the throwing of good money after bad (which again was a calculated risk in order to avoid an immediate default, and possibly to create an ability to repay both the old and new borrowing at some future date).

□ 6.13.2 Recent Developments

During 1983 and 1984 the IMF lent some $20 bn to 70 countries, although the effect was multiplied many times by the debt rescheduling which accompanied this lending, and the feared collapse among the banks whose balance sheets contained what, on any definition, were 'bad' debts in excess of their issued capital, was headed off. However, that is not the same thing as saying that the underlying problem went away, which it did not. The drop in the oil price provided some relief for the non-oil LDCs, although it also served to create problems for oil-producers such as Mexico and Nigeria, and the general upsurge in economic growth amongst the industrialised nations helped to boost world trade. Nevertheless, the scale of the problem remained severe.

Between 1982 and mid-1987 the 'Paris Club' creditor governments rescheduled $48 bn of debt for 39 countries, of which the UK's share was $4.5 bn. The problem for the banks, as indicated above, was their high exposure to 'non-performing' debt in relation to their capital base. They set out accordingly to strengthen their balance sheets. Between 1982 and 1986 the UK banks managed to reduce loans to problem debtors as a proportion of their total assets from 9.3 to 6.9 per cent. They simultaneously increased their capital as a proportion of problem loans from below 100 per cent to roughly 140 per cent. With the encouragement of the Bank of England the banks improved their provisions against the risk of bad debts.

Unfortunately, little parallel progress was made to reduce the indebtedness of the problem debtors where the ratio of debt to export earnings continued to rise. At meetings of the IMF and World Bank in April 1987 Nigel Lawson restated the UK's policy on international debt, the core of which was that in the long-term debtors must restore their creditworthiness so that they could once again borrow on world capital markets. This would necessitate policy reform in debtor countries and new finance should be conditional upon such reform. The weakening of conditions which Lawson detected should be reversed, and rescheduling held back until it was certain that new policies were operational.

One rather embarrassing aspect of the debt problem at the end of 1988 was the acknowledgement by the IMF that instead of the IMF financing the debtor nations, the debtor nations were financing the IMF. During the three years to April 1988 net repayments to the IMF totalled SDR 7 bn as a result of repayments of loans made in the early 1980s even though the debt burden of countries

Table 6.11   *20 LDC Debtors: Breakdown of Debt By Main Creditor Groups*[1], *1989*

	Bank Debt		Other Private		Official Debt		Total Debt
	$bn	% of total	$bn	% of total	$bn	% of total	$bn
Venezuela	25.4	79.4	2.1	6.4	4.6	14.2	32.0
Mexico	69.8	69.7	1.9	1.9	28.5	28.5	100.3
Brazil	77.2	68.7	6.3	5.6	28.8	25.7	112.3
Bulgaria	6.6	66.3	1.0	10.4	2.3	23.2	10.0
Argentina	36.8	64.6	3.4	5.9	16.8	29.5	56.9
Ecuador	6.1	54.5	0.4	3.7	4.7	41.8	11.2
Chile	9.9	52.3	2.6	13.8	6.4	34.0	19.0
Costa Rica	2.1	45.4	0.4	8.8	2.2	45.8	4.7
Colombia	7.6	43.6	1.5	8.5	8.3	47.8	17.3
Philippines	11.8	39.9	2.1	7.0	15.8	53.2	29.6
Peru	8.0	39.2	2.2	10.8	10.2	50.0	20.4
Yugoslavia	6.6	37.3	0.8	4.7	10.2	58.0	17.6
Uruguay	2.4	32.2	3.9	52.9	1.1	14.8	7.3
Poland	8.8	21.7	1.5	3.8	30.1	74.4	40.4
Nigeria	6.8	21.2	4.2	13.1	21.1	65.7	32.1
Cote d'Ivoire	3.2	20.8	4.1	27.3	7.9	51.8	15.2
Morocco	3.6	17.5	0.1	0.3	17.0	82.1	20.7
Egypt	4.1	11.1	2.1	5.5	30.9	83.4	37.1
Jamaica	0.4	10.6	0.3	6.4	3.4	83.0	4.2
Bolivia	0.4	10.3	0.0	1.1	3.6	88.5	4.1

Note:
[1] Listed in descending order, according to percentage of debt accounted for by banks.
Source: Barclays Bank Review (August 1990).

Figure 6.18   *LDC Interest Arrears, $bn*

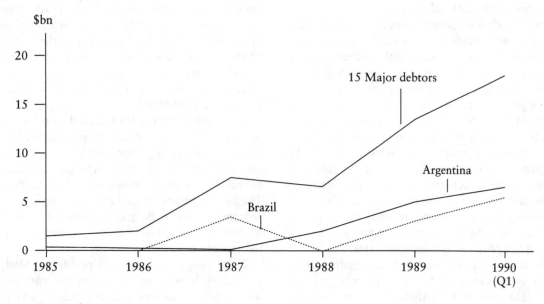

Source: Barclays Bank Review (August 1990).

making repayments was simultaneously rising. It is an irony of the nature of short-term lending that periods of heavy lending must inevitably be followed by periods of heavy repayments.

In early 1989 the debt problem was suddenly pushed back into prominence by rioting in Venezuela triggered by price rises introduced to qualify for new IMF loans. The US Treasury Secretary, Nicholas Brady, hastily cobbled together a plan, apparently without first consulting the President or Federal Reserve, which proposed that **commercial banks forgive** a part of their loans to Latin America, with the rest of the outstanding debt guaranteed by the World Bank and the IMF (in other words, by the nations contributing funds to these organisations).

In effect, the debtor nations demanded that resolution of their problems should be divorced from internal reform. This stirred up a storm of protest which centred around the argument that debtor countries should privatise their astonishingly inefficient State enterprises (as had been done in Chile), crack down on corruption and introduce market forces, in the absence of which residents of debtor countries had hidden away hard currency equal, in many cases, to a debtor's total external debts.

The refusal by debtor nations to implement structural reforms had previously caused the demise of the Baker Plan, and the softer line contained in the **Brady Plan** understandably resulted in a more positive reaction by debtor nations. However, no-one seemed anxious to come forward with new money or to offer to take the losses on existing loans.

By the end of 1990 three 'Brady-style' deals had been completed with Mexico, the Philippines and Costa Rica (see *Barclays Bank Review*, August 1990, pp. 30–2), three were pending with Venezuela, Uruguay and Morocco and others were in process. Unfortunately, this did not represent a big inroad into the overall problem which is depicted in **Table 6.11**.

As can be seen, there is considerable variability with respect to the creditor groups in each country. Argentina, Brazil and Mexico are heavily indebted to banks, and by March 1990 the first two had built up an arrears of interest payments of 65 per cent of the total $18 bn outstanding at that time. This had built up very rapidly since 1988, as can be seen in **Figure 6.18**, so it is understandable that the banks were in a less than forgiving mood, especially as they had come to believe that the IMF was giving the impression to debtor countries that failure to pay off the arrears would not disqualify them for further official assistance.

Faced with slow progress under the Brady Plan, attempts were made to enhance the existing secondary market in LDC debt with further financial innovations. By selling all of its outstanding debt a bank can clean up its balance sheet – but only by taking an actual rather than a theoretical loss. For the most part, the debt is bought by other banks which raise loans to pay for it. Brazil and Argentina introduced 'exit bonds' which if taken up relieved a bank of the obligation to supply new money. Some debtors such as Chile permitted debt to be converted into equity, whereas others ran auctions at which banks bid to swap their customers' foreign debt for local currency which they needed for projects in those countries.

Some of these schemes were successful. Chile, for example, raised its debt's value to 80 per cent of its face value in 1991 through a debt-to-equity scheme, but in almost every other case the secondary market value was lower in 1991 than in 1986 (although 1991 was commonly an improvement upon 1989). Since this was something of a deterrent to prospective purchases, action on the official debt seemed to be essential, and in June 1990 President Bush launched an 'Enterprise for the Americas' initiative involving partial forgiveness, on a case-by-case basis, of official bilateral debts for South American countries pursuing IMF/World Bank adjustment programmes.

There were also proposals for **debt-for-nature** deals whereby LDCs would be forgiven their debts provided they refrained from environmentally damaging activities such as chopping down rain forests. However, it simultaneously became evident that debt problems in Eastern Europe, which had previously attracted little attention, would also need to be addressed as a matter of some urgency, particularly in view of the overthrow of communist regimes in 1990. Eastern European debt rose from $70 bn in 1985 to $99 bn in 1987, and as shown in **Table 6.11**, Poland's debts alone amounted to $40 bn in 1989.

One major difference in the Polish case was that most of the debt was official ($33 bn out of $47 in 1991). Another was that it had instigated bold

economic reforms subsequent to the overthrow of communism. These considerations made it much easier to forgive the debt than in the case of other LDCs, and early in 1991 it was accordingly agreed by the Paris Club that one half of the official debt would immediately be forgiven (Egypt also attracted a similar deal in the light of its contribution to the Gulf War).

In March 1991 the USA agreed to write off 70 per cent of Poland's official bilateral debt, but the French, owed rather more, were reluctant to follow suit, and in April the Japanese blocked approval of a loan promised previously to Poland. The Brazilians and other LDCs were also less than enamoured about Poland's privileged treatment, so there is likely to be ongoing controversy for the foreseeable future.

If anything, the immediate problem is likely to worsen both because the dollar, the currency in which debt is normally denominated, has risen sharply in 1991 and because interest rates have not fallen as much as had been hoped. Whatever the outcome of short-term palliatives, the only long-term solution is to speed up the rate of growth in debtor nations so that they acquire the capacity to repay debts without eroding the existing standard of living of their inhabitants. There is clearly a strong case to be made out for requesting the industrialised nations to open up their markets, especially to agricultural products, and for the debtor countries to become more export-oriented. The debtor nations may well have a comparative advantage in food production, but world prices have long been poor because of protectionism in America, the EC and Japan. The discussion of the agricultural problem in Chapter 7 does not, however, hold out much hope in this respect.

References

Bank of England (1990) 'The External Balance Sheet of the United Kingdom: Recent Developments and Measurement Problems', *Bank of England Quarterly Bulletin* (November).

Coutts, K. and W. Godley (1990) 'Prosperity and Foreign Trade in the 1990s: Britain's Strategic Problem', *Oxford Review of Economic Policy*, 6(3).

Davies, G. (1990) 'The Capital Account and the Sustainability of the UK Trade Deficit', *Oxford Review of Economic Policy*, 6(3).

Muellbauer, J. A. and Murphy, A. 'Is the UK Balance of Payments Sustainable?', *Economic Policy* (October).

Rhys, D. (1990) 'The Motor Industry and the Balance of Payments', *Bank of Scotland Review* (December).

Pain, N. and P. Westaway (1990) 'Why the Capital Account Matters', *National Institute Economic Review* (February).

Holtham, G. (1990) 'World Current Account Balances', *Oxford Review of Economic Policy*, 6(3).

■ *Chapter 7* ■

External Relations

Peter Curwen

■ *7.1 Introduction*

The distinction between external transactions and external relations is necessarily a rather fine one, and there are clearly other ways to manage the division of material. Essentially, there seemed to be advantages in assembling together most of the material which impinges upon the role of the UK as a member of the EC (see **Table 7.1**) and Chapter 7 is broadly given over to this topic. This means that the issues pertaining to exchange rate relationships within the EC are also contained within Chapter 7, even though the more general discussion of exchange rates appears in Chapter 6. However, it is difficult to disentangle issues concerning the EMS, the EMU and the Single European Mar-

Table 7.1 *Growth of the EC*

1958 (6)	:	Belgium, France, Italy, Luxembourg, Netherlands, West Germany[1]
1973 (9)	:	Denmark, Ireland (Eire), United Kingdom
1981 (10)	:	Greece
1986 (12)	:	Spain, Portugal

Note:
[1] Now reunified with its eastern counterpart and referred to as 'Germany'.

ket, and these are accordingly dealt with in sequence at the beginning of the chapter. Chapter 7 then goes on to examine relationships between the EC and the rest of the world, treating the UK in its capacity of EC member, and finally looks in detail at the agricultural problem which is simultaneously an issue in terms of the UK's relationship with the EC and also in terms of the EC's relationship with other agricultural trading blocs.

■ *7.2 The Single European Market*

□ *7.2.1 SEA 1985*

During 1990–91 the issue of how best to create a single European market, in accordance with the **Single European Act** (SEA) 1985, has shot to prominence as the comparative immediacy of the implementation of the Act on **31 December 1992** has begun to permeate the consciousness of policymakers. This reflects, in part, the efforts of the incumbent President of the European Commission, Jacques Delors, who was reappointed in June 1988 to a second four-year term in office beginning in January 1989 (see **Table 7.2**). When he was first appointed in 1984, M. Delors considered carefully the areas in which to concentrate his

Table 7.2 *Institutions of the EC*

1	European Commission	17 members of whom 1 (Jacques Delors) is president. Commissioners are allocated by country. The UK has 2 – Sir Leon Brittan (competition policy) and Bruce Millan (regional policy). Ireland has 1 – Ray MacSharry (agriculture). The Commission is the EC's civil service – it has no direct political power. Its main role is to instigate proposals such as directives and see them through to acceptance or rejection (see **Figure 7.1**).
2	The Council of Ministers	Consists of 12 representatives, one from each member country. The make up of the Council varies according to the subject under discussion – 12 agricultural ministers if the subject is agriculture, and so forth. Voting is either **unanimous** or by **qualified majority**. Only the Council has the power to ratify a proposal. Grand strategy is left to the meeting of the 12 heads of state – the **European Council**.
3	European Parliament	518 Euro MEPs who sit according to their position on the political spectrum rather than by country. Main groups are socialists and Christian Democrats. The Parliament's powers have been enhanced under the new *co-operation procedure* (see **Figure 7.1**), but are not comparable to those of the Council.
4	The European Court of Justice	Consists of 13 judges and 5 advocates-general. The rulings of the Court are supra-national and take precedence over legal rulings in member countries.

attention. His first priority was to create an economic and monetary union within the EC, but neither the UK nor West Germany showed sufficient enthusiasm for that idea. He accordingly turned next to matters of foreign policy, but again found no takers for a policy of increased co-ordination. His third choice proved more inspired. Noting the movement towards deregulation and liberalisation in economic affairs, he advocated **freedom of movement for goods and services, people and financial flows throughout the EC**, now enshrined in Article 8A of the SEA 1985.

At the present time a number of developments are working their way through the complicated and time-consuming process of ratification by all EC members (see **Figure 7.1**). Most decisions are subject to **qualified** (weighted by size of country) **majority voting**, but some important ones – such as those concerned with **taxation** – require **unanimous** approval. The qualified majority is **54** votes out of a total of **76** (**Table 7.3**), of which the UK has **10**.

Roughly 300 measures, almost all in the form of **directives**,[1] have been tabled by the European Commission. Of these, **282** remain on the table in July 1991, as shown in **Table 7.4**, and of these **193** have (by May 1991) been voted into EC law by the co-operation process. As can be seen in **Table 7.4**, a large proportion of these concern the health of animals and plants. Progress has been quite good in respect of the removal of technical barriers, but the removal of fiscal barriers remains the real stumbling block. Some of the reasons for this have already been discussed in Chapter 4.

Table 7.3 *Qualified Majority Voting*

10 votes	Germany, France, Italy, UK
8 votes	Spain
5 votes	Belgium, Greece, Netherlands, Portugal
3 votes	Denmark, Ireland
2 votes	Luxembourg

76 votes in total : qualified majority = 54 votes

Figure 7.1   *Community Legislative Process: New Cooperation Procedure* [1]

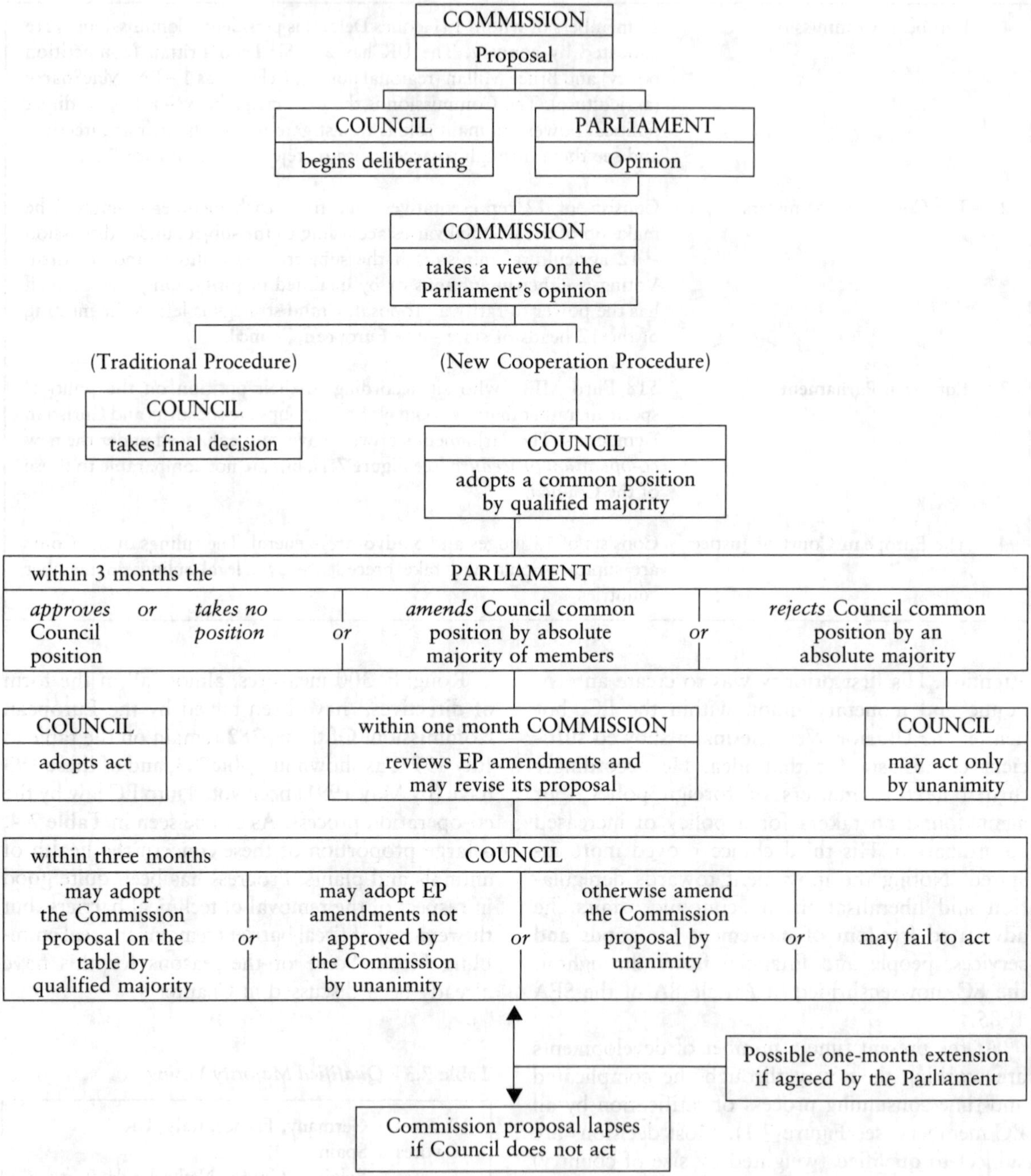

| COMMISSION |
| Proposal |

| COUNCIL | PARLIAMENT |
| begins deliberating | Opinion |

| COMMISSION |
| takes a view on the Parliament's opinion |

(Traditional Procedure)   (New Cooperation Procedure)

| COUNCIL |
| takes final decision |

| COUNCIL |
| adopts a common position by qualified majority |

| within 3 months the | PARLIAMENT | |
| *approves* or *takes no* Council *position* or position | *amends* Council common position by absolute majority of members | or | *rejects* Council common position by an absolute majority |

| COUNCIL | within one month COMMISSION | COUNCIL |
| adopts act | reviews EP amendments and may revise its proposal | may act only by unanimity |

| within three months | COUNCIL | | |
| may adopt the Commission proposal on the table by qualified majority | or | may adopt EP amendments not approved by the Commission by unanimity | or | otherwise amend the Commission proposal by unanimity | or | may fail to act |

| Possible one-month extension if agreed by the Parliament |

| Commission proposal lapses if Council does not act |

Note:
[1]   This has now been amended as part of the Maastricht Treaty on Economic and Political Union – see p. 250.
Source: The Single Market – the Facts (London: Department of Trade and Industry, 1990).

Table 7.4 *Progress Report on Measures as of 31 December 1990*

PROPOSALS	Adopted	Partially adopted	Common Positions Agreed	Other proposals in Council	Proposals still to be presented to Council
Part I: The removal of physical barriers					
I Control of Goods					
I.1 Various controls	7	1	–	2	–
I.2 Veterinary and phytosanitary controls	50	1	–	31	–
II Control of Individuals	4	–	1	3	–
Part II: The removal of technical barriers					
I Free movement of goods					
I-1 New approach to technical harmonisation and standards policy	10	–	1	–	–
I-2 Sectoral proposals	57	2	–	8	–
II Public procurement	4	–	–	2	–
III Free movement for labour and the professions	10	–	–	3	–
IV Common market for services					
IV-1 Financial services	17	–	–	7	–
IV-2 Transport	6	1	–	4	–
IV-3 New technologies and services	4	–	1	–	–
V Capital movements	3	–	–	–	–
VI Creation of suitable conditions for industrial co-operation					
VI-1 Company law	3	–	–	4	–
VI-2 Intellectual and industrial property	2	–	1	5	–
VI-3 Taxation (removing tax obstacles to co-operation between enterprises)	3	–	–	2	–
Part III: The removal of fiscal barriers					
VAT/Excise Duties	4	–	–	18	–
TOTAL 282	184[1]	5	4	89	0

Note:
[1] As of end-August 1991 the figure was 213.
Source: Department of Trade and Industry.

Once they become part of EC law, directives have to be placed upon the statute book of individual countries by a specified date. 137 measures were scheduled to have become national laws by the end of 1991. However, EC countries have varying difficulties in passing the necessary national laws. Despite its reputation as an EC lag-gard, the UK has an excellent record in implementing directives with 111 passed onto the statute book by the end of 1991. At that time only Denmark (125) and France (118) had a better record. Italy, by comparison, had managed only 74 and reappears regularly in the European Court to be reprimanded for its dilatory behaviour.

Figure 7.2 *Implementation Schedule of Directives[1] Adopted by 31 December 1990 [2,3]*

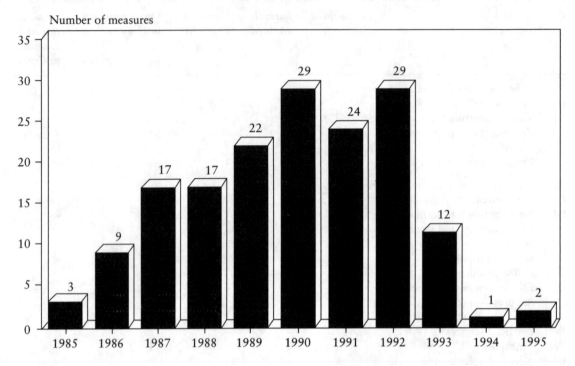

Notes:
[1] Includes all Directives adopted by the Council for which an implementation date has been fixed.
[2] Directives with implementation dates of 31 December have for presentation purposes been taken as entering into force on the first day of the new year.
[3] In some cases, implementation of a Directive is phased over several years.
Source: Department of Trade and Industry.

☐ 7.2.2 *Trade Flows Between Member States*

At this juncture we need to take a more general look at the **Single European Market,** concentrating in particular upon those aspects which affect trade flows between member states.

It has to be borne in mind that every step towards a single market implies a loss of national sovereignty on the part of member states. By a stroke of historic irony, the original impetus towards a Europe of nation-states came from de Gaulle in France, but when the French attempted to expand their way to prosperity in the early 1980s their failure caused them to become the arch advocates of the single market. The fact that M. Delors has maintained close links with the French Socialist Party has thus created a suspicion in other countries that he is over-keen on the French version of the single market. When he recently claimed that 80 per cent of economic legislation, and perhaps tax and social legislation, would be decided in Brussels within 10 years, he was rapidly brought to earth by Mrs Thatcher, who pointed out that she did not expect the loss of national sovereignty on such scale to take place during her lifetime.[2]

The evolution of the UK's attitude to European matters is discussed in the appropriate sections of the book (and see also the *Economist's* Survey of Europe's Internal Market on 8 July 1989). The UK has played a leading role in resolving disputes about the CAP and the EC Budget and has accepted the need for intervention in matters such as state aid and competition policy. It stands prepared to move in gradual stages (see, for example, the discussion of the Bank of England's role in fostering the use of the ECU for international finance on **p. 118**), but not in leaps and bounds. This, understandably, sometimes gives the impression that the UK has severe reservations about the whole idea of European co-operation, but it is fair to say that most other members support the UK's gradualist approach.

7.2.3 Harmonisation and Mutual Recognition

One of the primary reasons underlying the failure of the EC to develop much beyond the running of the CAP prior to the 1980s was the issue of **harmonisation**. By insisting, for example, that imports of beer would have to match the purity of the domestic product, the West Germans were able to create an effective non-tariff barrier against imports. Attempts by the European Commission to introduce rules which, if adhered to, would make products universally acceptable throughout the EC, foundered constantly because member states with the highest standards tried to harmonise the proposed EC-wide standards with their own.

The pointer to a way out of this dilemma came in the form of the *Cassis de Dijon Judgement* of the European Court of Justice. This ruled that if a product satisfied the laws governing its production and sale in one member State, then it could also be sold in an identical form in any other member State even if the laws of these states prohibited its domestic production in that form. Importation of the product would not affect domestic laws, so it would remain illegal to make the product domestically. In this respect 'domestic' was taken to mean production by a national company, its subsidiaries and branches and subsidiaries of foreign companies operating within the boundaries of that nation.

Up to that point products which were exported had to be compatible with the laws of the **importing** country. It was now proposed by the European Commission that they had to be compatible only with the laws of the **exporting** country. This is known as **mutual recognition,** and it obviously simplified enormously the problems facing a company wishing to engage in intra-EC trade. If an exporter was already making products in conformity with the laws of the importing country he could either continue to do so or opt to produce in conformity with domestic laws. One situation where an exporter would wish to continue to adhere to the laws of the importing country would be where the product exported was illegal in the domestic economy.

This begged the question as to whether a product exported from country A (where it was illegal) to country B (where it was legal) could also be sold without restriction elsewhere in the EC. The European Commission ruled that a product could not be marketed throughout the EC unless it satisfied the laws of the country of origin, although it could obviously be sold in any individual EC country where it was compatible with their laws even if prohibited in the domestic market.

Whilst it appeared to be reasonable, this ruling was not without its own problems. In the first place, once frontier controls are dismantled it becomes relatively easy to move a product from a country where it is legal to one where it is not. Secondly, the ruling favours imports from outside the EC altogether. Once imported legally into any one EC country these can, in accordance with Article 9 of the Treaty of Rome, be sold in every EC country without restriction. Hence, an importer has only to get his product accepted in an EC country of his choosing to gain access to countries where the product cannot legally be produced for domestic consumption.

Under certain circumstances prescribed in the Treaty of Rome or in judgements of the European Court of Justice (for example, concerning health and safety) a member state can prohibit imports from any source. However, these circumstances are much less pervasive than might be imagined. In the example cited above the West Germans were unable to prohibit imports of beer on the grounds that they were adulterated and hence harmful to health, and the same principle was applied when the Italians tried to prohibit imports of pasta. In both cases the Court of Justice ruled that the health of consumers was not seriously threatened and that their interests could be adequately protected by labelling clearly the contents of the products.

It is interesting to speculate whether mutual recognition will bring about a condition akin to total harmonisation. It is evident that a country which prohibits the domestic manufacture of a product cannot exclude the importation of that product in a form which is compatible with the laws of any other member state. Hence it follows that the domestic prohibition serves only to deny opportunities to domestic producers. Equally, if higher standards are required of a domestic producer than of producers who export from other states, the domestic producer must suffer some competitive disadvantages. It may accordingly make sense for prohibitions to be lifted and for exceptionally onerous domestic rules to be eased, not merely in order to permit domestic producers to reclaim the domestic market, but also to permit them to export successfully. Market forces may in this way harmonise national standards, albeit not in accordance with the preexisting highest standards of any individual country but in accordance with those set at a much less onerous level.

Unsurprisingly, this scenario holds little appeal for countries such as West Germany which can forsee their high quality domestic products driven out of both domestic and export markets by lower quality foreign products. Furthermore, in order to discover whether the foreign products should be sold in the domestic market, they must be checked not against the domestic standards, which are well-known, but against the standards set in each country of origin, which are unfamiliar. In order to avoid excessive bureaucracy an importer will generally have to trust the exporting country's own inspectorate, but it is understandable that, say, West Germans are suspicious of quality controls in Greece.

For these and other reasons, countries with high domestic standards have pressed for minimum standards to be continued by the Commission. A potential danger in this arrangement is that the Commission will bend under this pressure and both extend minimum standards to products where they previously did not apply, and also raise minimum standards for products where they already exist.

7.3 The European Community Budget and the UK

☐ 7.3.1 The EC Budget

The EC Budget is agreed annually between the Council of Ministers and the European Parliament on the basis of a draft by the European Commission. It is formally adopted by the Parliament which has the final say on 'non-compulsory expenditure' whereas the Council has the final say on 'compulsory' expenditure.

Total expenditure planned for 1991 is roughly ECU 56 bn. This represents about 1 per cent of the EC's combined GNP and about 3 per cent of member states' public expenditure. In cash terms it has grown very rapidly over the past decade and is nearly three times larger than in 1981. Spending which is **compulsory** is that which arises directly from provisions in the Treaty of Rome or from other Acts adopted in accordance with the Treaty. In practice it is almost all related to agricultural support and overseas aid. Spending which is **non-compulsory** includes spending on regional development and social policies.

In 1991 agriculture support is expected to constitute 57 per cent of total expenditure, as shown in **Figure 7.3**. This spending, together with the Regional Development Fund, the Social Fund and grants to farmers for modernisation or environmentally beneficial projects is known as the **structural funds**.

The EC Budget relies, apart from periodic intergovernmental agreements (IGAs) upon its **own resources**. These comprise (1) duties and levies on goods imported from non-EC countries (net of a 10 per cent contribution to cover collection and administration costs); (2) agricultural levies on imported produce; (3) the amount which would be raised if VAT up to a maximum specified rate (1.4 per cent) were levied on the same basket of spending on goods and services in each member state (itself worth a maximum of 55 per cent of GNP); (4) payments related to each member state's GNP, set at a level sufficient to bridge the gap between total expenditure and the yield of the three other own resources. There is a legally-binding ceiling on the total own resources available to finance the

Figure 7.3   *The EC Budget, 1991, bn ECU*

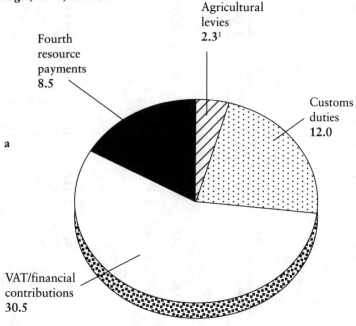

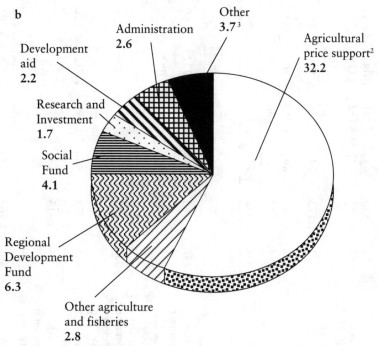

Notes:

1   Also includes levies raised on sugar and isoglucose.
2   Includes allowance for depreciation of produce held in storage.
3   Includes 1 billion ECU monetary reserve to allow for the effects of exchange rate fluctuations between the ECU and the US$.

a   Revenue, bn ECU.
b   Expenditure, bn ECU.

Source: Statement on the 1991 Community Budget.

Table 7.5   *General Government Transactions with the Institutions of the EC, £ mn*[1]

	1979	1980	1981	1982	1983	1984	1985	1986	1987	1988	1989	1990
EUROPEAN COMMUNITY BUDGET												
UK CREDITS												
Services	115	112	122	150	148	186	157	157	126	85	5	5
Transfers												
EAGGF	371	550	683	791	1 082	1 353	1 151	1 385	1 345	1 379	1 315	1 496
Social Fund	87	95	107	152	128	283	256	335	428	277	406	225
Regional Development Fund	71	173	145	111	139	184	274	298	404	370	347	441
Negotiated refunds[2]	–	98	693	1 019	807	528	61	–	–	–	–	–
Other	14	34	27	36	24	11	15	41	42	72	43	16
TOTAL	658	1 062	1 777	2 259	2 328	2 545	1 914	2 216	2 345	2 183	2 116	2 183
UK DEBITS												
Transfers												
Agriculture and sugar levies	246	260	218	307	232	260	189	244	354	226	192	135
Customs protective duties	868	861	861	1 001	1 075	1 276	1 291	1 244	1 417	1 521	1 638	1 555
GNP financial contribution	–	–	–	–	–	–	–	–	–	–	–	–
Budget adjustments[3]	–352	–95	–	–	–	–	–	–	–	–	–	–
VAT-gross before abatement/adjustments	844	728	960	1 497	1 712	1 720	1 930	2 742	3 347	2 886	3 444	4 149
Abatement[2]	–	–	–	–	–	–	–166	–1 701	–1 153	–1 595	–1 156	–1 697
Adjustments[3]	–	13	135	57	–43	–55	145	263	84	–127	311	516
Inter-governmental agreements	–	–	–	–	–	–	370	–	–	613	–	–
TOTAL	1 606	1 767	2 174	2 862	2 976	3 201	3 759	2 792	4 049	3 525	4 431	4 658
BALANCE	–948	–705	–397	–603	–648	–656	–1 845	–576	–1 704	–1 342	–2 315	–2 475

Notes:

1   For all years sterling figures reflect actual payments made during the year, not payments in respect of particular Budgets.

2   Refunds and abatements received in respect of the UK's excess net contributions to EC Budgets in earlier years.

3   Adjustments reflecting reassessments of the gross contributions required for the EC Budgets for the previous years.

Source: UK National Accounts 'Pink Book' (CSO, 1991) Table 9.2.

Budget which is expressed as a proportion of EC GNP (1.19 per cent for 1991 and 1.2 per cent for subsequent years).

The Budget is set initially to provide some leeway below the legal maximum, but if there are problems with, for example, the CAP, that leeway can rapidly be eroded (see **pp. 275–6**). The various contributions made by the UK are itemised as UK debts in **Table 7.5**. In return for these the UK receives credits, primarily from the European Agricultural Guarantee and Guidance Fund (EAGGF), the Social Fund and the Regional Development Fund. The difference between debits and credits represents the UK's net contribution to the EC Budget.

Gross of any abatements, the UK's share of total own resources in 1990 was roughly 20 per cent. This can be compared with the fact that the UK accounts for roughly 16 per cent of EC GNP. More importantly, however, the UK receives back only 7–8 per cent of total EC expenditure. It is not surprising, therefore, that the UK is a major net contributor to the EC Budget, as shown in **Table 7.5**. This arises because agricultural and other levies and duties are boosted by the UK's relatively heavy dependence on non-EC imports, because UK citizens' high propensity to spend generates large amounts of VAT and because the UK's relatively efficient agricultural sector attracts only modest levels of support.

In 1979 debits were 2.5 times as large as credits, and the net contribution amounted to almost £1 bn. As a consequence the UK Government sought, and obtained, agreement for a series of annual **refunds** based upon the UK's excess net contributions to EC Budgets in earlier years. In addition, certain modest **adjustments** were made with respect to previous years' gross contributions. In 1984, at the Fontainebleau Summit, an **abatement** mechanism was negotiated (now formally part of EC law). Under this agreement the UK's **gross** contribution to the Budget in any given year is currently abated by an amount which is broadly equivalent to two-thirds of the UK's **net** contribution in the previous year.

The UK's net contribution in financial year 1990–91 is estimated at £1.9 bn. This is expected to fall to £1.0 bn in 1991–92 before rising to £2.9 bn in 1992–93. This erratic pattern arises because of the need to make adjustments for inaccurate forecasts in previous years. The key issue is that whereas the EC Budget has risen on average by 4.3 per cent each year since 1979, the UK's contribution has only risen by an average of 0.5 per cent. A tough bargainer, that Thatcher woman!

□ 7.3.2 EC Structural Funds

EC structural funds, intended to boost development in backward and industrially declining regions, were doubled to ECU 63 bn for 1989–93, of which the UK was allocated ECU 3.9 bn, the same as prior to the doubling. The European Commission attached a condition of **additionality** to the new money in 1988, which meant that EC funds should supplement, and not replace, existing local and central government commitments to the projects selected.

The UK Government, however, proposed to add EC funds to the general spending pot, arguing that there was no additionality clause attached to pre-1988 structural funds and that the UK was spending only funds committed prior to that date.

The Commission argued that there was no longer any means of ensuring that the funds would retain their 'deliberately discriminatory effect', and although there was no explicit sanction for misuse of aid written in when the structural funds were reformed in 1988, withheld £100 mn of grants for coal mining communities in January 1991. This dispute has yet to be resolved.

Meanwhile Spain, which currently receives roughly one-quarter of the structural funds, has stepped in with a demand that, in return for the acquiescence of the poorer southern EC members in monetary and political union (see below), the structural funds should be much enlarged and (1) an equalising budgetary fund or 'inter-state compensation fund' should be set up to invest in physical and human capital in member states where GDP per head is below 90 per cent of the EC average (Greece, Spain, Ireland and Portugal currently average 70 per cent); (2) contributions to the EC Budget to be based upon a progressive tax regime measured by 'relatively prosperity'; (3) the

Table 7.6   *EC Budget 1989, ECU mn*

	Contributions	Total expenditure	(Agriculture budget)
Germany	11,110	4,580	(3,700)
France	8,623	5,677	(4,606)
Italy	7,606	6,177	(4,506)
UK	6,568	3,214	(1,797)
Spain	3,575	3,544	(1,850)
Netherlands	2,700	3,830	(3,469)
Belgium	1,807	683	(546)
Denmark	871	1,045	(977)
Greece	566	2,565	(1,701)
Portugal	458	946	(174)
Ireland	371	1,712	(1,072)
Luxembourg	73	8	(2)
Unattributable[1]		10,348	(3)
EC 12	**44,329**	**44,329**	**(24,403)**

Note:
[1]   Includes overseas aid.
Source: EC Court of Auditors.

Budget to be much enlarged and expenditure redirected towards southern members.

Spain was a marginal net contributor to the EC Budget in 1989, but did badly in respect of agriculture, as shown in **Table 7.6**. The European Commission has responded primarily by offering a 50 per cent increase in the structural funds when the current Budget runs out in 1993. It is unlikely that the IGCs will do anything other than defer Spain's demands to a Budget Summit in 1992, but it does look as though the UK will be paying out ever larger net amounts to the EC as the decade proceeds.

▌7.4 The European Monetary System (EMS)

In the Treaty of Rome, which originally set up the EEC in 1957, a target of 12 years was set by which time all tariffs and quotas were to be removed between EEC members. This proved to be more than a little unrealistic, since it became clear that individual countries were in no rush to give up their national sovereignty. However, an attempt was made to take a major step forward with the publication of the Werner Report in 1970, which proposed the setting up of a European Monetary Union (EMU). Initially, this took the form of a narrowly constrained adjustable peg mechanism linked to the existing adjustable peg based on the dollar.

The widening of the dollar-based peg in 1971 resulted in the EMU taking the form of the '**snake in the tunnel**', whereby each EMU member's currency was allowed to fluctuate only narrowly around its own par value, thereby restricting the gap between the strongest and weakest currency to no more than 2.25 per cent, whilst the EMU currencies **taken as a whole** were permitted to fluctuate against the dollar within a 4.5 per cent band.

The EMU, operated by the original six EEC members from the beginning of 1972, and also by the UK for one month in May 1972, quickly fell apart at the seams. In part this reflected the continuing precedence of national interests over monetary union, but the EMU also, by chance, coincided historically with the demise of the adjustable peg system (the UK dropping out of both when it floated in June 1972). Other EMU members either withdrew permanently, or moved in and out of the system, and by the mid-1970s it was regarded as terminated in practice even if not in principle.

The idea of monetary union was resurrected at the Bremen Summit in July 1978, which resulted in the setting up of the EMS in March 1979. The idea behind the EMS, apart from the longer-term objective of an economic and monetary union within the EC (a still elusive goal, as discussed below), was firstly to promote economic convergence in the EC by inducing member governments to adopt the sorts of policies being implemented by its most successful member, West Germany, and in particular to bring inflation down to the West German level, and secondly to create a 'zone of monetary stability' which would facilitate trade between EC members whilst providing insulation against the erratic behaviour of the dollar.

7.4.1 The European Currency Unit

The major innovation of the EMS was the introduction in 1979 of a new European currency, the **European Currency Unit** (ECU). This is a weighted average of the EMS currencies (and therefore has to be recalculated when new members join, as with the Greek drachma in September 1984), where the weights are calculated according to the relative importance of the individual currencies in terms of key indicators such as national output and the volume of trade with other members. The contribution of different currencies to the ECU is shown, in October 1990, in **Table 7.7**. It should be noted that there are normally eleven contributing currencies as Belgium and Luxembourg are treated as a single entity. As can be seen, the Deutsche Mark dominates the ECU, with the Franc also a significant contributor, whilst the Portuguese, Greek and Irish currencies are almost irrelevant. In respect of

the above the 'official' ECU performs the function of unit of account to the exchange rate mechanism described below, and also provides a currency which can circulate between central banks throughout the EC. In recent years there has also developed a separate private market for securities denominated in ECU, but, as noted previously, this has yet to form more than a marginal part of the total Eurocurrency markets.

The most recent five-yearly recomposition of the ECU took place in September 1989. The European Commission decided in June 1989 that the currencies of members admitted since 1984, namely Spain and Portugal, should be included in the make-up of the ECU, the weight which was to be assigned to them and from which other currencies to transfer it (as shown in **Table 7.7**). Clearly this was as much a matter of political infighting as straightforward assessment of relative economic strength. The 1984 recomposition gave rather too much weight to the Deutsche Mark and Guilder,

Table 7.7 *The Composition of an ECU*

	Amount of each currency in basket[1]	Weight % of currency in basket[2]	Value of ECU in national currency (central rate)[3]
Deutsche Mark	0.6242	30.1	2.05586
Sterling	0.08784	13.0	0.696904
French franc	1.332	19.0	6.89509
Italian lira	151.8	10.15	1538.24
Dutch guilder	0.2198	9.4	2.31643
Belgian/Luxembourg franc	3.431	7.9	42.4032
Danish krone	0.1976	2.45	7.84195
Irish punt	0.008552	1.1	0.767417
Greek drachma	1.440	0.8	205.311
Spanish peseta	6.885	5.3	133.631
Portuguese escudo	1.393	0.8	178.735

Notes:

[1] Fixed for a five year period on 20 September 1989.

[2] The currency amounts in the ECU must be reviewed every five years, or on request if the weight of any currency has changed more than 25% since the last revision. Weights change with exchange rate movements of component currencies.

[3] As of 8 October 1990.

Source: Eurostat.

and rather too little to the Lira, in relation to their relative economic strength at the time, and the weight of the DM should in principle have been reduced to roughly 24 per cent in order to make way for the new currencies and also to adjust for slow growth in the West German economy. This unsurprisingly proved objectionable to the West Germans, so the readjustment was in practice rather more modest. It is also the case that since bonds issued in each ECU contributor's own currency yield different interest rates, altering the balance of the ECU necessarily also affects the yield of bonds denominated in ECU. Considerable instability in the ECU bond market will therefore result from a major restructuring of the ECU, and this is always likely to operate to keep any restructuring within modest bounds.

7.4.2 The Exchange Rate Mechanism

The second element of the EMS is the **exchange rate mechanism** (ERM). Sterling joined the ERM on **8 October 1990**. Members of the EMS can contribute to the ECU without being members of the ERM, as was previously the case for the UK and is currently still the case for Portugal and Greece. The ERM is a dual mechanism similar to, but more complex than, the old-style adjustable peg. In the first place, the member countries are slotted into a **parity grid** (**Table 7.8**) which summarises the bilateral central and intervention rates. In the case of the UK the key central rate is to be found in the C row for Germany, namely £1 = DM 2.95.

Each currency is normally permitted to move bilaterally against any other currency in the grid by up to 2.25 per cent in either direction (the narrow band). In the case of the peseta and the £ the permitted movement is 6 per cent in either direction (the wide band). It is important to note, however, that a currency must stay within its permitted band against **all other currencies simultaneously**. In other words, sterling can never be more than 6 per cent above the weakest currency nor 6 per cent below the strongest. The **effective** limits in

relation to all other currencies are accordingly **less than 6** per cent.

In principle, the £ can move up only from DM 2.7780 (6 per cent below the DM central rate) to DM 3.1320 (6 per cent above it) if in the process it does not reach its upper limit against any other currency before it reaches its upper limit against the DM. In general, the scope for appreciation is limited by the weakest currency in the band, whilst the scope for depreciation is limited by the strongest. It is the custom for the likes of the *Financial Times* to show the parity grid in terms of the deviations from the weakest currency which is set at 0.

When any two currencies reach their compulsory intervention rates against each other the two central banks concerned are obliged to meet all bids/offers made to them at the relevant limit rate. In principle, currencies should not reach their effective limits because of the existence of the **divergence indicators**. Whenever a currency 'diverges' by more than 75 per cent from its central rate against the ECU (the divergence threshold) it is supposed to act as an early warning device which sets in motion a change in the way in which the country in question is conducting its economic policy. Where the divergence is below the central rate a suitable response might be a tightening of interest rates, and where it is above the central rate it might be a relaxation of fiscal policy. It should be noted that the permitted divergences are all different. This is because, when a currency's central rate moves, it also alters the value of the ECU. Hence, for example, the heavily weighted DM can move only by less than 1.5 per cent before the gap between it and some other currency becomes excessive. The formula determining the limit to divergence is ± 2.25 (1 − weight) per cent. However, the £ and peseta warrant exceptional treatment.

If the early warning system is effective it should prevent the currency running up against its upper or lower limit on the parity grid, although the speed of response to signs of excessive divergence has in practice been too slow to achieve much in this respect. Hence, there have been a number of occasions when currencies have run up against the limits of the parity grid without either adjustment of domestic policies or intervention by central banks

Table 7.8 Bilateral Central Rates and Selling and Buying Rates in the EMS Exchange Rate Mechanism from 8 October 1990[1]

		BFc/LFc 100	DKr 100	FrFc 100	DM 100	I£1	Lit 1,000	Fl 100	Pts 100	£1
Belgium/Luxembourg:		=				=	=	=	=	=
BFc/LFc	S	–	553.000	628.970	2109.50	56.5115	28.1930	1872.15	33.6930	64.6050
	C	–	540.723	614.977	2062.55	55.2545	27.5661	1830.54	31.7316	60.8451
	B	–	528.700	601.295	2016.55	54.0250	26.9530	1789.85	29.8850	57.3035
Denmark:	S	18.9143	–	116.320	390.160	10.4511	5.21400	346.240	6.23100	11.9479
DKr	C	18.4938	–	113.732	381.443	10.2186	5.09803	338.537	5.86837	11.2526
	B	18.0831	–	111.200	373.000	9.9913	4.98500	331.020	5.52600	10.5976
France:	S	16.6310	89.9250	–	343.050	9.18900	4.58450	304.440	5.47850	10.50550
FrFc	C	16.2608	87.9257	–	335.386	8.98480	4.48247	297.661	5.15981	9.89389
	B	15.8990	85.9700	–	327.920	8.78500	4.38300	291.040	4.85950	9.31800
Germany:	S	4.95900	26.8100	30.4950	–	2.74000	1.36700	90.7700	1.63300	3.13200
DM	C	4.84837	26.2162	29.8164	–	2.67894	1.33651	88.7526	1.53847	2.95000
	B	4.74000	25.6300	29.1500	–	2.61900	1.30650	86.7800	1.44900	2.77800
Ireland:	S	1.85100	10.00870	11.3830	38.1825	–	0.510246	33.8868	0.609772	1.16920
I£	C	1.80981	9.78604	11.1299	37.3281	–	0.498895	33.1293	0.574281	1.10118
	B	1.76950	9.56830	10.8825	36.4964	–	0.487799	32.3939	0.540858	1.03710
Italy:	S	3710.20	20062.0	22817.0	76540.0	2050.03	–	67912.0	1222.30	2343.62
Lit	C	3627.64	19615.4	22309.1	74821.7	2004.43	–	66405.3	1151.11	2207.25
	B	3546.90	19179.0	21813.0	73157.0	1959.84	–	64928.0	1084.10	2078.79
Netherlands:	S	5.58700	30.2100	34.3600	115.2350	3.08700	1.54000	–	1.84050	3.52950
Fl	C	5.46286	29.5389	33.5953	112.6730	3.01848	1.50590	–	1.73345	3.32389
	B	5.34150	28.8825	32.8475	110.1675	2.95100	1.47250	–	1.63250	3.13050
Spain:	S	334.619	1809.40	2057.80	6901.70	184.892	92.2400	6125.30	–	203.600
Pts	C	315.143	1704.05	1938.06	6500.00	174.131	86.8726	5768.83	–	191.750
	B	296.802	1604.90	1825.30	6121.70	163.997	81.8200	5433.10	–	180.590
United Kingdom:	S	1.74510	9.43610	10.7320	35.9970	0.964240	0.481050	31.9450	0.553740	–
£	C	1.64352	8.88687	10.1073	33.8984	0.908116	0.453053	30.0853	0.521514	–
	B	1.54790	8.36970	9.5190	31.9280	0.855260	0.426690	28.3340	0.491160	–

S = Exchange rate at which the central bank of the country in the left hand column will sell the currency identified in the row at the top of the table.
C = Bilateral central rate.
B = Exchange rate at which the central bank of the country in the left hand column will buy the currency identified in the row at the top of the table.

Note:
[1] The lower and upper bilateral intervention rates (at which central banks are obliged to buy and sell, respectively, the relevant foreign currency in exchange for their own) are derived for the narrow band by multiplying the central rates by factors of 0.977753 for the compulsory buying rates and 1.022753 for the compulsory selling rates. For the wide band currencies, the factors are 0.941798 and 1.061798 respectively. These factors are chosen so as to ensure that central bank A's buying rate for currency B is the same as central bank B's selling rate for currency A. The corresponding margins are –2.2247% and +2.2753% and –5.8202% and +6.1798%. Due to market convention, the intervention rates are normally not exact reciprocals but are rounded to convenient figures. These differences are, however, insignificant in practice.

Source: Bank of England Quarterly Bulletin (November 1990) p. 479.

Table 7.9 *Central Parity Realignments*[1] *Within the EMS, %*

	September 1979	November 1979	March 1981	October 1981	February 1982	June 1982	March 1983	July 1985	April 1986	August 1986	January 1987	January 1990
Deutsche Mark	+2.0			+5.5		+4.25	+5.5	+2.0	+3.0		+3.0	
French franc				−3.0		−5.75	−2.5	+2.0	−3.0			
Guilder				+5.5		+4.25	+3.5	+2.0	+3.0		+3.0	
Lira			−6.0	−3.0		−2.75	−2.5	−6.0				−3.7[2]
Belgian/ Lux. franc					−8.5		+1.5	+2.0	+1.0		+2.0	
Krone	−3.0	−5.0			−3.0		+2.5	+2.0	+1.0			
Irish £							−3.5	+2.0		−8.0		

Notes:

[1] + indicates a revaluation, − indicates a devaluation.

[2] When Italy moved from the wide band to the narrow band in January 1990, it moved the central parity down towards the existing lower limit, thereby substracting 3.75% (6% − 2.25%) from its value. Technically, this does not count as a realignment.

Source: European Commission.

proving sufficient to prevent these limits being breached. As a consequence, both devaluations and revaluations have occurred, as set out in **Table 7.9**.

Given that remedial action was expected to be taken at two prior stages, a currency realignment was intended to be very much a last resort operation, and a total of eleven realignments does, therefore, appear superficially to represent a rather excessive use of this ultimate remedy. However, as **Table 7.9** shows clearly, realignments mostly took place in the early days of the EMS when it was moving towards a longer-term equilibrium, and the system has been much more settled since 1983. As explained above, it was a characteristic of the adjustable peg that currencies were almost always devalued rather than revalued, whereas there have been more revaluations than devaluations under the EMS. This has reflected, in particular, a general tendency for the Deutsche Mark to rise, mirrored by the guilder, and for the French franc and the lira to decline.

It has nevertheless been argued that the weaker members of the ERM have borne most of the burden of adjustment because bilateral parities with the DM rather than the ECU have been crucial, and in order to dampen pressure for realignment weaker currency countries have had to adjust their interest rates relative to the static German rate.

7.4.3 European Monetary Co-operation Fund

The other major component of the EMS is the European Monetary Co-operation Fund (EMCF), the purpose of which is to provide funds to assist with the stabilisation of exchange rates. At the inception of the EMS, members were required to deposit 20 per cent of their gold and dollar reserves with the EMCF (which the UK does also), in return for which they received a credit in ECUs which they could then use to settle indebtness with other members or for intervention purposes. It was originally anticipated that this would evolve into a fully fledged European Monetary Fund as a major step on the path to monetary union, but this never developed as intended. The EMCF uses funds

deposited with it to offer a range of credit facilities, responding to requests by individual countries rather than to policy adjustments jointly agreed by all members. Virtually unlimited funds are available on a very-short-term basis. The very-short-term financing (VSTF) facility has been available since the advent of the Basle–Nyborg Accord in November 1987. However, only modest amounts, measured in ECUs, can be provided on either a short-term (up to nine months) or medium-term (two to four years) basis. In the case of the UK these latter credit facilities are virtually an irrelevance, in the first place because the UK has not borrowed from an international institution since 1977, and in the second place because it already has much larger credit facilities lying untouched at the IMF.

7.4.4 The EMS in Operation

It is possible to interpret the pattern shown in **Table 7.9** as indicating that in the early stages of the EMS there was a hard currency option offered by the West German Bundesbank and a soft currency option offered by the Banque de France (Weber, 1991). The guilder stayed with the DM whereas the other currencies first devalued against the DM then interspersed devaluations with periods of stability from 1983 onwards (except the lira which fell continuously relative to the DM until 1990). What this suggests is that the latter countries, by effectively adopting an adjustable peg against the DM, chose to forgo the tough anti-inflationary stance of West Germany in favour of the less rigorous approach espoused by France. For this reason, although there was a tendency for inflation to fall in all EMS countries during the early 1980s, convergence on the German rate was quite slow and unsteady until 1985.

It is interesting to compare the abrupt and rapid fall in inflation in the UK and USA after 1980 with the much slower fall in other EMS countries. However, after 1985 the hard currency option offered by the Bundesbank became the dominant influence, and disinflation in the EMS continued with a noticeable convergence upon the German inflation rate. What should not, incidentally, be forgotten, is that this was not a costless experience for all participants. In France, for example, unemployment remained at a very high level throughout the 1980s whereas, as shown in Chapter 8, it fell steadily in the UK from 1986 onwards.

The general tendency for inflation rates among ERM countries to converge was constantly reiterated as a major benefit of UK membership of the ERM once inflation in the UK began to rise again in the late 1980s. Nevertheless, it has never been proved satisfactorily whether this convergence was specific to ERM **arrangements** or whether it was a general feature of the **period**[3] during which both ERM and non-ERM countries such as the UK and USA committed themselves in their macroeconomic strategies to conquering inflation (see Haldane, 1991 and Weber, 1991). It is also notable that the anti-inflationary anchor provided by Germany has slipped in recent years, especially in the period since July 1990 when monetary union between East and West Germany took place. Indeed, it would appear that the inflation rate in Germany rose above that in France in June 1991 and that it is currently higher than in four other member states (to which the UK may soon be added).

As noted in Haldane (1991, p. 76) and Artis (1991, p. 11), there is evidence to support the argument that the ERM has helped to stabilise both nominal and real intra-ERM bilateral exchange rates, but it has had much less effect upon the stability of members' global EERs. The recent sharp fluctuation of the dollar is an obvious case in point since the dollar has not moved consistently against all ERM currencies.

A related issue is whether lower intra-ERM exchange rate volatility has been achieved at the cost of greater short-term interest rate variability. It would appear to be the case (Weber, 1991, p. 82) that during the early EMS period (1979–83) highly volatile movements at relatively high levels of interest rates corresponded to speculative attacks upon the currencies which were devalued. Disinflation, capital controls and policy adjustments in the following period (1983–87) reduced this volatility markedly whilst also exerting downwards pressure on interest rates generally. The period post-1987 has seen rates move more or less in line, but mostly in an upwards direction. Here again, the influence of Germany appears to be crucial.

The decision to remove all capital controls, with the deadline for all EC countries set for the end of 1992 (to match the commencement of the SEM) but achieved by all major countries by 1991, is often held to have heralded the coming of the 'new EMS' (Haldane, 1991, p. 79). Because speculative capital flows had been such an destabilising force under the adjustable peg, steps were taken

Table 7.10   *Key dates for EMS and EMU*[1]

Mar 1979	ERM begins. ECU consists of DM 32%; Ffr 19%; UK£ 15%; Lira 10.2%; Florin 10.1%; Bfr 8.5%; DKr 2.7%; Drachma 1.3%; I£ 1.2%
Mar 1981	Belgian and Luxembourg currencies at fixed parity
Sept 1987	Basle–Nyborg Agreement
Apr 1989	Delors Committee Report proposes three-stage transition to EMU
Jun 1989	Spain enters ERM on wide band
Jun 1989	European Council decides to begin 1st stage of EMU on 1 July 1990
Sept 1989	Revision of currency weights for ECU as in **Table 7.7**
Jan 1990	Lira moves to narrow band
Jul 1990	Removal of all capital controls for EMS members except Ireland, Spain, Portugal and Greece (deadline 1992)
Jul 1990	Monetary union in Germany
Oct 1990	Germany reunified
Oct 1990	UK enters ERM on wide band

Note:
[1]   Other than realignments as detailed in **Table 7.9**.

under the Basle–Nyburg Agreement in September 1987 to offset these through, for example, the introduction of the VSTF. Furthermore, realignments of ERM currencies were put into effective abeyance as the message was sent out to the financial markets that the ERM countries would act in concert to maintain exchange rate stability and to base their macroeconomic policy upon that in Germany.

So successful was this policy that the paradox of **excess credibility** became apparent. High inflation countries such as Spain and Italy needed to maintain high interest rates to keep inflation under control. As noted previously, inflows of hot money, attracted by these interest rates, would normally be discouraged by the exchange rate risk involved (see **p. 207**), but this risk was no longer serious for ERM currencies, especially those in the narrow band. Hence, hot money flooded into Spain and Italy, driving the lira and peseta to the top of the grid and, as for example in March 1991, causing the peseta to hit its ceiling against the French franc. The possibility that a high inflation country could end up at the top of the grid rather than, more logically, at the bottom, was of particular interest to the UK Government given that the UK had joined the ERM in October 1990 on the wide band (see **Table 7.10**).

□ 7.4.5 Sterling and the ERM

In the course of the first edition we discussed at length whether the UK should join the ERM. That discussion is no longer of any direct relevance since the UK is currently a member. This does not imply, however, that the controversy engendered prior to entry has died down, not least because, as discussed below, the controversy has shifted to Economic and Monetary Union (EMU).

One issue which was understandably controversial at the time of entry to the ERM was whether the £ was overvalued in terms of the DM. It is necessary to adjust for inflation when seeking to address such a question, which can be done using different deflators. If unit labour costs are used as the deflator then on that basis it would appear that the rate at entry was sustainable, as indeed it would have been had it been either slightly higher or slightly lower (see *Financial Times*, 14 February 1991).

However, it was subsequently counter-argued that the EER should be used rather than the DM, and that it should be deflated by export unit values. On that basis the real EER was well above its long-term average on entry, and this allegedly speeded up the descent into recession. But whereas the debate over the correctness or otherwise of the

Figure 7.4 *DM per £, 1980–90*

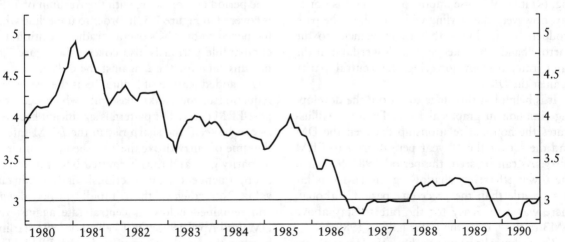

Source: CSO.

Figure 7.5   *DM per £, 1990–91*

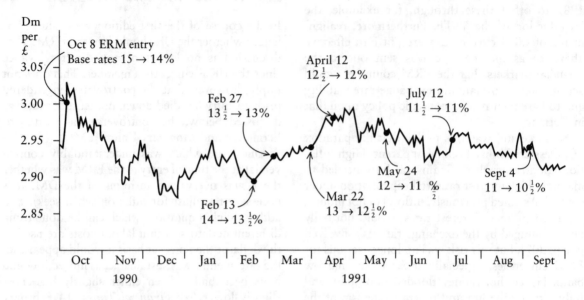

Source: Daily rates posted in *The Times*.

rate at entry has a certain fascination, the key issue is whether or not anything is going to be done actively to change it during 1991 – to which the answer is clearly in the negative. Whilst it is technically possible for sterling to devalue within the ERM, it is not going to happen because (1) no currency has devalued for four years; (2) the path to EMU requires currencies to move towards totally fixed rates; (3) it would be politically damaging; (4) it would raise import prices. This is not to say, however, that sterling will not follow the path trodden by the lira – that is, movement to the narrow band whilst keeping the lower limit at the same rate, thereby lowering the central parity against the DM.

It is helpful at this stage to set out the developing situation in graphical form. **Figure 7.4** illustrates the nominal relationship between the DM and the £ over the 10-year period prior to ERM entry. As can be seen, the period 1987–90 when the £ was effectively shadowing the DM was far less volatile than the preceding period, although there was a tendency for the rate to stay above DM3 to the £ until the latter half of 1989.

The technical arguments about the 'correct' rate of entry, which in any event fell somewhat short of

proof, played little part in influencing opinion outside the Treasury. The central parity chosen, namely DM2.95 to the £, did not appear to be particularly high taking a superficial longer-term perspective as in **Figure 7.4**. Nevertheless, the rate **had** been somewhat lower during the first half of 1990, and there were many who felt that the UK should have entered at a lower rate simply in order to give industry a competitive advantage. The period commencing with the Autumn of 1990 is covered in **Figure 7.5**. In order to underline what happened to the UK's overall trading position, the comparable period is also covered in **Figure 7.6**, but this time for the £ against the dollar.

An added feature of **Figure 7.5** is the sequential reduction in the banks' base rate which occurred post-ERM entry. The pattern is significant because, as can be seen, the sharp rise in the £/DM rate at the time of entry drove the £ to the upper limit of its parity grid and thus permitted base rates to be cut by 1 per cent without seriously undermining its value. Nevertheless, the £ rapidly turned down, and remained below its central rate against the DM until April 1991. On 1 February 1991 sterling became the weakest currency in the ERM. The authorities understandably felt unable to make any

Figure 7.6   *$ per £, 1990–91*

Source: Daily rates posted in *The Times*.

further dramatic cuts in interest rates, but rather chose to engage in a succession of half-point reductions as the £ rose steadily from mid-February to May. Given the strength of the recession this may be viewed as ultra-cautious, especially as, in practice, the £ was not adversely affected by each sequential reduction.

The strength of sterling reflected the unexpected combination of a rapidly strengthening dollar, as shown in **Figure 7.6**, which benefited UK exporters, and a declining DM. At the end of March the £ was the second strongest currency in the ERM, and remained there until the end of May when it succumbed to bad economic news and fear of an incoming Labour Government. By mid-June it had become the third weakest currency in the ERM, but was still trading comfortably within its permitted range. This temporarily ruled out further interest rate reductions – at least from the perspective of the Bank of England – and it is important to remind ourselves that the problem for sterling was

not its value against the DM, which remained comfortably above its bilateral floor of DM 2.778 to the £, but its value against the peseta which remained persistently at or near its maximum permitted bilateral limit against the weakest currency, the French franc.

7.4.6 Implications of ERM Membership

Monetary and Exchange Rate Policy

If we take other than a short-term perspective (which is admittedly difficult given the necessity of a general election in 1992), we must first take note of the fact that sterling will have to move to the narrow band before the end of 1993 when Stage 1 of the Delors Plan (discussed below) comes to an end. At this point, and subsequently, the £ will be closely tied to the DM.

Figure 7.7 *UK/German Interest Rate Gap* [1]

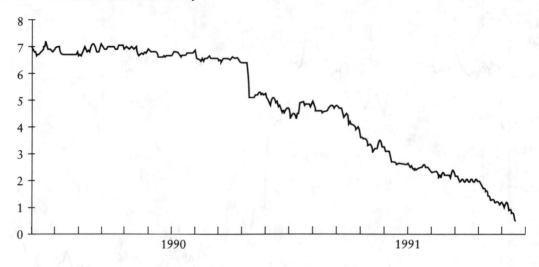

Note:
[1] 3-month sterling interbank rate *minus* 3-month Deutsche Mark interbank rate (%).
Source: Daily rates posted in the *Financial Times*.

By implication, significant capital flows of hot money will have to be avoided since they will serve to drive the £ beyond its bilateral limits with the DM, which in turn implies that UK and German interest rates will have to move in line with one another. As it happens, this should be relatively straightforward because UK rates have come down in response to the recession whereas German rates have risen in response to inflationary fears engendered by the cost of reunification. Given that the German difficulties will not go away in the forseeable future, either German interest rates will have to remain high by historical standards in order to finance fiscal deficits or the German inflation rate will rise, or both. As sterling is unlikely to shed fully its perceived exchange rate risk relative to the DM, UK interest rates can be expected to remain slightly above German rates although as shown in **Figure 7.7** the gap between UK and German rates has virtually disappeared, at least temporarily. One minor source of relief in this respect is that since short-term interest rates are currently higher than long-term rates (the so-called inverted yield curve), they can fall somewhat from their current level without much upset to financial markets.

Fiscal Policy

Given that the hands of the authorities are largely tied in respect of monetary policy, it follows that fiscal policy will have to play a bigger role in managing demand in the short term, especially with respect to the balance of trade. Since this appears to be on the mend (if only temporarily) there is currently no reason to expect that a choice will have to be made between devaluation and a very tight fiscal policy. It is notable that fiscal profligacy in Italy has not prevented the lira from settling at the top end of the ERM, and the UK Government's current fiscal stance cannot be viewed as unreasonable given the state of the economic cycle.

■ 7.5 EMU and EPU

7.5.1 Economic and Monetary Union

Whilst the EMS is generally held to have been a success, it was always seen in many quarters as simply a necessary step on the road to a 'United

States of Europe', incorporating a single European currency in an EMU structure. The Single European Act refers to EMU as 'cooperation in economic and monetary policy' and talks about 'EMU's progressive realisation'. These are sentiments with which even Mrs Thatcher was happy to comply.

Economic and monetary union involves two rather different concepts. **Economic** union is essentially concerned with the Single European Market – that is, a common market with an element of economic policy co-ordination between member states. **Monetary** union is essentially concerned with a single currency area with a common monetary policy.

The **Delors Committee** was set up in 1985 to recommend how best to proceed towards eventual EMU. It proposed a three-stage process.

Stage 1 : (i) completion of the SEM by the end of 1992
(ii) all member states join the ERM
Stage 2 : (i) co-ordination of monetary policy by member states
(ii) co-ordination to be overseen by new body with suggested title of **European System of Central Banks** (ESCB)
(iii) member states retain own currencies
(iv) no currency realignments except under severe duress (implying that currencies are within the narrow band by this stage)
Stage 3 : (i) irreversible fixity of EC currencies
(ii) at some point a single currency, possibly the ECU, to replace national currencies

In order to operate Stage 3 it will be necessary to set up a **European Central Bank** (ECB or **EuroFed**). Its job will be to issue the common currency; to conduct monetary policy; to act as lender of last resort to all European banks; and to manage the exchange rate for the common currency. In order to permit the EuroFed to conduct monetary policy on behalf of all member states **these must necessarily surrender some political sovereignty**. It was this issue which Mrs Thatcher could not stomach.

At the Madrid Summit at the end of June 1989 an attempt was made to set a rigid timetable for the full implementation of EMU. However, Mrs Thatcher managed to turn the tables by offering to join the ERM (in other words, to embark upon Stage 1) at such time as the rest of the EC fulfilled its obligations for 'the removal of all exchange controls, the full implementation of a free market in financial services and strengthening of competition policy'.

This apparently innocuous statement was expected to justify the postponement of the introduction of EMU for quite some time. Had Mrs Thatcher remained in power it is probable that she would have continued to insist that these conditions be met. Capital controls have largely gone now, but EC countries are proving very reluctant to enjoy the fruits of open competition in financial services with their more efficient UK counterparts. But that, as they say, is history. Mr Major has replaced Mrs Thatcher and intends to be a better European – up to a point. That point lies beyond joining the ERM, so Stage 1 of the Delors Plan is no longer at issue anywhere in the EC.

The timetable for the other stages was controversial. There was agreement on 1 January 1994 as the entry date into Stage 2. The suggested date for entering into Stage 3 was January 1997, although that was felt to be too early for the UK because of the controversies with respect to:

1 *The EuroFed*: the French were pressing to set up a central bank at the beginning of Stage 2, on the ground that delays would cause the momentum needed to complete all three stages to be lost. Germany was ambivalent, mainly because the Bundesbank, which expected to become the EuroFed for all practical purposes (and thereby to retain its anti-inflation remit and its independence from political interference), was unhappy. The Bundesbank argued that Germany's current problems, arising from reunification, had thrown the German fiscal strategy off course, and that the situation should be allowed to settle down fully before Germany ceded to the EuroFed (which might not be a reincarnated Bundesbank and hence less anti-inflationary in its approach because

the UK, among others, insisted that it be 'demo-cratically accountable') the right to regulate its domestic policies.

2   *One Speed or two speed*: most of the major EC countries had converged with respect to, for example, their rates of inflation. They were accordingly ready to link themselves together to a greater degree. The UK found conver-gence more problematic, as did southern EC members. It was therefore proposed that progress towards full EMU would be permit-ted **at two speeds**.

3   *The role of the ECU*: the UK proposed that, rather than set up a central bank in Stage 2, a European Monetary Fund be created to ad-minister a new common currency, the **hard ECU**. This would provide the necessary ex-perience of using a common currency in paral-lel with existing currencies prior to moving to a single currency. This proposal was strongly opposed by Germany.

4   *Fiscal policy*: for some, the EuroFed was insuf-ficient. They also wanted a centralised ap-proach to fiscal policy and centralised control of inter-governmental transfers designed to ensure that northern members subsidise south-ern members. At present, regional transfers are much larger within member states than between them. Poorer members can no longer devalue to assist with competitiveness and hence growth, and so they argued that with-out increased transfers they would be con-demned to permanently high unemployment. The UK was among the northern member states which opposed a major increase in such trans-fers.

The UK also expressed its forthright oppo-sition to 'binding fiscal rules', especially if the European Council were to be allowed to exer-cise ultimate authority over national fiscal policies by qualified majority vote. Germany was, not unreasonably, concerned that the fiscal profligacy of the likes of Greece could create debts which would then become the ultimate responsibility of richer EC members if the EC was not to be allowed to disintegrate – unless the Greeks could be prevented from running up the debts in the first place.

The British Parliament, however, had no in-tention of yielding up its centuries-old control over the nation's finances, especially not by January 1994.

This was a far greater threat to parliamen-tary sovereignty that full EMU at some as yet unspecific future date. The pragmatic view was that the UK should sign the new treaty and then ignore the bits it did not like in the Italian style.

☐ 7.5.2 The Maastricht IGCs

In December 1991 there was a double inter-governmental conference (IGC) held at Maastricht under the auspices of the Dutch presidency of the EC. These IGCs were instigated at the Rome Sum-mit in December 1990. The French were very keen to introduce EMU in order to offset what they saw as the dominant role of the Deutsche Mark and the Bundesbank. In return the Germans persuaded the French that this would work better if there was also closer political integration and more demo-cratic control over EC decision-making. Afraid that combining the two sets of issues together would delay his pet project of EMU, Delors in-sisted that they be discussed separately.

The two IGCs, one on EMU and the other on political union (EPU) took place simultaneously. The agenda for the Maastricht IGCs was (more or less) settled in the course of the Luxembourg Sum-mit in June 1991.

The Economic and Monetary Union IGC

Most of the issues relating to EMU have already been discussed above. At the Luxembourg Summit a formula was proposed for further discussion at Maastricht which would allow the UK to post-pone a decision on whether to join a single cur-rency. This formula contained three safeguard clauses:

1   no country would be able to prevent its part-ners from establishing a single currency if they had met certain criteria for the convergence of their economic performance

2   no country which had met these criteria could be excluded

3 no country could be compelled to join.

This formula was an advance on previous negotiations in that it met Mr Major's demand that any changes to the Treaty of Rome must not result in the imposition of a single currency without a separate decision by the British Parliament. At the same time it did not refer explicitly to a two-speed EMU with the UK as a laggard. However, it also prevented the UK from vetoing the entire proceedings.

The Political Union IGC

The previous IGC led to the 1985 SEA. The 1991 IGC was unlikely to be as dramatic, but it was once again to consider the relationship and the balance of power between the Council, the Commission, the Parliament and the Court of Justice. The outcome was to be a Treaty similar to the SEA, containing some amendments to the Treaty of Rome, plus a number of agreements outside the Community Treaties proper (see *Financial Times*, 28 June 1991).

There were four main areas of discussion, all given an airing at the Luxembourg Summit.

1 *Common foreign and security policy* (CFSP): the SEA enshrines political co-operation on foreign policy; it was proposed that this should become a common foreign and security policy.

2 *Democratic legitimacy*: the Parliament had been pushing hard for a bigger say in the legislative process, and also wanted a bigger role in appointing and monitoring the Commission.

3 *Extension of EC competence*: the Treaty of Rome covers commercial activity in a fairly non-specific manner, so it was proposed that it be amended specifically to include new areas such as telecommunications and consumer protection.

4 *Efficiency of EC institutions*: it was proposed that qualified majority voting be extended to matters which currently require unanimity; it was also proposed, for example, that EC expenditure be more closely monitored and that Court of Justice rulings be adhered to more strictly.

It may be noted that the above discussion omits any reference to **social policy** which is discussed at the end of Chapter 9.

□ 7.5.3 *Federalism*

In a draft preamble to a rewritten Treaty of Rome drawn up by the Luxembourg presidency the phrase 'a union with a federal goal' appeared for the first time as a description of the EC. The UK Foreign Secretary, Douglas Hurd, promptly rejected this on the grounds that whilst the world 'federal' might mean different things to different nationalities, 'it has come to mean something tight and integrated in English'. Oddly enough the term 'federal' means **decentralisation** in some countries even though it means **centralisation** in English. Denmark and Portugal were also less than keen on the term, so it needed to be written out of the new treaty.

Given the unfortunate recent history of such federations as the USSR, Yugoslavia and India, the UK's objection was not altogether surprising. However, the Treaty of Rome already commits the UK to 'an ever closer union', which in theory at least commits the UK to forge more and more links with other EC members, so a federal structure in which the UK's sovereign rights are more or less permanently defined might even seem to be the lesser of two evils.

□ 7.5.4 *The Maastricht Treaty*

The new Treaty hammered out at Maastricht will, once suitably tidied up, be signed by the twelve EC governments in the Spring of 1992. It will subsequently need to be ratified by every national parliament, and possibly also have to survive a referendum in Denmark and Ireland. All being well, it will come into force at the end of the year.

The *EMU* sections began by stating that:

The activities of the member states and the Community shall . . . include:
- the irrevocable fixing of exchange rates leading to the introduction of a single currency, the ECU;
- the definition and conduct of a single monetary policy and exchange rate policy the

primary objective of both of which shall be to maintain price stability;
- and, without prejudice to this objective, to support the general economic policies in the Community in accordance with the principle of an open market economy with free competition.

It then went on to state that:

A European System of Central Banks (ESCB) and the European Central Bank (ECB) shall be established in accordance with the procedures laid down in this Treaty . . . The basic tasks to be carried out through the ESCB shall be:
- to define and implement the monetary policy of the Community;
- to conduct foreign exchange operations consistent with the provisions of Article 109;
- to hold and manage the official foreign reserves of the Member States.
The ESCB shall be composed of the ECB and of the central banks of the member states.

The ECB was to be established before the end of 1992. Neither it nor the ESCB, nor individual central banks were to seek or take instructions from Community institutions or bodies, or from any government of a member state, thereby guaranteeing independence.

The core of the Treaty concerned the path of EMU. This was expressed in terms of 'a high degree of sustainable convergence' which itself required the following criteria to be satisfied:

- that a currency should not have devalued for at least two years, nor had great difficulty in staying within its ERM fluctuation margins;
- that the consumer price index should be close to that of at most the three best performing member states in terms of price stability over the past year;
- that the planned or actual government deficit should not exceed 3 per cent of GDP at market prices;
- that the ratio of general government debt to GDP at market prices should not exceed 60 per cent;
- that over the past year the average nominal long-term government bond rate should not ex-

ceed by more than 2 per cent that of at most the three best performing member states in terms of price stability.

Prior to the second stage of EMU, commencing 1 January 1994, all EC members will be obliged to abolish all restrictions on the movement of capital and set their economic houses in order. Once stage 2 begins a European Monetary Institute will be set up to

- strengthen co-operation between central banks;
- strengthen coordination of monetary policies;
- replace the European Monetary Cooperation Fund;
- monitor the functioning of the EMS;
- facilitate the use of the ECU.

By the end of 1996 the EMI will be obliged to specify the regulatory, organisational and logistical framework for the ESCB.

During stage 2 the European Commission will monitor the progress towards convergence of each country and, if the Council of Ministers so recommends on the basis of a qualified majority, on a date no later than 31 December 1996 the European Council (composed of Heads of State or of Government) will be obliged to consider

- whether a majority of the member states fulfils the necessary conditions for the adoption of a single currency;
- whether it is appropriate for the Community to enter the third stage of EMU, and if so, when.

If this date cannot be fixed before the end of 1997 then stage 3 will automatically begin on 1 January 1999. The Council's decision will be by qualified majority, as will be the decision concerning which countries will be permitted to proceed to full EMU, and which are to be given a derogation. At least once every two years, or at the request of a member state with a derogation, the Commission and the ECB will recommend to the European Council whether other countries have met the convergence criteria.

At the beginning of stage 3, all member states which qualify for full EMU will adopt the conversion rates at which their currencies will be irrevocably fixed in terms of the ECU which will then become a currency in its own right.

It is worthy of note that it is not essential that a country meets all of the five convergence criteria simultaneously since it would appear to be possible for the European Council to bend the rules somewhat in practice when deciding which countries qualify. This is probably just as well in view of the fact that as of the end of 1991 only France and Luxembourg met all five criteria as shown in Table 7.11.

It is a touch ironic that Germany is not currently ready for full EMU. It is frankly doubtful whether Italy, Greece or Portugal ever will be. Denmark may be obliged to hold a referendum before taking part in stage 3, and if it votes not to do so it will not count when calculating the necessary majority. As for the UK, it insisted on an 'opt-out clause' to the effect that:

> The UK shall not be obliged or committed to move to the third stage of economic and monetary union without a separate decision to do so by its government and Parliament.

If the UK does opt out then it will not count when calculating the majority needed to proceed to full EMU. It is, however, a touch ironic that if the UK were to move to the narrow band of the ERM, and to keep itself there for two years, it would be one of the leading contenders for full EMU. On the whole it is rather unlikely that the UK will opt out if it does indeed meet the convergence critera at the relevant time.

Table 7.11 *EMU Convergence Criteria*

	Exch. rate	Price index	Budget	Public debt	Bond rate	Score
F	Yes	Yes	Yes	Yes	Yes	5
L	Yes	Yes	Yes	Yes	Yes	5
DK	Yes	Yes	Yes	No	Yes	4
UK	No	Yes	Yes	Yes	Yes	4
FRG	Yes	No	No	Yes	Yes	3
B	Yes	Yes	No	No	Yes	3
IRL	Yes	Yes	No	No	Yes	3
NL	Yes	No	No	No	Yes	2
IT	Yes	No	No	No	No	1
S	No	No	No	Yes	No	1
GR	No	No	No	No	No	0
P	No	No	No	No	No	0

The *EPU* sections began by stating that:

> By this Treaty, the High Contracting Parties establish among themselves a European Union. . . . This Treaty marks a new stage in the process creating an ever closer Union among the peoples of Europe, where decisions are taken as closely as possible to the citizens.

The preamble then goes on to refer to the issue of 'subsidiarity' which is defined for the first time in article 3b as follows:

> the Community shall take action . . . only if and insofar as the objectives of the proposed action cannot be sufficiently achieved by the member states and can therefore, by reason of the scale or effects of the proposed action, be better achieved by the Community.

It is to be expected that the UK will adhere very strongly to the letter of this definition in order to restrict the powers of the Commission. However, the new Treaty both amends and extends the list of activities as set out in the Treaty of Rome and the SEA which fall within the competence of the Commission. This encompasses:

- The strengthening of economic and social cohesion.
- Measures concerning the entry and movement of persons in the internal market.
- A policy in the sphere of the environment.
- The promotion of research and technological development.
- Measures in the spheres of energy, consumer protection, civil protection and tourism.
- Contribution to the attainment of a high level of health protection.
- Contribution to education and training of high quality, and to the flowering of the cultures of the member states.

As noted above, cohesion essentially means a transfer of resources from north to south, which will be costly for the UK as a net contributor to the EC Budget. It is also worth observing that this extension of powers will make it harder for expiring members to reach EC standards unless, like Austria, they already meet most of them.

Readers will, perhaps, be pleased to learn that

they are now 'citizens of the Union', a title awarded in the Treaty to all EC nationals who 'shall have the right to move and reside freely within the territory of the Member States'.

The Treaty enchances the powers of the European Parliament. Whereas, as shown in **Figure 7.1**, the Parliament previously needed the Commission's backing to get its amendments through the Council, it now has the right to negotiate directly with the relevant ministers the changes that it wants to make, and to reject any proposed legislation that does not contain them. This was originally to be called the 'co-decision' process, but this was vetoed by the UK on the grounds that it smacked of loss of sovereignty, and it will be known as 'the procedure laid down in Article 189b'! It covers laws on the internal market; consumer protection; the free circulation of labour; the right of individuals and companies to establish themselves in other member states; the treatment of foreigners; vocational training; public health; and trans-European infrastructure.

In respect of foreign policy the Parliament has also now to give its assent to such matters as the objectives of the Structural Funds and the rights of citizenship created by the Treaty. The Treaty is due to be reviewed in 1996.

■ 7.6 The Demise of Free Trade?

Government policies in all the OECD countries have been moving in a market-oriented direction in recent years. There is, however, one rather notable exception to this general trend, which is in respect of international trade. The trade regimes of most OECD countries are currently less liberal than they were 10 years ago. In a survey carried out by the *Harvard Business Review*, some 11,700 managers in 25 countries proved themselves generally to be as two-faced about free trade as politicians (cause and effect?). 83 per cent of British managers, for example, supported the idea of free trade along with minimal protection for domestic firms – but 80 per cent went on to support the idea that governments should actively assist domestic firms in international markets (see *The Economist*, 11 May 1991, p. 96). South Koreans were, how-

ever, all in favour of protectionism whereas the Japanese claimed to be much more in favour of free trade than managers in the USA and the EC!

Free trade is easy to justify – even if one's trading partners do not consider it to be to their advantage. Suppose, for example, the Japanese refuse to buy UK products but have themselves developed a life-saving drug. Should the UK refuse to purchase it on a tit-for-tat basis? Clearly, welfare in the UK will be enhanced if the drug is bought **no matter what the Japanese choose to do**. Bilateral free trade is better than unilateral free trade, but unilateral free trade is much better than no trade at all.

Once upon a time there was an enormously strong trading nation called Great Britain which considered that its best interests were served by free trade, and thrived mightily on account of it. But when the Germans and Americans began to take over its markets it began to wonder whether it was such a good idea after all. After the recession of the 1930s, when the collapse of trade was instrumental in prolonging and worsening the recession, another great trading nation, the USA, considered that its best interests were served by free trade. Because of its economic strength it was able to impose its will upon other, less enthusiastic, nations, but all came to appreciate that removal of trade barriers would be in their **mutual** best interests.

Even the oil shocks of the 1970s failed to push the USA off course, but its confidence was steadily being damaged by the rapid trading progress of Japan. In this respect, democracy can be flawed. Free trade provides benefits to all of society, but these benefits are hard to quantify. If import barriers are erected they bring large benefits to small groups who accordingly lobby endlessly for their introduction. If introduced, they affect individual consumers so little that they rarely complain. The die is accordingly cast in favour of protectionism, and governments must show determination to set their faces against the lobbying.

Two issues about free trade need to be appreciated. In the first place, few businessmen and politicians appreciate that the classical case for free trade emphasised the merits of **unilateral** free trade. During the postwar period the USA pro-

Table 7.12 *The Pros and Cons of Protectionism*

PROS:
1 If cheap foreign imports are destroying domestic industries, they must be kept out to preserve domestic jobs and acceptable levels of domestic wages
2 If goods are being 'dumped' in the domestic market, they must be kept out to preserve output and jobs in what may be efficient domestic businesses
3 If other countries are introducing protectionist devices, retaliation is necessary to level the playing field
4 Protectionism is needed for 'infant industries' until such time as they are of a sufficient size to compete in international markets
5 Protectionism is a legitimate device to prevent the sudden collapse of an industry and to enable an orderly transfer to other activities to take place
6 Protectionism is justified if a country has a permanent balance of trade problem which it has been unable to resolve in more acceptable ways

CONS:
1 Since protectionism inevitably inspires retaliation, it causes a reduction in the volume of international trade, thereby causing damage to the economies of all nations dependent upon such trade for improvements in economic welfare
2 Because of retaliation, protectionism is not going to be successful anyway
3 Arguments over protectionism create political illwill between nations which may have maleffects beyond the trade sector

---

moted free trade primarily by promoting the idea of an **exchange of concessions** through the General Agreement on Tariffs and Trade (GATT). In the modern world, countries **expect to be compensated** for removing barriers to trade.

Secondly, it is evident that free trade is not universally the best solution, and even the classical economists admitted as much. For example, the need to protect 'infant industries' is an idea dating back to Adam Smith which is probably familiar to most readers (see Crook, 1990, p. 16). A brief summary of the pros and cons of protectionism is set out in **Table 7.12**. The important point to bear in mind, however, is that whilst new theories of trade which emphasise imperfect competition and externalities do provide some justification for export subsidies and tariffs, they do so in **only a limited number of cases**, and not as a general rule.

Managed trade should not, therefore, be dismissed out of hand. But it must also be borne in mind that if it is to be managed then its management must be **in the interests of society as a whole**. Needless to say, this is not what happens in practice, and it was the usurping of the intellectual defence for managed trade by lobbyists in the USA, as it progressively lost its markets to Japanese and other products, which lies at the roots of the current malaise in trade affairs.

Unfortunately, as anyone who has read about the 1930s will know, this is no laughing matter. In most years, recessions excepted, the increase in the volume of merchandise trade provides a major driving force promoting the growth of world output, as shown in **Figure 7.8** for the period 1980–90. The scale of world trade flows and their broad pattern is illustrated in **Figure 7.9**.

In recent years the USA and (West) Germany have vied for the title of the world's greatest ex-

Figure 7.8 *World Trade, Annual % Change*

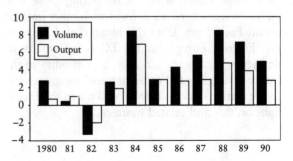

Source: GATT.

Figure 7.9   *World Trade Flows, 1989, $ bn*

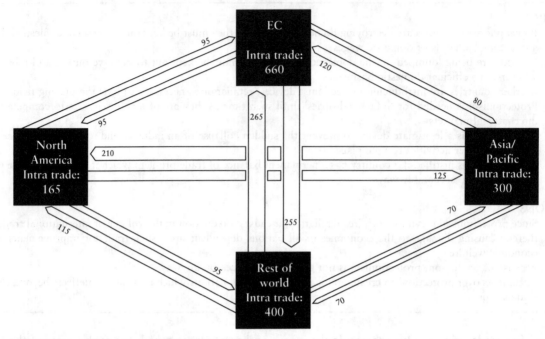

Source: The Economist, based upon GATT and OECD data.

porting nation, and the latter currently has its nose in front as shown in **Figure 7.10**. Great Britain sits a comfortable fifth in the list, and consequently has much to lose through a decline in world trade.

What **Figure 7.9** suggests is that the world is divided up into four main trading groups. In practice the 'rest of world' group is disparate and unwieldy whereas the other three are busy forming strong internal alliances. The EC has its 1992 project, and the US Government, having already formed a free trade relationship with Canada, is currently discussing similar links with Mexico. Meanwhile Japan, which is managing quite well on its own, is interested in links with other nations on the Pacific rim. Does this mean that, for example, **Fortress Europe** (as the EC is known by its detractors) is already a reality, a possibility in the future or a figment of other nations' imaginations? In the sections that follow we will try to shed some light on this and related matters.

Figure 7.10   *World Merchandise Exports, 1990*[1]

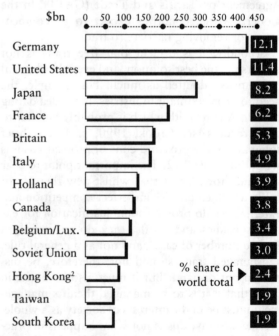

Notes:
[1]   The total value of world merchandise trade in 1990 was $3.5 trillion.
[2]   Including re-exports.
Source: The Economist.

■ 7.7 Protectionism

□ 7.7.1 Forms of Protectionism

Protectionism has become a matter of controversy primarily because of the difficulties which the US Government has had in reducing its enormous BoP deficit by more acceptable means. All countries operate some protectionist policies, but it is fair to say that the UK was one of the less protectionist-minded of the industrial countries throughout the 1980s. Protectionism is generally a negative-sum game, in that once the process is set in motion in one country its main trading partners usually respond with offsetting measures of their own, thereby causing all of them to lose out. It is therefore possible that the UK will be drawn into protectionism if it is instigated elsewhere on a sufficiently large scale.

Until fairly recently the commonest form of protectionism was the **tariff**, which is a tax imposed on imports either as a lump sum or as a percentage of their value. This drives up domestic prices, which is not particularly desirable, but the government obtains an additional source of revenue to fund its expenditure and the illusion is given that the foreign exporter is suffering most because he is virtually forced to pay the tax.

Tariffs have been restricted because major industrial countries have agreed to abide by the GATT rules (see below) which greatly limit their use, but in any event their inflationary consequences are undesirable and can apparently be avoided by resort to other non-tariff barriers. Of these the commonest are **quotas**, which serve to limit the access of overseas producers to the domestic market. The quotas are generally fixed in terms of the **number** or **value** of imports to be permitted. Inflationary consequences might still arise if the importer takes advantage of the artificial shortage of the product to put up its price, in which case it is the private sector, rather than the government, which gets the extra revenue, but the government could obtain extra revenue by auctioning import licences. In recent years many countries have preferred to avoid overt confrontation by 'requesting' foreign governments to limit their exports of particular products. In the case of cars, for example, both the EC and USA have agreed import quotas with Japan during the 1980s.

Underlying such **voluntary export restraints** (VERs) is an unspoken threat of 'official' quotas if compliance if not adhered to. It is alleged that the Japanese impose unofficial quotas by requiring foreign products such as cars to meet specifications, for safety or other reasons, which they cannot meet without expensive modifications. The Japanese counter-argument is, naturally, that products of 'inferior' quality simply do not sell on their domestic market.

Occasionally certain imports and/or exports are embargoed (given **a zero quota**). This is usually to 'punish' a country, such as South Africa, which is pursuing domestic policies unacceptable to the wider political community. The present UK Government has never favoured such methods of dealing with errant regimes, but irrespective of the moral issues it has to be said that embargoes are constantly being broken.

A rather more subtle procedure is to **subsidise exports**. This obviously costs the government a good deal of money, but protects jobs and hence, indirectly, the **tax base of the domestic economy**. An industry which is subsidised almost everywhere is the shipbuilding industry, which has long suffered from chronic world overcapacity. These subsidies are more subtle in the sense that they can be disguised as regional development grants or 'infant industry' support. The UK also operates **export credit guarantees** which insure exports against default by overseas buyers.

Finally, there is the possibility of introducing various forms of **exchange control**. Exchange controls operated in the UK until 1979. Such controls were philosophically incompatible with the free-market beliefs of the new Conservative Government, and their abolition was the first major step along the path to widespread deregulation. However, there was also an underlying economic rationale to abolition. At the time, the balance of payments on current account was about to improve markedly as a result of North Sea oil coming on stream. This was bound to exert strong upward pressure on the exchange rate, and whilst the government did not wish to intervene to keep the rate down, it was realised that the abolition of exchange controls would result in a huge outflow of capital, mostly for long-term investment, and that this would help to limit the appreciation of sterling. Furthermore, there would be a net inflow of interest and dividends in later years.

Other major countries have followed the UK example, but there is still pressure in certain circles to reinstate exchange controls on the grounds that the capital being exported could be better used within the UK. Such controls could be reimposed in a variety of forms. In the past there have been controls both on capital inflows, for example by suspending the convertibility of foreign currency into sterling, and upon capital outflows, for example by routeing requests to obtain foreign currency via the central bank which has the right to refuse authorisation, or by refusing permission for private individuals to export capital other than in small amounts.

It is worth observing, by way of conclusion, that most of the forms of protection discussed above were developed during the era of fixed exchange rates. Obviously, if exports are uncompetitive the simplest ways to deal with the problem where the exchange rate can float are to allow the currency to depreciate or to intervene to force down the exchange rate. This is much less likely to invite retaliation, although competitive depreciation is by no means unknown, but it has to be said that this policy can help only those industries which are close to being competitive at the higher exchange rate. Where an industry, such as shipbuilding, is regularly being undercut by up to 50 per cent, selective assistance, whatever its merits, is the only solution if it is to survive.

☐ 7.7.2 *Effects of Protectionism*

In a major review the OECD (1985) concluded that non-inflationary growth was being impeded by protectionism. The simple Keynesian model indicates that if one country refuses to buy the exports of another country, then the latter will suffer a reduction in its national income and hence reduce its own imports. The original country thus protects jobs in its industries previously losing out to import substitution, but suffers job losses in

industries dependent upon exporting. One might have thought that this lesson was learned in the 1930s following the US Smoot-Hawley Tariff of 1930, but regrettably this is not the case. In the first place, the jobs saved by protectionism are more immediate and more visible than the jobs lost as exports subsequently suffer. Secondly, as noted previously, it is easy to organise a combined lobby of politicians, businessmen and trade unions to support an endangered local industry.

The GATT regulations on trade barriers are based upon 'reciprocity'. **First-difference reciprocity** aims to reduce trade barriers through the requirement that a country provides a tariff reduction **comparable in value** to that introduced by a trading partner. In the USA, however, there has recently been a movement towards the principle of **full reciprocity**. This requires **equal access**, which is measured by the balance of trade both overall and/or in specific sectors. A trade deficit is taken to be evidence of unequal access and to justify retaliation. The worst offender is, as usual, claimed to be Japan, and the UK Government has also recently had cause to make representations about reciprocal access to financial markets in Japan. If this approach becomes more prevalent, the movement towards a more protectionist environment may become an unstoppable force. It is, perhaps, naive to point out that bilateral trade balances are rarely in equilibrium in the normal course of events, because even if the UK is in overall equilibrium it will almost certainly be in surplus with, for example, the USA whilst simultaneously in deficit with, for example, Japan. Indeed, the principle of comparative advantage should bring about precisely such an outcome.

This may not, however, be sufficient to prevent the reappearance of protectionism for the reasons cited above, as has been confirmed, for example, by the dispute over growth hormones in meat. Hormones are used in livestock production in most non-EC meat producing countries, including the USA, but were banned in the EC in December 1985. Fedesa, the association representing the veterinary pharmaceutical industry in Europe, claimed that the ban was based on dubious scientific evidence and did not originally relate to hormones used in the USA, and the European

Commission accepted privately that this was indeed the case. However, they claimed in public that it was an issue of consumer concern, and that the ban was applied in a non-discriminatory way in much the same way as the USA unilaterally introduced rigorous emission standards for cars.

The USA, in its turn claimed that the ban (introduced on 1 January 1988 but one year later in the case of American meat) represented an unfair barrier to trade. Hence, although the ban affected only $120 mn of US exports, it responded by imposing a 100 per cent duty on an equal value of food imports from the EC (see *Financial Times*, 20 December 1988 for details). The EC immediately threatened counter-retaliation of equal value, but held back from its implementation. The ban was upheld by the European Court of Justice in November 1990.

■ 7.8 1992 and EC Trade

If all goes according to plan, all border restrictions on trade between member countries of the EC will be discarded at the end of 1992. Goods and services, labour and capital, will flow freely across national borders. In principle, there is already free movement between member countries, and there is already a common external tariff. However, this is not exactly the case in practice. There are, *inter alia*, a host of protectionist agreements involving individual EC members and non-EC countries. There is, for example, a quota regulating the importation of Japanese cars into the UK. Furthermore, Article 115 of the EC prevents prospective importers from obtaining goods subject to restricted entry in their own country by routeing them via another EC country where they are imported freely. The SEM necessarily spells out the abolition of Article 115, and the erection of truly common external trade barriers. Some EC members want these to be as high as possible in order to keep the internal market as a near-exclusive preserve for members, whilst others, including the UK, consider that the net effect should be to reduce protectionism for the sake of the world economy.

From the viewpoint of consumers there is a clear gain where the common external tariff (CET)

Figure 7.11 *State Aid to Manufacturing, Annual Average, ECU bn, 1986–88*

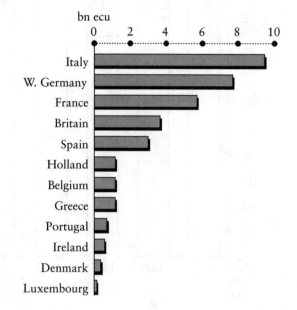

Source: The Economist.

Figure 7.12 *Subsidies as % of GDP*

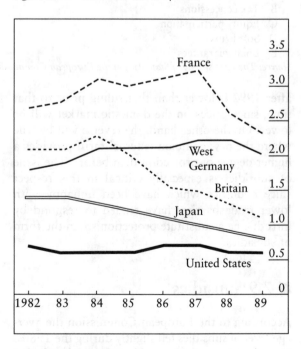

Source: The Economist.

Figure 7.13   *Subsidies to Industry, EEC 10, % of Total Support by Type, 1981–86 Average*

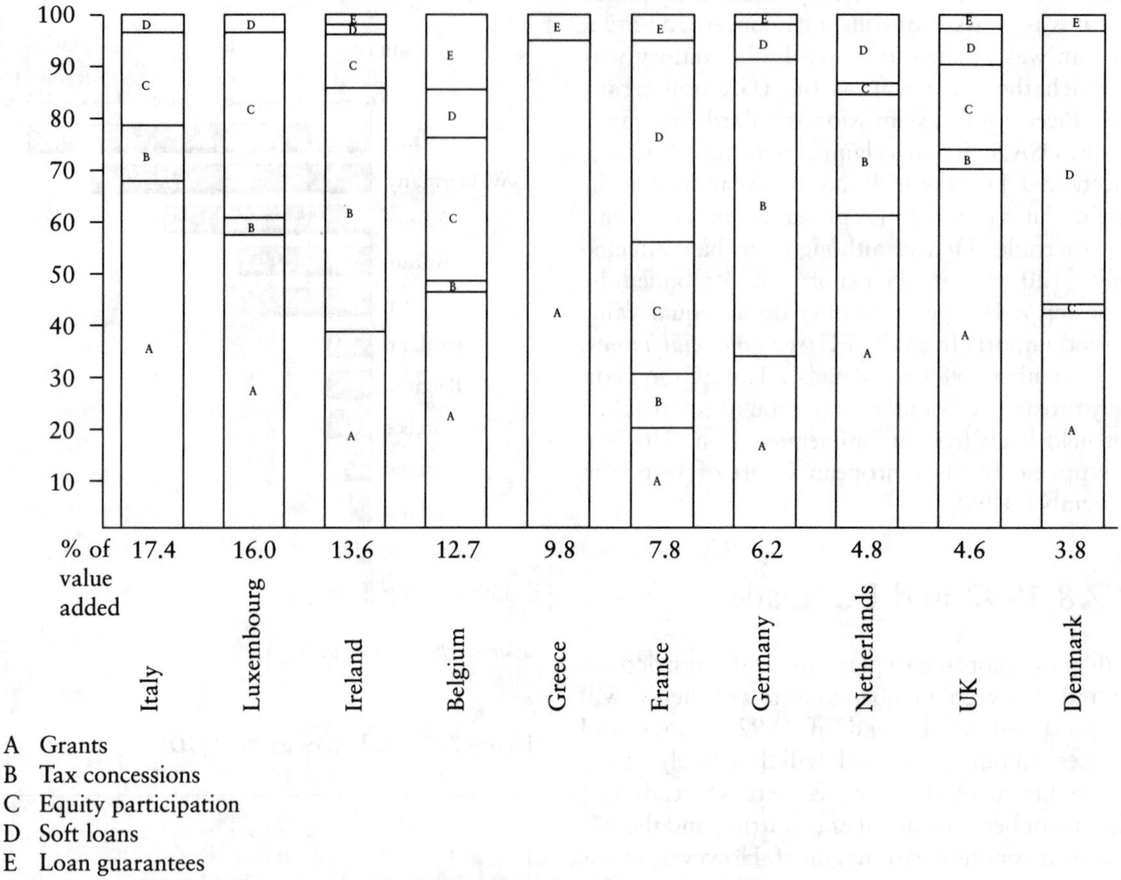

% of value added	17.4	16.0	13.6	12.7	9.8	7.8	6.2	4.8	4.6	3.8

Italy, Luxembourg, Ireland, Belgium, Greece, France, Germany, Netherlands, UK, Denmark

A   Grants
B   Tax concessions
C   Equity participation
D   Soft loans
E   Loan guarantees

Source: The First Survey of State Aids in the European Communities (Brussels: Commission of the European Communities, 1989).

after 1992 is lower than that ruling prior to that time, since prices on the domestic market will be lower. On the other hand, the reverse will be true where the new common external tariff provides a higher degree of protection than before. The issue of subsidies is especially critical in this respect since countries which have been unhappy with lower trade barriers have tended to respond by introducing a substitute protectionism in the form of subsidies.

■ 7.9 Subsidies

According to the European Commission the average level of subsidies fell slightly during the 1980s. The EC 10 averaged roughly ECU 89 bn during 1981–86 and the EC 12 roughly ECU 82 bn dur-

ing 1986–88. Of this sum ECU 11 bn was accounted for by agriculture; ECU 13 bn by coal; ECU 26 bn by railways; and the rest by industry.

These figures appear to be very high when compared to OECD data which, while it is consistently defined and illustrates a similar pattern during the 1980s, as shown in **Figure 7.12**, covers only direct grant aid. If other forms of aid are included the pattern changes considerably for industrial countries, as shown in **Figure 7.13**. It is very unlikely that, despite years of research, the Commission has managed to unearth the most opaque forms of assistance. Were it to do so, the position of the UK would look even more favourable since its subsidy policy is relatively transparent. During the 1980s the Thatcherite approach was to reduce aid to 'lame ducks' and to cut back severely on regional policy. In Germany, prior to reunification, independent estimates by the Kiel Institute and others suggest that 4 per cent of GNP was devoted to subsidies (financed by commensurately high levels of taxation). The situation is likely to deteriorate rapidly now that the former, hopelessly inefficient, industrial sectors of East Germany have been drawn into the fold, and even Italy will have to look to its laurels as the EC's subsidiser-in-chief, as shown in **Figure 7.11**.

Under the circumstances, the key issue is whether or not the EC competition commissioner, Leon Brittan, can stem the tide. He is certainly trying hard. In the first five months of 1991 he launched 15 investigations into alleged cases of unfair subsidies. Many of these, such as the French decision to inject hundreds of millions of pounds into Groupe Bull, a state-owned computer-maker and Thomson, a state defence and electronics group; the Belgian plan to recapitalise Sabena, its state-owned airline; and the use of Franch state-owned companies to channel aid to firms in poorer regions, certainly appear to fall foul of Brittan's premise that an illegal subsidy is one which involves any action whereby the state, as owner, acts differently from a private investor.

The awkward problem this raises is that state ownership becomes pointless if the state must run its firms as though they were private. The UK crossed swords with Brittan on this issue when he ordered British Aerospace in June 1990 to repay the £44 mn it had received from the state as part of its purchase of the Rover group – on appeal, BAe won on a technicality. Another well-publicised case in 1990 involved the repayment of state aid to Renault of France.

Unlike the UK, France has as yet failed to privatise in a meaningful way, which is why the current spate of investigations involves so many Franch companies. The DTI recently referred several deals involving links between foreign (mainly French) state-owned companies and companies in the UK to the Monopolies and Mergers Commission, much to the displeasure of the European Commission – but failed to get adverse judgements. It is probable that problems with balancing budgets will stem the subsidy tide rather than any overt desire to bend to the will of the Commission in this respect (see Giles, 1991).

▌ 7.10 The General Agreement on Tariffs and Trade (GATT)

The GATT was originally signed in 1947 by 23 countries (currently 100) determined to avoid a repetition of the worst consequences of protectionism evidenced during the 1930s. Its aims were to reduce existing barriers to free trade (but excluding agriculture and services, which are not covered); to eliminate trade discrimination; and to curb the reintroduction of protectionist measures by requiring member countries to consult together prior to such action. A critical principle was the **'most-favoured-nation' clause**, whereby any member country offering a tariff reduction to another country was obliged to offer the same reduction to all other member countries.

It may be argued that the oddest thing about the GATT was the need for anyone to join. Given that members already accepted the principle that more trade was better than less trade, it had to be in their mutual self-interest to lower tariff barriers. The necessity to treat a tariff reduction as a concession requiring reciprocity would seem to be redundant when self-interest dictates that tariff reductions should anyway be pursued, since bilateral tariff reductions should be taking place in the absence of reciprocity conditions. However, as discussed above, the economic virtues of free trade are not always self-evident to interest groups when domestic industries are being 'destroyed' by imports, so governments needed to counteract this by reference to their obligations to maintain GATT rules. In any event, governments have always been afraid of appearing to be weak when allowing competitors free access to their markets in the absence of publically-stated reciprocity. In this re-

Table 7.13 *GATT Rounds*

Geneva	1947
Annecy	1948
Torquay	1950
Geneva	1956
Dillon	1960–61
Kennedy	1964–67
Tokyo	1973–79
Uruguay	1986–90

spect the attitude of the present UK Government is interesting, since it continues to play the reciprocity game even though, according to its economic philosophy, reciprocity cannot be a precondition for trade.

The GATT therefore exists as a precaution against the facile adoption of the 'imports are bad, exports are good' creed, a creed which is intuitively appealing to the proverbial man-in-the-street. A virtue of the most-favoured-nation clause in this respect is that if a tariff is raised against one competitor it has to be raised against them all, thereby greatly increasing the risk of retaliation – an argument which the government can fall back on when pressed to protect a specific bilateral trade. This is bolstered by the principle of reciprocity, since it becomes possible to counter the argument that tariff reductions will damage domestic industries with the claim that benefits of equal value will accrue to exporting industries.

☐ 7.10.1 The Tokyo Round

The seventh, Tokyo Round began in 1973 (see **Table 7.13**). New or reinforced agreements called 'codes' were established in respect of subsidies and countervailing duties; government procurement; technical standards; import licensing procedures; customs valuation; and anti-dumping.

The code on subsidies and countervailing duties prohibits direct export subsidies other than in agriculture. Given the widespread use of subsidies a distinction is made between domestic and export subsidies. A domestic subsidy that treats domestic and export sales in a neutral way is normally permissible under GATT rules. However, a tariff designed to offset an export subsidy given to a foreign supplier – known as a **countervailing duty** – is prohibited unless domestic producers can be shown to have suffered (or are expected to suffer) 'material' injury as a consequence. Additionally a country can seek redress against another when the latter's subsidised exports have replaced the former's sales in a third country.

The code on government procurement states that in respect to qualifying non-military purchases,

governments and organisations under their control must treat domestic and foreign producers in the same way.

The anti-dumping code sets out rules for anti-dumping investigations, the imposition of anti-dumpling duties and the settlement of disputes. A method for assessing the degree of injury sustained is set out. Developing countries are expected to be given preferential treatment by developed countries.

☐ 7.10.2 The Uruguay Round

The oil price shocks and unflationary conditions of the 1970s, followed by the 1980–81 recession, made trading conditions problematic for many countries.

Understandably, no country, least of all the USA which had been instrumental in using the GATT as the vehicle for liberalising world trade, wished to flout GATT rules in an open manner. Thus the favoured tactic was to 'bend' the rules in such a way as to offer some degree of protection to domestic industries threatened by imports, particularly those originating in Japan. In place of the **multilateral** agreements previously negotiated in the GATT, the USA and the EC began increasingly

Figure 7.14 *Industrialised Countries, Average Tariffs, %*

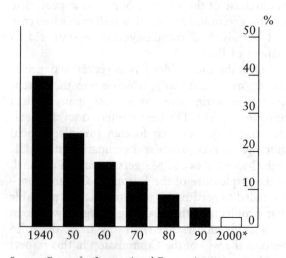

Source: Centre for International Economics.

to negotiate **bilateral** arrangements, many of which took the form of VERs. By and large the Japanese were happy to go along with these arrangements since it enabled them to concentrate on selling top of the range, high value-added products which could be sold very profitably in competition with high-priced, uncompetitive domestic products.

Governments also resorted increasingly to **subsidies** which they alleged did not infringe the rules of the GATT, and the tactic grew up during the 1980s of imposing **anti-dumping duties** on manufactured products, especially those originating in Japan and the Far East, on the alleged grounds that they were being sold for less than was being charged on the exporter's home market.

In some ways this behaviour was not altogether unexpected given that tariffs on the importation of manufactured goods had fallen to an average of less than 5 per cent (**Figure 7.14**) thereby offering inefficient domestic producers very little protection against imports. The proliferation of restraints on trade, which could be said to be compatible with the rules of the GATT only by exercising a good deal of imagination, nevertheless posed a severe threat to its continued role as the instrument for trade liberalisation.

Furthermore, the Japanese and West German onslaught had served in part to reduce the dependence of other countries, and especially of the USA, upon domestically produced manufactured goods. The service sectors which grew up in their place did not fall under the rules of the GATT since they were traditionally regarded as domestic rather than suitable for international trade. However, they were increasingly becoming the driving force underlying economic growth in countries such as the USA,

Table 7.14 *The Uruguay Round: State of Play in the 15 Areas under Negotiation*

OPENING MARKETS

Tariffs – still well short of 33 per cent overall reduction in duties

Non-Tariff barriers – real bargaining over reductions not started; deals may be struck on rules of origin and pre-shipment inspection of goods

Natural resource-based products – waiting for results from other areas

Tropical products – developed countries stalling on promise of full liberalisation; linked to progress in agriculture talks

Agriculture – key to whole Round; enormous gap between USA and EC; needs top-level governmental decisions

Textiles and clothing – serious discussion on liberalisation now under way; defeat of US textile industry lobby vital to success

IMPROVING GATT

Amending GATT articles – impasse over developing countries' right to protect markets when facing balance of payments difficulties

GATT codes – Japan and other Asian exporters confront USA and EC over anti-dumping measures; new rules for government procurement required

Safeguard measures (against unexpected surges in imports) – EC holding out for right to take selective action against offenders

Subsidies – US and EC have hardened positions but deal limiting industrial subsidies within sight

GATT dispute settlement – close to agreement on faster mechanism with new appeals body

Functioning of GATT – agreement to improve GATT surveillance of trade policies; disagreement over greater role for trade ministers and over new world trade organisation

EXPANDING GATT

To cover **intellectual property rights** – conflict between industrial nations and developing countries calls for top-level political decisions

Trade-related investment – agreement to remove some restrictions on foreign investment possible

Trade in services – blocked over the scope of a new general agreement and for which sectors exemptions or special reservations may be allowed

---

and these countries wished to exploit their comparative advantage in the service sectors in international trade in return for making further concessions with respect to manufactures.

Other deficiencies in the GATT also became increasingly evident. There was, for example, the issue of the sectors which, for various reasons, had been given special dispensations from the rules of the GATT. Of these the **Multi-Fibre Arrangement** (MFA) covering textiles and clothing was a particular irritant to developing countries whose access to the markets of advanced countries was limited by quotas. More importantly, there was the **agricultural sector** which was not covered at all by the rules of the GATT. Up until the end of the 1970s this had posed few problems since the EC had been a net importer of agricultural products, thereby allowing the USA to export its surpluses to everyones' mutual advantage. However, once the EC became a major net exporter in its own right, the agricultural sector became the battleground between the three dominant trading blocs – the EC, USA and Japan – without there being a set of GATT rules to determine fair conduct in the field.

The other outstanding problems are set out in **Table 7.14.** Given the proliferation of disputes, especially those relating to dumping, the inability of the GATT disputes settlement mechanism to act swiftly and to impose penalties with sufficient deterrent value to discourage deliberate abuse of the rules has also become of key importance. Equally, the expansion of the role of GATT not merely to cover trade in **services** but also **intellectual property rights** (IPRs) has come to the forefront of debate about the role of the GATT because in current circumstances it is too much to expect any country or trading bloc to make unilateral concessions.

The advanced nations are anxious that developing countries should open their markets to imports of services, and that they should honour intellectual property rights rather than turn a blind eye to outright piracy of patents and copyrights. In their turn, the LDCs want the advanced nations to open their markets to imports of textiles, clothing and agricultural commodities. Japan is unwilling to do anything much about its so-called 'structural impediments' to trade (for example, by allowing foreign firms to bid for public procurement contracts) unless the USA and the EC agree to curtail the stream of anti-dumping actions aimed at Japanese products. Almost everyone wants to stop the USA using the **super-301 provisions** of the 1988 Trade Act to take punitive action against them without recourse to the GATT, and so forth.

Because no country is prepared to make concessions without first securing the desired **reciprocity** from other countries, the Uruguay Round has dragged on for over four years without any real signs of progress. In particular, the dispute over agricultural reform has generated much intransigence, especially on the part of the EC as detailed below, and failure to resolve this dispute will probably consign the entire Uruguay Round to oblivion and usher in an era of increasing protectionism around the world.

7.10.3 The GATT and Protectionism

The move towards protectionism discussed above obviously threatens the foundations on which GATT is built. For several years now many countries have been busy negotiating bilateral agreements to the detriment of excluded countries. The Uruguay Round of trade talks, initiated at the end of 1986, has done little to stem the tide, with 23 non-tariff barriers coming into force in the six months subsequent to the start of the latest round of discussions in later 1987. One obvious difficulty is that the GATT secretariat has no resources to dispose to support its powers of persuasion, nor indeed any real sanctions other than adverse publicity, so it is obliged to fall back upon its stature as a body which exists to foster free trade without favour to any individual country. The trouble then, however, is that too-overt criticism of countries which are abusing the rules is likely to send their representatives scuttling home claiming unfair discrimination.

The very tricky question concerns bilateral agreements which are advocated on the grounds that they promote free trade between the signatories. A recent example is the agreement signed between the USA and Canada in 1988. The outcome is likely to be that the USA will buy certain products from Canada which were previously acquired from more expensive domestic sources. However, there is no most-favoured-nation clause which requires the treatment accorded to the most favoured trading partner to be made available to others, and it therefore follows that other products will be bought from Canada rather than, say, the UK, since they will now be cheaper from the former source on a tariff-free basis. This simply serves to **divert** trade rather than to **create** it, and indeed may result in the purchase of tariff-free products from an inefficient source being substituted for tariff-bearing products from a more efficient source.

The US-Canada trade zone is, fortunately, not dissimilar in its effects to the EC which has served more to create trade than to divert it, and it keeps to most of the GATT rules insofar as it covers 'substantially all trade' and does not result in the raising of tariff barriers against other countries.

At the end of the day, it all comes down to whether or not the US-Canada agreement is to be regarded as a special case. If the USA were to extend this type of agreement to other parts of the world, which it clearly has the economic muscle to do, then trade-diverting agreements may become the norm, with the destruction of the GATT an almost certain consequence.

A further awkward issue in respect of which the UK falls into line with the USA is in feeling that the GATT has gone too far along the road of permitting LDCs to be exempted from reciprocity in their trade relations with the industrialised nations. On the face of it, it is understandable that concessions were originally made, under the Generalised System of Preferences in 1971, since free access to the markets of the developed countries without the need for reciprocity appeared to guarantee an improvement in the balance of payments of the LDCs. However, it is unclear whether the LDCs actually benefit from their ability to produce goods domestically at much higher prices than they could have been obtained from elsewhere in the absence of tariffs, and it has left their export industries very vulnerable to the possibility that the industrialised nations will lose patience and impose reciprocal tariffs. In return for their compliance, the LDCs should be entitled to demand concessions on discriminatory non-tariff barriers such as the Multifibre Arrangement.

☐ 7.10.4 Anti-dumping Suits

Faced with breaking GATT rules if they are overtly protectionist, both the EC and the USA have resorted increasingly to a subtle, but no less effective, method of curbing Japanese and South Korean imports. This method is to threaten to take the exporters to court in an **anti-dumping suit**. Under the GATT's anti-dumping code, **dumping** is held to occur when a good is sold abroad at a price lower than that charged by the exporter for the same good in his home market, and it is permissible to impose penalties where deliberate underpricing is causing, or threatening to cause, **material injury** to producers in the importing countries.

By writing rules to regulate anti-dumping duties into the GATT during the Tokyo Round these duties were effectively legitimised, and have proliferated in a manner than was never the GATT's intention. In particular, anti-dumping suits are brought against specific countries in a deliberately discriminatory manner, and are often instigated with the intention of eliciting a voluntary restraint from the defendant.

The common rationale for an anti-dumping suit is that the exporter is engaged in predatory pricing designed to drive the domestic supplier out of the business. Nevertheless, for some unaccountable reason most EC anti-dumping suits are actually brought against exporters with a small share of the EC market! But then all the complainant has to demonstrate is that the exporter is either making a loss or selling at below the price in the exporter's home market, and that this is not helpful to the complainant.

Once a complaint has succeeded it becomes necessary to calculate the **dumping margin** – the difference between the price of a good in the exporter's home market and its price when exported. As Hindley has constantly pointed out (see, for example, *Financial Times*, 7 June 1991) both the EC and the USA are past masters at calculating preposterously high margins. Adding insult to injury, the USA has proposed that the GATT code be amended to include products which might exist if dumping were not taking place, whilst the EC's proposal is that if a rise in imports coincides with a fall in domestic production this should be taken as 'proof' of successful dumping.

In August 1988 the European Commission imposed duties on imported video-cassette recorders on the grounds that unless the EC could remain conversant with the technology it would lose the ability to develop new high-tech products. Whilst this could be construed as a legitimate aim of industrial policy, it is hardly surprising that the Japanese, who traditionally dislike airing trade disputes in public, felt compelled to complain to the GATT's anti-dumping committee that it could be regarded as evidence of dumping only by stretching GATT rules well beyond breaking point.

Much the same could be said about duties levied in April 1988 on typewriters and scales actually assembled in the EC by Japanese companies, which the European Commission claimed was simply a device to dodge the duties. The EC was particularly fond of the **screwdriver plant** ploy at this point in time, especially in respect of cars. The idea was that any imported components of Japanese products made in the EC could be saddled with anti-dumping duties unless more than a certain proportion of the total value of the end-product was added in the EC. Not surprisingly, most Japanese manufacturers adopted the line of least resistance and increased value-added in the EC. Nevertheless, a complaint to the GATT resulted in this rule being outlawed in 1990.

Undeterred, the Commission applied anti-dumping duties to Japanese audio-cassettes even though a substantial proportion were made in the EC and the share taken by the imports from Japan was falling. Furthermore, the Japanese products were actually more expensive than those made by EC companies. Indeed so, argued the Commission, but that was because the Japanese had 'forced the Community industry to undersell to hold its market share'.

The 'offending' Japanese producers have typically responded to these duties by holding prices constant and reducing profit margins. As what the Commission really wanted was for import prices

to rise they decided to introduce additional penalties where the duties are not added to the price. The reader may by now be beginning to wonder just how all of this benefits the consumer, but there really isn't any need to wonder – it doesn't! However, lest 'Fortress Europe' be taken too readily to be a fact of life, it is worth noting that in its first review of EC trade policy in April 1991 the GATT reported that, whilst the EC was excessively protectionist, this had not become materially worse since the introduction of the 1992 programme.

This may not last. The Commission initiated 43 dumping inquiries in 1990 compared to 27 in 1989, and the recent anti-Japanese rhetoric of Edith Cresson, the new French prime minister, is inauspicious.

□ *7.10.5 Future of the GATT*

Officially, time ran out on the Uruguay Round at the end of 1990. But it did not expire altogether. In the USA, the **fast track** authority, which requires that legislation implementing trade pacts be voted on by Congress as a package without amendment, was introduced at the beginning of the Tokyo Round. Its expiry date for the Uruguay Round was March 1991, at which point there was supposed to be a vote on the entire GATT package. In practice, there was no package because of the ongoing disputes about matters agricultural.

In principle agriculture, which accounts for only some 13 per cent of world trade, does not seem of sufficient importance to destroy the entire Round, but in practice many of the concessions which have been proposed in other areas are a quid pro quo for agricultural reform. The reasons for the agricultural disputes are discussed subsequently, but even though they remain unresolved the US Congress chose to extend the fast track authority in the hope of seeing the Round through to a successful conclusion.

US trade negotiators are thus much better placed than those representing the EC. The EC's position in each area inevitably reflects a series of compromises among its members, and hence its negotiators feel unable to budge from the agreed positions lest individual members withdraw their support.

To other countries this smacks of intransigence and a 'Fortress Europe' mentality. The only certain thing is that the future of the Round, and in many ways of the GATT itself, currently hangs in the balance.

■ 7.11 Agriculture

Whilst agriculture is a domestic industry, and could therefore be discussed in the context of Chapter 8 most of the issues which it raises are concerned with relationships both within the EC and between the EC and other trading blocs. It raises issues of protectionism and involves the GATT, and this section has, therefore, been placed in its entirety alongside the sections which deal with the latter topics.

The markets for agricultural products operate poorly in the absence of intervention. Demand tends to grow slowly over time, both because population growth in developed countries is very low, and because as incomes rise the extra money does not get spent on agricultural produce. Supply, on the other hand, grows rapidly as a consequence of mechanisation, improved crop strains and the intensive use of fertilisers. In a free market these forces would anyway tend to drive down prices – and hence also farmers' incomes – but the situation is further compounded by the unpredictable effects of climatic conditions and the small size of individual farms in relation to total supply, which conspire to leave farmers with very little control over the prices of their products.

□ 7.11.1 Rationale for Intervention

In practice, the governments of developed countries have, with few exceptions, been unwilling to let agricultural prices be determined by the forces of the free market during the postwar period. The rationale for intervention has taken a variety of forms, including the contribution of the sector to employment and to the balance of payments; the need for security of food supply in the event of external aggression; the need to protect the rural way of life; and the need to ensure delivery of the rural vote. Whilst many of these justifications cur-

rently have an archaic ring about them it must be recognised that, once a pressure group has been built up to keep them in the public eye, it becomes very difficult to persuade the public that they are no longer relevant.

Broadly speaking, farmers in any single domestic market, such as the UK, can be protected against the forces of the free market either by paying them subsidies, or by erecting a wall around the domestic market through which imports cannot pass at prices which undercut domestic suppliers. Given that the UK had traditional obligations towards the Commonwealth, which included the freedom for Commonwealth countries to export to the UK, the widespread use of tariff barriers or quotas was considered to be inappropriate, and those UK farmers who could not match import prices were therefore paid a subsidy known as a **deficiency payment**. The burden of financing such a payment fell upon the taxpayer, and not upon the consumer who paid a shop price based upon the costs of the cheapest world suppliers. As agricultural productivity rose, and world prices accordingly fell, the deficiency payments scheme became increasingly burdensome, and the government began to toy with the use of tariffs and quotas.

The supremacy of the latter form of protection came with the devising of the Common Agricultural Policy (CAP) in 1958 by the original six members of the EEC. At the time UK agriculture was considerably more efficient than its continental counterparts, in good part because the system of inheritance whereby land had been handed down to the eldest son, rather than dispersed among all male children as was the custom in, for example, France, had kept land holdings intact. Furthermore, UK farmers were used to competing in the open market unprotected by tariffs. As a consequence, a much smaller proportion of the UK population was employed in agriculture in 1960 than in continental Europe.

The objectives set out for the CAP under Article 39 of the Treaty of Rome were not, of themselves, incompatible with the objective of UK agricultural policy. They were (1) to increase agricultural productivity by promoting technical progress, and by ensuring the rational development of agricultural production and the optimum utilisation of the factors of production, in particular labour. (2) To ensure a fair standard of living for the agricultural community, in particular by increasing the individual earnings of persons engaged in agriculture. (3) To stabilise markets. (4) To guarantee the availability of supplies. (5) To ensure reasonable consumer prices. However, their implementation over the ensuing decade did create certain incompatibilities with UK practice, in particular the much greater emphasis upon import controls and, as a consequence, the payment by the consumer in the shop of a price sufficient to cover the full costs of operating the CAP.

It should be borne in mind that at the time of its inception the CAP was not expected to generate huge surpluses with their attendant difficulties. The reason for the rather dreadful mess in which it currently finds itself is that the EC sought to respond to the developing crisis of overproduction in a piecemeal way. It never sat down and tried to rethink the CAP from first principles in the light of the changes which had occurred in agricultural markets during the 1970s and 1980s. Hence reform has always been too little, too late.

Since 1958 the EC has acquired a further six members, amongst them the UK. Not surprisingly, the history of agriculture in the UK has created major disparities between the UK and other members, especially the most recent who have not as yet implemented the attempts at restructuring directed at the original six.

7.11.2 Overview of EC Agriculture

The Utilised Agricultural Area (UAA) is slowly but steadily decreasing as a proportion of total land use in the EC (excluding the former East Germany). It dropped below 60 per cent during the late 1980s and may well drop as far as 50 per cent during the 1990s. The proportion is unusually high in Ireland and the UK (**Table 7.15**). Approximately one-half of the UAA is arable land which is tilled and cultivated annually (ranging from 82 per cent in Ireland to 8 per cent in Denmark) and the other 10 per cent consists of permanent crops (orchards, vineyards and olive groves which are

prominent in southern Europe and almost non-existent in the north).

It is obvious from the above that there is considerable diversity in the patterns of agricultural output between different EC members, and that the addition of recent members has shifted the balance somewhat towards permanent crops and away from arable land. This has also served to reduce agricultural productivity, which was already relatively poor. Employment in agriculture provides 8 per cent of all jobs in the EC, but these workers contribute only 3 per cent of GDP. In the UK the proportions are both very low and very similar (between 2 and 3 per cent) whilst in Spain the latter proportion is high (at 5.7 per cent) but only one-third of the former.

Incomes from farming (defined as net value-added at factor cost and per annual work unit, adjusted for inflation) for the EC as a whole have remained constant since 1985. During the 1970s there was an appreciable decline, approximately half of which was recovered during the early 1980s, representing a loss of real incomes of roughly 10 per cent during the past two decades. As usual, individual EC members have shown great variability. In 1973, real incomes were particularly buoyant in the UK and West Germany, but in both cases these fell by roughly one-quarter during the remainder of the decade. France also suffered a big decline whilst incomes in Denmark remained constant and those in Greece actually rose sharply. During the 1980s incomes rose by one-half in Ireland and Luxembourg and by 40 per cent in Spain. Most of the other members exhibited modest upwards or downwards movements. Taking the past two decades as a whole, the heaviest losses have, therefore, been sustained in the UK and the biggest gains in Ireland and Luxembourg. Interestingly, despite these disparities, patterns of land use do not differ greatly in these countries.

The number of farms in the EC has fallen sharply over the past two decades to stand currently at a total of 6.9 mn. In Italy, Greece and Portugal there are almost as many farms as there were in 1970 and, predictably, as shown in **Table 7.15** these countries currently have average farm sizes significantly smaller than other EC members. By comparison, fewer than 60 per cent of farms in

Table 7.15 *EC Agricultural Statistics, 1989*

	EUR 12	B	DK	D	GR	E	F	IRL	I	L	NL	P	UK
UAA[5] (mn ha)	127.5[1]	1.4	2.8[1]	11.9	5.7	27.1	30.7	5.7[1]	17.3[1]	0.1	2.0[1]	4.5[1]	18.0[1]
% total area	56.5[1]	44.7	65.2[1]	47.8	43.5	53.7[1]	55.9	81.1[1]	57.4[1]	48.9	50.7[1]	49.2[1]	73.9[1]
Arable (%UAA)	52.9	52.2	91.7[1]	61.1	50.9	57.4[1]	57.5	18.1[1]	52.1	44.3	44.4[1]	64.1[1]	38.1
Grassland (%UAA)	n/a	45.1	n/a	37.1	n/a	24.6[2]	37.8	81.9	28.1	54.5	n/a	16.8[1]	63.4[1]
No. of farms[2] (000)	6929	79	86	671	704	1540	912	217	1974	4	117	384	243
1 – 5 ha (%)[2]	49.2	27.7	1.8	29.4	69.4	53.3	18.2	16.1	67.9	18.4	24.8	72.4	13.5
> 50 ha (%)[2]	6.8	5.9	17.2	6.1	0.8	6.0	18.1	9.0	1.9	26.3	4.4	1.9	33.3
Av. size (ha)[2]	n/a	17.3	32.5	17.6	5.3	16.0	30.7	22.7	7.7	33.2	17.2	8.3	68.9
Persons employed[4] (000)	9019	100	160	1010	965	1598	1381	163	1946	6	286	829	575
% employed working population	7.0	2.8	6.0	3.9	26.6[1]	13.0	6.4	15.1	9.3	3.4	4.7	18.9	2.2
Value of output ECU mn	175.7	6.1	6.9	28.9	8.0	23.4[1]	46.3	4.3	36.7	0.2	15.7	3.5	19.2
Share of agriculture in GDP (%)[1]	3.0	2.2	3.8	1.6	16.4	5.1	3.2	10.9	4.1	2.3	4.2	5.2	1.4

Notes:
[1] = 1988
[2] = 1987
[3] = 1986
[4] Includes all persons working for remuneration or self-employed, plus unpaid family workers; persons employed in more than one economic sector are counted only in the sector in which they mainly work.
[5] Utilised Agricultural Area.
Source: Eurostat.

Belgium and Luxembourg have survived since 1970, and fewer than two-thirds in Denmark, France and West Germany.

The typical EC farm has a UAA of 14 hectares (roughly 35 acres). On average, those in Denmark, Luxembourg and France are twice this size, but they in turn are half the size of the typical farm in the UK where in excess of 30 per cent of all farms have a UAA of at least 50 ha. Farms of this size are almost non-existent in Italy, Portugal and Greece where, as in Spain, farms of less than 5 ha predominate. It does not take much imagination to realise that this great diversity in farm sizes, combined with very different patterns of land use, represents a major difficulty in drawing up a common agricultural policy.

Between 1970 and 1987 the agricultural population in the EC fell by roughly one-quarter, with individual member variances ranging from a few per cent in the Netherlands to nearly 40 per cent in Luxembourg. There are currently roughly 9 mn agricultural workers in the EC, of whom roughly one-quarter work full time.

In part this, reflects the age structure of the agricultural population. Nearly one-half of all agricultural workers are age 55 or over, which in turn reflects a clearly expressed preference by younger generations to head for the towns and cities. It follows that in the course of time the retirement of large numbers of farm workers will create a much more efficient farming structure in many EC countries.

☐ 7.11.3 *Price Support*

The system of price support has two distinct strands, one applicable to EC products and the other to imports. At the apex of the price pyramid for EC products sits the **target** price, which is the notional market price negotiated annually by the Council of Agricultural Ministers for the place where a product is in shortest supply. For certain products the terms 'guide', 'norm' or 'basic' price are also used. In practice, a product's price will rise to its target level only at a time of great shortage, so target prices have little operational meaning. Of greater importance is the **intervention** price, which

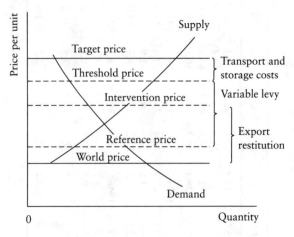

Figure 7.15   *Prices in the CAP*

is the lowest level to which product prices are permitted to fall before the relevant intervention agency is obliged to buy in all surplus supply. This price is fixed annually as a percentage of the target price by the Council of Ministers on an individual product basis. Payments are delayed to discourage selling into intervention. Should producers be willing to export, they are paid a subsidy, equal to the difference between the world price and the EC market price, in the form of an **export restitution**.

The position for imports is that, almost without exception, they must be sold in the EC at a **threshold** price which is equivalent to the target price adjusted for transport and storage costs. The minimum price at which non-EC products can be imported into the EC is known as the **reference** or sluice-gate price, and to this is added a **variable levy** in order to bring the actual import price (which may exceed the reference price) up to the threshold price (see **Figure 7.15**). All proceeds from the variable levy are paid into the EAGGF, often identified by its equivalent French initials as FEOGA, which uses roughly 95 per cent of the proceeds in order to fund intervention buying and export restitution payments (**guarantees**). The remaining 5 per cent is spent on **guidance**, largely to finance structural improvements. Guidance spending is discretionary, and EC funds usually have to be matched by recipient countries.

Since the inception of the CAP, the proportion of agricultural produce which has attracted some degree of price support has risen inexorably, and currently stands at roughly 90 per cent. However, it is significant that over 49 per cent of all price support expenditure goes upon milk, cereals and beef and veal, and that oils attract just under 19 per cent. This arises because all of these products are automatically bought into intervention. They represent almost 50 per cent of all output. The other 50 per cent attracts much less support spending and certain products – such as potatoes and flowers – are assisted only by the existence of the variable levy. Direct income support is used only at a modest level for small farmers producing specified products.

Intervention buying applies predominantly to products originating in northern Europe, and whilst guidance expenditure is directed largely to the more southerly members, the disparity between the guarantee and guidance funds represents a strong bias in favour of northern members.

☐ *7.11.4 Agri-money*

At the inception of the CAP it was intended that agricultural produce should have a common price throughout the EC. In a world of fixed exchange rates and zero inflation it is clearly possible to fix the price of, for example, wheat in several currencies, and to keep those prices constant for evermore. However, where exchange rates are subject to adjustment, and where different countries suffer different rates of inflation, common prices can be maintained only through the introduction of a complicated adjustment mechanism.

Agricultural products in the EC are priced in ECUs. These are converted into a number of units of a national currency at the prevailing exchange rate between that currency and the ECU, and the farmer then receives as payment the appropriate amount of his domestic currency. But if that currency is devalued against the ECU, then the farmer ends up with more of his domestic currency than before (less in the case of a revaluation) even though the price in ECUs has not altered. It was in order to avoid this outcome that 'green' currency was introduced.

Green currency has been in existence since 1969 when the French franc was devalued and the Deutsche Mark was revalued. The French were unhappy that this would cause the price of food to consumers to rise and the Germans were unhappy that this would cause the incomes of farmers to fall. It was accordingly agreed that the currency changes should apply to agricultural products only over a period of years during which an artificial exchange rate would apply, known as the representative or **green** rate.

This practice of using artificial exchange rates for agricultural products has now become institutionalised under the CAP. Some idea of its peculiarities can be seen by reference to the example in the box on **p. 268**. When a currency is revalued it is the custom to leave the green rate unchanged in order to protect the income of farmers. Hence the adjustment which involves MCAs in order to prevent consequent distortions of intra-country trade must operate such that: Green rate = Official rate *less* MCA. The MCA is thus positive and takes the form of a subsidy to that country's exports and a levy on imports from other countries. A positive MCA will disappear if the green rate is revalued, although, as indicated, this is never a popular policy.

On the other hand, if a currency is devalued, but the green rate either stays unchanged or is devalued by less, the adjustment which involves MCAs in order to prevent distortions of intra-country trade must operate such that: Green rate = Official rate *plus* MCA. the MCA is thus **negative** and takes the form of a levy on that country's exports and a subsidy to imports from other countries. A negative MCA will disappear if the green rate is devalued, which is generally acceptable since it raises farm prices (and consumers will probably not notice the slight rise in retail prices which results).

It was recognised that a system which had been introduced originally in order to permit an orderly movement towards official exchange rates had ended up, inevitably, as a permanent system of dual exchange rates, and the EC decided to bring it to an end. This partly reflected the fact that there was a good deal of cross-border smuggling in order to avoid MCA levies, but primarily it was a response to the fact that the concept of the Single European Market was incompatible with a system of dual exchange rates.

Green Currency and Monetary Compensatory Amounts (MCAs)

Begin with an official exchange rate of £ 1.00 = ECU = 10 francs

1   Assume value of £ **falls** to £ 1.20 = ECU 1 = 10 francs
    ECU 10 of farm produce is now worth £ 12 to UK farmers instead of £ 10
    Domestic French market is unaffected as franc/ECU rate unchanged
2   Assume value of £ **rises** to 80 pence = ECU 1 = 10 francs
    ECU 10 of farm produce is now worth £ 8 to UK farmer instead of £ 10
    Domestic French market is unaffected as franc/ECU rate unchanged

In order to protect incomes of UK farmers if condition **2** above prevails, an **artificial (green) exchange rate** is introduced of £ 1.00 = ECU = 10 francs. The UK farmer once again earns £ 10. However, if the French farmer exports ECU 10 of produce to the UK he receives £ 10 in return which he can convert back at the official exchange rate to yield 125 francs, an increase of 25 francs compared to previously.

In order to discourage this behaviour the MCA is used. An MCA **tax** equal to 25 francs will restore the value of ECU 10 of produce to 100 francs to the French farmer, the same as its value in the domestic market.

The UK farmer is not interested in exporting if ECU 10 of UK produce sold in France earns him only 100 francs, since converting it back into £ at the new official rate will yield only £ 8 whereas he gets £ 10 for ECU 10 of produce sold in the UK market at the green rate. He will wish to export only if he receives an MCA **subsidy** equal to £ 2 per ECU 10 of produce sold, thereby yielding a total of £ 10, the same as on the domestic market.

It follows from the above that the value of produce sold on the home market can be raised simply by **devaluing** the green rate instead of the official rate. The official rate of ECU 1 = £ 1.00 can be adjusted to ECU 1 = £ 1.20 for specified products. However, as noted above this will distort intra-EC product flows and require the introduction of new MCAs. It is also evident that no country will want to **revalue** its green rate (as against letting its official rate rise) since this will reduce the value of products sold by its farmers in its home market (which they will not find amusing).

It is frequently alleged that the CAP is the only element of the EC which can truely be called a common market, but this is demonstrably untrue since the common currency, the ECU, has two values, one official and one green, in respect of each currency.

The European Commission accordingly declared its intention to phase out all MCAs by the end of 1992. This always looked to be a touch optimistic since abolition of MCAs would leave agricultural prices at the mercy of currency fluctuations in the open market, and could potentially result in sharp fluctuations in retail food prices.

Nevertheless, from April 1987, no additional positive MCAs were to be created as a result of changes in central rates under the ERM. In effect, if a country revalued or if one country revalued by more than any others, its green rate would also revalue at the same time, and adjustments would be made to all other members' **negative** MCAs, thereby raising prices paid to farmers. Fortunately, in practice, such currency realignments have not been necessary since 1987 other than the band adjustment by Italy at the beginning of 1990. Unfortunately, the deliberate manipulation of green rates, independently of changes in official rates, has remained an integral part of the CAP, and the integration of East Germany into the EC in October 1990 may prove an excuse for maintaining MCAs beyond the end of 1992.

□ 7.11.5 *Mountains and Lakes*

In the UK, between 1975 and 1985, disposable incomes, prices in general and processed prices in particular rose at an almost identical rate. However, starting in 1978, farm-gate prices began to lag behind. This meant that the only way for farmers to maintain their incomes was to raise their output, which in turn meant more intensive use of fertilisers. However, the latter rose in price much faster than end-products, partly because of their oil-based content, and the ratio of producer prices to input prices fell sharply, both in the UK and in the EC as a whole, as depicted in **Table 7.16**.

This had a number of consequences. In the first place, **farmers' incomes,** as officially recorded, failed to keep pace with income in other sectors. However, it is important to note in this respect that very few studies have ever been done on agricultural incomes, so there is a great uncertainty about the validity of income comparisons; that those studies which exist indicate that farmers' incomes (though not those of their labourers) were on aver-

age well above the average for the whole economy before 1980 (although a large part of these incomes was a return on the ownership of land rather than on the farming of the land), and that the cost–price squeeze served merely to reduce this differential somewhat; that the indiscriminate nature of price support means that large-scale farmers never have been, nor are likely to be, near the breadline – on average, the wealthiest 25 per cent of farmers receive nearly ten times as much in subsidies as their poorer counterparts; and that whilst small-scale farmers may earn only modest incomes from their farms, they generally have other sources of income, and in many cases farming is a secondary rather than a primary occupation. Whilst this should not be taken to imply that there is no such thing as a poor farmer, it is clear that no-one really knows how to identify which farmers genuinely need help and which could survive quite happily with a reduced level of price support, or even with none at all.

In the second place, there is the problem of **vast overproduction,** and this in turn creates a major problem of storage. In early 1987, for example, EC butter stocks exceeded 1.3 mn tonnes, and those of skimmed milk powder just under 1 mn tonnes. In practice, these stocks can be disposed of only at prices well below those paid to buy them into intervention, and this difference is an im-

Table 7.16   *The 'Cost–price Squeeze': The Ratio of Producer Prices to Input Prices* [1]

	UK	EUR 10	EUR 12	D	F	IRL
1973	125.4	123.6	n/a	122.8	135.7	139.5
1981	106.2	103.7	n/a	97.1	105.3	108.1
1982	105.0	104.4	105.0	105.9	105.9	105.5
1983	102.1	102.3	102.3	101.1	105.3	105.7
1984	100.0	100.0	100.0	100.0	100.0	100.0
1985	96.5	100.7	100.0	100.8	103.1	95.1
1986	97.3	103.5	102.9	102.4	106.1	99.6
1987	102.5	104.0	104.0	103.4	105.3	109.7
1988	99.6	n/a	103.4	105.7	103.3	115.0
1989	101.2	n/a	n/a	112.1	106.1	115.3

Note:
[1]   This is calculated by dividing changes in the deflated index prices of the value of final agricultural production by changes in the deflated index prices of the value of inputs.
Source: Eurostat.

mense strain upon the EC Budget. In response to the **butter mountain**, the EC was obliged to sell over 500,000 tonnes to non-EC markets, 400,000 tonnes to the animal feed industry and 50,000 tonnes to be turned into concentrated butter. A further disposal of 100,000 tonnes to the USSR followed. As a result of these operations, and similar ones for skimmed milk, there was 'only' 300,000 tonnes of butter and 40,000 tonnes of skimmed

milk left in storage. However, the exercise cost ECU 3.2 bn (£2.1 bn), to be paid back in equal instalments out of EC own resources between 1989 and 1993.

The improvement in the storage position can be seen in **Figure 7.16**, but it was not to last. At the beginning of 1990 stocks of butter were only 20,000 tonnes, but this had risen to 350,000 tonnes by September. Skimmed milk stocks also rose from

Figure 7.16   *Intervention Stocks, End-year*

Note:
[1]   Forecast.
Source: European Commission.

virtually nil to 250,000 tonnes, fuelled by falling demand and the flooding of export markets by eastern European countries desperate to get their hands on hard currency.

The only customer for the butter stocks in early 1991 was the USSR (offering $1,100 per tonne for 200,000 tonnes at a cost to EC taxpayers of $580 mn), which was awkward given its unpopularity with EC countries due to its repressive approach to its breakaway republics.

Between June 1987 and June 1988 beef stocks rose from 637,000 to 760,000 tonnes, in good part as a result of the introduction of milk quotas (see below) which resulted in the wide-scale slaughter of cows no longer required for their milk. There is always a market for cheap beef, especially in the USSR, and it was possible to dispose of most of the stocks (at a big loss) by the end of 1989. New measures introduced in January 1989 to restrict intervention buying also helped to control stocks.

Unfortunately, an upturn in production in 1990 coincided with imports into the EC of live cattle from East Germany as dairy farmers there adjusted their herd sizes to keep within their new EC milk quotas; with consumers' fears brought on by BSE ('mad cow disease'); and with the loss of export markets in the Middle East when Iraq invaded Kuwait (which especially affected Irish exports). As a result prices fell so low in the UK and Ireland that the 'safety net' had to be brought into play in September 1990 which required the EC to accept unlimited quantities at 80 per cent of the official intervention price.

Attempts by UK and Irish farmers to offload their surpluses of beef and sheep into France brought French farmers into the streets in violent protests which included burning animals alive. Even the cereals situation once again gave cause for alarm. The poor EC harvest of 1987, followed by drought in the USA, pushed the world price of wheat up by nearly 50 per cent in 1988. As per usual, this stimulated more planting in 1989 in improved growing conditions, and the price fell back sharply through 1989 and 1990. Whilst EC stocks were very low, the reduction in the value of the dollar during 1990, together with aggressive export sales by the USA, meant that ECU 100 per tonne needed to be spent by the EC on subsidising export sales if an ever more expensive build up of stocks was to be avoided.

It also has to be remembered that the expansion of the EC to include additional southern members created surpluses in less traditional products. Between 1983 and 1988, for example, the EC paid out ECU 2 bn in order to turn unwanted wine into industrial alcohol, thereby creating a 750 mn litre 'lake'. Nevertheless, the apparent return of structural surpluses in a wide variety of products was not the only severe problem facing the EC at the end of the 1980s. A further important factor was that attempts to raise crop yields were doing a great deal of damage to the environment. Excessive use of the chemical fertilisers had long been a particular cause for concern, and the need to enlarge farms in order to permit mechanisation had produced a major change in the face of the countryside which few outside farming circles were inclined to regard as an improvement.

☐ 7.11.6 *Direct Income Aid*

Partly as a response to pressure exerted by the USA during the Uruguay Round to switch agricultural support onto a production neutral basis, the EC farm ministers agreed in January 1989 to the use of direct income aids to farmers. This scheme was strongly supported by Jacques Delors, although it was clear from the start that it would have to be introduced on a purely voluntary national basis.

A number of objections were raised, in particular by the UK. It was argued, first, that adequate and universally applicable social security systems already existed throughout the EC, so there was no need for a special scheme for farmers, especially one which would have to be paid for out of national taxation receipts. In any event, farmers themselves would prefer not to be singled out for special payments for fear of attracting further adverse publicity. It was also felt that the scheme could turn out to be yet another open-ended commitment, although this point was dealt with in practice by ring-fencing the scheme. The key elements of the scheme which became operational in 1991 are:

1 It is voluntary. If offered, any national scheme must be approved by the European Commission and must meet rules concerning eligibility and the level of funding.
2 Eligibility requires that a 'significant' (ill-defined) part of household income is derived from agriculture and that the total income is low relative to national *per capita* GNP.
3 Payments may be made for no more than five years, to any individual, commencing no later than four years after the scheme's inception.
4 Payments cannot exceed ECU 2500 per individual per year.
5 The EC contribution to the total aid paid is limited to 70 per cent of the total for the least developed member states and to no more than 25 per cent for the remaining member states.
6 Recipients must get decreasing amounts of aid each year, with the EC's contribution to be reduced by 15 per cent during each successive year of payment.

By late 1990 only two countries had adopted the scheme, namely France (despite its initial reservations) and the Netherlands. The EC capped its contribution at ECU 5.4 mn for 1991 rising to a ceiling of ECU 16.8 mn in 1994. However, these sums should prove adequate if there are few other takers. The UK, for one, is adamantly opposed to the scheme.

7.11.7 Producer and Consumer Subsidy Equivalents

The purpose of farm support is to transfer income from consumers to producers. The particular instruments chosen to effect that outcome are, however, inefficient and create a huge waste of resources. Hence, the policy-induced increase in the cost of food and taxation is much greater than the corresponding increase in farm incomes. There is a further distributional inefficiency insofar as a disproportionate share of payments to farmers go to the largest farm units.

The OECD calculates the effect of agricultural programmes on producers and consumers by recourse to **Producer Subsidy Equivalents** (PSEs) and **Consumer Subsidy Equivalents** (CSEs). A PSE is defined as 'the payment that would be required to compensate farmers for the loss of income resulting from the removal of a given policy measure. Expressed as a percentage, it represents that part of the value of output accounted for by assistance of various kinds'. A PSE cannot, however, incorporate intervention in the form of, for example, quotas which have no budgetary cost. A CSE corresponds to the implicit tax on (or subsidy to) consumption due to the payment both of higher domestic food prices and of taxes required to maintain farm incomes.

Table 7.17 *Effect of Agricultural Programmes on Domestic Farm Prices, 1980–82 Average and 1988 (Ratio of Producer to Border Prices)*

	United States		EC		Japan		All industrial economies	
	1980–82	1988	1980–82	1988	1980–82	1988	1980–82	1988
Wheat	1.15	2.20	1.40	3.40	3.90	8.00	1.25	2.45
Coarse grains	1.00	1.60	1.40	2.40	4.30	11.65	1.15	1.75
Rice	1.30	1.85	1.35	2.40	3.35	8.20	2.50	5.65
Beef and veal	1.10	1.30	1.95	2.75	2.80	5.40	1.50	2.05
Pork and poultry	1.00	1.00	1.25	1.60	1.50	1.90	1.20	1.40
Dairy	2.00	2.20	1.75	2.50	2.90	5.55	1.90	2.55
Sugar	1.40	2.05	1.50	2.80	3.00	7.10	1.50	2.60
Weighted average, all commodities	1.20	1.50	1.55	2.25	2.35	3.80	1.40	2.00

Source: Tyers and Anderson (1988) Table 1.

Table 7.18 *Producer Subsidy Equivalents*

	1987	1988	1989e	1990p
AUSTRALIA				
Net total PSE $ bn	1.10	1.23	1.25	1.30
Net percentage PSE	11	9	10	11
EUROPEAN COMMUNITY				
Net total PSE $ bn	72.95	70.48	61.49	81.62
Net percentage PSE	49	46	41	48
JAPAN				
Net total PSE $ bn	35.15	36.52	33.67	30.86
Net percentage PSE	76	74	71	68
UNITED STATES				
Net total PSE $ bn	45.07	37.21	33.42	35.93
Net percentage PSE	41	34	29	30
OECD				
Net total PSE $ bn	176.78	167.91	151.01	175.54
Net percentage PSE	50	46	41	44

Note: e = estimate; p = provisional.
Source: OECD (1991).

If we start by looking back at the position a decade ago (OECD, 1987) then the evidence shows clearly that Japan was much the worst offender in PSE terms, especially in respect of cereals. The EC also came out badly, its highest PSE being for dairy products. The USA came out well for all non-dairy products, although the PSE for sugar was surprisingly high.

CSEs for dairy products were almost identical in every case, indicating that consumers everywhere were paying one-quarter more than they would have done in a free market. The fact that the Japanese paid 45 per cent extra for their rice and 30 per cent extra for their beef was especially noteworthy. In the case of the EC the burden on consumers was fairly well spread out over different products, but was especially high for sugar (expensive domestically produced beet rather than cheap imported cane) and for coarse grains.

During the 1980s the situation worsened considerably. The OECD's calculation of PSEs for 1984–86 indicated a Japanese PSE of close to 70 per cent and a PSE for the USA up sharply to 28 per cent. The only exception was the EC where the PSE rose only by a few percentage points. A study by Tyers and Anderson (1988) concentrated upon the ratio of producer (domestic) prices to border (international) prices, as shown in **Table 7.17**. The ratio rises in line with policy-induced distortions to trade, and as can be seen the ratio for all industrial economies changed from a situation where domestic prices were on average 40 per cent higher than international prices in 1980–82 to a situation where they were twice as high in 1988.

The figures largely speak for themselves, but the marked deterioration in respect of wheat, rice and sugar is especially interesting. The study confirms the OECD's own conclusions that are summarised in **Table 7.18**. According to OECD (1991) the PSE for the OECD as a whole rose by 16 per cent in 1990 to $176 bn, equivalent to 44 per cent of the value of crops and livestock produced. After a run of good years, for reasons discussed in the previous section, the EC's net percentage PSE rose back almost to the 1987 level, whereas the USA managed to keep its PSE under control at a rate typical of the early 1980s and Japan managed a further reduction, albeit from a very high base. Lest it be assumed that PSEs must be a fact of life, a comparison with Australia is also included.

The OECD also noted that CSEs were increasingly taking the place of PSEs, rising overall by 18 per cent to $133 bn in 1990. With total subsidies amounting to $300 bn, it is hardly surprising that so much attention has been focussed upon agriculture in the Uruguay Round.

7.11.8 Refining the CAP: 1968–87

The CAP has been in a constant state of flux since its inception. Various reforms have been set in motion, but these have been wholly insufficient to prevent the current crisis during the Uruguay Round. The Mansholt Plan of 1968 was an early attempt to reform the CAP which recommended a reduction in land use for farming with the remaining land reorganised into fewer farms, thereby reaping economies of scale. The resultant unemployment would be resolved by finding new jobs for ex-farmers.

Disagreements among member states combined with a poor economic climate put paid to the Mansholt Plan, and it was not until 1981 that major reforms returned to the EC agenda with the publication of *Guidelines for European Agriculture* (EC, 1981). This proposed that prices should eventually be brought down to world market levels, and pointed out that 'it is neither economically sensible nor financially possible to give producers a full guarantee for products in structural surplus'. Subsequently price support was limited to pre-determined levels of production which, if exceeded, would cause a response in the form of, for example, a quota for sugar; a co-responsibility levy for milk, which taxed production in excess of quotas in order to help pay for its disposal; or a reduction in the intervention price for cereals.

Unfortunately, these restrictions were nothing like tough enough to prevent the piling up of surpluses, and the cost of financing these grew to the point at which, despite some creative accounting, the CAP had effectively bankrupted the EC. At a summit meeting at Fontainbleu in 1985 remedial action was taken to deal with this crisis which included action on the agricultural front to the effect that agricultural prices would not be allowed to rise as fast as inflation; MCAs would be phased out; and milk production would be limited by quotas (which became tradable the following year).

Quotas on milk production exemplified the problems of the CAP. With output rising faster than consumption during the early 1980s, the proportion of EAGGF guarantee spending devoted to dairy products stabilised at roughly 30 per cent. What was really needed was a price reduction of at least 10 per cent to discourage output, whereas the solution adopted in the form of quotas and co-responsibility levies failed utterly to resolve the problem because the quotas were set well above the level of self-sufficiency.

Quotas work inefficiently because, for example, farmers with expensive machinery cannot afford to leave it lying idle, and therefore seek to buy quotas from other farmers. Whilst this helps to unfreeze arbitrary market shares, which ironically are largest for these farmers who started with the largest surpluses, it often results in a farmer's milk quotas becoming more valuable than the land which he farms. Furthermore, cows no longer wanted for their milk will be slaughtered for beef, thereby adding to the beef mountain.

Although the initial quotas achieved very little, a tougher set, introduced in December 1986, combined with harsher penalties on overproduction, effected a noticeable improvement. In the UK farmers offered to pay up to 50 pence per litre for unused quotas in order to avoid the penalties. Nevertheless, the cost of supporting dairy and other surpluses remained excessive, and the political unwillingness by member states to allow their domestic farmers to suffer (whilst simultaneously extolling the virtues of austerity) once again left the CAP in a state of crisis in 1987.

The accession to the EC of Spain and Portugal in 1986 was a contributory factor in this respect, since they had inefficient agricultural sectors by EC standards and produced a range of products somewhat different to those grown in northern European which, since its inception, had attracted most CAP support. The CAP had thus to cope with a huge increase in the output of citrus fruits and olive oil, and to a lesser extent of wine and fresh vegetables.

■ *7.12* EC Budget Negotiations

The key Budget negotiations took place in 1988. These negotiations were, as usual, conducted in an atmosphere of impending crisis. On this occasion, however, there was clear evidence that previous measures to reduce both the degree of price sup-

port, and also surplus production, had failed to rein back expenditure on the CAP. In 1975 the EC Budget amounted to ECU 6.5 bn, of which ECU 4.5 bn went to the EAGGF. By 1980 the respective figures were ECU 16.3 bn and ECU 11.3 bn, subsequently rising to ECU 28 bn and ECU 19.7 bn respectively in 1985. In each case the percentage allocated to the EAGGF was 70 per cent. By 1987 the EAGGF allocation had risen to ECU 22.8 bn, but this represented only 63.5 per cent of the total Budget or ECU 36 bn, with an enlarged share of 18.3 per cent allocated to the Regional and Social Fund.

Figure 7.17 *EC Spending on Agriculture*

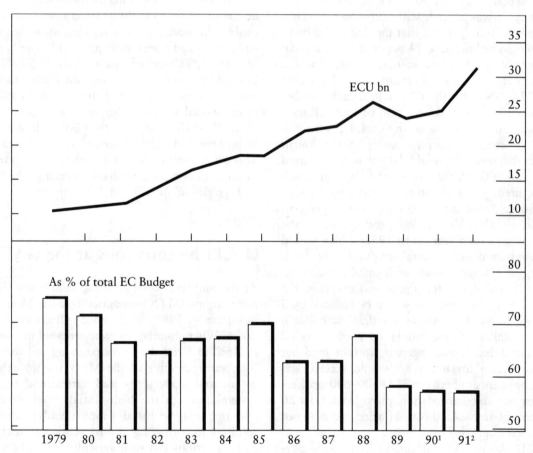

Notes:
[1] Estimate.
[2] Forecast.
Source: The Economist.

In the course of the negotiations, concern was expressed that the Budget should continue to be readjusted towards regional and social spending, and within the EAGGF towards structural support. These aims could be quite difficult to implement in practice given that allocations to the CAP are the only obligatory element in the EC Budget, and that the Council of Agricultural Ministers, backed by the business interests dependent upon agriculture, have a strong vested interest in maintaining the status quo. Nevertheless, the package put forward by M. Delors included a proposal to double the Regional and Social Fund by 1992.

A Summit was called in February 1988 to discuss the proposed package, and for once Mrs Thatcher was obliged to make significant concessions. It was agreed, with retrospective effect as from 1 January 1988, that the EAGGF growth rate would be limited to 74 per cent of the annual growth of EC GNP in volume terms; that the Budgets should absorb no more than 1.2 per cent of the EC GNP; that the VAT base of each member would be capped at 55 per cent of its GNP with the continuation of the ceiling of 1.4 per cent of VAT proceeds to be given over; that a fourth source of revenue should be introduced based on shares in GNP, the rate levied to be that which is required, given all other revenue, to balance the Budget;[4] that a production levy of 3 per cent would be placed on cereal production, at the beginning of each year up to 1992, which would be reimbursed only if total output fell below a ceiling of 160 mn tonnes (with small farmers exempted), and that if this figure was exceeded the price in the following year would be reduced by 3 per cent (a policy known as a budget '**Stabiliser**'); that a similar scheme would be applied to oil seeds; and that farmers agreeing to take land out of production for five years would receive **set-aside payments** of between ECU 100–600 per hectare by way of compensation, provided at least 20 per cent of arable land was set aside and also not reutilised as grazing.

ECU 600 mn was allocated for set-aside payments up to 1992, enough to fund 2 mn hectares, representing only 1.5 per cent of the total UAA. The EAGGF was also to be rebalanced, with 50 per cent of the funds being used for structural purposes by 1992, and with a greater proportion

directed towards the less developed members of the EC.

The various changes implemented in 1988 served to raise the Budget ceiling by roughly 40 per cent compared to what it would have been had the financial system which prevailed until 1985 not been changed. Whilst part of the intention was to provide funds other than for the CAP, it was ultimately the ongoing costs of the CAP which largely accounted for this substantial increase in budgetary resources. Nevertheless, the 'guideline' (binding ceiling) on farm spending built into the rules agreed in 1988 could not be breached without the **unanimous** agreement of the Council of Agricultural Ministers.

The 1989 and 1990 negotiations were as usual acrimonious, but for the reasons discussed previously CAP spending was reasonably under control. This can be seen in **Figure 7.17**. The 'guideline' for 1991 worked out at ECU 32.5 bn (£23 bn), up by a record 30 per cent on 1990, but with mountains and lakes reappearing (and an adjustment needed to allow for the incorporation of former East Germany into the CAP), it looked like being breached unless remedial action was taken. This action also needed to be other than a one-off in order to prevent a probable breach of the forecast 'guideline' of ECU 35.2 bn for 1992.

■ *7.13* Negotiations at the GATT

At the mid-term review of the multilateral trade negotiations (MTN) on agriculture (at Montreal, in December 1988), negotiations effectively broke down. When discussions were renewed in Geneva in April in 1989 the participants agreed that the long-term objective of the MTN was to achieve a 'fair and market oriented agricultural trading system' through the 'substantial progressive reduction in agricultural support and protection resulting in correcting and preventing restrictions and distortions in world agricultural markets'.

This wording was intended to permit short-term problems to be resolved whilst working towards long-term goals. The USA had previously insisted that it was unprepared to deal with immediate market imbalances until there was general agreement to abolish all trade-distorting policies. This latter objective was total anathema to the EC, which wanted to make some immediate progress by instituting a freeze on subsidies of all kinds. By agreeing 'substantial progressive reduction' it was possible for all parties to maintain that their own positions were still fully operative.

The USA submitted the first detailed proposal for agricultural reform in October 1989 which it refined progressively during 1990. In effect the amended proposal required the phasing out of all trade-distorting government interventions whether domestic or foreign. The key element in the proposal was **tariffication**. This meant that all non-tariff barriers to imports would be converted into tariffs and cut over 10 years to zero or very low rates. Tariffs would be 'bound', meaning that once introduced they could not be raised again. However, 'minimally trade distorting policies' would be permitted, as would direct supports not linked to production or marketing.

Tariffication was most obviously directed at the variable import levies used under the CAP and voluntary export restraints. A special **safeguard mechanism** would protect countries against import surges during the 10-year transition period. Governments would be permitted to revert to a higher level of tariff protection for the remainder of a year if imports exceeded specified proportions of the previous year's domestic consumption.

The USA proposed secondly that all **export subsidies** on a comprehensive list of farm products would be scrapped within five years. *Bona fide* food aid would be exempted provided new rules governing the granting of food aid were agreed. GATT rules permitting the restriction or prohibition of exports in short supply would be struck down.

The USA proposed thirdly that **domestic subsidies** should be subjected to a three-pronged attack. Policies such as government-administered pricing policies; income supports linked to production or marketing; transport subsidies; and any investment subsidy provided to producers and processors other than on an equal basis would be *prohibited* at the end of the 10-year adjustment period.

By way of contrast income supports not linked to production or marketing; environmental and conservation programmes; *bona fide* disaster as-sistance; and other minor items would be **fully permitted**. Finally, anything not covered by these two categories would be **subjected to GATT rules** designed to prevent them being used in ways that would cause prejudice or material injury to another country.

The final part of the US proposal dealt with sanitary measures, and was clearly intended as a reaction to the dispute over hormones in beef mentioned previously. The US proposed accordingly that any measures designed to protect health, human, animal or plant life should be consistent with 'sound scientific evidence'.

A key aspect of the US proposal was that its scope would encompass the USA's own non-tariff barriers in the sugar and dairy sectors, its export enhancement programme and possibly its deficiency payments scheme for grain farmers, although the latter were seen essentially as internal supports which did not distort trade. By and large the US proposal was unacceptable to the EC. The EC did not waver from its position that agriculture was a special case where the utopian level playing field, which would exist were all trade-distorting policies to be abolished, would do more damage than good. It much preferred to take an overall view of these policies, as reflected in an **Aggregate Measure of Support** (AMS) covering the first three elements of the US proposal – to be called a Support Measurement Unit (SMU) – which all parties would agree to reduce gradually over time. This would not rule out tariffication *per se*. Partial tariffication would be acceptable provided it encompassed US-style deficiency payments, but only one element of such a tariff would be fixed, which would be the part reflecting the difference between domestic and market prices. There would also need to be a flexible element (known as a 'corrective factor') which would take into account such factors as currency fluctuations and serious market disturbances. In return for its agreement to partial tariffication the EC insisted that 'rebalancing' be allowed. This meant that provided the overall trend was downwards, some subsidies could be increased at the same time as others were reduced.

The view in Brussels was that the US proposal was designed primarily as an attack upon EC export subsidies. The EC, however, was concerned about inroads being made into the animal foodstuffs market by cereal substitutes such as manioc or corn gluten feed, and hence wanted to **balance concessions** on lowering export subsidies on grains against increased protection for cereal substitutes.

With the divide between the EC and US proposals apparently unbridgeable, and with the Japanese continuing to insist that food security was of paramount importance, hopes faded of any resolution of the agricultural sector's problems by end-1990 when the Uruguay Round was due to come to a close. At the Summit meeting in Houston in early July, the leaders of the USA, EC nations and Japan tried to patch up their differences by signing an agreement that a future pact on agricultural trade 'should contain specific assurances that . . . participants would reduce not only internal support but also export subsidies and import protection in a related way'. This made the world's leaders feel happy because none of them had made any specific concessions whilst allegedly getting the others to agree to make them.

Suddenly, and without any prior discussion with, let alone the approval of, EC farms ministers, the EC Farm Commissioner, Raymond MacSharry, announced to a meeting of the 'Quint' (farm ministers from the EC, USA, Canada, Japan and Australia) on 31 July 1990 that he would cut EC support to farmers. Under his proposal EC farm support would reduced by 30 per cent over a 10-year reference period **commencing in 1986**. The programme of reductions would be retroactive so that the EC could claim credit for cuts already implemented since 1986. In the case of cereals these were alleged to amount to 10 per cent, and to amount to 15 per cent in respect of meat and dairy products.

Mr MacSharry insisted, however, that the EC would 'never' make specific commitments to cut support in the separate areas of domestic support, import barriers and export subsidies, but would continue to insist upon recourse to the aggregate measure of support. In mid-October the US Agriculture Secretary, Clayton Yeutter, formally tabled a new proposal which called for reductions of 90 per cent in export subsidies and of 75 per cent in import levies at borders and in internal supports for specific commodities (with an overall ceiling of

30 per cent in the latter case). The timescale for these reductions was a period of 10 years **commencing in 1991–2**.

Both the USA and the Cairns group of major food-exporting countries supported tariffication of non-tariff barriers followed by an overall tariff reduction of at least 75 per cent over 10 years, with no individual product permitted to carry a tariff in excess of 50 per cent at the end of the period. The adjustment period would be stretched to 15 years for LDCs, by which time they would be expected to have achieved an average tariff reduction of at least 45 per cent of that of the developed nations.

In order to protect farmers against sudden changes in prices or exchange rates the USA proposed, first, that governments would be permitted to levy a tariff surcharge if the volume of imports of a product exceeded 120 per cent of the imports of that product during the previous year. Secondly, governments would be able to impose a surcharge if the import price of a product fell below 75 per cent of the average import price for the product over the three preceding years.

Mr MacSharry's intransigence in the face of the US proposal created further tensions within the EC itself, since the Commissioner for External Relations, Frans Andriessen, with overall responsibility for the Uruguay Round, acknowledged that the US negotiators would utterly reject the idea of 'rebalancing'. Subsequently the EC Agriculture Council began to exhibit serious internal disarray. In certain quarters, most notably France and Germany, Mr MacSharry's proposals were considered to be overly harsh (the US proposals were simply regarded as beyond the pale!)

With the Uruguay Round officially at an end; the negotiations in all areas under discussion in abeyance pending the resolution (or otherwise) of the crisis in agriculture; the EC generally regarded as the main villain of the piece; and agricultural spending in the EC forecast to exceed its 'guideline' unless remedial action was taken, Mr MacSharry had little choice but to opt for a radical shake up of EC farming.

In effect a three-stage process was required (**1**) keeping within the 1991 Budget's 'guideline' for

CAP spending; (2) getting agreement by EC farm ministers to a reform package; (3) getting this package agreed in the GATT. Attempts to avoid (1) by raising the 'guideline' were frustrated by the UK and Dutch farm ministers, but by going to the limit of the 'guideline' and a little fiddling of the accounts the immediate crisis was resolved. Mr MacSharry's proposal for the longer-term was, first, that cereal prices would be cut by 35 per cent over a three-year period, with compensatory income support paid on a sliding scale. This compensation would be geared to a set-aside programme such that arable farmers with less than 20 ha would be exempt from set-aside; those with 20–50 ha would have to set-aside 15 per cent of their land to qualify for compensation but would also be compensated for the set-aside; those with in excess of 50 ha would be compensated only for a 15 per cent set-aside which did not attract further compensation. This was opposed by the UK on the grounds that it discriminated against relatively large UK farms; that the effect over the period to 1995 would be to bump up the cost of running the CAP (although savings might eventually emerge); and that the proposal was biased against northern farmers.

The proposed price reduction for beef was 15 per cent, and it was further proposed that the emergency safety net be abolished. In principle this could lead to the cessation of intervention buying of beef. Dairy farmers would face 4 per cent reductions in milk quotas, but the smallest producers would be exempt. Prices would also be cut for other products such as sugar and tobacco.

The proposed cut in the cost of EC feed grains would help beef farmers to absorb cuts in beef prices, but the Irish were unhappy because they rely upon the safety net and use relatively few feed grains. Most oddly of all, the German objection was that German farmers should be allowed to earn their living in the (non-existent) free market rather than from income supports.

A summit to discuss the proposals is scheduled for February 1992 after the usual long-winded negotiations on the reforms have taken place. 1992 is election year in the USA, so the US administra-tion is unlikely to sit quietly while the Uruguay Round awaits the EC's deliberations. The GATT stands at the edge of the precipice, but is there the political will anywhere in the world to haul it back from the brink?

Notes

1. A **directive** states the result that must be achieved within a stated period. It is left up to each member country to introduce or amend laws to bring about the desired effect. Failure to complement a directive may result in the Commission referring the matter to the European Court of Justice. This can be compared with a **regulation** which automatically applies to member countries and hence does not need to be ratified by national parliaments. Regulations take precedure over national laws.

2. In Bruges, attending the European Summit of September 1988, Mrs Thatcher caused something of a stir by stating 'We have not successfully rolled back the frontiers of the State in Britain only to see them reimposed at a European level . . . The Treaty of Rome was intended as a charter for economic liberty . . . Our aim should not be more and more detailed regulation from the centre: it should be to deregulate, to remove the constraints on trade and to open up'. She added that 'To try to suppress nationhood and concentrate power at the centre of a European conglomerate would be highly damaging'. Such opinions do not altogether project the image of the good European in the style of Edward Heath. On the other hand, Mrs Thatcher expressed reservations which other European leaders are afraid to voice in public because they are reliant upon coalition support to remain in power.

3. A very sceptical view of the value of the EMS for economic convergence is to be found in Bolongia (1988, pp. 19–29).

4. See Annex to *Statement on the 1989 Community Budget*, Cm 680 (HMSO, April 1989).

References

Adams, J. (1990) 'The Exchange Rate Mechanism of the European Monetary System', *Bank of England Quarterly Bulletin* (November).

Artis, M. (1991) 'The European Monetary System', *Economics* (Spring).

Barrell, R. (1990) 'Has the EMS Changed Wage and Price Behaviour in Europe?', *National Institute Economic Review* (November).

Bhagwati, J. (1989) 'United States Trade Policy at the Crossroads', *The World Economy* (December).

Bhagwati, J. (1990) 'Multilateralism at Risk. The GATT is Dead. Long Live the GATT', *The World Economy* (June).

Bolongia, M. (1988) 'Prospects for International Policy Coordination: Some Lessons from the EMS', *Federal Reserve Bank of St Louis Review* (July–August).

Canberra Centre for International Economics (1988) *Macroeconomic Consequences of Farm Support Policies* (Canberra: CIE).

Cm 88 (1985) *Decision of the Council of the European Communities on the System of the Communities' Own Resources* (London: HMSO, 7 May).

Cm 419 (1988) *Decision of the Council of the European Communities on the System of the Communities' Own Resources* (London: HMSO 24 June).

Cm 1059 (1990) *Statement on the 1990 Community Budget* (London: HMSO).

Crook, C. (1990) 'A Survey of World Trade', *The Economist* (22 September).

Curzon, G. and V. Curzon (1989) 'Non-Discrimination and the Rise of "Material Reciprocity"', *The World Economy* (December).

Devault, J. (1990) 'The Administration of US Anti-Dumping Duties: Some Empirical Observations', *The World Economy* (March).

Ford, R. (1990) 'The Cost of Subsidising Industry', *OECD Observer* (October/November).

Giles, M. (1991) 'Business in Europe', *The Economist* (8 June).

Haldane, A. (1991) 'The Exchange Rate Mechanism of the European Monetary System: a Review of the Literature', *Bank of England Quarterly Bulletin* (February).

Hoffman, S. (1989) 'The European Community and 1992', *Foreign Affairs* (Fall).

Main, D. (1991) 'Regional Policy Initiatives from Brussels', *The Royal Bank of Scotland Review* (March).

National Consumer Council (1985) *Consumers and the CAP* (London: HMSO).

National Westminister Quarterly Bank Review (May 1991) – articles by A. Adonis and A. Tyrie; F. Catherwood; D. Lomax; J. Stevens; and F. Vibert.

OECD (1985) *Costs and Benefits of Protection* (Paris: OECD)

OECD (1987) *National Policies and Agricultural Trade* (Paris: OECD).

OECD (1991) *Agricultural Policies, Markets and Trade. Monitoring Outlook, 1991* (Paris: OECD).

Tyers, R. and Anderson, K. (1988) 'Liberalizing OECD Agricultural Policies in the Uruguay Round: Effects on Trade and Welfare', *Journal of Agricultural Economics* (May).

Weber, A. (1991) Reputation and Credibility in the European Monetary System', *Economic Policy* (April).

Wolf, M. (1989) 'Why Voluntary Export Restraints? An Historical Analysis', *The World Economy* (September).

Zis, G. (1990) 'European Monetary Union: Policy and Institutional Implications', *Economics* (Autumn).

■ Chapter 8 ■

Employment and Unemployment

Peter Curwen

■ 8.1 Introduction

The purpose of this chapter and of Chapter 9 which follows is to examine the workings of the labour market in the UK. This divides into three main issues. First, there is the need to discuss **employment and unemployment** and the changes which have taken place in both, primarily in the period since 1979. Secondly, there is the need to examine the role played by the **trade unions** and to assess how they have fared since 1979. Thirdly, there is the need to assess the record with respect to **education and training**, the latter of which has been a central policy issue only since the early 1980s. Inevitably, all of these issues have something to do with the rewards to labour, and so we will need to say something about that also. However, wider issues concerning the distribution of income are left until Chapter 10.

The Thatcher era was undoubtedly one which has been closely associated in people's minds with attempts to improve the workings of the labour market although, as we will discover, not all such attempts were successful and hence we need to examine why this was so. Certainly, the 1980s witnessed many changes in the laws controlling the labour market, and these are set out below. Nevertheless, the first Thatcher Government had largely to live with the labour market as they found it in 1979, and a few remarks about the market prior to 1979 are therefore in order.

In the first place, there is the obvious contrast between the period of Keynesian 'full' employ-ment which lasted for over two decades after the end of the Second World War, and the period of protracted unemployment, even in years of buoyant demand, which began in the late 1970s and which looks to be a permanent feature of the UK economic life for the foreseeable future. These days few economists believe that governments can maintain full employment using predominantly fiscal instruments in the textbook Keynesian manner. Instead, they view the government's role as one of creating the appropriate climate for sustained investment by the private sector. The traditional method for achieving this was to declare that the government would do everything in its power to maintain full employment. Because of this firms were willing to invest to make goods and to provide services since they were assured that there would be no shortage of customers with incomes from employment to be spent. But the investment itself created jobs and incomes which could be spent on consumer goods, and so the expectation of buoyant demand became a self-fulfilling prophecy.

The housing market was also important in this respect since most people who buy a house take on a very long-term commitment in the form of a mortgage, and hence need to be fairly certain of remaining in constant employment whilst paying it off. Equally, the mortgage provider needs to believe that this will be so before making the loan, in order to avoid defaults. The expectation of full employment hence leads to buoyant demand for housing and creates demand, and hence jobs and incomes, in the construction sector, which again helps to ensure that full employment comes about.

The main drawback to this virtuous circle was that the trade unions ceased to fear the spectre of unemployment which had haunted them during the 1930s, the more so as the old-time union leaders faded away and were replaced by people who had never experienced anything other than an era of full employment. Wage demands accordingly began to escalate, accompanied by the threat of strike action, and employers generally gave in quickly, hoping to be able to pass on higher wages into higher prices. Full employment thus became a pre-condition for inflation, and also led to a deterioration in manufacturing standards because of the belief that there would always be ready buyers, even for poor quality products. The Japanese and West Germans were happy to disprove this hypothesis, in the process creating unpleasant problems for the UK's balance of payments.

Whilst there were various ways in which this combination of problems could have been tackled, Mrs Thatcher's chosen solution after being elected in 1979 was to discard any commitment to full employment and to engineer a recession which demonstrated that this was not mere bluff. The consequences of this changed approach forms a unifying trend in the discussion which follows.

There was also the matter of **workers' rights**. By and large the tradition in the UK up to the 1970s was to limit workers' rights to those who held specified types of jobs and who worked full-time. Compared to those available in other advanced countries, these rights were patchy at best. During the 1970s the situation was to a considerable extent remedied. A series of Acts of Parliament extended to workers the rights to a contract of employment; to notice before termination of con-tract; to appeal against unfair dismissal; to redundancy payments; to maternity leave; to protection against discrimination; and to participate in union activities.

Whenever possible employers responded by taking on workers who fell outside the limits fixed for access to these rights, resulting in an upsurge in female part-time labour. But for the purposes of our discussion below the key factor was that the Thatcher Government after 1979 set about limiting some of these rights. To some extent, as detailed below, this has come up against supra-national EC laws in recent years, but there can be no doubt that the balance of power has shifted from workers to employers during the past decade.

■ 8.2 Employment

□ 8.2.1 The Working Population

Table 8.1 illustrates that the total population of the **UK** grew steadily from 1957 to 1971 but has since grown more slowly. The 1990s are expected to exhibit a quickening of growth, but this is expected to fall off again early in the next century.

The number of children under 16 increased in the UK by over 1 mn between 1961 and 1971, but this was followed by a decline of just under 3 mn, to 11.5 mn, in 1989. However, during the period 1971–90 the younger adult (16 to 39) and pensioner (65 and over) age groups grew by 3 mn and 1.6 mn respectively. Between 1991 and 2011 the number of children is projected to rise modestly once again, whereas the number of younger adults is projected to fall back by 2 mn.

Table 8.1 *Population, UK, 1951–2011 and Great Britain, 1971–2001, mn*

	1951	1961	1971	1981	1985	1989	1991	1996	2001	2011
UK	50.3	52.8	55.9	56.4	56.6	57.2	57.5*	58.5*	59.2*	60.0*
Britain	–	–	40.6	42.7	43.7	44.5	44.7*	44.9*	45.4*	–

Note:
* Projections.
Source: Social Trends, 21 (1991 edn) Table 1.2; *Employment Gazette* (May 1991) pp. 272–3.

From the total population can be extracted a summary statistic known as the **population of working age**, which by convention encompasses males aged 16 to 64 and females aged 16 to 59. The population of working age comprises all those who might work and embodies those at school or in retirement. However, parts of the population of working age are economically inactive. Some are engaged in further and higher education, some in raising children and some are physically unable to work. On the other hand, by no means all who retire officially are economically inactive. By adjusting for these factors a further summary statistic is arrived at called the **labour force** (or the **civilian labour force** if those in the armed forces are excluded) which comprises those willing and able to work.

The civilian labour force in **Great Britain** was 24.9 mn in 1971 and 26.3 mn in 1981. However, it fell back to 25.9 mn by 1983, before rising once again to 26.9 mn in 1986 and 28.0 mn in 1989. It is not expected to rise to 29.0 mn until after the turn of the century (see *Employment Gazette*, May 1991, pp. 270–1). The population of working age is driven primarily by variations in the birth rate, which surged immediately after 1945 and hence created a cyclical effect approximately every two decades. However, it is also driven by retirements, which are dependent upon the birth rate six to seven decades previously. In its turn, the civilian labour force reflects changes in the **population of working age**.

However, as shown in **Figure 8.1**, this relationship has been fairly weak. Between 1951 and 1989 the civilian labour force grew by 3.1 mn, considerably faster than the population of working age. Furthermore, whereas the latter grew at much the same rate for males and females, almost 90 per cent of the growth in the civilian labour force comprised of females (see *Employment Gazette*, April 1990). This trend is projected to continue. During the current decade the number of males in the civilian labour force is expected to remain static at around 15.9 mn, whilst the number of females is projected to increase by 0.7 mn to reach 12.9 mn by the year 2000, at which point women will constitute 45 per cent of the civilian labour force.

In the early 1980s, as can be seen, a fairly large number of workers dropped out of the labour force, and the Labour Force Survey[1] estimated that 340,000 workers in total had become **discouraged** because they did not expect to get a job even if

Figure 8.1 *Civilian Labour Force of Working Age and Population of Working Age by Sex, Great Britain*

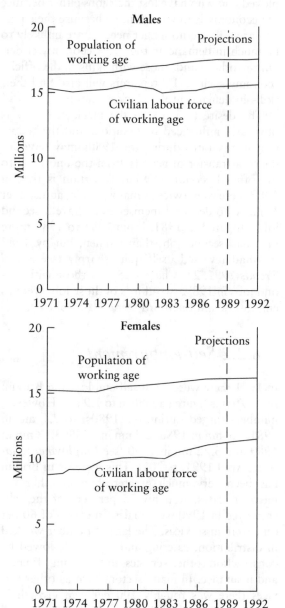

Sources: Social Trends; Employment Gazette.

they tried hard to do so. International Labour Office (ILO) estimates indicate 220,000 a year were discouraged during 1984–96 and 110,000 a year during 1988–90.

The notion of 'discouragement' is, however, somewhat ambiguous since some discouraged workers will have jobs in the unofficial, black economy. On the whole, those who are unemployed and who have lost their jobs either because the economy is in recession, or because their particular skills are no longer needed, are unlikely to be much in demand in the black economy either. On the other hand, those with skills in the official economy such as TV repairers will also find their skills in demand in the black economy.

The desire to work in the black economy is obviously influenced by taxation, and the reduction in tax rates during the 1980s may have induced a transfer of activity from the unofficial to the official economy. What is certain is that in 1989 there were twice as many people, at just over 1 mn, who declared themselves to have a second job compared to 1981. From 1981 to 1985 more men had second jobs than women, but by 1987 this had reversed itself quite sharply (see *Social Trends 1991*, 21, Chart 4.15). Of those with second jobs in 1989, two-thirds of those jobs were as employees and one-third were self-employed.

□ 8.2.2 Self-employment

In 1971 there were 2 mn self-employed in Britain. By 1979 this figure had fallen to 1.9 mn. However, numbers surged during the 1980s, to 2.1 mn in 1981; 2.6 mn in 1986; 2.9 mn in 1988; 3.18 mn in 1989 and 3.22 mn in 1990 (see *Employment Gazette*, April 1991, p. 201). This increase in Britain has been very much greater than in other EC member states. Roughly 75 per cent of the self-employed in 1990 were males. In excess of 60 per cent were in services. The largest number worked in distribution, catering and repairs, followed by construction, other services and banking, finance and insurance. In many sectors such as other services there was roughly 100 per cent growth in numbers between 1981 and 1990, but the overall average growth was only roughly 50 per cent be-

cause numbers were static in agriculture and forestry and grew only very modestly in distribution, the largest sector.

The rapid growth in self-employment is partly accounted for by the 1980–82 recession, which created a large pool of unemployment from which large numbers of individuals chose to emerge as self-employed. The government has fostered self-employment both through changes in the fiscal system and by its promotion of the joys of self-reliance. Start-up capital has also become more readily available. Needless to say the failure rate among the self-employed is very high, so the significant overall growth in numbers does indicate that the switch to self-employment is more than just a flash-in-the-pan consequence of the 1980–82 recession.

□ 8.2.3 Activity Rates

The proportion of the resident population who are in the civilian labour force is usually referred to as the **economic activity rate**. Activity rates have always been very different for males and females, but have been converging steadily during the postwar years. In the case of men the activity rate has been falling since the 1930s. In part, this has been due to an increase in the numbers staying on in further and higher education, although that factor was probably most important in the 1960s. More recently, the decline has been due to earlier retirements, stemming from improved pensions, and to the 'discouraged workers' effect.

In 1971 the activity rate in Britain for males of all ages was 80.5 per cent. Subsequently it fell to 74.2 per cent in 1983 (see *Employment Gazette*, May 1991, pp. 271–2) before rising back to 74.5 per cent in 1984, at which point there was a definitional changeover to the ILO/OECD system. On the latter basis, the male activity rate stood at 74.2 per cent in 1990 and is projected to fall back to 72.5 per cent by the year 2001.

The female activity rate in 1971 was only 43.9 per cent, but in spite of a setback during 1981–83 it had risen to 52.8 per cent in 1990, and is projected to rise further to 55.1 per cent by the year 2001. This increase in female activity rates

Figure 8.2   *Population of Working Age, by Sex and Economic Status*[1], *Great Britain, %*

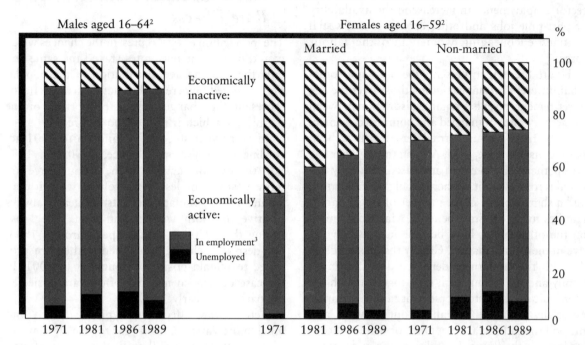

Notes:
[1] GB labour force definitions for 1981, ILO/OECD definitions for 1986 and 1989.
[2] Figures for 1971 relate to persons aged 15–59/64 (the school-leaving age was raised in 1972).
[3] Includes those on government schemes.
Source: Social Trends, 21 (1991 edn) Chart 4.2.

Table 8.2   *Women in the Labour Market*

According to analysis of the 1989 Labour Force Survey for Great Britain:

- Over 70 per cent of women of working age were active in the labour market in Spring 1989
- Between 1979 and 1989 the number of women in employment grew by just under 20 per cent
- In Spring 1989, over 40 per cent of employed people of working age were women; of these, just over 40 per cent worked part-time and a third had dependent children
- There were 750,000 self-employed women in Spring 1989, more than double the number in 1979
- In Spring 1989 the unemployment rate (on the ILO definition) among women of working age was 7.0 per cent, slightly below the rate for men
- The LFS identified 1 million lone mothers in Spring 1989 of whom just under one-half were active in the labour market
- 7 per cent of working wives (or co-habitees) had non-working husbands (or co-habitees)

Source: See *Employment Gazette* (December 1990) pp. 619–20. There is also some preliminary data on the 1990 Labour Force Survey in *Employment Gazette* (April 1991) and (May 1991).

has been due partly to the switch over to service sector employment, an increase in the availability of part-time jobs and other economic and social changes encouraging women into the labour force.

Figure 8.2, which presents the data in a somewhat different format excluding those over the age of retirement, reveals a notable distinction between the activity rates of married and unmarried women. Activity rates for unmarried females have been fairly constant since 1971. Among the younger age group there has been an increased tendency for females to stay on in further and higher education, and a sharp upturn in the number of single-parent families living off State benefits. Married women, on the other hand, have become increasingly active in the labour market. Clearly this has much to do with the modern tendency to delay having a family and the falling birth rate, together with the economic necessity to supplement family earnings, especially when the husband is out of work, and the widespread social acceptance of women working outside the home. In addition, the widespread introduction of labour-saving devices in the home has eased the burden of housework.

The most significant change in recent years has been in the proportion of women with a dependent child under 5 years of age who work. In 1984 this stood at 27 per cent whereas by 1989 it had risen to 40 per cent. This is the cause of some unease about the structure of modern society, but this goes beyond the scope of our present discussion. A summary of the role of women in the labour market is contained in Table 8.2.

Among the countries of the EC in 1988 the UK had the second highest economic activity rate behind Denmark. While UK men had the highest rate, UK women had the second highest rate. The difference between the sexes in Denmark was only 14 per cent, much smaller than in the UK, so there is some reason to expect the gap to narrow further in the UK over the coming decade. It would appear from this evidence that UK residents are relatively keen to work. Unfortunately, that does not necessarily mean that their time is used productively.

8.2.4 Population and Activity Rate Effects

The 'population effects' represent the changes which would occur if activity rates stayed the same and only the size and age distribution of the population changed, whereas the 'activity rate effects' represent the changes in the proportion of the population which is in the labour force.

In every year since 1971, and up to 2001 according to projections (Spence, 1990, pp. 188–90), the overall changes in the labour force are more positive (or less negative) for women than for men. The population effects are nearly always positive for both women and men. They rose during the 1970s to reach a peak around 1983, but despite declining subsequently they are projected to remain positive throughout to 2001. In the case of women negative effects are projected for part of the early 1990s.

Activity rate effects are typically larger, and much more variable, from year to year. It is movements in them, rather than in population effects, which explains both the fall in the labour force which occurred (even for women) between 1981 and 1983, and the large rises in 1983–84 and 1988–89. In most years they are positive for women but negative for men – in several years to such an extent as to outweigh the population effect and give falls in the male labour force, as in the projections for 1991–94.

8.2.5 Working Hours

Data on working hours are produced on a national basis and also on an internationally comparative basis by the EC and OECD. As a result of differences in definitions the data are not fully compatible, although the trends revealed are clearcut. Since the mid-1980s there has been a steady downwards trend in the number of hours worked in the UK, superimposed upon which has been a pro-cyclical pattern. The trend line is readily explained by the substitution effect – that is, the tendency for increasing number of workers to substitute leisure for working hours as their real incomes rise over time.

The tendency for hours worked to rise during booms and to fall during recession essentially reflects the volume of work on offer, and is much more marked in the manufacturing sector as compared to services, and among males as compared to females.

It is estimated from the Spring 1989 Labour Force Survey that four out of five male employees had basic usually weekly hours (that is **excluding** meal breaks and overtime) of between 35 and 45. Those at the lower end were mostly in white collar service jobs, whilst those at the upper end were mostly in manual jobs in manufacturing, energy and transport. Half of all female employees worked for less than 35 hours per week and over two-thirds for between 35 and 40 hours. For both sexes the self-employed worked longer hours than employees.

The official dividing line for part-time work is set at 30 hours per week. Women who work fewer hours invariably describe themselves as part-timers, but surveys reveal that 20 per cent of men who work fewer hours nevertheless describe themselves as full-time employees.

In 1979 the engineering working week was cut from 40 to 39 hours, and within three years a further 6 mn workers had won a similar reduction. In 1989 more than 600,000 manual workers in the engineering and water industries won the promise of a 37-hour week. Whilst there has been considerable reluctance in other industries to follow suit, this may happen a second time. For example, Rowntree Mackintosh have agreed to implement a 37-hour week by 1993 for craft workers provided productivity measures can be found to offset the costs, and British Rail and British Gas are involved in negotiations with a view to shortening the working week. In May 1991 British Nuclear Fuels offered its workers a 35-hour week subject to improved working practices which would make the deal self-financing.

International comparisons must be treated with care. Average weekly hours worked fell during the 1980s in most OECD countries, although Americans worked slightly longer and the Japanese exactly the same. Given the general tendency

Table 8.3 *Average Hours Usually Worked*[1] *per Week*[2]*, by Sex, EC Comparison, 1988*

	Males	Females	All Persons
United Kingdom	43.9	30.3	37.7
Belgium	38.1	32.5	36.0
Denmark	37.6	31.7	34.8
France	40.2	34.9	37.8
Germany (Fed. Rep.)	40.3	34.4	38.0
Greece	40.6	37.6	39.6
Irish Republic	41.0	35.5	38.8
Italy	39.4	35.3	38.0
Luxembourg	40.3	35.8	38.7
Netherlands	36.3	26.3	32.6
Portugal	43.2	38.6	41.4
Spain	40.9	37.2	39.8
EUR 12	40.7	33.4	37.8

Notes:
[1] Employees only.
[2] Excludes meal breaks but includes paid and unpaid overtime.
Source: Statistical Office of the European Communities.

for the statutory working week to be shortened, and for official holidays to be extended, this is not particularly surprising. What is surprising is the enormous disparity between the 34-hour Dutch working week and the 47-hour Japanese working week. This is, however, something of an illusion because the incidence of part-time relative to full-time work biases the data and Holland, for example, has proportionately twice as many part-timers (at 25 per cent of the workforce) as Japan. Equally, the Japanese holiday entitlement (typically at 2 weeks) is very low compared to that in Europe. Combining annual leave with public holidays yields 40 days' holiday for Germans, 36.5 days' for the French, 33.5 days' for Italians but only 31 days' for UK citizens (only the Irish get fewer at 28).

The latest year for which hours worked data are available officially for the whole of the European Community is 1988 (**Table 8.3**), and it should be noted that these data **include overtime**. Men in the UK (along with Portugal) worked longer hours than their European counterparts, whereas women worked fewer hours than elsewhere in the EC apart from The Netherlands. If hours worked are combined with holiday entitlement it becomes evident that Danes work far fewer hours per year than the Portuguese, and that UK citizens work many more hours than the French. Whilst this does not make much difference in any one year, it makes a huge difference over a 45-year working life. The combination of extended overtime working together with a heavy reliance upon part-time and temporary workers sets the UK aside from most comparable countries. In theory, at least, it suggests that the UK has a flexible labour market. Furthermore, there has been a noticeable tendency for firms to cease to do many jobs in-house and to sub-contract them to outside bodies as and when they are needed. This is a significant factor in explaining the switch from manufacturing to services in the national accounts, since a service provided in-house by a manufacturing concern is listed as a manufacturing activity, whilst the instant it is sub-contracted out it becomes listed as a service activity, even if it involves the identical group of workers.

From an economic perspective these developments obviously make sense for large companies, which thereby need to incur relatively little overheads and which can flex in line with the economic cycle. On the other hand, sub-contractors are increasingly vulnerable to economic downturns, and this helps to account for the exceptionally high number of bankruptcies during the 1990–91 recession.

The government has attempted through its own policies to foster **increased flexibility** in the workplace, in particular via the attack upon restrictive practices contained in the series of Employment Acts during the 1980s (see **pp. 325–7**). The Employment Act of 1989 was also notable for removing restrictions on the hours of work of young people and for abolishing most of the remaining legislation concerned with sex discrimination.

New contractual agreements introduced by Japanese companies are also of interest given their relative success in manufacturing. At the Nissan car plant in Sunderland the collective agreement specifies that 'there will be complete flexibility

and mobility of employees', and also that 'to ensure flexibility and change, employees will . . . undertake training for all work as required'. Despite union resistance elsewhere, these kinds of agreements are likely to become commonplace. Nevertheless, as demonstrated subsequently, the government (and its predecessors) have much to answer for in terms of their failure to create a system of education and training appropriate to the needs of the rapidly evolving labour market (for a full discussion of labour flexibility see Hill, Blyton and Gorham, 1989).

□ 8.2.6 The Demand for Labour

Changes in the size of the labour force and in activity rates are aspects of the supply of labour, although employment in total clearly has to do with the balance between supply and demand. Once the analysis turns to **unemployment** the demand side comes more into its own. Unemployment is associated in the Keynesian model with deficient demand for the goods and services in the production of which labour is used. A particular issue to which we will be referring below is the switch away from manufacturing and into services during the past two decades. This transfer has been common to all advanced economies, and indeed has proceeded much more rapidly in the USA than in the UK.

It was inevitably going to accelerate in the UK in the face of rising energy prices after 1975 and the exploitation of North Sea oil and gas which subsequently followed. The former produced a move away from energy-intensive manufacturing and towards services which were economical on energy use. In the latter respect it is often held that the benefits of North Sea oil were traded off (unwisely) in exchange for manufactured imports and an expansion of the internationally uncompetitive protected sectors of the economy.

The transfer of demand caused large numbers of jobs to be lost in manufacturing, as can be seen in **Table 8.4**, which analyses **employees in employment** by industry. Prior to 1979 the transfer from manufacturing to service sectors was proceeding fairly smoothly, but the 1980–81 recession bit

Table 8.4 *Employees in Employment, by Industry, UK, 000*[1]

	1971	1979	1981	1983	1986	1988[2]	1990[2]
Manufacturing							
Extraction of minerals and ores other than fuels, manufacture of metal, mineral products, and chemicals	1 282	1 147	939	817	729	688	n/a
Metal goods, engineering, and vehicle industries	3 709	3 374	2 923	2 548	2 372	2 366	n/a
Other	3 074	2 732	2 360	2 159	2 126	2 168	n/a
Total manufacturing	8 065	7 253	6 222	5 525	5 227	5 222	5 173
Services							
Distribution, hotels, catering, and repairs	3 686	4 257	4 172	4 118	4 298	4 442	n/a
Transport and communication	1 556	1 479	1 425	1 345	1 298	1 326	n/a
Banking, finance, insurance, business services, and leasing	1 336	1 647	1 739	1 875	2 166	2 475	n/a
Other	5 049	6 197	6 132	6 163	6 536	6 966	n/a
Total services	11 627	13 580	13 468	13 501	14 297	15 210	15 849
Agriculture, forestry, and fishing	450	380	363	350	329	313	n/a
Energy and water supply industries	798	722	710	648	545	487	451
Construction	1 198	1 239	1 130	1 044	989	1 044	n/a
All industries and services	22 139	23 173	21 892	21 067	21 387	22 276	22 864

Notes:
[1] As at June each year.
[2] The effect of revisions undertaken in 1991 impacted primarily on the 1989 and 1990 data.
Source: Social Trends, 21 (1991 edn), CSO, Table 4.11; *Employment Gazette* (April 1991) p. 201.

deeply into the manufacturing sectors without making any dent at all in service employment. By 1988 the total number of jobs stood once again at precisely the level of 1971 (and hence still well short of the 1979 aggregate). However, the manufacturing sectors employed exactly 3 mn less than in 1971 (5.2 mn) and the service sectors 3.5 mn more (15.2 mn). The reduction in each of the three manufacturing sectors was almost identical at 30 per cent, but the changes in the four service sectors were quite different, varying from a reduction of 12 per cent for transport to an increase of 85 per cent for banking and finance.

The missing 0.5 mn were lost in agriculture, energy and construction. Although this reduction was absolutely small, it represented a reduction of over 40 per cent in the energy sector.

It should be noted that the data on employees in employment underwent a significant revision early in 1991. The Census of Employment provides 'benchmark' figures on which to realign the estimates of employees in employment derived from the quarterly sample surveys of employers. The publication of the 1989 Census data, combined with information derived from the 1990 Labour Force Survey, indicated that previous estimates based upon the 1987 Census were too high for the period beginning June 1988. A significant difference emerged early in 1989, as indicated below.

Mar 1989 : – 45,000
Jun 1989 : – 87,000
Sept 1989 : – 138,000
Dec 1989 : – 209,000

Mar 1990 : − 273,000
Jun 1990 : − 365,000
Sept 1990 : − 432,000

By the end of 1990 there was a shortfall of roughly 500,000 – quite a lot of employees to misplace, all things considered. Whereas it had previously been estimated that the number of employees in employment grew by 2.23 mn between March 1983 and September 1990, this rise was now restricted to 1.80 mn. More importantly, the growth between September 1989 and September 1990 was revised downwards from 395,000 to 101,000.

An alternative approach is to conduct the analysis by splitting the workforce between **private** and **public** sectors (see *Social Trends*, 21, Table 4.44). The peak employment in the public sector (general government plus public corporations) occurred in 1979, but employment in general government remained constant from 1976 to 1989 and was untouched by the 1980–81 recession. The entire reduction of well over 1 mn from 1979–89 took place in the public corporations, initially as a consequence of recession and subsequently as a consequence of the privatisation programme (including the reclassification of 60,500 polytechnic staff in April 1989). Employment in the private sector

peaked in 1979, fell sharply, recovered to the 1979 level in 1986 and subsequently grew very strongly. As a consequence the public sector accounted for 30 per cent of the workforce in 1981, but had fallen back to 23 per cent by 1989.

Finally, it is possible to split employment down by **occupation** (see *Employment Gazette*, April 1991, p. 186). According to the 1990 Labour Force Survey 48 per cent of men and 69 per cent of women were in non-manual occupations. The main difference between the sexes was that 31 per cent of women were employed in clerical and related occupations compared to only 6 per cent of men, whereas 25 per cent of men were employed in craft or similar occupations compared to only 4 per cent of women. These percentages had changed little during the 1980s as a whole.

■ 8.3 Unemployment

The most important measure of the demand for labour is unemployment. This represents the difference between the **workforce in employment**, which consists of employees in employment, the self-employed, HM Forces and participants on work-related government training schemes, and

Figure 8.3   *Workforce and Workforce in Employment, UK, millions Seasonally Adjusted*

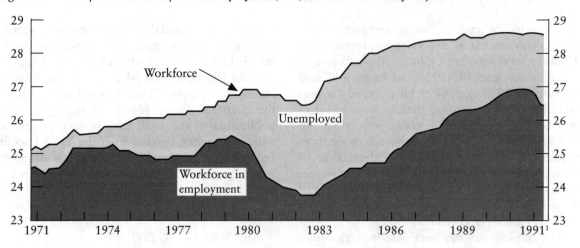

Note:
[1]   As revised (see *Employment Gazette*, April 1991, p. 199).
Sources: Social Trends, 19 (1989 edn) Chart 4.1; *Employment Gazette*.

the **workforce**[2] which also includes those people claiming benefit at Unemployment Benefit offices. This is illustrated in **Figure 8.3**, where the data has been adjusted to take account of the downwards revision referred to earlier with respect to employees in employment. However, in the case of the workforce in employment, the downwards revision between December 1988 and September 1990 amounted to 550,000, the extra reduction being accounted for by a sharp downward revision in the numbers of self-employed.

Between March 1983 and September 1990 the workforce in employment grew by 3.4 mn, of which 53 per cent represented part-time workers (1.72 mn). Included among the latter were 400,000 extra people on work-related government training programmes. Over the year to September 1990 part-time employment increased by 128,000, of whom 104,000 were females.

It is often argued that this preponderance of part-time work done by women results from market forces rather than from choice. However, the Labour Force Survey indicated to the contrary. In Spring 1990, 71.5 per cent of women stated that they took a part-time job because they did not want to work full-time, whereas only 14.3 per cent stated that it was because they could not find a full-time job (see *Employment Gazette*, April 1991, p. 179).

The trend in the number of unemployed can be seen more clearly in the form of **Figure 8.4** which also includes the number of vacancies notified to Job Centres. Unemployment is here measured according to the monthly claimant count (as reported in the newspapers – but see section on measuring unemployment below). The total number of unemployed on this definition reached 1 mn in December 1975, 2 mn in March 1981 and 3 mn in February 1985. The peak figure was 3.12 mn recorded in July 1986. Subsequently, the number unemployed fell for 44 successive months, reaching a low point of 1.60 mn in March 1990, since

Figure 8.4 *Unemployment*[1] *and Vacancies*[2,3]*, UK, 1971–91, mn*

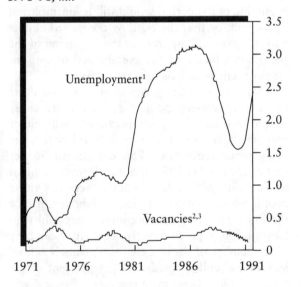

Notes:
[1] Seasonally adjusted unemployment (claimants aged 18 and over).
[2] About one-third of all vacancies are notified to Job Centres.
[3] Vacancy data prior to 1980 are not consistent with current coverage.
Source: Employment Gazette.

Figure 8.5 *Unemployment Rate*[1]*, Annual Averages, UK, %*

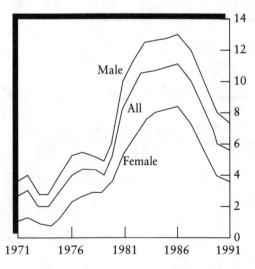

Note:
[1] The estimates used the seasonally adjusted series and are consistent with the current coverage of the claimant court.
Source: Department of Employment.

which point it has grown rapidly to reach well in excess of 2 mn.

An alternative way to express unemployment figures is as a **rate**, where the numbers in **Figure 8.4** are divided by the total workforce. This appears on an annual average basis in **Figure 8.5**, which also contains the unemployment rate for males and females separately.

The most notable features of **Figure 8.5** are, first, the very sharp upturn for males in 1980–81 (although the rate for females rose to a lesser degree) and, secondly, the sharp downturn from the 1986 peak for both males and females.

□ 8.3.1 *Stocks and Flows*

The total number of persons who are unemployed is counted at a point in time, and thus represents a stock which we can call the **unemployment pool** (**Figure 8.6**). It is, however, important to remember that even if the unemployment pool remains unchanged in size from one point in time to another (conventionally one month later) this does not mean that the **same people** are continuously unemployed. In the course of a year a very large number of people move in and out of employment, yet the unemployment pool will remain constant provided the inflow matches exactly the outflow.

In general, such exact matching does not occur either on a monthly or longer-term basis, as indicated in **Figure 8.7** which plots the inflow and outflow of both males and females combined during the period commencing February 1990. This was a period during which the total number of unemployed people first fell, then began to rise again in July 1990 on an unadjusted basis (when seasonally adjusted the turning point is April 1990). It can be seen that the numbers involved in these flows are very large in relation to the total unemployment pool of approximately 1.6 – 2.0 mn.

What **Figure 8.7** does not reveal is any information about the **characteristics** of those who entered and exited from the pool, nor the **reasons** why they did so. Nor does it tell us anything specific about the **duration of unemployment**, since it might be the case either that the outflow during the period comprised almost entirely those flowing in, in which case most of those unemployed at the beginning of the period would still be unemployed at the end, or that the outflow comprised almost entirely those unemployed at the beginning of the period, in which case the average duration of unemployment would be dropping rapidly.

There are two categories of people who enter the unemployment pool. First, there are those people who have lost a job previously held, either voluntarily by giving notice or involuntarily by being made redundant. This constituted 56 per cent of the total in 1990 although it was as high as 64 per cent in 1984. Secondly, there are those people who are either entering the labour force for the first time or re-entering after a gap and who have no job to go to directly. This latter category has a number of distinct elements, namely school leavers and college graduates (14 per cent of the total in 1990); those, most commonly housewives, who have been engaged in economic activity not recognised in official statistics as 'employment' (20 per cent of the total in 1990, but 46 per cent of all females); immigrants; the long-term sick and disabled; and those not wishing to work.

It is immediately evident that the unemployment pool cannot be held constant simply by creat-

Figure 8.6 *The Unemployment Pool*

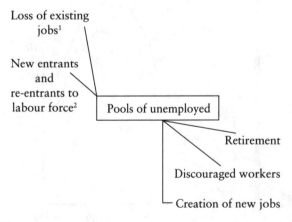

Notes:
[1] Loss of existing jobs can be voluntary or involuntary.
[2] New entrants and re-entrants consist of school leavers and college graduates; housewives; immigrants; the long-term sick and disabled; and those who do not wish to work.

Figure 8.7 *UK Unemployment Flows, February 1990–July 1991, 000* [1]

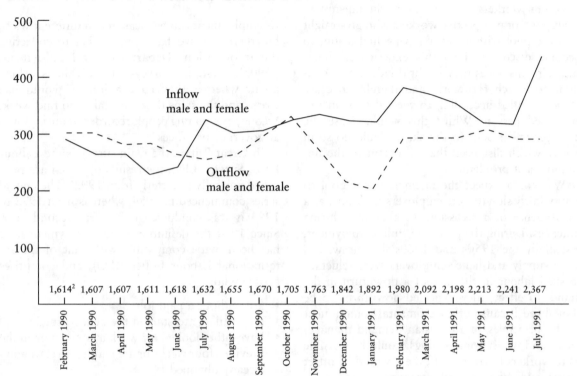

Notes:
[1] Not seasonally adjusted, standardised to 4⅓-week months.
[2] Number of unemployed, seasonally adjusted, 000.
Source: Employment Gazette, Tables 2.19 and 2.1.

ing a new job for each person who loses one. In order to achieve that objective the total outflow must equal the total inflow including those who have never previously been employed. In effect, jobs must be created much faster than they are being lost if the unemployment pool is not to grow. There are, admittedly, devices open to a government to mitigate this problem such as the obligation that a school leaver enter a training scheme, but the general proposition remains valid. It is, therefore, understandable that a recession causes the number of unemployed to rise sharply, since the unemployment pool is filling up both with those who have lost their jobs and with those who wish to enter the labour force for the first time. Equally, the pool will tend to empty fairly slowly since many of the jobs created as business picks up will be filled by new entrants to the labour force rather than by those already in the pool, especially where there is a mismatch in terms of skills, location, flexibility and so forth between the new jobs on offer and the workers in the unemployment pool.

The flow through the pool can also be affected by retirement of part of the existing workforce, either at the official retirement age or earlier. When a worker reaches retirement he or she may be replaced by another person, in which case the post will either be filled by employing someone who is not registered as unemployed (which will not affect the unemployment pool although the unemployment **rate** will fall) or by someone who is not registered as unemployed (which will reduce the unemployment pool and the unemployment rate). Where a retired person is not replaced the labour force will shrink, and since this will not affect the unemployment pool the unemployment rate will rise.

A further issue is concerned with the tendency of certain workers who end up in the unemployment pool, or prospective workers who go straight into the pool without ever having had a job, to become **discouraged** by this experience. Under such circumstances they might decide not to continue to search for work, and thereby to cease to be qualified according to the rules as an unemployed person. Whilst this would cause the unemployment pool to shrink, it would do so in a way which disguised the full extent of the unemployment problem.

We would expect the unemployment pool to empty fairly slowly were employers to decide, as a consequence of a recession, to alter their hiring practices. During the period of 'full' employment, essentially the 1950s and 1960s, labour was in short supply and hence employers were reluctant to shed labour in the face of a downturn in demand. In effect, they expected downturns to be short-lived because of governmental commitment to the principles of Keynesian demand management, and whilst some savings would be possible were workers to be laid off, these would be offset by any additional costs of retraining were the laid-off workers to have found alternative employment in the interim. In that sense **underemployment**, rather than unemployment, was a characteristic of periods of depressed demand.

However, once the commitment to 'full' employment has gone by the board, and a prolonged recession becomes a realistic scenario, it becomes more cost-effective to lay off workers than to hold them on the books. The election of the Thatcher Government in 1979 and the severe recession which followed understandably, therefore, caused a sharp upturn in official unemployment which reflected in part a decline in the hoarding of labour. Equally, when demand picked up again after 1981, most firms did not rush out to take on additional permanent full-time staff who might not be needed in the longer term, but rather preferred either to increase the hours worked by existing workers, to take on part-time workers or to sub-contract certain activities. As a result the unemployment pool was much slower to empty than in previous periods.

□ 8.3.2 Measuring Unemployment

Unemployment can be measured in different ways, but there are two basic approaches to collecting the information (Department of Employment, 1990b). First, by surveys of individuals asking about whether they have a job or would like work, and the steps they have taken to find work. Second, by counting people recorded as unemployed at government offices.

In Great Britain the main survey is the **Labour Force Survey** (LFS), the results of which are published annually (quarterly from 1992). The annual series commenced in 1984, whereas from 1973 to 1983 it was conducted only every second year. Since 1984 the definition of unemployment used has been made compatible with that of the International Labour Office (ILO), and comprises people who

- are without a paid job
- are available to start in the next fortnight
- have either looked for work at some time in the previous four weeks or are waiting to start a job already obtained.

The ILO definition is used both by the OECD and also the US Bureau of Labour Statistics, and hence provides a standardised basis for international comparisons of unemployment. The ILO's unemployment rate is expressed as a proportion of the corresponding estimate of economically active people (employed *plus* unemployed).

Since, however, surveys are expensive and take time to process the UK, in common with most EC countries, uses as its main monthly indicator of unemployment the count of those registered as unemployed. Since October 1982 the monthly figures have been based directly on the number of people claiming benefits at unemployment benefit offices, known as the **claimant count**. It is the frequency with which results are available that makes the monthly count the most widely quoted measure of unemployment.

'Claimants' include those people who claim Unemployment Benefit, Income Support and National Insurance Credits. They are counted in mid-month. Unemployment rates based on the

Figure 8.8 *The Monthly Claimant Count Compared with the ILO Measure of Unemployment* [1,2], *Spring 1989, Great Britain*

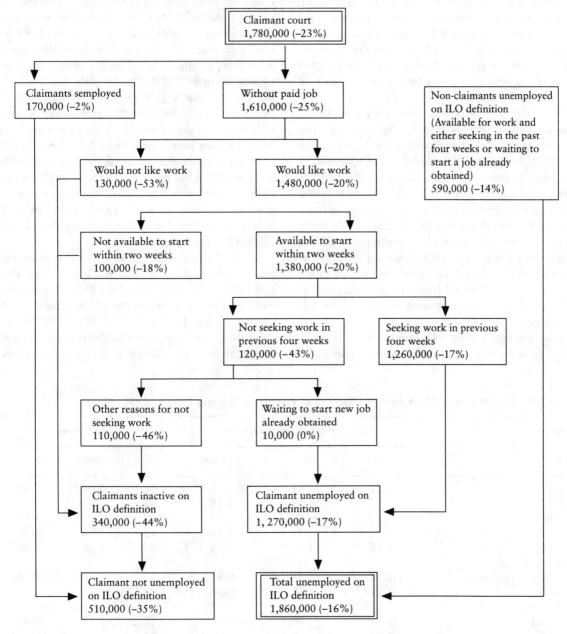

Notes:
1   % changes since Spring 1988 are shown in brackets.
2   The figures refer only to those aged 18 or over. This reflects the change in eligibility conditions for unemployment-related benefits for under-18 year olds in September 1988 which resulted in very few under-18 year olds remaining in the claimant court.

Source: Employment Gazette (October 1990) p. 508.

claimant count are expressed as a percentage of the corresponding mid-month estimate of the workforce (the sum of claimant unemployment, employees in employment, the self-employed, HM Forces and participants in work-related government training schemes). These rates are available on a seasonally adjusted basis going back to 1971 in a series which is **consistent with the current coverage of the count**.

The latest LFS which has been fully analysed at the time of writing is that for Spring 1989 (although there are some preliminary figures from the 1990 LFS). This indicated that there were 1.98 mn people unemployed. The corresponding claimant count was 1.78 mn (for Great Britain rather than the UK). However, in order to reconcile these numbers, unemployment must be confined to those aged 18 and over because in September 1988 a guaranteed place on a Youth Training scheme was offered to all 16 and 17 years old, which effectively removed them all from the claimant count. The LFS/ILO figure accordingly needs to be adjusted down to 1.86 mn.

The link between the two series is more complicated than expected, given the close proximity of the figures for Spring 1989, and is illustrated in **Figure 8.8**. As can be seen there were 570,000 claimants not classified as unemployed on the ILO measure whereas there were 590,000 who were unemployed according to the ILO measure but who were not claiming benefits. The difference of 80,000 represented the difference between the two aggregate figures. Of the 340,000 economically inactive claimants 130,000 did not wish to work (the men mostly because they were sick, disabled or retired and the women because they were looking after their family or home). A further 100,000 were temporarily unavailable for work and 110,000 were available but not looking for work. These are often referred as 'discouraged' workers if they express a belief that no work is expected to be available even if they look, but they numbered only 30,000 in Spring 1989.

Most of the claimants who said they were employed were doing so little work that they were still entitled to claim benefits, although a number were personally active in the black economy. On the other hand, 480,000 of the 590,000 unemployed who were not claimants were women, almost all married. Part-time and temporary work-

Table 8.5   *Comparison of Alternative Measures of Unemployment, Great Britain, 1984–89, mn*

Spring	ILO measure of unemployment			Claimant count[1]		
	All	Men	Women	All	Men	Women
1984	3.09	1.84	1.26	2.78	1.96	0.82
1985	2.97	1.79	1.18	2.92	2.03	0.89
1986	2.97	1.79	1.18	3.00	2.07	0.93
1987	2.88	1.72	1.16	2.82	1.96	0.86
1988	2.38	1.40	0.98	2.30	1.60	0.70
of which:						
aged 18 and over	(2.22)	(1.31)	(0.91)	(2.30)	(1.60)	(0.70)
1989	1.98	1.15	0.83	1.77	1.25	0.51
of which:						
aged 18 and over	(1.86)	(1.08)	(0.78)	(1.77)	(1.25)	(0.51)
1990[2]	1.87			1.52		

Notes:
[1]   Seasonally adjusted, consistent with current coverage. Excludes under 18 years old.
[2]   Preliminary.
Source: Employment Gazette (October 1990); preliminary figures for 1990 are in *Employment Gazette* (April 1991) and (May 1991).

Table 8.6   *Growth of Employment, 1984–90*

	Average increase 1984–88	Average increase 1984–90	Estimated increase 1988–89	Estimated increase 1989–90
All persons in employment	424,500	397,300	877,000	206,000
All full-timers	115,250	159,900	521,000	137,000
All part-timers	127,000	96,700	111,000	58,000

Source: Employment Gazette (April 1991) p. 179.

ers do not pay unemployment insurance premiums unless their earnings reach a certain level, and hence cannot claim benefits. It was notable that a majority of the unemployed non-claimant women were specifically seeking part-time work whereas the men were mainly seeking full-time work.

It is possible to make comparisons between the two measures over the period 1984–90, as shown in **Table 8.5**. **Table 8.5** shows that the claimant count carried on rising to Spring 1986, in total by 220,000. During the same period the ILO measure fell from its Spring 1984 peak by a total of nearly 130,000. However, almost all of this sharp divergence took place during 1984–85. During the period Spring 1986 to Spring 1989 the claimant count fell rapidly, by 1.23 mn in total, whereas the ILO measure fell by only 0.99 mn during the same period.

During 1987 and 1989 the numbers ceasing to search for work according to the ILO definition were heavily outweighed by the numbers ceasing to claim benefit. Preliminary estimates indicate that the claimant count fell by 240,000 whereas the ILO measure fell by only 110,000.

During 1988 and 1989, as shown in **Table 8.6**, there was a surge in the number of people taking up new full-time. jobs. When a claimant takes up employment he or she necessarily forgoes benefits. There is accordingly little financial advantage in taking up a part-time job. A drop in the number of claimants is therefore likely to be associated with growth in full-time rather than part-time jobs, and as shown above the number of claimants did fall sharply in 1988 and 1989.

The more modest reduction in the ILO data is unsurprising given that most of those searching

Table 8.7   *Changes in the Coverage of Unemployment Statistics, 1979–89*

Oct 1979	Fortnightly payment of benefits	+20 000
Nov 1981	Men over 60 offered higher supplementary benefit to leave the working population	−37 000
Oct 1982	Registration at Job Centres made voluntary	
	Computer count of benefit claimants substituted for clerical count of registrants	−190 000
Mar 1983	Men 60 and over given national insurance credits or higher supplementary benefit without claiming unemployment benefit	−162 000
Jul 1985	Discrepancies in Northern Ireland count corrected	−5 000
Mar 1986	Two-week delay in compilation of figures to reduce over-recording	−50 000
Jul 1986	Inclusion of self-employed and HM Forces in denominator of unemployment percentage (now working population)	−1.4%
Jul 1988	Inclusion of those on work-related government training schemes in the denominator of unemployment percentage	n/a
Sept 1988	Removal of all under 18s who have left school and not found a job but guaranteed a YTS place	−40 000
Jul 1989	Changes in conditions of the Redundant Mineworkers Payment Scheme	−15 500

Sources: Employment Gazette (September 1982); (December 1982); (July 1985); (March/April 1986); (December 1988); (December 1990).

but not eligible to claim will be women looking for part-time jobs, and these grew more slowly than in previous years from 1988 to 1990.

As can be seen, significant discrepancies between the different measures largely disappeared as they were progressively put onto a standardised basis, but the gap has apparently opened up again in 1989 and 1990. It is doubtful that the definitional issue will ever be fully laid to rest. Critics on the far right of the political spectrum argue that the unemployment should exclude all those who could be in education and training; all those who could have retired early; all women, or at least all who are married; and all those who have been unemployed for less than six months. On their reckoning, therefore, unemployment is largely an illusion. Critics on the far left argue, however, that unemployment is not merely real but understated. This is because many people do not choose to register as available to work, and also because the government deliberately distorts the official figures.

There can be no doubt that the government **has** changed the methods of recording unemployment statistics since it was first elected in 1979. **Table 8.7** offers one version of the most significant of these changes. In every case except one the redefinitions caused the numbers of unemployed to fall, so it is understandable that the government was constantly being accused of 'fiddling' the statistics. In point of fact many of the changes resulted from a desire to improve accuracy and to bring the statistics into line with international practice, and the charges of fiddling the numbers have largely lost their force. It has anyway to be borne in mind that even if the official figures are indeed understated, no account is taken of those who, despite being officially unemployed, are economically active in the black economy.

There are accordingly grounds for expecting the official figures to be simultaneously both overstated and understated. Assuming these effects cancel out to an considerable extent, this still leaves open the question as to how much of any reduction in unemployment is the result of government policy and how much is due to statistical chicanery. According to the Unemployment Unit there have been thirty changes in the way unemploy-

ment is measured since 1979. According to the government there have been only eight changes of any significance, of which two have been concerned with **redefining** unemployment *per se* whilst the other six have concerned the **rules that govern benefit entitlement** and thereby the number of people registering as unemployed (see *Employment Gazette*, December 1990, p. 608 for details).

The first official redefinition took place in October 1982 for two connected reasons. At this time the old system of registering at an unemployment centre for both benefits and another job was abolished. Under the old system an unemployed worker would receive benefits and might be offered a choice of three jobs from which to pick one. If he refused the job offers and could not find alternative work then he might forfeit benefits. The system thus contained an incentive to find work and not to stay unemployed unnecessarily. What the new system did was to split the payment of benefits (which was handed over to the DHSS) from the problem of finding a job. The argument for the changes was that it would improve efficiency by enabling the staff at Job Centres to concentrate on trying to fit workers to suitable jobs. But the split meant that there was no compulsion to register at the Centres and the effect was to decrease measured unemployment.

The second official redefinition took place in March 1986 when the production of the monthly figures was deferred by two weeks to take place three weeks instead of one week after the specified count date. The change was necessary to take account of those who had already ceased to be unemployed on the count day but had not yet been removed from the register.

According to the government there have only been six significant changes to the **rules** concerned with benefit entitlement. These are listed in **Table 8.7**. These six, plus the other two definitional changes, are accommodated in the consistent (seasonally adjusted) claimant count which goes back to 1971, and which it is claimed offers a distortion-free comparison over time. There have also been two changes to the way in which unemployment **rates** have been calculated. In July 1986 the denominator of the equation was expanded, in particular to take account of the much enlarged number of self-employed. This, given an unchanged numerator, inevitably caused the rate to fall. The denominator was expanded further in July 1988 with the inclusion of those on work-related government training schemes. However, this followed their inclusion in the statistics of the employed workforce and had very little effect on the rate of unemployment. These changes in the way unemployment rates have been calculated have not affected the **numbers** included in the unemployment count.

Many of the other changes cited by the Unemployment Unit are too insignificant to warrant further attention. Insofar as the accusation of fiddling the numbers can be made to stick it relates, firstly, to the introduction of the 'Restart' programme (see **p. 319**) and, secondly, to the introduction of tighter 'availability-for-work' tests in 1986 and in the Social Security Act 1989. These changes can be justified insofar as they weeded out people who should not have been on the unemployment register in the first place. They are excluded from **Table 8.7** because, effectively, they involved neither a change in rules nor a change in the coverage of the count. Nevertheless, they accounted for a reduction in the official count of the unemployed, and therefore created the reasonable suspicion that the government was trying simultaneously to claim credit both for generating a huge fall in unemployment and for cleaning up the statistics.

8.3.3 Unemployment by Age, Duration and Sex

The overall position as of July 1990, when there were 1.62 mn unemployed according to the claimant count, is shown in **Figure 8.9**. In each case the unemployed are broken down into three age groups, namely 18–24, 25–49 and over 50 respectively, and also according to the duration of unemployment, namely up to 25 weeks, 26–52 weeks and over 52 weeks respectively. Each sub-section thus represents a combination of a specific age group and duration. The proportion of all those who fell into each sub-section who were male is also specified (and hence by subtraction from 100 per cent

the proportion who were female can be deduced).

If one compares the situation in April 1987 when total unemployment stood at 3.1 mn, roughly twice the level in July 1990, it is interesting to note that the relationship between age and unemployment was relatively little affected by the sharp drop in unemployment. Taking the whole period from the upper turning point to the lower turning point of unemployment there is, however, some indication that unemployment fell relatively rapidly among those with the longest working lives ahead of them. Of greater importance was the change in duration. Whereas 38 per cent of the unemployed were unemployed for up to 26 weeks in April 1987, this had risen to 42 per cent in April 1989 and to 57 per cent in July 1990. For those unemployed between 26 and 52 weeks the percentage fell from 20 per cent in April 1987 to 18 per cent in 1989 and then only marginally to 17.5 per cent in July 1990. The really significant fall occurred among those unemployed for over one year, where the percentage fell from 42 per cent in April 1987 to 40 per cent in April 1989 and then to 31.5 per cent in July 1990.

This clearly demonstrates the **increasingly transient nature of unemployment** during a period of economic growth. Unfortunately, it also demonstrates that long-term unemployment is both far more pervasive than it was during the period of 'full' employment after 1945 and also that it is likely to stay that way in spite of the improvement during the late 1980s. Nevertheless, compared to other advanced economies the UK's record, as shown below, is by no means one of the worst.

Figure 8.9 also contains information on the relative incidence of unemployment on males and females. Most of the percentages fall within the 70–80 range, but it is notable that, first, females are disproportionately likely to be unemployed in the 18–24 age bracket for periods of up to six months, and disproportionately unlikely to be unemployed in the 25–49 age bracket for periods in excess of one year. The fact that, as a general rule of thumb, males are three times as likely to be unemployed as females, irrespective of age or duration of unemployment, is clearly less to do with aggregate numbers (see the earlier discussion on activity rates) than with the particular sectors in

Figure 8.9   *Unemployment by Age, Duration and Sex, July 1990, 000*

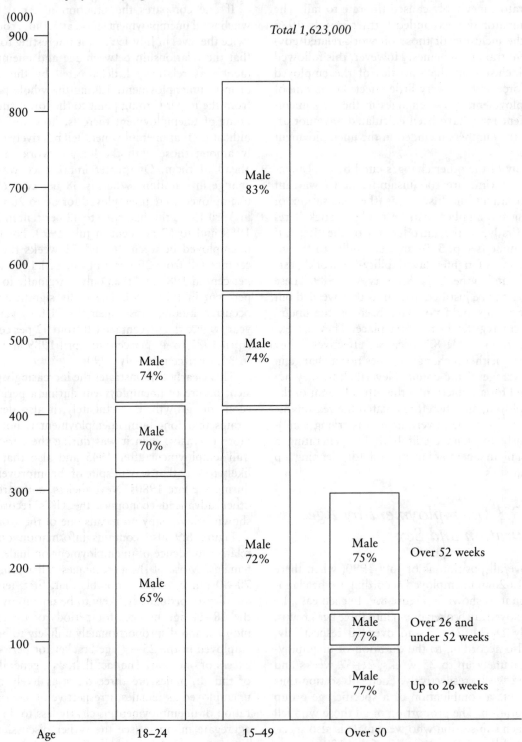

Source: Employment Gazette (November 1990) Table 2.5.

which redundancies occurred and with the willingness of females to take up part-time jobs which may be plentiful but nevertheless shunned by most unemployed males.

□ 8.3.4 Long-term Unemployment

Figure 8.10, based on standardised OECD data, is very revealing. As can be seen, there are tremendous variations between countries with respect to the proportion of total unemployment which is in excess of 12 months' duration. A number of EC countries were clustered in the 40–50 per cent range in 1988–89 but Ireland, Spain, Italy and Belgium had much higher proportions. These can be compared with the far lower proportions in the USA and Japan, and also with those EFTA countries such as Norway and Sweden which devote considerable resources to the prevention of long-term unemployment.

It is notable that far more Americans lose their job every month (roughly 2 per cent) than workers in the EC (roughly 0.3 per cent in France and Germany), yet they remain unemployed for an average of only 2.5 months, much less than is typical in the EC. This reflects the very fluid labour market in the USA where workers move rapidly from one relatively low-paid service sector job to another and where, for example, there is a tradition of working one's through college. This has helped to keep the US unemployment rate below that in the EC, where the immovable block of long-term unemployed typically creates a base level of 3 to 4 per cent unemployment.

Figure 8.10 *Long-term Unemployment as % of Total Unemployment*

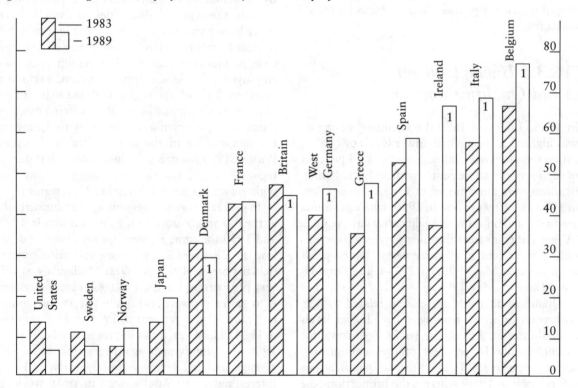

Note:
1 1988. The 1989 Labour Force Survey indicated that the rate had fallen by 4.6 per cent compared to 1 year earlier in the case of Britain.
Source: The Economist.

In most EC countries the problem of long-term unemployment got worse during the 1980s, in some cases (such as Ireland and Greece) markedly so. Only in Britain, where the 1983 rate was relatively high, though by no means the highest, did the problem improve noticeably after 1983 as the government began to address itself more seriously to the issue. A key issue is that the long-term unemployed must have an incentive to maintain active job status. In the early 1980s no such incentive existed, and numbers grew rapidly. The introduction of Restart interviews and tougher availability for work testing were crucial in the speed of the subsequent fall. However, toughness alone is clearly insufficient, and high quality training and job search programmes are also needed.

In the course of the 1990–91 recession the number of long-term unemployed is inevitably going to grow. However, the relatively rapid rise in the total number of mainly short-term unemployed will clearly provide the main focus for policy measures.

8.3.5 Unemployment and Qualifications

In 1988, 1989 and 1990 the unemployment rate was higher for people with lower levels of qualification than for well qualified people. 13.4 per cent of economically active people with no formal qualifications were unemployed in 1988, 11.3 per cent in 1989 and 10.9 per cent in 1990, whereas among graduates and others with qualifications above GCE 'A'-level or equivalent the unemployment rate was only 2.9 per cent in all three years (see *Employment Gazette*, May 1990, pp. 272–4, and *Employment Gazette*, May 1991, p. 300).

Qualification levels are closely related to age, with younger people tending to have higher levels of qualification. Among the 16–24 age group, for example, only 16 per cent of the economically active people in 1990 had no formal qualifications (19 per cent in 1989) whereas the proportion rose to 38 per cent for those aged between 45 and retirement age (42 per cent in 1989).

Among the unemployed, the proportions with no qualifications rose from 36 per cent for 16–24

year olds in 1990 to 53 per cent for those between 45 and retirement age. Those with higher levels of qualification tended to have been out of a job and looking for work for shorter periods than those with lesser qualifications or none. For example, roughly one-half of the unemployed who had no qualifications had been out of work and seeking a job for a year or more, compared to about a quarter of those with higher qualifications and about a third of those with other qualifications. This effect is much more marked for men than for women.

8.3.6 Regional Dispersion of Unemployment

Figure 8.11 illustrates the changing pattern of the regional dispersion of unemployment since 1985. By the standards of many other EC countries such as Italy the regional disparities in the UK have never been particularly severe, and it is reasonable to treat Northern Ireland as something of a special case, permanently marooned at the top of the unemployed pile. As an approximation, excluding Northern Ireland, the region with the highest rate of unemployment has since 1979 suffered twice as much unemployment as the region with the lowest rate irrespective of the stage in the trade cycle. Prior to 1979 the gap had closed somewhat due to regional policy, but this was largely allowed to wither away under the Thatcher Government.

In general, the same regions appear consistently at the top and bottom of the distribution. In 1979 and 1990 the same regions appear above and below the UK average – with one exception of particular note. In 1979 the West Midlands was still very prosperous, but the 1980–82 recession caused it to suffer a disproportionate rise in unemployment (up from 5 per cent in 1979 to 12.5 per cent in 1984). However, it has improved markedly since 1986, is currently once again very close to the UK average and fell below it briefly early in 1991. Interestingly, East Anglia (with its small working population) has for the past two years had less unemployment even than the South East, partly as a result of improved communications. Northern Ireland excepted, it is clear that the improvement

Figure 8.11 *Regional Unemployment Rates*[1], *1986–91*

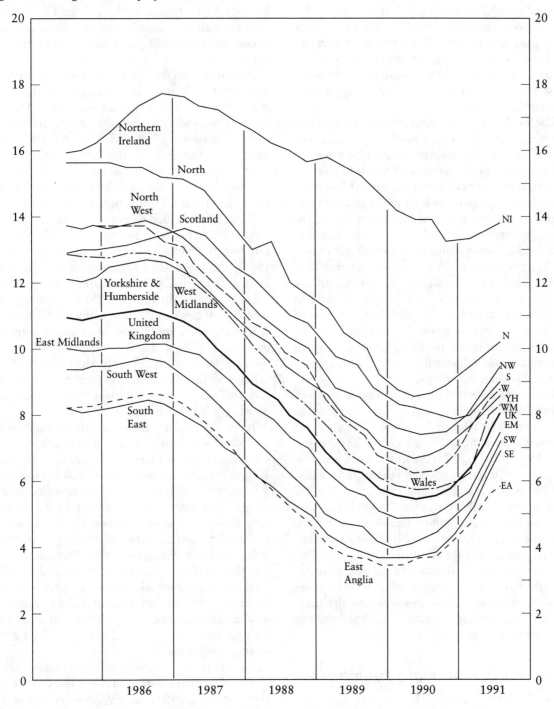

Note:
[1] Seasonally adjusted. Figures shown are at January, April, July and October.
Source: Employment Gazette.

in the employment situation to mid-1990 was fairly evenly dispersed. Nevertheless, it is very noticeable that whereas unemployment has risen everywhere during the first half of 1991, the rate of increase has been less severe in regions which are manufacturing for export than in the South East and South West which are far more dependent upon non-exportable services.

The evidence from **Figure 8.11** is that unemployment fans out along a north–south axis. For the UK as a whole, unemployment first began to fall during the third-quarter of 1986, whereas this occurred one-quarter later in the case of Northern Ireland and two-quarters later in the case of Scotland. The UK average turned up again during the second-quarter of 1990. In the South East and East Anglia, unemployment bottomed out during the fourth-quarter of 1989 and one-quarter later in the South West. By way of contrast it had not bottomed out until the third-quarter of 1990 in the North West and it was still falling in Scotland and Northern Ireland at the end of that year. The only real puzzle is that the first region to exhibit a reduction in unemployment was the North, a whole year earlier than in Scotland.

The consistency of the pecking order in terms of regional unemployment is a feature common to EC countries and Japan (with the UK exhibiting the most consistent order of all – see *The Economist*, 29 July 1989, p. 73) but not to the USA. This suggests that it has its roots in labour immobility, and hence that it will remain a feature of the UK economy until such time as local wage bargaining becomes widespread and/or regional house price differentials narrow considerably. Since these matters are not directly the concern of regional policy measures, it is understandable that attention has recently been focussed upon specific unemployment blackspots, such as towns where the main industry has gone into terminal decline, and the inner areas of large cities.

8.3.7 International Comparisons of Unemployment

It is possible to make international comparisons of unemployment using either national (but mostly incompatible) data or standardised data published by the OECD. **Figure 8.12** plots the OECD data over the past two decades for five major industrialised countries and for 8 members of the EC taken as an average.

As can be seen the UK's record was satisfactory until 1974, and, in relation to countries other than West Germany and Japan, no worse than average until 1980 when the recession began to bite in earnest. Between 1979 and 1983 the UK's rate more than doubled, but this was less out of line with experience elsewhere in the EC than is generally believed to be the case. The rate in Spain, for example, also doubled from 8.5 to 17.2 per cent, and indeed continued to rise to a peak of 21.4 per cent in 1985. Partly as a consequence (the rates in Eire and the Netherlands were also very high by 1983), the rapid fall in the rate in the UK after 1986 (the turning point measured using national data) brought it down below the EC average and indeed very close to the rate being experienced in West Germany. In France, after rising continuously from 1974 to 1987 (a fourfold rise overall), the rate remained stubbornly high, registering 9 per cent in July 1990. At that time the rate in Eire was 14.7 per cent and in Spain 16 per cent, compared to 6.2 per cent in the UK.

It would appear, therefore, that countries in the EC which chose not to engineer such a severe recession as was suffered by the UK during 1980–82 had initially made the wiser choice. However, the UK appeared to be reaping benefits in the longer term once unemployment began to fall after 1986. Countries elsewhere in the EC which preferred to protect jobs rather than restructure their economies during the early 1980s, discovered that their problems did not go away, and that the need, as in the case of France, to bring inflation down to West German levels in order to stave off continual devaluation in the EMS meant maintaining tight control on demand and hence high rates of unemployment.

Now that the UK also finds itself under a similar constraint the UK rate has risen back to the EC average during 1991. Clearly, however, unusually high rates of unemployment by historical standards are not a peculiarly UK affliction. What is particularly interesting is why they do not afflict

Figure 8.12   *Unemployment Rates, International Comparisons, 1970–91, %*

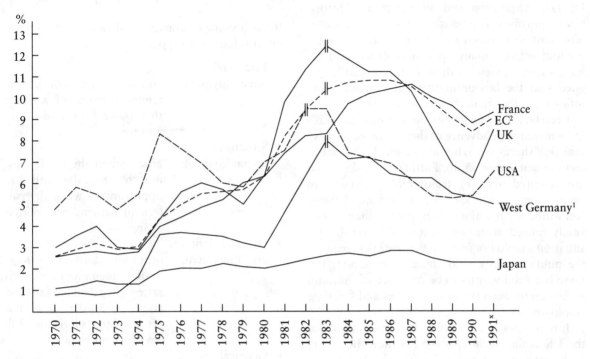

Notes:
[1]   German unification took place at the end of 1990.   ˣ Forecast
[2]   Germany, France, UK, Italy, Belgium, Netherlands, Portugal and Spain.   ‖ Discontinuity
Source: OECD *Economic Outlook*, 47 (June 1990) Table R18; *Employment Gazette*.

Japan. Part of the answer is, as usual, a matter of statistical definition since it is far less common for part-time workers who lose their jobs in Japan to be recorded as actively seeking a new job than it is in the EC. More importantly, in terms of potential lessons for the UK, is the degree of **wage flexibility** in the Japanese labour market.

In Japan a significant element in the total wage bill consists of bonuses which are cut sharply during times of recession. This reduction in wages makes it possible for Japanese employers to keep their employees in work, and indeed in many cases to offer a virtual guarantee of life-long employment. In effect, rising wages are traded off against job security. Unfortunately, such an idea is entirely alien to the culture of the UK labour market, although the 1990–91 recession has seen some Japanese-style agreements. So long as workers in the UK regard an annual pay rise as their unalienable

right, and furthermore a rise as large as that awarded to 'comparable' groups of workers, the UK's rate of unemployment will remain stubbornly high by Japanese standards.

☐ 8.3.8 Labour Market Flexibility

As we have seen, the UK labour market appears to have become more flexible during the 1980s given the evidence of increased overtime working, part-time working and self-employment. Nevertheless, such a conclusion is by no means self-evident.

In the first place, it can be argued that temporary work may indeed be precisely that, and may lead subsequently to a (further) period of unemployment rather than to a permanent job. Secondly, part-time jobs, mostly undertaken by females, neither utilise properly such skills as the workforce possess nor offer many opportunities for skill acquisition and advancement. Thirdly, self-employment is primarily a response to unemployment and utilises such skills as already exist without offering many opportunities for skill enhancement. In view of these factors it can be argued that the labour market has become more inflexible rather than the opposite.

Clearly, a flexible labour market requires skills to be acquired **in advance of** their being needed, so that skill shortages do not automatically appear as soon as demand picks up. Furthermore, skills that are acquired must be **transferable**, rather than occupation or firm specific. During the 1980–1 recession, when training was predominantly privately funded, it mostly went by the board. This situation should not recur to the same degree given the public funding of training programmes, but there is a good way to go before there is a smooth transition between such programmes and full-time employment.

It may anyway be argued that the key issue for the UK is that what is needed is more flexibility with respect to **pay** rather than to jobs. During the 1980–82 recession wages remained too high and the recession manifested itself via a sharp upturn in unemployment. As noted elsewhere, this is not what happens in Japan where bonuses are cut rather than jobs when demand falls back.

Much of the problem lies with the fact that in the UK higher productivity is passed on as higher wages rather than as lower prices combined with job security. Whilst this can be justified for the individual firm, it is an undesirable outcome for the economy as a whole. This is firstly because higher wages inevitably leak into sectors where productivity is not rising, and therefore cause rising prices in these sectors. Secondly, it is preferable that the real wage of workers should be increased by combining modest wage rises with constant or falling prices rather than by combining much higher wages with somewhat more slowly rising prices. Such a conclusion does not need to be spelled out in competing countries such as West Germany, but even a decade of Thatcherism has, at least until recently, failed to get the message through in the UK.

□ 8.3.9 Types of Unemployment

It has become customary to divide unemployment up into four main types:

- **Frictional unemployment:** consists mainly of people temporarily out of work as they move from one job to another

- **Structural unemployment:** arises when there is a mismatch of skills and job opportunities when the pattern of demand and output changes

- **Demand-deficient unemployment:** otherwise known as Keynesian unemployment, this arises when demand falls and wages and prices have not yet adjusted to restore full employment

- **Classical unemployment:** arises when the wage level stays above that at which the labour market will clear, possibly as a result of the exercise of union power or the existence of minimum wages legislation.

Unemployment can also be seasonal, but the unemployment data is normally 'seasonally-adjusted' to prevent this from showing up independently.

However, the current debate about unemployment is usually conducted in terms of whether it is **voluntary** or **involuntary**, although the distinction is not as clear-cut as it might seem at first sight. Unemployment is 'voluntary' if a worker is offered a job but is unwilling to accept it at the real wage on offer. Clearly, frictional unemployment is voluntary because the workers concerned have chosen to be temporarily unemployed whilst moving from one job to another (and it is anyway evident that such unemployment does not merit a policy response by the government to eliminate it – indeed, if it did not exist the economy could not evolve to meet changing patterns of demand). Structural unemployment can also be regarded as voluntary insofar as any worker who has become unemployed in one industry or occupation refuses to accept a job which is on offer in another occupation. The fact that the worker may find the job unappealing, or may consider the wage on offer to be lower than is acceptable, does not detract from the fact that such behaviour is voluntary.

Classical unemployment is also voluntary insofar as it occurs when a worker – or more likely a group of workers organised in a trade union – refuse to accept the wage on offer for existing or potential jobs. However, this is strictly true only if the trade union has been mandated by the workforce to seek a wage higher than the firm is willing to pay whilst keeping them all in employment. If an individual worker who is willing to work for a lower wage rather than become redundant is prevented from so doing through the behaviour of a union which he does not support, then he can be said to be 'involuntarily' unemployed. Nevertheless, **involuntary** unemployment is **predominantly caused by a deficiency of demand** such as occurs during the downswing of the economic cycle.

Given the above distinction, it is possible to envisage the labour market when unemployment is purely **voluntary**. In other words, the level of demand is sufficiently high to provide a job for everyone who is willing to work at whatever real wage results from the equilibrium between the demand for and supply of labour in the labour market. In such circumstances it is reasonable to consider employment to be 'full'. However, this does not mean that, as was true during the 1950s when voluntary unemployment was predominantly frictional, fewer than half a million workers would currently be unemployed if demand was not deficient because, for various reasons, the numbers of those unwilling to work at the market clearing real wage may have increased substantially.

The gap between the rate of unemployment which would exist were the labour market to be in equilibrium and the rate which actually exists at any point in time is known as the **natural rate of unemployment**. The natural rate cannot, by implication, be eliminated through a policy of gener-

ating additional demand. It is a problem which is created on the supply side of the economy, and hence can be tackled only using *supply-side* measures.

8.3.10 Why is Unemployment so High?

At the beginning of the 1980s unemployment was approximately ten times as high as it had been two decades earlier, and it has remained very high by postwar standards for the past decade. In many ways it is easier to explain what did **not** cause this long-term adjustment to happen than to explain what did.

For example, it had very little to do with the **growth in the labour force**. In the short-term, an increase in activity rates or in the number of school leavers can create an excess supply of labour, but past experience in the UK as well as experience overseas demonstrates that demand adjusts to supply changes within a few years. Nor was **insufficient investment** to blame. It is evident that a given stock of capital can be combined with a variable number of workers by working it for longer hours. In any event, when capacity becomes scarce there is typically a surge in investment to enhance the capital stock, as in 1988. It is also foolish to imagine that **machines replace labour**, although new technology does cause temporary structural unemployment. If, for example, the typewriter was supposed to destroy the jobs of all those clerks inefficiently wielding quill pens, where did all the clerical jobs come from which the advent of the computer was subsequently supposed to destroy? As information processing speeds up, so more information gets processed!

On a more positive note, Layard and Nickell (1986), examining male unemployment from 1956 to 1983, concluded that there were seven major contributory reasons for the upturn in unemployment, as shown in **Table 8.8**.

There was considerable variation in the contribution made by each factor cited, and during sub-periods several appeared to have had the effect of reducing unemployment. During the period up to

Table 8.8 *The Causes of Male Unemployment in the UK*

Changes In	Effect on Unemployment Rate (%)		
	1956–66 to 1967–74	1967–74 to 1975–79	1975–79 to 1980–83
Employers' labour taxes	0.25	0.38	0.44
Unemployment benefit	0.54	−0.09	−0.10
Trade union power	1.18	1.17	0.80
Real import prices	−0.58	1.47	−0.93
Mismatch of skills	0.16	0.20	0.49
Incomes policy	–	−0.36	0.49
Demand factors	0.12	0.54	6.56
	1956–66	1967–74	1975–79	1980–83
Estimated 'natural' rate of unemployment	2.0	4.2	7.6	9.1
Actual rate of unemployment	2.0	3.8	6.8	13.8

Source: Layard and Nickell (1986).

the early 1970s the second strongest influence was exerted by unemployment benefit. In other words, as the **replacement rate** – the ratio of unemployment benefit to wages – rises, so workers become more selective about the jobs they are prepared to accept. However, it is notable that from the mid-1970s onwards this ceased to be a factor in rising unemployment because benefits ceased to rise relative to wages. Until 1974 only trade union power exerted a stronger influence, and one that remained constant up to the end of the decade, although by then it was making a proportionately smaller contribution to the higher level of unemployment. During the early 1980s, however, it became much less significant, which is unsurprising given the effects of the recession and the attack on union powers and privileges by the Thatcher Government.

Throughout the period employers' labour taxes remained a positive factor contributing to unemployment. This was only to be expected given that labour taxes have the effect of raising the marginal cost of employing additional workers. The mismatch of skills also continued to exert a positive influence which grew modestly throughout the period, but which in aggregate accounted for well under 10 per cent of male unemployment. Incomes policies made little contribution in any sub-period, and were neutral taking the period as a whole.

During the middle sub-period the biggest contribution was made by rising real import prices. Given the quadrupling in the price of oil and sharp increases in other commodity prices, it is hardly surprising that many firms responded to rising costs by laying off workers. However, real import prices also tend to fall significantly at times, and as can be seen reductions in real import prices were a factor – much the most significant factor – contributing to the maintenance of employment during the other sub-periods. Hence, in the long term, it is not to be expected that real import prices will have a strong uni-directional force upon unemployment.

Prior to the latter part of the 1970s demand management was used primarily to sustain employment, although to increasingly less effect as inflation came progressively to be regarded as a more important policy objective. By the end of the decade it had effectively been discarded as a means to maintain employment, and it was viciously reined back by the incoming Thatcher Government. As **Table 8.8** shows, this swamped out all other factors contributing to the rise in unemployment at that time.

As can be seen in the lower part of **Table 8.8**, there was little difference between measured unemployment and estimates of the natural rate until the end of the 1970s. In other words, the slow but almost continuous rise in measured unemployment had little to do with a deficiency of demand and could largely be explained by supply-side factors. These factors also served to maintain the rise in unemployment during the early 1980s but were temporarily swamped by a massive dose of deflation, so it is hardly surprising that unemployment followed the pattern illustrated previously.

The natural rate is by its very nature a difficult concept to measure accurately, and there is no unanimity about Layard and Nickell's calculations (see Dawson, 1990). Nevertheless, the natural rate almost certainly began to fall after 1983, and there was subsequently, as we have seen, a four-year period during which measured unemployment fell continuously. The gap between the natural rate and actual unemployment is important because if actual unemployment exceeds the natural rate then the gap can be bridged by expanding demand without setting off an inflationary spiral, whilst if there is no gap an expansion of supply must precede any increase in demand if an inflationary spiral is to be avoided.

The relationship between inflation and unemployment can be used as an alternative way to identify the natural rate. When actual unemployment is less than the natural rate and there is excess demand in the labour market, inflation will tend to **accelerate** – in other words, it will be higher in one time period than in the preceding period irrespective of what the rate was in the earlier period. Equally, when actual unemployment is greater than the natural rate, and there is excess supply in the labour market, inflation will tend to **decelerate**. When the two rates are identical, and the labour market is in equilibrium, inflation will consequently remain steady **at whatever rate exists at the time**. This is known as the NAIRU – **the non-accelerating inflation rate of unemployment**. Thus, in principle, the natural rate can be identified by the fact that the rate of inflation is neither rising nor falling.

This may not in practice be easy to pin down. What is certain is that the natural rate shifted considerably during the 1980s as the supply conditions of the economy evolved under a variety of pressures. A number of these are discussed in Chapter 9, such as the concerted attack upon trade union power and the insider-outsider distinction. Others were referred to in the earlier section on supply-side economics.

If the supply-side measures have been successful then the natural rate should be permanently lower in the 1990s compared to the 1980s. Nevertheless, one problem which has, if anything, become harder to resolve is the mismatch between job-seekers and vacancies. Whilst this could have something to do with increasing choosiness about jobs by those out of work, this is unlikely given the increasingly tight rules to qualify for unemployment benefit. It is much more likely to be due to imperfections in the housing market where there are big differences in house prices in different regions, and where jobs are most plentiful in areas where house prices are relatively high. The reduction in private sector rentals and the difficulties of exchanging council houses only make the problem worse.

8.3.11 Unemployment and Real Wages

During the 1980s real wages rose exceptionally fast in the UK whilst they fell in the USA. However, this may simply have reflected relative productivity. Rising real wages which are wholly offset by rising productivity do not eat into profits, in which case there should be no need for firms to shed labour.

We have examined the trend in productivity in Chapter 3 (see **pp. 62–5**), but what exactly is the link to real wages and jobs? Poret (1990) seeks to answer this question by setting real wages against productivity. Real wages are defined as nominal wages deflated by the private consumption deflator, whilst labour efficiency is defined as output per employee adjusted for the replacement of workers by increased capital investment. Poret divides the former by the latter and expresses this ratio as an index with the average value of the ratio for 1960–89 set at 100.

The ratio fell during the 1980s in virtually every OECD country. In 1989 the ratio was below its 1960–89 average with very few exceptions, among which the most prominent was Britain. From 1983–87 the ratio remained steady in Britain at around 95, but in 1989 it rose back up to 100, where it had previously been in 1981. So why was Britain so different?

The OECD study discovered that the biggest single factor in explaining the slower growth in real wages during the 1980s was basically the higher unemployment sustained during that decade. The study measured this using the gap between actual unemployment and the NAIRU (defined as the level at which unemployment exerts neither upwards nor downwards pressure on real wages relative to labour efficiency. As a proxy measure for this gap the study used a measure based on a moving average of actual unemployment.

After 1982 the gap opened up throughout the OECD. In 1989 it still existed in France (where, as we have noted, unemployment grew steadily during the 1980s), whereas in Britain, by 1989, the gap had become negative (actual unemployment less than the NAIRU, which was calculated at the time as 8 per cent) by two percentage points. This was the largest negative gap anywhere in the OECD. What this indicates is that unless unemployment is allowed to rise to at least the NAIRU then real wages in Britain are going to exceed what is warranted by productivity. Supply-side reforms do not appear on this evidence to have affected this conclusion, which also held good during the 1960s and 1970s.

8.3.12 The Reduction of Unemployment

The problem of unemployment is complex, and there can therefore be no simple nostrum to make it disappear. What we have established so far is that sharp, short-term changes in unemployment are normally demand driven, whilst the medium to long-term adjustment takes place on the supply-side.

The use of demand management when demand is deficient in the short term is appropriate where the initial unemployment rate exceeds the NAIRU. For obvious reasons, it is undesirable to use it if there is subsequently going to be an inflationary spiral. Hence, insofar as additional demand is to created, it must be targeted towards those parts of the economy where there is the greatest excess supply. Clearly, however, whenever the actual unemployment rate remains below the NAIRU, the appropriate response must be to improve supply conditions in the labour market.

The range of possibilities is too great to warrant detailed coverage in this section. Some, like incomes policy, are popular in certain quarters, although only in a more flexible form than has been customary in the past. It is unlikely, however, that they will find favour in Conservative Party circles. Others, like training vouchers, are too new to be assessed (but see the discussion in *Economic Affairs*, April 1991, pp. 16–18). Another possibility is to reduce taxation – or perhaps more appropriately, given the need to reduce labour costs, to reduce NICs, either for all workers in regions suffering severe unemployment or for all very low-paid workers. The payment of a working wage combined with minimal NICs is to be preferred to a policy of low wages combined with income support measures, although both may need to be used in practice.

Jobs can be increased by providing subsidies, although an awkward problem in practice is to ensure that subsidies are not offered to an employer to provide jobs which he intended to fill in any case. Equally, subsidies should be directed only towards the provision of the kinds of high-skill jobs which are comparatively rare in the UK compared to its main competitors. Furthermore, subsidies should not be provided simply to deal with short-term problems, but should be associated with the provision of jobs which will be needed over the longer term.

Given that the low skills ethos in much of British industry has something to do with the influx into the labour market of ill-prepared 18 year olds and part-time women workers, it is evident that something needs to be done to improve the long-term career aspirations of these groups. One of the key issues here is to ensure that the basic education, whether academic or vocational, provided both for school children and for those who re-enter the education system as mature entrants is comparable to that provided in successful competitors such as Germany.

All of this may appear rather grandiose in relation to the apparent ability of governments to reform UK institutions in the past, although matters are in hand and are considerably more realistic than President Bush's aspirations to improve education in the USA. Understandably, therefore, there are those who believe that the solution which can be effected very quickly is to introduce a harsher regime for those who are out of work. In fact, as we have noted, the rules relating to eligibility for benefit have been tightened up considerably during the 1980s, and the replacement rate, which stood at nearly 70 per cent in 1970 and remained well above 60 per cent until 1978, fell sharply to 59 per cent in 1979 and to only 41 per cent in 1982. It is currently even lower, and it seems unlikely that 'living off the dole' is any longer a comfortable prospect. Whether the unemployed should be 'forced' to do some kind of 'work' if they are to be entitled to any help from the State at all is even more controversial and unlikely to be implemented.

It is also of crucial importance that information about the availability of jobs is circulated as efficiently as possible. During the 1970s, as disclosed previously, the provision of information about jobs was divorced from the payment of benefits. Job information came to be provided by the Job Centres which at that time were responsible to the MSC, and the payment of benefits was handed over to the DHSS. On the face of it, the Job Centres were very efficient. 40 per cent of vacancies were filled within one day and 68 per cent were filled within two weeks. However, employers notified only those vacancies to Job Centres which they thought they could deal with efficiently and, as noted in **Figure 8.4**, only about one-third of all vacancies are notified to Job Centres.

Information is available on the job search methods of the unemployed from the Labour Force Survey (see *Employment Gazette*, May 1991, pp. 299–300). In 1990, 30 per cent visited a Job

Centre as their main method of job search, 3 per cent less than the proportion that relied primarily upon studying situations vacant columns in newspapers. Answering advertisements and personal contacts each accounted for a further 10 per cent, and direct approaches to firms and employers for 8 per cent. Private agencies were used by only a small minority.

Job Centres were favoured particularly by the younger job seekers, whilst the use of situations vacant columns increased with age and was particularly favoured by married women. Job Centres are used most frequently by the unskilled. As workers grow older and acquire some skills they turn increasingly to the newspapers. In effect, the state appears to provide a subsidised information service for low-income groups.

During the 1970s and well into the 1980s, Job Centres were ill-equipped to deal with the unemployed. One reason for their failure was the divorce of information transmission from both the provision of training and unemployment benefits. In an ideal system, these three functions would be brought together in an effort to assist the unemployed because the three functions address four issues – namely, the matching of an unemployed person with a vacancy; the length of time that a job is likely to last; the savings to the community of a person being permanently employed or placed on a training programme; and the costs to the community of a person being permanently unemployed. Unfortunately, the issues became separated in the 1970s, when the payment of unemployment benefit was handed over to the DHSS and there was no compulsion on the unemployed to use Job Centres. Moreover, when attempts were made to improve the efficiency of Job Centres by cutting costs, the Centres reacted by reducing the amount of assistance to the long-term unemployed, and as a result many of the costs of unemployment were transferred to the DHSS. In 1987, an attempt was made to improve the efficiency of Job Centres by linking advice and assistance through the Job Restart Scheme which was introduced to do something for the long-term unemployed. Nevertheless, there is room for further improvement in methods of information dissemination in the labour market. Layard (*Financial Times*, 27 February 1991) recommends either that the TECs be put in charge of Job Centres or that Job Centres be made responsible for spending the training budget, possibly via the TECs.

Finally, it is worthy of note that reducing the level of unemployment can be made more difficult by legislation introduced for other purposes. For example, the incentive to work has been affected adversely by the Social Security Act 1988. In the housing market the philosophy has been to allow rents to be set at market-clearing levels, both in the private and public rental sectors, and to target subsidies more narrowly upon those **families** unable to afford these rents, rather than to offer subsidies on all rented **houses** via, for example, rent controls. Under the 1988 Act, rent is determined by family income and circumstances, and hence when it rises so does housing benefit paid to eligible families.

As a consequence, recipients of benefit have no incentive to quibble over rent increases. More importantly, where family income rises by £1 there is a deduction of 65 pence in housing benefit and of 15 pence in respect of Community Charge. This obviously creates a severe poverty trap even where incomes are reasonably high if, as in London, rents are also very high.

□ 8.3.13 *Into the 1990s*

As we have seen in **Figure 8.4**, the unemployment rate has turned up again and it is expected to rise sharply during 1991. Both the UK and USA appear to be ahead of other advanced economies in terms of their economic cycle, as can be seen in **Figure 8.13**.

Between 1986 and 1989 employment grew exceptionally rapidly in the UK. During 1988 it began to slow down perceptibly at a time when it was still rising in Japan, France and West Germany (although not in the EC as a whole). During 1990 it collapsed back so rapidly that it fell below the EC average, where it has stayed during 1991. However, the cyclical rebound is also likely to be earlier than elsewhere, and the upturn, when it comes, should cut rapidly into unemploy-

Figure 8.13 *Growth of Unemployment in Selected Countries*[1], *%, 1987–90*

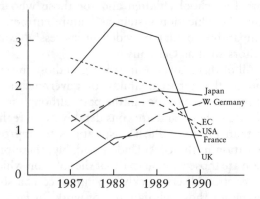

Note:
[1]   Total economy, % changes from previous period, seasonally adjusted at annual rates.
Source: OECD.

ment. Nevertheless, the 1990–91 recession, like that of 1980–82, is certain to result in a further restructuring of the labour market in respect of such matters as manufacturing versus services, male versus female and full-time versus part-time workers.

One thing known with reasonable certainty about the unemployment consequences of the 1990–91 recession is its **regional distribution**. Between April 1990, when unemployment began to rise, and March 1991 unemployment in the South-East rose by almost exactly one-half from 3.6 per cent to 5.5 per cent. Rises of over 40 per cent were sustained in East Anglia and the South-West, and of just under 40 per cent in Greater London. The Midlands suffered rises of roughly one-quarter, with the proportionate rise diminishing strictly in a northerly direction. Indeed, employment actually rose by 0.2 per cent in Scotland and by 0.8 per cent in Northern Ireland.

The unemployment statistics do not reveal the nature of jobs previously held by the newly unemployed. However, it was initially believed that there was a key difference between the 1980–81 recession and that of 1990–91. In the former case, unemployment arose primarily in the northern-based manufacturing sectors, whereas southern-based service sectors emerged largely unscathed. During 1990–91, however, the worst effects were felt in the south with white collar jobs in sectors such as banking and sales particularly hard hit.

Nevertheless, it had become clear by the end of 1990 that manufacturing was sustaining its fair share, if not the majority, of job losses once again. The number of workers in the manufacturing sector fell below 5 mn in February 1991, the lowest level recorded since records began in 1959, when the number stood at just under 8 mn. In particular, it appeared that defence and electronics were especially hard hit, with job losses at least proportionately comparable to those in banking, transport and energy. Redundancies and vacancies notified to the Department of Employment also indicated severe job losses in engineering.

The comparative resilience of the service sector is, however, somewhat misleading because many service sector employers such as banks prefer to slim down by a combination of natural wastage and non-replacement rather than by firing employees, the tactic commonly preferred by manufacturing concerns.

During the 1980–81 recession the vast majority of job losses were sustained by full-time male employees. Not surprisingly, given the huge growth of part-time female jobs during the 1980s, these have been lost in disproportionate numbers during the 1990–91 recession. In February 1991, 0.5 mn females were claiming unemployment benefit compared to 1.5 mn males, but this understates job losses among females since many who lose their jobs are ineligible to claim benefit.

Job losses among different age groups seem to have been fairly evenly dispersed during 1990, with some tendency for 18 and 19 years old to be disproportionately affected. All in all, therefore, it would appear that the structural shift in the pattern of employment brought on by the 1980–81 recession itself ensured that the pattern of rising unemployment would never again be repeated. Nevertheless, it is clearly wishful thinking to believe that the manufacturing concerns which survived that recession have thereby been rendered recession proof.

Finally, it would appear that the onset of recession has had a lagged and rather weak effect upon wage bargaining. As business confidence collapsed

Figure 8.14 *Underlying Earnings, % Change on a Year Earlier*

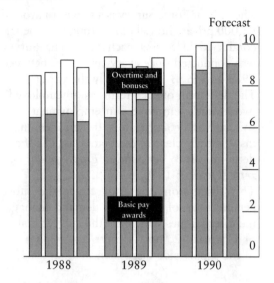

Source: UBS Phillips & Drew.

in Autumn 1990 pay settlements moved in the opposite direction. A survey by Industrial Relation Services of 300 businesses, almost 70 per cent of companies with wage settlements under negotiation, indicated a willingness to give bigger raises than they had a year earlier. Much the same was true of companies expecting to settle early in 1991. The effects can be seen in **Figure 8.14**.

Part of the reason for the escalation in basic pay could be found in evidence that managers and directors were setting a bad example by awarding themselves double-digit salary increases. Quite clearly, also, the prospect of a sharp downturn in corporate profitability had less influence on wage bargaining than a determination to be recompensed for increases in the then rising cost of living. The severe recession of 1980–81 was expected to drive this mentality out of existence once and for all. As inflation has fallen, on certain measures at least, during 1991, earnings have at last began to follow suit. Unfortunately, whilst the short-term battle was won in 1980–88 and may eventually be won again by 1992, the probability is that the ingrained habits of the postwar years were reassert themselves as soon as the recession is over.

Notes

1. The Labour Force Survey is a survey of around 65,000 private households throughout the UK conducted in Spring each year. The Survey was conducted once every two years between 1973 and 1983 and annually thereafter.
2. The definition of such terms as 'unemployed', 'workforce', 'employees in employment' and so forth can be ambiguous. If their meaning is insufficiently clear in the text, a list of official definitions is to be found in *Employment Gazette* (October 1989, p. 567).
3. This discussion does not cover the more general issue of the use of demand management techniques which are the subject matter of Chapter 12, nor is there any replication of the supply-side discussion in Chapter 3.

References

Bird, D. (1990) 'Membership of Trade Unions in 1988', *Employment Gazette* (May).

Bird, D. (1991) 'Industrial Stoppages in 1990', *Employment Gazette* (July).

Bird, D., M. Stevens and A. Yates (1991) 'Membership of Trade Unions in 1989', *Employment Gazette* (June).

Blanchflower, D. (1984) 'Union Relative Wage Effects', *British Journal of Industrial Relations*, pp. 311–22.

Blanchflower, D., N. Millward and A. Oswald (1988) 'Unionisation and Employment Behaviour', *CLE Discussion Paper*, 339.

Brown, W. and S. Wadhwani (1990) 'The Economic Effects of Industrial Relations Legislation Since 1979', *National Institute Economic Review* (February).

Confederation of British Industry (1988) *The Structure and Processes of Pay Determination in the Private Sector* (CBI).

Dawson, G. (1990) 'Interpretation of the Natural Rate of Unemployment', *Economics* (Summer).

Department of Employment (1990a) 'Measures of Unemployment', *Employment Gazette* (October).

Department of Employment (1990b) 'Provisions of the Employment Act 1990', *Employment Gazette* (November).

Disney, G. (1990) 'Trade Union Membership', *British Journal of Industrial Relations* (July).

Freeman, R. and J. Pelletier (1990) 'The Impact of Industrial Relations Legislation on British Trade Union Density', *British Journal of Industrial Relations* (July).

Gregg, P. (1990) 'The Evolution of Special Employment Measures', *National Institute Economic Review* (May).

Hill, S., P. Blyton and A. Gorham (1989) 'The Economics of Manpower Flexibility', *Royal Bank of Scotland Review* (September).

Kelly, J. and R. Bailey (1989) 'British Trade Union Membership, Density and Decline in the 1980s', *Industrial Relations Journal* (Spring).

Layard R. and S. Nickell (1986) 'Unemployment in Britain', *Economica*, 53 (Supplement) S121–S169.

Machin, S. and Wadhwani, S. (1989) 'The Effects of Unions on Organizational Change, Investment and Employment', *CLE Discussion Paper* 335.

Metcalf, D. (1988) 'Trade Unions and Economic Performance: the British Evidence', *London School of Economics*.

Metcalf, D. (1991) 'British Unions: Dissolution or Resurgence?', *Oxford Review of Economic Policy*, 7(1).

Millward, N. and M. Stevens (1986) *British Workplace Industrial Relations 1980–84* (Gower).

Nickell, S. and S. Wadhwani (1989) 'Insider Forces and Wage Determination', *Economic Journal* (June).

Poret, P. (1990) 'The "Puzzle" of Wage Moderation in the 1980s', *OECD Working Paper*, 87 (Paris: OECD).

Spence, A. (1990) 'Labour Force Outlook to 2001', *Employment Gazette* (April).

Stevens, M. and A. Wareing (1990) 'Union Density and Workforce Composition', *Employment Gazette* (November).

■ *Chapter 9* ■

The Labour Market

Peter Curwen

■ *9.1* Education and Training

In the UK there is continuous public debate about how to improve the quality of education and training, and to transform it into something suitable 'for the coming decade'. When the next decade comes along, it is almost universally agreed (except, perhaps by some of the providers who have a vested interest in prolonging existing practices) that education and training have not been transformed and the debate starts up again. By historical standards, technological change has become increasingly rapid of late, and no industrialised country can afford to go without a well educated, well trained workforce. However, it is by no means easy to identify the precise source of the problem, and what should be done to resolve it.

□ *9.1.1 Education*

Up the age of 16 education is **compulsory**. The school leaving age is currently at its highest ever level, partly in order to keep down the numbers of unemployed. It is primarily provided by public sector institutions which for older children conform to a common pattern known as comprehensives. The growth of the independent, private sector attests to widespread dissatisfaction with the quality of primary and secondary education. At the beginning of 1991 Her Majesty's Inspectors of Education reported that the teaching of reading was 'less than satisfactory' in a fifth of the institutions of lower learning which they had visited. At the same time a report by the National Foundation for Educational Research indicated that since 1965 there had been a fall in the reading standards achieved by seven year olds.

Clearly, something is seriously wrong with the state of educational provision, but what exactly, and what should be done to remedy it? It may be argued that parents do most damage by ignoring their children's pre-school education. Certainly, although the school leaving age is quite late by international standards, very few children **volunteer** to continue their education beyond the age of 16. Table 9.1 indicates that until recently just over 30 per cent of 16 year olds have continued their education. In Japan the figure is nearer 70 per cent, and it is also very high in the USA – although there are severe quality problems there also.

Until very recently it was customary to sit either Ordinary ('O)-level or Certificate of Secondary Education (CSE) examinations at the age of 15 or 16. 'O'-levels were 'academic' and seen as the test of suitability for further years spent in school, whereas CSE candidates were mostly expected to move straight out into the labour market. On the whole, it was generally accepted that these school leavers were insufficiently educated for the needs of an advanced society.

All school children now sit a common General

Table 9.1   *Education and Labour Market Status of Young People, %, 1984–89, Great Britain*

	1984	1985	1986	1987	1988	1989	1990
16–18 year olds							
Total population[1]	100	100	100	100	100	100	100
Full-time education							
School[2]	17.2	17.1	17.1	16.9	17.2	18.4	19.3
Further education[3]	13.7	13.8	14.0	14.4	15.0	15.5	17.1
All	30.9	30.8	31.1	31.3	32.2	33.9	36.4
On YTS[4]	10.1	10.3	10.4	12.3	15.4	15.7	14.8
Other young people:							
Unemployed[5]	16.7	16.2	15.2	13.4	10.1	n/a	n/a
Other (mainly in employment)	42.3	42.6	43.2	42.9	42.3	n/a	n/a
All	59.0	58.9	58.5	56.3	52.4	50.4	48.8

Notes:
[1]   Measured in January of each year. Ages as at 31 August of previous year.
[2]   Including independent, maintained and special schools.
[3]   Full-time and sandwich including higher education; excludes those on YTS within colleges.
[4]   Includes those in further education on YTS courses.
[5]   Claimant unemployment; change of definition affects figures from 1989.
Source: Employment Gazette (December 1991) p. 666.

Certificate in Secondary Education (GCSE), but problems remain. For example, despite the great scientific and engineering traditions of nineteenth century Britain, there has developed a strong bias towards arts subject since the war. Compared to countries such as Germany, engineers are held in relatively low esteem and are relatively badly paid in the UK. A weakness in mathematics also goes hand in hand with a weakness in English. One often gets the impression that the inhabitants of countries, especially in Northern Europe where English is a compulsory second language, speak better English than the British.

Stung by these kinds of criticisms the Third Thatcher Government passed an Education Act in 1988 which, although highly controversial, may ultimately be seen as one of its greatest achievements. The underlying premise behind the Act was that control over teaching had to be taken away from the teachers who, in the course of applying 'fashionable' theories about education, were (with the exception of those who use this book!) failing to deliver the well educated workforce which was so desperately needed. During its first two terms in office the Thatcher Government had held off from reform. Now it began the process by introducing a basic core curriculum designed to give all children skills in reading, writing and arithmetic and a passing acquaintance with science. The 10-subject core would be 'assessed' at ages, 7, 11, 14 and 16.

It is noteworthy that the words 'tested' and 'examined' were studiously avoided for fear of an adverse response from the teaching profession. An administrative apparatus was constructed, but this proved too unwieldy because of the excessive burden of assessment. Subsequently, therefore, it was decreed that at the ages of 7 and 11 the national assessments would apply only to 'key aspects' of mathematics, science and English, and that the other seven subjects would be assessed by teachers without the control of a national standard test. Since November 1990 the number of attainment targets in each subject has been reduced, and the 10-subject compulsory GCSE at 16 whittled down. English, mathematics and science are designated core subjects; art and music are no longer compulsory after the age of 14; and history and geography are alternatives in later years.

The target date for completion of these developments is Summer 1997. Meanwhile the teaching profession fights a rearguard action to hold back change, but the battle is lost if only because the prospective Labour government seems intent upon an even tougher regime, including assessment of teachers' performance in the classroom. The key question nevertheless remains to be addressed, namely how to give parity of esteem to technical and vocational subjects so that even those school-children intent upon higher education come to perceive them as more worthy of consideration. In February 1991, the government proposed that 16 year olds could leave school with vocational quali-fications instead of GCSEs. Up to 70 per cent of class time beyond the age of 14 could be spent on vocational study, but this would be of equal rigour to academic study. If this comes to pass the 1988 Act will have evolved considerably from its origi-nal conception.

Given that post-16 education is **voluntary**, there is a choice to be made between continuing in edu-cation, either taking Advanced ('A')-levels in a narrow set of subjects (usually 3) with a view to entry into a university or polytechnic, or a BTEC (Business and Technician Education Council) na-tional diploma of a multi-disciplinary nature. The latter are provided in further education colleges and are intended as an introduction to subjects of relevance in a work environment whereas 'A'-levels are much less work-specific.

The decision to stay on in education is much affected by parental ambitions – graduate parents expect their children to get a degree – and by the relative pay of those who go to work at 16 and those who enter the workforce with qualifications at a later age. The amount of state and parental financial support for those who stay on is also a major factor. Unlike in the USA there is no tradi-tion of 'working one's way through college'. 'A'-levels and degrees are generally done on a full-time attendance basis. The 1980–81 recession also served to drive home the realisation that unemployment typically affects the unskilled and unqualified more harshly than the skilled and those with educa-tional qualifications.

The highly specialised nature of 'A'-level courses is peculiar to Britain (it is broader based in Scot-land than England) and is a major deterrent to those wishing to stay on at school. The proportion of the age cohort who enrol on degree programmes at universities and polytechnics is exceptionally low by international standards. The virtue of this system is that those who take British degrees are on average superior to their counterparts almost everywhere else since excess demand is used to ration by academic quality rather than by price. In addition, the system is very efficient, with a low cost per graduate, since it has a very low drop-out rate by international standards.

The drawbacks are that the system is physically constrained, over-specialised and inflexible, with the consequence that unless a school child does sufficiently well at GCSE to stand a sporting chance of a place on a degree course, or for that matter a place on a BTEC course, he or she tends to drop out as soon as the rules allow.

Further and higher education have also remained very much a middle-class preserve despite the abolition of grammar schools and attempts to im-prove opportunities for children from working-class backgrounds.

The government has been particularly concerned to expand the numbers of those who stay on in mathematics and the sciences. Unfortunately, most of those who stay on are concerned about their job prospects and future incomes, and hence opt for courses in business studies and the professions. Presumably, if there really was a severe shortage of science graduates then relative pay would rise to clear the market, but there is little sign of this happening so far. On the other hand, there is undoubtedly a need for more qualified technicians, and it may be argued that insufficient resources have been invested in further education to meet this objective.

In line with their general philosophy the gov-ernment have tried to make further and higher education more responsive to the market place. There has been a considerable expansion of provi-sion on the basis of reduced fees paid for incre-mental students, although the longer-term effects upon quality are as yet uncertain. However, the physical capacity of the system is the ultimate constraint. Public funding has been progressively withdrawn, forcing institutions to earn their keep in the market place via research, consultancy and full-cost courses. The polytechnics have been re-leased from the grasp of local government and further education colleges seem set to follow suit.

A White Paper in Spring 1991 proposed that higher education should be restructured in order to improve access.

9.1.2 Government Spending on Labour-market Policies

Public sector labour-market measures encompass unemployment pay and 'active employment measures' such as training. The latter have been primarily a phenomenon of the past decade and their incidence is patchy in relation to GDP. On the face of it, as shown in **Figure 9.1**, their incidence is considerably patchier outside the EC (compare Sweden with the USA) than within it. To some extent this latter difference can be ascribed to a preference for private provision within the USA and Japan. It is also evident that the balance between the two kinds of measures is exceptional in Sweden. This does not seem to reduce the overall cost in relation to GDP, at least in the short term, but it may be seen as preferable from a social welfare perspective.

Unemployment benefits do not correlate at all closely with the rate of unemployment. The rate of unemployment in Denmark is roughly average for the EC, but unemployment benefits are set at a very high level. By comparison, Italy appears to be positively mean (a more easily forgiven deficiency in the case of much poorer countries such as Greece and Portugal). Britain's spending on training is widely criticised domestically, but as can be seen it

Figure 9.1   *Government Spending on Labour Market Policies as % of GDP*[1]

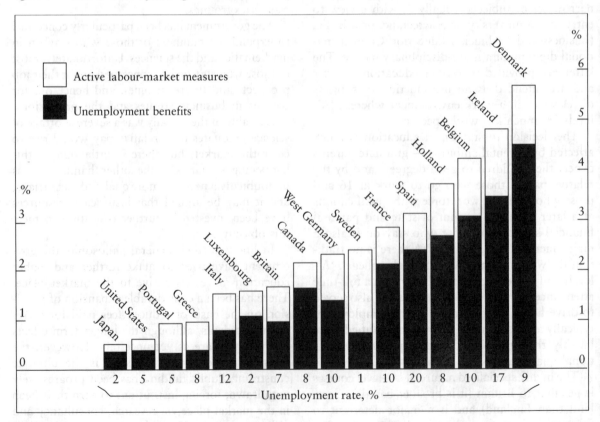

Note:
[1]   1989 or latest.
Source: The Economist.

Table 9.2 *Training Expenditure, £ mn*

	Cash Prices	Constant (1990–91) Prices
1975–76	171.7	620.2
1978–79	377.3	954.3
1989–90	2658.8	2871.5

Source: Employment Gazette (January 1991) p. 39.

is not unfavourable **in relation to the rate of unemployment** compared to most of the EC.

Table 9.2 indicates the scale of publically funded expenditure on training in both nominal and real terms in various years. As can be seen it has escalated rapidly over the past decade. This is a little surprising given the government's preference for market solutions to problems such as a shortfall in skills. However, if companies are reluctant to instigate training programmes on a voluntary basis, and if the government is unwilling to compel them to do so, then either much training is publically funded or it is non-existent.

Traditionally, training in the UK took place 'on the job'. In the case of craftsmen this involved an apprenticeship supplemented by City and Guilds examinations. The first significant state intervention came with the Industrial Training Act 1964. This Act created **training boards** which were to be financed mainly by levies on firms with a supplement from the State. The boards consisted of representatives of employers, trade unions and civil servants.

The justification for the levies was that instead of training their own workers many firms preferred to poach workers from other firms that did. The levies could then be returned only to those firms that incurred training costs by way of compensation for the benefits transferred to the poachers. However, the levies were generally unpopular with employers who argued that investment in training would be worthwhile only if the skills acquired by their workers were specific to their particular business, since such skills could not, by definition, be poached. Where skills were general, and hence could be used in a variety of firms and industries, it would not be sensible for an individual firm to invest heavily in training since trained workers would subsequently be able to sell their skills to the highest bidder. In effect, the investment yielded benefits to the individual rather than to the firm.

But even if poaching could be prevented it might not pay a firm to invest in training. If workers are performing well in their present jobs they will often want to move on to more challenging tasks. Yet if they are trained to do them, they may simply become even more anxious to move on to yet more demanding jobs which are unavailable unless the workers move to other firms. The lack of **transferable skills** may be the only thing which keeps workers from quitting many firms.

It may be argued that any workers who realise that the acquisition of skills will result in a much higher wage will finance their acquisition themselves. However, this will often be successful only if their firms allow them time off to train, if the unions lend their support and if there are readily available funds for this purpose. Government help to overcome these potential hurdles may thus be more sensible than trying to browbeat reluctant employers into policies which they do not perceive as self-serving.

Given the attitude of many employers it is hardly surprising that the shortage of trained workers proved to be persistent, and the decision was taken in the early 1970s to create a national training programme under the umbrella of the Manpower Services Commission (MSC), a semi-autonomous body set up separately from the Department of Employment in 1973. The MSC operated a corporatist strategy in that it tried to obtain a consensus view about what the problems were and what should be done about them, rather than attempting to force its own strategy upon reluctant employers and unions. The system it created was that inherited by the Thatcher Government in 1979.

The history of labour-market measures since 1975 is summarised in **Table 9.3**. Most of these measure have been terminated, and space does not permit a detailed discussion of their contents (but see Gregg, 1990, pp. 49–52).

From 1974 to 1979 the Labour Government concentrated upon the traditional approach of creating more demand for labour, especially for spe-

Table 9.3   Employment and Training Schemes, Great Britain, 1975/76 to 1990/91

Scheme	Incentives for employers to maintain current employment	Incentives for employers to raise employment	Direct employment by government or its agencies	Work sharing or reducing labour supply	Training-based schemes	Other	Initials	Introduced in	Phased out in	Replaced by	Live Cases. 1 July 1991 (000)
Restart Interviews						✓	RI	86/87	Live	X	890
Employment Training Scheme					✓		ET	88/89	Live	X	240
Job Training Scheme					✓		JTS	85/86	88/89	ET	
Youth Training Scheme					✓		YTS	83/84	Live	X	400
Work Experience Programme					✓		WEP	76/77	78/79	YOP	
Jobshare				✓			JS	87/88	Live	X	0.1
Job Release Scheme				✓			JRS	76/77	Live	X	1.1
Community Programme			✓				CP	82/83	88/89	ET	
Community Enterprise Programme			✓				CEP	81/82	82/83	CP	
Special Temporary Employment Progamme			✓				STEP	78/79	81/82	CEP	
Job Creation Programme			✓				JCP	75/76	78/79	STEP	
Jobstart Allowance		✓					JA		Live	X	0.5
Enterprise Allowance Scheme		✓					EAS	82/83	Live	X	50
New Workers Scheme		✓					NWS	86/87	88/89	X	
Young Workers Scheme		✓					YWS	81/82	86/87	NWS	
Small Firms Employment Subsidy		✓					SFES	77/78	80/81	X	
Youth Opportunities Programme		✓					YOP	78/79	82/83	YTS	
Youth Employment Subsidy		✓					YES	77/78	78/79	YOP	
Recruitment Subsidy for School Leavers		✓					RSSL	75/76	76/77	YES	
Temporary Short-Time Working Compensation Scheme	✓						TSTWC	78/79	84/85	X	
Temporary Employment Scheme	✓						TES	75/76	78/79	TSTWC	

Note:

[1]   This is not by any means a complete version; see example, *Training Statistics 1990* (HMSO) p. 35.

Source: Department of Employment; Gregg (1990).

cific groups of workers and in specific locations. Subsidies such as the Temporary Employment Scheme (TES), Youth Employment Subsidy (YES) and Small Firms Employment Subsidy (SFES) were the primary instrument to achieve this, with a little help from the Job Release Scheme (JRS) on the supply side. The use of training-based schemes was very modest until the Youth Training Scheme (YTS) was initiated in 1983.

The Thatcher Government largely forsook the traditional approach, which raised the demand for labour at the existing wage, in favour of wage flexibility designed to match supply and demand at an acceptable level of employment. This initially involved the Young Workers' Scheme (YWS) followed by the New Workers' Scheme (NWS). From 1983 onwards it placed considerable emphasis upon training-based schemes, primarily the YTS, but for adults also after the inception of the Job Training Scheme (JTS) in 1986.

Coupled with Restart and benefit regulations that require active job search, as noted by Gregg (1990) 'it produces a consistent policy response if the problem of unemployment persistence is too high reservation wages and too little job search by the unemployed, coupled with growing problems with skill acquisition by the young, skill maintenance when unemployed and a skills mismatch'.

The **Restart Programme** was introduced in 1986, and was aimed at the long-term unemployed. Initially, anyone unemployed for one year or longer was invited to an interview at a Job Centre and offered opportunities designed to help him or her back to employment. In 1987 coverage was extended to anyone unemployed for six months or longer. Currently, the opportunities on offer include an interview for a job; a place on Employment Training; a place on a Restart Course; a Jobstart Allowance; a place on an Enterprise Allowance Scheme; or a place in a Jobclub. **Jobclubs** aim to help people who have been unemployed for six months or more by providing help in finding jobs and free facilities such as telephones and stationery.

The particular problems of **youth unemployment**, which arose in the late 1970s, led initially to the Youth Opportunity Programme (YOP). In 1983 this was replaced by the YTS and was expanded to cover almost all 16 year olds not in education. The YTS placed greater emphasis upon training at employers' premises. In 1986 the YTS was itself expanded to provide a two-year structured period of training and work experience for 16 year old school leavers and a one-year period for 17 year old school leavers. Subsequently, benefit entitlement was withdrawn for those who did not participate, effectively compelling all those eligible to join.

In 1990 the YTS comprised the largest of the three main strands of government policy in the labour market. The second was the **Enterprise Allowance Scheme** (EAS), first introduced on a national scale in 1983 to help those setting up their own business. It provides a weekly subsidy for up to a year for a claimant who must invest modestly in his or her own business. About one-half of EAS ventures last six months beyond the termination of the subsidy.

The dominant adult scheme in current usage is **Employment Training** (ET), introduced in September 1988 with the slogan 'Training the workers without jobs to do the jobs without workers'. ET replaced 34 pre-existing schemes, but only two were nationally significant, namely the Community Programme (CP) and the Job Training Scheme (JTS). ET inherited some 250,000 people from these schemes. Its objectives were, firstly, to give the long-term unemployed the skills which they needed to get and keep jobs and, secondly, to guarantee a training opportunity for all those aged 18 to 24 who had been unemployed for between six and twelve months and for all those aged 18 to 50 who had been unemployed for more than two years.

The scheme normally runs for six months, occasionally for twelve, so the 300,000 places were expected to handle roughly 550,000 people a year.

The unemployed are allocated to training agents (who may be employees' or employers' organisations) and whilst on ET continue to receive benefits as though they were unemployed plus a training allowances and, if eligible, Income Support and travelling expenses. In addition, training managers are allowed to make discretionary payments without affecting benefits or liabilities for tax.

As noted previously, ET is closely tied up with the Restart Programme. Of the 890,000 interviewed in January 1991, the largest proportion of those (roughly 75 per cent) who took up an offer of some kind ended up in ET. An assessment of ET based upon the follow up survey of scheme leavers can be found in *Labour Market Quarterly Review* (November 1990).

The MSC subsequently evolved into the **Training Commission**. In 1987 the government proposed a New Training Initiative which the unions objected to on the grounds of under-funding. As a result, the government decided in September 1988 to absorb the former MSC within the Department of Employment under the umbrella of a new **Training Agency**. This Agency would operate in tandem with the **Employment Service** formed in 1987 to bring together unemployment benefit, Job Centre and other services centred on the unemployed.

In the White Paper on training (*Employment for the 1990s*, Cmnd 540, 1988) the government went a stage further by setting in motion a restructuring of training through the establishment of 82 locally based, employer-led **Training and Enterprise Councils** (TECs) in England and Wales, together with 70 local councils in Scotland. The Department of Employment then invited local groups of employers to submit proposals for setting up the TECs which were given responsibility for drawing up local training programmes, arranging for their delivery by signing up providers including voluntary organisations, stimulating enterprise and building better industry/education links. TECs started off by signing a contract with the Training Agency. All 82 TECs were contracted up by October 1990, with 31 fully operational and 51 in the development phase, some two years ahead of schedule. At least two-thirds of a TEC Board of Directors must be top private sector business leaders with the balance drawn from local authorities, trade unions, the voluntary sector, education and others.

In November 1990, the Treasury announced that, because of a simultaneous fall in the numbers of unemployed and of teenagers, expenditure per head on training had been growing rapidly since the mid-1980s and that this growth needed to be restrained. They accordingly proposed to cut the Department of Employment's budget by £120mn in 1990–91 and by in excess of £300mn in 1991–92, with the biggest reductions falling on the programmes for training unemployed adults. The rationale for this was that many of the long-term unemployed did not benefit from training: rather, they needed help and encouragement with job search. The dumbstruck TEC directors were then recommended to make up the shortfall by raising money from the private sector just as a recession was officially recognised to be in existence.

TEC directors were left facing difficult choices. They were unenthusiastic about using up their funds, at a time of rising unemployment, solely on managing anti-unemployment schemes such as ET and YTS. On the other hand, few felt themselves to be in a strong position to raise private finance for innovatory programmes. Given that one-quarter of TEC income is to be related to the gaining of qualifications, fears were expressed that TECs would concentrate upon the provision of intensive courses for people who are easy to train, and largely ignore the needs of the handicapped and ex-prisoners who need basic, expensive education if they are to become employable.

Subsequently, there was a heated debate about the extent of the cuts. In March 1991 The Employment Secretary, in the face of a barrage of criticism, restored £120mn to ET financing, and then claimed the remaining cuts amounted to only a 4 per cent reduction after adjusting for start-up costs. Everyone else quoted much larger reductions. In late March a further £55mn was allocated to the Employment Service in order to improve the interface between claimants and benefits staff, as well as to provide interviews to claimants who want them after 13 weeks instead of the present Restart interviews provided only after six months of unemployment.

A £340mn temporary work scheme was also proposed, but the Treasury pulled back on the grounds that it was an inappropriate way to deal with long-term unemployment. In any event, the Department of Employment had been unable to obtain a consensus with the TECs as to whether the scheme should include training and whether it should be run by the TECs or the Employment Service.

The issue of qualifications also generated much debate. The **National Council for Vocational Qualifications** (NCVQ) was set up in 1986 to accredit and standardise qualifications awarded by others, roughly in line with practices elsewhere in the EC. Unfortunately, because it has been poorly publicised; appears not to be independent of those it is assessing; has opted to rationalise rather than to replace the existing chaotic system of qualifications; and over-grades (NVQ levels from 1 to 5) compared to, for example, West Germany, it has failed to make much impression so far (see also *National Institute Economic Review*, August 1990, pp. 56–7 for a discussion of Britain's inadequacies compared to France).

On 1 April 1991, the Department of Employment handed over control of its training budget to the TECs. It simultaneously (27 March 1991) launched a £120mn scheme to give adolescents in 11 areas training vouchers called Training Credits, worth from £500 to £5000, to spend on an approved training scheme of their choice (*Employment Gazette*, May 1991, p. 248). Under the provisions of the 1991 Budget income tax relief was introduced for vocational training.

In May a White Paper was published entitled *Education and Training for the 21st Century*. Its main proposals were (**1**) to extend the provision of Training Credits to every 16 and 17 year old by 1996; (**2**) to introduce two new diplomas – one Ordinary and one Advanced – which will combine academic and work-related qualifications; (**3**) to extend the use of the National Record of Achievement for school leavers.

In July the Employment Secretary announced a new package of measures to help the unemployed. A new programme called **Unemployment Action** will offer up to 60,000 long-term unemployed people in a full year the chance to keep their skills up to date by work experience on local projects. It will pay only state benefits plus £10 a week, and be administered by the TECs. The rest of the package will provide (**1**) new help for more than 100,000 people a year in finding a job (primarily the newly unemployed); (**2**) 15,000 extra places on Employment Training; (**3**) 100,000 extra opportunities in the Jobclub programme; (**4**) expansion of Restart courses. As a result help will be provided for 900,000 unemployed people in 1992–93 at an additional cost of £230 mn. An additional £110 mn is also being made available in 1991–92.

9.1.3 *Skill Shortages and Their Consequences*

The only consistent indicator of skill shortages comes from the CBI Quarterly Industrial Trends Survey which covers Great Britain. What this showed, as in **Figure 9.2**, on the face of it perversely, was that as unemployment rose rapidly during the first half of the 1980s so did shortages of skills. In 1982 roughly 2.5 per cent of manufacturing companies cited skill shortages as a constraint on output. By October 1988 this figure had risen to 28 per cent. By this time unemployment was falling progressively, yet in January 1991 the figure had fallen back to 6 per cent.

Skill shortages are location specific, and are understandably most acute in newly established high-technology companies. In the face of an inflexible supply of qualified personnel companies respond either by bidding workers away from one another, which is something of a zero-sum game, the main consequence of which is to escalate wage inflation, or by resorting to extensive overtime. If the response of the government to such upwards pressures on wages is to curb demand to the point of generating widespread unemployment, then skill shortages can be viewed as a primary cause of the deterioration in the unemployment/inflation trade-off previously discussed.

What is evident is that, first, the disappearance of skill shortages during the period 1988–1990 did not result in any downwards pressure on earnings growth. Secondly, the high of 28 per cent in 1988 was nevertheless well below the peaks recorded in the 1960s and early 1970s, whilst the low of 6 per cent was only just above the 5 per cent recorded in July 1980. Given that July 1980 and January 1991 represent almost identical points in successive eco-

Figure 9.2   *Expectations of Skill Shortages* [1,2], *Great Britain, 1972–90*

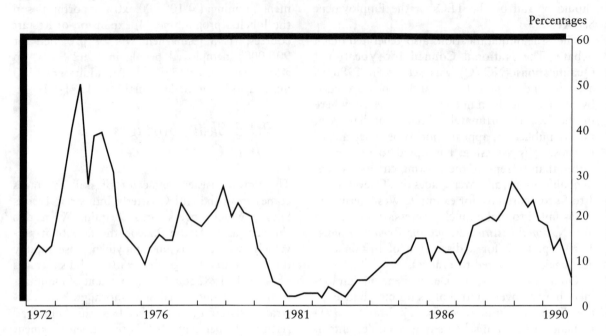

Percentages

Notes:
[1]   % of manufacturing firms expecting skill shortages to limit output over the next 4 months.
[2]   The survey is carried out in January, April, July and October of each year.
Source: CBI Quarterly Industrial Trends Survey.

nomic cycles, it is evident that the pattern of skill shortages is consistent over time and cannot, therefore, have had more than a marginal impact upon the unemployment/inflation trade-off. It therefore follows that this trade-off will not be improved other than marginally through improved training.

It is further alleged that the UK's relatively poor productivity performance can be blamed, in good part, upon the shortage of skills. This is a highly contentious matter since there must inevitably be considerable uncertainty over the boost to productivity to be expected from a given programme of education and/or training. This is not to downplay the virtues of education and training: rather it is to remind ourselves that they cannot provide a miracle cure for the economy's ills in isolation. If they are combined with a German system of collective bargaining then the effects are going to be rather better than where they are combined with the system in the UK.

■ 9.2 Trade Unions

In their manifesto of 1979 the Conservative party stated that 'a fair balance between the rights and objectives of unions, management and the community in which they work is essential to economic recovery'. By this, they meant that the balance needed to be tilted away from the unions and towards management and the community. As the manifesto went on to say: 'We cannot go on, year after year, tearing ourselves apart in increasingly bitter and calamitous industrial disputes. In bringing about economic recovery, we should all be on the same side'.

It is not difficult to discern why the manifesto inferred that everyone was not on the same side in 1979. Trade unionism is essentially a twentieth century phenomenon. Illegal prior to 1824, unions spent the first 50 years of their legal existence primarily as organisations of craft workers. Hence membership grew slowly despite the widespread

Figure 9.3   *Trade Union Membership, UK, 1901–91, mn*

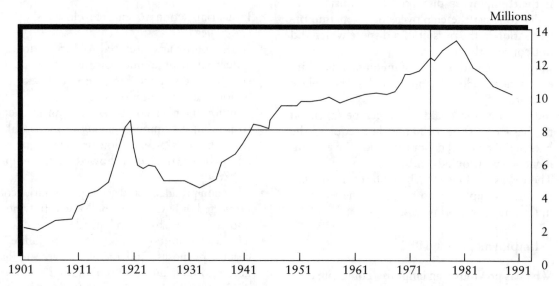

Source: Department of Employment; Certification Office.

onset of industrialisation. At the turn of the century, where we pick up the data on union membership in **Figure 9.3** above, membership was still modest, but the unions were beginning to make their voices heard in the face of the adverse trading conditions faced by the UK economy at the time. The erosion of the UK's pre-eminent position as a producer and exporter of manufactures, combined with the massive transfer of workers out of agriculture, depressed wages and caused unemployment.

During the period 1906–13 the government granted immunities to unions from damages incurred in contemplation or furtherance of trade disputes and introduced minimum wage legislation. After 1914 unionism spread rapidly into the transport, energy and iron and steel industries, and unions secured a political power base by putting their voting power behind the newly formed Labour party. During the 1920s unions flexed their muscles, as in the General Strike of 1926 which, whilst it was a failure, established the political power of organised labour.

During the decades after 1945 the trade union movement grew enormously in both economic and political strength such that, by the 1970s, it effectively held the Labour party in thrall and demanded a say in the governing of the country. The attempt by the Labour party to disengage, in accordance with the conditions imposed by the International Monetary Fund in 1976, eventually led to the 'Winter of Discontent' which ushered in the first Thatcher Government.

This government had no intention of allowing the unions any say in the political process. On the other hand, it could do little immediately to strip the unions of their accumulated privileges and immunities. A more immediate weapon was the 1980–81 recession which caused vast numbers of union members to lose their jobs, causing union membership to fall away progressively from its 1979 peak (see **Figure 9.3**).

During the 1980s the successive Thatcher Governments put in place a new legislative framework which redefined, in a cumulative fashion, the role of unions in the economy. There were six main pieces of legislation.

The Employment Act 1980

- Employers were given the power to take legal action where strikers sought to disrupt business at a workplace other than their own – known as **secondary picketing**.

- They were also empowered to take legal action if their employees disrupted their business in order to assist the employees of a separate organisation in the pursuit of a dispute which did not concern them directly.
- Employees could opt out of union membership, even where a closed shop existed at their place of work.
- Industrial action could no longer be taken on the basis of a show of hands, but required the backing of a postal ballot for which the government would provide funds.
- There was no longer to be a statutory obligation upon employers to recognise the rights of unions at their workplaces.

The Employment Act 1982

- Whereas previously an employer could cite only individual union organisers when taking legal action in respect of disruptions to his business, he could now take action against the union itself.
- Where a strike was **political** – that is, it involved neither employment matters nor a dispute between an employer and his own employees – an employer could seek redress from his striking employees.
- Any contract which sought to enforce the exclusive use of union members would be deemed to be illegal.
- Where a closed shop had not been approved by an overwhelming majority of the workforce, its provisions could not be legally enforced upon either an employer or dissenting employees.

The Trade Union Act 1984

- All elections for senior union posts would have to be by secret (generally postal) ballot.
- Unless a strike ballot was held by means of a secret vote, an employer could sue the organising union for damages.
- A union would be required to ballot its members every 10 years if it wished to maintain a fund for political purposes.

The Employment Act 1988

- Industrial action to enforce closed shops became illegal.
- If a union member refused to participate in an industrial dispute, and his union subsequently sought to discipline him, he could take legal action against the union.
- A union member could take out an injunction to prevent his union engaging in industrial action without a prior ballot, or engaging in such action before the ballot showed a clear majority in favour.
- All union presidents and general secretaries could be elected only where the ballot was fully postal and supervised by an independent body.
- The use of union funds was to be limited to certain purposes, and members were to have access to their union's accounts.
- A Commission for Union Affairs was to be established in order to finance union members wishing to take legal action against their union.

The Employment Act 1989

The 1978 Employment Protection (Consolidation) Act was amended to limit the duties in respect of which an employer was required to allow officials of a recognised trade union time off with pay. The Act was also amended to ease other burdens on employers.

The Employment Act 1990

This Act was passed on 1 November 1990, and contained the following key provisions (*Employment Gazette*, November 1990, pp. 567–70):

- It became unlawful to refuse to employ a person because he or she is, or is not, a trade union member, or because he or she will not agree to become or cease to be a member, and that any person refused employment for such a reason may complain to an industrial tribunal.
- It removed the immunities under section 13 of the Trade Union and Labour Relations Act 1974 for acts in contemplation or furtherance of trade disputes involving calling for, or otherwise or-

ganising, 'secondary' action unless made in the course of peaceful picketing as the law allows.

- It extended existing legislation which enabled employees (and others) to take action in tort against a union which calls for industrial action without holding a proper secret ballot.
- It extended section 15 of the Employment Act 1982, which prescribed circumstances in which a union is legally responsible for organising industrial action. In particular, if any union shop steward calls for industrial action, his union will be liable unless and until it effectively repudiates what he has done as soon as reasonably practicable.
- It gave employers greater freedom to dismiss employees taking part in unofficial action.

□ 9.2.1 Trade Union Membership

A list of trade unions is maintained by the Certification Office of Trade Unions and Employers' Associations in accordance with section 8 of the Trade Union and Labour Relations Act 1974. Section 28 contains the definition of a union, primarily in terms of a requirement that it is an organisation of workers which has the regulation of relations between workers and employers as one of its principal purposes. All listed and unlisted unions are required under section 11 to submit annual returns, which include membership figures, to the Certification Officer.

The number of unions recorded by the Certification Office is somewhat different from that recorded by the Employment Department (which we use below) because the latter counts only 'parent' unions, such as the National Union of Mineworkers, and includes unions with their head office in Northern Ireland.

Figures for union membership are those provided by the Employment Department which are compatible with those of the Certification Office for the UK as a whole. However, membership figures which are also now available, as a result of a question included for the first time on the 1989 Labour Force Survey, are calculated in a manner which gave a membership figure for Spring 1989 as 9.1 mn compared to the Employment Depart-

ment's figure of 10.2 mn. The 1.1 mn discrepancy arises because the LFS count excludes those who were unemployed, wholly retired or overseas at the time of counting. In addition, the LFS counts individuals in membership rather than individual memberships, whereas the Certification Office counts the number of memberships even if individuals belong to more than one union.

Figure 9.3 illustrates the long-term membership trend. As can be seen, although membership slumped during the 1920s for reasons indicated in Chapter 1, it rose steadily from the early 1930s to a peak of 13.3 mn in 1979. Subsequently, it has been downhill all the way, with the 1990 figure standing at an estimated 10.0 mn, a reduction of 25 per cent from the peak figure.

Table 9.4 provides data for both union membership and the number of unions for the period after 1974. The sharp downturn in membership during 1981 and 1982 comes as no surprise given the severity of the recession at the beginning of the decade, but it is surprising to note that the previously noted upturn in employment from 1986 onwards failed to reverse the downwards trend.

In part, this can be attributed to inefficient practices among the unions themselves. Workplaces where unions are recognised encompass roughly 60 per cent of the workforce, yet one-third of these workers are not union members. Under such circumstances it is easy to give up union membership without the expectation of disapproval by fellow workers. It is also the case that entrepreneurial (and, often, medium-sized) firms are neglected by union officials who prefer to service existing agreements with larger companies. The old-style bargaining methods utilised by male officials are also unlikely to strike a sympathetic chord in a modern factory full of female part-time workers.

It is reasonable to argue that the growth of female part-time workers and of small companies would have caused some erosion of union membership even if officials had tried harder to recruit in non-traditional ways. Nevertheless, there is evidence to suggest that the attitude towards unions in different types of workplace is a more critical factor. In general, managers in large companies with full-time workforces are happy to foster union membership in order to simplify bargaining

Table 9.4   *Trade Unions: Numbers and Membership, UK, 1974–89*

	No. of Unions	Total Membership Mn	As a % of Civilian Workforce in Employment [1]	% Change in Membership Since Previous Year
1974	507	11.8	47.6	+2.7
1975[2]	501	12.2	49.4	+3.6
1975	470	12.0	48.6	n/a
1976	473	12.4	50.5	+3.0
1977	481	12.8	52.4	+3.7
1978	462	13.1	52.6	+2.1
1979	453	13.3	52.8	+1.3
1980	438	12.9	52.9	−2.6
1981	414	12.1	51.0	−6.5
1982	408	11.6	49.8	−4.2
1983	394	11.2	47.4	−3.1
1984	375	11.0	45.6	−2.2
1985	370	10.8	44.6	−1.6
1986	335	10.5	43.2	−2.6
1987	330	10.5	41.5	−0.6
1988	315	10.4	39.8	−0.9
1989	309	10.2	37.9	−2.1

Notes:
[1]   As at December for years 1978 onwards, previously based on mid-year estimates.
[2]   31 organisations previously regarded as trade unions are excluded from 1975 onwards because they failed to satisfy the statutory definition of a trade union in section 28 of the Trade Union and Labour Relations Act 1974.
Source: Department of Employment.

arrangements. Where the employers in small companies also seek to encourage unions there is typically an equally high membership ratio. Where, however, such companies – almost all of which operate in the private sector whereas many of the largest employers operate in the public sector – discourage membership it is typically only one-third as high.

It is often believed that workers are much more likely to join unions in the traditional manufacturing regions as compared to the south east. However, the significant switch of employment to the south east does not, of itself, seem to have had much effect upon union membership. Rather, the explanation is to be found in the points outlined above, namely that the type of company shedding labour in the north is much more likely to encourage membership than the newer companies taking on labour in the south east.

Furthermore, there is no reason to attribute the decline in membership to the switch from unskilled to relatively skilled and managerial occupations. If anything, the latter group appear to have a more favourable image of unions than their unskilled counterparts. On the other hand, as suggested above, the unions themselves may show less enthusiasm for recruiting among their ranks.

In recent years a number of highly publicised confrontations, such as the 1980 dispute at News International, have given the impression that attempts by employers to derecognise unions have accounted for a major decline in membership. Such incidents, however, have been relatively rare and the effects of derecognition correspondingly insignificant.

It would appear, therefore, that the switch from public sector to private sector employment, from manufacturing to services, and from male to female employment has been instrumental in loosening the grip of unions on the workforce, and that the unions themselves have done little to counteract these trends. It should also be noted that the unions are not perceived by their members as delivering a satisfactory service. Only about one in ten workers, whether unionised or not, believes that unions are successful in defending the rights of workers. Nevertheless, this does not appear to make workers feel hostile towards unions, nor does it appear to explain why more than a modest proportion – roughly 15 per cent according to a 1989 Nuffield College study – give up their membership.

In conclusion, it would appear to be the case that, as the industrial structure has evolved, employees have become increasingly disenchanted with traditional trade unionism and that the unions have failed to respond to the challenge. During the latter part of the 1980s the environment was at least modestly positive for a turnaround in the trend of membership decline, but the opportunity was not grasped and is unlikely to recur in 1990s.

□ 9.2.2 Trade Union Numbers

As shown in **Table 9.4**, the number of unions has fallen from roughly 500 in 1975 to roughly 300 in 1990. The number peaked at 1384 in 1920, and numbers fell steadily thereafter with the exception of 1973 and 1977 when small increases were recorded. In fact, new unions are constantly being formed – there were 10 in 1988 – but mergers and transfers of membership have been the dominant factor throughout the period.

Figure 9.4 *Membership and Number of Unions, by Size, 1989*

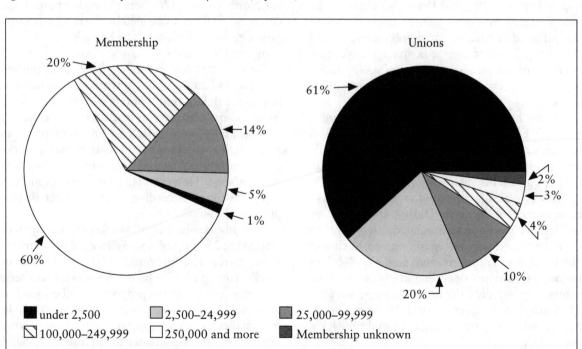

Source: Employment Gazette (June 1991) p. 339.

Even today most unions are small. In 1989 almost one-half of all unions had fewer than 1000 members, accounting for 0.3 per cent of total membership. By way of contrast the 23 largest unions, each with more than 100,000 members, accounted for 81 per cent of total membership and the 10 largest unions, each with more than 250,000 members, accounted for 60 per cent of total membership. The most recently available data are presented in **Figure 9.4**.

□ 9.2.3 Trade Union Finances

Falling memberships, coupled with a failure to raise subscriptions as a proportion of members' earnings, have resulted in a steady decline in the primary source of income for virtually all unions. Whether this creates severe financial problems depends, however, upon their spending. Where unions take on large numbers of full-time officials and push for expansion, as in the 1970s, spending tends to outrun revenue and causes a reduction in real net worth (which almost halved for registered unions between 1965 and 1980). Whereas real net worth rose by over one-quarter during the 1980s, this reflected in part, as noted previously, the failure by the unions to engage in an aggressive membership drive in smaller workplaces where, due to lack of co-operation by management, recruitment was costly.

Unions have sought to save costs by merging together, but this has often been a financial disaster due to inaccuracies in the accounts of smaller unions and their tendency to exaggerate their memberships and hence their subscription income. The salaries of officials also tend to be boosted as a consequence of mergers. During the 1980s the careful investment of accumulated reserves helped to offset these costs, but many unions, even such giants as the Transport and General Workers' Union, are currently operating at a loss and hence eating very rapidly into those reserves, which in 1988 stood at an average of 1.25 times average expenditure compared with a multiple of 4.1 in the early 1950s.

As a consequence, the unions will have to pull in their horns during the 1990s and cannot be expected to try and enlarge their membership, although there are exceptions, typically in the public sector such as NALGO, which are still very prosperous. Equally, spending on benefits, which constituted 32 per cent of total spending in 1950, will continue to decline from the 12 per cent recorded in 1986.

□ 9.2.4 Union Density

'Union density' is simply the number of individuals in each category who are members of either a trade union, staff association, or both, expressed as a percentage of all individuals in that category. It is possible to obtain data using this 'tight' definition through the Labour Force Survey (LFS), although alternative measures are also available using somewhat different definitions (see *Employment Gazette*, August 1990, p. 413).

Table 9.5 summarises the data on union density in Spring 1989 for Great Britain and Northern Ireland separately. The overall density for employees in Britain was 39 per cent. It was 49 per cent for Northern Ireland, where the higher percentage can most easily be explained by the relatively large public sector (which tends to be highly unionised) compared to Britain.

Density was higher among males than among females, and among manual workers compared to non-manual. Full-time workers were twice as likely to be union members as part-time workers. All these findings were closely in line with previous research. The difference in density between workers in manufacturing and non-manufacturing was quite modest. However, sharp differences in density were found according to the number of employees per workplace.

Roughly one-half of all workers in workplaces employing 25 or more employees were union members, twice the proportion to be found in workplaces employing between 6 and 24 workers, and over four times the proportion to be found in workplaces employing fewer than 6 workers. In the smallest workplaces male density rates were one and a half times greater than those for females (14 per cent as against 9 per cent), but the overall density is depressed by the relatively high propor-

Table 9.5   *Union Density in the UK, Spring 1989, %*

	Great Britain		Northern Ireland	
	No. 000	Density %	No. 000	Density %
Male	11 862	44	262	51
Female	10 187	33	226	47
Non-manual	12 357	35	249	51
Manual	9 659	43	235	47
Manufacturing				
(2–4)	5 434	41	106	55
Non-manufacturing				
(0, 1, 5–9)	16 584	37	379	47
Full-time[1]	17 051	43	397	54
Part-time[1]	4 995	22	91	28
Size of workplace:				
Under 6 employees	2 407	11	}170	}25
6–24 employees	4 378	23		
25 or more employees	14 465	48	316	62
All employees[2]	22 049	39	488	49
Self-employed	3 425	9	87	4
All in employment[3]	25 962	34	595	42

[1]   The definition of full-time and part-time is based on the respondent's own assessment, not on the number of hours usually worked.

[2]   Includes those who did not provide information on one or more of the dimensions reported in the table.

[3]   Includes those on government employment and training programmes and those who did not report their employment status.

[4]   Sample size too small for reliable estimate.

Sources: 1989 Labour Force Survey estimates. *Employment Gazette* (August 1990) p. 404.

tion of females who work in small workplaces. The only density rate which was found to be lower was, predictably enough, among the self-employed.

The LFS estimates revealed (*Employment Gazette*, August 1990, p. 406) that female part-time employees were roughly twice as likely as their male counterparts to be union members. This appeared to arise because these females were predominantly middle-aged married women who stayed with the same employers for long periods of time, whilst the part-time males tended to be either relatively young or relatively old and treated their jobs in a much more transient manner. The LBS estimates also revealed that whereas West Indian/Guyanese males and females were noticeably more likely to be union members than their white counterparts, the opposite held true for other ethnic origins for males whereas differences for females were insignificant.

According to the LFS, 74 per cent of union members were 30 years of age or older in 1989 compared to 65 per cent of employees in employment, whereas 14 per cent of union members were under 25 compared to 22 per cent of all employees. Interestingly, in 1989 less than one-fifth of all union members (who were employees) were skilled craftsmen, whereas 30 per cent were in managerial and professional occupations. In part, this reflected the high proportion of women in the latter groups (almost 50 per cent) who were members, a higher density both compared to their male counterparts (36 per cent) and especially compared to females in manual occupations (*Employment Gazette*, August 1990, p. 407).

Looked at from an occupational perspective, union densities varied from 69 per cent among education professionals down to 14 per cent for those engaged in selling. Nevertheless, the union movement still consists predominantly of workers in occupations such as clerical and catering where union densities are relatively low.

It is possible to take a more sanguine view of the above when account is taken of the somewhat lower densities in most other EC member countries, and of the overall density of 17 per cent in the USA. It is significant, however, that 60 per cent of US union members work in the private sector whilst the comparable figure for Britain is probably only 27 per cent. Clearly, the unions in the UK need to recruit amongst workers in the private sector, yet that is far harder than in the public sector. On the whole, the evidence indicates that in the private sector non-union plants are more productive and more profitable than their unionised counterparts. Hence non-union workers tend to be better rewarded and to enjoy better relations with

Table 9.6   *Stoppages[1] in Progress, UK, 1967–90*

Year	No. of Recorded Stoppages in Progress	Workers involved in Period (000)	Working Days Lost (000)	Working Days Lost per 1000 Employees[2]
1967	2 133	734	2 787	122
1968	2 390	2 258	4 690	207
1969	3 146	1 665	6 846	303
1970	3 943	1 801	10 980	489
1971	2 263	1 178	13 551	612
1972	2 530	1 734	23 909	1 080
1973	2 902	1 528	7 197	317
1974	2 946	1 626	14 750	647
1975	2 332	809	6 012	265
1976	2 034	668	3 284	146
1977	2 737	1 166	10 142	448
1978	2 498	1 041	9 405	413
1979	2 125	4 608	29 474	1 273
1980	1 348	834	11 964	521
1981	1 344	1 513	4 266	195
1982	1 538	2 103	5 313	248
1983	1 364	574	3 754	178
1984	1 221	1 464	27 135	1 278
1985	903	791	6 402	299
1986	1 074	720	1 920	90
1987	1 016	887	3 546	164
1988	781	790	3 702	166
1989	701	727	4 128	182
1990	630	298	1 903	83

Notes:
[1] The statistics relate to stoppages of work in the UK due to industrial disputes between employers and workers, or between workers and other workers, connected with terms and conditions of employment. Work to rules and go-slows are not included nor are stoppages involving fewer than ten workers or lasting less than one day unless the total number of workers' days lost in the dispute exceeds 100. The statistics include lock-outs and unlawful strikes (see *Employment Gazette*, July 1989, p. 359).

[2] Based on the latest available mid-year (June) estimate of employees in employment.

Sources: Employment Gazette; Bird *et al.* (1991).

management. Their employers understandably often refuse to recognise unions, and derecognition may occur. Unless statutory recognition is introduced, which is Labour party policy, the union movement is likely to concede further ground. Certainly, it is notable that there are currently virtually no disputes about union recognition.

□ *9.2.5 Industrial Disputes*

Table 9.6 contains data on industrial disputes in the UK covering a period of two decades. As can be seen, there are various ways of measuring the incidence of disputes and the various series tell a somewhat different story. For the purpose of making international comparisons it is customary to use the number of working days lost per 1000 employees, although there are definitional ambiguities (for example, only the UK and USA exclude data on political stoppages – see *Employment Gazette*, December 1990, p. 610).

What the data shows fairly unambiguously is that the number of stoppages has fallen noticeably since 1979. Excluding the effects of the Winter of Discontent in 1979–80, which effectively preceded the Thatcher Government, the number of working days lost per 1000 employees has also tended to be lower during the 1980s with the exception of 1984, due to the miners' strike discussed below – and, less obviously, 1986 where the printers' strike does not show up in the data.

□ *9.2.6 Key Disputes and Data Distortion*

In interpreting the data care has to be exercised in respect of the two key disputes during the 1980s. The first of these, the miners' strike of 1984–85, caused an enormous increase in the number of days lost through strikes in 1984 even though the number of stoppages was relatively modest. By way of contrast, the print union strike of 1986–87, which was almost comparable in its intensity, does not show up at all in the data for days lost because the workers involved had lost their

jobs although the company, News International, carried on production.

It is interesting to relate these disputes to the union law then in existence. In the case of the miners, their defeat can most obviously be ascribed to a determined government, astute planning by the Coal Board and an unsympathetic public, rather than to the use of the new laws which were largely ignored. On the other hand, it is possible that the failure of the National Union of Mineworkers to involve other unions in the dispute may have had something to do with the law on secondary picketing and their fear of having their funds sequestered.

In the case of the dispute between News International and the National Geographical Association and SOGAT 82, the dismissal of the strikers took place under the terms of pre-1979 legislation, but injunctions were also taken out to prevent secondary picketing and secondary action by other union members to disrupt the company's business. Perhaps the crucial matter arising out of these disputes is that certain unions, whether newly formed in the case of the Union of Democratic Mineworkers or longstanding in the case of the EEPTU, have now decided to act wholly in accordance with the new laws and to use this as a lever to gain recognition in place of other unions, such as the NUM and SOGAT, which are wholly opposed to them. The new Acts have, therefore, served to weaken the union movement primarily by dividing it from within.

□ *9.2.7 Are Strikes a Thing of the Past?*

In 1990 the number of stoppages in progress was the lowest for more than 50 years, as it was in 1989, although the exclusion of some of the smallest stoppages from the recorded data in recent years casts some doubt over this conclusion. On the other hand, the number of working days lost rose slightly for four successive years from 1985 before falling back sharply in 1990. Throughout the 1980s four sectors of industry were especially prone to disputes – namely mining and quarrying, manufacturing, construction and transport and communication, both in the UK and elsewhere (although the UK in particular suffered relatively due to the 1984–85 miners' strike – see *Employment Gazette*, December 1990), p. 611. In other sectors strikes are therefore of little economic significance, and even in the more troublesome sectors the period 1985–90 was a huge improvement compared both to 1980–84 and to 1970–79.

On the whole, bearing in mind that the 1980s were a decade during which there was a good deal of disruptive restructuring, there is reason for a cautiously optimistic response to the above question in the sense that, whilst industrial disputes will always remain with us, their incidence and economic effects do seem to have reached an equilibrium at an acceptable level.

1991 started off on a promising footing with the lowest monthly total number of stoppages in progress (26) since 1934.

9.2.8 Effects of Legislation Upon Union Behaviour

It is generally believed that the huge improvement in corporate performance after the end of the 1980–81 recession can be ascribed to the stream of anti-union legislative emanating from the various Thatcher Governments. It is difficult to 'prove' the precise form of the relationship between the two, but such evidence as exists (in particular the work of the Centre for Labour Economics at the London School of Economics) lends little support to the popular view that unions deter investment and hold back productivity growth thereby creating unemployment (their effects upon wage differentials are discussed separately below).

What the studies show (see also the *Financial Times*, 29 August 1989) is that the 1980–81 recession would have created a positive climate for change even in the absence of supporting legislation, since it threatened union members with unemployment and companies with bankruptcy unless they improved their performance in quick time. What it is certainly fair to say is that there was a great deal of potential for such an improvement at the turn of the decade, and that the con-

servative attitudes of unions during the 1970s in resisting change had a great deal to do with this fact.

The British tradition was that in a bargaining situation the union was concerned only with pay and job security, whereas management was concerned with efficiency and productivity. One obvious consequence was the debilitating miners' strike of 1984–85 which was fought in order to preserve jobs in arguably the least pleasant occupation on offer, rather than to ensure that miners' sons could be found something else to do of a less arduous kind.

Irrespective of cause, however, the studies showed that unionised companies seemed to have more organisational change, higher investment and higher productivity growth after 1981 without the unions seeking to oppose these developments. The comparison of productivity growth between highly unionised companies, with more than half the workforce in a union, and companies with little or no union representation is especially interesting. Throughout the 1970s neither group held the ascendency for other than short periods and each held it for roughly half the period. From 1981 to 1985, however, the highly unionised group performed much better, especially from 1983 to 1985. Unfortunately, it is as yet unclear whether this trend, which came to an end during 1985, was simply a one-off response to the recession or is a more permanent feature of the industrial landscape.

Insofar as the government chose to believe that their anti-union legislation was responsible for this improved performance, it is understandable that they chose to introduce several more Acts, set out above, during the latter part of the decade. The interesting question (to be addressed hopefully in a subsequent edition) is, therefore, whether this legislation is mere overkill, although it is certainly electorally popular which may prove to be its sole justification.

9.2.9 The Closed Shop

Closed shops come in two varieties – namely **pre-entry** whereby a worker cannot be hired unless he or she is already a member of a union with nego-tiating rights at the workplace where employment is sought, and **post-entry** whereby it becomes a condition for being hired that a worker joins an appropriate union as soon as possible after being given a job. It is argued that closed shops are only fair because otherwise non-members will be able to 'free-ride' on the backs of members and secure the same improvements in terms and conditions which the members pay for via their subscriptions to the union.

It is also the case that closed shops typically come into existence only when union density has reached a high level, and that many employers look upon them with favour, particularly in the public sector, because they find it much easier to enter into collective agreements with a specific union. During the 1960s and 1970s closed shops became increasingly popular, and at their peak in 1978 they covered in excess of 5 mn workers. Subsequently, however, partly as a result of the Thatcher Government's labour legislation and the efforts of the 1980–81 recession, numbers em-ployed in closed shops fell away sharply to a total of roughly 3.5 mn in 1985, of whom roughly 0.5 mn were covered by a pre-entry shop according to the Workplace Industrial Relations Survey (WIRS).

Further research by the government undertaken as a prelude to the Employment Act 1990 indi-cated that there were only 2.6 mn workers in closed shops in 1989, although rather more than had been thought appeared to be in pre-entry shops. The closed shop, therefore, appeared to be fading away without any further assistance, but the 1990 Act, as we have seen, nevertheless made it illegal to refuse to employ a worker who neither was, nor wished to become, a union member. This arose largely because, prior to the Act, a worker who believed that he had been refused a job simply because he was not a union member could obtain no redress against the company in question. The European Court has also ruled that it is unfair to dismiss workers who refuse to join a union, but these are sentiments which may not appeal to a future Labour Government.

□ 9.2.10 The Union Mark-up

In an ideal world the success or otherwise of a union can be judged by its ability to raise the pay of its members above levels ruling for non-union members whilst simultaneously maintaining full employment for its members. In certain industries and during certain periods this happy combination (from the union's perspective since it is unlikely to be conducive to improved profitability – ask any newspaper owner) was achieved.

In general the 1970s were a good decade for the unions, with income rising at the expense of prof-its and with the incomes of union members rising faster than those of non-union members. A com-parison of unionised sectors with non-unionised sectors during the period 1964–79 by Minford indicated an enormous differential in favour of union members. However, it is more customary to treat the mark-up as the difference in pay for two workers doing exactly the same kind of work, but where one belongs to a union and the other does not. Defined in this way the mark-up appears to have risen, on average, only from roughly 5 per cent to 10 per cent during this period, but also to have shown considerable variability as between different occupations and industries. One study (Blanchflower, 1984) reached the somewhat sur-prising conclusion that whereas the mark-up was only approximately 1 per cent for skilled workers in 1980, it was roughly 10 per cent for semi-skilled manual workers. (For a summary of other studies see Brown and Wadhwani, 1990, pp. 65–8.)

Intra-industry variability is to be expected be-cause of significant differences which exist in prod-uct markets. By and large unions cannot establish much of a differential where there is intense prod-uct market competition, especially from foreign companies, whereas a protected home market com-bined with a closed shop necessarily greatly strengthens the union's hand. For our purposes the most interesting questions are whether the 1980–81 recession eroded differentials and whether these were restrained further by the anti-union legislation.

The initial impact of the recession was undoubtedly minor. Faced by the choice between taking a reduction in pay or accepting the loss of jobs which could no longer be justified at existing wage levels, unions almost invariably preferred the latter to the former. Eventually, the sheer scale of job losses, wholesale plant closures and the onset of legislation ate significantly into differentials, but the buoyant employment situation during the latter part of the decade did much to restore what had been lost. When compared to the effect exerted by changing market forces, the effect of anti-union legislation appears to have been minor (see Brown and Wadhwani, 1990, pp. 68–9).

☐ 9.2.11 Insiders and Outsiders

The sluggish response of differentials to the rapid rise in unemployment during the early 1980s – and, indeed, their continued existence, albeit at somewhat reduced levels, at a time when between 2 mn and 3 mn people were unemployed – is something of a puzzle. Clearly, the labour market is imperfect in its operation, and a convincing explanation for why that is so can be found by reference to the distinction between **insiders** and **outsiders**.

Insiders' comprise those people who are either in work or who have recently lost their jobs but who retain valuable skills. A significant proportion among them will belong to unions. 'Outsiders', by way of contrast, comprise those people who have lost their jobs recently but whose skills are largely non-transferable, those who lost their jobs more than a year ago (the long-term unemployed) and those who have never held a job at all (school leavers and housewives).

Outsiders may become very numerous, but they may nevertheless have little effect upon the labour market. In the first place, unions may be more concerned with protecting the position of their members who are still employed than with the interests of the unemployed (who will tend to let their membership lapse). Secondly, employers will not be interested in taking on workers with redundant skills, or none at all, unless absolutely necessary. Thirdly, some outsiders will be content to live off social security, at least for a time. Under

these circumstances an upturn in demand is likely to lead to overtime working and the re-employment of skilled workers only recently laid off. As a consequence, wages will continue to rise despite the existence of a large pool of unemployed workers. This becomes even more probable where there is a geographic imbalance between the places where the unemployed reside and the places where demand is growing.

In general, it is fair to say that any convincing analysis of how the labour market works must contain some elements of the insider/outsider dichotomy. Nevertheless, it is also fair to say that it explains persistently high unemployment more easily than changes in unemployment.

☐ 9.2.12 Political Levies

It is hardly surprising that the Thatcher Government heartily disliked union political funds since they provided the main source of revenue for the Labour party. What rankled above all else was the fact that large numbers of union members were voting for the Conservative party whereas the unions' political funds were being passed in their entirety to the opposition. Allowing members to 'contract out' of making payments into a political fund was a step in the right direction, but inertia combined with a preference not to be at loggerheads with fellow workers meant that relatively few took up this option.

The government accordingly made it obligatory under the Trade Union Act 1984 for unions to hold a ballot on the question of whether or not to have a political fund. However, much to the government's annoyance, the answer in almost every case was in the affirmative.

■ 9.3 Recent Labour Market Controversies

☐ 9.3.1 Equal Pay

The Equal Pay Act 1975 required that women who performed similar tasks to men should be treated equally. The Sex Discrimination Act 1975 further required that men and women should be guaranteed equality of opportunity. In 1970, womens' hourly earnings relative to those of men, as calculated from data in the annual New Earnings Survey, stood at 63.1 per cent. In 1975 the comparable figure was 72.1 per cent and in 1976 it was 75.1 per cent. It is reasonable to attribute most of the increase to the existence of these Acts. All alternative explanations, such as the existence of flat-rate incomes policies, an upturn in the demand for female labour or a reduction in the supply of female labour lack explanatory power, either because they did not happen (the reduction in supply); because they were not permanent yet there was no reversal of the relative earnings ratio when they ceased to apply (incomes policies); or because they were permanent (the increased demand for female labour) yet the earnings differential ceased to narrow after 1977.

In fact, the differential has yet to return to its peak value achieved in 1977. On the other hand, it has never subsequently fallen back below 73 per cent. This suggests strongly that it was the pre-1977 changes which were critical. Nevertheless, the obvious lack of progress since 1977 is an indictment of government policy in this respect.

Some actions to improve things have, however, been taken. In 1983, for example, the European Court of Justice ruled that the UK was in contravention of EC legislation which defined equal pay in terms of equal value. The Equal Pay (Amendment) Regulations were speedily enacted to bring the UK into line with this ruling. Unfortunately, this did not resolve the precise meaning of the term 'equal value', and a body of case law has had to be accumulated for this purpose.

In the case of *Hayward* v. *Cammell Laird Shipbuilders* (1980), for example, the House of Lords eventually ruled that equal pay literally meant equal money wages, and chose to disregard differences in perks. In June 1989 a woman records assistant employed by Northern Ireland Electricity was awarded equal pay with a male manual worker by a Belfast tribunal in the first case in which parity was established between white collar and blue collar jobs. An important current case revolves around

a claim first lodged in 1985 by a district speech therapist against Frenchay District Health Authority claiming parity with clinical psychologists and hospital pharmacists. The initial ruling that the speech therapist had no case was upheld by an appeals tribunal in January 1991.

This judgement means that separate collective bargaining arrangements which result in unequal pay between men and women cannot be challenged under equal pay laws unless it can be shown that the arrangements are **directly** discriminatory. Cases are typically based on claims of **indirect** discrimination. There is likely to be an appeal to the House of Lords followed, if necessary, by an appeal to the European Court of Justice.

□ 9.3.2 *Pension Equality*

The key case involved a gentleman called Mr Barber who was made redundant by the Guardian Royal Exchange Assurance at the age of 52. Under the GRE severance scheme men and women made redundant 10 years before the scheme's normal retirement ages would be treated as taking early retirement, thus qualifying for an immediate pension. Mr Barber received a deferred pension and redundancy compensation whereas a woman of the same age would have received an immediate pension. Mr Barber made a claim on the grounds of sex discrimination to an industrial tribunal and the Employment Appeal Tribunal, but both dismissed his claim.

On appeal, the Court of Appeal referred the case to the European Court of Justice to give a preliminary ruling as to whether the benefits received in connection with compulsory redundancy in the circumstances of the case constituted 'pay' within Article 119 of the Treaty of Rome, and accordingly whether they had to be equal for men and women.

The UK Government argued that the benefits paid from a pension scheme fell within Articles 117 and 118, not Article 119. The Court of Justice gave judgement on 17 May 1990, ruling that (i) the benefits paid by an employer to a worker in connection with redundancy fall within Article 119;

(ii) pensions paid under occupational pension schemes, including contracted out schemes, fall within Article 119; (iii) equal treatment must apply to each component part of remuneration including components of a pension; (iv) Article 119 has direct effect and does not apply to state social security benefits.

The situation has been further complicated by a ruling made by a Manchester tribunal in March 1991. A Mr Roscoe retired at age 60 after 40 years of service with Hick Hargreaves and only a few weeks after the Barber judgement. The company took the view that it need equalise the pension rights only accruing from the date of the judgement, rather than over the full 40-year period (to provide a full pension at age 60). The tribunal ruled that since Mr Roscoe retired after the judgement he should have received a full pension comparable with a woman with 40 years' service.

If this case ends up before the Court of Justice, and if the Court rules in favour of Mr Roscoe, it could cost the pension industry £13 bn a year to supplement the pensions of all men who retired after the Barber judgement.

In December 1990, the Equal Opportunities Commission prevailed upon the government to ask the High Court to obtain a ruling from the Court of Justice as to whether existing pension rules breached the European Social Security Directive. Although the EC directive allows member states to keep different pension ages for men and women, the Commission argues that National Insurance Contribution arrangements are not covered by the exemption.

At present, men have to pay contributions for at least 44 years to qualify for a full State pension compared to 39 years for women. Even if a man has paid contributions for 44 years, he still has to continue making contributions until he retires or reaches 65, whereas women stop paying at 60. The Court of Justice is almost certain to rule against the UK Government despite its claim that the UK is not out of line with practices elsewhere in the EC. Only in France do both sexes qualify for a state pension at 60. In West Germany, Eire, Spain, the Netherlands and Luxembourg both sexes qualify at 65, and in Denmark both qualify at 67.

Belgium and Greece have the same rules as the UK. In Portugal men qualify at 65 and women at 62.

For the UK Government to lower the male retirement age to 60 would be hugely costly (at £3 bn a year). Raising the retirement age to 65 for women would save money but be damaging politically. A common age of 63 could provide a potential compromise with the adjustment phased in over a period of years.

□ 9.3.3 *Absenteeism and Sick Pay*

Absenteeism through sickness is a costly problem. According to the CBI unauthorised absenteeism costs industry up to 30 times more working days than strikes, currently around £5 bn a year. British companies have traditionally been lax in investigating such absenteeism whereas a number of Japanese and US companies operating in Britain have managed to reduce absenteeism by insisting upon a doctor's note and an interview upon return to work.

Currently, statutory sick pay is financed entirely through employers' and employees' NICs. It is an insured scheme and contributors are entitled to claim, initially from the employer who is reimbursed by the state. In addition, a majority of employers also provide occupational sick pay arrangements. Interpreting this as an indication that employers were becoming more willing to foot the bill for sick pay, and anxious to impose a penalty upon companies that manage absenteeism badly, the government decided at the end of 1990 to introduce a Statutory Sick Pay Bill. This provided that an employer would be able to reclaim from the state only 80 per cent of what he had paid out to an employee, and also that this rate could be varied (downwards) without returning to Parliament for debated approval to do so.

The Bill was rushed through Parliament, but when it came before the House of Lords it met with concerted opposition on the grounds that the existing system worked well and that the Bill had not been subjected to a proper parliamentary debate. The Lords raised the reimbursement rate to 91 per cent and threw out the right to vary the rate at will on subsequent occasions. There was also concern expressed about the financial consequences for small businesses. In the latter regard the government subsequently agreed to exempt small businesses from the changes only if an employee was off sick for more than eight weeks, but this amendment was also defeated in the Lords at the end of January 1991.

At present, 6 bn payments are made annually at a total cost to the exchequer of just under £1 bn. Whilst there is a reasonable case to be made for trying to economise in this area by inducing employers to tighten up on absenteeism, it is clear that the current proposals are deeply unpopular.

9.3.4 The Child Care Debate

In the course of the 1990 Budget the then Chancellor, John Major, stated that 'it is not for the Government to encourage or discourage women with children to go out to work.' This did not, however, prevent him from exempting workplace nurseries from taxation as a benefit in kind.

The underlying presumption behind the offering of a subsidy is that it is necessary if a problem is to be overcome. The problem in this case is that there is allegedly going to be a shortage of labour due to the reduction in the number of young people entering the labour market; that this needs to be overcome by attracting married women with young children to fill the employment void; and that this is best achieved by providing better child care facilities.

Certain commentators find this argument unappealing (see, for example, Martin Wolf in the *Financial Times*, 9 April 1990, p. 17). In Wolf's view, if there is truly a shortage of labour then the wages on offer will rise and bring the labour market back into equilibrium. Furthermore, he sees this as the only logical way to overcome pay differentials between men and women. He sees little point in attracting more women into the labour market when the female activity rate in the UK is already the second highest in the EC.

In response, it is alleged that the lack of child care facilities is instrumental in preventing women from working full-time, and hence in preventing them from realising their true potential. Unfortunately, this does not accord with the facts. According to the 1989 Labour Force Survey, fewer than one in twenty married women and one in eight single women were working part-time because they could not find a full-time job. For the great majority, part-time work was the preferred alternative.

■ 9.4 The European Dimension

9.4.1 The Single European Market (SEM)

It would go beyond our immediate purpose to examine in detail the implications of the SEM for the UK labour market. Nevertheless, a number of comments are in order.

In the first place, the SEM is likely to have consequences for union structures. The idea of pan-European unions in specific sectors must inevitably hold some appeal for unions which are facing an adverse climate in the UK. However, this may prove difficult to realise in practice because, for example, most other EC countries are less highly unionised; the industries in decline in the UK are generally also in decline elsewhere; there are political and cultural differences to overcome; and there is the small matter of linguistic difficulties, at least for UK union leaders.

Secondly, there are implications for the structure of wage bargaining. Those EC countries, including the UK, where unions are big enough to influence wages but too small to care about their effect on the whole economy, have generally performed worse than countries where either bargaining is centrally organised, and hence unions have to take into account the effects of their actions on the economy as a whole, or bargaining is highly decentralised and unions are too weak to affect wage levels. Insofar as the SEM will open up EC markets to greater internal competition it will weaken the power of unions, especially those in previously sheltered industries. By implication this should yield benefits for the performance of the UK economy.

Thirdly, there is the matter of the European Community Charter of Workers' Fundamental Social Rights, better known as the **Social Charter**, which was first approved by the European Commission in May 1989. Its purpose is to guarantee the basic rights of workers in the EC and it covers, *inter alia*, employment and remuneration, living and working conditions and information, consultation and participation. It is proceeding primarily via the issuing of directives, known as the **Social Action Programme**, which must eventually be translated into national law once they are ratified by the Council of Ministers.

The Programme got fully into its stride in June 1990 with a draft directive giving the same rights, such as training and holidays, to **part-time and temporary workers** as to full-time workers. In July a draft directive appeared on working hours. Among the 12 EC members only Denmark and the UK do not regulate the maximum daily working period, but this is of little relevance since actual working hours for full-time employees are in most cases well below the maximum set. The UK is also unusual insofar as it is one of only two countries which do not regulate overtime. This is because the ideal UK working week is seen as one where official working hours are short – the lowest in the EC in many industries – but there is plenty of overtime available at higher rates of pay.

This directive is accordingly concerned with shift and night work. On average, 20 per cent of EC employees do shift work, with the highest rates in the UK and Spain (29 per cent). The directive proposes that every worker will be entitled to at least 11 hours of rest in 24 hours and an average of one rest day a week. Night work will be limited to eight hours a day, averaged over two weeks. Although there will be exemptions, these rules will cause a good deal of disruption to working patterns in the UK, and hence raise unit labour costs, if they need to be implemented. In September a further draft directive on **maternity leave** was issued. This proposes that women will get 14 weeks' maternity leave (already normal in most EC States) at full salary (compared to the 70 or 80 per cent of salary currently the norm in most states). Jobs will be protected during this period. In aggregate, these measures are more generous than those ruling in member states such as the UK, where women currently have rights to maternity leave and reinstatement only when they have held a job for two years.

A draft directive on a European **minimum wage** is expected shortly. This will probably fix the minimum at a level in excess of two-thirds of an EC member's average manufacturing wage, with enforcement left up to each member state. Small and medium sized companies in the services sector understandably feel threatened by these developments.

Finally there are moves afoot to require **worker representation** on boards of directors of companies with more than 1000 employees and where at least 100 of them work in each of two EC countries. Also, any EC company with subsidiaries in more than one country will probably be required to set up a 'European works council', effectively a consultative council at group level where strategic decisions will be discussed which touch on plant closures and employment contracts.

Mrs Papendreou, the Social Affairs Commissioner, is anxious to turn these directives into European law, and has put them forward as health and safety directives which can be passed by a majority vote. This is almost certainly necessary if they are to be passed because the UK Government is adamantly opposed to these directives, arguing that such matters are best dealt with at a purely national level, and that the directives will impose costs running into billions upon UK industry, with consequent serious damage to its competitiveness.

At a meeting of the Social Affairs Council in December 1990 a majority of member states supported the UK in respect of the directive on part-time workers, both on a substantive and legal basis, arguing in particular that it should not have been presented in a form that required majority voting but in one that required unanimity. At the Maastricht IGC the UK refused to accept the inclusion of a 'Social Chapter', and this accordingly had to be omitted from the new Treaty even though the UK was isolated. The Social Charter will nevertheless proceed.

References

Bean, C., R. Layard and S. Nickell (eds) (1986) *The Rise in Unemployment* (Oxford: Blackwell).

Bean, R. (ed.) (1989) *International Labour Statistics* (London: Routledge).

Blanchflower, D. (1984) 'Union Relative Wage Effects', *British Journal of Industrial Relations*, pp. 311–22.

Bird, D., M. Stevens and A. Yates (1991) 'Membership of Trade Unions in 1989', *Employment Gazette* (June).

Brown, W. and S. Wadhwani (1990) 'The Economic Effects of Industrial Relations Legislation since 1979', *National Institute Economic Review* (February).

Dawson, G. (1990) 'Interpretation of the Natural Rate of Unemployment', *Economics* (Summer).

Department of Employment (1990a) 'Measures of Unemployment', *Employment Gazette* (October).

Department of Employment (1990b) 'Provisions of the Employment Act 1990', *Employment Gazette* (November).

Department of Employment (1991) 'Characteristics of the Unemployed', *Employment Gazette* (May)

Gregg, P (1990) 'The Evolution of Special Employment Measures', *Royal Bank of Scotland Review* (September).

Hall, S. *et al.* (1987) 'The UK Labour Market', *Lloyds Bank Review* (July).

Lawlor, J. (1990) 'Monthly Unemployment Statistics: Maintaining a Consistent Series', *Employment Gazette* (December).

Layard, R. and S. Nickell (1986) 'Unemployment in Britain', *Economica*, 53 (Supplement) S121-S169.

Poret, P. (1990) 'The "Puzzle" of Wage Moderation in the 1980s', *OECD Working Paper*, 87 (Paris: OECD).

Spence, A. (1990) 'Labour Force Outlook to 2001', *Employment Gazette* (April).

Chapter 10

Welfare: Inequality and Poverty

Paul Marshall

▌ *10.1* Inequality and Income Distribution

Even at the crudest level no assessment of the well-being of a society can have much credibility unless it takes some account of the distribution of income as well as its aggregate total (Morris and Preston, 1986).

This quotation is from a study of income distribution over time. Even for a simple economy, measuring the distribution of economic gain is very difficult; for a large, developed, mixed economy, in which both public and private sectors exert their influences on income distribution, the complications of measuring distribution patterns are endless. The study from which the quotation is taken is of income distribution in the UK and covers a period during which there were major structural changes to the economy, several exogenous shocks (including the oil price hike of the early 1970s) and major social and political upheavals, including three changes of government. Nevertheless, as the quotation underlines, if we are interested in measuring economic welfare, and its tendency to change over time, we must take account of the **distribution of the gains from economic processes** no matter how complicated or dynamic they may be.

In the case of a mixed economy like the UK the role of government is a crucial influence upon the distribution of income and wealth and this will be emphasised in the course of this chapter, particularly in relation to government's objective of reducing inequality. Within the government spending section of the national accounts are many items which relate to programmes aimed at improvements in individual welfare. The range of such programmes is considerable, spanning subsidies to both production (for example, farm income support programmes) and consumption (for example, household income maintenance programmes). Indeed, such is the range that any overview must be selective. For present purposes the selection concentrates on issues which lie at the heart of government aims to reduce inequalities in the distribution of income and wealth, issues which are often subsumed under the heading of 'social policy'. **Why** governments need to finance and /or provide such programmes and to **what extent** they should do so are extremely difficult questions to answer and this chapter can do more more than shed some light on the policy debate.

So far as economists are concerned the issues to be discussed concern individual 'welfare' — whether welfare is maximised for everyone through the market system or whether market determined incomes require alteration by state action and, if so, how the alteration is to be achieved. Clearly, the welfare of individuals depends upon a multitude of things and not simply on the acquisition of material goods and services; it is the search for an understanding of the characteristics of, and the influences exerted by, this multitude that forms the basis of enquiry in social science. Within social science it is Economics which has concentrated on the material aspects of well-being, but it is difficult to maintain a strict divorce between Economics and other disciplines when trying to analyse the causes of the distribution of material consumption.

10.1.1 The Efficiency/Equity Trade-off

As an analytical concept, and as an aim of government policy, **efficiency** holds centre stage throughout this book, reflecting the main preoccupation of economists. But questions of welfare relate often to **equity** as well as to efficiency, and here lies a problem for both the analyst and the policymaker: **it is rare for an efficiency objective to be achieved without an inequality being created.** Indeed, to recognise the reality of the problem of managing a mixed economy is to see it as a search for acceptable **trade-offs** between equity and efficiency. What the trade-offs look like is a major question for research into the evaluation of government expenditure programmes. What the trade-offs **should** look like is part of a normative debate which manifests itself in the varying policies advanced from different political standpoints. Thus, for some observers, the question of equity should be at the forefront of political debate and should be the primary consideration in the formation of government expenditure plans. This argument may stem from altruism but it may also be based on pragmatism — if 'the system' creates too much inequality it may invite violent political upheaval, or revolution! On the other hand, some observers argue that efficiency should be always the main criterion for judging public expenditure programmes since only if the economy is efficient in every respect can the income available for redistribution be maximised — in other words reducing inequality depends on reducing inefficiency! The issue of the trade-off will recur throughout this chapter and is often illustrated by the characteristics of the social policies implemented by different governments.

10.1.2 The Concept of Inequality

Using the term 'inequality' in the present context is intended as a comment upon the extent to which the rewards of the market place, supplemented and modified by government tax/transfer programmes, are distributed equally throughout the population. To measure inequality in this way is very difficult for reasons of practical computation and for reasons of principle. Practical difficulties loom large when choosing appropriate data from which to analyse distributions. In the UK, for example, official estimates of income distribution are often derived from Inland Revenue returns whereby the definition of 'income' is that used for the purposes of income taxation. Since income defined for tax purposes may exclude some important sources of income (for example capital gains, imputed income from home production and property ownership, fringe benefits and certain government transfers), measures of distribution based on this definition may be inaccurate.

But even if comprehensive measures of income were available and distributions were to be computed accurately, there remains a difficult issue of principle – namely, how to **judge** distributions as 'equal' or 'unequal'. Certainly, we know what an equal distribution of incomes looks like – one in which **every income unit** (individual or household) has the **same income as any other unit**. We might be tempted to say, therefore, that any distribution in which at least one income unit has more or less than each of the other units is unequal. But this is not very helpful when looking at a world of many distributions in which the **degree** of inequality differs; it is this very question of degree which makes the measurement problem so difficult to resolve. If we are interested in comparing distributions at a point in time, or assessing changes in inequality over time, the problem becomes acute.

The crux of the problem lies in the fact that while it is possible always to describe different patterns of income distribution, it is not possible often to describe different patterns of **inequality** without invoking a value judgement. Suppose, for example, that a change in government policy makes the top 10 per cent of income recipients slightly better off, the next 80 per cent much better off and the bottom 10 per cent slightly worse off. Has the policy change effected a more equal distribution of income? How is the small loss suffered by the bottom 10 per cent of income recipients to be weighed against the large gain to the majority of the population? What comment can we make about a change which has made the bottom 10 per cent of income recipients worse off while raising the incomes received by the top 10 per cent?

Clearly, for an observer to describe one pattern of income distribution as more or less equal than another, reference must be made to an accepted concept of **social justice**, a rule by which any pattern of shares may be judged. Later on we shall concentrate on **poverty** as an important manifestation of inequality, and this issue of social justice takes on more obvious relevance when we try to make judgements about government measures to improve the relative positions of individuals or households at the bottom of the income distribution. But we must not lose sight of the fact that to compare distributions may involve comparisons of gains and losses – that is, altered distributional positions for different percentile groupings – in which case judgements about which is more equal or even, perhaps, 'preferred' cannot be made on any objective criteria. The history of 'Welfare Economics' has been written in terms of a search for an objective criterion by which to judge the outcome of economic processes but the question of social justice does not reside exclusively within the domain of academic reasoning. Indeed, the very question of a trade-off between equity and efficiency, discussed earlier and to be returned to later, lies (again) at the heart of real-world government decisions affecting the distribution of income. Both government expenditures and methods of raising revenue affect income distribution; a government implementing policies to promote efficiency at the expense of equity will be more likely to create inequalities than a government opting to sacrifice efficiency gains for equity goals.

10.1.3 The Measurement of Inequality

The problem of trying to judge between alternative distributions is illustrated clearly by the statistical summary measures most favoured by both private researchers and government reports: the **Lorenz curve** and the **Gini coefficient**. The Lorenz curve offers a pictorial representation of inequality. The Gini coefficient, which is the measure favoured by statisticians and often used in government reports, provides a numerical summary measure of inequality.

The Lorenz curve is used for **comparative** analysis – for example comparing income distributions between countries at some point in time or between different points in time in a given country. The curve shows cumulative percentage income shares: the bottom 10 per cent of the population (income units) receive x per cent of income, the bottom 20 per cent receive y per cent, where y is greater than x, and so on. When there is perfect equality – when every n per cent of the population receives n per cent of total income – the Lorenz curve is a 45° line or **line of income equality**. Such a line thus operates as a yardstick by which to gauge the inequality in any given distribution. If there is inequality the Lorenz curve lies below the 45° line, and the more unequal the distribution the further away from the 45° line lies the Lorenz curve. **Figure 10.1(a)** shows two hypothetical Lorenz curves with the distribution in year t represented as more equal than that in year t–50.

It is possible to draw unambiguous conclusions from **Figure 10.1(a)** because one Lorenz curve lies completely outside the other. But let us examine **Figure 10.1(b)** where the two Lorenz curves cross. Are we still able to judge which of the two distributions is most equal? The Lorenz curves show that for all percentile groups up to the bottom 40 per cent their share in total income was higher in year t–50 than in year t, but above this point shares were higher in year t. A measure of inequality which gives a greater weight to improvements in the share of total income enjoyed by the lower income groups would register t–50 as the year of greater equality; a measure of inequality

Figure 10.1 *Hypothetical Lorenz Curves and the Measurement of Inequality*

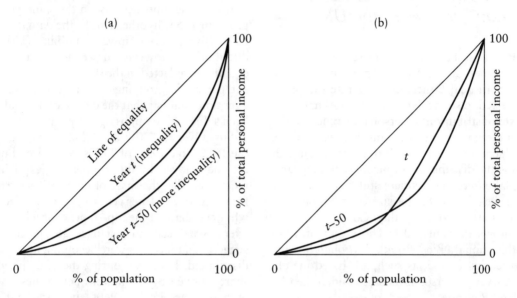

which gives a greater weight to improvements in upper income group shares would yield a preference for year *t*.

The same problem arises when using the Gini coefficient. This numerical measure of inequality is based on the relationship between the Lorenz curve and the line of income equality; it measures the ratio of the area between the Lorenz curve and the diagonal (the line of income equality) to the total area beneath the diagonal. In **Figure 10.2** the Gini coefficient is measured as the ratio A/(A+B).

It can be seen from **Figure 10.2** that when the Lorenz curve follows the diagonal, when incomes are equally distributed, the Gini coefficient has a value of 0(A=0). At the other extreme, when all income is held by one individual (B=0), the Gini coefficient has a value of 1. Thus for purposes of comparison, the nearer the Gini coefficient is to 0 the more equal the distribution may be considered to be. However, when two Lorenz curves cross how can we draw an unambiguous conclusion regarding relative inequalities? Consider **Figure 10.1(b)** again: the Gini coefficient suggests that incomes are more equally distributed in year *t* but this obscures the fact that from the viewpoint of the bottom four deciles year *t–50* is more equal.

It would seem, then, that when measuring the degree of inequality in income distribution we cannot avoid introducing value judgements about the

'desired' state of distribution. Any two observers with different views on the weight which should be given by society to improvements in the position of the lower income groups could place two different interpretations on any decrease in the value of the Gini coefficient between two points in time. Only if the Gini coefficient is used in conjunction with the original data on percentile shares is an adequate comparative picture likely to emerge.

Figure 10.2 *Measuring the Gini Coefficient From the Lorenz Curve*

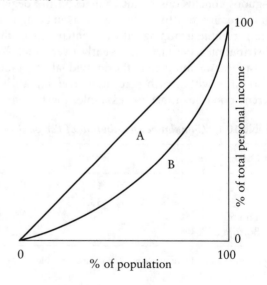

10.1.4 The Distribution of Pre-tax Incomes in the UK

The official estimates of the distribution of personal incomes in the UK are published by the Central Statistical Office and illustrate the problems referred to so far. Note that the estimates are of the **size** distribution of **personal** incomes. In the modern economy the distinctions between factors of production are rather blurred, and although analysing the distribution of incomes among capitalists, labourers and rentiers still has its uses, it tends to be inferior to the size distribution as a summary measure of inequality. Consider the estimates shown in **Table 10.1**. Those estimates are from the annual 'Blue Book', *National Income and Expenditure*, and, as such, are based mainly on the Survey of Personal Incomes undertaken by the Inland Revenue.

So what do the data suggest? If the period since the Second World War has been one of rising prosperity for the UK how has this prosperity been shared out among the population? The data show clearly that pre-tax income has not been shared equally at any point in time. Insofar as pre-tax incomes reflect a market determined set of rewards, this is to be expected. But what about shares over time – have pre-tax incomes become more or less equally shared?

The data suggest that we cannot draw unambiguous conclusions about changes in the degree of inequality over time, the main reason being that the percentile groupings at different points in the distribution have fared differently over time. We must bear in mind that the individual tax units also differ within each percentile grouping at different points in time: for example, the tax units

comprising the top 10 per cent group in 1985 are not the same units as those in the same percentile group in 1955. In other words, the data do not tell us anything about upward mobility within the distribution. However, if we do accept that inequality is reflected in the shares enjoyed by different percentile groupings, looking at these shares over time suggests that the degree of inequality has been subjected to opposing forces, at least until the 1980s. Over the 30-year period, from the end of the 1940s to the end of 1970s, the share of pre-tax income enjoyed by the top percentiles of income recipients fell – the share of the top 1 per cent fell, from just over 11 per cent to just over 5 per cent, while the share of the top 10 per cent fell from just over 33 per cent to just over 26 per cent. This suggests that incomes were becoming more equally distributed. However, during the same period the share enjoyed by the bottom percentiles also fell, with recovery in the 1960s and early/mid-1970s proving insufficient to regain the share enjoyed at the end of the 1940s, suggesting that incomes became more unequally distributed over the period.

How are we to weigh these opposing forces? It would appear that the Lorenz curves at different points of time are crossed and we cannot make a clear judgement about overall inequality without reference to a specific concept of social justice – the very problem discussed earlier. The only firm conclusion which might be drawn from the data is that whatever redistribution of pre-tax incomes has taken place, it has done so from the top to the middle.

Similar difficulties face us when trying to assess the changing degree of inequality throughout the 1980s – that is, some percentile groupings fared better than others in the overall distribution of incomes. The task of measuring changes in in-

Table 10.1   *Cumulative Distribution of Personal Income before Tax, UK, 1949–85 selected years*

Quantile Groups	1949	1959	1967	1975–76	1984–85
Top 1%	11.2	8.4	7.4	5.7	6.4
Top 10%	33.2	29.4	28.0	26.2	29.4
Top 50%	76.3	76.9	76.0	76.2	77.7
Bottom 50%	23.7	23.1	24.0	23.8	22.3

Sources: Diamond Commission, Report no. 1, Table 15; *Social Trends*, 19 (1989 edn).

equality over the decade was made particularly difficult by the fact that the Royal Commission on the Distribution of Income and Wealth was disbanded shortly after the Conservatives came to power in 1979 and then, following the 1987 election victory, the Conservative Government abolished the official poverty statistics. However, the CSO estimates do suggest (see **Table 10.1**) that over the first half of the decade there was no reduction in the degree of inequality in the distribution of pre-tax incomes; indeed the share enjoyed by the top half of the distribution increased while the share of the bottom half decreased.

Further evidence that inequality might have increased over the same decade has been offered by Jenkins (1991), who has calculated that most of the real income growth during the 1980s took place in the upper income bands with little gain being enjoyed by those in the lower bands. According to Jenkins: 'in 1967 the richest 10 per cent had an income almost 10 times that of the poorest band. In 1978, the ratio was just more than 10, but in 1988, it was almost 18'. In his updating of the work of the Royal Commission, Stark (1990) has also added fuel to the argument that income inequality worsened over the 1980s. According to Stark, the income of the top 10 per cent increased by 43 per cent while the bottom 40 per cent suffered a decrease of up to 8 per cent.

☐ 10.1.5 Trends in Factor Incomes

To explain the causes of the observed changes in the distribution of pre-tax incomes over the period in question requires an understanding of highly complicated and interrelated forces. Not all of these forces are economic, although for present purposes we shall look in more detail at the distribution of factor market incomes. Social and demographic factors play their part in altering income shares over time. In the 1970s the Royal Commission on the Distribution of Income and Wealth (the Diamond Commission) identified four major forces: changes in the age structure of the population; changes in the activity rates of various sectors of the population; changes in marital patterns; and changes in education patterns. Not surprisingly,

the Commission concluded that alterations to the pattern of income distribution were often attributable to some combination of these separately identified factors (Diamond Commission, 1975). For present purposes we shall let the observation rest there, although we shall return to the age factor when we consider the incidence of poverty and the problem of intergenerational finance of social security arrangements. Several relevant observations on activity rates (for example, labour force participation of married women) are also made in Chapter 8 (see **pp. 284–6**).

So far as economic forces are concerned, we can usefully begin with a closer look at factor market patterns. When a mixed economy allocates resources it determines rewards to factors of production in both private and public sectors, while the state's tax-transfer mechanism provides income maintenance for those who are eligible. We shall leave the distribution of state transfers until later and concentrate first on factor incomes as an indication of how rewards are shared out on the supply side of the economy, the many determinants of this distribution being discussed in every other chapter of this book.

☐ 10.1.6 The Distribution of Factor Rewards

Whatever the nature of social and demographic changes, the distribution of rewards in a market-oriented economy must reflect the nature of markets. Thus, there are at least two important questions to address: how are the total rewards from economic processes shared out among the various factors of production and, if one type of reward dominates, what forces help to determine **its** distribution? The answer to the first question offers a guide to answering the second. To understand the forces which determine the distribution of incomes we need to know the dominant source of income; an increase in the share going to capital is likely to have an impact on overall size distribution which is different from that resulting from an increase in the share enjoyed by labour. Furthermore, if one component of income accounts for, say, more than half the rewards in an economy, then any change in the dispersion of that component will result in a change in the overall dispersion of incomes. **Table 10.2** shows the relative shares of the main components of total household income in the UK for the period 1971–89.

As can be seen from **Table 10.2** the largest component of household incomes in the UK is **income from employment**. Researchers into the distribution of incomes have seen the changes in this large component as indicators of both the overall state of the economy and the prevailing degree of inequality. Lydall, for example, discerned a trend towards equality in the distribution of incomes, from the immediate postwar years until the later 1950s, and argued that this trend owed much to postwar economic expansion and the improving fortunes of labour (Lydall, 1959). According to Lydall, the sustained high level of employment during the period meant that earned income rose faster than any other form of personal income, and that such a trend would be a major force towards equality. However, as calculated by Nicholson, this pattern changed during the period 1957–63 with the rate of growth of employment income slowing down relative to that of self-employment (and, within employment income, the rate of growth of wages slowed down relative to that of salaries). During this period rent, dividends and interest became the most rapidly growing sector of personal income. The result, according to Nicholson, was a slowing down in any trend towards equality (Nicholson, 1967).

According to official estimates the downward slide in the share of labour income continued into the 1970s, when it steadied before resuming its downward trend during the early 1980s – from 73 per cent in 1978 to 69 per cent by 1985, since when it has remained almost constant. Nevertheless, the trend over the long run remains in labour's favour. By itself this long-term trend reduces inequality if the gains are equally distributed among labour units. However, over time such redistribution has not been equal. Earnings (wages and salaries) constitute the largest proportion of factor incomes, yet there are forces at work to prevent an equal distribution of earnings among earners.

Between the sexes there is considerable inequality. **Figure 10.3** plots the weekly earnings enjoyed by the extremes of the earnings distribution for each sex over the decade 1977–87. The observed pattern is one of persistent inequality.

There are two main conclusions to be drawn from **Figure 10.3**. In the first place, the top male earners consistently earn more than the top female earners. Secondly, the difference between the highest female earnings and the lowest male earnings is consistently less than that between highest and lowest female earnings. It should be noted that a similar pattern emerges in the case of hourly earnings and that differences in earnings performance are equally marked for the other percentile groupings in the distributions (of both weekly and hourly earnings). For example, in 1987 the weekly earnings figure for the highest female decile (full-time) was only about 15 per cent higher than the median for men (full-time), while the median for women was only some 70 per cent of that for men. Such inequalities have persisted despite the flurry of legislation on equal pay and sex discrimination

Table 10.2   *% Shares of Main Components in Total Household Income, UK, 1971–89*[1]

	1971	1976	1981	1986	1989
Wages and salaries	68	67	64	59	59
Income from self-employment	9	9	9	10	11
Rent, interest and dividends	6	6	6	7	8
Private pensions, annuities, etc.	5	5	6	8	8
Social security benefits	10	11	13	13	11
Other current transfers	2	2	2	3	3

Note:
[1] Figures to nearest whole numbers
Source: Social Trends, 21 (1991 edn) Table 5.2.

Figure 10.3 *Dispersion of Gross Weekly Earnings, 1977–87*[1,2,3]

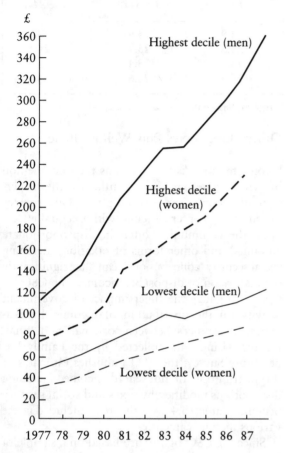

Notes:
[1] Of full-time adults whose pay was not affected by absence.
[2] From 1977 to 1983 adult rates on the basis of males aged 21 and over and females aged 18 and over.
[3] From 1984 onwards on the basis of all on adult rates.
Source: New Earnings Survey 1987, Table 30.

documented in Chapter 8. Another significant inequality persists between manual and non-manual earners (regardless of sex), with non-manual earnings consistently outstripping manual earnings in all deciles within the two distributions.

The share of personal income going to rents, dividends and interest behaved more erratically during the period from 1960. Throughout the 1960s this share fell steadily before 'hitting bottom' in

the early 1970s, since when it has climbed again, particularly during the 1980s (although the ramifications of the 1987 stock market crash and the subsequent recovery have yet to show up in the official data).

Looking at the shares accruing to the major components of personal income cannot 'explain' changes in inequality. There is much more to the story than this. However, the broad categories which we have considered do give some strong indications of what is happening to the degree of inequality associated with the overall distribution of personal incomes. In particular, it is difficult to avoid the conclusion that during the first two terms of the present government the increased share in pre-tax income enjoyed by the highest percentiles in the distribution resulted, in part, from an increased concentration of earned income due to a rise in the proportions of the population who were unemployed or retired.

10.1.7 The Distributional Impact of Taxes and Transfers

Income Tax

When considering how UK Governments have influenced the pattern of personal income distribution over the period since 1945 we must concentrate on two things: the effect of progressive income taxation and the effect of Welfare State transfers. A progressive tax structure smooths out the dispersion of incomes after tax and works towards a more equal distribution. Welfare State benefits, in principle, are transfers of income both in cash and in kind to the poorest percentiles in the distribution and, hence, a force towards reducing inequality.

In practice, the evidence suggests that it is only the benefits side of the tax/transfer mechanism which has worked to reduce inequality. Consider first the distribution of post-tax income as shown in **Table 10.3**.

Taking first the period from the end of the 1940s up to the end of the 1970s, two observations can be made. First, income tax does indeed reduce the income dispersion at any point in time.

Table 10.3 *Cumulative Distribution of Personal Income after Income Tax, UK, 1949–85 Selected Years*

Quantile Groups	1949	1959	1967	1975–76	1984–85
Top 1%	6.4	5.3	4.9	3.9	4.9
Top 10%	27.1	25.9	24.3	23.1	26.5
Top 50%	73.5	74.8	73.2	73.4	75.1
Bottom 50%	26.5	25.2	26.8	26.6	24.9

Sources: Diamond Commission, Report no. 1, Table 15; *Social Trends*, 19 (1989 edn).

Second, over time the post-tax dispersion of income alters in roughly the same directions as the pre-tax dispersion. In other words the redistribution of post-tax income has been from the top of the distribution towards the middle rather than towards the bottom. It would thus appear to be the case that, for the period in question, income tax was progressive and a force for equality but that its progressivity altered little over time.

What about the period since 1979? The most obvious point to make is that for the first time since the Second World War the share of post-tax income enjoyed by the top 10 per cent of the distribution has begun to rise. The share of the top 50 per cent of the distribution has also risen steadily during the period since 1979. For the most part, these trends are a reflection of the same patterns emerging in the distribution of pre-tax incomes. However, an additional factor is that, successive governments since 1979 have set out to reduce the burden of direct taxation, either by raising tax thresholds or by reducing the tax rates. Since 1979 both these changes have been implemented on several occasions, the most dramatic being the reduction in the standard rate of income tax from 33 per cent to 25 per cent by the end of 1988. Raising the tax threshold takes some income earners out of the income tax net, but it does nothing positive to improve the relative positions of those whose earned incomes are initially to low to be liable for income tax. Reducing the standard rate of income tax affects only taxpayers, and cannot be considered a force to reduce inequality in post-tax income distribution. It must be noted also that the 1980s have seen a massive reduction in higher rates of income tax – from 83 per cent to 40 per cent on earned income.

Other Direct taxes Plus Welfare Benefits

Income taxation is by no means the only method by which governments can influence the dispersion of income and consumption. Government expenditures confer benefits (with unequal effects upon the community, often in disproportionate amounts) and other forms of taxation, including social security 'contributions', can alter significantly the dispersion of disposable income. The CSO attempts to gauge the fuller impact of government activity on the distribution of incomes by estimating differences between 'original' and 'final' income. Using data collected by the Family Expenditure Survey, the CSO publishes estimates of the distribution of **household** income, including distributions modified by taxes and social security benefits. **Table 10.4** gives the items included in the various income categories.

Since the CSO figures are based on a sample of households and upon an assumed incidence of taxes and benefits, they provide estimates rather than hard facts about income redistribution through state action. What do the estimates suggest? **Table 10.5** gives a summary of CSO findings for the period 1976 to 1986.

On the basis of the CSO estimates we can make two important observations. In the first place, throughout the whole of the period covered by the estimates, the combined impact of taxes and benefits has been to reduce inequality at any point in time. Secondly, the combined influence of taxes and benefits has not prevented a widening of the gap between the very top and the very bottom of the distribution.

The first observation stems from the fact that while the distribution of original income in **Table**

Table 10.4 *Household Definitions used by CSO in Estimates of Income Distribution as Modified by State Tax/Transfer Programmes, 1989*

Income Concept	Definition
Original income	Earnings *plus* Occupational pensions *plus* Annuities, *plus* Investment income *plus* Other income
Disposable income	Original income *plus* Cash benefits *minus* Income tax *minus* National insurance contributions
Final income	Disposable income *minus* Indirect taxes *plus* Benefits in kind (Education, National Health Service, Travel subsidies, Housing subsidy and Welfare foods)

10.5 shows a pattern very similar to that of the distribution of pre-tax incomes in **Table 10.1**, the dispersion in the shares of disposable and final incomes are much less marked at any point in time. In 1986, for example, the top fifth enjoyed 50.7 per cent of original income but only 42.2 per cent of disposable income and 41.7 per cent of final income, while the negligible share of the bottom fifth in original income rose to 5.9 per cent of disposable income and final income. The second

observation is based on the wider dispersions in disposable and final incomes in 1986 as compared with 1976. In terms of percentage points, in 1976 the gap in shares of original income between the bottom and top fifths was 43.6, for disposable income it was 31.1 and for final income it was 30.5; whereas in 1996 the respective gaps were 50.4, 36.3 and 35.8.

Thus, over the decade in question, so far as the extremes of the distribution were concerned, there was a trend towards greater inequality not only in the distribution of original income but also in the distribution of incomes after adjustments for taxes paid and benefits received. This conclusion is endorsed by the more detailed study of the longer period, from 1968–83, undertaken by Morris and Preston using the raw data of the Family Expenditure Survey rather than the published group data. The results are calculated using the Institute for Fiscal Studies' tax and benefit model, which adopts income definitions similar to those used by the CSO. The authors found that both the Lorenz curve and the Gini coefficient give reliable results for the period studied, concluding that their calculations show 'an unambiguous outward movement taking the curve completely beyond that of 1968 and *creating a clear-cut rise in inequality over the 1968–83 period*' (present author's italics). **Figure 10.4** gives a summary of the Morris and Preston findings.

This trend towards greater inequality was to continue throughout the second half of the 1980s. Following the 1991 Budget, the IFS model was used to estimate the cumulative effect of tax and

Table 10.5 *Cumulative Distribution of Original, Disposable and Final Household Income, UK, 1976–86*

Quantile Group	Original Income			Disposable Income			Final Income		
	1976	1981	1986	1976	1981	1986	1976	1981	1986
Top 20%	44.4	46.4	50.7	38.1	39.4	42.2	37.9	38.6	41.7
Top 40%	71.0	73.3	77.6	62.2	63.5	66.3	61.9	62.6	65.6
Top 60%	89.8	91.3	94.0	80.4	81.2	83.2	79.9	80.5	82.6
Bottom 40%	10.2	8.7	6.0	19.6	18.8	16.9	20.1	19.5	17.3
Bottom 20%	0.8	0.6	0.3	7.0	6.7	5.9	7.4	7.1	5.9

Source: Social Trends, 19 (1989 edn).

Figure 10.4 *Lorenz Curves as Calculated by Morris and Preston (1986)*

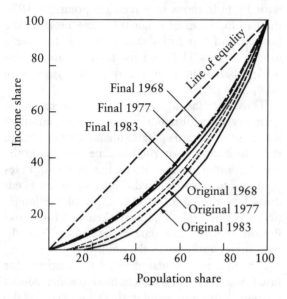

Source: *Fiscal Studies* (1987).

benefit changes since 1979 on household disposable incomes. The model showed that while the combined changes had, on average, produced gains (averaging about £11 per household per week), the distribution of these gains was uneven and the top decile of income earners gained a rise of £95 per week whereas the bottom five deciles actually lost on average over the period (Johnson, Stark and Webb, 1991).

10.2 The Concentration of Wealth

In the view of many observers the distribution of wealth shares within a society gives a more accurate picture of the degree of inequality, because the full extent of individuals' economic power is determined ultimately by their potential command over available resources and this must reflect ownership of assets as well as current income. It is thus held that any society concerned with social justice will be concerned about both wealth and income shares. Unfortunately, when it comes to measuring wealth shares, obstacles are met which are even

bigger than those encountered in the estimation of income distributions. This is true even though wealth and income are but different dimensions of a common set of means by which individuals satisfy their wants. **Wealth** refers to the **stock** of means available, while **income** refers to the **flow** of means from the given stock. Another term for wealth is 'net worth' which underlines the fact that wealth relates to a **net stock** – the difference between a set of assets and a set of liabilities.

10.2.1 The Definition and Measurement of Wealth

Given that any stock of means is measured by the total (capitalised) value of the various items within the stock, the essential preliminary step in empirical work is to determine which assets are to be included in the definition of the wealth stock. Some researchers see the crux of the problem in the relationship between 'value' and 'ownership', the key concept being that of 'marketability'. An individual may own the right to an income flow from a given asset, yet he or she may not be able to realise the market value of that asset because it is **non-transferable**. A prime example of this is the state pension – the asset has a value to its owner because it bestows income, but the pension right cannot be traded in the market-place. Should such rights be included in the calculation of a comprehensive wealth stock? Less difficult to handle in empirical work are those assets which confer income benefits upon their owner and are disposable at an **exchange price** – cash, bank deposits, company shares, government bonds, dwellings and so forth. Clearly, such assets must be included in any definition of personal wealth.

Official measures of wealth distribution in the UK represent **estimates** of wealth holdings since the Inland Revenue does not undertake a regular survey of such holdings in the way that it does for personal incomes. This is because the UK fiscal system does not include a comprehensive wealth tax; it does include capital taxes but those relate to disposals or transfers of assets rather than holdings (see **pp. 154–6**). This means that estimates of

Table 10.6   *The Distribution of Wealth in Great Britain, 1911–60 and the UK, 1966–88*[1]

Quantile Group	% Share of Wealth, GB			% Share of Wealth, UK			
	1911–13	*1936–8*	*1960*	*1966*[2]	*1976*	*1986*	*1988*
Top 1%	69	56	42	33	24	18	17
Top 5%	87	78	75	56	45	36	38
Top 10%	92	88	83	69	60	50	53
Top 25%				87	84	73	75
Top 50%				97	95	92	94

Note:
[1] Figures to nearest whole number.
[2] Using 'estate multiplier' method.
Sources: Diamond Commission, Report no. 1, Table 41 for figures for Great Britain only; *Social Trends*, 21 (1991 edn) Table 5.20 for UK figures.

holdings are made from too narrow a definition of wealth since transfers of 'capital', as defined for tax purposes, exclude some forms of wealth. Prior to the 1960s no official estimates of wealth distribution appeared in government statistical publications, but since then such estimates have been published annually. From 1962 to 1978 the Inland Revenue published annual estimates of both total wealth holdings and the distribution of those holdings based on the 'estate multiplier' method, whereby the estates of persons who die in a given year are used as the sample base for estimating the wealth of the living in that year. From the mid-1970s the CSO published their estimates of wealth holdings based on calculations of the aggregates of assets *minus* liabilities owned by individuals – the so-called 'balance-sheet' approach. From 1978 the Inland Revenue combined these two approaches to produce a new annual series which is also published by the CSO in *Social Trends*.

Needless to say, the methods adopted by government statisticians are disputed by other researchers, and a comprehensive survey must include these alternative estimates. For present purposes we shall confine ourselves to official estimates. For estimates of wealth distribution prior to the 1960s we shall refer to the calculations of Professor Jack Revell who pioneered the balance-sheet approach, later taken up by the CSO. This was the line taken by the Diamond Commission in the mid-1970s and, following the Commission, we can present

the trends in wealth concentration in two distinct periods with 1960 as the watershed. **Table 10.6** presents the various estimates of the distribution of **marketable wealth** – that is, excluding pension rights (both state and occupational).

Table 10.6 suggests that over the course of this century there has been a considerable levelling down of shares in marketable wealth from the very top of the distribution but, overall, the majority of wealth-holdings have remained concentrated in the hands of a minority of wealth-holders. The share of the top 10 per cent of the population fell, from over 90 per cent around 1911 to 50 per cent by 1987. However, in 1987, over 90 per cent of wealth was still owned by the wealthiest 50 per cent of the population. Measured in terms of the rate of decline in wealth shares at the **top** of the distribution, any movement towards equality quickened pace between 1960 and 1980 but slowed down considerably between 1980 and 1988. Since 1960 the Gini coefficient for wealth has been falling but the fall in shares around the middle of the distribution has been sluggish.

If we take account of pension rights the distribution pattern becomes more equal in terms of reducing the shares enjoyed by the top percentiles. **Figure 10.5** shows the changes brought about by including both occupational and state pension rights.

As **Figure 10.5** shows, the share enjoyed by the top 1 per cent was almost halved between 1971

Figure 10.5 *Distribution of Wealth, UK, 1971–87, Selected Years*

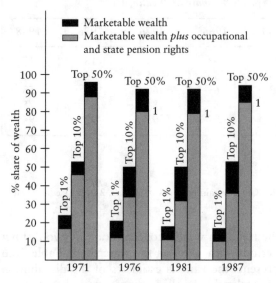

Note:
[1] Depends upon assumptions. Variability = ± 3%.
Source: Social Trends.

and 1988, while that of the top 10 per cent fell from 65 per cent to 36 per cent over the same period. But note that the fall in share of the top 19 per cent was less dramatic than that of the top 1 per cent – the redistribution was taking place **among the wealthiest percentiles**. Note also that in 1987 over 80 per cent of wealth, even when defined to include pension rights, was held by the wealthiest 50 per cent of the population.

The growth and spread of pension rights has been very much a feature of the pattern of wealth ownership over the time period since the Second World War, following the introduction of the State retirement pension under the Nation Insurance Scheme and the later growth in occupational pensions. We shall consider this feature again in the later discussion of poverty. Other important changes have taken place during the same period in the ownership of property (dwellings) and of financial assets, and we shall discuss these presently. But it must be appreciated that over the longer period the break-up of wealth concentration tends to be slow because the interplay of social, demographic and economic influences upon such concentrations is a long process.

Observers of this interplay have concentrated on three important features: the forces of accumulation, the patterns of mating and fertility and the mode of inheritance.

Accumulation Patterns

Analysis of the determinants of accumulation is complex and difficult; it includes exploration of **savings functions** – the relative propensities to save out of income in different property regimes, the relative influences of earnings and profit, and so on. This is not the place to attempt such analysis, but it must be borne in mind. What we can note, however, is that, other things remaining unchanged, an increase in the spread of ownership of property will break down any concentration in property incomes. Part of the explanation of the break-up of wealth concentration in the top half of the distribution in the UK lies in the increased share of the value of dwellings in the composition of net wealth. **Figure 10.6** plots the main patterns in wealth composition between 1971 and 1987.

In 1971 the net value of dwellings made up just over one-fifth of total net wealth in the UK but only sixteen years later this proportion had increased to one-third. The increase was most noticeable during the 1970s following the very sharp rise in house prices during the early years of that decade. Another very sharp rise in house prices during 1987–88 followed by the slump in 1990–91 will no doubt have a significant impact on the final picture for the 1980s.

An increase in the proportional value of dwellings does not, however, reduce inequality in wealth-holdings unless accompanied by an increased spread of ownership. Over the period since the Second World War the UK has increasingly become a 'property-owning democracy' – over the quarter of a century after 1960 the number of owner-occupied dwellings in the UK housing stock actually doubled and, currently, about 67 per cent of households are owner-occupied.

The direction of influence of other major components of net wealth is less certain and there are likely to have been forces pulling in opposite directions. For example, while the proportion of wealth accounted for by building society shares increased steadily between 1971 and 1986, that of national

Figure 10.6 *Composition of Net Wealth of Personal Sector, UK, 1971–87*

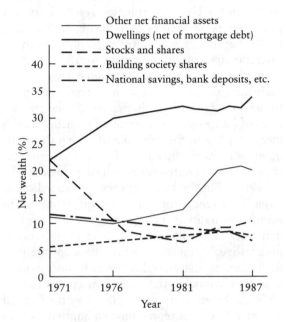

Source: *Social Trends*, 21 (1991 edn).

savings and bank deposits fell markedly. The combined effect of these movements on the overall concentration of wealth will depend upon the extent to which they represent switching among 'popular' assets compared with changes in relative patterns of ownership.

Nor do the trends exhibited by stocks and shares suggest an obvious influence on concentration. The proportion of wealth held in this form fell considerably after the stock market collapse of the early 1970s (the fall in share prices in 1974 was 42 per cent – much greater than in any of the previous 14 years). Between 1971 and 1976 the proportional value of wealth held in the form of stocks and shares fell from 21.7 per cent to 8.2 per cent and by 1981 the proportion was down to 7.0 per cent. However, during the early to mid-1980s this trend changed direction as the proportional value of stocks and shares rose to 10.3 per cent by 1987. During the same period stocks and shares became a more popular form of wealth-holding as the proportion of the adult population owning shares increased from 6 per cent in 1984 to over 20 per cent by the beginning of 1988. Much im-

petus to this increase in share ownership was given by the privatisation of state-owned enterprises such as British Telecom in 1984, and the Trustee Savings Bank and British Gas in 1986. Clearly stocks and shares became a more popular form of asset during the 1980s but this trend does not tell us anything about **relative values of individual share holdings**. What has happened to such values and how they were affected by the impact of the stock market crash of Autumn 1987 will leave a firm mark on the overall pattern of inequality for the 1980s.

Socio-demographic Patterns

Strong influences on the long-term distribution of wealth are exerted by the extent to which the rich marry the rich and the poor marry the poor and by differential fertility – if the rich have fewer children than the poor then concentration increases and vice versa. These are very important considerations, but we do not have the space here to discuss them further. However, one socio-demographic factor which we must look at more closely is that of inheritance patterns. One custom which works strongly against the dispersion of wealth is that of **primogeniture**, strictly the passing on of wealth to the first-born child (although, historically, this has been interpreted as the first born son). If inheritance were not an important determinant of the degree of wealth concentration then such a custom would assume less importance. However, available evidence suggests that inheritance is a major factor in the self-perpetuating cycle of wealth determination.

Much of the evidence collected for the United Kingdom is found in the important work of C.D Harbury and his collaborators. In 1962, Harbury published the results of an attempt to quantify the effect of inheritance on the distribution of wealth (Harbury, 1962). The attempt was based largely on an examination of the relationship between estates left by top wealth-holders and the estates left by their fathers, using a sample of large estates left in the years 1956 and 1957. Among other things, the study found that around two thirds of rich sons (estates over £100,000) had fathers who were in the top 0.25 per cent of wealth-holders, and that the 'self-made man' was in a small minority. In comparing Harbury's study with an earlier one undertaken by Wedgwood for the years 1924–6, Atkinson found that, in spite of social upheavals, inflation, estate duty and so on, there was no clear decline in the importance of inheritance during the first half of the twentieth century (Atkinson, 1972). Later empirical work by Harbury suggested that this view should be qualified somewhat, because inheritance had declined in importance since the earlier studies, but nevertheless the basic argument remains that inheritance is a prime factor in determining wealth. Thus Harbury and McMahon found that over 50 per cent of sons leaving over £100,000 had fathers who had done the same, (Harbury and McMahon, 1973) while Harbury and Hitchens found that some 58 per cent of those who died wealthy had themselves inherited large fortunes (Harbury and Hitchens, 1976).

On 6 April 1991 the *Financial Times* quoted an estimate by Mintel that the total wealth passed from one generation to another in 1990–91 was £8.1 bn, a figure projected to rise to £13 bn by the year 2000, and argued that the reasons are clear: (*i*) inheritances have never been taxed more leniently and (*ii*) the sharp rise in property values in the second half of the 1980s combined with the growth of home ownership. As far as the future is concerned this inheritance factor will work in conjunction with the 'property-owning democracy' to spread inheritance across more of the population, but the impact of this on the degree of inequality in the distribution of wealth will depend, among other things, upon the degree of inequality in the initial distribution of property.

10.2.2 Wealth Taxation: Inheritance and Concentration

If inheritance is such an important determinant of wealth concentration, and if government had a serious commitment to reducing inequality, one might expect that the fiscal system would be used to discourage the concentration of inheritances. So

far in the UK, however, this has not been the case.

Until 1974 Estate Duty was the main tax on wealth in the UK. Unfortunately, estate duty was not a noteworthy success in reducing inequalities, partly because it was never applied properly to discretionary trusts, and partly because the rules permitted exemption of gifts *inter vivos* unless such transfers took place within seven years prior to the donor's death. Perhaps, though, the greatest fault of estate duty as a means of reducing wealth inequality lay in the principle of taxing the value of an estate rather than the value of an inheritance. It is not large estates *per se* which perpetuate inequalities, but the fact that they are passed on as large inheritances and the most efficient way to promote equality by taxing wealth is to tax inherited receipts. Furthermore, if its rates structure is progressive, an inheritance tax offers an incentive to donors to disperse their wealth more widely than they would in the face of an estates tax. In 1974 the Estate Duty was replaced by the Capital Transfer Tax. This represented an improvement in that the new tax was levied on a cumulative basis, not just on wealth at death but also on gifts and bequests *inter vivos*. However, the Capital Transfer Tax was still based on the estate principle and not levied on receipts on transfer, and thus did not provide the additional incentive to disperse wealth that is offered by an inheritance tax.

The Finance Act of 1986 brought in yet another change, with Capital Transfer Tax being replaced by the Inheritance Tax. As in the cases of Estate Duty and Capital Transfer Tax, the new levy was hedged by a long list of wealth exemptions. Further, although the tax is cumulative, no tax is payable on the first part of the cumulative total, an exemption which is increased in April of each year, in line with the rise in the Retail Prices Index. Finally, once again (despite its name) the Inheritance Tax is levied on the value of a gift or an estate and not the amount received or inherited; the main charge under the tax arises on transfers made by an individual on death, or within seven years of death. As with its predecessors, there is no incentive provided under this tax for a wider dispersal of inheritances.

10.3 Poverty and Income Maintenance

10.3.1 'Absolute' versus 'Relative' Definitions

While the discussion of distribution and inequality referred mainly to a summary index, the Gini coefficient, important occasional use was made of the comparison between extremes in a distribution. We turn now to this question of extremes in more detail as we consider poverty as a manifestation of inequality. However, while 'poverty' is indeed a reflection of 'inequality', the two concepts are quite separate and have different meanings. It is a tautology to state that where incomes are unequally distributed the poorest members of the population will be found at the bottom of the distribution. But it may be that these poor individuals are rich indeed when compared with those in the bottom percentile (or even the top percentile) of the income distribution in some other population. In other words, we might judge, say, the bottom 20 per cent of any population to be 'poor' but this may be true in only a relative sense, rather than an absolute one.

The question of relative versus absolute makes it difficult to identify the poor in an empirical sense. If we could rely on an absolute (an objective) measure we could estimate poverty simply by counting the individuals (or the households) who do not possess the means of achieving the absolute minimum standard of living. An absolute yardstick can also be applied over time and, hence, offers the means of checking whether or not the incidence of poverty is changing. So why not rely on an absolute measure of poverty? To answer this question, we must consider carefully what is meant by an 'absolute standard of poverty'. Such a measure would attempt to define a minimum level of subsistence for the chosen income unit (individual or household) and to determine the level of income necessary to guarantee that such a minimum can be enjoyed. Thus, 'the poor' would be those units with incomes short of the minimum level. It should be easy to appreciate that defining absolute subsistence is difficult and not very helpful in the formulation of social policy.

One obvious criticism of absolute measures is that any population is likely to be heterogeneous in terms of minimum requirements. Compare, for example, the basic food and clothing requirements of an 18-year old male who is tall and heavy and whose occupation is felling trees, with those of a retired female schoolteacher who is small and light. But a more fundamental criticism is that 'poverty' can be defined only in relation to prevailing social conventions and available 'life-styles', that is by comparing the differing living standards enjoyed by different units in the population. But this, in turn, causes further difficulties for empirical measurement. What is the minimum living standard for a UK household in 1992? For example, should every household be expected to own a television set? Many social observers have wrestled with the problems of defining minimum relative living standards (and, hence, standards of 'relative deprivation') but none has yet derived a definition which has proved universally acceptable.

10.3.2 Income or Expenditure? Individual or Household?

Another difficult theoretical issue which has very serious implications for empirical work is the question of whether poverty should be defined by reference to **income** or **expenditure**. Some researchers argue that individuals' incomes indicate whether or not they are poor because incomes determine consumption potential. Other researchers argue that this is not the case and that consumption is determined by expenditure which, in turn, is determined not only by income but also by wealth (past savings) and by borrowing – an individual who can dip into past savings and/or can borrow is less constrained in current spending then someone who depends solely on current income to finance current expenditure.

There is also the issue as to whether the reference unit for determining living standards should be seen as the **household** rather than the **individual**. Some researchers argue that choosing the individual as the basic reference unit loses sight of the fact that many individuals live in a household where incomes are pooled and shared, thus permitting some household members to have access to a higher level and range of consumption than that determined by individual income. On the other hand, it can be argued that households vary in size, age and gender structure, with a consequent variable network of dependents, and that such dependency must be recognised when calculating real incomes or expenditures and, therefore, real poverty.

Nor do the problems for researchers end here. For example, another difficult question to answer is whether or not poverty is manifested by individuals' **total** expenditure or by their **specific** expenditures – the actual goods and services purchased. Some researchers have emphasised the need to consider specific expenditures (or, strictly, consumption of specific commodities) and, historically, state welfare programmes have subsidised consumption of specific goods – for example, milk and orange juice. The difficulties for social commentators raised by such considerations are akin to those raised by the concept of **merit goods**, namely that attempts by government to subsidise specific consumption can interfere with individuals' exercise of free choice. For example, a wealthy individual might choose to eat a diet which, taken in isolation, would identify him as poor.

☐ 10.3.3 Poverty Estimates

Given the problems associated with defining minimum standards, most researchers into the incidence of poverty rely on the definition accepted for determining levels of income maintenance under state tax/transfer programmes. This is not to say that state minima are 'correct', but they do provide a benchmark against which successive government programmes might be assessed, at least so long as the minima remain constant in real terms. When the minima themselves are shifting over time, appropriate adjustments must be made if the incidence of poverty is to be tracked across time. For example Abel-Smith and Townsend have estimated that 1.2 per cent of the population were living below National Assistance level in 1953,

while official estimates for 1983 suggest that 5.3 per cent were then living in families with incomes below the Supplementary Benefit levels (Abel-Smith and Townsend, 1965).

Does this means that over that 30-year period there was a more than a fourfold increase in poverty, despite the impressive improvements in living standards for the bulk of the population during the same period? One obvious reason why poverty may not have increased on this sort of scale over the period is that the 'poverty line' was itself raised by successive governments, and the more generous the poverty line the more people become classified as 'poor'.

Another problem to be faced when trying to trace the extent and incidence of poverty over time is that researchers have not used a consistent data base, nor have they maintained a consistent definition of the income unit. For example, Abel-Smith and Townsend, in their comparative study of 1953 and 1960, used the Family Expenditure Survey (FES) and based their findings on expenditure data for 1953 and income data for 1960. Since 1972 the DHSS has also used the FES for its own estimates of the numbers in poverty. However, while Abel-Smith and Townsend based their analysis on the 'household' as the income of expenditure unit, later studies by the DHSS adopt the 'family' which usually means 'tax unit' or 'budget unit' and, therefore, constitutes a narrower income/expenditure unit. Since broader units, like households, offer greater access to shared resources than do narrower units like the family and the tax unit, it is not surprising that the extent of poverty is relatively greater when measured across the narrower units.

The two difficulties emphasised are but examples of many differences in the way researchers have tried to estimate the extent of poverty. Some studies have used the General Household Survey as their data base; studies differ in their definition of disposable income and the items to be offset against gross income; studies differ in their treatment of 'necessary' expenditure on children's welfare; and so on. Thus, taking account of the many different approaches, it is not surprising that estimates of, say, individuals in poverty can vary from 1.2 per cent to 12.3 per cent for 1953/54 and between 2.3 per cent and 11.3 per cent for 1975 (Hemming, 1984)

One way to achieve a consistent measure of the extent of poverty has been suggested by Piachaud who uses a poverty line which remains constant relative to prevailing living standards (Piachaud, 1988). Piachaud's guideline is the level of personal disposable income *per capita* which includes all forms of money income and is not directly affected by changes in the composition of households. Thus, if the poverty line keeps pace with this guideline, then the relative poverty level can be said to have remained constant. Using this index Piachaud is able to adjust both the findings of Abel-Smith and Townsend and the later estimates of the DHSS to make them directly comparable. His findings suggest a four-fold increase in poverty over the 30-year period from 1953 to 1983, insofar as they identify 6.2 per cent of households in 1953 and 23.3 per cent of families in 1983. If we use Piachaud's findings for families only, covering the decade 1973–83, the increase in poverty is very much smaller over the shorter period – from 19.4 per cent to 23.3 per cent.

The most graphic recent example of how conflicting conclusions can be drawn from very similar data bases was provided by three studies which published their findings within a few weeks of each other early in 1991. These were (i) a report (Townsend, 1991) for the Statistical Monitoring Unit at the University of Bristol, (ii) the EC's re-port on its second anti-poverty programme (EC, 1991) and (iii) a report published by the Institute for Fiscal Studies (IFS) of a study carried out on behalf of the House of Commons Social Security Select Committee (Social Security Select Committee, 1991). The Townsend study concluded that income inequality had increased in the UK over the decade of the 1980s and also that the poorest 20 per cent of the population were worse off at the end of that decade (after adjusting for inflation). A similarly depressing conclusion was drawn by the EC report which claimed that there were more individuals living in relative poverty in the UK than in any other country within the EC. By way of contrast, however, not only did the approach adopted by the Department of Social Security (DSS), and reviewed in the IFS report for the Select Committee, arrive at different numbers for those on low incomes from the findings of the EC report, but it also concluded, in contrast to Townsend's findings, that the real incomes of the poorest 10 per cent of the population may have **increased** (by up to 10 per cent) over the decade of the 1980s.

This is not the place to explore the fine details of such different findings, but they are referred to here to underline the difficulties in discovering the truth about poverty and its incidence. The reader is recommended to study the excellent analysis of the three studies published by the IFS in May 1991 (Johnson and Webb, 1991). As a final illustration of the nuances in definition and consequent modi-

Table 10.7 *Summary of Main Characteristics of Three Major Surveys of Poverty Published in 1991*

	Townsend	EC	DSS
Area covered	UK	UK/EC	GB
Data source	FES reports	FES micro-data	FES micro-data
Period	1979–89	1975/80/85	1979–88
Unit of measurement	Disposable income[1]	Expenditure	Income before/after housing costs
Definition of poverty	Poorest quintile	Expenditure <50% of national average	No explicit poverty line
Adjustments for household size (equivalisation)	None	OECD scales	McClements scales

Notes:
[1] Including housing help to SB recipients pre-1983.
Source: Johnson and Webb (1991) Table 2.

fications to data bases, a summary table from the analysis by Johnson and Webb is reproduced as **Table 10.7**.

But while there is no agreement among empirical observers on the magnitude of changes in the extent of poverty in the UK, there is unanimity on the observation that poverty has remained a stubbornly persistent feature of UK society. This feature was justly highlighted by the sociologists Abel-Smith and Townsend, and came as a major surprise to a society which had undergone significant restructuring of its public sector, including its system of income maintenance, shortly after the Second World War, and which had enjoyed, in the aggregate, the fruits of considerable economic growth over the first two postwar decades. The Abel-Smith and Townsend findings were to inspire the many further efforts to monitor the scale and incidence of poverty over the next 20 years and more as the extent of poverty became once again a major concern of social policy.

☐ 10.3.4 The Origins of the Present System

For most of the period since the Second World War anti-poverty legislation in the UK has built on the foundations laid down in the Beveridge Report of 1942, subject to occasional modification (Cmd 6404, 1942). There was no attempt at a comprehensive overhaul of the Beveridge system until the Conservative Government's White Paper in 1985 and the subsequent reforms embodied in the 1986 Social Security Act (implemented fully only in 1988). The primary aim of the Beveridge Plan was to eradicate all want by concentrating on its causes: loss of work through unemployment or sickness, cessation of work through retirement and the drain on household resources created by large numbers of dependents. The main instrument of the system was a comprehensive programme of social (or 'national') insurance, offering flat-rate benefits to the

Table 10.8 *The 1940s Foundations of the Welfare State in the UK*

Social Security	*Beveridge Report* (1942)
	Social Insurance White Paper (1944)
	Accepted most of Beveridge's recommendations
	Family Allowance Act 1945
	National Insurance Act 1946
	Based on 1944 White Paper
	National Insurance (Industrial Injuries) Act 1946
	National Assistance Act 1948
Employment	*Employment Policy White Paper* (1944)
	Committed government to maintaining a high (and stable) level of employment through deficit spending when necessary
Health	*National Health Service White Paper* (1944)
	Set plans for comprehensive health care for all, free of direct user charge and financed out of general taxation
	National Health Service Act 1946
	Based on 1944 White Paper
Education	*Educational Reconstruction White Paper* (1943)
	Set out plans for comprehensive national system of primary, secondary and further education, primary and secondary education to be free of direct user charge and financed out of general taxation
	Education Act 1946
	Based on 1943 White Paper

unemployed and the sick and flat-rate retirement pensions, financed mainly by weekly contributions from those covered by the scheme. This programme was supported by Family Allowances (later to become Child Benefits) payable on behalf of all children except the first born. As a minimum income guarantee the programme include National Assistance (later Supplementary Benefit and the Income Supplement) for those whose needs could not be met by the insurance scheme. The insurance benefits were intended to be sufficient to satisfy subsistence needs, and the role of National Assistance was anticipated to be minimal.

The optimism underlying the anticipation of such a minimal role for National Assistance was founded on an assumption that full employment would prevail. This optimism was reflected also in the fact that Family Allowance was not to be payable for the first child in a family since the family wage in a fully employed economy would be sufficient to support one child. It must be remembered that the Beveridge scheme was introduced at a time when government believed that management of aggregate demand would in future ensure that the evil of mass unemployment did not return. This new-found faith in demand management was to be enshrined in the famous White Paper of 1944 (UK, 1944, Cmd 6527). It is worth remembering also that the years 1945–50 witnessed the introduction of other 'social welfare' programmes to complete a massive frontal attack on the main causes of deprivation; in particular the Education Act 1944 and the National Health Service Act 1946 were meant to add significant firepower to the state's armoury. **Table 10.8** summarises the flurry of State activity in the 1940s which provided the foundations to what came to be known as the 'Welfare State'.

☐ 10.3.5 Socio-economic Changes and the Incidence of Poverty

Although not intended by Beveridge, the social security system in the UK grew steadily over the decades following the Second World War until, by the mid-1980s, it was accounting for almost one-third of all public expenditure. Over this same period the importance of social security benefits as a component of personal incomes grew dramatically, from less than 10 per cent in the mid-1950s to over 20 per cent by the mid-1980s. According to its critics, this relative growth of the social security system is further testimony to its failure, brought about by its intrinsic nature and by the fact that its basic philosophy has been interpreted differently by successive governments.

So large a scheme, covering so many categories of want through state discretion, is likely to be slow to adapt to changes in the social and economic structure. The period after the Second World War has seen many demographic changes. In particular it has seen proportional increases in the dependent sectors of the population, as well as changes in the scale and incidence of unemployment and changes in the occupational wage structure. One result of the many changes unforeseen by Beveridge has been the heavy dependency upon the role of the so-called 'safety net' of National Assistance/Supplementary Benefit/Income Supplement. The Beveridge intention that the safety net would play a minimal role has not been realised, a problem compounded by government's refusals to guarantee that National Insurance benefits at least be equal to subsistence requirements.

In terms of demographic and structural changes, the three most significant ones have been in the number of aged people, family composition, and the level and incidence of unemployment.

☐ 10.3.6 Poverty and Old Age

The population of the UK, like that of the rest of Europe and other parts of the developed world, has been getting older and is expected to continue doing so well into the foreseeable future. In the UK at the beginning of the 1950s the proportion of the population aged 65 and over was just under 11 per cent, but by the middle of the 1980s it had risen to just under 15 per cent. Projections published by the OECD, and reproduced in **Table 10.9**, suggest that by the middle of the next century the elderly populations of the UK and several other developed countries will have doubled their proportional sizes.

Table 10.9 *Projections of the Elderly Population, UK and Selected Countries, % of Population Aged 65 and Over*

	UK	US	Japan	Canada	France	W. Germany	Italy
1980[1]	14.9	11.3	9.1	9.5	14.0	15.5	13.5
1985[1]	15.1	11.9	10.2	10.4	13.0	14.8	12.9
2000	14.5	12.1	15.2	12.8	15.3	17.1	15.3
2020	18.7	17.2	22.9	20.0	21.2	23.5	20.7
2040	26.4	25.3	29.2	29.2	29.7	34.1	29.1
2050	28.7	29.0	33.1	33.0	34.0	36.2	31.0

Note:
[1] Actual.
Source: Financial Times (6 July 1988, using OECD Demographic Data Files).

The projections in **Table 10.9** suggest severe implications for future income maintenance arrangements (and for the health care of the elderly) in the light of their performance in the face of the ageing of the population to date. One vivid representation of the burden placed on the system so far is that around 16 per cent of the social security budget in the mid-1980s would not have been required if the benefit then had been payable to the number of pensioners alive in the early 1950s. (Dilnot, Kay and Morris, 1984). This is not to say that the burden of the elderly had been completely unanticipated by Beveridge. Indeed the Report envisaged that over the 'transitional period' up to 1965, social security costs would rise by some 25 per cent due to the increasing burden of retirement pensions. However, over the course of the transitional period the cost of retirement pensions, in real terms, was twice as high as Beveridge had envisaged.

Poverty among old people is not a new feature of society, but it has been a notorious contributor to total domestic poverty over the course of the twentieth century. The famous surveys of poverty in York undertaken by Rowntree found that old age was the major cause of poverty in under 5 per cent of poor households in 1899 whereas in 1951 old age was estimated to be the cause of poverty in two-thirds of poor households. Rowntree's explanation of this trend included the increase in the relative size of the aged population and the increase tendency for the aged to live alone rather than with their families. As we have seen, the proportion of old people in the population has increased markedly since Rowntree's last survey.

Income sources for the aged are based less on market earnings than is the case with younger age groups. Labour market activity rates for pensioner households have fallen dramatically since the beginning of the twentieth century, and retirement pensions, both state and private, have become the main source of income for such households. Some indication of how this reliance on pension income affects living standards for old people can be taken from a comprehensive survey of poverty in the early 1970s which found a 17 per cent risk of poverty for the elderly compared with only 2.5 per cent of other adults (the risk for old people living alone was calculated to be as high as 30 per cent) and that, in total, elderly households accounted for approximately 42 per cent of the poverty among the sample (Fiegehen, Lamsley and Smith, 1977).

While the risk factor remains high for old people, recent government estimates suggest that old age has diminished as a factor in poverty since the beginning of the 1970s. New legislation to combat poverty introduced in the mid-1980s gave more emphasis to the burden of pensions on taxpayers than to the burden of poverty on pensioners, against the background of a fall in the proportion of pensioners in the poorest fifth of the population from 35 per cent to 19 per cent between 1971 and 1982. Nevertheless, such an estimate still suggests that roughly one in five of the poorest fifth were pensioners at the start of the 1980s.

☐ *10.3.7 Family Poverty*

The other major component of the dependency sector of the population is children. Various surveys of poverty in the years before the Second World War had identified the number of children in a family as a major determinant of family poverty. In recent years concern has arisen again over this issue. Despite a fall in the proportion of households with dependent children from 39 per cent to 32 per cent over the period 1971–85, the proportion of couples with children, together with single parents, rose from 48 per cent to 58 per cent among the poorest fifth of the population over roughly the same period (1971–82). One estimate has claimed that between £1.5 bn and £2 bn of social security expenditure in the mid-1980s was due to trends in the number of children wholly or partly within the social security system's responsibility (Berthoud 1985). The increase in the number of single parents has been a particular cause for concern. According to official estimates the rise in divorces, the increasing incidence of illegitimate births and fewer illegitimate children being put forward for adoption, all contributed to the proportion of people living in one-parent families with children doubling from 2.5 per cent in 1961 to 5 per cent by 1985. It must be said that the one-parent family was a problem identified by Beveridge, but its increase on such a scale was not anticipated.

☐ *10.3.8 Lower Earnings and Unemployment*

The Beveridge Report paid a lot of attention to the problems created by unemployment, taking account of the history of the labour market and, in particular, the 1930s. However, in this one respect, the experience of the first three decades after Beveridge seemed to suggest that full employment was not the norm and unemployment was, indeed, a contingency. The reality after 1970 was to shatter this illusion as unemployment rose to over 13 per cent by 1984, including a dramatic increase in the numbers of long-term unemployed which

swelled the numbers in receipt of Supplementary Benefit following the exhaustion of rights to Unemployment Benefit.

However, unemployment has not been the sole economic cause of poverty among families. Another problem which Beveridge failed to anticipate was the high incidence of low earnings among households in poverty after the Second World War. Beveridge virtually took it for granted that earnings in a fully employed labour market would be sufficient to support a dependent spouse and one child – this was the main reason why Family Allowance was to be for the second and any further children in a family.

However, the general increase in living standards which has pushed up the poverty line has left behind certain groups in low-paid employment. In 1986 there were 290,000 families (680,000 persons including children) with incomes below Supplementary Benefit level despite the family head being in full-time employment.

▮ *10.4 The Response from the System*

☐ *10.4.1 Poverty Among the Aged*

How well has the system copied with these social and economic pressures? Given the numbers remaining in poverty, particularly in specific groups of dependents, the UK's social security programme has been found wanting. Some observers have blamed successive governments for failing to implement fully the Beveridge proposals, while others have emphasised that the cause of the problem lies in the nature of social insurance programmes. One important principle of the Beveridge scheme which has not been adhered to consistently is that National Insurance benefits should be at least equal to the basic poverty standard. On this principle was based the expectation that National Assistance (now Income Support) would be a genuine 'safety net'. Yet for long periods throughout the post-Beveridge years this principle was not adhered to in the categories of pensioners and children. Many pensioner households have had to rely on a flat-rate state retirement pension which has not been maintained at all times at a level above the state minimum. Hence those pensioner households totally depend on the state retirement pension have required supplementation to their flat-rate benefit and even in the early 1980s more than a fifth of pensioners were supported by Supplementary Benefit. Until Child Benefits were introduced in 1977, direct state income support for children was founded on Family Allowances, where the rate payable to the first eligible child was raised only twice between 1945 and 1975. Indeed, over the period 1948–67 the real value of Family Allowances declined by 22 per cent.

The most important determinant of the system's response to changes in the socio-economic structure has been the fact that benefit levels and eligibility conditions have been at the discretion of government. Social security budgeting has had to take its place in the ranking of expenditure priorities, set against available government revenues. Recall that the Beveridge perception of social security was one of insurance against contingencies like unemployment and sickness, and against loss of earnings on retirement, with earmarked benefits for children and all supported by National Assistance for those not catered for within the insurance scheme. The Beveridge programme of income maintenance was thus founded on a relationship between the principles of 'contribution' (the insurance part) and 'eligibility' (or means-testing, for the assistance part). This has given rise to two difficulties for governments. In the first place, social insurance is not very flexible; because its benefits depend on past contributions it reacts slowly to socio-economic change. Secondly, the relationship between contribution record and means testing for supplementation is very difficult to maintain.

To try and resolve the first difficulty, successive UK Governments added on several new measures to the fundamental, Beveridge-based, social security programme. Inevitably, this increased the scheme's complexity. Significant steps were taken to modify provision in the three main areas outlined earlier: retirement, family size and low earnings. The increase in the number of pensioners was to put pressure on the social security system in

terms of both the increasing costs of providing Beveridge-style retirement pensions and the need to make adequate provision for pensioners as living standards rose for the population as a whole. The year 1961 saw the introduction of a graduated pension, financed by a graduated contribution (a scheme which was extended to earnings-related supplements to unemployment benefit, sickness benefit and maternity allowances in 1966). Those employees with occupational pension rights considered by the authorities to be 'adequate' were permitted to 'contract out' of the graduated pensions scheme, another significant factor leading, by the end of the 1960s, to a situation wherein the cost of benefits had risen significantly in relation to the size of the potential 'tax base'. From 1969 onwards graduated contributions financed more and more of the flat-rate benefits.

However, the major change in state pension arrangements was to come in the Social Security Pensions Act 1975 and its implementation in April 1978. This legislation introduced the State Earnings Related Pension Scheme (SERPS) under which retirement pensions were to comprise an earnings-related addition to the basic flat-rate benefit (once again provision was made for adequate occupational pension schemes to be 'contracted out' of SERPS). Early fears about the full cost of SERPS led to a proposal for its abandonment in a government Green Paper published only seven years after its introduction. However, the ensuing White Paper of 1986 retained SERPS with modifications designed to reduce its long-term cost – the 1986 White Paper will be considered in more detail later.

10.4.2 Insurance or 'Pay as you go'

On the question of pensions, the second difficulty referred to earlier links closely with the first since the problem of the ever increasing costs of pensions has arisen mainly because public preoccupation has been with the income maintenance aspect of pensions rather than the principle of insurance. It is difficult to see how this could be otherwise in a state-provided scheme. To try and appreciate this point it might help to rehearse the arguments for state involvement in provisions for retirement.

Microeconomic theory depicts the individual as maximising the satisfaction which he or she derives from consuming goods (including leisure) and services, according to taste and subject to various constraints. Since the rational individual is interested in lifetime utility, he or she will attach relative weights to present and future consumption levels according to his or her time-preference pattern of consumption, and attempt to maximise satisfaction subject to both present and expected future constraints. Given that individuals do behave in this way, a state programme of compulsory provision for old age may distort the individual's 'optimal' (from the point of view of his or her own time-preference pattern) allocation of consumption between time periods. The individual with positive time preference is forced to increase future consumption at the expense of the present, and even the individual who places a greater weight upon future consumption is satisfied only if the level of state provision accords with his or her own expectations and desires.

The counter-argument is that the time preferences of most individuals are such that they make inadequate provision for old age for two main reasons, namely widespread myopia, intensified by the difficulties of decision-making which takes account of the distant future, and a lack of means by which to plan a consumption pattern over more than one time period. Even if the state could mitigate the latter part of the problem by providing those without means with a margin of saving over current consumption, this would be fruitful only if the first part of the problem could be solved.

Thus, given that individuals are improvident, or find the calculus of optimisation concerning future income streams, investment yields, family circumstances, likelihood of employment and so on beyond their mental powers, the state assumes a paternalistic role via the compulsory purchase of annuities so as to protect the individual. If the individual does not want this protection – for example, if he or she has a very strong positive time preference for consumption – the state justifies its interference on the grounds of social costs. While concern for others might lead society to help the myopic and improvident, it does not prevent society from taking steps to ensure that the need for such aid is minimised. Furthermore, it is reasonable to expect that the working population at any point in time might wish to minimise the likelihood of their children having to support the retired population at some future date and demand that individuals be compelled to make proper provision for their retirement needs.

It must be admitted that even if a case exists for compulsory insurance, itself debatable, it is by no means obvious that this requires the compulsory purchase of state annuities. But assuming that this method of protection is adopted, should a state scheme be organised, as far as possible, on an insurance basis? The pension problem is an intergenerational one. If we accept that the sole rationale for intervention is to protect a future generation of tax-payers (the assumption we made above), then the state has a duty to organise its scheme on a funded basis, that is to ensure its actuarial soundness. To protect current policy-holders against the possibility of receipts being less than adequate to cover benefit payments at some future date, a reserve fund would be accumulated on behalf of all insured persons. To create such a reserve, premiums would be set at a sufficiently high level; if the individual wants the promise of a higher level of benefit, or more comprehensive coverage than is allowed by the original contract, he or she must be prepared to pay a higher premium. In this way, then, a reserve is accumulated for each individual, and it follows that an increase in the number of people insured must mean an increase in total reserves.

However, if we modify the rationale of intervention to one of protecting all generations, including current taxpayers, then the state has no need to organise its scheme on a funded basis (even assuming it could do so), but can make use of its coercive powers to establish the programme on a 'pay-as-you-go' basis, whereby current beneficiaries are supported by current contributions. In other words, an 'acceptable' tax/transfer plan can be devised. This argument is based on two assumptions – namely, that the scheme is financed by compulsory contributions and that future governments maintain the compulsion. Given these conditions, we can view social 'insurance' as a form of social contract whereby the young are prepared to support the old on the guarantee that a future generation of taxpayers will do the same for them when they grow old.

But what happens if the age structure of the population changes? In particular, what happens if the proportion of the retired population increases significantly? In order to maintain the same level of pension per head of the retired population the contributory costs on the active population must rise. If this situation persists, and these costs continue to rise, the contract is very much weakened and is likely to be modified by government action. This problem appears even with real incomes growing over time if pension levels are to be determined relative to current living standards. In other words, the insurance system collapses into the government's general tax/transfer programme.

The consequences of accepting the provision of income maintenance for retired people as part of a state tax/transfer mechanism are many. One important feature at the time of inception is that 'pensions' can be paid immediately – that is, contributions do not have to grow on a funded basis before an individual enjoys the fruits of entitlement. But the most important, if obvious, consequence is that pension arrangements as part of a wider tax/transfer mechanism are decided by government and become the subject of political as well as financial constraints. One area where this can raise difficult problems is in respect of inequality – what should be the 'reasonable' level for state pension benefits given the benefits enjoyed by those in receipt of occupational pensions? And how should state retirement transfer compare with, say, transfers to the temporarily sick or unemployed?

These very questions have been discussed constantly in the debate over pensions in the UK. At the same time eligibility for retirement pension has been, and continues to be, based on contribution records. From the very start the post-Beveridge scheme of national insurance was not funded on an actuarial basis. Even in its early years current contributions from employees and employers comprised a very large proportion of the total current receipts of the National Insurance Fund, and by the mid-1960s this proportion had risen to 80 per cent with contributions from interest income and exchequer grants having fallen dramatically.

Clearly, the social security system has moved a long way from the insurance principles recommended in the Beveridge Report. As one research report puts it, 'in introducing full-rate pensions straight away, the Government acknowledged a funding deficiency to be met from general taxation. When the time came to pay the subsidy on any substantial scale, the pledge was abandoned and a "pay as you go" basis adopted. The National Insurance Fund was reduced to meaningless accounting and the actuarial link between contribution and benefits abandoned' (Dilnot, Kay and Morris, 1984). Yet, as the same report points out, 'contribution records' are still the basis of eligibility (at substantial administrative cost). Whether or not this is because governments still believe (as Beveridge did) that individuals are more willing to pay 'contributions' than 'taxes' is debatable. Of course if governments do believe this to be so they might also believe that their capacity for raising revenue without generating too much political 'heat' is enhanced.

10.4.3 Poverty Among Families With Children

In the area of family poverty too there have been major changes. We have mentioned the long-term decline in the real value of Family Allowances. In 1957 child tax allowances were reintroduced (first used in 1909 but removed when the Family Allowance was introduced) whereby deductions could be allowed from income for tax purposes at rates varying according to the age of the child. While such allowances offered indirect help to families with children, their distributional consequences differed from those of direct benefits. To see this more clearly consider the situation after 1968 when Family Allowances became classified as taxable income and hence subject to reclamation by the Inland Revenue (the 'claw-back' principle). This clawing-back meant that the real value of the Family Allowance rose as family income fell. Tax allowances, on the other hand, increased in value as family income rose because of the rate structure of income tax. This meant that families with incomes so low as to be unaffected by income tax did not receive any real benefit from the tax allowances, and the benefits enjoyed by tax-paying families favoured the higher income groups.

Both tax allowances and Family Allowance were merged in the Child Benefit Act 1975 which introduced a **flat-rate benefit** on behalf of each child in a family and paid at a higher rate for one-parent families, the latter in recognition of the growth in single parenthood. Child Benefit, like the Family Allowance, is a 'universal' benefit – that is, payable to every family unit with children irrespective of the income of that family unit. As such it remains a contentious issue and we shall return to it shortly when considering the vexed question of how to make social security more efficient.

The other main cause of family poverty discussed earlier was that of earnings too low to support a spouse and child, contrary to the assumption of the Beveridge Report. This problem was brought to governments' attention on several occasions by various lobbies, in particular by the Child Poverty Action Group. A response was offered by the Conservative Government of 1971 when it introduced Family Income Supplement (FIS), a means-tested benefit specifically aimed at those families where the family head was in full-time employment but whose earnings were below the 'prescribed amount'. FIS was welcomed with great optimiam, but its effects were disappointing and it was replaced in 1988 by **Family Credits**.

There were many other modifications and additions to the social security over the post-Beveridge period. We cannot enter into the details of the main 'piecemeal' changes, but we should note here that help with housing costs was another major source of help offered to low-income families. Rate rebates were introduced in 1968, and a national scheme of rent rebates and allowances was introduced in 1972 following years of development in local authority schemes in the 1950s and 1960s. In 1983 **Housing Benefit** was introduced to replace these earlier arrangements. The other major change to note is the extension of the principle of earnings-related income maintenance, not only from the supplement offered under the 1961 graduated pension scheme to the later pension arrangements

already discussed, but also to other national insurance benefits in 1966 and 1975. By 1985 the social security system offered a complex array of 30 separate benefits with differing structures and rationales and costing over £2 bn annually to administer.

□ *10.4.4 The Problem of 'Take-up'*

We turn now to a question which has so far only been hinted at. While the pressures on the social security system go some of the way to explain why so many individuals have had to rely on the safety net of benefit supplementations, they do not explain why so many have fallen **below** the poverty line. The main reason why so many fall below this line is because they are not in receipt of full income supplementations **even when entitled to them**. This is the infamous problem of low 'take-up' thought, by most commentators, to be due to two causes: the complexity of the social security system and the stigma which attaches to receipt of means-tested benefits. The complexity of the system was underlined earlier. Not only is there a plethora of benefits for claimants to consider, but there is also a detailed and, for many claimants, difficult application procedure. Part of the difficulty lies in the detail required in order to assess the means and needs of claimants but this very enquiry is also considered to be degrading by many potential claimants. As a consequence, many eligible individuals refrain from claiming means-tested benefits.

A government inquiry in 1965 found that one-third of pensioners were ignorant of the availability of National Assistance, while 30 per cent of married couples and 20 per cent of single men and women indicated that pride prevented them from applying for supplementary help. Family Income Supplement at the end of the 1970s was being taken up by only 50 per cent out of those eligible while, at the same time, the take-up rate for Supplementary Benefit was around 74 per cent and that for Rent and Rates Rebates in the region of 70 per cent, all according to government estimates. In 1987 Fry and Stark published a comparison of their own estimates of Supplementary Benefit take-up and those of the DHSS for a period covering

Table 10.10 *Estimates of Supplementary Benefit Take-up*

Study	Year	Take-up rate		
		Pensioners	*Non-pensioners*	*All*
DHSS	1977	0.72	0.79	–
DHSS	1979	0.65	0.78	0.70
DHSS	1981	0.67	0.75	0.71
Fry and Stark	1984	0.87	0.81	0.83
Fry and Stark[1]	1984	0.66	0.78	0.74

Note:
[1] Estimates on 'DHSS basis'.
Source: Fry and Stark (1986).

the end of the 1950s to the middle of the 1980s (Fry and Stark, 1987). Their findings, reproduced in **Table 10.10** underline the fact that take-up of the 'bottom line' income support for the period in question was well short of 100 per cent.

Low take-up of means-tested benefits creates two serious problems for income maintenance programmes. An obvious, but important consequences of low take-up among means-tested households is that income support is not being given to many of the households most in need of it. A second consequence, creating a problem for the longer run, is that low take-up rates affect the accuracy of policy planning because they influence the outcome of benefit expenditure by the government. For example, a reduction in universal benefits and an increase in selective or 'targeted' (means-tested) benefits should, in principle, result in a more equal distribution of final incomes, but, if the former type of benefit has a high take-up rate and the latter a low one, the move towards equality is lessened. This is a problem we shall return to later.

10.4.5 *The Social Security 'Traps'*

Another reason advanced to explain high numbers remaining in poverty, even during a time of economic growth for the country as a whole, relates to the implicit taxation of earned income in a social security system which relies on means-tested benefits, for basic income support. This implicit taxation arises from the interaction among means-tested benefits and between them and the income tax system. As the number of means-tested benefits rose over the decades following the Beveridge Report this was to become an increasing problem.

The various means-tested benefits and the social security programme are, in fact, examples of the principle of 'negative (income) taxation' in the sense that principles governing the receipt of benefit include elements of tax as well as welfare payment. These separable elements emerge from both the direction of the **total** resource flow involved and the nature of the impact at the **margin** of economic activity. Taking the case of a family unit of given size, we can demonstrate this point by assuming eligibility for weekly benefit to be determined by the amount of weekly income earned by the unit from other sources, say from earned income. Thus, at the margin, the net flow of resources is from the private sector to the government. In other words, the family unit is being taxed on **additional earnings**. However, the total flow of resources remains in the opposite direction to that of a tax since the net overall effect of the scheme is a supplement to the income of the family unit.

We may also note at this stage that the structure of means-tested benefits, as in this example, usually bears the other hallmarks of a taxation scheme. Benefit is paid to, or withheld from, a defined tax unit (say, head of household plus dependants); is determined by reference to a defined base (say, earned income); and the benefit payable in any period depends on income received by the tax unit from the base source during that same period. There is, however, one feature of means-tested social security benefits which does set them apart from usual tax conventions: the marginal rate of tax applied to low levels of income is often very high because state supplements to income are a substitute for a lack of income from other sources within the tax base. Hence, as other income rises, the supplement is withdrawn. The rationale for this may lie in the philosophy behind the system (only those who have a genuine need for state help can receive it) and/or a lack of resources in society to permit a more generous redistribution of resources towards the lower income groups.

The propensity for claimants to incur high marginal tax rates, is, of course, increased by interaction between the benefits system and the income tax. The so-called **poverty trap** operates usually when an increase in earnings offers only a small increase in final income because of simultaneous lower benefit receipt and higher taxes and National Insurance contributions; in its most extreme form it has affected families in work so as to make them **worse off** by earning an extra £1 of income. While the withdrawal of means-tested benefits has placed claimants on high marginal rates of (implicit) tax throughout the post-Beveridge period, the piecemeal additions to the benefit system served to intensify the problem. In particular, the introduction of FIS and its resulting interaction with housing subsidies was to become the main reason for poor households facing marginal rates of tax in excess of 100 per cent: the numbers of families in this severe form of the poverty trap was estimated by the Treasury and Civil Service Committee in 1982 to have increased from 15,000 in early 1974 to 105,600 by the end of 1981.

The **unemployment trap** operates when low-earning households find that they are either financially better off depending on state benefits than in paid employment, or that the difference in living standards offered by the two choices is so small that the incentive to find paid work is very small. This particular problem was considered to be severe by the 1970s in the case of the short-term unemployed. It has been estimated that in 1978

about 21 per cent of the heads of working families would have received more than 90 per cent of their weekly income if, instead, they had been unemployed for a short time (Dilnot, Kay and Morris, 1984). This was probably due to the availability of earnings-related benefit supplements and the fact that tax rebates were received during unemployment of short duration. In 1982, Unemployment Benefit was made taxable and earnings-related benefit supplement was abolished earlier in the same year. It has been estimated that only 2.9 per cent of people would have been able to enjoy more than 90 per cent of their income in work during a short spell of unemployment (Dilnot, Kay and Morris, 1984).

10.4.6 *Fairness, Incentives and Supply-side Effects*

High marginal rates of tax on the earnings of poor individuals or households are considered to be undesirable for reasons of equity as well as efficiency. When a tax system, like that of the UK, is based on a principle of 'ability to pay' supported by a progressive rates structure, it is absurd as well as unfair for the tax system to combine with the social security programme and impose higher marginal rates of tax on low income groups than on higher income groups. While most observers agree about the inequity of the system's regressive rates structure, there is less agreement on the extent to which means-testing creates genuine disincentives to effort. Government preoccupation with the question of work disincentives has been a constant feature of social security in the UK, although this concern has been dressed up in different language from time to time. Hence, 'less eligibility' was the principle behind the nineteenth-century Poor Law condition that state aid to the unemployed should be less than the lowest earnings rate; the same principle supported the 'wages stop' of the post-Beveridge Unemployment Benefit programme; and the need to minimise the 'disincentive to effort' became an essential ingredient of government policies on supply-side economics during the 1970s and 1980s.

The increasing government preoccupation with supply-side economics has encouraged several investigations by economists into household reactions to changes in the relative costs of work and leisure. These have concentrated more on changes in the marginal rate of taxation, and less on the average rate which affects disposable incomes and is more significant when considering Keynesian demand-side policy. If marginal tax rates are reduced, households are faced with an increase in the monetary reward for extra time at work. But microeconomic theory suggests that the resulting change in labour supply will depend upon the directions and relative strengths of **income and substitution effects**; the former is an inducement to substitute work for the now relatively more expensive leisure, while the latter may encourage the household to work less hours and enjoy some of its increase in real income in the form of leisure. Thus, if the substitution effect dominates, households will supply more work, but if the income effect dominates more leisure might be consumed.

The likely outcome to a change in marginal rates of tax is clearly an empirical question, but one which has proved difficult to answer, and research into labour supply reactions has unearthed evidence of both incentives and disincentives arising from alterations in the marginal net income of households (see **pp. 82–3**). However, so far as the poverty trap is concerned, since the effective marginal tax rates can be so high it is difficult to assume that disincentives to effort do not exist in and around the trap, and government concern has accordingly centred on how many individuals are actively caught in the trap.

In looking at the unemployment trap, empirical work has tended to concentrate on the estimation of the **replacement rate** – that is, the ratio of net income out of work to net income in work, for various household categories. Our earlier reference to relative returns from working and living on state benefit before and after 1978 took account of replacement rates. The estimate quoted there of the proportions affected by high replacement rates was but one of several attempts to measure the supply-side disincentives of the benefit system before and after the 1978 changes. As with the poverty trap, estimation of the impact of

the unemployment trap have proved difficult, and there is by no means a consensus on the issue of whether or not the benefit system has induced unemployment. A correlation of the benefit-income rates to unemployment for the period up to the end of the 1970s has been calculated by Hemming which suggests that, on the whole, both increased from 1948 to the end of the period. In particular, large increase in the benefit-income ratio after the introduction of the earnings-related supplement in 1966 is worthy of note (Hemming, 1984).

10.4.7 *The Conservative Reforms of the 1980s*

As part of its comprehensive reappraisal of the relative roles of public and private sector in the mixed economy, and in its determination to ensure that government spending is 'efficient', the Conservative Government turned its attentions to issues of social security in the mid-1980s. A Green Paper in June 1985 outlined the main points at issue and was followed by a White Paper later the same year containing detailed proposals for major reforms of the social security system. The resulting parliamentary debate led to the Social Security Act 1986, which introduced several major changes to the benefit side of social security arrangements, and full implementation of these reforms took place in April 1988. What we see in both the debate and the subsequent reforms is clear recognition of the list of problems discussed so far in this chapter, with added emphasis on the efficiency-equity trade-off referred to at the outset. The main defects of the system, as identified by the 1985 White Paper, were deemed to be its complexity, its failure to give proper support to those most in need, the problems created by the poverty and unemployment 'traps' and the burden of costs on future generations of taxpayers. In addition, the White Paper emphasised the government's concern about the restrictions on individual choice on the matter of pensions.

The response to the problems identified in the White Paper was set out in the 1986 Act, and centred on changes to the income-related benefits.

The Green Paper had, in fact, proposed the abolition of SERPS, but this met with stiff opposition and the Act, instead, set out modifications aimed at reducing its cost on future generations. Supplementary Benefit was replaced by **Income Support**; Family Income Support was replaced by **Family Credit**; and a new **Housing Benefit** replaced the previous two-part scheme (one for recipients of Supplementary Benefit and one for all others on low incomes). But these changes were not in name only. The new system rationalised the relationship between these three main income-related benefits and established their entitlements on the same basis for the first time. At the same time, the changes represented a shift in resources towards Income Support and Family Credit and away from Housing Benefit which, in effect meant a **shift of emphasis in the system towards families with children and away from pensioners**. Income Support could continue to be the main benefit for those not in full-time work, offering a benefit of a personal allowance plus increases for dependents. Under the new benefit there would be no additions for specific needs whether 'one-off' or longer term. Instead, such needs would be met out of a new Social Fund. Like its predecessor, Family Credit was designed to offer supplements to low-income families in full-time work and with children to support; it is designed also to be more extensive in its coverage than was FIS.

The issue of whether or not the provisions in the 1986 Act would be likely to achieve the objective laid down in the earlier White Paper initially provoked a mixed response. It was true that the social security system was **simplified**, but it was **not made simple**. In particular, the reforms offered no structural alterations which might improve take-up – even the White Paper optimism had been limited to an assumed take-up rate of 60 per cent for Family Credit. In respect to helping those most in need, initial estimates suggested that the majority of couples with children and single parents were made better off by the reforms while about three-quarters of pensioners were either unaffected or made worse off. Finally, on the question of the social security traps, the position was ambiguous. The unemployment trap should have been eased and the extreme form of the poverty trap was virtually eliminated (no more marginal tax rates of 100 per cent or greater). However, the extension of cover offered under the Family Credit arrangements was to face many more individuals than previously with marginal tax rates around 80 per cent (Dilnot and Webb, 1988).

The reforms of the mid-1980s were aimed to combine with the income and wealth creating effects of the freer market economy encouraged by the government's general economic programme of the period following 1979, a programme which came to be labelled 'Thatcherism'. This combination should have provided a major force for the eradication of poverty – the 'trickle down' effect of wealth creation supported by a more efficient social security system. Unfortunately, the expected result was not forthcoming by the beginning of the 1990s. On the contrary, as we saw in the early section on income distribution, the signs were suggesting an increase in inequality.

As far as the absolute position of the poor was concerned, researchers were unable to find any evidence of a significant improvement. According to one estimate (Jenkins, 1991) average **real** incomes for the poorest 10 per cent of households were about the same in 1988 as they had been 20 years previously, and were actually lower than they had been 10 years previously. As discussed earlier, Townsend was also to argue that the real incomes of the poorest two deciles had fallen over the decade 1979–89 (Townsend, 1991), and even though Johnson and Webb were to modify Townsend's findings, showing that by removing an inconsistency in Townsend's income definition the real incomes of the poorest two deciles had **risen** by 5 per cent, the same authors could not escape the conclusion that as far as the poorest groups are concerned 'it is clear that even on a consistent definition of income their living standards have grown only slowly over the last decade' (Johnson and Webb, 1991).

■ 10.5 A European Perspective

How does the UK poverty picture compare with that in the rest of Europe? To answer this question properly and fully would require us to reconsider all of the methodological issues raised so far in order to attempt any comments about the pattern of poverty across a population totalling more than 350 million individuals.

One attempt which caused considerable controversy on publication, but which did give rise to real concern about the UK's record on poverty *vis à vis* its European partners, was the EC report on the second anti-poverty programme, published in April 1991 (EC, 1991). The stark conclusion of this report was that in 1985 the UK had the fifth highest 'poverty rate' in Europe behind Portugal, Ireland, Spain and Greece, and that the percentage in poverty (both individuals and households) in the UK had risen between 1980 and 1985, the two reference dates used in the report. Not only did such findings give cause for concern to policy-makers, but they also created considerable controversy because they were based on **relative** measures and, hence, emphasised inequalities in income distribution rather than poverty in any **absolute** sense.

Estimating for both individuals and households, the EC report measured poverty in relation to both national and EC criteria. Using expenditure, rather than income, as the guide, the report defined as 'poor' by the **national** criterion, any individual or household spending less than 50 per cent of the national average for any given period. Using a **EC** criterion, an individual or household was classified as 'poor' when spending less than 50 per cent of average EC spending (measured by a purchasing power standard) for any given period. In each case 'adult equivalent' scales were used to take account of differences in household size and composition.

☐ 10.5.1 Using a National Criterion

The Overall Picture

The picture presented by using a national criterion was a depressing one, suggesting that in 1985 some 50 mn persons in the EC (about 16 mn households) were poor, and that this represented very little change in the total number of poor in the EC since 1980. The findings suggested, how-

Figure 10.7 *Changes in the Number of Poor Persons in the EC, 1980–85*[1]

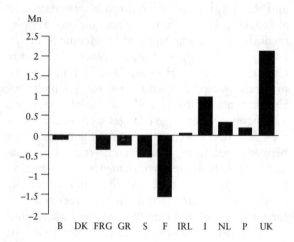

Note:
[1] National criteria.
Source: EC (1991).

ever, that there **had** been changes in the proportions of poor found in individual countries, with some faring better and some worse between the two years. **Figure 10.7** presents a clear and stark impression of the relative changes in numbers of poor persons experienced by eleven of the twelve members over the five-year period (there were no survey returns for Luxembourg) with the biggest increase in numbers seen to be in the UK.

High Risk Groups

- **Children and elderly:** The findings of the EC report emphasised yet again that the very young and the very old are particularly vulnerable to poverty. We saw earlier how these distinct groupings have emerged time and again from UK studies, and the evidence from across Europe confirms that throughout all EC countries children and the aged form consistently high risk groups in relation to poverty. **Table 10.11** gives data from the report which show that, with the exceptions of Greece in 1980 and Italy in 1985, the index of poverty among children was positive everywhere in both years and, with the exception of the Netherlands, the poverty index for the elderly was positive everywhere in both

Table 10.11 *Poverty Among Children and the Elderly in the EC*

	Children			Elderly		
	Poverty Index (National Poverty Rate = 100)		Variation in the Absolute Number of Poor (%)	Poverty Index (National Poverty Rate = 100)		Variation in the Absolute Number of Poor (%)
	1980	1985		1980	1985	
Belgium	113	114	–20.3	175	181	–17.7
Denmark	110	114	–5.4	238	255	12.1
F.R. of Germany	110	138	3.5	136	141	–8.1
Greece	96	103	–16.5	145	153	–2.9
Spain	106	107	–14.5	157	125	–21.7
France	108	124	–6.6	159	136	–31.2
Ireland	122	143	23.8	163	73	–50.5
Italy	114	97	–14.4	132	129	1.5
Netherlands	136	155	25.6	44	46	31.9
Portugal	112	112	–2.3	139	139	8.1
United Kingdom	138	132	12.2	163	119	–7.1

Source: EC (1991).

1980 and 1985. **Table 10.11** shows also that in most countries (exceptions being Italy and the UK) the poverty index either stayed the same or worsened for children between 1980 and 1985, while for the elderly it either stayed the same or worsened in six of the eleven countries surveyed over the same period.

As a final point in relation to **Table 10.11** we should remind ourselves that insofar as the ageing of the European populations is a contributor to the large number of poor persons also being elderly persons, the problem is unlikely to diminish (as shown in **Table 10.9**).

- **Others:** The EC report also highlighted the other socio-economic groups most vulnerable to poverty, and again we can see the parallels between the UK picture, as discussed earlier in the chapter, and the rest of the EC. In particular, we can observe the prevalence of poverty among single-parent (particularly female) households and among households with low educational attainment and/or low economic activity of the household head.

☐ *10.5.2 Using an EC Criterion*

Using average household, or individual, income or expenditure as the poverty yardstick for each EC member produces 12 different poverty lines (only 11 in the 1991 report, given no returns for Luxembourg). What happens to the picture if we apply just one EC poverty line, that is if poverty is defined with reference to some notion of an EC average income or expenditure for households and individuals? The question is addressed in the 1991 report by referring to any household (or individual) as being 'poor' if expenditure is less than 50 per cent of the EC average household expenditure (per adult equivalent) for the period in question. As with the measures for individual countries, this poverty line was calculated by reference to data from national family budget surveys. The survey suggests that the fundamental extent and causes of poverty changes only slightly but the **distribution** of EC poverty changes dramatically.

Table 10.12, taken from the EC report, suggests that, measured against an EC poverty line, overall poverty fell slightly between 1980 and 1985

Table 10.12   *EC Poverty Incidence, in 1980 and 1985*

	1980		1985	
	%	mn	%	mn
Households	14.8	16.4	14.4	16.2
Persons	16.8	52.9	15.9	51.3
Children	19.7	13.5	19.4	12.3
Elderly (65+)	22.5	9.9	19.6	8.5

Source: EC (1991).

and that it fell slightly also for the high risk groups of children and the elderly across the whole of the EC. That EC-wide poverty was reduced during the period 1980–85 was welcome news for the makers of European social policy, but the size of the reduction was not impressive and begged questions about the efficiency of the EC's general social programme. We shall address some aspects of this shortly but first we should also consider the dramatic changes in the geographical distribution of poverty which result from adopting a poverty line. **Figure 10.8** gives a very clear impression of how the geographical distribution of poverty responds to changing the poverty line from a national to an EC criterion.

Figure 10.8   *% of Poor EC Households Located in Each Member Country*

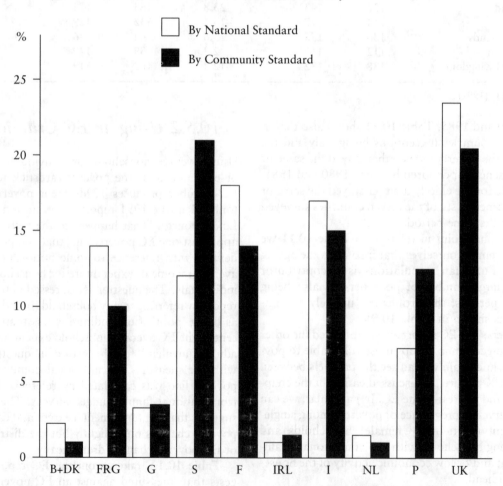

Source: EC (1991).

From the viewpoint of the UK the initial comparison is not very favourable. Using the national poverty line as the criterion, the UK had the biggest share of the community's poor in 1985 at 23.5 per cent, with France next at about 18.3 per cent followed by Italy (17.1 per cent), West Germany (14.3 per cent) and Spain (11.9 per cent). National poverty lines obviously do not take account of relative living standards outside national boundaries and, as we saw early in this chapter, a cohort of 'poor' according to a national poverty line might appear (relatively) 'rich' according to some other nation's poverty line. So how does adopting the EC poverty line change poverty rankings? As **Figure 10.8** illustrates, the UK is overtaken by Spain but the gap is very narrow and remains potentially embarrassing for UK policymakers. The proportion of the EC's poor who are resident in the UK does fall, but it also falls in Italy, France and West Germany whereas only Spain suffers an increase (a fairly dramatic one in fact, from 11.9 to 20.9 per cent).

It could be argued, however, that measuring poverty distribution on the basis of population percentages is very unfair to countries with large populations because this increases the likelihood of larger numbers in poverty. Thus, to counteract the population effect, the EC report offered a picture of the geographical distribution of poverty that results from assuming the EC's population to be equally distributed. One obvious effect of this is to offer a picture as if some of the households from the more densely populated and more industrial countries had been relocated into previously less dense and more agrarian countries. As one would expect, the poverty percentage now rises dramatically in countries like Portugal and Ireland and falls dramatically in the UK, France and Italy.

☐ 10.5.3 EC Action to Combat Poverty

Every country within the EC has adopted some form of the mixed enterprise economy and, in line with this, some variant of the 'Welfare State' model of social policy whereby markets reward individuals and households according to the market value

of their productivities and the state offers income supplementation when market earnings are low and also when there are no market earnings, as in the case, for example, of children, the retired and those whose skills are obsolete. Hence, as we saw earlier in the case of the UK, researching all the reasons for a country's poverty profile requires analysis of both market patterns, state tax-transfer programmes and labour market legislation. Clearly, we cannot begin here to explore the details of each of the other eleven countries within the EC. However, we can at least offer some comment on the **collective action** taken so far by the EC to combat the considerable poverty in its midst.

The EC programme to combat poverty is piecemeal, but it is possible to single out three main prongs of attack on both inequality and poverty.

1 The collective commitment by EC members to develop **social** as well as economic policy
2 The European Social Fund
3 The Anti-Poverty Programme.

The Commitment to Social Policy

Article 2 of The Treaty of Rome specifies an objective of an accelerated raising of the standard of living across the EC – that is, it makes it clear that the EC's objectives are **social** as well as economic. To this end, the EC has developed policies and provided finance for projects relating to: unemployment; training; equal opportunities (to include policies relating to regions as well as gender); improving working conditions; families and the elderly; immigrants; handicapped people; social security and public health. Many of these areas have received significant funding for many years.

The European Social Fund

Many of the real commitments to development of social policy are made through this Fund, representing a massive injection of finance mainly into the improvement of labour market returns. The list of commitments made under the Social Fund is large but its three major categories are:

• training and employment of young people (under 25s) – about 75 per cent of the Fund's resources are put to this end

- helping disadvantaged regions via a geographical concentration of the Fund's activities, with targeted regions so far including all of Greece, Ireland and Portugal and specific areas of Italy, Spain and Northern Ireland
- helping specific adult groups – for example, the long-term unemployed; women returning to work; handicapped people who are capable of work in the labour market; immigrant workers; individuals suitable for re-training for new technologies; and persons working in the promotion of employment (for example, in vocational training and recruitment). By the second half of the 1980s the expenditure in these various areas was accounting for 7 per cent of the EC budget and covered some 2.5 million people (approximately 85 per cent of them under 25 years of age were benefiting from the Social Fund).

The Specific Anti-poverty Programme

In addition to its efforts on the supply side of the European market based economies, the EC has also addressed the issue of poverty created by absence of any access to labour markets. There have been two major programmes launched, each one concerned primarily with the gathering of information about poverty and inequality and with measuring poverty incidence. The initial programme for the period 1975–80, very much concerned with gathering information about poverty, was superseded in 1984 by a new programme of more specific EC action for the period up to 1988 coupled with further research into and measurement of the incidence of poverty. The EC report referred to earlier is part of the culmination of this research. The various projects under the second programme were to concentrate on testing new methods of helping the poor and on the dissemination and exchange of knowledge about the extent and incidence of poverty and on the evaluation of projects. In terms of target areas, the distribution of activities can be seen from the pie chart published by the EC in 1987, and reproduced as **Figure 10.9**.

Figure 10.9   *EC Anti-poverty Programme*[1]

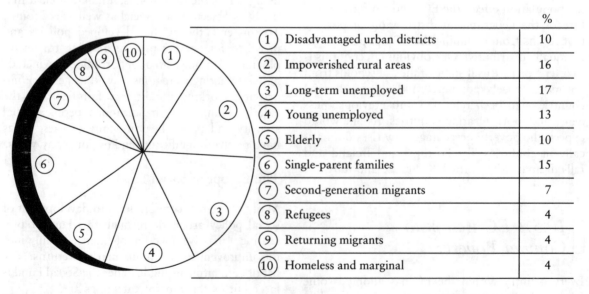

		%
①	Disadvantaged urban districts	10
②	Impoverished rural areas	16
③	Long-term unemployed	17
④	Young unemployed	13
⑤	Elderly	10
⑥	Single-parent families	15
⑦	Second-generation migrants	7
⑧	Refugees	4
⑨	Returning migrants	4
⑩	Homeless and marginal	4

Note:
[1]   Excluding Spanish and Portuguese projects selected in 1987.
Source: Commission of the European Communities, DG V.

10.5.4 Recent Debate and the Future of Social Security

What emerges from both the findings of the EC report and the nature of the categories within the EC's anti-poverty programme is an awareness of what has been labelled by some observers as the 'new poverty'. As we have seen in previous sections of this chapter, what might be termed the 'old poverty' was concentrated mainly in two broad categories: dependent children (and their families), and old people. Both of these categories remain at the core of poverty problem in both the UK and throughout the EC. But a new category of poor has emerged who are more diverse in nature and belong perhaps to what is regarded as society's periphery rather than its core: immigrant workers (who usually earn low wages and suffer intermittent unemployment); single parents; ethnic minorities (who might suffer the additional burdens of prejudice and discrimination); the mentally and physically handicapped; and longer-term unemployed young people. As the 'service economy' emerged throughout the 1970s and 1980s there was rapid growth throughout the EC in both part-time working and in home-based work and small-scale self-employment, and many of these opportunities offered no more than relatively low and often temporary returns for labour.

According to one eminent poverty analyst, the sufferers of the 'old poverty' were a large proportion of the working class who were able 'to mobilise particularly through labour and socialist movements, to form alliances with the liberal middle class, and to build the defences which eventually came to be called the "Welfare State"' (Donnison, 1991). The same observer sees no similar socio-political solution to the problems of the 'new poor' because they are so diverse and scattered and, therefore, do not form a cohesive political lobby – indeed, they 'share nothing but their exclusion from the mainstream of society'.

Whether or not one agrees with this socio-political analysis, it is clearly being recognised to some extent in the categorisation of aid objectives within the European Social Fund. But as far as social policy in individual countries is concerned, the 'new poverty' adds yet another dimension to an already difficult policy agenda – if households or families comprise low earners who find only intermittent employment to supplement, say, one mainstream household income, then both the poverty and the employment traps discussed earlier pose severe disincentive effects unless combined incomes lift the whole family or household well above state assistance levels.

It is not surprising, therefore, to find that the issue of 'universal' versus 'selective' benefits remains at the centre of debate on social security. The UK government has placed **efficiency** at the forefront of economic objectives, and increasingly blurred the distinctions between economic and social issues. Since universal benefits are made available to all, regardless of means, they are deemed to be a less efficient means of income redistribution than selective benefits which, by definition, are targeted on those recipients most in need. This issue underpinned the 1986 reforms but the argument has continued. Nowhere has the debate been more intense than over the issue of Child Benefit. When Mr John Moore announced to the House of Commons in October 1988 that child Benefit was to be frozen for the second year running, the howls of protest were confined mainly to the Opposition benches only because the proposed freeze was to be part of a package of anti-poverty measures to be available **only to those who were most in need of Child Benefit**. In other words, poor families with children were to be given special benefit rises (of up to 9.3 per cent) but they were to be targeted (means-tested).

This proposal for a resource switch, and consequent denial of the fundamental Beveridge principle of providing a flat-rate benefit for all families with children, represented a significant denial of 'universality' as a cornerstone of the social security system. The door was now opened wider to make possible further 'selective' arrangements. It could be argued, for example, that future tax/transfer support of the aged will be modified along similar lines. Bearing in mind the burden on future generations of working taxpayers of providing income support to a proportionally growing retired population, many of whom will be enjoying the fruits of their occupational pension schemes, the demand by voters for more selective measures to concentrate transfers on the 'genuinely needy' within the retired population is likely to grow. Increased awareness that the UK state pension scheme has not been 'as of right' but 'pay as you go' is likely to fuel such demands.

The debate over selectivity in the social security system brings us back, full circle, to the efficiency/equity trade-off. On the one hand is a concern for efficiency and the removal of disincentives in tax/transfer programmes while, on the other, is a concern for the welfare of the poor. A problem for the party image-makers in the 1980s was how the present the government as a 'caring' administration as well as one which promoted efficiency and increased incentives. The solution to the problem for the future lies in persuading the electorate that 'targeting' is 'cost-effective caring'.

So to persuade the electorate is conditional on achieving two related objectives, namely finding a way to much simpler means-testing and improving markedly the take-up of available benefits. One way to reach these goals which has received a lot of attention from economists and which enjoys a degree of consensus among political opinions, is to introduce some form of **truly comprehensive negative income tax** which would follow the principles outlined earlier but would combine social security benefits and income tax payments in a single system of redistribution, centrally administered. To date no government has gone that far in its legislation (although a variant was proposed in a Green Paper published by the Health-led Conservative Government of 1972) and Mr Fowler's overhaul of the mid-1980s fell a long way short of such radicalism.

To date, the concept of a 'European Social Dividend' available to all (but subject to means) and across national boundaries has not appeared as a serious item on the politico-economic agenda for post-1992 Europe.

References

Abel-Smith, B. and P. Townsend (1965)*The Poor and the Poorest* (London: Bell & Sons).

Atkinson, A. B. (1972) *Unequal Shares* (London: Allen Lane, The Penguin Press).

Berthoud, R. (1985) 'Mr Fowler's Examination', *Catalyst* (Autumn).

Cmd 6404 (1942) *Social Insurance and Allied Services* (The Beveridge Report) (London: HMSO).

Cmd 6527 (1944) *Employment Policy* (London: HMSO).

Diamond Commission (Royal Commission on the Distribution of Income and Wealth), *Report No. 1* (1975). Cmnd 6171 (London: HMSO); *Report No. 4* (1976) Cmnd 6626 (London: HMSO).

Dilnot, A. W., J. A. Kay and C. N. Morris (1984) *The Reform of Social Security* (Oxford, London: Clarendon Press, for the Institute of Fiscal Studies).

Dilnot, A. W. and S. Webb (1988) 'The 1988 Social Security Reforms', *Fiscal Studies* (August).

Donnison, D. (1991) 'Squeezed and Broken on the Brink', *The Times Higher Education Supplement* (April 19, p. 13).

EC (1991) *Final Report on the Second European Poverty Programme* (Brussels: Commission of the European Communities).

Fiegehen, G. C., P. S. Lansley and A. D. Smith (1977) *Poverty and Progress in Britain, 1953–73* (Cambridge: Cambridge University Press).

Fry, V. and G. Stark (1986) 'The Take-Up of Supplementary Benefit: Gaps in the "Safety Net"?', *Fiscal Studies* (November).

Harbury, C. D. (1962) 'Inheritance in the Distribution of Personal Wealth', *Economic Journal* (December).

Harbury, C. D. and D. M. Hitchens (1976) 'The Inheritance of Top Wealth Leavers', *Economic Journal*, 86.

Harbury, C. D. and P. C. McMahon (1973) 'Inheritance and the Distribution of Personal Wealth in Britain', *Economic Journal*, 83.

Hemming, R. (1984) *Poverty and Incentives* (Oxford: Oxford University Press).

Jenkins, S. (1991) 'Living Standards and the Diverging "Thatcher" Effect', *The Guardian* (15 April, p. 13).

Johnson, P. and S. Webb (1991) *UK Poverty Statistics: A Comparative Study*, Institute for Fiscal Studies, Commentary, 27.

Johnson, P., G. Stark and S. Webb (1991) 'A Decade of Taxation Gains and Losses', *The Financial Times* (20 March, p. 23).

Lydall, H. F. (1959) 'The Long Term Trend in the Size Distribution of Income', *Journal of the Royal Statistical Society* (Series A, 122, Part 1).

Morris, N. and I. Preston (1986) 'Taxes, Benefits and the Distribution of Income 1968–83', *Fiscal Studies* (November).

Nicholson, R. J. (1967) 'The Distribution of Personal Income', *Lloyds Bank Review* (January).

Piachaud, D. (1988) 'Poverty in Britain 1899 to 1983', *Journal of Social Policy*, 17 (3).

Social Security Select Committee (1991) *Low Income Statistics: Households Below Average Income Tables 1988*, First Report 1990–91, House of Commons.

Stark, T. (1990) *Income and Wealth in the 1980s* (London: Fabian Society).

Townsend, P. (1991) *The Poor are Poorer: A Statistical Report on Changes in the Living Standards of Rich and Poor in the United Kingdom 1979–1989*, Statistical Monitoring Unit, University of Bristol.

■ Chapter 11 ■

Industry and Policy

Keith Hartley and Nick Hooper

■ 11.1 Introduction: the Policy Issues

Industrial policy has been the victim of various definitions reflecting different views about the role, extent and appropriate form of state intervention in the economy. At the one extreme, interventionists favour an active role with governments intervening throughout the economy at the industry and, ultimately, the firm level. The other extreme takes a laissez-faire approach leaving everything to market forces. In the UK, these alternative views about industrial policy have been reflected in continuing controversy between the major political parties.

During the 1970s and 1980s controversy raged over policy towards manufacturing industry and over the size of the public sector, reflecting concern about crowding-out, deindustrialisation and the decline of the UK's manufacturing industrial base. Aspects of this controversy were apparent in debates about state rescue operations for companies such as British Leyland (now Rover), Chrysler, Rolls Royce 1971 and the Westland helicopter company. In the 1980s the debate focused on the decision to sell off valuable national assets such as British Aerospace, British Telecom, British Steel and the Royal Ordnance Factories; the sale of public utilities such as gas, electricity and water; and whether major government de-

fence contracts should be used to support British industry (Nimrod AEW, tanks). On such issues the major political parties have differed in their views on the extent and appropriate form of state intervention.

The Labour Government of the 1970s (1974–79) favoured interventionist policies in the form of an industrial strategy. This strategy was supported by an interventionist state agency (the National Enterprise Board); state ownership; planning agreements; industrial democracy; a policy of 'selecting the winners'; and an extensive system of financial subsidies to firms, industries and regions. In contrast, the Conservative Government of the 1980s and early 1990s has relied on market forces as its preferred industrial policy. Its emphasis has been on supply-side policies with a smaller public sector and reduced state intervention reflected in privatisation; contracting-out; deregulation; the withdrawal of industrial and regional subsidies; and more emphasis on competition policy and support for small firms. This policy aims to replace a 'culture of dependency' with an 'enterprise culture' based on profitability and lower personal taxation, offering greater incentives for managers, workers, shareholders and new businesses.

The policy agenda for the 1990s is likely to depart from that of previous decades. Changes in the electorate, political parties and their leaders will mean a continued search for new solutions to the UK's economic problems reflected in its growth, inflation, unemployment and balance of payments performance. Events in Eastern Europe and the Soviet Union during the late 1980s and early 1990s have also raised serious doubts about the performance of centralised planning and collectivist solutions to economic problems. Furthermore, the European dimension is becoming increasingly important, with the EC's 1992 Single Market initiative (Gowland and James, 1991).

The framework of the likely future debate about industrial policy was outlined in the 1991 policy statements of the major political parties. The Liberal Democrats were committed to creating a **liberal market economy** based on efficiency and social justice. They aimed for a more rigorous competition policy through strengthening competition mechanisms and discouraging unproductive merger mania by requiring hostile bidders to prove that a takeover would be beneficial. They also favoured 'green' taxes on finite materials and carbon taxes on pollutants. Labour's focus is on creating a **high-technology manufacturing economy** with Regional Development Agencies and a National Investment Bank to promote increased investment and research and development. A new national technology body (British Technology Enterprise) would be created to develop, patent and licence innovations, whilst Technology Trusts would be created to encourage closer links between universities, industry and government to facilitate both innovation and its rapid diffusion throughout the economy. Finally, the Conserva-

tives are committed to the **enterprise economy** with further privatisation (for example, of British Coal and the Royal Mail), contracting-out, and deregulation, the 'hiving-off' of state agencies and the introduction of a Citizens' Charter for public sector activities.

Whilst governments have differed in their approach towards UK industry, policy performance can be assessed against some broad indicators of the trends in manufacturing, its productivity and its export and import record. A starting point is the changing role of manufacturing in the economy. The overall picture is of a continuing shift away from an economy dominated by industry to one based on services. As shown in **Table 11.1**, the manufacturing share of gross domestic product has fallen from a third in 1969 to well under a quarter in 1990. Over this period activity shifted towards services, with private services rising from 38 per cent to 47 per cent of total output and public services from 12 per cent to 16 per cent of GDP. Inevitably, concern has been expressed about the contraction in manufacturing industry reflected in deindustrialisation and its possible adverse effects upon the economy's investment and export performance. Various explanations have been advanced, ranging from rising government spending 'crowding-out' private sector investment to the long-run decline in the competitiveness of UK industry (as in Blackaby, 1979).

The falling share of manufacturing is reflected in steadily declining industrial employment. In 1990

Table 11.1 *Contribution to GDP by Sector, %*

	1969	1980	1985	1989	1990
Manufacturing	34.1	26.8	23.9	23.1	22.4
Agriculture	3.1	2.1	1.9	1.6	1.5
Energy	4.9	9.7	10.6	5.2	5.1
Construction	7.0	6.1	5.8	7.4	7.6
Private services	38.5	39.0	42.1	46.6	47.4
Public services	12.4	16.3	15.7	16.1	16.0
	100.0	100.0	100.0	100.0	100.0

Source: UK National Accounts 'Blue Book' (CSO, 1991) Table 16.4.

manufacturing employment was 72 per cent of its 1979 level. Part of the fall in manufacturing employment over this period was due to productivity gains. Labour productivity in manufacturing grew faster than in the whole economy, as shown in **Table 11.2**. Indeed, the substantial UK productivity gains in the 1980s raise questions as to whether the Conservative Government has succeeded since 1979 in reversing permanently the UK's relative economic decline.

The changing position of manufacturing in the UK economy has been reflected internationally in the pattern and balance of trade. The manufacturing share of UK exports fell from 76 per cent in 1979 to shares ranging from 62 per cent to 67 per cent between 1981 and 1985, rising to 81 per cent between 1988 and 1990. In addition, between 1979 and 1990 the proportion of sales going to exports rose from 24 per cent to some 30 per cent.

Similarly, between 1979 and 1990, the manufacturing share of imports rose from 63 per cent to 78 per cent, and during the same period, the balance of visible trade in manufactures shifted from a surplus to a substantial deficit. Such stylised facts raise questions about the performance of UK manufacturing industry, and whether public policy can improve its performance.

The contribution which economists can make to this debate about industrial policy is to subject myths and special pleading to economic analysis and critical appraisal, and to confront the arguments with the available evidence. Some of the major issues are now apparent, and we must ask whether economic theory offers any guidelines for a public policy towards industry. What, for example, are the implications of the analysis for the size, structure, location, ownership and performance of UK industries? In particular, how can economic

Table 11.2 *Employment, Productivity and External Trade*

Index numbers 1985 = 100	1979	1982	1984	1988	1990
Employment					
Manufacturing	132.6	107.5	100.5	98.2	97.4
Total labour force	103.8	97.7	98.9	105.2	108.4
Productivity (output per person)					
Manufacturing	81.9	84.7	97.0	116.2	121.4
Total labour force	90.8	93.1	97.6	107.5	107.4
Employees in employment, GB (000)					
Manufacturing	7 053	5 751	5 302	5 116	5 046
Services	13 578	13 117	13 503	14 853	15 497
All industries and services	22 587	20 916	20 741	21 760	22 325
External trade (£mn)					
Total UK visible exports	40 637	55 538	70 374	82 098	103 882
of which manufacturing	30 870	37 316	46 668	66 194	84 469
Total UK visible imports	46 925	56 940	78 760	106 572	126 135
of which manufacturing	29 689	37 083	52 982	83 484	98 191

Source: Monthly Digest of Statistics; Employment Gazette.

theory be used to evaluate specific industrial policies such as policy towards competition, subsidies, privatisation and the role of government purchasing?

■ *11.2* Theory and Industrial Policy

□ *11.2.1 Introduction*

Questions about the proper role of government in the economy dominate policy debates. In relation to industry, it has to be asked whether there are any economic arguments for government intervention, and if so, to what extent should the state intervene and in what form? For example, should the state favour British manufacturing industry? Should policy be applied to all firms or to a selected group (selected by industry or region)? Should intervention be in the form of subsidies (to firms, capital, labour or R & D); import controls; a buy-British government purchasing policy; competition and merger policy; nationalisation; or privatisation with state regulation? These are the general issues behind such specific examples as the UK Ministry of Defence decision to buy US Boeing AWACS aircraft and to cancel the British Nimrod AEW project; to bring Rolls Royce into public ownership in 1971 rather than to bail out the privately-owned company through subsidies; and to replace publicly-owned enterprises such as British Telecom, British Gas and Electricity with privately-owned companies subject to state regulation.

The methodology of economic policy provides a framework for analysing industrial policy issues. The approach requires economists to seek answers to three questions:

1   **What is the policy problem** and what are governments seeking to achieve? Usually, the underlying problem worrying policy-makers can be deduced from the government's stated objectives (and vice versa). For example, in 1991, the Conservative Government's Department of Trade and Industry aimed to achieve wealth creation through open and competitive markets both at home and overseas.

2   **Why is there a problem?** Economists use their theories to explain the causes of problems which are worrying governments. For example, British industry's declining international competitiveness might result from a structure of too many small firms unable to undertake the necessary R & D and thus obtain the scale economies required to compete in world markets, or it might reflect a comparative advantage in areas other than manufacturing. Alternatively, it might be due to general inefficiency reflecting the motivation and attitudes of managers and workers (a culture of dependency rather than enterprise), or it could reflect interest rate and exchange rate policy. The choice between these alternative theories depends on which best explains the facts.

3   **What can be done to solve the problem?** Usually, there are alternative policy solutions. To improve the performance of UK manufacturing industry might require an industrial strategy; better management; the creation of labour-managed firms; or a competition policy. Private monopolies could be controlled through nationalisation, by creating contestable markets, or by state regulation of prices or profits. Governments might promote technical progress through subsidising R & D, by training more scientists or through placing contracts with UK firms for advanced technology equipment (such as computers, Concorde, nuclear power stations and space satellites). Theories can be used to predict the likely effects of alternative policy solutions, with governments having to choose between the alternatives. Such choices will reflect the governing party's values and ideology, its possible interest in maximising the welfare of the community and its immediate concern with votes and re-election.

Economic theory approaches industrial policy issues from the starting point of Paretian welfare economics. It is assumed that society aims to maximise welfare by achieving an **optimum allocation of resources** (that is, a Pareto optimum occurs where it is impossible to make one person better off without making someone else worse off). In private enterprise economy, the Paretian model suggests that properly-functioning competitive markets are socially desirable since perfectly competitive markets result in a Pareto optimum allocation of resources. On this basis, market forces determine the optimum size of the manufacturing sector. The model provides some broad guidelines for industrial policy. State intervention is required whenever markets are failing to work properly (that is where there are substantial departures from the competitive ideal). This approach suggests that industrial policy is a means of correcting for major market failures. The obvious focus is on the operation of product markets, although it has to be recognised that failures can occur in markets for capital, labour, money and foreign exchange.

There are two general sources of market failure, namely (a) imperfections in the form of monopoly, oligopoly, restrictive practices and entry barriers, and (b) beneficial or harmful externalities, including public goods (for example defence). Externalities mean that, left to themselves, private competitive markets might provide too little of some socially desirable activities (such as information, basic R & D) and too much of some socially undesirable products such as pollution, noise and traffic congestion. Here, however, economists have to be careful in distinguishing between the technical issues concerned with the causes of market failure, and the policy issues concerned with the choice of the most appropriate solution. For example, even if imperfections are identified as the main source of market failure, governments have to choose between such alternative policies as increased competition, reduced tariff barriers and the state regulation of monopoly prices and profits. Similarly, externalities might be corrected through taxes and subsidies, public ownership or by legislative changes in property rights allowing the courts to determine compensation for the victims of spillovers.

The 1990s are also likely to see a continued and increased concern with **protecting the environment**. Worries have been expressed about the environmental impact of acid rain, ozone depletion, deforestation, the greenhouse effect, the need to preserve the natural environment and fears about the exhaustion of natural resources. Industry is seen as a major cause of pollution and environ-mental destruction. Profit-conscious firms seeking to minimise costs have every incentive to adopt cheap production methods and to produce outputs which might impose harm and costs on the rest of society (harmful externalities). Examples include atmospheric pollution from smoking chimneys, from petrol-driven motor cars and from cooling towers at electricity power stations; water pollution from waste disposal and oil spillages; and noise from jet aircraft. Various policy solutions have been proposed, including **market incentives** in the form of environmental taxes imposed on firms and 'harmful' products as well as tradable permits allowing firms to pollute. Alternatively, regulations can impose either limits or a complete ban on certain socially undesirable activities (for example, smoke-free zones; restrictions on airport opening hours); and governments might support basic research into new, cleaner, environmentally-friendly production methods. However, environmental problems are not created solely by industry. Consumers also create external effects as in the case of tourism with its possible destruction of the natural environment. All of the above raise questions as to whether environment issues are the proper concern of the Department of Trade and Industry or the Department of the Environment or, ultimately, consumers themselves.

In analysing policy issues, care must also be taken to distinguish between efficiency issues concerned with market failure, and equity issues where the outcomes are socially unacceptable. Finally, a Pareto optimum allocation of resources might be achieved through either a perfectly competitive private enterprise economy or by direct controls and commands in a centrally-planned economy.

11.2.2 The Structure–Conduct–Performance Paradigm

In examining the causes of market failure and the range of policy solutions, we also need to be aware of the standard tool kit of industrial economists, namely, the structure–conduct–performance framework. This states that industrial performance depends ultimately upon industry structure where the variables in the model are structure, conduct and performance.

Structure

Structure comprises the number and size distribution of firms in an industry and the conditions governing the entry of new firms. There are two extremes – **perfect competition** and **monopoly** – with the intermediate and often typical cases of **monopolistic competition** and **oligopoly**. With this approach industry concentration is determined by economies of scale, the size of the market (the number of firms of optimal scale it will support) and entry barriers. Perfectly competitive markets are characterised by free entry, with large numbers of relatively small firms each operating at optimal scale.

Conduct

Conduct embraces the pricing, advertising, marketing, R & D and product differentiation aspects of firm behaviour (in other words, price and non-price competition), as well as the possibilities for collusion and restrictive agreements.

Performance

Performance is measured by technical and allocative efficiency. In this context, a concern with a Pareto optimum allocation of resources requires that prices equal marginal cost throughout the economy. Applied to a private enterprise competitive economy, the result would be firms which are technically efficient so that X-inefficiency (organisational slack) is absent and, in the long run,

Table 11.3 *A Taxonomy of Industrial Policy*

Industry Features	Main Characteristics	Examples of Industrial Policy Options
1. **Structure**	Number of firms Size of firms Entry conditions	Monopoly, mergers and restrictive practices policies in UK and EEC Tariff policy; government contracts
2. **Conduct**	Pricing Advertising Marketing Product differentiation Research and development Collusion and restrictive agreements	Monopoly and restrictive practices policy Regulation of prices and advertising Consumer protection policy Regulation of new products and standards Restrictive practices policy
3. **Location**	Regional Towns Inner cities Rural areas	Subsidies to firms and labour Location of industry policy Local authority planning controls Tourism policy; subsidies to rural industry and to agriculture

4. **Ownership**	Firm behaviour
	– profit maximisation
	– non-profit objectives
		Nationalisation of firms and industries
		Privatisation with or without:
		  a competition
		  b regulation

5. **Performance**	Efficiency – technical – allocative Profitability Growth	Monopoly, merger and competition policy State regulation of profits Industrial strategy; R&D and technology policy

Figure 11.1   *Mergers, Scale Economies and Competition*

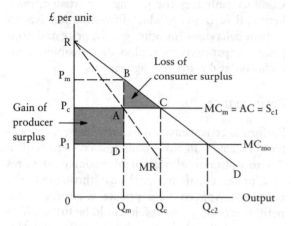

normal profits would be earned. On this basis, the efficiency of an economy's industries might be measured by such performance indicators as profitability, and by inter-firm and international comparisons of labour productivity and total factor productivity. However, the Pareto approach is static, and a society interested in growth will be concerned with the dynamic aspects of industrial performance as reflected in innovation and technical progress (see the taxonomy in **Table 11.3**).

The model in **Table 11.3** runs from industry structure to conduct to performance with the relationships depending on the assumptions about firm behaviour (that is, its objectives). The standard assumption is that firms are **profit maximisers**. On this basis, the neo-classical model shows that, for given demand and cost conditions, monopoly leads to a higher price and to a lower output than perfect competition. Also, since monopoly prices exceed marginal costs, Paretian welfare economics concludes that there will be a misallocation of resources and hence a market failure: monopoly is regarded as socially undesirable (see **Figure 11.1**). Estimates of the losses of consumer benefit due to monopoly have ranged from extremely small to up to 7 per cent of gross corporate product in the UK and up to 13 per cent of gross corporate output in the USA. However, the analysis can be modified to allow for a trade-off between the cost savings from mergers and economies of scale and the loss of consumer benefits due to monopoly. Alternative

approaches have also emerged involving contestability, transaction costs and the Austrian critique all of which are discussed in the sections which follow. Moreover, the theory of second-best shows the limited applicability of the Paretian model.

☐ 11.2.3 Trade-offs

Let us consider a competitive industry and ask whether such an industry should be monopolised through mergers? If we assume that a merger leads to economies of scale which would not otherwise be available to a competitive industry, then a merger to monopolise a competitive industry will result in cost savings. There will thus be a trade-off between the cost savings from scale economies and the loss of consumer benefit (surplus) due to the monopolisation of the competitive industry. Logically, the merger should be allowed to proceed if the additions to producer profits (surplus) exceeds the loss of consumer benefits (surplus) as shown in **Figure 11.1**.

This trade-off analysis is not, however, without its critics. It uses a modified form of Paretian welfare function which allows a comparison of gains and losses, but distributional issues cannot be ignored so that we must ask whether the same or different weights should be attached to changes in producer and consumer benefits. Moreover, after the merger has taken place, a profit-maximising monopolist will expand output (beyond OQ_m in **Figure 11.1**) so raising producer profits and reducing the loss of consumer surplus, resulting in an even stronger case for the merger. Nevertheless, the merger will continue to be associated with a misallocation of resources, with price greater than the new marginal costs. In the circumstances, consumers could in principle bribe the monopolist to produce at the new competitive price and output (Q_{c2} at P_1 in **Figure 11.1**): the monopoly would be no worse off since it would be compensated for its lost profits and consumers would be substantially better off. Such socially desirable compensation does not occur because substantial transaction costs make it too costly to negotiate such a solution between the consumers and the monopolist. Finally, once the merger has occurred, competitive pressures will be absent, allowing the firm to become technically inefficient which results in a departure from cost-minimising behaviour.

☐ 11.2.4 Contestable Markets

The concept of contestable markets represents a further modification to the standard structure-performance paradigm. A contestable market is one where there is the possibility and threat of entry by domestic and foreign firms, and therefore the **threat** of rivalry. A perfectly contestable market is one which has no entry barriers, where entry and exit are easy and costless, and which may or may not be characterised by economies of scale or economies of scope (that is, economies which result from the range or scope of a multi-product firm's activities). In contestable markets, potential entrants are attracted by opportunities for profits. 'Hit-and-run behaviour' is evident since new entrants are not at a cost disadvantage compared with established suppliers, and the absence of sunk (irrevocable) costs means that exit is costless. One of the major features and policy implications of this approach is that a contestable market need not be populated by a large number of firms (as in perfect competition). In fact, a contestable market may contain only one or a small number of firms. Thus, with contestable markets, economists no longer have to assume that efficient outcomes occur only where there are large numbers of firms as in perfect competition. Contestability, rather than structure, determines performance.

☐ 11.2.5 Transaction Costs

Economic activity and exchange is a transaction process in a world of imperfect information and knowledge. Producers do not have complete knowledge of production possibilities and market opportunities. Similarly, individuals as consumers lack information on the price and quality of goods and services on offer, and as workers they will have only limited information on the wages, employment conditions and career prospects available in the labour market. Further costs are incurred in completing a transaction or doing business. For instance, after searching the market for a new car, costs are incurred in negotiating a price, and then policing, monitoring and enforcing a contract. After all, if producers and consumers were perfectly informed, and there were no transaction costs, then markets would not fail since all opportunities for mutually advantageous trade and exchange would be fully exploited.

Transaction costs have been defined as the costs of running the economic system, and include all the costs involved in planning, bargaining, modifying, monitoring and enforcing an implicit or explicit contract (Williamson, 1981, p. 1544). On this approach, the modern corporation and other economic institutions reflect efforts to economise on transaction costs rather than to pursue anti-competitive practices and create monopolies. Two assumptions are central to transaction costs, namely **bounded rationality** and **opportunism**. Bounded rationality recognises that economic agents have a limited capacity to handle information and to solve complex problems. Opportunism recognises that individuals will affect transactions through pursuing self-interest by hoarding valuable information, distorting data and sending misleading messages.

Transaction cost economics offers some distinctive explanations and interpretations of economic organisations:

1 Transactions will be organised in markets unless market exchange creates substantial transaction cost penalties. On this basis, firms will be substituted for markets if it becomes too costly to use markets compared with the costs of managing a firm.
2 It explains decisions by firms to undertake activities in-house or to buy-in, as reflected in the extent of integration.
3 It explains the internal organisation of firms in the form of hierarchies, internal government and divisions. An example is the multi-divisional, or *M*-form, organisation which resembles a mini-capital market compared with the centralised, unitary or *U*-form structure. The success of the *M*-form was due to its ability to economise further on transaction costs.

4   It explains non-standard and unfamiliar forms of economic organisation such as conglomerates, multinationals and franchising.

This approach accepts that whilst firms seek to economise on transaction costs, they might also aim to become monopolists. However, the transactions school believes that monopolising behaviour is the exception. In advocating transaction cost economics, it has been suggested that it is the only hypothesis that is able to provide a discriminating rationale for the succession of organisational innovations that have occurred over the past 150 years and out of which the modern corporation has emerged (Williamson, 1981, p. 1564). However, critics claim that transaction costs are so general that they can be used to rationalise almost anything, and that the approach does not offer any testable and refutable predictions. The critics suggest that we have a simple proposition without any predictive content: firms are used whenever they are cheaper, all costs considered – and markets are used whenever they are cheaper, all costs considered. However, the notions of imperfect information and contestability are elements in the Austrian critique.

☐ *11.2.6 The Austrian Critique*

The Austrian economists (such as Hayek, Schumpeter and Kirzner) are critical of the structure–conduct–performance paradigm, with its underlying emphasis on perfect competition and equilibrium. They assert that actual economies consisting of real world firms and industries are never in equilibrium (that is, never at a state of rest). Instead, economies are characterised by **ignorance** and **uncertainty**, which leads to continuous change and continuous market disequilibrium. Ignorance and uncertainty create opportunities for profits and it is the entrepreneur's task to discover these profitable opportunities. To the Austrians, competition means continuous rivalry (contestability) with entrepreneurs searching for opportunities to make money before anyone else – all of which occurs in a world of ignorance and uncertainty where there is no such thing as perfect information and knowledge. To the Austrians, trial and error price adjust-

ments, and trial and error advertising and product variations are simply a **search and discovery process** – they are methods of trying to obtain market information in situations where knowledge is imperfect and costly to acquire. But conventional theory regards these actions by a businessman as evidence that he possesses some monopoly power. In other words, the competitive process which we witness in the high street seems alien to our model of a perfectly competitive equilibrium. In the high street, the trial and error price cuts made by businessmen are simply examples of the way they try to gain information on their profit-maximising price (they are searching for profits).

The public policy implications of the Austrian approach concern two major issues in particular. In the first place, they concern the role of **profits**. At any given moment, profits may seem to be monopolistic resulting from output restrictions – the monopoly problem. Austrians, however, regard high profits as temporary since rival entrepreneurs will be attracted into the relatively profitable activity. Austrians suggest that monopoly control regulations should involve an assessment of profits over the **long run** (whatever that might be). They believe that any public policy which minimises the rewards of entrepreneurship will **reduce** future entrepreneurial effort, with adverse effects on the competitive process.

Secondly, they concern **industrial organisation**. Austrians believe that policy-makers should avoid making statements either about the most efficient form of industrial organisation or about the wastes of advertising, product differentiation and duplication. Austrians claim that no one has sufficient knowledge and competence to judge which form of market structure is the most efficient for meeting **tomorrow's** consumer needs (given that some of today's sunrise industries will almost certainly have to be tomorrow's dinosaurs and smokestack industries). Entrepreneurs do not have perfect foresight, but they do have a greater motivation than politicians and bureaucrats to meet new and unexpected consumer demands – namely, their desire to seek out profitable opportunities. Critics, though, say that the Austrian approach ignores completely the costs and time required for an economy to adjust and respond to free market forces, and that such costs and time might be unacceptable to society and to vote-conscious governments.

11.2.7 The Theory of Second-best

There is a further problem in using the Paretian model. It requires that all the conditions for an optimum are satisfied simultaneously throughout the whole of the economy. For example, optimality requires that all markets be perfectly competitive throughout the economy. However, consider the case where perfect competition exists in only a limited section of the economy, but not everywhere. Assume also that there is a constraint in the form of at least one private market which is monopolistic and which can **never** be made perfectly competitive. In these circumstances, it does not follow that policy efforts to introduce perfect competition into some, but not all, of the private markets will necessarily move the economy towards an optimum position. It might, but it might also either leave welfare and/or efficiency unchanged or affect them adversely. Thus, given a constraint such that the rules for optimum resource allocation cannot be satisfied throughout the economy, it becomes necessary to resort to a next-best or **second-best** solution, in which efforts are made to make the best of the existing situation. A second-best solution is likely to involve a complete departure from the conditions required for optimum resource allocation. In the example given above, the second-best policy rule might require the departure from perfect competition in those markets where it already exists. Similar examples apply to other Paretian-type, piecemeal policy recommendations involving proposals for more marginal cost pricing, more centralisation or more free trade.

Given the importance of constraints preventing the achievement of a first-best or Pareto optimum, questions arise about their nature. Constraints can be policy-created, such as a government's support for 'national champions' or domestic monopoly defence contractors, or its desire to protect newly-privatised state industries from competition. But such policy-created constraints can always be re-moved by changing public policy! Presumably therefore, governments are reluctant to change policy because of the likely effects on their popularity. If so, an alternative theory of industrial policy is required which embraces voters and political parties, and which recognises the role of the political market place.

11.2.8 A Public Choice Approach

Traditionally, state intervention in an economy was rationalised on grounds of market failure. Governments and bureaucracies were assumed to formulate policies to correct such market failures. Government was regarded as a black box and was not analysed using the same self-interest, maximising and exchange concepts which had been applied extensively to households, firms and markets in capitalist economies. Instead, elected politicians and bureaucracies were assumed, somewhat simplistically, to pursue the public interest and to implement the will of the people. By way of contrast, public choice analysis is concerned with collective non-market decision-making. It applies neo-classical concepts of exchange and self-interest to the political market place of voters, political parties, governments, bureaucracies and interest groups.

Voters are assumed to act like consumers and to maximise their expected benefit or utility from the policies offered by rival politicians and political parties. Similarly, political parties resemble firms and seek to maximise votes. Parties compete in market structures ranging from small to large numbers of rivals, where new parties can enter or threaten to enter the market. The majority party forms the government and obtains the entire market. Its policies will be implemented through bureaucracies which are monopoly suppliers of information and services, aiming to maximise their budgets. In the UK, the Department of Trade and Industry has a central role in policy towards industry, including aerospace, shipbuilding and steel manufacture, together with support for regions, inner cities and industrial innovation. Other departments with an involvement in industrial policy include Defence (R & D and equipment procurement); Employment (enterprise schemes, small firms, tourism and health and safety at work); Energy, (coal and nuclear R & D); Environment (environmental protection); the Home Office (fraud); Transport (civil aviation and bus and rail services); the local authorities (for example, industrial estates); and the state regulatory agencies (for example, the Office of Fair Trading (OFT), the Office of Gas Supply (OFGAS), and the Office of Telecommunications (OFTEL)).

In the course of formulating and implementing policies, governments and bureaucracies are lobbied by pressure groups pursuing their own self-interest by trying to influence policy in their favour (so introducing contestability into the political market). With the intention of safeguarding or improving their incomes, producer groups of management, professional associations and trade unions lobby governments for contracts (to buy British), subsidies, laws to licence and restrict entry and for protection from foreign competition Producer groups are willing to allocate resources in their efforts to persuade governments to create or protect monopoly rights – sometimes referred to as rent seeking and rent protection. For example, producers in a competitive industry will seek to obtain monopoly profits by persuading the government to introduce economic regulation of their industry, perhaps by pointing to the wastes and duplication of competition and to the fragmented nature of competitive industries. Presumably, they would be willing to invest resources in order to capture monopoly profits. At the limit, they would spend P_m B A P_c in **Figure 11.1**, so that the social cost of monopoly is the sizeable area P_m B C P_c.

It happens that not all the lobbying costs are wasted. Politicians and officials may receive payments in kind in the form of expenses-paid trips or free meals. In some cases, the market may be provided with valuable information. Nevertheless, the producer group and rent-seeking approach to government explains public policies in terms of **wealth transfers**. Government is a mechanism for promoting exchanges of wealth or rents, the aim being to take wealth from some groups and to transfer it to others. On this view, industrial policy is about which firms, industries and regions gain from policy and about who loses and who has to pay. Such

wealth transfers and rent-seeking occurs in a political market place where the rules and constraints on behaviour are determined by the constitution, which is itself the result of exchanges within the political market.

When the various agents in the political market place are recognised, it is perhaps not surprising that governments often seem to ignore obvious opportunities for making people better off. Many economists are fond of advocating public policies which expand the opportunities for consumer choice by promoting competition and mutually advantageous trade and exchange both within and between nations. But if such policies are socially desirable, why do governments frequently ignore them? Why the use of tariffs to protect British industry, regulations to prevent entry and a preference to buy defence equipment from higher cost domestic firms? Changes and policies which appear so attractive to economists often fail to recognise the influence of the different agents in the political market place and their impact on policy formulation. **Figure 11.2** presents a framework for identifying and mapping the various linkages within the political market. It takes the example of government policy towards cigarette smoking and shows the agents which will try to influence and modify government policy in their favour.

The economics of politics and bureaucracies provides predictions which are relevant to explaining UK industrial policy (Downs, 1957 and Niskanen, 1971):

1   In a two-party democracy, both parties agree on any issues which are strongly favoured by a majority of voters. As a result, party policies will be more vague, more similar to those of the other party (consensus politics) and less directly linked to an ideology than in a multiparty system.

2   Political parties will attempt to differentiate their policies, but movements towards the political extremes of total laissez faire or complete collectivism are likely to be constrained by the potential losses of moderate voters.

3   Government is more attentive to producers than consumers when it formulates policies. Producer groups dominate both because they can afford to invest in the specialised informa-

Figure 11.2 *Linkages¹ in the Political Market: the Example of Smoking*

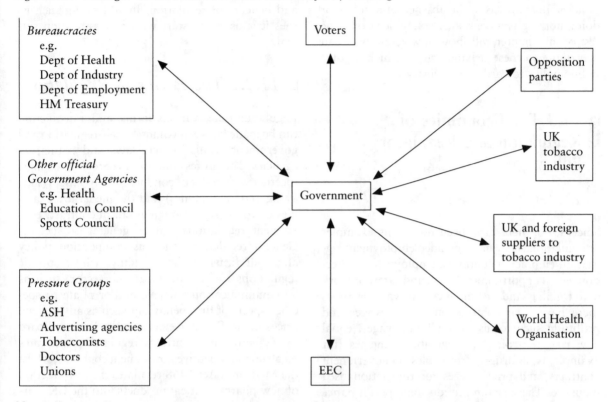

Note:
¹ For simplicity, most of the linkages shown by the arrows focus on the government. Other inter-relationships
   are possible.

tion needed to influence government and also because they have the most to gain from influencing public policy in their favour. As a result, government policies tend to favour producers more than consumers.

4 Bureaucracies aiming to maximise their budgets will be inefficient in supplying a given output and will overspend. Their budgets are likely to be too large as they exaggerate the demand for their services and underestimate the costs of their preferred activities. This affects the way in which information is presented to politicians. In bidding for a larger budget, a bureaucracy can stress how the funds will contribute to social benefits in the form of, say, jobs, high technology and exports.

The public choice approach shows that the form and extent of state intervention as reflected

in industrial policy cannot be divorced from the motives and behaviour of politicians, bureaucracies and interest groups. The traditional market failure analysis suggested that state intervention was needed to correct market failure and to improve the operation of markets. By way of contrast, the public choice approach recognises that governments and state intervention can also fail!

These approaches to analysing aspects of industrial policy will now be applied to a set of issues which dominate current debates: should governments regulate the economy and is competition policy an effective regulatory instrument? Alternatively, should policy focus on ownership, choosing between private or public ownership? Can firm behaviour and performance be sufficiently influenced by subsidies? It should be borne in mind that governments can affect industrial performance directly through their public purchasing policies. In some cases, the absence of a policy or doing nothing is a conscious policy decision. The rest of this chapter will show how economists can contribute to these debates, all of which involve public policy towards UK industry.

11.3 The Economics of Regulation and Regulatory Policy

☐ 11.3.1 The Issues

Since 1960, there have been numerous examples of regulation. They have included employment legislation embracing contracts; employment protection; equal opportunities; health and safety at work and training and redundancy. At various times there have been controls on prices, wages and profits in such forms as minimum wages; equal pay; rent control; price regulation schemes (for example, NHS drugs); profit rules on government contracts; and price freezes for the nationalised industries. The structure, conduct and performance of industry have been regulated by monopolies, mergers and restrictive practices policy. Regulation has also taken the form of government licensing of entry as with patents; public houses; taxis; television companies; road and air transport; and new pharmaceutical products. Finally, output is regulated through such forms as pollution controls and safety standards, as in the case of food products and passenger transport (for example, speed restrictions; vehicle testing; and airliner safety).

The 1980s have been characterised by a mix of both regulation and deregulation, which can be linked to a broad interpretation of privatisation (see **Figure 11.3, p. 407**). The privatisation of public monopolies such as British Telecom, gas, electricity and water has resulted in the creation of industry-specific regulatory agencies (for example OFTEL). At the same time, the Government has **deregulated** some markets such as bus transport and financial services. All of this raises general issues concerning the rationale for regulation, the likely response of firms to regulatory constraints

on their behaviour and the calculation of the costs and benefits of regulation. In addressing such issues it is useful to start with a classification system.

☐ 11.3.2 The Forms of Regulation

Regulation takes various forms, and a distinction can be made between voluntary self-regulation and government regulation via laws and regulatory agencies. The professions and the Stock Exchange, together with codes of conduct for advertisers (such as cigarette companies) and the media are examples of voluntary self-regulation. In contrast, government regulations can be general or specific. General regulations such as competition policy affect all firms in the economy, whilst specific regulations can be aimed at one sector, such as telecommunications or gas, and/or relate to specific aspects of firm behaviour such as advertising, prices or profits. For example, the Review Board for Government Contracts regulates profit rates on all non-competitive government contracts, whilst the Medicines Act 1968 regulates the introduction of new pharmaceutical products into the UK market. In these various forms, regulations affect aspects of structure through entry conditions, as well as conduct (advertising, R & D) and performance (prices, profits). Whatever its form, the central issue is **why regulation is needed**.

11.3.3 The Rationale for Regulation

Economic theory suggests that regulation is a means of correcting for market failure, thereby improving the operation of markets. State regulation might, for example, be a means of controlling private monopoly power or, alternatively, a means of controlling harmful externalities. An alternative public choice view suggests that government regulation benefits producers rather than consumers. Firms will devote resources to lobbying governments to introduce favourable policies such as regulating entry, on the pretext of protecting consumers from cowboy operators and from cheap, inferior and unsafe foreign products. Regulators will have only limited information about producers. The possibility arises of new or existing regulatory agencies being captured by the industry and persuaded to act in favour of producers rather than consumers. Senior officials in the regulatory agency might seek employment in their regulated industry (for example defence and pharmaceuticals).

Firms also have an incentive to persuade the regulatory agency that its required standards can be met voluntarily, claiming that excessively high standards will lead to bankruptcy with implications for plant closures, unemployment and a government's popularity. Alternatively, firms might accept the costs of government regulations in return for more beneficial policies elsewhere such as restrictions on new entry. Certainly, firms are unlikely to be passive–mechanistic agents, but will seek to change regulations and to adapt to them. This, in turn, requires an explanation of how firms are likely to respond to different regulatory rules.

☐ 11.3.4 The Response of Firms

Regulation can take various forms such as licence requirements; certification; entry fees; inspection systems and fines for breaching regulations; the auctioning of rights; and controls on prices and profits. In choosing between these alternatives policy-makers need to know what they are trying to achieve, and how firms are likely to respond to different regulatory instruments.

At the outset, it has to be recognised that regulators do not have perfect information about producers in the regulated industry. For example, a regulator trying to enforce cost-based prices incorporating an average profit rate does not know whether a firm's costs reflect efficient behaviour or X-inefficiency. In these circumstances, regulators have to formulate incentives which will change firm behaviour in certain socially desirable directions, but some incentives can have unexpected and undesirable results. A state-determined limit on profits might, for example, induce a firm to pursue objectives other than maximum profits, so substituting expenditure on staff, or other discretionary items such as luxury offices, for profits.

Alternatively , if the profit controls take the form of a maximum rate of return earned on capital, the regulated firm may use increasingly capital-intensive production methods. Regulatory controls on advertising may encourage a firm to expand its unregulated marketing inputs, for example by employing more salesmen or introducing new sponsorship schemes (as with sports sponsorship). In other words, firms may respond to regulatory constraints by seeking alternative ways of making money, thereby raising questions about the effectiveness of regulation.

☐ 11.3.5 The Desirability of Regulation

Some governments, politicians and civil servants are fond of proposing regulation – they seem to believe that all regulation is good and that more is desirable regardless of cost. However, regulation is not costless, so it is necessary to examine the likely costs and benefits and to assess any evidence, particularly on costs and benefits at the **margin**, in order to enable a choice to be made about the **optimal amount** of regulation.

Regulation involves substantial transaction costs in negotiating, monitoring and enforcing regulatory rules. Staff are needed by the regulatory agency and costs are imposed on producers in responding to the regulator's requirements. For example, a monopoly inquiry involves substantial inputs by members of the inquiry team and corresponding inputs by the monopolist. Specialist witnesses will also be hired by both parties, and the monopolist might devote resources to a public relations campaign and to lobbying politicians. There are also possible indirect costs which need to be included in the analysis. For example, regulatory requirements for the introduction of new drugs into the NHS might lead to longer development periods, so delaying the introduction of new pharmaceutical products. There might also be adverse effects on innovation with fewer new drugs being marketed, and firms might shift their R & D activities to foreign locations where there are fewer regulatory restrictions. In the meantime, delays in the introduction of new drugs can have harmful effects on patients in the form of prolonged suffering and death which might have been avoided by the earlier use of the new product. Questions then arise as to whether the delays are beneficial insofar as they protect consumers from the unforeseen and possibly harmful side effects of new drugs: a classic trade-off situation.

A cost–benefit analysis of regulation must also take account of its potential benefits. Regulatory agencies which aim to remove market failures will introduce policies to correct for externalities or to change the structure, conduct or performance of markets with the ultimate objective of improving consumer welfare. But can society assess the output or performance of a regulatory agency? Various performance indicators have been suggested, not all of which can be easily related to consumer satisfaction. For example, agencies are likely to emphasise the number of inquiries and reports; the number of licences issued, the number of inspections; the number of prosecutions; and the size of the regulatory authority. The Director–General of Fair Trading will refer to the number of monopoly inquiries; the number of merger investigations; reports issued; and the number of cases brought before the Restrictive Practices Court. Similarly, in regulating the introduction of new drugs, the Medicines Division of the Department of Health will eagerly report the number of licences awarded; the time taken to process applications; the introduction of any new testing requirements; inspection and enforcement activities; and the number of statutory orders.

The various performance indicators **appear** impressive, indicating a lively, active and vigorous regulatory authority. However, many of the indicators measure inputs or intermediate output, rather than **final output**: they do not indicate the effects on consumers and how highly consumers might value such effects. Supporters of regulation will obviously claim that it results in substantial social benefits. However, a regulatory agency aiming to maximise its size or budget will exaggerate the social benefits of its activities (such as improved product safety) and underestimate or ignore the costs of regulation. A regulatory agency will also favour independent fund-raising powers in the form of, say, licence fees which enable it to finance

inefficiency, labour hoarding and discretionary activities such as luxury headquarters and offices. Some of these arguments about regulation will now be applied to UK competition policy, which is a classic example of a general form of regulatory policy.

■ 11.4 Competition Policy

□ 11.4.1 *The Economic Rationale*

Competition policy is a classic example of general regulatory arrangements applying to all firms in the UK economy. It embraces policy towards monopolies, mergers and restrictive practices. In this context, standard economic theory offers some clear policy guidelines suggesting that monopoly and other imperfections result in market failure and hence are socially undesirable (see **Figure 11.1, p. 386**). Theory defines monopoly as a single seller of a product with no close substitutes. This model indicates that policy-makers need to focus on structural characteristics, the resulting performance reflected in the relationship between price and marginal cost and whether excessive profits are earned in the long run. However, theory also recognises that small numbers of firms constituting an oligopoly can have market power and that groups of firms acting together through collective agreements (cartels) can behave like a monopolist. As a result, policy needs to focus on mergers creating oligopoly or monopoly situations; on the conduct of firms in relation to entry barriers (for example, advertising); and on collective agreements which restrict competition in an industry. How far have such guidelines from economic theory influenced UK competition policy?

□ 11.4.2 *UK Practice*

UK competition policy is based on various pieces of legislation dating from 1948, concerned with monopolies, mergers, restrictive practices, resale price maintenance (RPM) and consumer protection. Monopolies and mergers may be referred for investigation by the Monopolies and Mergers Commission (MMC) whilst restrictive practices including RPM are the subject of legal procedures in the Restrictive Practices Court (see **Table 11.4**). Specific reference to consumer protection was first incorporated in the 1973 Fair Trading Act.

Current policy towards monopolies and mergers is based on Acts of 1973 and 1980. The Fair Trading Act 1973 created an Office of Fair Trading with a Director-General and cases **selected for investigation** referred to the MMC. Where a monopoly situation appears to exist, both the Director-General of Fair Trading and the Secretary of State for Trade and Industry can refer cases to the MMC. A monopoly is defined as one firm or a group of firms acting together (called a complex monopoly) accounting for **at least 25 per cent** of the relevant **local** or **national** market. **Selected** mergers are referred to the MMC by the Secretary of State for Trade and Industry. Mergers **may be** investigated where they involve a 25 per cent or more market share or **at least £30 mn worth of assets are taken over**. These definitions are interesting. The market share criterion contrasts with the economist's definition of monopoly as a single seller. Whilst the policy definition embraces oligopoly, it also implies that as the number of similar-sized firms declines from 5 to 4 a market changes from competition to a monopoly situation constituting a policy-relevant imperfection. Moreover, the value of assets taken over figure for mergers introduces an absolute size of firm criterion into the policy definition of monopoly. This contrasts with the economist's emphasis on market share. However, an absolute size criterion allows vertical and conglomerate mergers to be investigated. It might also reflect a public choice perspective, whereby large size can create dominant producer groups capable of influencing government purchasing and regulatory policies: hence, large firms might be undesirable.

In its investigations, the MMC has to determine whether a monopoly or proposed merger operates or is likely to operate **against the public interest**. In the case of both monopolies and mergers which are contrary to the public interest the MMC can recommend appropriate action to be taken, but cannot itself enforce a remedy. Only the relevant Secretary of State can enforce remedies against monopolies and can choose to prohibit a merger or to allow it to proceed unconditionally or subject to conditions. For the first time, the 1973 Act defined the public interest to include the desirability of maintaining and promoting competition. However, the public interest definition is wide-ranging. It includes a concern with consumer interests in relation to price, quality and variety; encouraging cost reductions, technical progress and new entry; a consideration of the international competitive position of UK producers; and promoting a balanced distribution of industry and employment. It is not at all obvious that some of these elements such as a balanced distribution of industry – itself an ambiguous term – are the proper concern of competition policy. Moreover, the MMC retains substantial discretion since it is allowed to take into account any factors which it deems to be relevant in determining the public interest! This is, in fact, a distinctive feature of UK policy towards monopolies and mergers.

Whilst standard economic theory suggests that competition is socially desirable, UK policy has not condemned monopolies and mergers as undesirable. A discretionary cost–benefit approach is adopted, **with each case examined on its merits**. Policy recognises that monopolies and mergers involve a trade-off between the costs of reduced competition, including X-inefficiency, and the potential benefits through scale economies and technical progress (see **Figure 11.1, p. 386**). Moreover, existing UK monopolies and mergers policy might be rationalised on second-best grounds. The standard welfare economics case for competition has to be modified where governments accept as policy-created constraints the continued existence of monopolies in parts of the economy. Alternatively, a public choice approach would explain current policy, with its wide-ranging public interest criterion and a reluctance to act against monopolies, as reflecting the influence of producer groups.

UK policy towards restrictive practices and RPM has taken a different approach. The Restrictive Practices Act 1976 and the Resale Prices Act 1976 consolidated the prior legislation of 1956, 1964 and 1968. Restrictive practices legislation applies to the supply of both goods and services. It is concerned with agreements which restrict prices,

Table 11.4 *Major Competition Policy Measures*

Legislation	Agencies	Features
Monopolies and Restrictive Practices Act 1948	Monopolies Commission	Monopoly = one-third or more of a market
Restrictive Trade Practices Act 1956	Registrar and Restrictive Practices Court	Restrictive agreements illegal but exemptions (gateways); if agreement passes through a gateway it still has to satisfy a public interest criterion
Resale Prices Act 1964	Restrictive Practices Court	RPM declared illegal subject to exemptions (gateways) and ultimate public interest test
Monopolies and Mergers Act 1965	Board of Trade mergers panel Monopolies Commission	Mergers to be reviewed involving one-third or more market share, or where value of assets taken over exceeded £5 mn
Restrictive Trade Practices Act 1968	Registrar and Restrictive Practices Court	Amendment of 1956 Act to incorporate information agreements
Fair Trading Act 1973	Director-General of Fair Trading Monopolies and Mergers Commission Consumer Protection Advisory Committee	Replaced 1948 and 1965 Acts Monopoly = 25 per cent or more of a local or national market. Mergers to be reviewed involving one-quarter or more market share or value of assets taken over exceeded £15 mn (increased to £30 mn in 1984) Public interest defined to include competition Reference to consumer protection
Restrictive Trade Practices Act 1976	Director-General of Fair Trading Restrictive Practices Court	Consolidated previous legislation (1956, 1968) with an extension to services Agreements registered with Director-General of Fair Trading
Resale Prices Act 1976	Director-General of Fair Trading Restrictive Practices Court	Consolidated previous legislation (1964), banning RPM

Table 11.4 *Major Competition Policy Measures (cont'd)*

Legislation	Agencies	Features
Competition Act 1980	Director-General of Fair Trading Monopolies and Mergers Commission	Deals with anti-competitive practices and extended monopoly control to public sector bodies and nationalised industries
EC Articles 85 and 86 of Treaty of Rome	Directorate General for Competition (European Commission) European Court of Justice	Applies only where trade between member states is affected Article 85 deals with restrictive practices and allows exemptions Article 86 originally applied to monopolies; but extended to prohibit mergers
EC merger regulation 1990	Directorate-General for Competition (European Commission) European Court of Justice	Aggregate world-wide turnover above ECU 5 bn and other requirements

conditions of sale and quantities to be supplied, and which lead firms to exchange information on prices and costs. Restrictive agreements have to be registered, and are presumed to be illegal and against the public interest unless the parties can establish a case for exemption before the Restrictive Practices Court. To be exempted, an agreement has to pass through one or more of eight **gateways**. For example, it has to be shown that an agreement protects the public against injury; that it provides substantial benefits to the public as purchasers, consumers or users; that it acts as a countervailing power against the anti-competitive practices of third parties; or that its removal would result in serious and persistent local unemployment or a substantial reduction in exports. Once again, some of these gateways, such as the concern with employment and exports, are rather odd aims for competition policy. However, even if an agreement passes through the gateways, it still has to satisfy the tailpiece or public interest test. The Court has to determine whether both currently and in the future, the benefits to the public on balance outweigh the detriments or costs.

The Resale Prices Act 1976 controls RPM in the same way as restrictive agreements. There is a general presumption that RPM is contrary to the public interest unless a supplier can gain exemption through one or more of five gateways. RPM might be allowed if its abolition would substantially reduce the quality and variety of goods for sale; if there would be a substantial reduction in the number of retail outlets; if there was likely to be a long-run increase in retail prices; or where there might be dangers to health or a substantial reduction in necessary point-of-sale sale or after-sales services. Once through a gateway, it is still necessary to satisfy the tailpiece where the Court has to consider the balance of benefits and detriments.

The Competition Act 1980 complemented existing legislation and takes a different approach from that of both 1976 Acts. It is concerned with the anti-competitive practices of individual firms supplying goods or services which have the effect of restricting, distorting or preventing competition. Examples include price discrimination, predatory pricing, exclusive supply and rental-only contracts, all of which are aspects of a firm's **conduct**. The 1980 Act also extended monopoly control to include the nationalised industries and other public sector bodies (for example, the bus companies, and water authorities). The 1980 procedure requires the Director-General of Fair Trading to investigate alleged anti-competitive practices. Where such a practice exists, the Director-General can either require the firm to discontinue the practice or it can be referred to the MMC which will apply the 1973 public interest test.

As a member of the EC, the UK is also subject to European competition law, reflected in Articles 85 and 86 of the Rome Treaty which are enforced by the European Commission. Article 85 prohibits restrictive agreements and practices which prevent, restrict or distort competition within the EC and which affect trade between member states. Examples include price-fixing, market-sharing and limitations of production, technical progress and investment. As in the UK, agreements may be exempted where they improve production, distribution or technical progress, subject to the requirement that these benefits must not be outweighed by other detriments associated with reduced competition. The European Commission has the power to impose heavy fines on the guilty parties to a restrictive agreement.

Article 86 originally applied to monopolies but has since been extended to mergers. It deals with situations where trade between member states might be affected by one or more enterprises taking improper advantage of a dominant position. Examples of improper practices include the imposition of inequitable purchase or selling prices, or limiting production, markets or technical developments. However, questions arise as to what constitutes a firm with a dominant position. In the case of mergers, the position is clearer. Under a 1990 regulation, the European Commission can control and prohibit mergers which have a Community dimension. These are defined as mergers where the **aggregate world-wide turnover** of the firms involved is above ECU 5 bn (approximately £3.5 bn), and **Community-wide turnover** of each of at least two of the firms is above ECU 250 mn (approximately £175 mn), unless two-thirds of that turnover is within one member state. Such mergers must be notified and will be prohibited if they create or strengthen a dominant position so that effective competition is impeded. All other mergers falling

outside this regulation will be dealt with by national governments. Firms and member states can appeal to the European Court of Justice against decisions of the European Commission. Clearly, European competition policy and its relationship with national policy will become a more important issue with the creation of the Single European Market in 1992.

Three issues are likely to dominate the evolution of an EC competition policy required for achieving a genuinely free internal market from 1992 onwards. First, there is likely to be a continued concern with the Community's merger regulations and their potential conflict with national merger policy. Indeed, the 1990 EC regulation on mergers reflected unanimous voting with some countries objecting to limits lower than the ECU 5 bn threshold. Second, the European Commission has become increasingly concerned about the competition implications of state subsidies and other forms of government protectionism. An example was the European Commission's requirement that the UK government reduce the amount of state aid offered as part of British Aerospace's acquisition of the Rover Group. Third, the European Commission is likely to become more actively involved in policy towards cartels and restrictive policies, particularly in the services sector and in markets dominated by state-owned industries.

□ 11.4.3 The Results of Competition Policy

Any evaluation of UK competition policy needs to focus on final output indicators in terms of the effects of policy on market structure, conduct and, ultimately, performance. Such an appraisal requires a model of structure, conduct and performance which holds constant all other relevant influences and identifies the contribution of competition policy. Other influences such as newly-industrialising nations, international trade, membership of the EC, technical progress, oil price shocks and the general level of aggregate demand and expectations in the UK economy cannot be ignored.

Competition policy can be evaluated against the general evidence on trends in the size of firms and industry structure in the UK economy. **Table 11.5** shows data on aggregate concentration in the form of the share of the 100 largest enterprises in manufacturing output. Aggregate concentration rose significantly from a pre-1939 figure of some 25 per cent to about 40 per cent by the late 1960s. However, since 1970, aggregate concentration has remained relatively stable – a feature which shows the uncertainties involved in predicting future trends. Interestingly, in 1987, about 10 per cent of the top 100 enterprises were the leading alcohol and tobacco companies such as BAT Industries, Grand-Metropolitan, Hanson Trust (Imperial), Allied Lyons, Gallaher, Bass and Guinness. At the same time, small firms are important. By 1987, there were 2.5 million firms in the UK, with 96 per cent employing fewer than 20 people and such small firms accounted for 36 per cent of total employment.

The extent of competition in a single market is usually shown by a **5-firm** concentration ratio which measures the proportion of industry output accounted for by the five largest firms in the industry. Evidence on concentration ratios is shown in **Table 11.5**. Following a small rise in the early 1970s, industry concentration declined up to the mid-1980s. Indeed, once the ratios are adjusted

for foreign trade, industry concentration actually declined between 1970 and 1984. Interestingly, even after allowing for foreign trade, a number of UK manufacturing industries remain highly concentrated, with 5-firm concentration ratios exceeding 75 per cent in 1984. Examples include asbestos; biscuits; cement; fertilisers; glass; locomotives; margarine; ordnance and tobacco. Inevitably, such data raise questions about the role and effects of monopoly policy.

By 1990, the MMC had issued over 60 reports on UK monopoly situations. Examples included the supply of beer (tied houses); cigarettes; soap and detergents; postal franking machines; animal waste; credit card services; the supply of petrol; cross channel ferries and travel agency services for tour operators. There have also been investigations of professional services (for example, of architects, surveyors and solicitors) and such public sector activities as British Rail computer services, some water authorities and the National Coal Board. Various monopoly situations and practices have been found to be against the public interest.

In its judgements, the MMC assesses monopolies in terms of their policies and their effects on prices; advertising; marketing; new entrants and, ultimately, profitability. For example, in 1989, the

Table 11.5 *Firm Size and Market Structures*

	1970	1974	1975	1979	1980	1984
100 largest enterprises share in manufacturing output (%)	39.3	42.1	n.a.	n.a.	40.5[1]	38.7
Unadjusted 5-firm CR[2,3] (%)	49.0	50.9	48.5	51.4	n.a.	49.1
Adjusted 5-firm CR[3] (%)	41.3	40.9	36.5	39.3	n.a.	33.8
Mergers[4]						
Number of companies acquired	793.0	504.0	534.0	–	469.0	568.0
Expenditure on acquisitions (£ bn at 1986 prices)	5.9	1.7	2.8	–	2.1	5.9

Notes:
[1] Change in definition after 1980.
[2] 5-firm concentration ratios (CR) based on a sample of 93 comparable industries 1970–9 and a sample of 195 comparable industries 1979–84.
[3] Unadjusted 5-firm CR is unadjusted for foreign trade while the adjusted CR allows for foreign trade.
[4] Mergers refer to acquisitions and mergers by UK industrial and commercial companies.
Source: DTI (1988).

MMC found that certain restrictions on advertising by the professions acted against the public interest and the Director-General of Fair Trading was asked to seek assurances that the professions would modify their behaviour. Similarly, the 1989 report on the supply of beer found that six brewers produced 75 per cent of beer sold and owned 75 per cent of all tied houses. An earlier 1969 report on the supply of beer had already concluded that the tied house system operated against the public interest. In its 1989 report, the Commission found a complex monopoly situation in brewing (mainly through tied houses) which restricted competition and was against the public interest. Unusually for the Commission, it recommended a series of **structural** changes to achieve a more competitive regime. These included a ceiling of 2000 on the number of tied premises owned by a brewer; allowing tied tenants to sell a 'guest' draught beer; and also allowing them to buy non-alcoholic and low alcohol drinks as well as wines and some other drinks from the lowest-cost suppliers (Cmnd 651, 1989; also Cmnd 216, 1969).

The concern of UK monopoly policy with prices, entry, profitability and consumers has a possible economic basis in models of perfect competition and contestable markets. But such models do not provide operational guidelines for determining when prices are too high and profits become excessive. Are prices too high if they result in abnormal profits and, if so, how is it possible to distinguish abnormal from normal profits? Austrian economists would adopt a different approach suggesting that market power is usually transitory and that so-called monopoly profits are the temporary reward of successful entrepreneurship. To the Austrians, an innovating monopolist generates a **social gain** represented by the firm's profits and the resulting consumer surplus: without the innovation a new product such as a microcomputer would never have been produced so there is no question of a deadweight loss due to a departure from the perfectly competitive output. Such contrasting interpretations of monopoly makes life extremely difficult and complicated for governments who have to determine a monopoly policy!

Critics of UK monopoly policy claim that it is slow and ineffective. Typically, a MMC enquiry might take 2–3 years. Few reports are issued in any one year and, to date, the total number of monopoly investigations represents only a small part of the UK's monopoly and oligopoly industries (although the presence of the MMC might have a deterrent effect). Moreover, governments are often reluctant to take effective remedial action against monopolies, preferring to rely on informal undertakings, which may reflect pressure from producer groups and the possibility that the regulatory agency has been captured by producers. The result is that UK monopoly policy has not achieved any major changes in either the structure or the conduct of monopoly industries which have been investigated.

Even the 1989 MMC recommendations for structural change in the brewing industry were modified by successive Secretaries of State. Clearly, the brewers represent a powerful producer group which lobbied the government not to implement or to modify or delay the recommendations of the MMC. In the event, the MMC's recommendations were modified, so that brewers were required to sell or place at 'arm's length' **half** of the pubs they owned above the 2000 ceiling (for example, Bass with 7300 pubs has to sell 2650 rather than 5300). At the same time, the brewers have responded to the new regulatory requirements in ways which are to their benefit and which might conflict with the aims of the MMC's 1989 report. For example, Grand Metropolitan and Courage agreed to a pubs-for-breweries exchange with Grand Met ceasing to make beer and a new jointly-owned company running the pubs. Some brewers have stopped brewing and retained their pubs (for example, Greenalls). Elsewhere, pubs have been sold and then converted to private houses. And examples have arisen where sales representatives of the big brewers have intimidated tenants not to take a guest beer or have made it difficult to stock a guest beer (for example, by threatening rent increases or eviction).

Cases continue to arise and the issues are not diminishing. In 1989, the Competition Act 1980 was applied to Black and Decker. The company's policy of refusing to supply retailers who sold its products below a particular price was found to be anti-competitive and against the public interest.

The government's initiatives on privatisation, deregulation, contracting-out and public purchasing policy are likely to create new demands on the UK's competition agencies. Also, mergers are contributing to major structural changes in the UK economy, with substantial numbers of mergers being of the horizontal and conglomerate types.

Between 1964 and 1989, the annual rate of mergers within the UK varied between 315 and some 1200 per annum, with a similar variation in annual expenditure on acquisitions of between £0.8 bn and some £22 bn at 1986 prices. Peaks of merger activity in terms of numbers and expenditure occurred in 1965, 1972–73, 1986–87 and 1989. Despite the high level of activity, relatively few qualifying mergers, typically well under 5 per cent, are actually referred to the MMC (for example, 1.2 per cent in 1987). Of those referred, not all are found to be contrary to the public interest. For example, between 1984 and 1986, there were 13 merger reports from the MMC, of which only four references were declared to be against the public interest. However, by the mid-1980s concern was expressed over the continued merger boom, allegations of asset stripping and especially the size of some acquisitions and their controversial nature (for example GEC-Plessey and Nestlé–Rowntree). As a result, the Government reviewed its merger policy and published the results in 1988 (DTI, 1988).

The 1988 government review of merger policy examined two performance indicators – namely, **trends in concentration ratios** and **post-merger performance**. Whilst evidence showed a substantial increase in industry concentration in the 1950s and 1960s, it seems that between 1970 and 1984 concentration ratios adjusted for foreign trade actually declined, as shown in **Table 11.5**. The 1988 review also confirmed the earlier findings of poor, disappointing or inconclusive post-merger performance (for example, with respect to profitability). Such evidence has been used to suggest that mergers were failing to provide economic benefits. Nevertheless, the government review reaffirmed its policy of leaving most merger decisions to the market: 'the vast majority of mergers raise no competition or other objections, and are rightly left free to be decided by the market' (DTI, 1988, p. 7). The review also confirmed that the main,

though not the only, factor in determining whether a merger should be referred to the MMC should be its **potential effects on competition in the UK market.**

However, to allow for a few exceptional cases (such as foreign ownership of UK companies or the level of any state ownership in the acquiring company), an open-ended public interest criterion was retained in the legislation. Finally, the 1988 review proposed two legislative changes to improve the speed and flexibility of merger policy. Both changes were incorporated in the Companies Act 1989. In the first place, a procedure for voluntary pre-notification was introduced, which is designed to obtain faster clearance of mergers involving no major public interest issues. Secondly, where a proposed or completed merger gives rise to concern about loss of competition, the merging parties can give a binding undertaking for the divestment of part of the merged company's business, as an alternative to a reference. The Companies Act 1989 also introduced a charging system to cover the costs of public sector merger control work. Even so, there is continued concern over mergers. Worries have been expressed about asset stripping, that foreign competitors are taking advantage of the UK's open door policy and that industrial structure is determined by short-termism (see Peacock and Bannock, 1991).

Restrictive practices legislation has been extremely effective in removing certain restrictive agreements which were the basis for the widespread cartelisation of UK industry in the 1950s. By 1988, some 6650 agreements had been registered, over 70 per cent of which were goods agreements. A substantial number of agreements have been abandoned, and many have been modified to remove any anti-competitive effects. Interestingly, it is possible that restrictive practices legislation, originally introduced in 1956, might have contributed to the high rate of merger activity in the 1960s. Nevertheless, evidence shows that the legislation resulted in new entry, increased competition, lower prices and generally contributed to its main objective of improving industrial efficiency (Cmnd 331, 1988).

Similarly, legislation was effective against resale price maintenance. In 1960 RPM applied to about 20–25 per cent of consumer expenditure; by

1979, it was restricted to net books and medicines, representing under 2 per cent of consumer expenditure. The result was improved efficiency in retailing and lower prices, although the efforts were smaller than expected and some groups such as small independent retailers and their customers had to bear the costs of the change. Nevertheless, the Resale Prices Act has made a major contribution to increased competition in retailing to the general benefit of consumers.

By the late 1980s, there were serious doubts about the effectiveness of restrictive practices legislation in tackling cartels. A government review suggested that 'the Act must now appear a relatively weak piece of legislation' (Cmnd 331, 1988, p. 29). It is criticised because potential colluders are unlikely to be detected (for example, the secret price-fixing agreements amongst ready-mixed concrete companies in 1991); penalties for ignoring the law are not sufficiently heavy to act as a deterrent; it catches trivia by including agreements which do not restrict competition; there are too many exemptions; and the whole registration process is costly and a waste of resources.

Instead, it was proposed that the registration system be abolished and **any agreement with anticompetitive effects was to be prohibited (illegal)**. Examples of anti-competitive agreements include the price fixing of goods and services, collusive tendering, market sharing, restrictions on advertising and collective refusals to supply. Exemptions would be allowed using a broad test similar to Article 85 (3) of the Treaty of Rome. The new policy would be administered by a competition authority as part of the Office of Fair Trading. The authority would have to determine whether an agreement is anti-competitive and, if so, whether it qualifies for an exemption. It was proposed that fines be imposed by the authority up to a maximum of 10 per cent of a firm's turnover. Appeals on prohibitions and exemptions would be made to the Restrictive Practices Court, which would also have the power to impose fines above the competition authority's maximum limit (Cmnd 331, 1988). However, whilst a White Paper was issued, none of the proposals had been incorporated into the legislation by late 1991.

11.4.4 The Single European Market

In addition to competition policy within the UK market, a major change is planned which will affect competition and contestability within the EC. Whilst there are no tariffs between member states of the EC, there remain a number of substantial and costly non-tariff barriers. Physical, technical and fiscal barriers mean that the EC consists of twelve fragmented national markets separated by frontier controls, public procurement practices and different product and technical standards, all of which hinder trade in goods and services between member states. The EC aims to remove these various barriers and to create a single internal market by the end of 1992.

It is estimated that the single European market will result in potential gains of over ECU 200 bn, equivalent to 5.3 per cent of EC GDP in 1988 (Cecchini, 1988, p. 84). Such gains will result from lower costs due to the abolition of frontier barriers, removing the barriers to entry into national markets (for example, for public procurement), exploiting scale economies and a general increase in competitive pressures in both goods and services markets. Currently, for example, cross-frontier trade is hindered by administrative formalities and border controls (red tape and delays); public procurement protects national industries from foreign competition; and divergent technical regulations, standards and certification procedures means costly market fragmentation (as in the case of financial services and telecommunications). However, the estimated benefits from abolishing non-tariff barriers will not be achieved immediately in 1993: it will take time for economies to adjust and adapt to the new market conditions, and the adjustment will not be costless.

Critics claim that the likely benefits have been exaggerated, that they are based on a simple perfectly competitive model which will never be achieved and that most of the worthwhile economies of scale have already been exploited. Further gains are also available from opening-up national defence equipment markets, an area currently outside the remit of the EC. Moreover, efforts to exploit any potential scale economies within the EC will probably require mergers, leading to possible conflicts with competition policy: the price of efficient scale might be monopoly which would benefit producer groups rather than consumers. Similar worries about the potential gainers and the potential losers from policy changes have dominated the debate about UK privatisation policy. Indeed, privatisation involves issues of ownership, monopoly, regulation and market competition. We must, therefore, turn to examine the relative merits of public versus private ownership and the role of ownership in enterprise performance.

■ *11.5 Ownership*

□ *11.5.1 The Nationalised Industries*

The UK economy consists of a mix of publicly- and privately-owned firms and industries. Within the public sector, public corporations, including nationalised industries, are state-owned bodies accountable to government but with a substantial degree of independence, and whose activities in the case of nationalised industries are financed largely by the consumers of their goods and services rather than by the taxpayer. These industries have been the focal point of continuing debate between the political parties with Labour governments traditionally preferring state ownership of the means of production. Since 1945, UK industries such as aerospace, airlines, coal, gas, electricity, rail, shipbuilding, steel and telecommunications have at various times been state-owned, as too have individual firms such as British Leyland, British Petroleum, Rolls Royce and the Royal Ordnance. However, since 1979, a substantial number of nationalised industries and state-owned companies have been privatised, raising debates about whether ownership is an important determinant of enterprise performance.

Various economic arguments have been used to explain and justify nationalisation. After 1945, much emphasis was placed on the need to control private monopoly power; to plan and control the commanding heights of the economy; to include social costs and benefits into decision-making; and to improve industrial relations by removing the traditional conflict between labour and capital. In the 1970s, state ownership of firms such as British Leyland and Rolls Royce was justified as a rescue operation to save strategically and economically important companies and to prevent substantial job losses. Nationalisation, however, is not without its problems. Objectives have to be specified, pricing, investment and financial rules are required, and performance has to be monitored. Problems have often arisen because of the lack of clearly specified objectives or because of changing and conflicting aims, resulting from the need to balance a concern with economic efficiency, technical efficiency, anti-inflationary pricing policies, social objectives and financial targets.

Economists seeking economically efficient solutions are fond of proposing marginal cost pricing rules for nationalised industries, requiring them to set price equal to long run marginal cost. However, 'marginal cost' has to be defined and measured, and difficulties arise where state industries are monopolies not subject to competitive pressures. In such circumstances, the lack of contestability is likely to be associated with organisational slack and X-inefficiency: marginal cost is whatever the Chairman of the nationalised industry says it is! Moreover, in decreasing cost industries, marginal cost pricing will be associated with losses. In such circumstances, losses are consistent with an economically-efficient solution and are not an indication of inefficiency. However, marginal cost pricing is further criticised on second-best grounds. Where prices do not equal marginal cost throughout the economy, the appropriate second-best pricing rule for a nationalised industry is likely to require a departure from strict marginal cost pricing.

Actual pricing policies for the UK nationalised industries have varied from a requirement to break-even (that is, average cost pricing), to marginal cost pricing and to a requirement to act commercially. Marginal cost pricing was introduced following a 1967 White Paper. In a 1978 White Paper a further element was introduced requiring nationalised industries to aim at a **real rate of return** on their new investment programmes of 5 per cent (8 per cent in 1991). The required rate of return is reviewed periodically and is related to the return achieved by private companies, thereby ensuring that the nationalised industries do not divert resources away from more valuable alternatives. Also, since 1976, the nationalised industries and most other public corporations have been subject to **external financing limits** (EFLs) which control the amount of finance, whether grants or borrowing, which an industry may raise during the financial year to supplement its income from normal trading.

Since 1979 the government has been concerned about the efficiency and losses incurred by the nationalised industries and has sought to reduce the size of this sector through denationalisation or privatisation. By 1989, the government's major aim for the nationalised industries was to 'ensure their effectiveness and efficiency as commercial concerns and to strengthen them to the point where they can be transferred to the private sector or, where necessary, remain as successful businesses within the public sector' (Cmnd 621, 1989, p. 62). As a successful public sector business, they are expected to minimise the burden on the taxpayer (via subsidies), earn an economic return on their assets, and improve their commercial performance. In other words, the remaining nationalised industries are to act commercially. If such an objective is interpreted as profit maximisation, it will promote technical efficiency but, in the absence of competition, it will not produce allocative efficiency.

During the 1980s, a substantial number of nationalised industries have been privatised. In 1979, the nationalised industries accounted for some 9 per cent of GDP and employed over 1.8 million people; by 1989, the corresponding figures were 3.5 per cent and some 700,000 employees. During this period, the productivity of the nationalised industries increased substantially, reflecting efficiency improvements, reductions in overmanning and the incentive of possible privatisation. Between 1979 and 1990 the average annual productivity growth of the nationalised industries was 4.4 per cent, exceeding that both for manufacturing (4.1 per cent) and for the economy as a whole (1.9 per cent). By 1991, the remaining UK nationalised industries were British Coal, British Rail, British

Waterways, the Civil Aviation Authority, London Transport, Nuclear Electric and the Post Office, together with such public corporations as the BBC, the Commonwealth Development Corporation and the Urban Development Corporations.

11.5.2 Privatisation: a Classification System

Privatisation has been a central feature of the successive Conservative Governments elected since 1979. The policy has embraced denationalisation or selling-off state assets, deregulation (liberalisation) and competitive tendering. Public sector assets have been sold to the private sector in the form of both share issues and private sales. Examples include British Aerospace, British Airways, British Gas, British Steel, British Telecom, Cable and Wireless, Electricity, the National Freight Corporation, Rolls Royce, the Royal Ordnance Factories and Water (see **Table 11.6**). Currently, there are plans to privatise British Rail. A number of markets have been deregulated, thereby reducing or removing restrictions on new entrants. Examples include short and long-distance bus services (Transport Act 1980 and 1985), the Stock Exchange, opticians, building societies offering banking services, together with the emergence of Mercury as a rival supplier of telecommunications services. Finally, a range of services provided by central and local government, by the NHS and by the Armed Forces have been exposed to rivalry through competitive tendering and contracting-out. Examples include catering, cleaning and laundry services, refuse collection and the maintenance of grounds and vehicles (Bishop and Kay, 1988).

The distinction between government (public) and private finance and provision can be used to classify the different forms of UK privatisation policy. Such a classification system is shown in **Figure 11.3** which provides a useful starting point for analysis and also allows the rival advocates of private and state ownership to contemplate horizontal, vertical and diagonal movements between the boxes. Inevitably, **Figure 11.3** is only a broad classification system. For instance, state-owned

Table 11.6   *UK Privatisations*

Year	Type of Sale	% Sold	Proceeds[3] £ bn (1988–89 Prices)
1979			0.8
British Petroleum (phase 1)	S[1]	17.0	
ICL	P[2]		
1980			0.4
Fairey Engineering	P		
Ferranti	P		
1981			0.8
British Aerospace (phase 1)	S	51.0	
British Petroleum (phase 2)	S	5.0	
Cable & Wireless (phase 1)	S	49.0	
1982			0.7
Amersham International	S	100.0	
Britoil (phase 1)	S	51.0	
National Freight Corporation	P		
1983			1.6
Associated British Ports (phase 1)	S	51.5	
British Petroleum (phase 3)	S	7.0	
BR Hotels	P		
Cable & Wireless (phase 2)	S	22.0	
International Aeradio	P		
1984			2.7
Associated British Ports (phase 2)	S	48.5	
British Telecom	S	50.2	
Enterprise Oil	S	100.0	
Inmos	P		
Jaguar	S	99.0	
Scott Lithgow	P		
Sealink	P		
Wytch Farm	P		
1985			3.4
British Aerospace (phase 2)	S	49.0	
Britoil (phase 2)	S	48.0	
Cable & Wireless (phase 3)	S	31.0	
Vosper Thorneycroft	P		
Yarrow Shipbuilders	P		
1986			5.4
BA Helicopters	P		
British Gas	S	97.0	
Hall Russell	P		
National Bus Company	P		
Royal Ordnance (phase 1)	P		
Swan Hunter	P		
Vickers Shipbuilding	P		

Table 11.6   *UK Privatisations (cont'd)*

Year	Type of Sale	% Sold	Proceeds[3] £ bn (1988–89 Prices)
1987			5.9
British Airports Authority	S	100.0	
British Airways	S	100.0	
British Petroleum (phase 4)	S	36.8	
DAB	P		
Istel	P		
Leyland Bus Company	P		
Rolls Royce	S	100.0	
Royal Ordnance (phase 2)	P		
Unipart	P		
1988			7.5
British Steel	S	100.0	
Rover Group	P		
1989			4.2
Harland and Wolff	P		
Short Bros	P		
Regional Water companies	S	100.0	
1990			4.9
Regional Electricity companies	S	100.0	
Electricity generation (Powergen and National Power)	S	100.0	
1991			n/a
Scottish Power and Hydro-Electric	S	100.0	
British Telecom (phase 2)	S	28.0	

Notes:

[1] S = privatisation by share issue: those sold in phases reflect flotation of government holdings in the private companies.

[2] P = private sale of company – for example, National Freight was sold to its employees; Royal Ordnance and Rover were sold to British Aerospace; in all cases the entire company was disposed of.

[3] Proceeds are based on financial years – for example, 1979 is 1979–80, and include sales phased over a number of years.

Sources: Public Expenditure White Paper 1991.

enterprises selling products to private markets may also receive subsidies (British Coal and British Rail) and there are privately-owned schools and hospitals. In addition, monopolies transferred from the public to the private sector are subject to regulatory constraints. In the case of airports and the privatised utilities such as gas and telecommunications, the regulatory agencies impose a pricing rule known as **RPI-X**, where RPI is the retail prices index and X is a percentage figure. This rule imposes a ceiling on the annual increase in a firm's prices which will always be X per cent below the general inflation rate. Even so, the 1990 financial results of the major privatised utilities led to public criticism of excessive profits and over-charging reflecting their monopoly power.

11.5.3 Objectives of Privatisation Policy

Current privatisation policy has been associated with various objectives, some of which are in conflict. Consumers are expected to benefit from

Figure 11.3 *Classifying Privatisation*

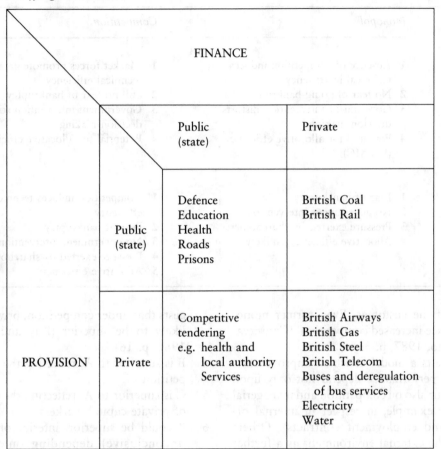

rivalry, more choice, greater efficiency and innovation. The policy is also aimed at reducing the size of the public sector through denationalisation, and reducing public sector borrowing. Furthermore, it has been associated with a desire for wider share ownership. Suggestions have also been made that the real purpose of the policy is to reduce the monopoly power of trade unions. There are conflicts between some of these objectives. For example, reducing the size of the public sector and maximising Treasury income from selling public assets can be achieved by transferring monopoly power from the public to the private sector without increasing rivalry. It is, of course, likely that the actual extent and form of privatisation policy will reflect the influence of agents in the political market place – namely, governments seeking votes and established interest groups (managers and workers) trying to protect their positions, especially their income and on-the-job leisure.

The debate about privatisation in its wider aspects raises the general question of whether ownership is an important determinant of economic performance. During the 1980s the government claimed that, following privatisation, productivity and profitability in the newly-privatised companies increased dramatically (as in the case, for example, of British Aerospace, Jaguar and the National Freight Consortium). The official explanation offered was that 'the overwhelming majority of employees have become shareholders in the newly privatised companies. They want their companies to succeed. Their companies have been released from the detailed controls of Whitehall and given more freedom to manage their own affairs. And they have been exposed to the full commercial

Table 11.7   *Ownership and Market Structure: a Taxonomy*

	Monopoly	Competition
Public Ownership	*A* 1 Absence of competition induces technical inefficiency 2 No fear of going bankrupt 3 Government intervention distorts decision-making 4 Potential for allocative efficiency (P = MC)	*B* 1 Market forces promote greater technical efficiency 2 Still no fear of bankruptcy 3 Government intervention still distorts decision-making 4 Potential for allocative efficiency
Private Ownership	*C* 1 Fear of bankruptcy 2 No government intervention 3 Pressure exerted by shareholders 4 Allocative efficiency unlikely	*D* 1 Competition induces technical efficiency 2 Fear of bankruptcy 3 No government intervention 4 Pressure exerted by shareholders 5 Allocative efficiency

disciplines of the customer. Even former monopolies now face increased competition' (Conservative Manifesto, 1987, p. 36).

This suggests a model in which improvements in economic performance depend not only upon ownership, but also on competition and managerial freedom (for example, in respect of internal organisation and employment contracts). Others would add the external environment as a further variable in the model in the form of, for example, the Thatcher effect via Rayner scrutinies, Financial Management Initiatives and the withdrawal of subsidies providing a shock effect throughout the public and private sectors (Dunsire *et al.*, 1988). Some of these complex and sometimes interdependent issues can be simplified into a two-variable model showing the impact of ownership and market structure on efficiency. A framework is shown in **Table 11.7**, where the following hypotheses on enterprise performance or efficiency can be formulated:

1   D is superior to A, where D represents private ownership and a competitive product market.
2   D is superior to C – neo-classical economics favours competition.
3   D is equal to, or superior to, B – does ownership matter? One review of the evidence suggests that under competition, private firms are likely to be superior (Kay and Thompson, 1986, p. 16).
4   B is superior to A, reflecting the role of competition.
5   C is superior to A, reflecting the policing role of private capital markets.
6   B could be superior, inferior or equal to C (inconclusive) depending on the relative strengths of competition and ownership.

Testing hypotheses about the effects of ownership and market structure on enterprise performance and efficiency is not without its problems. Indicators are required to measure enterprise performance and, ultimately, economic efficiency. Some crude performance indicators are readily available such as profitability, labour productivity and international competitiveness, and tests can be undertaken to determine whether performance improves following a change from public to private ownership, *ceteris paribus*. It should be borne in mind that an increase in profitability might reflect the exercise of market power by a newly-privatised monopolist, and higher labour productivity could reflect investment in new equipment. Moreover, empirical tests of performance before and after an ownership change need to allow for what would have happened without the change, and the distinct possibility that a transfer of ownership will result in the pursuit of different objectives. There are, however, alternative policies for influencing enterprise performance, with subsidies as an obvious option.

■ 11.6 Subsidy Policy

□ 11.6.1 A Classification System

At their simplest, subsidies are payments by government to producers which are designed to reduce prices. Such a definition can be modified to allow for payments to firms and industries to ensure their survival or to prevent contraction. More generally, subsidies are a means of affecting the **allocation and use of resources** in the economy, thereby interfering in the operation of markets. The issue is, however, whether such interference is desirable.

Over time, British governments have offered various subsidies to firms, industries, regions and to factors of production. Examples have included private firms such as British Leyland and Chrysler, private and state industries such as aerospace, computers, cotton, steel and shipbuilding, as well as high unemployment regions, namely development areas. Subsidies have been used to achieve specific policy objectives such as maintaining or increasing employment, assisting the balance of payments through export promotion and import saving and encouraging growth through supporting high technology. At times, the range of industrial subsidies has been bewildering, and so extensive that questions have arisen as to whether there are any economic activities in the UK which should not qualify for a subsidy!

As a starting point in analysing subsidies, a classification system is required. Subsidies can be classified in at least three related ways.

General and Specific Types

General schemes offer subsidies to all firms satisfying certain conditions which might relate to investment, location, employment, size of firm or type of activity (for example, agriculture, manufacturing or tourism). General schemes have been the traditional method of subsidising UK industry. They are automatic and aim to influence industry decisions and hence the operation of markets without involving substantial transaction costs. In contrast, specific or discretionary schemes are designed for an individual firm or project with subsidies being used to prevent bankruptcy and plant closure or to promote reorganisation, re-equipment and restructuring. Or specific subsidies might be offered for the development of a new high-technology project such as a supersonic airliner or a new generation of computer. In principle, specific schemes aim at fine tuning by setting the subsidy at the minimum level required to influence a firm's decisions. However, this approach involves substantial transaction costs. It requires detailed information about a firm's costs and its efficiency, and it assumes that civil servants will be motivated to negotiate the minimum subsidy. Further costs will be incurred in bargaining, monitoring and policing. Critics claim that public servants may be influenced in their decisions by the prospect of employment in industry or that specific subsidies result in an undesirable cosiness between civil servants and the firms with which they negotiate.

The Production Function Approach

A distinction can be made between subsidies for outputs and for factor inputs. Farmers, for example, receive output subsidies. Factor inputs can also be subsidised, the aim being to encourage and increase the use of relatively cheaper (subsidised) factors. Input subsidies embrace capital, labour and technology. Examples include incentives to invest in new plant and machinery, to substitute labour for capital and to increase research and development.

The Geographic or Location Dimension

Subsidies in their general and specific forms, for inputs and outputs, can be tied to specially designated areas of the country embracing development areas, intermediate areas, enterprise zones, free ports and inner cities.

Table 11.8   *DTI Programmes*

DTI Expenditure	1985–6	1986–7	1987–8	1988–9	1989–90	1990–1	1993–4 (Plans)
£ bn at 1989–90 prices							
Total expenditure	2.3	2.7	0.9	1.6	1.6	1.5	0.7
Privatisation proceeds	3.4	5.4	5.9	7.5	4.2	4.9	4.4
Expenditure on major programmes (£ mn at constant prices)							
Regional and general industrial support	947	1 049	787	929	843	879	720
Support for aerospace, shipbuilding, coal, steel and vehicle manufacture	764	1 540	456	1 286	708	390	70
Scientific and technological assistance	533	531	502	577	503	576	590
DTI total expenditure	1 809	2 261	821	1 460	1 648	1 630	910
Government subsidies	5 285	4 677	4 885	4 050	4 503	5 636	5 110
GDP deflator (1989–90 = 100)	80.3	83.1	87.6	94.0	100.0	108.0	124.1
Subsidies as % of public expenditure	4.0	3.4	3.4	2.8	2.8	3.1	2.3

Source: HM Treasury, *The Government's Expenditure Plans*, 1991.

During the 1960s and 1970s, UK expenditure on subsidies increased substantially, from under 2 per cent of GDP at market prices and around 4 per cent of government expenditure in 1965 to corresponding figures of almost 4 per cent and around 7–8 per cent respectively in 1975. The government since 1979 has taken a different attitude towards a general and massive subsidy policy. Indeed, **Table 11.8** shows the declining trend in government subsidies between 1985 and 1994. As a further indication of the government's industrial policy, the annual level of real spending by the Department of Trade and Industry declined substantially after the mid-1980s, whilst privatisation proceeds were much greater than the Department's budget. In view of the major contrasts between the 1970s and 1980s, questions have to be asked about the economic logic of UK subsidy policy.

11.6.2 Economic Theory and Subsidies

A market failure approach suggests that subsidies are required whenever there are substantial and beneficial externalities or social benefits. Alternatively, subsidies might be required to cover the losses associated with marginal cost pricing applied to a decreasing cost industry. Whilst a number of UK firms and nationalised industries have received subsidies to reduce losses and to prevent closure, these have usually not been associated with marginal cost pricing and decreasing costs. Instead, subsidies have more often been justified on grounds of social benefits. The argument is that private markets, if left to themselves, will provide too little of some socially desirable activities and subsidies are required to correct this market failure. Typically, governments have used the social benefits argument to justify subsidies to protect jobs, to promote high technology and to support the balance of payments, all of which are deemed to be in the national or public interest. Economists need to assess these arguments critically, subjecting them to economic analysis and empirical evidence.

The methodology of economic policy can be applied to subsidy policy, although critics might claim that it is a counsel of perfection. The objectives of policy have to be clearly stated. The causes of the policy problem have to be identified, and it needs to be shown that subsidies are the most appropriate and efficient solution from the available alternatives. For example, with regional policy the aim might be to increase employment in the high unemployment areas of the country. However, this might conflict with the objective of promoting a reallocation of resources from declining to expanding regions and with encouraging firms to locate in their most efficient areas. Questions then arise about the causes of local unemployment. Is it, for example, due to high wages failing to reflect local labour scarcities; do firms elsewhere lack information about local labour supplies; are there infrastructure deficiencies which raise the costs to firms locating in the area; is the housing market impairing labour mobility; or is the capital market failing to finance worthwhile human investments in mobility and training? From this analysis of causes, it does not follow that subsidies to firms in high unemployment areas are the most appropriate and efficient solution. Questions have to be asked about the effectiveness of policy: has it achieved its objectives? If so, at what cost? Regional policy which offers a variety of incentives and subsidies to firms located in high unemployment areas is an obvious candidate for evaluation.

☐ 11.6.3 Regional Policy

Markets are changing continuously and the results of change are reflected in the expansion and decline of different regions in the UK. High unemployment areas in northern England, Scotland, Wales and Northern Ireland are associated with the decline of the UK's traditional smokestack industries such as coal, shipbuilding, steel and textiles. Sunrise industries such as electronics have developed elsewhere. In the 1990s, cuts in defence budgets will mean that UK and other EC regions dependent on defence industries and bases will be vulnerable to job losses.

The regional policy problem arises because markets do not adjust instantly, and because private markets do not consider the social costs and benefits of their activities (externalities). Successive UK governments have thus intervened to correct regional imbalances by seeking to reduce the regional differentials in unemployment rates. However, problems have arisen because the objectives of regional policy are often social and political rather than economic. Budget-conscious government departments can offer schemes to solve regional unemployment which will be supported by producers likely to benefit and by governments attracted by the likely favourable effects on votes.

A new UK regional policy was introduced in 1984. This was a result of substantial economic changes which had occurred in the 1970s, with UK membership of the EC, the oil crisis and higher national unemployment. It was estimated that between 1972 and 1983, the previous regional policy created some 500,000 more jobs in the assisted areas at an Exchequer expenditure of £35,000 per job (at 1982 prices). Nevertheless, it was felt that the 1970s' regional policy was not cost-effective; was not sufficiently selective; discriminated against services; favoured capital-intensive projects, and often resulted in a transfer of jobs and a failure to emphasise job creation.

Under the policy introduced in 1984 there were two types of regions (namely development areas and intermediate areas) together with two types of grants (namely, **regional development grants (RDGs)** and **regional selective assistance (RSA)**). Firms in development areas qualified for both RDGs and RSA. RDGs were automatic and paid at 15 per cent of eligible capital expenditure subject to a cost ceiling per job or, where higher, at £3000 for each new full-time job created (at 1989 prices). In 1988–89, it was estimated that RDGs led to some

56,000 jobs for an Exchequer outlay of £220 mn. The RDG scheme was phased-out in 1988. In future, RSA will be the main form of regional industrial assistance. RSA grants are discretionary and are available to firms in both development and intermediate areas. They are provided for projects which maintain employment or create additional jobs, the aim being to provide the minimum assistance needed for the project to proceed in an assisted area. In 1988–89, RSA was reputed to have created over 32,000 new jobs and safeguarded almost 9000 others for an Exchequer outlay of £93 mn.

Further regional assistance is available. In April 1988, **Regional Enterprise Grants** were introduced for development areas. These are available to firms with under 25 employees and they offer limited grants for investment projects and innovations. In addition, UK government support is available for inner cities, enterprise zones and free ports. Finally, regional support is also provided through the European Community's Regional Development Fund.

Critics of current UK regional policy claim that it represents a move towards a free market approach, with reductions in special support for the regions and an emphasis on improving the operation of product and factor (including labour) markets throughout the economy. They claim that there will be too little government assistance and financial support to solve the regional problem, and they also assert that there is a need for more policy instruments. In particular, supporters of an interventionist policy favour **Industrial Development Certificates** (IDCs) as a means of controlling new factory buildings and extensions, thereby influencing the location decisions of firms. Originally, IDCs were used to reduce congestion in London and the South-East and to promote activity in the assisted areas, but they were no longer used after 1982.

Nonetheless, whether an interventionist or laissez faire approach is preferred, there remain some outstanding issues for regional policy. Questions arise about the aims of policy and the potential conflicts between efficiency and social objectives; about whether policy is simply transferring jobs between different parts of the country; and ultimately, about the beneficiaries from the policy.

But regional policy is not the only form of support for UK industry. The DTI also offers selective assistance to individual firms and industries (for example, aerospace, shipbuilding and steel); it encourages business to develop a positive and competitive response to environmental issues; and there is a major programme of support for industrial innovation.

□ *11.6.4 Technology Policy*

Government support for science, technology and R & D is designed to improve the efficiency, competitiveness and innovative capacity of the UK (Cmnd 621, 1989, p. 25). But why is state intervention required? Here, the argument is that R & D is risky, it may take a long time to produce marketable results and the benefits are likely to extend far beyond a single innovating firm. On this basis, it is argued that if left to themselves, private markets will fail to provide the socially desirable amount of R & D and will encourage the hoarding of valuable ideas, so resulting in too little innovation and its dissemination, with adverse effects on economic growth. Such market failure reflects at least three factors. In the first place, a belief that capital markets will fail to finance large-scale, risky and long-term projects. Secondly, it might reflect the costs of establishing property rights in valuable ideas. Thirdly, the pursuit of profits might lead to the hoarding of valuable ideas and a failure to generate the socially desirable transfer of knowledge throughout the economy.

Persuasive though these arguments appear, they are often long on emotion and short on economic analysis, critical content and empirical evidence. For example, what might appear to be market failures in research and scientific activity might simply reflect the diversity of solutions adopted by firms to economise on transaction costs. Similarly, it is not sufficiently convincing evidence of a capital market failure to claim that it failed to provide funds for such high-technology projects as Airbus and Concorde. In such cases, the capital market might be working properly and judging that the projects are likely to be unprofitable. After all, the UK capital market has funded large-scale, long-term and risky projects such as the Channel Tunnel and the North Sea oil fields. Nor does it follow that state intervention will take an impartial long-term view, independently of the political market including a government's need to be re-elected. In fact, public choice analysis predicts that governments can also fail.

Once governments decide to intervene in research and scientific markets they are faced with a complex choice set. Decisions are needed on support for basic or applied research and technology transfer; on training the appropriate number and mix of different types of scientists and engineers; and on whether to offer support in the form of cash incentives (such as subsidies), tariff protection, patent legislation, or public procurement. Further choices are required on whether to support key high-technology industries such as aerospace, electronics and telecommunications and, if so, whether to favour small or large firms and a competitive, oligopolistic or monopoly industry structure. Here, the evidence suggests that an industry with many moderate-to-large firms of relatively similar size will be the most technically pro-

gressive, and that a market structure intermediate between monopoly and perfect competition will promote the highest rate of inventive activity (Kamien and Schwartz, 1982, p. 3).

Some of the results of UK government choices on science and technology policy are shown in **Table 11.9**. Defence is the largest programme, followed by Education and Science (including the universities), DTI and Energy (including atomic energy). Within defence R & D, some 60 per cent of expenditure is allocated to the aerospace and electronics industries. Moreover, the large share of defence in government spending on science and technology led the Ministry of Defence in 1987 to admit that defence R & D may crowd-out valuable investment in the civil sector, so impairing industry's ability to compete in international markets for civil high-technology products. Interestingly, though, since 1987 there has been no dramatic shift in the relative shares of government spending on military and civil technology.

The DTI has a major programme of assistance for industrial innovation. In recent years, policy has changed from support for near-market R & D

Table 11.9 *Government Spending on Science and Technology*

Department [1]	Expenditure (current prices £ mn)							
	1982–83	1985–86	1986–87	1987–88	1988–89	1989–90	1990–91	1993–94 (Plans)
Defence	1 765	2 266	2 186	2 156	2 123	2 350	2 558	2 670
Education & Science	1 135	1 260	1 316	1 440	1 575	1 722	1 878	2 070
DTI	327	458	462	418	411	404	411	260
Energy (incl. nuclear)	250	206	171	161	194	180	189	160
Total	3 839	4 581	4 578	4 614	4 775	5 154	5 549	5 740
of which: Civil science and technology	2 074	2 315	2 392	2 458	2 652	2 804	2 991	3 070
% civil	54	51	52	53	56	54	54	54

Note:
[1] Only major spending departments are shown.
Source: Cmnd 1504, 1991.

to support for long-term research collaboration and technology transfer. The DTI has encouraged collaborative programmes involving European firms (Eureka), as well as collaboration between government, industry and higher education. It has also promoted technology transfer where the market may be slow to adapt (Cmnd 605, 1989, p. 7). In addition, the DTI has provided further support for specific sectors, namely aircraft, aeroengine and civil space research programmes together with launch aid for civil aerospace projects. Interestingly, both the defence and DTI R & D programmes offer substantial public sector support to the UK aerospace industry. In evaluating government support for civil aircraft programmes, one study concluded that between 1945 and 1975 the net effect of aerospace launching aid has been a net loss of national welfare (Gardner, 1976, p. 149).

☐ 11.6.5 European Collaboration

The trend towards the rising costs of some advanced technology projects means that the minimum entry costs are so high that it is necessary for a number of large firms or even nations to combine. Even before the completion of the single internal market in the EC, there have been some notable examples of European government involvement in collaborative programmes. These include Airbus, Concorde, the European Centre for Nuclear Research, ESPRIT (an IT programme), the European Space Agency and a series of joint defence ventures mainly involving military aircraft, helicopters and missiles such as the three-nation Tornado and the four-nation European Fighter Aircraft. For these projects, European collaboration reflects the fact that independence based on small national markets is too costly.

Europe's high-technology industries such as aerospace, defence, electronics and telecommunications are frequently criticised for the wasteful duplication of costly R & D and for the relatively short production runs resulting from a dependence on a small domestic market. International collaboration is often presented as the appropriate solution leading, so it is claimed, to the eventual creation of European-wide high technology industries capable of competing with Japan and the USA in world markets. Supporters of European collaboration in high technology claim a variety of benefits, as indicated below:

1 Cost savings for both R & D and production
2 The sharing of risks and costs allows projects to be undertaken which would be too costly on an independent national basis (for example, space satellites and supersonic airliner).
3 The creation of a European industry able to compete in world markets for high-technology products, so avoiding Europe becoming a nation of metal bashers.
4 A set of general economic and political benefits in the form of domestic jobs, the balance of payments, rivalry in ideas and the creation of a united Europe through reducing national barriers and prejudice.

The simple economics of collaboration are shown in **Figure 11.4**. Consider the case of a two-nation collaborative military aircraft project based on equal sharing of R & D costs and a pooling of national orders. In the ideal case, each nation bears only 50 per cent of the development costs compared with an independent national venture and gains from the doubling of output which, through learning economies, will reduce unit production costs by about 10 per cent. However, collaboration has some disadvantages and costs leading to departures from the ideal model. Where governments are involved, substantial transaction costs arise as each partner nation seeks to establish property rights in the joint programme. Bargaining between partner governments, their bureaucracies and customers (such as the armed forces), together with lobbying from producer groups of scientists and contractors, can lead to substantial inefficiencies. Work might be shared on political, equity and bargaining criteria and not on the basis of efficiency and competition. Each partner will demand its fair share of high-technology work. Also, there might be substantial administrative costs in the form of duplicate organisations, frequent committee meetings, delays in decision-making and excessive government involvement in monitoring and policing international contracts. As a result,

Figure 11.4 *The Economics of Collaboration*

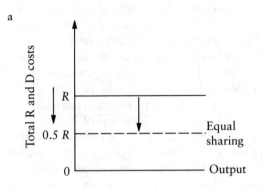

a

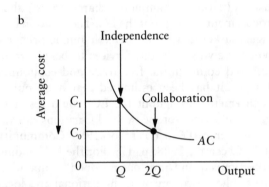

b

a R & D Costs
b Unit Production Costs

collaborative programmes involving governments might lead to higher costs and take longer to develop than a national project. Government involvement in collaboration also raises wider issues of public purchasing, and we must accordingly turn to consider the likely effects of government purchasing on industrial performance.

■ *11.7* Public Purchasing

☐ *11.7.1 Scope of Government Procurement*

Government purchasing is big business. In 1988–89, central and local government purchases of assets, goods and services was almost £39 bn, representing about 25 per cent of public expenditure.

Government purchases range from standard items such as clothing, paper clips, furniture, motor cars, office equipment and accommodation, to more complex products such as computers, space satellites, nuclear power stations and Trident submarines. Such purchases have the potential for influencing industrial performance. Defence and Health are the major spending departments, purchasing from industries such as aerospace, electronics, ordnance, shipbuilding, pharmaceuticals and medical equipment.

Government purchasing from private and state-owned enterprises involves choices about a product, a contractor and a contract. Decisions are required on the type of goods and services to be purchased, the selection of a contractor and the choice of a contract. Often such choices provide scope for governments to pursue wider economic and social objectives and not simply the acquisition of goods and services. Considerations of the national interest might lead a government to purchase from higher-cost domestic suppliers so as to protect a nation's key strategic industries, its technology, jobs and the balance of payments. The pursuit of such wider ends makes it difficult for Parliament and independent analysts to determine whether public procurement is giving good value for money. However, privatisation results in the transfer of purchasing from the public to the private sector where commercial criteria rather than wider public interest considerations dominate procurement choices.

The range and complexity of public procurement choices can be illustrated by considering two limiting models. At one extreme, the government as the buyer knows what it wants, the products exist and they are being traded in competitive-type markets. In these circumstances, the state acts as a competitive buyer, specifies its requirements, invites competitive tenders and awards a fixed price contract to the lowest bidder. Problems arise at the other extreme where the government is the only buyer, it is uncertain about its requirements, and the product does not yet exist (as is often the case for high-technology products such as defence equipment and telecommunications). Moreover, the domestic market might contain only one or relatively few actual or potential suppliers. The government as the major, or only, buyer might have to select a contractor and to write a contract for a project which either does not exist, might involve a major jump in the state of the art and where the contractor requires a cost-based contract with a substantial proportion of the risks borne by the state. Contracts for such advanced technology projects are often associated with cost overruns, time slippages and major modifications and sometimes with cancellations (for example the Nimrod AEW project) leading to allegations of waste, incompetence and contractor inefficiency.

Where a government department is a major buyer, as with defence equipment, the NHS, nuclear power and railway equipment, its procurement choices and contracting policies can have a decisive effect on an industry's size, structure, entry and exit, technical progress, efficiency, prices and profitability. For example, non-competitive government contracts, as with some defence equipment and pharmaceuticals for the NHS, are subject to state regulatory constraints. A Review Board for Non-Competitive Government Contracts and a Pharmaceutical Profit Regulation Scheme are designed to ensure that government contractors receive a reasonable rate of return on capital, where 'reasonable' usually means a profit rate similar to the average return earned by British industry. However, firms respond and adapt to regulatory constraints. The possibility of post-costing and renegotiation of excessive profits provides firms with an inducement to sacrifice profits for expenditures which give satisfaction (utility) to the company's managers, such as company cars, luxury offices and the hoarding of scientists.

For many years, there have been continued debates about whether co-ordinated government purchasing might improve industrial performance through, for example, exploiting the economies of scale associated with combining and standardising orders from different state agencies. Since 1979, the emphasis has been on achieving better value for money from public purchasing. Government departments have been subject to Rayner scrutinies, budgets have been cash limited, civil service manpower has been reduced and functions traditionally undertaken in-house have been contracted-out to private firms. Also, in 1984, an official review

concluded that government procurement was costing the taxpayer too much, mainly due to administration costs and because the prices paid were often higher than necessary. At the same time, defence has been the focus of a major initiative in the form of its competitive procurement policy which was launched officially in 1984.

Evidence suggests that there is substantial scope for improving the efficiency of public procurement, not only in the UK but throughout the EC. As the only or major buyer, governments will be lobbied to buy British, thereby preventing foreign firms bidding for UK government contracts. In fact, protectionism and support for domestic industries (national champions) characterises public procurement throughout the EC. The creation of a single market in 1992 will enable public procurement for civil goods and services to benefit from increased competition, free trade and economies of scale. It has been estimated that open public procurement throughout the EC would result in aggregate savings for the twelve EC nations equivalent to some 0.6 per cent of 1986 Community GDP (Cecchini, 1988, p. 17). For the UK, ending protectionism and introducing open competition into public procurement at the national and local levels would produce price savings of 25 per cent in coal and 40 per cent in pharmaceuticals. (Cecchini, 1988, pp. 19–20). The UK's experience with competitive tendering further illustrates the potential gains from a more competitive public procurement policy.

□ 11.7.2 Competitive Tendering

Competitive tendering and contracting-out is potentially a vast area covering the possible use of private contractors for a whole range of public sector services. Contracting-out is one element of the current government's privatisation policy. It is concerned with the central or local government financing of services which could be supplied by private contractors. By the late 1980s, it was the focus of major policy initiatives in local government, the NHS, defence and other parts of central government. Cleaning, catering, laundry, refuse collection, maintenance and security services are

Table 11.10 *Contracting-out: Progress and Potential*

Local Authorities

---

1 Since legislation in 1980, direct labour organisations are required to compete with private firms for most of their construction and maintenance work
2 The Local Government Act 1988 extended compulsory tendering to refuse collection, catering, cleaning streets and buildings, the maintenance of grounds and vehicles and the management of local authority sport and leisure facilities
3 Other possibilities for contracting-out might include accountancy, architectural services, careers advice, computer and data processing services, housing sales and fire protection

NHS
1 Currently there is a major DHSS policy initiative to introduce competitive tendering for hospital catering, cleaning and laundry services (domestic services)
2 Other possibilities could include ambulance and transport services, the contracting-out of major surgery and patient care to private hospitals, together with hospital management, and care for the elderly, disabled and mentally handicapped

---

Ministry of Defence

Current examples include catering and cleaning at defence establishments, the refitting of warships (traditionally undertaken in the Royal Dockyards), some limited aircraft servicing and vehicle repair, air transport and the management of stores

---

popular examples (see **Table 11.10**). With its emphasis on better value for money, government policy aims to extend the use of private contractors by public bodies where this will increase their economy, efficiency and effectiveness.

Contracting-out can be viewed as an aspect of public procurement policy since it involves the public sector purchasing goods and services from private firms. As such, the debate about contracting-out is not new. For example, within the NHS there is a tradition of buying pharmaceutical products, high-technology medical equipment and buildings from private firms. Similarly, within defence there is a long tradition of buying weapons and equipment from private firms.

Consideration now needs to be given to the basic policy problem, which is the means by which public bodies such as NHS hospitals can assess the efficiency of their direct labour departments and in-house services. The starting point is that direct labour departments are usually monopoly suppliers of services protected from possible public and private sector rivals. In the absence of competition from rival departments and from private contrac-

tors, there are no alternative sources of information and no alternative cost yardsticks to assess the efficiency of a public agency. Here, efficiency is defined to embrace two aspects. In the first place, it is concerned with the lowest-cost method of supplying a **given** quantity and quality of service. Secondly, it is also concerned with the lowest-cost method of supplying **different** levels of service. This second aspect of efficiency enables a local authority or hospital to determine whether its existing level of service is worthwhile. For example, a lower level of service might be so much cheaper that the extra cost of the existing provision is deemed not to be worthwhile.

Contracting-out is offered as a solution to the problem of public sector monopolies which are criticised as inefficient bureaucracies responding to the wishes of producer groups rather than consumers. To its supporters, competitive tendering, or even the threat of rivalry means improved efficiency and cost savings. It allows public procurement agents to recontract with different suppliers and for different levels of service. Competition between rival suppliers leads to the introduction of new ideas, the latest management techniques and modern equipment, thereby resulting in major changes in established and traditional methods of working. New equipment might replace labour; manning levels can be reassessed; and part-time workers might replace full-timers. Successful firms in a competition are also subject to the incentives and penalties of a fixed price contract so that there is no open-ended financial commitment, as can arise with in-house units.

The opponents of contracting-out claim that it leads to a poor quality and unreliable service. Examples are given of dirty streets, schools and hospital wards, and of penalty clauses being imposed on contractors. Proposals for privately-managed prisons have been condemned because of fears of lower standards and conditions in prisons, with discipline determined by profit-conscious managers. Private contractors are also believed to be less reliable than in-house units. For example, it is suggested that they are less able to respond to emergencies; that they are liable to default and bankruptcy; and that the award of a contract to a private firm leads to industrial relations problems and strikes. On the issue of cost savings, critics claim that these are short-lived. Low bids can be used to buy into an attractive new contract and eliminate the in-house capacity, so that the public

authority loses its bargaining power. As a result, it becomes dependent on a private monopoly which, in the long run, means higher prices, a lack of dynamism and a poor quality service. Competitive tendering also involves substantial transaction costs which are often ignored by the supporters of contracting-out. Moreover, critics claim that any cost savings from contracting-out are achieved at at the expense of the poorly paid members of society, so that the policy cannot avoid equity issues and debates about the distribution of income. The various arguments are summarised in **Table 11.11**.

The arguments for and against provide extensive opportunities for critical analysis and evaluation. Some of the arguments obviously represent special pleading by those interest groups most likely to gain or lose from the policy. However, many of the arguments for and against contracting-out can be resolved by empirical testing. UK studies suggest for a given level of service, annual cost savings of some 25 per cent over a range of hospital and local authority activities and 20 per cent for refuse collection (Domberger *et al.*, 1986 and Hartley and Huby, 1985).

If society wants improved efficiency, then privatisation and contracting-out are not sufficient: competition is also required. However, competitive tendering is likely to be associated with con-

Table 11.11 *Contracting-out: the Arguments*

The Case for Contracting-out	The Case Against Contracting-out
1 Public sector in-house monopolies are inefficient bureaucracies	1 Private contractors offer a poor quality and unreliable service
2 Competition allows regular recontracting by public procurement agents	2 Private contractors are liable to default, bankruptcy, and are less able to respond to emergencies
3 Competition leads to new ideas, modern equipment and changes in traditional methods of working	3 Contractors use low bids to buy into attractive contracts and eliminate the in-house capacity so that public authority becomes dependent on a private monopoly
4 Successful firms in a competition are subject to the incentives and penalties of a fixed price contract	4 Private contractors achieve cost savings by cutting jobs, reducing wages and worsening working conditions

tractors lobbying for public sector business and for entry barriers to protect their existing markets and profits. Inevitably, there will be opposition from established interest groups likely to lose from the policy. Opponents of the policy can impose delays by insisting upon discussions with all interested parties; the timing of any change can be inappropriate; administrative time might be unavailable to prepare the tender documents and to undertake the necessary comparative studies, especially in an era of manpower cuts; and an authority might be reluctant to face a confrontation with the trade unions leading to major industrial relations problems. There is also a more fundamental worry. With competitive tendering, choices about the quantity and quality of service provision are ultimately made by elected representatives whose preferences are unlikely to reflect the diversity of preferences of large numbers of individual consumers in properly functioning markets. The government's commitment to better value for money in public purchasing has also been reflected in its new competitive procurement policy for defence equipment.

11.7.3 A Competitive Procurement Policy: the Case of Defence

The Ministry of Defence (MoD) is the largest single customer for the products of British industry, with its purchases ranging from simple items such as batteries, cars and furniture to highly complex equipment such as missiles, submarines and advanced combat aircraft. For 1990–91, expenditure on defence equipment totalled £8.3 bn, with a further £4.2 bn spent on other items such as works, buildings and stores. About 75 per cent of the MoD's defence equipment is purchased directly from UK industry; a further 15 per cent benefits domestic industry through its participation in collaborative programmes; and the remaining 10 per cent is imported. Within the UK, MoD purchases about 60 per cent of the output of the ordnance industry, 50 per cent of the output of the aerospace industry, 40 per cent of shipbuilding output

and 20 per cent of 1989–90 electronics' output. In 1989–90, the leading UK defence equipment contractors, which were each paid over £250 mn by the MoD, were British Aerospace (including the Royal Ordnance), GEC, Rolls Royce, Vickers Shipbuilding and Engineering and Devonport Management.

R & D also forms a substantial part of the defence equipment programme through which it can have a major impact on technical progress in specific sectors of the UK economy, particularly aerospace, electronics and shipbuilding. It is often also claimed that there are additional economic benefits associated with spin-off and technology transfer from defence to the civil sector of the economy. However, the government has announced that necessary investment in defence R & D may crowd-out valuable investment in the civil sector and that restraints on government-funded defence R & D spending were required to free resources for civil work (Cmnd 101–I, 1987, p. 48). Nevertheless, such a proposition needs to be carefully assessed, particularly the evidence on crowding-out and whether the UK's commitment to defence R & D has affected adversely its international competitiveness. Furthermore, where there is evidence of these adverse effects, it is necessary to discover whether they have arisen because, in the past, cost-plus defence contracts have tended to reduce a firm's innovative drive, and whether the situation will change now that the MoD operates a competitive procurement policy. Issues also arise as to what happens to the resources released from defence R & D – whether they are used in civil technology or elsewhere in the civil sector in the UK; whether they remain unemployed or whether they emigrate. It is evident that, in the long run, reduced defence R & D sends out clear signals to the labour market about future employment prospects in military technology work.

Traditionally, MoD procurement policy was characterised by support for UK industry, by non-competitive cost-plus or cost-based contracts, and by contractors bearing none of the risks of the project. Defence contractors were often criticised for cost escalation, delays, labour hoarding, inefficiency and project failures. In 1984, the MoD introduced a new competitive procurement policy in an effort to change the traditional dependency relationship in which defence business was regarded as 'lucrative, not very competitive and a cosy relationship' (HCP 392, 1988). The MoD became a more demanding customer, introducing and extending competition and encouraging new entrants, especially small firms. Risks are being shifted from the MoD to industry, with a greater use of firm or fixed price contracts rather than cost-plus contracting. In 1988, a further extension of competition occurred when the MoD announced that it was more willing to purchase equipment from overseas sources where they were likely to offer greater value for money.

The published results of the new competition policy are impressive. In 1979–80, 30 per cent of MoD contracts by value were awarded on a competitive basis and 22 per cent were cost plus a percentage fee contracts; by 1989–90, the corresponding figures were 67 per cent and 4 per cent respectively. At the outset of the new policy, a target was announced for achieving cost savings of 10 per cent on the total equipment budget. Some of the actual results of competition have been impressive, with cost savings ranging from 10 per cent to 70 per cent, all of which might be taken as indicators of monopoly pricing and/or inefficiency in UK defence industries. In 1987–88, for example, the median cost saving on a group of 13 equipment projects was 40 per cent, giving total savings of over £100 mn. Similarly, there are examples where competition resulted in savings of over £400 mn from 10 projects originally expected to cost £2.4 bn. Some examples are shown in **Table 11.12**.

Competition policy as implemented by the MoD is not without its problems and it is subject to both constraints and conflicts. A potential constraint arises if the MoD or the government is unwilling to impose the ultimate sanction on poor performance by a major contractor – namely, bankruptcy. Until 1988, there was a further constraint in that domestic monopolies dominated the high technology and costly equipment programmes. These comprise British Aerospace (aircraft, missiles, ordnance and small arms), Rolls Royce (aeroengines), Westland (helicopters), GEC (torpedoes), Vickers Shipbuilding (nuclear-powered submarines) and

Table 11.12   *Savings from Competition*

Project	% Savings
Harrier GR5 airframe fatigue testing	70
Watchman airfield radar	66
Missile pallets	50
Tucano trainer simulator	40
RAF trainer aircraft	35
Sample quoted in SDE 1984	30+
Armoured repair and recovery vehicles	20
Combat vehicle MCV 80	12
Minehunter vessels	10

Source: Cmnd 344, 1988, vol. 1, p. 37.

Vickers (tanks). However, the 1988 announcement that the MoD is willing to buy from overseas means that the threat of competition is likely to increase the contestability of those UK defence markets dominated by domestic monopolies. But conflicts arise between competition policy leading to foreign purchases and support for the UK defence industrial base which appears to offer attractive wider economic and social benefits in the form of security, independence, jobs, technology and an improved balance of payments.

11.7.4 The UK Defence Industrial Base

The debate in 1985–86 over the future of the Westland helicopter company was a classic example of the arguments about the need for a defence industrial base (DIB). It was claimed that the UK needed a strong DIB for strategic objectives and for national economic benefits. The strategic benefits included security of supply in times of tension and war (an insurance policy), the need for equipment designed specially for national requirements and the capability to respond to emergencies (such as the Falklands crisis and Gulf conflict). There are also claimed to be national economic benefits in the form of employment, foreign exchange savings and earnings and the development of high technology, including spin-offs to the civil sector. Certainly, defence sales are a major source of industrial employment, accounting for 585,000 jobs in 1990. The result is a significant pressure group which will seek to persuade governments to spend more on defence equipment and to buy British. Large producers with domestic monopolies will use their political influence and lobbying to oppose foreign purchases (of, for example, Boeing AWACS and tanks). Stress will be placed on job losses, possibly in marginal constituencies, the loss of a vital defence capability and the dangers of depending on foreigners.

Many of the arguments for a DIB are vague and emotive and are used to rationalise and justify the status quo. Costs are ignored. Informed public choice on the appropriate or optimal size and composition of the UK's DIB needs answers to three questions. In the first place, what is meant by the DIB and why is it needed? Secondly, what is the minimum size and composition of the DIB? For example, should it comprise only an R & D capability in certain key technologies (which?) and what would be the costs and benefits if the current DIB were reduced by, say, 10 per cent or 20 per cent? Thirdly, how much are the Armed Forces willing to pay for retaining key UK industrial capabilities for military objectives? Any wider economic benefits such as jobs and advanced technology should be charged to other government departments (for example Employment and Trade and Industry). Indeed, the point has to be made that there are usually alternative ways of achieving employment, technology and balance of payments objectives.

Buying British is not costless. It can mean paying more for equipment (perhaps an extra 25 per cent or more), and waiting longer for delivery (as was the case for the Nimrod AEW and torpedoes). The result is smaller defence forces and less protection. Ultimately, it is necessary to ask what the defence budget is buying: protection for UK citizens or protection for UK defence industries? Each option involves different sets of costs and benefits and, once again, choices cannot be avoided.

Major changes are likely in the 1990s as UK defence contractors adjust to the prospects of substantial reductions in British defence spending (the peace dividend). Faced with a reduced demand for new equipment (fewer new projects; shorter production runs), defence firms will respond by seek-

ing new military and civil markets at home and overseas. Mergers are likely both nationally and internationally, especially within the EC; and, of course, there will be job losses, plant closures and exits from the industry. The question then arises as to whether governments should leave the adjustment process to market forces. Furthermore, should they intervene either to encourage a reallocation of resources from declining defence industries to expanding sectors or more directly to assist the conversion of defence plants to civil activities (swords to ploughshares)? Whichever policy option is chosen, the required reallocation of resources from defence to civil activities will involve time and substantial adjustment costs: any peace dividend will not be an instant free gift.

■ *11.8* Conclusion

Economics is the study of choices and industrial policy is a classic example of choices under uncertainty. Economists contribute to policy debates by focussing on policy objectives, by applying their theories and by identifying alternative policy solutions. They are also concerned about the economic welfare implications of alternative policies. Increasingly, though, it is recognised that this ideal approach to policy issues cannot be divorced from the realities of the political market; nor can it ignore the institutional framework of the economy. Moreover, many of the traditional certainties in industrial economics are now being challenged. New models of the supply side are being developed and applied, all of which makes it more difficult for economists to be confident about the advice which can be offered to policy-makers.

References

Bishop, M. and J. Kay (1988) *Does Privatization Work?* (London Business School).

Blackaby, F. (ed.) (1979) *De-industrialisation* (London: Heinemann).

Cecchini, P. (1988) *The European Challenge 1992*

(London: Wildwood House).

Cmnd 216 (1969) *Report on the Supply of Beer* (Monopolies Commission) (London: HMSO).

Cmnd 101 (1987) *Statement on the Defence Estimates 1987*, I (London: HMSO).

Cmnd 331 (1988) *Review of Restrictive Trade Practices Policy*, Department of Trade and Industry (London: HMSO) (March).

Cmnd 344 (1988) *Statement on the Defence Estimates 1988*, I (London: HMSO).

Cmnd 605, 621 (1989) *The Government's Expenditure Plans 1989–90 to 1991–92* (London: HSMO).

Cmnd 651 (1989) *The Supply of Beer* (Monopolies and Mergers Commission) (London: HMSO).

Conservative Party (1987) *The Next Move Forward* (Conservative Political Centre).

Department of Trade and Industry (DTI) (1988) *Mergers Policy* (London: HMSO).

Domberger, S., D. Meadowcroft and D. Thompson (1986) 'Competitive Tendering and Efficiency: the Case of Refuse Collection', *Fiscal Studies*, 7, pp. 69–87.

Downs, A. (1957) *An Economic Theory of Democracy* (New York: Harper and Row).

Dunsire, A., K. Hartley, D. Parker and B. Dimitriou (1988) 'Organizational Status and Performance', *Public Administration* (Winter) pp. 343–58.

Gardner, N. (1976) 'Economics of Launching Aid', in A. Whiting (ed.), *The Economics of Industrial Subsidies* (London: HMSO).

Gowland, D. and S. James (1991) *Economic Policy After 1992* (Dartmouth).

Hartley, K. and M. Huby (1985) 'Contracting-out in Health and Local Authorities', *Public Money* (September) pp. 23–6.

HCP 392 (1988) Defence Committee, *Business Appointments* (London: HMSO) (March).

Kamien, M. I. and N. L. Schwartz (1982) *Market Structure and Innovation* (Cambridge: Cambridge University Press).

Kay, J. and D. Thompson (1986) *Privatization and Regulation: the UK Experience* (Oxford: Clarendon Press).

Niskanen, W. A. (1971) *Bureaucracy and Representative Government* (London: Aldine Atherton).

Peacock, Sir A. and G. Bannock (1991) *Corporate Takeovers and the Public Interest* (Aberdeen: Aberdeen University Press).

Williamson, O. E. (1981) 'The Modern Corporation: Origins, Evolution, Attributes', *Journal of Economic Literature* (December) pp. 1537–68.

■ *Chapter 12* ■

Macroeconomic Policy

David Gowland and Stephen James

■ *12.1* Introduction

In the course of this chapter many of the threads which run through earlier chapters will be pulled together with a view to explaining the evolution of macroeconomic policy in the UK. The purpose is both to examine the theoretical models which at various times have been adhered to with varying degrees of conviction by UK Governments, and also at the empirical assessment of the outcomes from their use. This chapter necessarily contains a more wide-ranging historical perspective than most others, but in common with them it concentrates upon the evolution of theory and practice over the past two decades. In setting this discussion at the end of the book, rather than at the beginning as is commonly the case in other texts, the problem of introducing many matters as yet unfamiliar to some readers, such as the exchange rate, is avoided. To retain the continuity of the narrative it is assumed that the reader has indeed read the previous chapters, but where necessary he or she is referred back to the discussion earlier in the book. Thus there is, for example, no attempt to replicate the discussion of supply-side economics in Chapter 3, but models such as New Classical macroeconomics, which were mentioned only briefly in Chapter 1, are spelled out in some detail.

Virtually everything mentioned in this chapter is in some way controversial. Some controversies are concerned with matters of theory such as the debate about expectations, and some with the interpretation of the statistical data. These controversies are ongoing, and it is not the purpose of this chapter to do other than to spell out the key issues and to form a reasoned judgement to guide the reader through the debate. As in certain other chapters, this one ends by addressing specific controversies which are currently at the forefront of the policy debate in the UK – in particular, whether credit controls have any useful role to play as an alternative to interest rates, and whether the government is justified in running a continuing Budget surplus.

■ *12.2* Macroeconomic Policy

The phrase **macroeconomic policy** is used to describe the actions of governments when they seek to manipulate the economy so as to influence the level of inflation and unemployment. Sometimes macroeconomic policy is used to try to stimulate the level of economic activity so as to increase the level of output and employment and so reduce unemployment. These policies are usually referred to as **expansionary**, or **reflationary**. However, critics of such policies point out that they sometimes lead to inflation and so term them 'inflationary policies'. On other occasions governments seek to reduce the level of economic activity in an attempt to reduce inflation. These policies are referred to as **deflationary** (or occasionally disinflationary). In the United Kingdom the government first started to pursue active macroeconomic policies in 1941. As the date suggests this was part of their effort to manage the economy so as to win the Second World War in the most efficient and equitable manner. For most of the period since 1941 governments have frequently referred to macroeconomic policy as **stabilisation** policy. This presumed that the level of economic activity was likely to fluctuate. Hence the role of macroeconomic policy was to be to minimise the fluctuations of output around its long-run trend level.

Logically, the term macroeconomic policy could be used to refer either to policies which sought to influence aggregate supply or to policies which sought to influence aggregate demand. In practice, however, the term was traditionally used to refer only to **demand management policies**, although in recent years there has been a revival of supply-side policies. The underlying objective of governments in formulating macroeconomic policy is to achieve the best available (that is, the **optimal**) combination of output, inflation, employment and other desirable objectives (such as the distribution of income, or, more generally, equity). These are also known alternatively as the goals or final targets of economic policy.

In Chapter 2 we considered the role of instruments, intermediate targets and objectives in our macroeconomic model (see **pp. 19–24**). Tinbergen's law states that a government can achieve as many objectives as it has independent instruments: with five instruments a government can achieve five objectives, **but no more**. In practice, however, due to uncertainty, it is much harder to make economic policy than Tinbergen's law suggests. Attempts to modify this approach to incorporate uncertainty and other real world complexities are called **optimal control**. A number of economists have worked on this for several years, but with little result so far.

There are two crucial issues in macroeconomic policy:

- **Rules or discretion?** Keynes and his followers argued that governments should actively manage the economy. This means that they should vary their instruments of policy so as to stabilise output whenever the economy suffers a shock. The alternate view, whose most famous advocate is Milton Friedman, argues that this is not possible. Instead, governments should set their instruments so as to keep an intermediate target at a constant level.
- **Which target?** A **rule** might be set in terms of, for example, the exchange rate, the Budget deficit or the money supply. Similarly the government might choose to vary any of these three as part of a discretionary policy. In practice, the choice has usually been restricted either to an external target (normally the exchange rate) or to an internal one such as the money supply. This debate is totally independent of that in the issue above. Both Friedman and Keynes have taken the same side in this debate in that both have argued passionately in favour of an internal rather than an external target.

These debates were inaugurated by Ricardo in 1817. He persuaded the UK Government to return to the gold standard. This fixed exchange rate meant that the government had accepted a **rule** and an **external** target. Most economists supported this view until the 1920s when Keynes argued in favour of **discretion** and an **internal** target. In the 1950s, Friedman argued in favour of an internal target and a rule in the form of a fixed rate of money supply growth. The decision by the UK Government to join the Exchange Rate Mechanism (ERM) of the EMS was the latest round in this long-running debate. Despite the preference of economists for an internal target, governments have usually preferred an external one. The only periods when clear precedence has been given to internal targets were 1931–39 and 1971–90.

There are various ways in which instruments can influence objectives. It is useful to group these into three forms of economic policy– direct controls; Keynesian policy (fiscal policy is the best known form of this); and financial policy (monetary policy is one form of financial policy).

☐ 12.2.1 Direct Controls

Direct, or one-stage, controls are so named because they operate **directly upon objectives**. For example, a government seeking to control inflation might issue an ordinance setting out maximum prices and Draconian penalties for charging in excess of them (the penalty in Stalin's Russia was death). Such policies are easy to understand because it is clear to the general public how they are intended to work. However, economists believe they are generally ineffective because of the problem of *black markets* – the control creates an incentive to set up an unofficial market in which mutually beneficial exchanges can be made in violation of the control. In the UK the only direct control used in the last twenty years has been incomes policy. The general form of an incomes policy consisted of a direct attempt by the government to reduce the level of wage settlement. It thereby hoped, through various mechanisms, to reduce not only the level of wages but also the level of prices and to increase the level of output. The present government immediately abandoned incomes policy when it came into power in 1979. However, its critics feel that this was a mistake, and the issue of incomes policy still forms one of the major issues dividing Thatcherite opinion from its opponents.

☐ 12.2.2 Keynesian Policy

Keynesian policy consists of using instruments in the **goods market**: the government operates so as to change demand in the goods market. Keynesian policy thus involves two stages: the instrument is used to influence the goods market which, in turn, is used to influence the objective variable. For example, if the government sought to reduce inflation it would use its instruments to reduce demand in the goods market (the 'real sector') and would hope that lower demand would reduce the price level (below the level at which it would otherwise

have been). Hence Keynesian policy can fail if either:

(a) the government's instruments do not influence demand in the predicted fashion, or
(b) the reduction in demand does not influence price (or output) as intended, for example because (aggregate) supply shifts.

☐ 12.2.3 Financial Policy

Financial policy is the most indirect of the three forms of economic policy, involving three stages, hence Milton Friedman's famous aphorism that monetary policy would operate only with a long and variable lag. The three stages are, respectively:

1. The monetary authorities (an umbrella term to describe all branches of government including the Bank of England) **do something**. This disturbs the financial system in a way which can be analysed using supply and demand curves. This disturbance is often called a 'shock' because it disturbs equilibrium. This stage involves the use of an instrument of policy. In the case of monetary policy, narrowly defined, this is called a **technique of monetary control**.
2. The purpose of stage 1 is to change either **price** or **quantity in financial markets**. The quantity might be the quantity of money or of credit (see below). The price might be the price of borrowing (the rate of interest) or the price of foreign currency (the exchange rate). This variable is called the **intermediate target**. The arguments for the money supply being the most appropriate intermediate target are examined below.
3. The purpose of stage 2 is to influence the **real sector**, the goods or labour market. In this way a government hopes to achieve its ultimate objective.

Because three stages are involved, the possibility of error is much greater than with direct or Keynesian policy. This does not mean that financial policy is necessarily less effective or less important – indeed the contrary may be the case. It does, however, mean that greater care in its use is essential. The crucial feature of the analysis of financial policy is to examine the means by which changes in financial markets influence developments in the real sector – how stage 2 leads on to stage 3. This is usually called the **transmission mechanism** of monetary policy – the means by which developments in financial markets are passed on to (transmitted to) the real sector.

It is important to distinguish between *direct* and *indirect* transmission mechanisms since the core of the monetarist position is a belief in a direct transmission mechanism whereas Keynesians believe in an indirect one. This means that they accept that money influences income but only through its effect on **some other variable**. Young Keynesians believe that this variable is the exchange rate, whereas older Keynesians believe it is the rate of interest. All Keynesians believe that government policy should focus on these variables. Monetarists, on the other hand, believe that money has a direct impact on income and hence that monetary policy should be used.

12.2.4 Financial, Monetary and Credit Policy

It is important to distinguish financial policy in general from monetary policy. Narrowly used, the phrase **monetary policy** refers to control of the **money supply**. Financial policy encompasses not only monetary policy but also credit policy, interest rate policy and exchange rate policy. The latter two terms are quite straightforward. Exchange rate policy occurs when a government seeks to control the exchange rate. This policy has both micro- and macroeconomic aspects, some of which were analysed in Chapter 6. Interest rate policy is mainly concerned with influencing the level and structure of interest rates, and thereby influencing the rate of interest which firms and persons pay when they borrow to finance expenditure.

Credit policy, however, is more complicated and more controversial. The distinction between money and credit is straightforward. **Money** is an asset which a person owns, whereas **credit** is a liability which a person owes. It is not hard to tell the difference! Monetarists believe that a person's actions are largely influenced by the amount of money which he has – that, as the proverb puts it, 'money burns a hole in one's pocket'. Keynesians, on the other hand, emphasise the importance of credit. Keynesians believe that consumers' expenditure is very likely to be influenced by the cost and availability of credit to the personal sector. If the cost of borrowing falls then Keynesians expect expenditure to rise. Moreover, if individuals are allowed to borrow more, then their expenditure will rise. Such a general increase in borrowing possibilities occurred in the UK in the 1980s due to financial innovation. Keynesians believe that credit-availability is critically important in economic analysis because they believe that individuals are rarely able to borrow as much as they would wish to. Consequently, any relaxation in credit limits is likely to lead to increased spending. Monetarists, on the other hand, usually believe that this would have little effect in itself.

In seeking to clarify the relationship between instruments and objectives many economists and most governments believe that it is useful to introduce a further concept, the **intermediate target**. The idea is that a government should use its instruments to control the intermediate target, and rely upon the effect of the intermediate target in attaining its objectives. Economists tend to have some of their fiercest debates about the question as to which is the most appropriate intermediate target. Monetarism is defined by most authors as being belief in a monetarist target – in other words that the money supply should be the intermediate target. It is consequently important to distinguish between a belief in the use of financial or even monetary policy and monetarism itself. Monetarism is a belief that the best intermediate target is the *money supply*, and that a government should sacrifice other variables such as government spending, tax rates, interest rates and exchange rates to as to ensure that the money supply performs this function.

Monetary policy is one of the means by which governments can seek to manipulate the economy so as to influence inflation and unemployment. In 1960 it was unfashionable in the UK, and regarded as of little importance. Thereafter, its importance grew steadily until 1981, especially after the adoption of monetary targets (defined below) in June 1976. Since 1981, the Conservative Government has de-emphasised the role of monetary policy, particularly after Mr Lawson became Chancellor of the Exchequer. Similar developments have occurred in other countries, but the extent of the controversy has been much greater in the UK. Some critics believe that the government was wrong to abandon monetary targets. In their view the price for this mistake could be seen in 1988 with rising inflation, soaring house prices and an enormous and growing balance of payments deficit. Their view was put eloquently by Sir Alan Walters, a close associate of Mrs Thatcher (Walters, 1986). In this view, the need to increase interest rates nine times (by 5 per cent in all) in the second half of 1988 was a belated attempt to correct for the error, although perhaps too late. At the least, the need for such strong medicine showed to monetarists the extent of the error in abandoning their nostrum.

Other critics argued that the government had been wrong to put as much emphasis on money as it had. Instead it should have sought to manage – and indeed to stabilise – the exchange rate. Many such critics believed that the attempt to control the money supply in 1978–81 led to an excessively high exchange rate and so to deindustrialisation. Some argued that membership of the EMS was the best form of exchange rate policy – keen supporters of the EC believed that it was inevitable anyway, so the sooner the UK joined the better.

They argued that the problems of the late 1980s would have been avoided if the government had joined the ERM in 1985. These arguments caused serious divisions within the Conservative Government. Nigel Lawson resigned in consequence as Chancellor in 1989. finally, this controversy led to a successful challenge to Mrs Thatcher's leadership of the Party, but even before this Mrs Thatcher had been forced to agree to UK membership of the ERM on 6 October 1990.

■ 12.3 A Framework for Analysis

The same macroeconomic instrument may have both a direct (Keynesian) impact on the goods market, and also an indirect one through its effect on financial markets. For example, in increase of £100 mn in government expenditure on currently produced goods and services can be regarded as a Keynesian policy designed to raise the level of planned injections (exports plus investment plus government spending) at each level of income, and so to raise the equilibrium level of income. However, ceteris paribus, such a policy also increases the money supply permanently by £100 mn – that is by the exact amount of the spending – and is therefore also an instrument of monetary policy. In whichever way the instrument is regarded, its effect is nevertheless to **raise income**. However, the amount and duration of the change in income may depend crucially on how it is viewed. The **interdependence of policy instruments**, as it is usually called, is thus essential to understanding macroeconomic policy. It is the source of both theoretical and practical controversies in economics, because it means that it is usually impossible for a government to achieve all of its intermediate targets simultaneously. If one target variable is too high (for example, the money supply) and one too low (for example, a measure of fiscal policy) then the use of an instrument which will bring the first back on course (lower government spending) will tend to depress the other (fiscal) target still more and so cause it to move even further away from its desired value.

12.3.1 The Supply-side Counterpart Equation

It is therefore necessary to have some sort of conceptual framework both in order to elucidate this interrelationship between variables and also to analyse their impact. The most useful such framework is the flow-of-funds or supply-side counterpart equation. This uses the orthodox definition of the change in (Δ) the money supply as:

Δ Money Supply = Δ Currency held by the non-bank private sector
+
Δ Bank Deposits

This is a very general definition of money. In practice, a number of definitions of money are consist-

Figure 12.1 *Relationships Between the Monetary Aggregates and Their Components*[1]

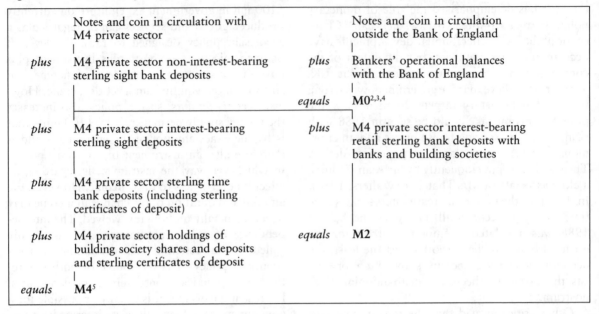

Notes:

[1] The Abbey National Building Society was authorised under the Banking Act 1987 as from the date of its conversion to a public limited company on 12 July 1989. From the end of July onwards its assets were transferred into the category of retail banks and ceased to be included in the building societies category. The amount of assets transferred (£32 bn) were such as to cause a major discontinuity in the series which included bank deposits but excluded building society deposits (namely M1, M3 and $M3_C$) and these were accordingly terminated as of June 1989. In aggregate M2, M4 and M5 were unaffected as there were equal and offsetting changes in the bank and building society contribution to each aggregate. There was a small but easy to adjust for statistical break in M0 due to the appearance of bankers' deposits at the Bank of England placed by the Abbey National, and an insignificant break in nib M1. The disappearance of $M3_C$ was compensated by the creation of a new definition $M4_C$ which included certain deposits in currencies other than sterling placed with UK banks and building societies by the rest of the UK private sector.

The term 'non-bank private sector' is used throughout this text to refer to the sector comprising UK residents other than the public sector and banks. The increasingly blurred distinction between banks and building societies has resulted in the increased use of the term 'M4 private sector' to indicate that both banks *and* building societies are excluded.

In the light of the statistical discussion paper (Bank of England 1990a) and the subsequent responses to it, the August 1990 *Bank of England Quarterly Bulletin* (pp. 336–7) announced the Bank's intention of replacing the monetary aggregates $M4_C$ and M5 by data for a range of liquid assets outside M4. These were also discussed in the May 1991 *Quarterly Bulletin* (pp. 263–6).

As a consequence the definition of 'broad' money is now confined to M4, and has as its base 'notes and coin in circulation with the M4 private sector' as shown in the Figure.

[2] M0 is calculated on a weekly averaged basis. All other aggregates are calculated at end-months.

[3] The stock of M0 outstanding at the end of June 1991 was £18 mn while that of M4 was £455 bn.

[4] Bank of England equations suggest that a 1 per cent increase in consumption will raise M0 by 0.2 per cent in the current quarter and by 1 per cent in the long run. A permanent 1 per cent increase in interest rates will lower M0 by 0.1 per cent in the current quarter, and in the long run will lower the growth of M0 by 0.5 per cent per annum.

[5] Over the last decade M4 deposits have grown broadly in line with total gross wealth. See *Bank of England Quarterly Bulletin* (August 1990) pp. 381–2.

Source: Bank of England

ent with it; UK policy makers currently use 3, US ones over 40. Until the end of July 1989 the UK definitions were MO; non-interest bearing M1 (nib M1); M1; M2; M3; M3c; M4; and M5. M1, M3 and M3c were dropped but were replaced by M4c. Then, in August 1990, M4c and M5 were replaced by data for a range of liquid assets outside M4. The reason for this multiplicity of definitions is that it is not clear in practice which institutions are banks (see **p. 86**). Given that a building society is similar, but not identical, to a clearing bank, it is treated as a bank for some definitions but not for others. The Abbey National Building Society's conversion to a bank on 12 July 1989 triggered an alteration in definitions of money because it caused a huge switch of assets from the building society to the banking sector.

There are similar difficulties over the definition of a deposit. As a concept it is an 'almost perfectly liquid' claim on a bank. However, it is unclear whether a 7-day account is 'almost perfectly liquid', or indeed whether such a term can be applied to funds which can be obtained instantly, but subject only to the payment of a penalty. Different answers to these issues produce different definitions of money. It is preferable to examine a range of definitions rather than to risk being misled by a single one. The full range, both current and recent, is set out in **Figure 12.1**.

It is important to see whether different money indicators give different signals about the nature of the economy, a matter to which we will return below.

The basic definition of money in **Figure 12.1** (deposits plus currency) is often used by economists to analyse financial developments, and is referred to as **demand-side analysis**. However, supply-side analysis is more common. The supply-side counterpart equation is derived by two substitutions into the definition of money:

(a) **the bank balance sheet equation**: bank assets are equal to liabilities so loans (assets) can be substituted for deposits (liabilities)
(b) **the government finance equation**: bank loans to the government are replaced by a rearrangement of the government finance equation:

$$\text{PSBR} = \Delta \text{ Bank loans to the government}$$
$$+$$
$$\Delta \text{ Non-bank private sector loans to the government}$$
$$+$$
$$\Delta \text{ Non-bank private sector holdings of currency}$$

These substitutions are merely rearrangements of accounting identities. When the government runs a surplus called a Public Sector Debt Repayment the relationship still holds: (–PSDR) replaces PSBR. The purpose is to derive a useful and economically meaningful relationship, which now takes the form:

$$\Delta \text{ Money Supply} = \text{Public Sector Borrowing Requirement}$$
$$+$$
$$\text{Bank loans to the non-bank private sector}$$
$$-$$
$$\text{Non-bank private sector loans to the public sector (government)}$$
$$+$$
$$\text{Overseas effect}$$

The supply-side counterpart is thus the key to the analysis of macroeconomic policy-making in the UK.

☐ 12.3.2 Intermediate Targets

Many of the rival candidates for the role of intermediate targets can be identified from this equation. They are respectively

(a) **Money supply**: this, the preferred target of monetarists such as Milton Friedman, is the sum of the four supply-side counterparts.

(b) **Domestic Credit Expansion (DCE)**: this is the domestic component of money creation, that is the first three of the supply-side counterparts.

(c) **Public Sector Borrowing Requirement**: Mr Lawson had a variety of targets for the PSBR. From 1985–88 his target was a PSBR equal to

1 per cent of GDP. Thereafter his target was for a substantial surplus. Mr Lawson indicated that in the long run he might revert to a balanced budget (Mr Lamont's decision now).

(d) **Measures of fiscal policy**: the PSBR is equal to:
- Government spending (a Keynesian injection)
    −
- taxation (a Keynesian withdrawal)
    −
- asset sales by the public sector
    +
- public sector loans to the rest of the economy

By an accounting quirk the last category includes nationalised industries' profits and losses. Losses appear as loans by the National Loans Funds to the industry concerned; a profit as a notional repayment.

Keynesian measures of fiscal policy could be weighted averages of the first, second and fourth of these. For example, 'fiscal leverage' might be government spending −0.7 taxation +0.5 public sector loans (Musgrave's values for 1967). Moreover, Keynesians might disaggregate some components further − government spending might be divided into expenditure on goods and services and on transfers, with a higher weight given to the former.

(e) **Credit**: credit, the preferred target of both Ben Friedman and other Keynesians, is measured by the second supply-side counterpart: bank lending to the non-bank private sector.

(f) **Interest rates**: the level of interest rates influences both bank lending and non-bank private sector purchases of public sector securities (National Savings and gilt-edged). Higher rates reduce the demand for bank loans and increase the demand for public sector debt. Hence the level and structure of interest rates are critical determinants of these supply-side counterparts.

(g) **Exchange rate**: the overseas influence on the money supply, the fourth of the supply-side counterparts, is closely related to the balance of payments surplus − hence exchange rate policy will be reflected in monetary developments and vice versa.

This framework can be used to analyse a large number, indeed virtually all, issues in UK macroeconomic policy. More importantly, perhaps, it has been used by policy-makers in formulating their policy. Hence the use of flow-of-funds analysis is crucial to an understanding of the origins and objectives of economic policy. For example, the Conservative government used it to devise the Medium Term Financial Strategy in 1979. The government purported to commit itself to setting the key values of economic policy for a period of four years in advance; the purpose was to give the private sector information about macroeconomic policy and to increase the credibility of economic policy. It did this by announcing its target values for the key flow-of-funds variables − especially money supply and PSBR. However, the values included in the MTFS bore no relationship to the actual outturn as shown in **Table 12.3 pp. 447–8**. Hence they were useless both as forecasts and as targets. Thus, while the government continued to publish the MTFS in order to avoid losing face, neither it nor its critics regarded it as of any importance.

12.4 Methods of Monetary Control

A very useful and fruitful use of supply-side counterpart or flow-of-funds analysis is in analysing the methods of monetary control used in the UK. In presenting the range of options open to the monetary authorities textbooks frequently emphasise the reserve ratio/reserve base system whereby a change in either the quantity of reserve assets or the reserve ratio leads to a corresponding change in the money supply. It does this by either forcing banks to lend less or making it possible for them to lend more through the workings of the credit multiplier. Such a system has never been used in the UK, though the government might have chosen to introduce it and did consider doing so in 1979–80. There have been various reserve ratios in the UK but they were neither designed to − nor did they −

work in the textbook fashion. In the reserve ratio method of monetary control a bank lends whenever, **but only when**, it has the necessary reserve assets. In other words, the direction of causality runs from reserves to loans. In the UK there has been no attempt to control the volume of reserves and the direction of causality has run from loans to reserves – in other words banks lent because they wanted to (usually because it was profitable) and then acquired the necessary reserves. This meant that the various ratios were partly prudential (to reduce the risk of bank failure) and partly devices to increase the authorities' control of short-term interest rates – an intention made clear in *Competition and Credit Control* in 1971 and repeated in *Monetary Control* (Cmnd 7858) in 1980. However, as was also made clear in the latter, these devices did not work very well. Hence neither the introduction of a 12.5 per cent minimum liquid assets ratio in 1971 nor its abolition (in stages) in 1980–81 was of much importance.

12.4.1 The ERM and Monetary Policy

It is necessary to distinguish the analysis of the economic **effect** of something from the **motive** for carrying it out. This is very important in the case of the ERM. It is easy to establish that most of the actors are influenced by political rather than economic considerations. Indeed, this is a difference between Anglo–Saxon politicians and their continental equivalents since the former are normally far more influenced by narrow economic considerations.

In the case of EMU, as so often, it is quite easy to agree on economic analysis but not necessarily on the consequent policy implications. For example, it is easy to agree that monetary union will lead to unemployment in some regions of Europe. Governments will be powerless to do anything about this. Mrs Thatcher believes that this is an argument against monetary union. Jacques Delors argues that this is a reason for a much enlarged European Social fund, and for greater *dirigiste* activity generally.

The underlying issues raised in switching from a floating to a semi-fixed exchange rate have been discussed in an earlier chapter (see **pp. 212–6**) and do not need to be reiterated at this juncture. It is interesting to note that Keynes himself argued that adjustable parity systems were undesirable in that they deprived domestic monetary authorities of the autonomy to pursue the policy they wished. Keynesians frequently argued the case for autonomy in the 1960s. It is ironic that the only remaining prominent upholder of this position is Mrs Thatcher. In many ways she is the last remaining Keynesian, arguing for political control of economic policy (discretion), rather than for exogenous discipline. Indeed autonomy and discipline/credibility are the key elements in any analysis of the ERM. The argument about autonomy is also the argument against accepting narrower bands within membership of the ERM and against membership of a monetary union.

A monetary union exists when:

(a) there are no exchange controls or other inhibitions on movements of money and

(b) when exchange rates are fixed permanently **and** are believed by all market participants to be fixed forever.

Within such a system, it would not seem to matter whether there was one currency or many currencies. In these circumstances, one currency is always a perfect substitute for another. If £1 is always worth 3 Marks then it is a matter of indifference whether it says on a pound coin '£1' or '3 Marks'. This was illustrated in the nineteenth century when gold coins from different countries were treated as perfect substitutes. A contemporary example is Italy, the Vatican and San Marino. These three countries form a monetary union and coins from each of the three are used in the other two. Similar considerations applied between Ireland and the UK prior to 1979. However, there are two economic reasons why the one currency issue is thought to be important in addition to symbolic arguments.

1 **Seigniorage**, the profit on issuing currency. This was analysed by classical economists in the eighteenth and nineteenth centuries and then disappeared from the textbooks until re-

Figure 12.2   *The Effect of the Exchange Rate on the Economy*

(a)   Short term

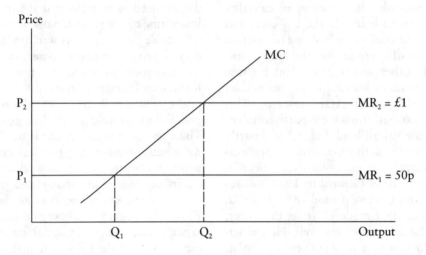

(b)   Long term

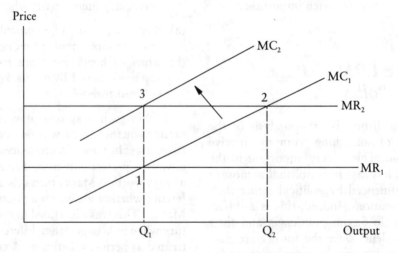

cently. This is one of the many contexts in which it is of contemporary importance.

2   **Fixed exchange rates.** The crucial word in the definition of a monetary union is 'believed to be fixed forever'. Jacques Delors argues that if currencies remain distinct, then there will always be a possibility that their parity will change. Only a single currency can ensure permanent locking of exchange rates. Tyrie argues that even this is not sufficient. Nevertheless, it is clearly much easier to break a monetary union if separate currencies remain. This is illustrated by the ease with which

the Republic of Ireland broke away from its monetary union with sterling in 1979 after 58 years.

There are three pieces of economic analysis that are relevant to analysis of the UK position within a fixed exchange rate system.

Exchange Rates and the Domestic Economy

The first concerns the impact of exchange rate changes upon a small economy – that is, one unable to influence world prices. The question of whether the UK is a small economy is considered below.

The effect of a variation in the exchange rate is illustrated in **Figure 12.2**. The underlying idea behind this analysis is that most UK firms are price takers in markets (both in the UK and abroad) in which the price at which they sell is determined by the world price and the exchange rate. (The world market may be competitive or the UK producers may be relatively small firms in a market in which a foreign price leader or cartel determines the price.) **Figure 12.2** illustrates this for a representative UK producer – and thus for the entire UK economy. The diagram shows the marginal cost and revenue curves for a producer of a representative good, 'leets'. 'Leets' have a world price of $1. Originally the exchange rate is $2 = £1, so the world price expressed in pounds is 50p, the world price divided by the exchange rate. The UK producer faces a perfectly elastic demand and marginal revenue curve at this price. Hence his output of leets is Q_1 at a price of P_1 (50p).

The exchange rate then falls to $1 = £1. The world price expressed in sterling is now £1. Hence the fall in the exchange rate causes the *MR* curve to shift upwards to *MR* = £1. Output of leets rises to Q_2 and price to P_2 (£1). This can be generalised:

> a fall (rise) in the exchange rate will lead domestic producers to increase (decrease) their output and prices. Hence a fall in the exchange rate increases output (and so reduces unemployment) but at the cost of higher prices (more inflation); a rise in the exchange rate will reduce inflation but at the price of more unemployment.

Figure 12.3   *The UK Economy in the 1980s*

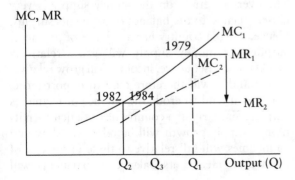

However, this result applies only in the short term. The lower exchange rate causes a rise in prices. This means domestic producers will face a rise in costs because:

(a) **Costs of raw materials and inputs have risen.** If they are imports, they obviously rise by an amount determined by the depreciation. If they are domestically produced, then their price rises in exactly the same way as the good analysed in **Figure 12.2**. British Steel raises its prices by exactly the same amount as Austin-Rover and for exactly the same reasons. Thus, the steel purchased by Austin-Rover rises in price by exactly the same amount as the price of cars.

And, much more importantly.

(b) **Real wages are lower and marginal value product higher.** Hence, whatever model of the labour market is used, wages will rise.

The rise in marginal cost is shown in **Figure 12.2**. The MC curve shifts upwards from MC_1 and ultimately reaches MC_2, where output has fallen back to Q_1 – that is, the economy moves from 1 to 2 to 3. This diagram can be reversed to show the effect of an appreciation. This is one way to illustrate the UK economy in the 1980s (see **Figure 12.3**). The appreciation in sterling from 1979–81 caused a fall in output and price, hence the economy reached the point marked '1982' in that year. Thereafter the supply curve shifted rightwards as marginal cost was below the level it would otherwise have been and output rose steadily until the inflationary effects of Mr Lawson's policy changes in 1985 worked through. The spirit of this model has influenced UK governments since 1974. Whenever they have wanted to reduce inflation they have sought a high exchange rate (1974–75, 1977–78, 1979–80, 1988–89). On other occasions they have sought a lower rate to reduce unemployment (1976, 1985). This is of considerable relevance at the moment because the UK has not got out of a depression in the last 30 years without a devaluation.

The above analysis thus illustrates the proposition that membership of the ERM deprives a country of autonomy of domestic policy. It can no longer use the exchange rate to counter unemployment and inflation.

It also illustrates the other proposition about the ERM, that it leads to lower inflation. In this model, the UK price level is determined by the exchange rate and world prices. Within the ERM, world prices means German prices. If the exchange rate is fixed, then a necessary consequence is that prices are equal to world (German) ones. It is usually assumed that the other members of the ERM will move to Germany's low inflation rate. As Karl Pohl pointed out it is equally possible that the reverse might occur. This is as good a way as any of introducing the possible need for an independent central bank.

One may argue about the precise relevance of this model. It is arguable that the UK is a medium-sized economy and that therefore one needs to use both traditional large economy models as well as this one. Certainly, however, the UK is in this sense much 'smaller' than it used to be and the model is becoming ever more relevant.

Optimal Currency Areas

The argument above is one way of illustrating a crucial problem:

Within a fixed exchange rate system, balance of payments problems show up as unemployment.

If the exchange rate is fixed, then if a random shock occurs in the above model, its impact will be to shift the *MC* curve and so to cause a change in output. If this leads to a fall in output, the consequence will be unemployment. This analysis has been standard in textbooks for 30 years to explain regional unemployment. The reason that unemployment persists in, say, Scotland is that Scotland cannot devalue its £ against the rest of the UK. The proposition is generally accepted, but the policy implications vary (see above).

The above analysis leads to a discussion of optimal currency areas. The theoretical conclusion is that an optimal currency area exists if factors are perfectly mobile within it. The world would thus be divided into optimal currency areas; goods, but not factors of production, would be mobile between these blocks; exchange rate variations could

then eliminate unemployment. This analysis reappears frequently in John Major's speeches. It is cited as being a necessary condition of moving towards EMU.

It is worth pointing out that **existing** currency areas are **not** optimal. Almost certainly there should be a different currency for Scotland and England. It is arguable that the optimal currency areas are even smaller. It is also conceivable that optimal currency areas cross existing national frontiers. A half-serious study by an American Federal Reserve Bank pointed out that Scotland and Northern Ireland should be part of the same currency area as the Republic of Ireland! On the other hand, in their model Brittany was annexed by the £ sterling area, rather than the French franc.

Finally, it is worth emphasising that theoretical analysis suggests that factor mobility is as important a consideration as inflation convergence in deciding when the time is ripe for monetary union. This is one way in which the SEM is viewed as being a natural precursor to monetary union.

DCE and Related Matters

One of the many virtues of flow-of-funds analysis is that it makes it possible to break down the sources of the supply of money into a **domestic** (DCE) and an **overseas** (Ov) component. The change in the money supply is necessarily equal to

$$M = DCE + Ov$$

The significance of this is that a necessary condition of membership of an exchange rate fixing mechanism is that a DCE target must be maintained. The IMF have, in consequence, always preferred DCE targets. The rationale is simple. The overseas effect on the money supply is very closely related to the balance of payments surplus. Hence, when a country has a balance of payments surplus, its money supply will grow relatively quickly. In consequence, incomes will grow relatively fast and it will therefore tend to import more, which will tend to erode the balance of payments surplus. Similarly, if a country has a deficit then its money supply growth will be relatively slow and so incomes will fall relative to these in the rest of the world. Hence, its balance of payments will improve. DCE targets are therefore stability conditions for any fixed exchange rate system.

This is one way of emphasising Minford's objection to the ERM, which is that ERM membership is inconsistent with a monetary target. Membership of the ERM necessarily involves a DCE target. Overseas flows will therefore determine short-term fluctuations of the money supply and mean that no monetary target can be met. This is reinforced by the fact that any intervention in the foreign exchange market by the government will also affect the size of this overseas influence on the money supply. Intervention must be such as to maintain the parity within the prescribed bounds. In other words, the money supply can no longer be controlled by the authorities.

12.4.2 The Consequences of Membership

Membership of an exchange rate fixing agreement involves a commitment to support one's currency. If the parity is fixed at £1 = DM3 then every time anyone presents the Bank of England with £1, it must be exchanged for DM3 (or the appropriate amount of other currencies in the ERM). This means that the UK needs sufficient foreign exchange to meet all such demands. Usually there is little problem in keeping a currency within its limits, but occasionally there is a widespread view that it is overvalued and there is an excess of sell orders. This is called a crisis of confidence.

This is an especial problem for the UK given that the pound is held internationally on a far wider scale than continental European currencies. This is why the UK Government argued that a necessary condition for UK membership (and why it now argues that a wide band is necessary) was that its inflation rate be equal to that of Germany. In the latter case it is reasonable to expect the pound to maintain its value against the DM, so there is little incentive to convert pounds into DM. Were this not achieved, the government has argued, membership would involve excessive heavy expenditure in buying DM in exchange for pounds which would not be successful.

If a country does not have enough reserves on such occasions it has three options – to leave the ERM, to impose direct exchange controls or to change its economic policy in such a way that it convinces people that the currency is worth holding. This leads to five arguments.

British Membership of the ERM Could Prove an Expensive Fiasco

The UK joined the previous version of the ERM in 1972 and has to leave after a few weeks because it did not have enough reserves. The effect was not only to humiliate the UK but also to set back the cause of European economic integration.

The government, in consequence, only joined the wide band. Experience since October 1990 suggests that the Bank of England is sufficiently adept at exchange rate management to avoid a recurrence of the 1972 crisis, but there are those who have yet to be convinced on that score.

Membership may Involve Actions that Impede European Economic Integration

To ease the problem described above, most of the members of the EC have used exchange controls – that is, regulations which forbid some or all transactions in a foreign currency. An Italian, for example, could not have a UK or German bank account, nor any other sterling or DM asset without government permission until 1990. Hence he could not convert lira into DM so it was much easier to support the lira's value against the DM. These restrictions impeded the EC's goal of a single market and led to the UK's requirement that the remaining members of the EC abandon their exchange controls before the UK joined the ERM. They promised to do this at Hanover in June 1988 (with a waiver for Italy until 1992 and for Portugal, Spain and Greece until 1995). Following further British pressure at the Madrid summit in 1989, France and Italy abandoned their exchange controls in the first half of 1990. It remains to be seen how the ERM will function without it. There may, in other words, be a conflict between the two aspects of a move towards monetary union:

permanent exchange rate fixity and freedom of capital movement.

A Country may be Forced to Change its Macroeconomic Policy so as to Remain a member of the ERM

For example, the French Government in 1983 had to abandon a Keynesian policy of reflation adopted after the election of President Mitterand. Usually this is regarded as a consequence of the wider proposition that the UK's membership of the **ERM** will cause a loss of autonomy over **domestic policy**. The exchange rate is linked to the money supply (and other domestic targets such as interest rates). Hence if the exchange rate is fixed it becomes impossible to retain complete control over the other variables, just as a monetary target involves the sacrifice of other objectives, and the UK government will not be able to manage the UK economy.

The Bundesbank will Manage the UK Economy Better than UK Politicians

Many economists and people in the City welcome this loss of autonomy. They argue that if membership of the ERM involves management of the UK economy by the Bundesbank then this can be seen only as an improvement.

Membership of the ERM will Increase the Credibility of UK Anti-inflation Policy

Given the importance of expectations in determining inflation, it is desirable if people expect a low rate of inflation. This means that inflation policy will work only if people have confidence in it. This is called 'credibility.' Membership of the ERM may have increased the credibility of anti-inflation policy in France.

Almost all economic theories involve either an aggregate supply curve or a Phillips' Curve incorporating an expected inflation mechanism (see below). Within such a model, it is desirable to reduce inflationary expectations. This makes it possible to reduce unemployment without an inflation cost. Similarly, it is desirable to stop inflationary expectations rising if there is a rise in

inflation rate, otherwise there can be adverse long-term consequences following upon a short-term shock to the economy – exemplified by increases in oil prices or VAT. In effect, the argument for ERM membership was that these could be achieved. Economic agents would form future expectations of **British** inflation by reference to performance in Germany. The Bundesbank has credibility in the sense that short-term shocks do not raise inflationary expectations. The UK could obtain this by surrendering control of its economic policy. This is, in fact, the most common way of testing for the impact of the ERM on a country's economic management. It is hypothesised that inflationary expectations bear a growing dependence on German and a declining dependence upon domestic inflation.

The above argument can, however, be reversed. It is conceivable that German inflation will rise to British levels rather than vice versa, as indeed it has done during the later half of 1991. In other words, how can the Bundesbank retain its credibility within a ERM or EMU? Such doubts are reinforced by Pohl's resignation and by the events surrounding German reunification. The answer proposed by European Central Banks is that it is necessary to have an independent Central Bank.

12.4.3 Economic Policy Within the ERM

It is useful to go through the various aspects of economic policy and see how much, if any, scope is left to the domestic authorities.

Monetary Policy

It was argued above that it is impossible to control the money supply and the exchange rate simultaneously. The one exception is if **exchange control** is used.

Interest Rate Policy

There are two problems with the use of interest rates as an instrument of economic management. The first arises if they are assigned to management of the exchange rate. It is normally presumed that if a country's currency is under pressure then its interest rate will be raised, and vice versa. However, there is a more fundamental problem: **the Walters critique**.

Walters's argument, which is generally accepted although it is not clear how relevant it is, is that given freedom of capital movements, interest rates in each country will differ only by the amount of the **expected change in the exchange rate**. This is necessary to ensure an equality of expected returns. If such a condition is not met, there will be capital flows until it is. Within a monetary union exchange rates are therefore equalised. Walters goes on to point out that it will be true within an ERM, at least for short-term interest rates. If no-one expects the pound to be devalued within the next six months then UK interest rates will equal German ones. This is incontrovertible and has happened to a significant extent elsewhere in the EC. Walters points out that this means that real interest rates will necessarily be low in the countries in which inflation is high, and vice versa. As a consequence, the effect of interest rates will be destabilising. A low real interest rate tends to be expansionary and to cause inflation to rise, and vice versa.

Fiscal Policy

It is generally accepted (see above) that even an ERM requires a DCE target. If one examines the three components of DCE, then either the authorities must be able to influence bank lending and debt sales **or** they will no longer have autonomy over fiscal policy. It would appear to be the case that the inability to use interest rate policy or, alternatively, the fact that it will be destabilising lends to the conclusion that the implication of a DCE target may be the necessity to surrender autonomy over fiscal policy. Mrs Thatcher and Jacques Delors would agree with this whereas Minford would disagree. The one exception to this is where it is possible to use **direct credit controls** to influence DCE. This highlights the continued relevance of the domestic debate between the Labour and Conservative Parties about whether such policy instruments are viable.

It is important to try to identify the precise scope of domestic economic management within ERM or EMU. In the light of the above discussion, there does not seem to be very much left, and this can be taken to highlight the importance of one final point, namely that:

> **Within an EMU most traditional issues of economic policy are still relevant, but are now relevant at the level of the European Community.**

The IGCs (Inter-Governmental Conferences) have recently taken place in Rome to consider many of the issues that are traditionally looked at in elementary economics. These include whether the money supply should be controlled, and if so how; how should credibility be maintained, and so forth. Within the UK, the residents of York have to accept the general price level. The price level in York is determined by the price level in the UK and by the fact that the York pound is irrevocably linked to the UK pound. The same argument will eventually apply to the UK pound within an EMU. Thus, it will be necessary to apply traditional macroeconomics at the level of the EC to see what determines its rate of inflation.

▌ 12.5 Monetary Policy in the UK 1971–91

▯ 12.5.1 Competition and Credit Control

Instead of relying on a reserve base system the authorities sought to control the money supply through the various items of the flow-of-funds equation. The five crucial flow-of-funds variables are bank deposits (from the demand side) and the four supply-side variables: PSBR, bank lending, non-bank lending to the public sector and overseas effect. The PSBR can be influenced in a variety of ways, such as via changes in government spending, tax rates and asset sales (privatisation). The remaining variables can be influenced by either quantity controls or price devices. The latter work by seeking to induce economic agents to change their behaviour – in other words, to move along a demand curve. Quantity controls, in contrast, seek to override demand by official fiat.

Prior to 1971 monetary policy was in effect credit policy since the principal tool of monetary policy was a number of quantity controls on bank lending and other forms of credit, notably hire purchase instalment credit. The quantity control on bank lending took the form of 'ceilings' whereby the Bank of England set a maximum level of lending (the 'ceiling') for each bank. The ceiling took two forms – **quantitative** in the form of a ceiling on overall lending, and **qualitative** in the form of restrictions on lending to certain categories of borrower, especially personal customers and property companies. Any form of rationing or quantity control will create an incentive to evade it – the familiar 'black market' argument of elementary microeconomics. Financial markets are no exception; new institutions, notably secondary banks, grew up whose main purpose was to evade the controls. The extent of evasion is still unclear but this is not very important. What is relevant is that the authorities were convinced that their ceilings were no longer effective, and this regime of monetary control, the 'old approach', was abandoned in 1971.

Its replacement was known as either the 'new approach' (1971–73) or 'Competition and Credit Control'. Its principal feature was a decision to seek to control bank lending solely by means of **interest rates**. If the money supply grew too quickly then interest rates would be raised so as to reduce the demand for bank loans and thus the money supply. In December 1973 monetary policy seemed to be a shambles – for example, £M3 had grown by over 60 per cent in 27 months. The effects of this explosion were clearly seen in accelerating inflation, a massive balance of payments deficit and massive growth in house prices. Monetary policy had failed. However, it is still not clear why. To some extent the new approach was flawed technically, since the authorities had less control over bank base rates than they had anticipated. Largely, however, the problem was a lack of political will by Mr Heath and his Chancellor, Mr Barber: they were unwilling to change interest rates often enough, or by a large enough amount.

It fell to the incoming Labour Government to devise a new regime of monetary control early in 1974. It had three instruments of control: a ceiling on interest-bearing eligible liabilities (IBELs), an aggressive debt management policy and manipulation of the PSBR for monetary purposes. The latter was accomplished by a combination of tax increases, public expenditure cuts and, after 1977, asset sales – mainly of BP shares and government holdings of private sector loans. Such policies were continued after 1979 by the incoming Conservative Government and were largely successful as macroeconomic tools. Debt management policy was similarly successful, especially through selling National Savings Securities to the private sector. The controversial element of the package was the ceiling on IBELs (a legal term for bank deposits), often called the 'corset'. This ceiling was reinforced by a system of penalties whereby a bank whose deposits grew faster than permitted had to deposit a proportion of the excess interest-free with the Bank of England. This interest-free deposit was termed a 'supplementary special deposit'. Initially the ceiling held, but it was later evaded on a massive scale; in other words the black market problem was once more evident.

□ 12.5.2 Policy After 1979

Monetary policy was reasonably successful under the 1974–79 Labour Government but the breakdown of the IBELs ceiling, and the election of a new Conservative Government in 1979 headed by Mrs Thatcher, led to a reappraisal of monetary policy. The PSBR and debt management instruments of monetary policy remained, although the latter was abandoned in November 1985. However, the IBELs ceiling was dropped in June 1980 and replaced by a plethora of new instruments:

(a) A reiteration of the **interest rate weapon** as a tool to control bank lending, as in the 'new approach'.
(b) Use of the **exchange rate** to influence overseas flows, especially in 1979. Later the exchange rate was an intermediate target rather than an instrument of monetary policy. The idea was

that a high exchange rate made foreign assets cheaper. UK citizens and financial institutions would buy them and the resultant capital account deficit would reduce the money supply. This mechanism was the centrepiece of criticism of the government by moderate left and 'young Keynesians' who argued that the consequent high level of the exchange rate was a major cause of deindustrialisation.

(c) The **abolition of exchange controls** in November 1979. This mechanism was similar to (b) in that a balance of payments deficit on capital account would reduce monetary growth. The Labour party made this the centrepiece of their criticism of the government. £100 bn of capital was exported during 1979–86 which, they argued, reduced domestic investment and hence caused unemployment to rise.

In addition the government made a number of technical changes in monetary policy in 1980–81. The most important was the replacement of minimum lending rate (MLR) by the much more flexible 'intervention rate'. In all western countries the banking system normally borrows from the central bank. The central bank uses variations in the cost and terms of such borrowing as a means of controlling the short-term rate of interest. The Bank of England has made a number of changes in this system since 1971. Their goal has been a system in which the rate at which the banking system borrowed could be changed frequently – if necessary several times a day. They wished such changes to be viewed as normal, minor technical acts of policy rather than as major changes. In some countries, as in the UK prior to 1971, publicity is sought for such changes so as to reinforce their impact through changing expectations. At the present time the Bank prefers the flexibility of frequent unobtrusive changes.

12.6 The 1950s and 1960s: The Age of Demand Management

☐ 12.6.1 The Development Phase

This period constituted the high years of demand management in the UK. In retrospect, at least from the standpoint of the recession of the early 1980s, these years seemed to be a time when economic principles were successfully applied so as to achieve high employment, moderate growth and reasonably stable prices. Granted, the growth rate was moderate by comparison with other European countries and it gave rise to increasing concern as time wore on. Periodic balance of payments and sterling crises and inflationary spurts required the application of the economic brakes to the extent that the booms and slumps of earlier periods became the policy-induced stop-go cycle. Nevertheless, it was a a period in which unemployment never rose above 2.4 per cent, GDP grew at an average rate of 2.7 per cent per annum, and inflation – at least until the late 1960s – fluctuated in the range of 1 to 5 per cent per annum. **Table 12.1** gives a summary of the economic performance.

The consensus view that it was the responsibility of the government to regulate demand grew out

Table 12.1 *GDP, Inflation and Unemployment, 1950–79, Selected Years, %*

	1950–69	1950–59	1960–69	1970–79	1970–73	1974–79
Real GDP growth (annual average)	2.7	2.4	3.1	1.8	2.9	0.5
Inflation (annual average)	3.1	2.7	3.5	12.6	8.0	15.7
Unemployment (% of employed labour force)	1.7	1.5	1.9	4.1	3.1	4.8

Source: Economic Trends, Annual Supplements.

of the inter-war experience and the development of Keynesian macroeconomics. The policy can be characterised as the short-term management of the level of demand through the use of fiscal and monetary policies in order to iron out fluctuations in the level of economic activity, thereby maintaining the economy at or near its full employment level. In the extreme the policy becomes one of 'fine tuning' whereby frequent adjustments are made to keep the economy on course. The principal instrument was to be fiscal policy, and in particular the adjustment of **tax rates**. Public expenditure was regarded as less flexible in the short term and in any case was determined by long-term factors. Monetary policy played a subsidiary and supportive role, mainly through the use of direct control on credit. Interest rates were primarily deployed in defending the exchange rate. The economy fluctuated in a fairly regular pattern, with a cycle of around four to five years duration, that is from peak to peak or trough to trough. Policy was adjusted in a **counter-cyclical fashion**, becoming contractionary in times of current account deficit and rising inflation, and expansionary when unemployment rose.

It was not until the boom associated with the Korean War in 1951 that this form of demand management became the major preoccupation of economic policy. Then commodity price rises and defence spending commitments resulted in severe inflationary pressure to the extent that in both 1951 and 1952 retail price rises were in excess of 9 per cent, and the current balance moved into serious deficit – £307 mn in 1951. The first Bank Rate rise since 1939 and the introduction of hire-purchase (HP) controls for the first time constituted the main acts of demand management, along with the introduction of import controls. As the economy slowed expansionary measures followed; in 1953 there were reductions in direct and indirect taxes and HP controls were removed in 1954.

1955 saw the first major piece of economic mismanagement (or misjudgement). In his Spring Budget, shortly before an election, R. A. Butler lowered tax rates, instituting, at the same time, a restrictive monetary policy to hold back demand. Inflation accelerated and the current account moved into deficit shortly afterwards. Following an election in May, the Chancellor was forced into taking supplementary restrictive measures in the Autumn. Whether Mr Butler was politically unscrupulous or economically naive about the potency of monetary policy (or possibly both), this episode discredited monetary policy for nearly twenty years.

12.6.2 *Fiscal Policy in the Ascendant*

Demand management was in future operated primarily through **fiscal policy**, with interest rates directed towards influencing the capital account of the balance of payments. This latter policy became apparent in 1956, and more so in 1957 when the Bank Rate was raised to 7 per cent in the face of heavy speculation against the currency. It was to become a regular feature in the 1960s.

In terms of the flow-of-funds equation the authorities relied during the period 1951–55 on the manipulation of the bank lending term, but from 1955 they relied primarily on adjustment of the PSBR term through tax changes. The failure to look at economic policy as a whole – that is, at all four parts of the equation simultaneously – handicapped policy considerably.

The 'stop' period of the mid-1950s cycle lasted from 1956 to 1958, as Budgets remained relatively neutral or mildly contractionary in demand management terms, until the Budgets of 1958 and 1959 reversed the policy and once again expanded demand. The result was the familiar, repeated pattern: accelerating real GDP growth – 4.6 per cent and 5.3 per cent in 1959 and 1960 respectively – combined with declining unemployment but ending in overexpansion with a current account deficit in 1960, rising inflation and contractionary Budget measures. In prospect was another sterling crisis, and the neutral Budget of Spring 1961 had to be followed by a July package aimed primarily at the balance of payments and at defending the value of sterling. As well as fiscal contraction and a rise in the Bank Rate to 7 per cent, there was a public sector incomes policy – a 'pay pause' and, for the first time, a call for special deposits.

By the beginning of the 1960s it had become apparent that the management of demand alone was not sufficient to achieve all macroeconomic objectives simultaneously, and the authorities began to look for alternatives to supplement their fiscal instruments. On the one hand, there was an experiment with supply-side policies with a shift to planning, first with the establishment of the National Economic Development Council (NEDC) and later with Labour's Department of Economic Affairs and its National Plan. Attempts were made to control inflationary pressure through various prices and incomes policies, monitored from 1964–70 by the National Board for Prices and Incomes (NBPI). Overall, the period 1964 to 1970 was, however, mostly dominated by the balance of payments and the attempt to maintain the exchange rate (Blackaby, 1978).

12.6.3 The First Wilson Government

On its accession to office Harold Wilson's first government faced what appeared at the time to be a major current account deficit (but one which subsequently has been shown not to have been so bad) and initiated deflationary measures. Further restrictive action was taken in response to the three successive sterling crises (November 1964, July 1965 and July 1966) that ultimately led to the 1967 devaluation. The packages comprised the conventional adjustments: rises in the Bank Rate and intervention in the currency markets to protect sterling, and on the domestic side the tightening of controls on HP and bank lending and the raising of tax rates via the 'Regulator', a device to raise indirect taxes without a separate Finance Act.

When in November 1967, **devaluation** finally came it was accompanied and followed soon after by further deflation as the current account failed to respond in the way the government had expected and as set out in the Letter of Intent to the IMF in November 1967. Moreover, speculative pressures on sterling continued. 1968 witnessed the most deflationary Budget since the War, which included significant cuts in public spending.

It was backed up with additional monetary tightening throughout the year. This was mainly achieved by 'import deposits' – a requirement to lodge 50 per cent of the cost of imports with the Bank of England for six months as a condition of importing goods into the UK. This acted as a fixed loan to the government. The government was now acting on three of the flow-of-funds items – PSBR via budgetary policy, bank lending via ceilings and private lending to the government via import deposits. Compared to the 1950s and earlier 1960s the use of policy instruments was more co-ordinated and hence more successful.

The restrictive policy stance continued into 1969 when the current account finally responded and moved into surplus. The costs of the balance of payments improvement were, however, in terms of rising unemployment (2.4 per cent in 1969) and the slowing down in the growth of output to 2 per cent in 1969 and 1.7 per cent in 1970. It is evident that by the end of the period the focus of demand management policies had shifted from maintaining internal to external balance although, by comparison with previous years, unemployment, at over 500,000 was high. However, the authorities had been successful in achieving their objective after the half-hearted drift of the 1960s, largely because of their improved co-ordination of economic policy.

■ 12.7 The 1970s

The 1970s were a time of major and repeated crises in the UK economy. During this period macroeconomic policy lurched from overexpansion to crisis management as the governments of Heath, Wilson and Callaghan attempted to cope with major developments, both within the UK and in the world economy. In common with the latter part of the 1960s demand management alone proved insufficient, and during much of the period governments attempted to control wage inflationary pressures by the use of income policies, either as voluntary agreements or imposed by statute. Furthermore, in the desire to release economic policy from the constraint of maintaining the value of sterling, it was allowed to float from 1972 although this owed much to the developments in international monetary relations (see **pp. 216–18**).

The period can be usefully divided into a number of sub-periods, although the division is somewhat arbitrary:

- **1970–71:** A short-lived market experiment, with no active demand management policy
- **1971– early 1974:** An initial period of over-expansion ending in the chaos of a wage-price spiral, a major external shock to the economy and 'stagflation' (often referred to as Barberism after the then Chancellor)
- **early 1974– mid-1975:** A time without major policy initiatives during a major crisis as the new Labour Government consolidated on re-election
- **mid-1975–77:** Labour's deflationist period
- **1977–79:** A time of misjudgement on major policy issues.

☐ *12.7.1 The Heath Government*

Table 12.1 provides a summary of the economic performance over the decade. In the first year of the 1970–74 Conservative Government there were no major policy initiatives in managing the economy: policy was primarily aimed at reducing the involvement of government in economic life. This followed the 'Selsdon' philosophy announced by Edward Heath during the Conservatives' last months in opposition. On the other hand, subsequent action would seem to imply that the government had by no means given up its commitment to maintaining high employment. As output stagnated and unemployment rose towards the 1 million mark, the government's policy shifted from neutral to expansionary, culminating in the infamous Barber Budget in the spring of 1972 and the Barber boom that followed.

The 1972 Budget was designed to raise the annual rate of growth of output to 5 per cent over the ensuing 18 months, and its main measures were significant tax reductions (achieved by raising allowances and cutting purchase tax) since they were faster acting than increases in public expenditure. They were also more in line with the government's philosophy. In addition, the Chancellor announced that monetary growth was to be allowed to accelerate in order to accommodate this expansion, and that an unrealistic exchange rate would not be maintained if it meant unacceptable distortion to the domestic economy. This was the first public indication that the government might permit the exchange rate to fall if the current account of the balance of payments constrained the growth of the economy.

This Budget has often been presented as a U-turn in policy: it is probably truer to say that the U-turn best describes the shift in the government's attitude to intervention at the microeconomic level – notably that of supporting lame ducks. It also marks the embarkation on a prices and incomes policy as a solution to the growing inflation problem.

This 'dash for growth' Budget was almost certainly misconceived. Not only had fiscal policy become steadily reflationary from mid-1971, but output had begun to rise, unemployment was expected to stabilise by the end of the year and significant underlying inflationary pressure was building up in the economy. In 1970 the inflation rate had been 6.3 per cent but by the end of 1971 it had accelerated to 9.4 per cent. More importantly, monetary policy had become expansionary from the early summer of 1971. The abolition of direct controls on bank lending under the new monetary control framework ('Competition and Credit Control') had led to a surge in bank lending, partly the result of reintermediation – that is, the re-entry into the banking system of lending that had been forced out of the officially regulated banking sector by the operation of credit ceilings – and partly as a result of the fact that banks were now able to satisfy previously frustrated demand for credit. The latter added directly to demand, which was stoked further by the lowering of interest rates and the ending of the agreement by which banks collectively fixed interest rates on deposits which restricted their ability to bid competitively for funds in order to finance lending.

Credit was made even more attractive by the reintroduction of the relief on loan interest in the 1972 Budget. In the event, the money supply expanded wildly out of control, growing by 60 per cent in 1972 and 1973 and by 80 per cent from 1971 to 1973.

The effects of such monetary laxity soon became apparent in the inflation figures. One of the major routes for the transmission of the inflationary effects came through the **property market** where there was an enormous speculative bubble. Between 1970 and 1973, commercial property prices almost tripled and house prices rose by an annual average of 34 per cent in 1972 and 1973. There are numerous channels through which house price inflation may be linked to more general inflation, including the wealth effects on consumption or the cost and wage inflation impact of higher property prices (Gowland, 1984, pp. 127–31). For a monetarist the experience of the period provided an almost perfect fit for the proposition that an excessive expansion in the money supply would result in accelerating inflation after a lag of about 18 months to two years.

Further inflationary twists were added by a world-wide commodity price boom and the depreciation of sterling after it had been floated in 1972. Indeed, as in previous reflations there followed the characteristic sterling crises (in June 1972 and March 1973) and a marked worsening of the current account which went into deficit in 1973 and even more so in 1974. As if these developments were not sufficient, the 1973/74 oil crisis administered a severe supply-side shock to an already fragile economy. Whatever interpretation is put on the period – whether monetarist or Keynesian – such developments made the appearance of stagflation almost inevitable.

The authorities' response was slow in coming and may be seen as a classic case of 'too little too late' and of a misalignment of instruments and objectives. Attempts were made to hold back wage pressure by the use of a statutory prices and incomes policy (in three stages) whilst demand was kept at a level sufficient to reduce unemployment. By the end of 1973 interest rates had been raised significantly, and in December of that year 'Competition and Credit Control' was abandoned, being replaced by a new form of direct control on

bank liabilities called supplementary special deposits (the 'corset'). Monetary growth did indeed fall as bank lending was reduced under the new regime, but the growth in demand was enough to raise output by 5.2 per cent in 1973 and to cut unemployment to 2.6 per cent – at the cost of raising inflation to 10 per cent at an annual rate by the end of the year. In early 1974 the government, now facing a rapidly deteriorating economic climate, with a three-day week and a second miners' strike, panicked, called an early election and got thrown out of office for its pains.

□ 12.7.2 Labour Back in Power

Mindful perhaps of its tenuous position and the rapidly contracting economy during the year, the subsequent minority Labour Government took no major deflationary measure in 1974 despite four Budgets. Indeed, public spending rose by 28.3 per cent in 1974 and by 31.4 per cent in 1975: in cash terms it was out of control. The PSBR also soared to over £10 bn in 1975 (11 per cent of GDP) although its effect on monetary growth was offset by falling bank lending and a large negative overseas impact – the result of the sizeable balance of payments deficit. The £M3 measure of the money supply rose by only 10.4 per cent in 1974 and by 6.8 per cent in 1975.

In mid-1975 the government finally produced a coherent policy response to the economic crisis, and this date marks a watershed in postwar macroeconomic management. There are a number of main strands to consider. In the first place, **inflation** became the primary policy objective. As a consequence, the commitment to full employment, to be achieved by manipulating aggregate demand, was dropped. This is best summed up in the Prime Minister's (James Callaghan) famous speech to the Labour Party Conference in 1976 when he said:

> We used to think that you could just spend your way out of a recession, and increase employment, by cutting taxes and boosting government spending. I tell you in all candour that that option no longer exists, and that in so far as it ever did exist, it worked by injecting inflation into the economy.

Secondly, the principal instrument of policy was **incomes restraint** in the form of a notionally voluntary agreement with the trades unions – the Social Contract. Thirdly, a major role in the attack on inflation was assigned to **financial policy**, specifically controlling and targetting the money supply and manipulating the PSBR to this end.

Even if the adoption of a money supply policy did not represent a conversion to monetarism as such, it did indicate a recognition of the importance of the money supply in the inflationary process, possibly as a way of validating inflationary pressure. There are alternative justifications for the adoption of money supply targets. One is that, **ceteris paribus**, a money supply target implied a given PSBR and thus a given stance on public spending and taxation. Public expenditure, as a consequence, became easier to control. Another is that such targets were required to convince 'monetarist' financial markets of the government's resolve to combat inflation. A final possibility is that the targets were foisted on the UK by the IMF in 1976 after the collapse of sterling. This third explanation can be rejected as the government had shifted towards targetting before IMF involvement in the economy whereas to other two might well have been accepted by the authorities (Gowland, 1984, pp. 154–6). Moreover the IMF put the emphasis upon DCE rather than money.

Another important factor at that time which requires emphasis concerns the use of the PSBR as a means of controlling the money supply. This meant that fiscal and monetary policy became inextricably linked as part of the government's financial policy, and was a major change from the earlier demand management approach of the 1950s and 1960s when fiscal and monetary policy were seen as independent instruments with the former as the senior partner. Indeed, it was something of a role reversal. The authorities now used the flow-of-funds approach to guide policy with instruments aimed at each component. Macroeconomic or monetary policy had thus changed over twenty years from a naive Keynesian analysis of injections and withdrawals to a financial analysis of flow of funds and an emphasis upon the money supply as a summary indicator of this.

□ 12.7.3 The Deflationist Period

The first positive deflationary action was taken in the April Budget of 1975. There followed a pay freeze under a renegotiated Social Contract and further rounds of public expenditure cuts throughout 1976. In addition, cash limits were introduced to control the growth of public spending. On the monetary side, the first official money supply target was announced (July 1975) and there was a tightening of monetary policy, with rises in the MLR and the re-introduction of the supplementary special deposits scheme, particularly during 1976 as sterling began to slide in the foreign exchange markets. Following the fall in sterling to an

Table 12.2 *Monetary Targets and Outcomes, 1976–79*

Target set	Period Covered	Aggregate	Target Range (%)	Outturn (%)
December 1976	Financial year 1976/77	£M3	9–13	7.7
March 1977	Financial Year 1977/78	£M3	9–13	15.5
April 1978	Financial Year 1978/79	£M3	8–12	10.8
November 1978	12 Months to October 1979	£M3	8–12	13.1

Source: Bank of England.

all-time low against the dollar in October 1976 – a crisis that resulted from a mismanaged attempt to float the currency down to a more competitive level – and negotiations with the IMF for a loan, the Chancellor announced a further package of spending cuts along with targets for both £M3 and DCE.

There can be little doubt that these policies achieved their objectives, at least over the short term. £M3 growth was well within its target range for 1976/77 as shown in **Table 12.2** and DCE was some 45 per cent below its target level in the same period. Public spending growth fell to 5.8 per cent in 1977 and the PSBR was reduced to 4.7 per cent of GDP in the same year, the latter being significantly less than its forecast levels in the financial years 1976/77 and 1977/78. By mid-1978 inflation had fallen to 8 per cent at an annual rate, although unemployment remained intractably high despite the moderate growth of GDP in 1976 and 1977.

However, from late 1977 policy had become markedly more expansionary as monetary policy eased and public spending and the PSBR rose. This was largely a paradoxical by-product of the IMF agreement. The government, equipped with the IMF seal of approval, was less constrained and indeed was pressed by the IMF to reflate. £M3 also overshot its target range. This combination of circumstances produced a mini pre-election boom in 1978, but this was accompanied by consequent pressure on the housing market, inflation and the government's incomes policy. Indeed, it occurred just as the government was tightening that incomes policy, setting a 5 per cent guideline for settlements in the 1978/79 pay round. This was rather like trying to hold the lid on a saucepan whilst turning up the heat, albeit accidentally. Not only did the lid come off wages, which rose rapidly after the notorious 17 per cent Ford settlement in November 1978, but the government also got embroiled in the 'Winter of Discontent' which preceded its electoral defeat in May 1979. As in 1971–73, monetary expansion led to a house price explosion, a balance of payments problem and finally to rapid inflation.

One final aspect of policy of some importance at this time was the approach to the exchange rate,

that is the means of influencing the fourth flow-of-funds item. At first, in 1972, the exchange rate was floated in the hope that this would reduce the balance of payments constraint on expansion, but it subsequently became an **instrument** of demand management policy. As has been noted (Allsop and Mayes, 1985), it was argued by some economists, notably Kaldor, that the exchange rate could be depreciated in a controlled way, inducing expansion from the export sector and from import substitution. This is the well known 'export-led growth' policy. There would, therefore, be no need to compromise on the tight stance of domestic policy required to combat inflation. The experiment with this policy effectively came to an end with the sterling crisis in 1976: a managed depreciation was not quite so easy to accomplish in practice. Moreover, it was increasingly realised that the cost inflationary impact of a lower exchange rate would be faster working and more than outweigh the trade benefits of a lower exchange rate.

▌ *12.8* The 1980s: The Thatcher Years

During the years since 1979 discussion of economic policy in Britain has been dominated by 'Thatcherism', an economic doctrine that is wider in scope than the macroeconomy but which has particular relevance to it. While demand management is consistent with either more or less government involvement in economic life, and hence was acceptable to both Labour and Conservative Governments of the 1950s and 1960s, Thatcherism is consistent only with less involvement. Indeed, the reduction of government activity – or, more graphically, 'rolling back the frontiers of the state' – is one of the central tenets of this economic outlook.

It should be recognised that the **ultimate** objectives of government policy in the 1980s have not changed: that is, the aim of achieving a high growth in living standards combined with stable prices. What is distinctive are the methods by which these are to be achieved and the costs the government, and implicitly the British electorate, are prepared to accept in their pursuit.

The principal features of the approach can be identified as follows:

1   **The necessity of eradicating inflation** is of fundamental importance, not only for its own sake but because of its effects on the level of **unemployment**. In contrast to the more pragmatic policies of Denis Healey, who saw the abandonment of demand-managed full-employment, and the need for higher unemployment, as a requirement for bringing inflation under control, the major proposition of Thatcherism is that inflation has to be reduced as it is a major **cause** of rising unemployment. Thus, instead of a conventional Phillips Curve trade-off, or even a monetarist vertical long-run Phillips Curve, the government believed in an **upward sloping one**. Traditional demand management is rejected since it can have no beneficial long-term effect on the economy.

2   The emphasis of macroeconomic policy is to provide a **stable non-inflationary framework** within which the private sector of the economy can flourish. The means to this end is to exercise control over the growth in the money supply – the government, at least in its early years, was self-proclaimed monetarist. Furthermore, the policy is to be operated over the medium and long term. This ties in closely with the view, accepted by the government, that manipulation of policy for short-term stabilisation will have unpredictable and possibly destabilising effects on the economy.

3   **Free market supply-side policies** constitute the main weapons for tackling unemployment and raising the rate of growth of output. These include tax cuts to boost incentives, privatisation and deregulation to extract the state and its agencies from the economy, and especially a series of reforms in the labour market which have removed a number of trade union privileges (see Chapter 8). The aim of the last was both political and economic, the economic aim being to increase labour market flexibility. It is also interesting to note that the government is at pains to stress that the unions can not

only be held responsible for a significant part of the high unemployment – the 'pricing themselves out of a job' view – but also can increase the unemployment costs of the adjustment to a low inflation rate. Encouraging labour market flexibility is preferred to direct intervention via an incomes policy on two grounds. In the first place, such policies interfere with market forces. Secondly, it is maintained that the relaxation of the policy usually resulted in a 'catching-up' period, undoing any benefits that might have been produced during the time income restraint was in operation.

12.8.1 The Medium-Term Financial Strategy (MTFS)

The specific details of the government's macroeconomic policy intentions were enshrined in the MTFS, first published with the 1980 Budget and detailed in **Table 12.3**. The strategy set out a declining target for £M3 over the subsequent four years as the principal mechanism for reducing inflation.

The importance of the declining target lay not only in the government's attachment to a monetarist view of the inflation process but also for the supposed effects of such targets on inflation expectations. It was believed that by committing the government to the creation of a stable environment over the medium term, **wage and price expectations could be reduced**. The prime benefit was that the unemployment costs of the transition to a low inflation economy could be cut significantly.

Monetary policy was thus the dominant weapon in the government's array of macroeconomic policy instruments. Particular reliance was placed on the use of interest rates, the PSBR and debt sales to contain monetary growth. Direct controls were rejected on the grounds of their distortionary impact on the banking sector; they reduced the efficiency of the financial institutions and produced disintermediation (see **p. 128**).

The use of the PSBR as an instrument of monetary control continued the subordination of fiscal to monetary policy. The government aimed to decrease the PSBR because of its direct impact on the growth of £M3 and also because of the effect of financing a high PSBR on interest rates – the so-called 'crowding out' effect. As a result the MTFS and other government policy statements emphasised the need for consistency between the PSBR and monetary targets, and a series of projections (not targets) for the PSBR was announced in 1980 as shown in **Table 12.3**. It is worth emphasising that the achievement of a stable financial policy, summarised in the £M3 target, required a reduction in the PSBR if interest rates were to be prevented from rising to an excessive level because of the need to finance the deficit from debt sales. This is evident from the flow-of-funds money supply counterpart equation.

□ 12.8.2 Benefits of a MTFS Policy

For all the faults in its operation, the benefits of the principles of such an approach should be clear: it does attempt to produce harmonisation of the stance of macroeconomic policy which can be contrasted with the tight monetary but loose fiscal policy stance of the Reagan era in the USA. In practice however, the UK experience was the converse, combining a loose monetary with a tight fiscal policy. Another important feature of the government's policy as initially conceived was the eschewal of an exchange rate policy and the commitment to a market-determined, floating exchange rate. In the early years, at least, it was fortuitous that the commitment came at a time of a rising £; it was to provide the main mechanism through which monetary policy deflated the economy in 1979–81 and set the conditions for falling inflation rates. As the exchange rate environment changed so did the government's policy, shifting increasingly towards a managed exchange rate by the mid-1980s. Indeed, such was Mrs Thatcher's commitment to this that she became an adamant opponent of membership of the EMS. She wished to retain the freedom to depreciate if unemployment rose or to appreciate in order to combat inflation. Broadly speaking, such were the intentions of policy – to provide a non-inflationary environment in which an increasing market economy would flourish.

However, as is the case with all grand economic policy designs, the principles are more clear-cut than their application. The practice of the policy has, in fact, been laced with a good deal of pragmatism, if not some degree of opportunism as the government has had to respond to changing circumstances and failure, in many cases, to meet the intermediate policy targets that had been set as shown in **Table 12.3**. Such flexibility should not necessarily be held against the government: in an ever-changing world economic policy clearly must adapt and targets set at one time may not be relevant at another. Examples of shifts in emphasis in policy include the move from a single money supply target to multiple targets, and their subsequent abandonment. Another is the adoption of an exchange rate target which later had to be revised upwards as domestic and external pressures clashed. A further one is the use of asset sales as a means of enabling the government simultaneously to reduce the PSBR and to cut personal tax rates.

Despite these changes the following quotation from the ex-Chancellor signifies that the broad thrust of the government's policy has remained remarkably similar over a decade. Thus:

The Government's job, in short, is to deal with the *financial* framework, which it *can* influence, rather than the activities of businesses and individuals within that framework . . . I would maintain that provided the overall fiscal, monetary and exchange rate framework is sound, and markets are working effectively, the results of the private sector's economic activity should not normally be something in which it is sensible for the Government to interfere (Lawson, 1988, p. 16).

■ 12.9 The Policy in Action

□ 12.9.1 The First Budget

The operation of policy and the fortunes of the economy can be divided for convenience into a number of phases:

Table 12.3   *Medium Term Financial Strategy, Target Ranges[1] and Outcomes, %*

	1979/80	1980/81	1981/82	1982/83	1983/84	1984/85	1985/86	1986/87	1987/88	1988/89	1989/90	1990/91	1991/92	1992/93
Money Supply: M0 (% change)														
March 1984						4-8	3-7[6]	2-6[6]	1-5[6]	0-4[6]				
March 1985							3-7	2-6	1-5[6]	0-4[6]				
March 1986								2-6	2-6	1-5[6]	1-5[6]			
March 1987									2-6	1-5	1-5			
March 1988										1-5	1-5	0-4	0-4	
March 1989											1-5	0-4	0-4	
March 1990												1-5	0-4	−1-3
March 1991													0-4	0-4
Outcome[5]	10	6½	0	3½	6¼	5½	3½	4	5	7	5¾	4½		
Money Supply: M1 (% change)														
March 1982				8-12	7-11									
March 1983					7-11									
Outcome[5]				11										
Money Supply: £M3 (% change)														
June 1979[2]	7-11													
March 1980		7-11	6-10	5-9	4-8									
March 1981			6-10	5-9[6]	4-8[6]									
March 1982				8-12	7-11	6-10								
March 1983					7-11	6-10	5-9[6]							
March 1984						6-10	5-9	4-8[6]	3-7[6]	2-6[6]				
March 1985[3]							5-9	4-8[6]	3-7[6]	2-6[6]				
March 1986								11-15						
Outcome[5]	16¼	19½	12¾	10	9¾	9½	14¾							
Money Supply: PSL1[1] (% change)														
March 1982				8-12	7-11									
March 1983					7-11									
Outcome				9	12⅓									

Table 12.3 *Medium Term Financial Strategy, Target Ranges*[1] *and Outcomes ,% (cont'd)*

	1979/80	1980/81	1981/82	1982/83	1983/84	1984/85	1985/86	1986/87	1987/88	1988/89	1989/90	1990/91	1991/92	1992/93
PSBR														
(% of GDP)														
June 1979	4½	*	*	*	*	*	*	*	*	*	*	*	*	*
March 1980	4¾	3¾	3	2¼	1½	*	*	*	*	*	*	*	*	*
March 1981	5	6	4¼	3¼	2	*	*	*	*	*	*	*	*	*
March 1982	*	5¾	4¼	3½	2¾	2	*	*	*	*	*	*	*	*
March 1983	*	*	3½	2¾	2¾	2½	2	*	*	*	*	*	*	*
March 1984	*	*	*	3⅓	3¼	2¼	2	2	1¾	1¾	*	*	*	*
March 1985	*	*	*	*	3¼	3¼	2	2	1¾	1¾	*	*	*	*
March 1986	*	*	*	*	*	3	2	1¾	1¾	1½	1½	*	*	*
March 1987	*	*	*	*	*	*	1½	1	1	1	1	1	*	*
March 1988	*	*	*	*	*	*	*	1	–¾	–¾	0	0	*	*
March 1989	*	*	*	*	*	*	*	*	–¾	–3	–2¾	–1¾	–1	–½
March 1990	*	*	*	*	*	*	*	*	*	*	–1¼	–1¼	–½	0
March 1991	*	*	*	*	*	*	*	*	*	*	–1½	–¼	1¼	2
Outcome	4¾	5½	3½	3¼	3¼	3	1½	1	–¾	–3	–1½[7]	–¼[7]	*	*
Money GDP														
(% change)														
March 1985	*	*	*	*	7¾	6¾ (8¼)[4]	8½ (7)[4]	6¾	5¾	5	*	*	*	*
March 1986	*	*	*	*	*	*	9½ (8¼)[4]	6¾	6½	6	5½	*	*	*
March 1987	*	*	*	*	*	*	*	6	7½	6½	6	*	*	*
March 1988	*	*	*	*	*	*	*	*	*	7½	6½	6	5½	*
March 1989	*	*	*	*	*	*	*	*	*	11	7¾	6	6	5½
March 1990	*	*	*	*	*	*	*	*	*	*	8½[7]	7½[7]	6¾[7]	6¼[7]
March 1991	*	*	*	*	*	*	*	*	*	*	*	7¼[7]	6[7]	7½[7]

Notes:

1. Targets are set for a 14-month period commencing in February.
2. Old definition including public sector deposits.
3. New definition excluding public sector deposits.
4. Adjusted for coal strike.
5. Data taken from source cited. Slightly different figures are cited elsewhere. Outcomes relate to a 12-month period commencing in February.
6. 'Illustrative range'.
7. Adjusted for distortions arising from the abolition of domestic rates.

Source: FSBR, 'Red Book', for each year, of which the most recent is that for 1991–92 HC^{300} (March 1991).

- **1979–81**
  A policy-induced recession as the government set up its anti-inflation strategy
- **1982–85**
  A period during which the authorities **abandoned a single monetary target** and experimented with multiple ones; as the inflation rate fell the policy stance eased, and the economy recovered slowly but steadily
- **November 1985–Summer 1988**
  A time when the focus of monetary policy switched to the **exchange rate**; policy was relaxed and the boom in the economy intensified
- **Summer 1988 onwards**
  A **tightening of policy** as the government attempted to deal with the effects of the boom.

Table 12.4 summarises the performance of the economy at this time.

Committed to an anti-inflationary strategy from the outset, the government began to tighten both fiscal and monetary policy almost immediately after taking office. The first Budget, in June 1979, saw the announcement of some £1.5 bn cuts in public expenditure and a planned fall in the PSBR from £9.2 bn to £8.2 bn over the year, reducing it from 5.5 per cent to 4.5 per cent of GDP. On the monetary side the MLR was raised by 2 per cent to 14 per cent and the £M3 target range of 8–10 per cent was adjusted to 7–11 per cent, although this was for the 10-month period to April 1980. For the time being the direct controls on the banking

Table 12.4 *The Performance of the Economy, 1979-88*

	1979–88	1979–83	1984–88
Real GDP growth (average % p.a.)	2.3	1	3.5
Inflation (average % p.a.)	8	11.2	4.7
Unemployment (average % of labour force)	9.3	8.4	10.3

Source: Economic Trends, Annual Supplement 1989.

system remained in place. More controversially, there was a major switch in **taxation policy**: income tax rates were reduced (the basic rate from 33 to 30 per cent and the top rate from 86 to 60 per cent) and VAT rates were raised to a uniform 15 per cent. At a time when inflation was rising, from 8.1 per cent in the fourth quarter in 1978 to 10.6 per cent by the second quarter of 1979, the policy can be seen as perverse since it added to the RPI, and thus to inflationary expectations. Some writers have dismissed such a view as confusing a once-and-for-all rise in prices with a persistent increase in the general price level. In the event inflation continued to accelerate, reaching a peak of almost 22 per cent by mid-1980. This aided by the government's commitment to meeting in full the Clegg Committee pay awards, established in the closing months of the Labour Government. The removal of subsidies to, and of price controls on, the nationalised industries was pursued vigorously. Nationalised industry prices rose by 25 per cent in 1980, by 19 per cent in 1981 and by 58 per cent between 1980 and 1982. This increased cost inflation but reduced demand inflation.

Further tightening occurred during 1979 with the MLR being raised to 17 per cent as the government attempted to cope with a policy that seemed to be going awry. By the end of the third quarter £M3 was growing at an annual rate of 14 per cent, well outside its target range, and the PSBR appeared to be on course for a major overshoot. It was only the abolition of exchange controls in July which prevented the money supply from rising completely out of control: the external impact in the third quarter of 1979 was £1.7 bn alone.

□ 12.9.2 Introducing the MTFS

The introduction of the MTFS in the Budget of 1980 saw the reaffirmation of the government's principal objective of attacking inflation by reducing the rate of growth of £M3. A declining target range for this broad money aggregate was announced (**Table 12.3**). The tightening of fiscal policy was reflected in a projected PSBR of £8.5 bn to be achieved through planned cuts in public spending and increases in taxation – the raising of excise duties and the abolition of the reduced income tax

Figure 12.4   *Bank Base Rates, 1977–91*

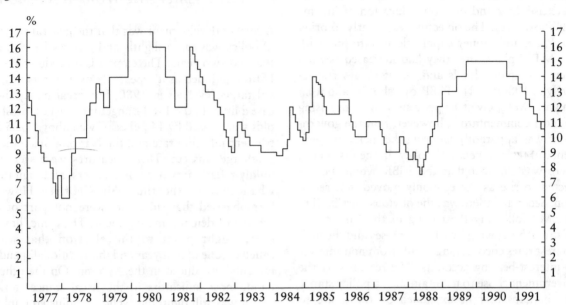

Source: Barclays Bank Review.

band of 25 per cent. There was also a projected decrease in the PSBR as a percentage of GDP over the next four years to 1.5 per cent of GDP (**Table 12.3**). The apparent monetary squeeze continued.

The MLR was maintained at an historically high level in nominal terms (although it was nevertheless negative in real terms) and by the end of 1980 stood at 14 per cent, having been reduced to 16 per cent in July and to 14 per cent in November. The general trend of interest rates can be seen in **Figure 12.4**. The exchange rate appreciated sharply and M1, a narrow money aggregate, slowed.

During 1980 it became clear that the economy had moved into a major downturn as output contracted rapidly and unemployment began to mount, rising to 1.7 million by the end of the year. It was to be the severest recession of the postwar period, reaching its depth in output terms sometime in the second quarter of 1981 with GDP 7.5 per cent below its previous peak two years earlier. Manufacturing output contracted by nearly 9 per cent in 1980 alone.

The most cogent explanation of the severity of the recession is that it was the effect of the extremely tight monetary policy on the exchange rate that produced such an intense squeeze on UK industry. Not only did sterling rise to over $2.40 in 1980, but the Exchange Rate Index in the second quarter of 1981 was also over 17 per cent above the level it had been two years before. (see **p. 211**). Coupled with the surge in domestic prices and costs, the real exchange rate was even higher. Domestic producers were caught between rising costs and interest rates at home and a major loss of competitiveness abroad. Exports held up surprisingly well; it was the **import-competing sector** that bore the brunt of the adjustment.

Other explanations of the contraction include the impact of oil on the exchange rate and the effect of the second oil price shock with the ensuing world-wide downturn in economic activity. Whilst these added to the UK's problems, some estimates suggest that North Sea oil contributed 8–12 per cent of the real appreciation whilst others suggest much less. As regards the international recession, the slowdown occurred rather later, in 1980/81, than the downturn in activity in the UK.

It was against such a background that the government tightened its fiscal policy further in the 1981 Budget. This was achieved primarily through significant rises in taxation, principally increases in excise duty and the non-indexation of income tax allowances. The objective was clearly to bring the PSBR and money supply closer into line with the MTFS plans after they had increased beyond their anticipated levels and target ranges respectively in 1980/81. The PSBR overshot by about £5 bn and £M3 grew at 19 per cent. It was surprising to most commentators, however, that the government was apparently ignoring the increasing evidence of the stringency of policy. In the first place, there was the fact that the PSBR would be expected to rise as the economy moved into recession. Secondly, there was the obvious unreliability of £M3 following the ending of the Corset, the 'distress' borrowing by UK businesses and the high interest rates encouraging a shift from non-interest to interest-bearing accounts. The reason why the government chose to maintain such a policy stance can perhaps best be explained by the desire to retain the credibility of its anti-inflation commitment. Undoubtedly the 1981 Budget was an act of considerable political and economic courage, and almost certainly it paved the way for the successes of subsequent years.

Towards the end of 1981 economic activity reached a lower turning point and there were some signs of an incipient recovery in output despite the fact that unemployment was rising inexorably to over 2.5 million by the end of the year. The anti-inflationary policy was also beginning to show its first fruits as the annual rate fell to 12 per cent. From this time a number of changes in policy became apparent. One was the beginning of the disillusionment with £M3 as the proximate target for economic policy. In the 1982 Budget target ranges were set for M1 and a broader aggregate PSL2. There was also an indication that some account would be taken of the exchange rate in the operation of monetary policy. Another change was a switch in emphasis to nominal (money) GDP as the target for economic policy, with projections set for four years ahead as part of the MTFS. The basis of the GDP target was that if inflation showed signs of reaccelerating it would not be accommodated: policy would be adjusted to keep money GDP in the target range, and output would decline until price inflation fell.

□ 12.9.3 Emerging from Recession

A further development was that the general stance of policy was eased slightly and progressively over the next two years. The emphasis on reducing the PSBR continued as it repeatedly overshot its original target level set in 1980, but fiscal policy did ease a little. In the 1983 Budget income tax thresholds were raised by 14 per cent, well above the 5.5 per cent inflation rate and the National Insurance surcharge was cut. These measures were seen as mildly reflationary in some quarters, although the Chancellor of the time, Sir Geoffrey Howe, reemphasised that such cuts were not part of a scheme of demand management. The cynic, however, might point to the election that was called in June of that year and the additional spending cuts introduced in the Autumn. On the other hand, most indicators of the fiscal stance show that it was still tight; the cyclically adjusted public sector balance suggested that there was a real structural budget surplus (Dornbusch and Layard, 1987, p. 37).

The main easing came through the monetary side, the money supply targets notwithstanding. By the Autumn of 1982 interest rates, as measured by short-term money market rates, had fallen to 9 per cent (**Figure 12.4**) and despite a sharp increase in the Winter of 1982/83 to prevent too fast a fall in the exchange rate, interest rates remained in the 8–9 per cent range until June 1984. It was this monetary relaxation, and the corresponding fall in the exchange rate, as interest rates rose abroad, which provided some of the stimulus to growth. But the main impetus came from consumers' expenditure. This was boosted by the rise in real incomes as earnings grew faster than prices, a credit boom inspired by deregulation and the effects of falling inflation on the saving ratio via a wealth effect. At the end of 1983 the inflation rate had fallen to 4.5 per cent per annum, and GDP grew by 1.9 per cent in 1982 and 3.7 per cent in 1983.

Under a new Chancellor, Mr Lawson (1983), the monetariest strategy, though not the other elements of Thatcherism, was finally abandoned. The official date is November 1985 when it was announced that £M3 was to be downgraded from a target variable to a monitored one. Since 1987, M0 has been the only targeted monetary aggregate. Monetary policy reverted to influencing the exchange rate; this had been evident for some time before the official abandonment of monetary targets. In June 1984, for example, the Bank of England signalled a rise in interest rates, which persisted until the Autumn, as sterling fell to 76 per cent of its 1980 level. More dramatic were the events of January 1985. At a time of increasing uncertainty over oil prices, the UK's balance of payments and the government's resolve to maintain its anti-inflation policy – inflation had begun to accelerate during 1984 and the government had shown increasing concern over the serious unemployment problem – sterling fell sharply. At one time it went below the $1.10 level. The government responded by reintroducing the MLR at 12 per cent for a short period and interest rates remained high for most of 1985 (**Figure 12.4**).

The reasons for the shift in monetary policy towards the exchange rate lay in an increasing concern that exchange rate volatility affected adversely the trade performance of UK industry, and an acceptance of the view that exchange rate depreciation was the main mechanism through which inflation was transmitted to the domestic economy. With regard to the latter it was maintained that if the value of sterling could be tied to the currency of a stable, low inflation economy this would provide an 'anchor' for the UK's inflation rate. For this reason the government operated an unofficial exchange rate target of £1 = DM 3, later amended to DM 3.10 and then DM 3.20. It was at this time that the appropriateness of the UK's entry into the EMS's exchange rate mechanism became an issue of increasing topicality.

Just as the concentration on a single internal monetary target in the early years of the government led to an excessively tight monetary policy, so the emphasis on a single external target – the £:DM exchange rate – resulted in an over-relaxation of the monetary stance. The upshot was the 'Lawson Boom' which exhibited many, though not all, of the marks of previous expansions. It has been likened to the ill-fated 'Barber Boom' 15 years previously. Some details of the boom are given in **Table 12.5**.

One difference was that the public sector moved into considerable surplus as higher levels of economic activity increased tax revenues even after privatisation revenues have been accounted for.

In fact the fiscal position can be said to have remained relatively tight despite the reflationary effects of a series of income tax cuts in the 1986, 1987 and 1988 Budgets. The rise in productivity has also been cited as a significant change from the earlier boom (Minford, 1989). But whilst productivity rose by 19 per cent between 1985 and the third quarter of 1988, the rise in productivity from 1970 up to the third quarter of 1973 was 21 per cent.

☐ 12.9.4 Overheating

In many respects the similarities are more striking – the rapid expansion in consumer credit, a house price boom, a surge in consumer spending and the deterioration in the current account are all characteristic symptoms of overheating in the UK economy. If nothing else, they are certainly reminiscent of an earlier age.

By far the most important contributor to the boom was the continued rise in consumers' expenditure, which grew at an average rate of 6.2 per cent per year between 1985 and 1988, as shown in **Table 12.5**. In particular, the housing market once again provided a graphic indicator of the loosening of money and credit policy. House prices rose at an average of nearly 16 per cent per annum in both 1986 and 1987; by 1988 they had accelerated to 38 per cent. Inflation followed suit. After reaching a low of 2.6 per cent per annum in the third quarter of 1986, rising demand began to feed through to higher inflation figures during 1987 and especially in 1988, rising to 6.5 per cent by the year's end. The unfolding of events at this time is instructive since it reveals the government's attempt to deal with a major policy dilemma.

Policy entered a critical phase early in 1988 after interest rates had been cut in the wake of the Stock Exchange collapse of the previous October as shown in **Figure 12.4** and **Table 12.6**, below. Upward pressure on sterling forced further interest rate cuts as the government attempted to hold

Table 12.5   *The Lawson Boom – Selected Indicators, 1985–88*

		Real GDP Growth (% p.a.[1])	Inflation (% p.a.)	Average Earnings (% p.a.)	Real Consumers' Expenditure (%)	Consumer Credit (%)	M3 (% p.a.)	Current Balance[2] £ mn
1986	I	3.1	5.0	8.3	5.0	43.0	16.9	1250
	II	2.8	2.9	8.1	7.8	50.0	18.9	56
	III	3.9	2.7	7.4	6.2	43.1	19.1	−693
	IV	4.4	3.5	7.9	6.2	36.9	19.1	−679
1987	I	3.8	3.8	7.0	6.6	12.4	19.7	293
	II	4.0	4.2	7.5	3.8	20.1	19.8	−947
	III	4.9	4.2	7.7	5.5	21.2	20.2	−1249
	IV	4.6	3.8	8.4	6.4	29.2	22.8	−2419
1988	I	5.6	3.4	8.9	8.0	30.4	21.0	−3168
	II	4.5	4.3	8.2	6.8	25.0	20.1	−3144
	III	3.7	5.6	8.7	6.9	27.9	22.5	−3261
	IV	3.4	6.5	–	6.1	18.4	20.3	−5812

Notes:
[1]   All % changes are year on year.
[2]   Seasonally adjusted.
Source: Economic Trends, (June 1991); *Bank of England Quarterly Bulletin* (February 1989); *National Institute Economic Review, various issues.*

Table 12.6   *Representative[1] Money Market Interest Rates, %*

	USA	Germany	Japan	UK		USA	Germany	Japan	UK
Annual Averages					Monthly Averages 1990/91				
1978	8.2	3.7	4.4	9.2	1990 August	8.0	8.3	7.4	15.0
1979	11.2	6.7	5.9	13.7	September	8.1	8.4	7.6	14.9
1980	13.1	9.5	10.9	16.6	October	8.1	8.5	7.7	14.0
1981	15.9	12.1	7.4	13.9	November	8.1	8.7	7.9	13.7
1982	12.3	8.8	6.9	12.3	December	7.9	9.1	8.1	13.8
1983	9.1	5.8	6.4	10.1	1991 January	7.3	9.2	8.1	13.9
1984	10.4	6.0	6.1	10.0	February	6.6	9.0	8.1	13.2
1985	8.1	5.4	6.5	12.2	March	6.5	9.0	8.3	12.4
1986	6.5	4.6	4.8	10.9	April	6.2	9.1	8.2	11.9
1987	6.9	4.0	3.5	9.7	May	6.0	9.0	8.0	11.5
1988	7.7	4.3	3.7	10.3	June	6.2	8.9	8.0	11.2
1989	9.1	7.0	4.9	13.9	July	6.1	9.0	7.4	11.1
1990	8.0	8.4	7.2	14.7					

Note:
[1]   USA – 3 months' CD rate; Germany – 3-month inter-bank; Japan – Call money; UK – 3-month inter-bank.
Source: Barclays Economic Review (August 1991).

sterling at its DM3 target. Even after sterling had been 'uncapped' in March 1988, further interest rate reductions were required in order to prevent too fast an appreciation. On the domestic front, however, there were signs of too rapid an expansion. Either the exchange rate target would have to be sacrificed or interest rates would have to fall further, but at the risk of fuelling further domestic demand. By mid-Summer the problem resolved itself. The evidence of overheating had become incontrovertible as measured by any indicator of the level of economic activity – be it the current account, inflation, consumer credit, average earnings, or the government's sole remaining monetary target M0. Compared with its target range of 1–5 per cent, M0 grew by 7.7 per cent between June 1987 and June 1988. Interest rates were raised progressively through the Autumn and the exchange rate permitted to rise as the government sought to slow the pace of expansion. Base rates reached 13 per cent in November and mortgage rates followed suit.

Nigel Lawson, the ex-Chancellor, emphasised on numerous occasions (for example, Lawson, 1988) that short-term interest rates were regarded as the only effective instrument of monetary policy and hence the best way of affecting demand. This clearly indicated that demand management was by no means dead; during much of the 1980s it was actively pursued. What is different is that greater importance was given, at least verbally, to the **control of inflation** rather than the regulation of employment as in earlier decades. Furthermore, fiscal policy as ostensibly used as a supply-side instrument as well as a demand-side one.

In reflecting on the 1980s it is possible to identify two sharply contrasting ways of looking at the experience of the UK economy. The first is that because of the shake-up that has been administered by the tight anti-inflationary policy of the early years (1979–81), the prudent fiscal policy and the continuing emphasis on free market supply-side measures, the economy emerged as more robust and flexible. The consequence was that economic growth was now more sustainable. The second, more pessimistic interpretation is that in spite of the growth performance in 1986–88, much of the improvement represents a catching-up

period after a time of severe recession and the result of the operation of policy in a way rather different from its original conception. Moreover, many of the inherent weaknesses still remained and would resurface given the right conditions.

However, both these views are too extreme. The period produced some positive benefits – for example, in the marked improvement in the trend growth of productivity and the competitiveness of the manufacturing sector. On the other hand, such achievements were obtained at the cost of heavy unemployment and lost output. As is the case with all economic adjustments, the costs have not been shared equally. In addition, there was ample evidence of the resurgence of some of the underlying problems of the UK economy – the current account deterioration, rising inflation and the behaviour of earnings.

12.9.5 From Boom to Bust . . . Again

Economists are justifiably sceptical of the existence of obvious symmetries in the historical development of economies. It is, however, more than just a cruel coincidence that the 1980s ended and the 1990s began with the UK economy exhibiting some of the same problems that had existed a decade earlier, and which the Thatcher Government had set out to remedy in the certainty that its approach was correct. Thus the large current account deficit of £15 bn in 1988 had worsened to nearly £20 bn by 1989 and, by the early Autumn of 1990, inflation had accelerated to just short of 11 per cent.

The policy response, that of raising interest rates progressively from Summer 1988 (when bank base rates were at a low of 7.5 per cent) to October 1990 (when base rates reached 15 per cent), was relatively slow to take effect. This was especially true on the inflation front. The inflation rate continued to rise despite the slowing of the economy, and this was irrespective of whether inflation was measured by the full RPI – the headline rate – or the 'underlying' rate which excludes the effects of mortgage interest rates (see **pp. 66–72**).

Table 12.7   *Into recession, 1989–91*

		Real GDP Growth (% p.a.)	Inflation (% p.a.)	Unemployment (%)	Manufacturing Productivity (% change p.a.)	Current Balance £ mn
1989	I	2.7	7.7	7.0	6.5	–4 323
	II	1.9	8.2	6.5	5.8	–5 346
	III	1.3	7.7	6.2	3.3	–6 783
	IV	1.3	7.6	5.9	2.5	–3 194
1990	I	1.2	7.8	5.7	0.9	–5 523
	II	2.0	9.7	5.6	2.2	–5 400
	III	0.1	10.4	5.7	0.1	–2 891
	IV	–1.3	10.0	6.0	–1.7	15
1991	I	–3.5	8.7	6.7	–0.9	–3 152
	II			7.6		

Source: Economic Trends.

As was the case a decade earlier, inflation once again became the principal objective of macroeconomic policy. For example, the mounting current account deficit was variously dismissed as either symptomatic of overheating, the result of unreliable statistics as indicated by the massive balancing item, or a temporary phenomenon that would be self-correcting.

In the early days of the operation of the restrictive policy, much was made of the likelihood of a 'soft landing', where the economy would adjust with relatively little cost in terms of lost output and of unemployment. The reality was quite the reverse as the details in **Table 12.7** indicate. From around the third quarter of 1990 the UK entered a major recession.

ERM Entry

Of central importance to the operation of macroeconomic policy at this time was the debate – indeed split – within the government over the causes of the inflation and the related and critical issue of the appropriate policy response. It is a debate that led to the resignation of a Chancellor (Lawson) and the wider aspects of which brought about the departure of a Foreign Secretary (Howe) and a Prime Minister (Thatcher).

As regards the causes of the inflation, one explanation offered was that of the Thatcher–Walters camp. This view maintained that the policy of shadowing the Deutsche Mark from 1987 resulted in excessive monetary expansion as the authorities sold sterling on the foreign exchange markets and lowered interest rates to prevent the pound from rising above its DM 3 target. For a monetarist such as Walters, the excessive money supply increases could lead only to an acceleration in inflation at some later date.

Opposing this view was Lawson and the EMS camp. Their argument was that had the UK entered the Exchange Rate Mechanism of the EMS at an earlier date, say in 1985, this would have provided a credible anchor for UK inflation.

In brief, the policy works by tying the pound to the Deutsche Mark and thus not permitting faster inflation in the UK relative to Germany being offset by a currency depreciation (see pp. 243–5). As long as wage bargainers and price setters have confidence in the authorities' determination to maintain the exchange rate, expectations should adjust and the UK inflation rate ultimately converge on the German rate. A failure of expectations to adjust, and the persistence of higher inflation in the UK, can lead only to a loss of competitiveness.

Ultimately, the discipline of the ERM forces a convergence of inflation rates either through the effect of reduced competitiveness producing a rise in unemployment, or because the authorities have to raise interest rates in order to maintain the exchange rate, or both. To support their case the proponents of ERM entry cited the superior inflation performance of countries such as France and Italy.

The policy implications of the two views should be reasonably clear. In the Thatcher–Walters version, the best indicators of inflationary pressure are the **domestic monetary statistics**, especially the narrow monetary base (MO). As a consequence, policy should be targeted to maintain a steady non-inflationary growth of these aggregates. By contrast, the government settled finally upon the ERM approach, joining the wide band in October 1990 at a central rate of £1 = DM2.95.

Although entry can be seen partly as a victory for the supporters of the ERM approach to inflation control following the disappointing response of domestic inflation to high interest rates, there were other factors at work. In the first place, the victory had in essence already been won in June 1989 when Mrs Thatcher gave a conditional commitment to join the ERM. Secondly, the pressure to join was intensifying following the increasing integration of the EC economies as a result of the 1992 programme and the proposals for monetary union.

An important aspect of exchange rate regimes such as the ERM is that they reduce greatly a government's freedom in the domestic monetary sphere. Interest rates cannot be set solely with reference to domestic developments, but must be directed to maintaining the pound within its ERM band. This provides one possible explanation of why interest rates were maintained at so high a level for so long at this time. A rapid cut in interest rates immediately after ERM entry could have undermined confidence in the government's commitment to a stringent anti-inflationary stance, and any pressure on the pound resulting in an early realignment would have eroded credibility altogether.

As a result, interest rates were reduced by only 1 per cent on entry. It was not until the rate of increase in the RPI began to fall back in late 1990 and early 1991, and the severity of the downturn became evident as the level of economic activity plunged, that the government felt confident enough to cut interest rates. Base rates subsequently fell from 14 per cent in January 1991 to 11 per cent in July of that year.

ERM entry alone cannot explain why the government maintained high interest rates for so long in the 1988–91 period, since the policy had operated for at least two years prior to entry. Furthermore, the downward trend in interest rates began after October 1990, albeit slowly and in line with falling inflation. One possible explanation is the already noted slowness of the economy to respond to the monetary squeeze. A second possibility is that the government misjudged the seriousness of the recession. Even though growth had slowed down from its high levels in early 1988, and unemployment had started to rise from the low point of 1.6 mn in March 1990, GDP was still growing at an annual rate of 1–2 per cent up until the second quarter of 1990. It was not until the third quarter of that year that, in the colourful language of City commentators, the economy 'fell off the edge'. GDP growth halted and subsequently fell precipitously (see **Table 12.7**). This abrupt plunge probably arose from the combination of a slump in consumer and business expectations after a protracted period of high interest rates and rising inflation, combined with high levels of indebtedness following the credit boom earlier in the decade.

Another likely explanation is that the government over-corrected, squeezing the economy too hard – a reaction to the laxity in monetary policy that had allowed the boom to run on too long in 1987–88. Faulty statistics may have had some part to play in misjudging the boom, as perhaps did a misplaced belief in the productivity 'miracle'. Nevertheless, errors of policy in the upswing of the cycle should not be used as an excuse for over-reacting in the downturn.

A further, and important, aspect of ERM entry is the question of whether the UK entered at too high a level for the pound. This is a view shared by monetarist critics such as Walters and Keynesians (for example, the National Institute) alike. Both have emphasised the long-term loss of competitiveness and the consequent unemployment problems that arise from an overvalued exchange rate. It imparts a recessionary bias into the economy, a problem which may become greater in the UK unless inflation falls to, or below, the EMS average. For monetarists such as Walters, interest rates were held at too high a level throughout 1990. In their view the monetary indicators showed that the battle against inflation had already been won and that policy needed to be relaxed significantly if a serious recession was to be avoided. As a consequence, ERM entry could only make things worse.

Political considerations notwithstanding, a possible justification for the government's decision to enter at its chosen rate is that any lowering of the rate on entry would have threatened the strict anti-inflationary stance of policy. A relatively high pound had the benefit of reaffirming this policy, possibly having a beneficial effect on expectations. In addition, the rate gave the government the option of devaluing at a later date after inflation had been brought under control, which could then be used to provide a stimulus to the domestic economy.

Fiscal Policy

In terms of the counterpart equation outlined at the beginning of this chapter, policy during the period 1988–91 has operated primarily on the credit term; interest rates have been used to reduce the growth of bank and building society lending. As it had during the first half of the 1980s, the government continued the break with the earlier Keynesian tradition and did not use fiscal policy (measured by the PSBR in the counterpart equation) as a discretionary counter-cyclical measure. As a consequence, the PSBR tended to move with the cycle. Thus, despite reductions in tax rates, the buoyant economy of the mid-to-late 1980s produced sizeable public sector surpluses. In 1989 the PSDR reached £11.8 bn. As the pace of economic activity slowed, the PSDR declined so that by the end of the 1990/91 financial year it was only roughly £0.5 bn.

The recession has caused the PSBR to reappear. However, unlike the policy of the early 1980s

when the government sought to cut the deficit in a recession, the intention as stated in the 1991 FSBR was to permit the deficit to move with the economic cycle. This may well provide the economy with some automatic stabilisation, although of a very limited kind.

In summary, the past several years provide a classic demonstration of a fundamental difficulty of macroeconomic policy – it is rarely possible to achieve **all policy objectives at the same time**. A traditional explanation for this is that to hit more than one policy target requires more than one policy instrument. Policy during this period has been compared to a golfer using only one club. Another, less emphasised, aspect is the problem of economic dynamics – that is, the way an economy develops over time. In the first place, it takes time for a policy measure to take effect. Thus the timing of an increase or reduction in interest rates is critical to the effect of the policy on inflation and growth. Secondly, when an economy recovers after a period of disinflation, the level of economic activity, and especially the rate of unemployment, may remain at undesirable levels for some time. It is this latter problem that was beginning to dog the government from about the middle of 1991.

■ *12.10* The Decline of Keynesianism

□ *12.10.1 Self-fulfilling Beliefs*

In the 1950s the average level of unemployment was about 250,000, only a tenth the level of the 1980s and about one-eighth that of the 1930s. The low level of unemployment was almost universally attributed to Keynesian economic management as economists complacently congratulated themselves as having rid the world of the scourge of unemployment. Any appraisal of economic policy in the 1980s must, therefore, start by asking why the techniques that worked so well in the 1950s were not even tried in the 1980s – and whether, if tried, they would have worked.

Full employment in the 1950s and 1960s was the result of the **private sector's response** to the government policy of the time, not directly of what the governments did. In particular, because the private sector believed in full employment it changed its behaviour and invested more. The critical act of government was to commit itself to a policy of **full employment**. Full employment implied that demand and expenditure (and hence future sales) would remain high. It would thus be profitable to invest to satisfy this demand. Moreover, a belief in full employment boosted such intangible forces as business confidence, and so caused a further rise in investment.

One category of investment does not depend in any way on expectations of future sales. This is housebuilding, which is of especial importance because some studies suggest that it was a major cause of the high levels of employment experienced in the late 1950s – that this was, in Keynesian terms, the injection which kept the economy at a high level of demand. However, the housebuilding boom depended in large apart on the enormous personal sector demand for housing which was matched by a willingness to accept long-term mortgage commitments to finance house purchase. Keynesian economists argue plausibly that the belief in full employment was at least a necessary condition for people to be prepared to do this. If someone takes out a mortgage they are committing themselves to making repayments over a period of at least 20 years. No-one would do this if he or she feared that they were likely to lose their job in the near future, nor for that matter would any building societies (which had a monopoly of mortgage lending in the 1950s) lend to him or her. Moreover, house purchasers have to consider the prospects of resale, which depend upon both the state of the economy in general and upon other people's willingness to take out mortgages in particular. Hence, the **belief** in full employment was again one of the causes of extra demand.

These Keynesian arguments can be challenged, but it is generally accepted that they have some force and that belief in the efficiency of activist government policy boosted employment in the 1950s. The reasons for its apparent failure in the 1960s and 1970s are more controversial. Keynesians cite two factors – a decline in the belief in full employment and the adverse consequences of the belief in full employment.

☐ *12.10.2 The Erosion of Belief*

Belief in the continuation of full employment, and in particular of the ability of government to maintain it, declined from about 1965 because:

(a) of criticism of the theory of demand management, especially those made by Friedman; this has led some prominent Keynesians (such as Hahn) mischievously and humourously to suggest that such views should be suppressed even if they are right and Keynesianism promoted even if wrong

(b) governments seemed to give less prominence to full employment as a goal of economic policy after 1964 (when the Labour Government gave priority to the balance of payments)

(c) as unemployment rose after 1965, faith in the efficiency of full employment policies declined.

The Keynesian account is thus of a **cumulative process**. Full employment would continue only so long as people believed that it would. As faith declined so unemployment rose and faith declined further and so on *ad infinitum*.

Most Keynesian analysts, however, give much more weight to the adverse effects of a belief in full employment rather than to the decline in the belief itself. In particular, because trade union leaders believed in full employment, they ceased to believe that the threat of unemployment need constrain wage demands. Hence they asked for large-scale wage demands. Employers acceded to these demands – in part because their belief in full employment created the expectation in their minds that they would be able to pass the wage increases on as price increases, and consequent high demand. Hence the belief in full employment led firstly to cost inflation, and so to upward movements of aggregate supply curves, and secondly to employers substituting capital for labour. The premise of activist demand management was that the demand for labour would fluctuate only according to output. This was no longer so. Some Keynesians regarded this as an argument for incomes policy.

What is relevant is that the achievement of full employment depended on a belief that it **could and would be achieved**. This was because investment was much higher as a consequence of the belief in the effectiveness of government policy. Such beliefs, however, also had adverse effects which made the continuation of full employment much harder to achieve – indeed perhaps impossible. In summary, belief that governments could achieve and maintain full employment was self-fulfilling in the 1950s, but problems also arose both because this confidence declined and because of the management and trade union movement's response to its belief in full employment.

It was certainly the case that full employment policies encouraged complacency and inefficient management of firms. Firms expected to sell their products irrespective of quality, design or reliability, so they had no incentive to produce reliable, high quality goods. Hence the two aspects of the 'English disease' arose as a consequence – bad management and aggressive unions which resisted innovation and demanded high wages.

■ *12.11* Friedman's Critique

The most important omission from the elementary Keynesian theory of demand management is **inflationary expectations**. In essence, the idea underlying this concept is very simple: if economic agents expect inflation, they will change their behaviour such that there will be inflation. Although originally introduced into economic analysis by Friedman, the concept is now central to all economic models whether Keynesian, monetarist, post-Keynesian, New Classical or anything else.

Let us suppose that the government decides to pursue an expansionary policy which can be represented by an outward shift of the aggregate demand curve for the whole economy. Output will rise, and so will inflation. In the Keynesian model this is the end of the story, whereas Friedman argues:

1   that the higher rate of inflation will generate higher expectations as to the future rate of inflation
2   that this will cause the aggregate supply (AS) curve to shift up and to the left
3   that ultimately the AS curve will come to rest such that output falls to its original level and

inflation is ongoing at the rate determined by the point of intersection of aggregate demand and aggregate supply.

If Friedman is right, then obviously activist demand management will work in the short run but not in the long run. However, the reader may very well ask two pertinent questions, namely

- Why does a rise in inflationary expectations cause the AS curve to shift upwards?
- Why is this shift exactly enough such that output reverts to its original level?

The answer to the first question is most easily answered by considering underlying microeconomic behaviour. Firms make decisions about their prices on the basis of costs and demand (marginal and average revenue). However, all of these have to be based on their beliefs about these variables since in the real world they cannot be known with certainty. In many cases, prices are fixed for a period of time so these beliefs are **expectations about the future**. For example, when Hoover are deciding what price to charge for washing machines, they need to determine the demand for their product. This will depend on such matters as the price of substitutes. If Hoover believe that rivals are going to increase their prices then their demand curve

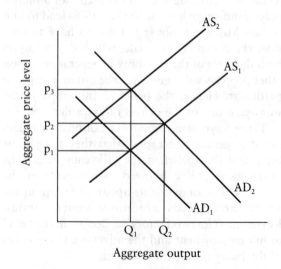

Figure 12.5 *Aggregate Demand, Aggregate Supply and Inflation*

moves further to the right. Hoover's expectations about price increases by rivals will thus determine the position of their demand curve and hence their price. If every firm expects every other firm to charge more, the belief is self-fulfilling. Moreover, a higher price for the same output is a definition of an upward shift in a supply curve, aggregate or otherwise.

The argument is even simpler in the labour market. The perceived shift in the demand for goods causes a shift in the demand for the labour which made them. A higher expected level of prices causes a fall in perceived real wages, and so leads to an inward shift in the supply of labour. Supply moves in and demand moves out, hence wages rise at each level of employment. All of these shifts can be represented at an aggregate level by a shift of the AS curve. Higher inflationary expectations thus lead to an upward shift of the AS curve.

Friedman's argument is that higher inflation leads to a higher expected level of inflation and so to an adverse shift of the AS curve. The extent of this shift of the AS curve depends upon how expectations of inflation respond to actual inflation. There can be little doubt that there is some response, since if inflation is high or rising it is unreasonable not to expect it to be higher in future than one would if inflation were low. Friedman's analysis is, however, a special case in that he assumes that the rise in the expected rate of inflation is exactly equal to the current rise in inflation. Thus if inflation rose from 4 to 5 per cent, expected inflation would follow suit (at least in the long run). If this is so, the shift in aggregate supply is exactly enough for output to fall to its original level, that is for aggregate supply to shift from AS_1 to AS_2 in **Figure 12.5**.

Friedman's analysis can be presented in another way:

$Inflation_t$ = Expected inflation$_t$ + Demand inflation

Expected Inflation$_t$ = Inflation$_{t-1}$

so Inflation$_t$ = Inflation$_{t-1}$ + Demand inflation

It is the linkage between **inflation and past inflation** which is one of the achievements of Friedman's model. By so doing, it explains inflation as a **continuing increase in prices**, rather than as a once-and-for-all rise in price. In the orthodox model there is an inverse relationship between inflation and unemployment. In Friedman's model the inverse relationship is between **demand** inflation and unemployment. The cost of a lower level of unemployment is demand inflation and hence an accelerating, rising level of total inflation – whenever there is demand inflation, inflation is necessarily higher than in the previous year (inflation falls only when demand inflation is negative).

In brief, Friedman's argument is that activist demand management can keep unemployment at a low level only by accepting an accelerating level of inflation. This is likely to be both unacceptable and probably uncontainable.

Since his earliest writings in the late 1940s, Friedman has emphasised a simple point: that the theory of (Keynesian) activist demand management was based upon an **assumption of omniscience**. Activist demand management assumes that governments know both the entire structure of the economy and the shocks that it will face. Friedman stressed the enormous amount of knowledge of behaviour required to write even the simple consumption function and other relationships discussed in Chapter 3 above. The government is unlikely, in Friedman's view, to know the value of the marginal propensity to save, with the result it cannot carry out the calculations necessary to manage the economy. Behaviour, Friedman argued, is much more complex and difficult to predict than the activists had assumed.

Similarly, to use stabilisation policy to offset shocks as described above, governments must be able to **predict them**. Friedman argued that any government which believed it had such knowledge was living in a fools' paradise. In this respect Friedman was echoing Keynes who had based his analysis on the threat posed by the 'dark forces of ignorance and uncertainty'. Keynes was, however, by temperament an activist and an optimist who believed that governments could reduce the consequences of the dark forces. Friedman, by nature a pessimist, believed that they could not.

Opponents of demand management have continued to stress these Friedmanite arguments.

Laidler, for many years the most prominent of UK monetarists, recently described it as 'the bottom line' of his moderate Friedmanite-monetarist position, the foundation on which he rested his opposition to activist policy.

Friedman went on to argue that activist demand management policies would confuse the private sector and introduce an element of unpredictability into private sector decision-making – for example about tax rates. In Friedman's view this would have two adverse effects:

(a) it would render private sector behaviour less efficient: with less knowledge upon which to base their decisions, economic agents would inevitably make worse decisions; hence, the economy would be less efficient – in the terms of the analysis used in this book, the AS curve would shift upwards

(b) it would render private sector behaviour less stable and so contradict the goals of demand management; private sector behaviour would respond to contra-cyclical policy by being more erratic, and so income would vary more than without government action designed to reduce such fluctuations.

To summarise Friedman's argument: activist demand management is possible only with a degree of knowledge and predictive ability that is normally unattainable. However, for a variety of temporary reasons it seemed in the 1950s that such omniscience was the case. The 1960s and 1970s revealed the hollowness of this claim.

12.12 New Classical and Radical Critiques

So far in this chapter, the analysis has concentrated upon Friedman's critique of the theory and practice of Keynesian demand management. The contrast between these is marked when the analysis of the effect of an increase in aggregate demand on the economy is considered.

In **Figure 12.6** this is shown using both AD/AS analysis and Phillips Curves. The naive Keynesian model says that the expansionary policy, represented by a shift in the AD curve from AD_1 to AD_2, will move the economy from 1 to 2, that is it will reduce unemployment albeit at a cost in terms of inflation. Friedman argues that the result is only a short-run one. The higher inflation will generate expectations of higher inflation which will cause the AS or Phillips Curve to shift such that the economy finishes at point 3. For Friedman, then, acceptance of a higher rate of inflation buys only a transient fall in unemployment. The only way to reduce unemployment permanently is to accept accelerating inflation. Sophisticated Keynesians accept the essence of Friedman's analysis, but suggest econometric or theoretical reasons why the AS or Phillips Curve will not shift as far as in Friedman's analysis – thus the economy will finally come to rest at K. In this case there is still a long-run trade-off between unemployment and inflation, albeit a much more expensive one that in the naive Keynesian model.

Figure 12.6   *Aggregate Demand, Aggregate Supply and Phillips Curves*

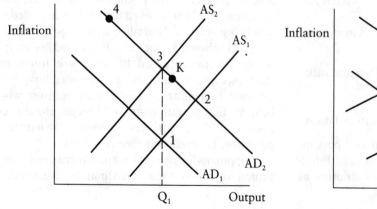
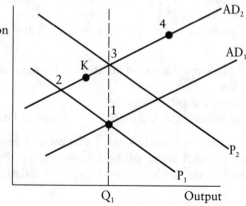

Many economists reject both the Keynesian and Friedmanite analysis. Indeed, they are both regarded as being very similar and open to the same objections. These critics take various positions, but all deny the Keynesian-Friedman model as 'orthodox' or some such similar term which they regard as pejorative. These critiques will now be analysed.

12.12.1 New Classical Macroeconomics

The New Classical school focus upon the formation of inflationary expectations in Friedman's model. He argues that people usually expect inflation to be what it was in the previous period. This is regarded as irrational by the New Classical school because it introduces a systematic error. If inflation is rising, then in Friedman's world economic agents **always underpredict**. If inflation is falling, they **always overpredict**. On either statistical or common sense grounds it is easy to see that a better predictor could be devised. For example, if inflation has risen from 4 to 6 per cent, it is more plausible to expect 8 per cent in the following year rather than 6. Once this point is accepted then there is no reason for the 1–2–3 route shown in **Figure 12.6**. Indeed, 4 is just as likely as 2 as a response to an increase in aggregate demand.

The above analysis is often called 'rational expectations'. The argument is that a rational efficient prediction is equally likely to be right or wrong in either duration. Constant underprediction can be eliminated merely by adding a constant to the model. There is also another sense of rational expectations, that expectations should be model-consistent. The proposition is that if economic modellers believe that the final resting place of the economy in **Figure 12.4** is 3, they should assume that economic agents will also be able to calculate this.

In its simplest and most plausible form, the New Classical critique argues that Friedman's model is just as mechanistic and illogical as the Keynesian analysis. Some New Classical economists, however, go on to argue that since it is known that the real wage will not rise even though money wages are being bid up, there is simply an instantaneous movement up the long-run Phillips Curve without the short-run curve coming into play. This would happen only if the government were deliberately to introduce an unpredictable policy change, but this is rarely possible.

12.12.2 Radical Critiques

Some New Classical economists argue for the 'clean kill' – that is, an instantaneous reduction in inflation with a minimal cut in unemployment. It should be possible for the government to send out unambiguous signals about its intention to cut the money supply with a view to reducing inflation, causing an instantaneous movement down the **AS** curve or the long-run Phillips Curve – in other words reducing inflation without creating unemployment in the process. But such a policy is unlikely to be practicable since it depends upon a government's credibility – economic agents have to believe that the government has both the power and the intention to execute such a policy. Even in 1979–82 the government faced major credibility problems even though its strategy was much less extreme than the 'clean kill' strategy.

Although there are other unorthodox right-wing critiques of the Keynesian-Friedmanite analysis, more attention has been paid to self-styled radical critiques. Radicals draw inspiration from Marx, Kalecki and the 'fundamentalist' interpretation of Keynes advanced by Shackle, Joan Robinson and Paul Davidson. There are many different streams of radical thought. Some radicals – part-Keynesians – stress the significance of speculation and argue that in consequence financial markets are inherently unstable. 'Black Monday' in October 1987 fitted their theories but the ease with which the world economy adjusted to the shock came close to refuting this line of thought. Other radicals stress that apparently economic decisions are frequently weapons in a class or sectoral conflict. Inflation may be the by-product of such conflict. If a group of workers wish to increase their share of real income they can do this only by bidding for higher nominal wages. The response by an opposed group will similarly be to raise its prices or to ask for higher wages. Such conflict theories are but some of a whole army of sociological theories of inflation. However, it is the premise of this book that economic models suffice without recourse to sociology.

A less radical but more influential approach emphasises the role of organised labour. It is argued that trade union bargain for a money wage compatible with their real wage aspirations, after which employers simply add a mark-up to the wage cost in order to cover other costs and to provide an acceptable profit margin. This mark-up is not influenced by the demand for the end-product, hence an increase in demand will not cause money wages and prices to rise or fall relative to their previous levels. In this way of thinking the problem created by raising demand is not that it will fail to be matched by greater supply, hence creating inflation, but rather that UK firms are too uncompetitive to be the preferred source of the things demanded with the result that the excess demand gets side-tracked into imports. This leads to a justification for import controls, which were an integral part of the New Cambridge model once favoured by Radical Keynesians.

12.13 Financial Policy in the Ascendant

12.13.1 The Loss of Faith in Incomes Policy

In the 1980s the government were reliant upon financial policy and largely ignored direct and Keynesian instruments. The merits of that policy are reviewed in this section. The argument for an incomes policy is that it can reduce inflationary expectations and so reduce the unemployment cost of fighting inflation by shifting AS curves onwards. This effect depends upon economic agents having faith in the government to achieve its objectives. Such faith may be rare in the 1990s. Moreover, a full-blooded Thatcherite would argue that there is no hope that an incomes policy can shift the aggregate supply curve outwards, although the evidence on the effects of incomes policy is unclear. The Thatcherite view is that, if after 30 years of effort success had not yet been achieved, it was time to abandon the experiment of incomes policy. The essence of the Thatcherite view is that incomes

Table 12.8 *Incomes Policies*

1	Cripps – TUC Pact	February 1948–1950
2	Selwyn Lloyd Pay Pause	July 1961–March 1962
3	Guiding Light	April 1962–October 1964

The Labour government 1964–70 had an incomes policy which changed its name and form

4	Statement of Intent	December 1964–July 1966
5	The Freeze	July 1966–December 1966
6	Severe restraint	January 1967–July 1967
7	Continued restraint	July 1967–April 1968
8	Reserved restraint	April 1968–June 1970

The Conservative Government (1972–4) had an incomes policy divided into 3 stages

9	Stage 1	November 1972–January 1973
10	Stage 2	February 1973–October 1973
11	Stage 3	November 1973–February 1974
12	Social Contract	March 1974–July 1975
13	Compulsory non-statutory incomes policy	July 1975–May 1979

Source: Gowland (1989).

policy has an adverse effect on aggregate supply –
that is, it causes the AS curve to shift inwards not
outwards as the postwar orthodoxy suggested. The
argument is simple:

1   incomes policies interfere with the workings
    of market forces
2   market forces ensure efficiency
3   therefore, **incomes policy reduces efficiency**; in
    other words they cause the aggregate supply
    curve to shift inwards.

Perhaps, the key feature of this argument is that
incomes policies may be malign as well as benign.
The full list of postwar incomes policies is set out
in **Table 12.8**. The contrast between Thatcherism
and the frequent use of incomes policy during the
Keynesian era is clear to see.

12.13.2 *The Loss of Faith in Fiscal Policy*

The Thatcher era has also seen the (temporary?)
end of the use of Keynesian fiscal policy. It has
been argued that Keynesian demand management
policies carry the seeds of their own destruction
because after a while fiscal devices cease to influence aggregate demand. The argument is that, once
individuals and companies realise that governments
are seeking to use the tools of demand management to influence their behaviour, the private sector will change its behaviour. A special and much
publicised example of this is the 'rational expectations' model but, in fact, the argument is both
more general and more widely accepted.

It is clear that private sector behaviour does
depend upon its perceptions of government policy
as well as upon objective reality. Sometimes such
behaviour can reinforce the workings of policy, as
suggested above, because if businessmen believe
that governments will maintain a high level of
demand they will invest more, which leads to a
high level of demand.

However, in most cases the effect on policy is
counter-productive. The following example illustrates the use of one tool of fiscal policy: to vary
income tax rates so as to vary personal disposable
income (PDI) and hence, given an orthodox
Keynesian consumption function, consumers' expenditure. The idea behind this is the manipulation of consumers' expenditure so as to offset
fluctuations in investment and exports, and so
maintain a stable full employment level of output.
As a consequence, the private sector will have a
fluctuating level of consumption. An example of
this is shown in **Table 12.9**, in which consumers
always have a pre-tax income of 100 and always
choose to spend 75 per cent of their post-tax income. The government can then adjust tax rates so
as to attain the level of consumers' expenditure
necessary for the success of its demand management policy.

Table 12.9 *Stabilisation Policy*

		Income	Tax	PDI	Consumers' Expenditure	Saving
1	**Initially**					
	1	100	44	56	42	14
	2	100	0	100	75	25
	3	100	20	80	60	20
2	**Once consumers react to policy**					
	1	100	44	56	59	–3
	2	100	0	100	59	41
	3	100	20	80	59	21

In each of 3 years, consumers' income is 100. The government's stabilisation goals require that consumers' spending be 42, 75 and 60 in the successive years. Believing that the consumption function is such that expenditure is 0.75 of PDI, the government sets taxes at 44 per cent, 0 per cent and 20 per cent. In consequence, personal disposable income is 56, 100 and 80 and so consumers' expenditure is 42, 75 and 60. Stabilisation policy is thus effective. However, the personal sector would prefer a stable path of consumers' expenditure, if only because of the **diminishing marginal utility of consumption**. This principle states that a consumer will obtain less pleasure from consuming a ninth pint of beer than he or she obtained from the eighth. In consequence *ceteris paribus*, they would rather drink 8 pints of beer on each of two successive nights than 7 on one night and 9 on the other (since the extra benefit – an eighth pint – produces more pleasure than the cost, the foregone ninth).

By extension to the macroeconomic level it is reasonable to assume that, *ceteris paribus*, consumers would like to spend the same amount in real terms each year. Once consumers realise the nature of policy – and the consequent fluctuations in their incomes and consumption that it induces – they will react by adjusting their borrowing and saving plans. The personal sector will maintain a constant path of consumers' expenditure and pay for any extra taxes by drawing upon savings, which will be replenished when taxation is low. This case is illustrated in the lower part of **Table 12.9**. A consumption pattern of 10 in year 1 and 10 in year 2 gives more utility than 15 in year 1 and 5 in year 2 (diminishing marginal utility means that the benefits of consuming 6–10 are greater than 11–15). Consumers will thus borrow and save such that, so far as is possible, they can achieve this. Once they realise how government policy is working, they will adjust their behaviour such that if the policy is repeated it will not work, as set out in the lower part of **Table 12.9**. Consumers will spend 59 each year – and so maximise their utility – and vary their savings to achieve this.

If necessary they will dissave (borrow) in year 1 so as to achieve their welfare-maximising level of consumption. It is important to realise that consumers do not need to understand how government policy operates, but merely to observe that there are fluctuations in their tax bills which will cause their consumption to vary unless they respond by adjusting saving. In this case, when the government varies the size of one withdrawal (taxation) it is not income which adjusts (as in the simple model) but another withdrawal (saving) so demand management is ineffective. Hence, in the belief that direct controls and Keynesian instruments are ineffective, the government has relied upon financial policy since 1979.

12.14 The Desirability of Intermediate Targets

□ 12.14.1 The Case for Targets

From 1976 to 1985 UK governments pursued monetary targets. After that, until his resignation Mr Lawson argued against any effective target. It was his critics who argued for a restoration of some target: either the money supply or the exchange rate through membership of the EMS.

The most basic case for targets is that they give information about the **future behaviour of objectives**. In the UK, monetary developments in 1986–87 suggested that inflation would accelerate, eventually. It did in late 1988. Advance knowledge should make it possible to take corrective action. If this is done, less drastic measures will be needed than if action is delayed. The dramatic 5 per cent rise in UK interest rates in May–October 1988 would not have been necessary if the authorities had raised rates earlier – perhaps a 1 per cent increase in 1986 and 2 per cent in 1987 would have sufficed.

In addition, three arguments have been put in favour of targets. The first is an argument that a money supply target acts as an automatic stabiliser – that is, it will reduce the deviation of output from its trend level. This can be accepted by many Keynesians since it is agreed that the action necessary to meet a monetary target will frequently reduce the impact of shocks on output. The difference, of course, is that Friedman and Brunner have argued that this reduction of the impact of shocks is the most that is attainable, whereas Tobin and other self-styled Keynesians believe that more is possible. However, less emphasis is now given to this aspect of Keynesian beliefs, since the implicit fine-tuning discretionary policy is very hard to implement successfully.

The shock analysed for illustrative purposes is a fall in exports caused, for example, by a world recession. This will reduce the overseas effect below what it would otherwise be. In this case it is necessary to influence one of the other items so that it is larger (or less negative) than it otherwise would be, and thus offset the monetary effects of the fall in exports. Any action that would do this would be expansionary in any model – whether lower interest rates, higher public spending or a relaxation of credit ceilings. Consequently, the reduction in output and employment caused by a fall in exports would be offset. The monetarist argument is that setting the economy on an automatic course is better than letting the authorities use their judgement.

Hence, it is universally accepted that observance of a monetary target will be stabilising. However, whereas Brunner and Friedman argue that this is the maximum attainable degree of stability, Keynesian writers would either rely on discretionary action or on automatic stabilisers of a fiscal kind.

The second argument concerning monetary targets is beguilingly attractive. The private sector needs information about the public sector's behaviour if it is to plan its activities optimally. Information about government monetary policy is the most useful information that private sector agents can have, so a government should commit itself to a specific path of monetary growth. This proposition is very similar to the arguments put forward for indicative planning in the 1960s. The counter-arguments of opponents of monetary targets are that more useful information can be given – for example, a commitment to price stability or full employment or that the benefits of more information are less than the costs imposed by monetary targets.

However, much more attention has been given, at lest in the UK, to the more sophisticated argument of the role of the money supply in the formation of inflationary expectations. This argument can range from a purely economic argument, to one incorporating a large element of politics. Minford has argued that the function of monetary targets is to show that the government means 'business about inflation'.

The third argument for targets is that they are necessary to constrain or discipline governments. Buchanan has been a frequent proponent of this view, but it is even more closely associated with Friedman. This view can be put in a rather illiberal, undemocratic fashion: governments, left to themselves, will pursue policies that cause inflation, perhaps to buy votes, so it is necessary to find devices which will constrain them. This method of presentation is, however, unfair to its proponents who, to use Buchanan's terminology, want to see the introduction of an 'economic constitution'. Governments have enormous potential political power but accept constraints upon it, either through a written constitution as in the USA, or tacitly as in the UK. Such constraints involve both an acceptance of 'rules of the game' (the Opposition is not kept out of power by force) and of rights such as freedom of the press, as well as procedural safeguards, such as trial by jury. Buchanan and Friedman argue that it is equally necessary to constrain the economic power of government by similar devices. In this form the argument is not unreasonable, although one may argue that the majority's right to use economic power is sufficiently circumscribed by a political constitution. Nevertheless, it is worthy of note that this form of argument is new to monetarism in the twentieth century; traditionally monetarists believed in discretion not fixed rules, for example, in their contests in the nineteenth century with supporters of the gold standard.

To summarise, monetarists believe that governments should accept a commitment to a monetary target and should be prepared to make sacrifices to achieve it. This is justified because of the impact of monetary targets on expectations and because their adoption constrains governments and tends to stabilise output. None of these is without foundation. The 'automatic stabiliser' proposition is incontestably valid; the dispute is whether discretion or an alternative rule could do better. Monetary targets do convey information and influence expectations, but it is as easy to overstate as to ignore this case for their introduction.

Nevertheless, an issue which needs to be addressed is 'why money?' Similar arguments could be constructed for interest rate targets; other quantity targets; exchange rate targets; or more complex rules. This is seen most clearly in the discipline case. Buchanan acknowledges that a balanced budget rule (or a maximum tax: GDP ratio) or fixed exchange rates may be better constraints on governments. So what are the relative merits of monetary and other targets?

□ 12.14.2 Monetary Targets

Since Wicksell, in the 1880s, economists have argued that some quantity target, such as money, is necessary as well as a price target such as the rate of interest. Otherwise, the price level is indeterminate in theory and hyperinflation is possible in practice. However, while the system requires some anchor to avoid this, the institutional structure of the UK provides this without any target. Hence, whilst this argument is both reasonable and theoretically important, it has little practical relevance. Indeed, it was shown above that an exchange rate target ensures that prices grow at the world (German) rate. It is fanciful to imagine that this introduces a serious danger of hyperinflation.

It can be demonstrated that a money target is desirable if the economy is subject to shocks in domestic goods markets, and an interest rate target if it is subject to monetary shocks. Similarly, a money target is preferable if shocks come from foreign sources and an exchange rate target if they come from domestic sources. The predominant nature of uncertainty in the UK in the 1980s is probably from the foreign and goods rather than the domestic and monetary sectors.

The most interesting argument against monetary targets is the post-Keynesian critique. This argues that money is so powerful in its effects that control of the money supply is likely to have dramatic and unpredictable effects. It is better to let money adjust to shocks, especially to changes in

speculative sentiment, than to seek to control it. Money is the best buffer. Milton Friedman argues on similar lines that the best buffer is no change in money. In other words, post-Keynesians accept Friedman's argument for a neutral financial policy, but disagree about the meaning of neutrality. In the UK context the argument is that although the effects of no control have been devastating, the effects of trying to control money would have been still more destabilising.

Friedman has always argued that excess money growth causes high and variable (nominal) interest rates. Monetary growth raises inflation and inflationary expectations. Both cause interest rates to rise and the monetary authorities, moreover, have to increase rates still further to reduce inflation. Friedman could argue that the period 1984–88 in the UK proves his point.

12.14.3 The EMS and Monetary Targets

Many of the arguments for an exchange rate target closely mirror those for a monetary target. The arguments for the ERM, like monetarism, impose a form of discipline on economic management that is designed to induce lower inflation and greater stability. The statistical analysis presented above showed that, at least in the short run, the two indicators do present divergent signals about the behaviour of the economy. In 1991, the monetarist Patrick Minford argued that membership of the ERM was forcing the government to pursue a misguided monetary policy. He argued that the consequence was an excessively rapid rise in unemployment. This is a good example of the fact that in recent years arguments in favour of variable exchange rates (and so opposition to the EMS) have been based on domestic macroeconomic grounds. In its negative form, the argument is that exchange rate constraints may inhibit freedom to exercise domestic instruments to combat inflation and unemployment. The German authorities have found that trying to stabilise the DM tends to lead to excess monetary growth, because such intervention leads to a positive overseas impact on the money supply. In the UK the argument is usually more forcefully put; higher exchange rates reduce inflation, lower ones reduce unemployment. Hence a government needs the freedom to adjust exchange rates for domestic reasons – in late 1988 the UK authorities welcomed a higher exchange rate for anti-inflationary reasons. However, few would currently deny the merits of more fixed rates.

As previously noted, if the EMS is to survive there must be co-ordination of monetary policies – probably a common DCE target. Otherwise, differential macroeconomic policies will produce differential inflation and so mean that EMS rates cease to be in equilibria. Given that the UK's trade pattern is different from that of the rest of the EC, it will be harder to maintain EMS membership than for existing members. Hence the need for macro co-ordination is greater. Indeed for good or ill, EMS membership probably implies not only a monetary target but a common one with Germany.

■ *12.15* Direct Controls on Credit

The analysis presented above, the relationship between the EMS and monetary policy, stressed that direct controls on credit were one of the few instruments that might preserve the autonomy of domestic economic policy within a monetary union.

In 1988, with inflation accelerating and a £15 bn balance of payments deficit, it was clear that either money or credit, or both, needed to be controlled. Moreover, since the PSBR was already in surplus and the Government had in 1985 ruled out the use of debt sales as an instrument of monetary policy, it followed that to control money it was necessary to control bank lending. Thus Keynesians and monetarists were agreed about **what** was necessary, but not about **why**. Many critics suggested that it would be either necessary or desirable to use quantity ceilings or other direct controls on credit, but the Chancellor opted for the alternative of control on interest rates. The choices are illustrated in **Figure 12.7**. The authorities wish to reduce credit from Q_1 to Q_2. They can either ration credit and aim for point 2, or raise interest rates to

r_2 and aim for point 3.

In general the following considerations apply to the choice of methods.

- **Direct controls are ineffective**: Any form of rationing creates an incentive to evade it (profitably!) – the classic black market. Direct controls on credit led, during the 1960s, to black markets (called parallel markets) and to disintermediation (see **pp. 112** and **128**). Direct controls on bank deposits (the Corset) led similarly to evasion in the 1970s. The simplest form of evasion involves the use of the overseas sector, and involves a loan (or credit card) from, say, the Midland Bank of Paris rather than the Midland Bank of York. Evasion is a serious problem with direct controls but with personal sector credit they could probably be effective **for a time**.
- **Direct controls are (Pareto) inefficient**: Direct controls lead to a loss of economic welfare.
- **Direct controls are inequitable or unfair**: Some lenders and borrowers are far more adversely affected than others.
- **Direct controls distort official statistics**: This may not seem important, but it is probably one of the two main arguments against direct con-

Figure 12.7 *Alternative Approaches to Credit Control*

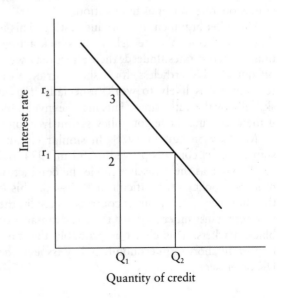

Quantity of credit

trols on credit. A direct control will probably be partially effective, but to an unknown extent. Hence it is no longer clear whether policy is too tight or too slack. For example, if the authorities wish the level of credit to be £250 bn and use direct controls, official statistics will understate the size of credit. Black market transactions are never included in official data, and rarely ever under official purview in the short term. Hence, if the official data show £240 bn it is not clear if official policy is too tight, too slack or about right – it depends on whether the black market is more or less than £10 bn.

Given these circumstances, the reader may wonder why anyone supports the use of direct controls. There are two main reasons. One is that rationing of any kind leads to a lower price – in this case interest rates – than would otherwise be the case. This may be thought desirable in its own right or as a means to a preferred redistribution. Lower interest rates help the rich, mortgagees, the young and debtors generally at the expense of the poor, the old and creditors generally.

More usually, lower interest rates are welcomed because they lead to a higher ratio of investment to consumers' expenditure. Investment is usually more interest-sensitive than consumers' expenditure in empirical studies, and moreover in theory a rise in interest rates has an ambiguous effect on consumers' expenditure since the income and substitution effects operate in opposite direction.

The other argument is more interesting. This is that direct controls are relatively quick-acting, unlike interest rates. Indeed, their effect may wear off quickly. Nevertheless, for a short period a direct control is likely to work, especially if used skilfully by the authorities. This may be invaluable if the authorities have got policy seriously wrong, as Mr Lawson had in 1988. In similar circumstances direct controls proved useful in 1974 and 1978, whereas their absence made the conduct of monetary policy very difficult in 1979–80. This is the choice concerning direct controls on credit: the fast-acting instrument against the disadvantages of black markets. This choice is probably the most important short-term economic policy issue in the UK at present.

∎ 12.16 Are Budget Surpluses Beneficial?

In his 1988 and 1989 Budget speeches, Mr Lawson took considerable pride in large Budget surpluses. Indeed, there was much press comment about the possibility and desirability of running Budget surpluses of sufficient size for sufficient time to pay off the National Debt. In favour of such a policy it can be argued that:

(a) It will benefit **future generations** at the expense of **present ones**. After centuries of argument, it has been agreed amongst economists that the National Debt is a burden and does impose costs on future generations.

(b) It **eliminates the danger of crowding-out**, which occurs when government spending or borrowing reduces private spending or borrowing in an undesirable way. There is no evidence that it has ever been a serious problem in the UK, but it is still of some relevance. In particular, the withdrawal by the government from the long-term bond market has led to an upsurge of private corporate bond issues.

(c) It **raises the saving ratio**. Private sector saving has fallen in the UK in recent years. A Budget deficit – public sector saving – may be a substitute for it (see **p. 48**).

However, these advantages are offset by the disadvantages of Mr Lawson's unbalanced policy – tight fiscal constraint with very slack monetary policy, even after the interest rate increases in 1988.

Governments have usually used monetary and fiscal policy at the same time. For example, during the Barber expansion (1971–73), the money supply grew rapidly **and** there was a record Budget deficit. During the Jenkins squeeze (1968–69) both monetary and fiscal indicators measured the tightness of policy (the first Budget surplus for 50 years, the smallest money supply growth for 15 years). On occasions governments used one instrument earlier than another (monetary policy was tightened in 1974, fiscal policy in 1975), or eased one without adjusting the other (monetary policy alone was eased in 1977–78). Nevertheless, the tools were always in approximate balance, whereas since 1980 government policy has been unbalanced. However, it is necessary to examine the impact of an unbalanced policy, combining a loose monetary policy with a tight fiscal policy. (It is interesting to note that at the same time the USA pursued an equally unbalanced policy the other way around.) The effects of this lack of balance mean that the basic assumptions of macroeconomics must be relaxed – the economy can no longer be treated as if it were producing a single good. Instead, it is both necessary and possible to examine the form and duration that the stimulus to demand takes.

Monetary policy operates through **changing the demand for assets** (for an expansionary policy):

(a) An increase in the money supply creates an excess of supply over demand in the money market.
(b) Some of the excess money is switched to those assets which are substitutes for money (say, houses, antiques and Spanish villas).
(c) This extra demand means that there is excess demand for these assets. Hence either their price rises (antiques), or their quantity (Spanish villas), depending on the elasticity of supply. The two examples cited are unusual examples of (almost) perfectly inelastic and elastic supply respectively, and rather more often both price and output rise (houses).

Some monetarists argue that supply is virtually inelastic (classical monetarism); others, including French monetarists, that it is perfectly elastic. Friedman takes the compromise position: output responds in the short run but price in the long run. Hence, to examine the effects of the imbalance, one must seek to list the assets that private sector economic agents, companies and persons wish to purchase with their excess money holdings:

(a) Foreign assets – factories, shares, property; from 1980–88 these totalled £100 bn.
(b) Consumer durables – (in particular) cars and electrical goods. Most of these came from abroad, so there was little effect on prices, but an enormous balance of payments deficit was created (£15 bn in 1988.)
(c) Shares and financial assets – hence one reason why in the boom prior to October 1979, share prices rose faster in the UK than elsewhere.

(d) Houses

Undoubtedly, the monetary expansion caused the explosion in house prices. This generated a rise in housebuilding but it also caused serious social problems as well as impeding labour mobility.

More generally unbalanced demand management led to the concentration of growth in a few sectors of the economy and a few regions, notably the South East. This is an excessive price to pay for the advantages of a Budget surplus.

References

Allsop, C. and D. Mayes (1985) Chapter 13 in D. Morris (ed,), *The Economic System in the UK* (Oxford: Oxford University Press) 3rd edn.

Bank of England (1971) 'Competition and Credit Control. The New Approach', *Bank of England Quarterly Bulletin* (December).

Bank of England (1990a) 'Monetary Aggregates in a Changing Environment: a Statistical Discussion Paper', *Discussion Paper*, 47 (March).

Bank of England (1990b) 'The determination of the Monetary Aggregates', *Bank of England Quarterly Bulletin* (August).

Bank of England (1991) 'Liquid Assets Outside M4', *Bank of England Quarterly Bulletin* (May).

Blackaby, F. (ed.), (1978) *British Economic Policy 1960–74* (London: Heinemann).

Cmnd 7858 (1980) *Monetary Control* (London: HMSO).

Dornbusch, R. and R. Layard, (1987) *The Performance of the British Economy* (Oxford: Oxford University Press).

Gowland, D. H. (1984) *Controlling the Money Supply* (London: Croom Helm) 2nd edn.

Gowland, D. H. (1989) *Whatever Happened to Demand Management?* (London: RJA Books).

Lawson, N. (1988) *The State of the Market* (London: IEA).

Minford, P. (1989) *The Sunday Telegraph* (5 March).

Shields, J. 'Controlling Household Credit', *NIER* (August).

Walters, A. (1986) *Britain's Economic Renaissance* (Oxford University Press).

Index